THE
MICRO ECONOMY
TODAY

Bradley R. Schiller
American University

David R. Sabiston
Mount Royal College

Laurie Craig Phipps
Camosun College

McGraw-Hill Ryerson

Toronto Montréal Boston Burr Ridge, IL Dubuque, IA Madison, WI New York San
Francisco St. Louis Bangkok Bogotá Caracas Kuala Lumpur Lisbon London Madrid
Mexico City Milan New Delhi Santiago Seoul Singapore Sydney Taipei

The Micro Economy Today
Canadian Edition

Copyright © 2008 by McGraw-Hill Ryerson Limited, a Subsidiary of The McGraw-Hill Companies. All rights reserved.
Copyright © 2006, 2003, 2000, 1997, 1994, 1991, 1989, 1986, 1983, 1980 by The McGraw-Hill Companies, Inc. All rights reserved. No part of this publication may be reproduced or transmitted in any form or by any means, or stored in a database or retrieval system, without the prior written permission of McGraw-Hill Ryerson Limited, or in the case of photocopying or other reprographic copying, a licence from The Canadian Copyright Licensing Agency (Access Copyright). For an Access Copyright licence, visit www.accesscopyright.ca or call toll free to 1-800-893-5777.

Statistics Canada information is used with the permission of Statistics Canada. Users are forbidden to copy this material and/or redisseminate the data, in an original or modified form, for commercial purposes, without the expressed permission of Statistics Canada. Information on the availability of the wide range of data from Statistics Canada can be obtained from Statistics Canada's Regional Offices, its World Wide Web site at http://www.statcan.ca and its toll-free access number 1-800-263-1136.

ISBN-13: 978-0-07-095654-4
ISBN-10: 0-07-095654-5

1 2 3 4 5 6 7 8 9 10 TCP 0 9 8

Printed and bound in Canada

Care has been taken to trace ownership of copyright material contained in this text; however, the publisher will welcome any information that enables them to rectify any reference or credit for subsequent editions.

Editorial Director: Joanna Cotton
Executive Sponsoring Editor: Leanna MacLean
Sponsoring Editor: Bruce McIntosh
Marketing Manager: Matthew Busbridge
iLearning Sales Specialist: Milene Fort, Laura Lazaruk
Senior Developmental Editor: Maria Chu
Associate Developmental Editor: Alison Derry
Editorial Associate: Stephanie Hess
Supervising Editor: Joanne Limebeer
Copy Editor: Cat Haggert
Senior Production Coordinator: Madeleine Harrington
Cover Design: Sharon Lucas Creative Services
Cover Image: © Photographer's Choice/Sylvain Grandadam
Interior Design: Sharon Lucas Creative Services
Page Layout: Aptara, Inc.
Printer: Transcontinental Printing Group

Library and Archives Canada Cataloguing in Publication Data

Schiller, Bradley R., 1943-
    The micro economy today / Bradley R. Schiller, David R. Sabiston, Laurie Craig Phipps. — 1st Canadian ed.

Includes bibliographical references and index.
ISBN 978-0-07-095654-4

    1. Microeconomics—Textbooks. I. Sabiston, David R., 1957- II. Phipps, Laurie Craig, 1952- III. Title.

HB172.S36 2008   338.5   C2007-905152-9

To my parents, Gordon and Alison, who, through example, taught us the value of an honest effort, the value of a kind gesture at the appropriate time, and the importance of accepting people at face value.

D.R.S.

To my brother, Jay, whose memory encourages me always; to my wife, Kate, who has convinced me that all things are possible—even co-authoring a text; and to the multitude of students at Camosun College who struggled with me to find a better way to help them learn economics and understand the passion I feel for the study.

L.C.P.

Bradley R. Schiller has over three decades of experience teaching introductory economics at American University, the University of California (Berkeley and Santa Cruz), and the University of Maryland. He has given guest lectures at more than 300 colleges ranging from Fresno, California, to Istanbul, Turkey. Dr. Schiller's unique contribution to teaching is his ability to relate basic principles to current socioeconomic problems, institutions, and public policy decisions. This perspective is evident throughout *The Micro Economy Today.*

Dr. Schiller derives this policy focus from his extensive experience as a Washington consultant. He has been a consultant to most major federal agencies, many congressional committees, and political candidates. In addition, he has evaluated scores of government programs and helped design others. His studies of discrimination, training programs, tax reform, pensions, welfare, Social Security, and lifetime wage patterns have appeared in both professional journals and popular media. Dr. Schiller is also a frequent commentator on economic policy for television, radio, and newspapers.

Dr. Schiller received his PhD from Harvard in 1969. He earned a BA degree, with great distinction, from the University of California (Berkeley) in 1965. He is now a professor of economics in the School of Public Affairs at American University in Washington, D.C.

David R. Sabiston received his PhD from the University of Ottawa in 1996 and has taught the principles courses on an annual basis since the early 1990s. He is currently a tenured faculty member with the Department of Policy Studies at Mount Royal College. Prior to joining MRC, he worked part-time at the Department of Finance during his graduate years and later taught at Laurentian University. His research interests lie in the field of international economics and in the pedagogical approaches to teaching economics. He teaches face-to-face, blended, and online sections of principle courses and acts as a consultant for the online assessment company associated with this text (Lyryx Learning Inc.).

Away from the office and the classroom, David enjoys an eclectic assortment of activities. When he is not repotting neglected orchids, replacing broken window cranks, or complaining about the colour of the walls in his bedroom, he may be on the links instructing his children on the finer aspects of the game of golf. He insists that his latest toy—a Ducati ST3—is not a mid-life crisis but rather a motorcycle invented by the Italians to help resolve the world's problems.

Laurie C. Phipps completed an MA in Economics from Queen's University, Kingston and has been a faculty member at Camosun College in Victoria, British Columbia since January, 1995. Over the past thirteen years, he has taught predominantly principles courses in microeconomics and macroeconomics along with some money and banking and quantitative methods courses.

His current focus is on the teaching and learning process and the role and potential of information and communication technologies within that process. To that end, he completed an MA in Distributed Learning from Royal Roads University in 2003 and is taking time this fall to begin PhD studies in Educational Technology and Learning Design at Simon Fraser University. He has worked with learners in both face-to-face and fully online courses, developing an introduction to economics course at the undergraduate level and co-developing a course in online facilitation at the master's level.

Away from the classroom, either as an instructor or student, Laurie takes advantage of beautiful British Columbia to hike in its parks and mountains, kayak its coastline, bike in and around Victoria, and become more acquainted with wines from each of British Columbia's wine-growing areas.

CONTENTS IN BRIEF

Preface   x

PART 1 BASIC CONCEPTS

CHAPTER 1 ECONOMICS: THE CORE ISSUES   2
Appendix: Using Graphs   22

CHAPTER 2 INTRODUCTION TO SUPPLY AND DEMAND   27
CHAPTER 3 THE PUBLIC SECTOR   51

PART 2 PRODUCT MARKETS: THE BASICS

CHAPTER 4 THE DEMAND FOR GOODS   70
Appendix: Indifference Curves   94

CHAPTER 5 THE COSTS OF PRODUCTION   101
Appendix: Productivity, Unit Costs, and Exchange Rates   124

PART 3 MARKET STRUCTURE

CHAPTER 6 THE COMPETITIVE FIRM   128
CHAPTER 7 COMPETITIVE MARKETS   151
CHAPTER 8 MONOPOLY   170
CHAPTER 9 OLIGOPOLY   192
CHAPTER 10 MONOPOLISTIC COMPETITION   217

PART 4 REGULATORY ISSUES

CHAPTER 11 (DE)REGULATION OF BUSINESS   230
CHAPTER 12 ENVIRONMENTAL PROTECTION   249

PART 5 FACTOR MARKETS: BASIC THEORY

CHAPTER 13 THE LABOUR MARKET   274
Appendix: A Backward Bending Individual Supply Curve?   300

CHAPTER 14 FINANCIAL MARKETS   302

PART 6 DISTRIBUTIONAL ISSUES

CHAPTER 15 TAXES: EQUITY VS. EFFICIENCY   322
CHAPTER 16 TRANSFER PAYMENTS: SOCIAL ASSISTANCE AND SOCIAL INSURANCE   340

PART 7 THE FOREIGN MARKET

CHAPTER 17 INTERNATIONAL TRADE   358

Glossary   384
Index   387
Student Problem Set   PS-1

CONTENTS

PREFACE X

PART 1 BASIC CONCEPTS

CHAPTER 1 ECONOMICS: THE CORE ISSUES 2

1.1 The Economy Is Us 4
1.2 Scarcity: The Core Problem 5
1.3 Production Possibilities 7
1.4 Basic Decisions 12
1.5 The Mechanisms of Choice 13
1.6 What Economics Is All About 17

World View:

  Cloudy Days in Tomorrowland 3
  India's Economy Gets a New Jolt from Mr. Sourie 11
  Index of Economic Freedom 15
  China's Leaders Back Private Property 18

Applications:

  Controversy over Ottawa's Rebate for Fuel-Efficient Cars 16

Summary 21

Appendix: Using Graphs 22

CHAPTER 2 INTRODUCTION TO SUPPLY AND DEMAND 27

2.1 Market Participants 28
2.2 The Circular Flow 29
2.3 Demand 31
2.4 Supply 38
2.5 Equilibrium 42
2.6 Market Outcomes 47

World View:

  Dining on the Downtick 49

Applications:

  Millions of Albertans Receive Prosperity Cheques 34
  Wheat Prices Increase as Disaster Hits Prairies 41
  Boxing Day Madness 44
  Canada's 1998 Ice Storm 48

Summary 49

CHAPTER 3 THE PUBLIC SECTOR 51

3.1 Market Failure 52
3.2 Government Failure 62

Applications:

  Napster Gets Napped 54
  Second-hand Smoke Hurts Others 56
  Labatt Pleads Guilty—Pays $250,000 Fine 59
  Auditor General "Blasts" Gun Registry 63

Summary 66

PART 2 PRODUCT MARKETS: THE BASICS

CHAPTER 4 THE DEMAND FOR GOODS 70

4.1 Determinants of Demand 71
4.2 Utility Theory and the Demand Curve 72
4.3 Price Elasticity 80
4.4 Price Elasticity and Total Revenue 86
4.5 Other Elasticities 88

World View:

  Where the Pitch Is Loudest 92

Applications:

  Canada's Consumption Patterns 71
  Teen Smoking Rate Drops Below that of General Population: StatsCan 84
  New York City's Costly Smokes 85
  Professor Becker Corrects President's Math 85

Summary 93

Appendix: Indifference Curves 94

CHAPTER 5 THE COSTS OF PRODUCTION 101

5.1 The Production Function 102
5.2 Marginal and Average Productivity 105
5.3 Resource Costs 107
5.4 Dollar Costs 109
5.5 Long-Run Costs 117
5.6 Economies of Scale 119

Applications:

  Alcan and Partners Build US$1.7 Billion Aluminum Smelter in Middle East 117
  Farm Size in Saskatchewan 120
  Bombardier Calls on Feds to Stabilize High Loonie 125

Summary 123

Appendix: Productivity, Unit Costs, and Exchange Rates 124

PART 3 MARKET STRUCTURE

CHAPTER 6 THE COMPETITIVE FIRM   128

6.1 The Profit Motive   129
6.2 Costs and Profits: Economic vs. Accounting   130
6.3 Market Structure   133
6.4 The Nature of Perfect Competition   134
6.5 The Production Decision   136
6.6 Profit-Maximizing Rule   138
6.7 The Shutdown Decision   143
6.8 The Investment Decision   145
6.9 Determinants of Supply   146

Applications:
 Are Profits Bad?   130
 Strawberry Fields Forever?   131
 T-Shirt Shop Owner's Lament: Too Many T-Shirt Shops   133
 Southern Farmers Hooked on New Cash Crop   141
 GM Plans Temporary Shutdown   145
 Wal-Mart's German Retreat   145
 E-Commerce Increasing Competition   149

Summary   149

CHAPTER 7 COMPETITIVE MARKETS   151

7.1 The Market Supply Curve   152
7.2 Competition at Work: Microcomputers   154
7.3 The Competitive Process   165

World View:
 Whiskered Catfish Stir a New Trade Controversy   152

Applications:
 Competition Helps Drop Laptop Prices: Worldwide Sales Jump 40%   155
 IBM to Halt PCjr Output Next Month   164
 Dell's Move to Embrace Retail Is a Sign of Changing Marketplace   165
 Attack of the iPod Clones   167

Summary   168

CHAPTER 8 MONOPOLY   170

8.1 Market Power   171
8.2 Market Power at Work: The Computer Market Revisited   174
8.3 A Comparative Perspective of Market Power   180
8.4 Pros and Cons of Market Power   184

World View:
 Foxy Soviets Pelt the West   174
 New Competition May Mean Bad News for CNN   188
 Europeans Come Down Hard on Microsoft   190

Applications:
 Concerts Becoming a Pricier Affair; Music Industry Consolidation Has Brought Higher Ticket Fees. Some Cry Foul   179
 Privatization of Alcohol Trade in Ontario and Quebec: Consumers Would Come out Ahead in an Alberta-style System, Says the MEI   183
 Pepsi Takes Coke to Court   184
 Jury Rules Magnetek Unit Is Liable for Keeping Technology off Market   185
 Competition Bureau Appeals Decision in Superior Propane Case   187
 Judge Says Microsoft Broke Antitrust Law   189

Summary   190

CHAPTER 9 OLIGOPOLY   192

9.1 Market Structure   193
9.2 Oligopoly Behaviour   196
9.3 The Kinked Demand Curve   200
9.4 Game Theory   202
9.5 Oligopoly vs. Competition   204
9.6 Coordination Problems   207
9.7 Barriers to Entry   210

World View:
 Putting Size in Global Perspective   196
 OPEC Cuts Oil Production by 1.2M Barrels   206

Applications:
 Mountain Crest Brewing Feud   200
 Airlines Drop Fare Hikes   202
 WestJet, Air Canada Raise Fares Due to Rising Fuel Prices   202
 Delta Cuts Fares 25 Percent; Rival Lines Follow Suit   202
 Coke and Pepsi May Call off Pricing Battle   204
 Competition Bureau Investigation Leads to Record Fine in Domestic Conspiracy   208
 Air Canada Using Predatory Pricing: CanJet   210
 Frito-Lay Devours Snack-Food Business   211

Summary   215

CHAPTER 10 MONOPOLISTIC COMPETITION   217

10.1 Structure   218
10.2 Behaviour   219

World View:

The Best Canadian and Global Brands   226

Applications:

Latte Letdown: Starbucks Set to Raise Prices   219
Water, Water Everywhere; Coke, Pepsi Unleash Flood of Ad Muscle   220
Who Can Be Loyal to a Trash Bag?   221

Summary   226

PART 4 REGULATORY ISSUES

CHAPTER 11 (DE)REGULATION OF BUSINESS   230

11.1 Competition Policy vs. Regulation   231
11.2 Natural Monopoly   231
11.3 Regulatory Options   233
11.4 The Costs of Regulation   235
11.5 Deregulation in Practice   237

World View:

Demise of Telephone Monopolies   240

Applications:

Costs of Trucking Seen Rising Under New Safety Rules   236
Crow's Nest Pass Agreement   238
Mergers and Mavericks in the Mobile Wireless Services   241
Financial Woes Heating Up   245
Electricity Price Options for Homeowners and Low-Volume Business Customers in Ontario   246

Summary   247

CHAPTER 12 ENVIRONMENTAL PROTECTION   249

12.1 The Environmental Threat   250
12.2 Pollution Damages   253
12.3 Market Incentives   255
12.4 Market Failure: External Costs   256
12.5 Regulatory Options   259
12.6 Balancing Benefits and Costs   265

World View:

Polluted Cities   251
Taxing Pollution   262
Scientists Issue Dire Prediction on Warming   269

Applications:

Can We Swim at the Beach?   252
Toronto's Talkin' Trash   253
Dirty Air Can Shorten Your Life   254
Quebec Imposes Carbon Tax: Motorists Wary of Pump Price   261
Auction: $156 to Emit a Ton of Pollutants   263
Two Economists Question Benefit of Cleaning Up a Major Air Pollutant   266
Forced Recycling Is a Waste   267

Summary   270

PART 5 FACTOR MARKETS: BASIC THEORY

CHAPTER 13 THE LABOUR MARKET   274

13.1 Individual Labour Supply   275
13.2 Market Supply   277
13.3 Labour Demand Under Perfect Competition   278
13.4 A Firm's Hiring Decision   282
13.5 Market Equilibrium   285
13.6 Choosing Among Inputs   286
13.7 Imperfect Competition—Labour Power   290
13.8 Imperfect Competition—Employer Power   294
13.9 Collective Bargaining   296

World View:

In Moscow, 25,000 Apply for 630 Jobs at McDonald's   275

Applications:

MBA Grads Seek Challenge at Work, Not Just Big Bucks   276
Blue Jays Sign Vernon Wells to Long-Term Contract   284
David Beckham Scores Again—and Again   284
Stern Gets Sirius Payday: $83 Million   289
Union Membership   291
Bettman Puts NHL on Ice   296
Canada Ranks High on the List of Work-Shy   300

Summary   298

Appendix: A Backward Bending Individual Supply Curve?   300

CHAPTER 14 FINANCIAL MARKETS   302

14.1 The Role of Financial Markets   303
14.2 The Present Value of Future Profits   306
14.3 The Stock Market   309
14.4 The Bond Market   317

Applications:

*Venture Capital Falls 72 Percent from
Last Year 305*

*Growth Undergirds Google's Pricey IPO But Can It
Keep Up? 314*

Market Battered, but Intact 316

Summary 320

PART 6 DISTRIBUTIONAL ISSUES

CHAPTER 15 TAXES: EQUITY VS. EFFICIENCY 322

15.1 What Is *Income?* 323
15.2 The Size Distribution of Income 325
15.3 The Federal Income Tax 327
15.4 Provincial, Municipal, and Payroll Taxes 331
15.5 Taxes and Inequality 334

World View:

*Stones Keep England off '98 Tour to
Avoid Tax 329*

Top Tax Rates 336

Applications:

*More Working Poor Relying on Food Banks Despite
an 8.5% Drop in Overall Use 323*

Summary 338

CHAPTER 16 TRANSFER PAYMENTS: SOCIAL ASSISTANCE AND SOCIAL INSURANCE 340

16.1 Major Transfer Programs 341
16.2 Social Assistance Programs 344
16.3 Social Insurance—Pension Plans 349

World View:

An Aging World 352

Summary 354

PART 7 THE FOREIGN MARKET

CHAPTER 17 INTERNATIONAL TRADE 358

17.1 Trade Patterns 359
17.2 Motivation to Trade 361
17.3 Pursuit of Comparative Advantage 365
17.4 Terms of Trade 366
17.5 Protectionist Pressures 368
17.6 Barriers to Trade 372
17.7 International Institutions 378

World View:

Export and Import Ratios (2005) 360
Farmers Stage Protests over Import of Products 372
Inuit Call for Rethink of Seal-Ban Proposal 373
"Beggar-Thy-Neighbour" Policies in the 1930s 374
High Court Opens U.S. Roads to Mexican Trucks 377

Applications:

Chrysler Deals to Get Small Cars from China 369
U.S. Appliance Firms Guilty of Dumping in Canada 371
*Ottawa Moves on Dairy Protection: Import
Restriction 375*
B.C. Premier Shines Spotlight on Free Trade 377
*DOHA Talks in Danger of Collapse; Subsidies at Issue:
Rich, Poor Countries Remain at Odds 379*
*Emerson Touts Trade Agreement with EFTA; Other
Talks to Start 380*
*Free Trade, Human Rights Top Harper's Columbian
Agenda 381*
Living off the Land 381

Summary 382

GLOSSARY 384

INDEX 387

STUDENT PROBLEM SET PS-1

THE 24/7 ECONOMY

24/7. That's the way the economy works. While you're sleeping, workers in Malaysia are assembling the electronic circuits that will instruct your alarm clock to go off, relay the news via satellite TV or radio, enable video presentations in class or at remote locations, and help retrieve music files on the iPod you carry around. If you live in eastern Canada, Norwegian and Algerian oil workers are pumping oil that will fuel your drive to class. Ethiopian farmers are harvesting the coffee beans that will help keep you alert. Traders in London, Hong Kong, and Tokyo are pushing the value of the dollar up or down, changing the cost of travel and trade. In an increasingly globalized economy, the economy truly never sleeps. It's in motion 24 hours a day, 7 days a week.

All of this perpetual motion makes teaching economics increasingly difficult. The parameters of the economy are constantly changing. Interest rates are up one day, down the next. The same with oil prices. Inflation looks worrisome one month and benign the next. Job growth looks great one month, then dismal the next. Even economists at Canada's central bank—the Bank of Canada—have trouble keeping track of all these (changing) data, much less divining the implied direction of the economy.

At the micro level, incessant changes in the economy create similar problems. Market structures are continuously evolving. Products are always changing. With those changes, even market boundaries are on the move. Is your local cable franchise really a monopoly when satellite and Internet companies offer virtually identical products? Will Apple Computer, Inc., with a 70 percent market share in the portable MP3-player market, behave more like a monopolist or like a perfect competitor? With the Internet creating *global* shopping malls, how should industry concentration ratios be calculated? Canadian regulatory agencies are continuously challenged by ever-changing market boundaries and structures.

Coping with Change

So how do we cope with all this flux in the classroom? Or, for that matter, in a textbook that will be in print for three years? We could ignore the complexities of the real world and focus exclusively on abstract principles, perhaps "enlivening" the presentation with fables about the Acme Widget Company or the Jack and Jill Water Company. That approach not only bores students, but it also solidifies the misperception that economics is irrelevant to their daily life. Alternatively, we could spend countless hours reporting and discussing the economic news of the day. But that approach transforms the principles course into a current-events symposium.

The Micro Economy Today pursues a different strategy. We are convinced that economics is an exciting and extremely relevant field of study and have felt this way since our first undergraduate principles course. For at least two of us, we somehow discerned that economics could be an interesting topic despite an overbearing textbook and a super-sized class (over 250 students). All it needed was a commitment to merging theoretical insights with the daily realities of shopping malls, stock markets, global integration, and policy development. Whew!

What Makes Economies Tick

How does this lofty ambition translate into the nuts and bolts of teaching? It starts by infusing the textbook and the course with a purposeful theme. Spotlighting scarcity and the necessity for choice is not enough; there's a much bigger picture. It's really about why some nations prosper while others languish. As we look around the world, how can we explain why millionaires abound in Canada, the United States, Hong Kong, the United Kingdom, and Australia, while 2.8 *billion* people live on less than $2 a day? How is it that affluent consumers in developed nations carry around videophones while one-fourth of the world's population has never made a phone call? Surely, the way an economy is structured has something to do with this. At the micro level, Adam Smith taught us long ago that the degree of competition in product markets affects the quantity, quality, and price of consumer products.

At the aggregate level, we've also seen that macro structure matters. Specifically, we recognize that the degree of government intervention in an economy is a critical determinant of its performance. The Chinese Communist Party once thought that central control of an economy would not only reduce inequalities but also accelerate growth. Since decentralizing parts of its economy, freeing up some markets, and even legalizing private property (see the World View box, p. 18), China has become the world's fastest-growing economy. India has heeded China's experience and is also pursuing a massive privatization and deregulation strategy (World View, p. 11).

This doesn't imply that *laissez faire* is the answer to all of our economic problems. What it does emphasize, however, is how important the choice between market reliance and government dependence can be.

We know that the three core questions in economics are WHAT, HOW, and FOR WHOM to produce. Instead of discussing them in a political and institutional void, we should energize these issues with more real-world context. We should also ask who should resolve these core questions, the governments or the marketplace? Where, when, and why do we expect market failure—suboptimal answers to the WHAT, HOW, and FOR WHOM questions? Where, when, and why can we expect government intervention to give us better answers—or to fail? This theme of market reliance versus government dependence runs through every chapter of *The Micro Economy Today.*

Within the two-dimensional framework of three core questions and markets-versus-governments decision making, *The Micro Economy Today* pursues basic principles in an unwavering real-world context. The commitment to relevance is evident from the get-go. At the outset, DaimlerChrysler's tradeoff between producing gas-guzzling SUVs or gas-sipping subcompact cars (p. 4) illustrates the concept of opportunity cost in a meaningful context. The discussion also highlights the "economic way of thinking" by documenting the relevant information required to make an informed decision. The recent controversy surrounding the federal government's decision to offer rebates to fuel-efficient automobiles (see the Applications box, p.16) integrates the market reliance vs. government dependence theme. In an effort to provide consumers with an incentive to reduce pollution, has the policy inadvertently favoured one automobile manufacturer over another? These kinds of concrete, page-one examples motivate students to learn *and retain* core economic principles.

The Micro Economy Today emphasizes real world applications. Nowhere is this more evident than in the discussion of market structure. Chapter 6 offers the typical depiction of the perfectly competitive firm in static equilibrium (albeit illustrated with real-world catfish farmers). Then comes a *second* chapter on perfect competition which turns the spotlight on the competitive dynamics that power market-based economies. The reality of market structures is that they typically evolve—sometimes at lightening speed. In 1977, Apple Computer, Inc., had a virtual monopoly on personal computers; in 2001 it had a lock on portable, digital music players (iPods). In both cases, a swarm of wannabes transformed the market into more competitive structures. In the process, the products improved, sales volumes increased, and prices fell at extraordinary rates of speed. By emphasizing the *behaviour* of a competitive market rather than just the *structure* of static equilibrium, Chapter 7 injects excitement into the discussion of market structures. The section at the end of Chapter 7 (p. 167) explains why iPods are likely to cost only $49 within a few years. Understanding how competitive markets make this happen is probably the most important insight in microeconomics. By building on student experience with music downloads and MP3 players, *The Micro Economy Today* helps students acquire that insight.

The central theme of government dependence versus market reliance is particularly evident in Chapter 11, "(De)Regulation." When the lights went out in California, a lot of people blamed "power pirates." They wanted the government to more closely regulate electricity markets. Others protested that government regulation (e.g., price controls, environmental standards) had *caused* the brownouts and blackouts. They advocated *less* government intervention and more reliance on the market mechanism. Chapter 11 uses the experience of (de)regulation in the rail, air, electricity, and telecommunications industries to highlight unique features of natural monopoly and the possibilities of both market and government failures.

The FOR WHOM question is one of the three core issues in economics, but it typically gets scant treatment in a principles course. *The Micro Economy Today* tries to remedy this shortfall with companion chapters on taxes (Chapter 15) and income transfers (16). The chapters emphasize the key economic concepts (e.g., marginal tax rates, tax elasticity of labour supply, moral hazard) that are common to both sides of the tax-transfer redistribution system. By presenting the most recent federal *and* provincial marginal tax rates (Table 15.5, p. 332), students are able to see the regional tax disparities across Canada. By reviewing trends in aging and labour-force participation rates (Figures 16.7 and 16.8, p. 351), they may realize how Social Insurance, employer pension plans, the state of the Canadian economy, and other factors alter work incentives and behaviour.

International Realities

The International Trade chapter (17) not only introduces students to a basic model of trade and explains the core concepts of comparative advantage and absolute advantage, but does so by incorporating concerns for globalization, climate change, poverty, and increasing development and opportunity for those around the world who don't share the standard of living many of us take for granted. By identifying the vested interests, political compromises, and the myths that support resistance to trade, *The Micro Economy Today* bridges the gap between abstract free-trade models and real-world trade disputes. Students see not only why trade can be a solution rather than a problem, but also how and why we pay for trade barriers.

The bottom line here is simple and straightforward: *by infusing the presentation of core concepts with a unifying theme and pervasive real-world application,* The Micro Economy Today *offers an exciting and motivated introduction to microeconomics.* This is the kind of reality-based instruction today's students need to be able to think about newspaper headlines through the critical context *thinking like an economist* can bring.

EFFECTIVE PEDAGOGY

Clean, Clear Theory

Despite the abundance of real-world applications, this is at heart a *principles* text, not a compendium of issues. Good theory and interesting applications are not mutually exclusive. This is a text that wants to *teach microeconomics,* not just increase awareness of policy issues. To that end, *The Micro Economy Today* provides a logically organized and uncluttered theoretical structure for macro, micro, and international theory. What distinguishes this text from others on the market is that it conveys theory in a lively, student-friendly manner.

Concept Reinforcement

Student comprehension of core theory is facilitated with careful, consistent, and effective pedagogy. This distinctive pedagogy includes the following features:

Self-Explanatory Graphs and Tables

Graphs are *completely* labelled, colourful, and positioned on background grids. Because students often enter the principles course as graph-phobics, graphs are frequently accompanied by synchronized tabular data. Every table is also annotated. This shouldn't be a product-differentiating feature but, sadly, it is. Putting a table in a textbook without an annotation is akin to writing a cluster of numbers on the board, then leaving the classroom without any explanation.

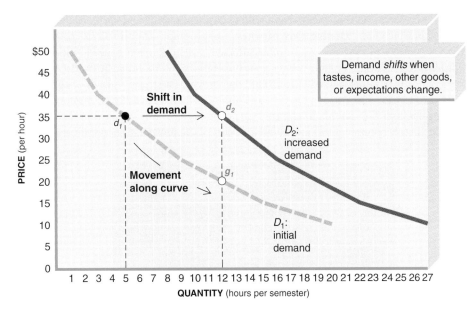

Demand *shifts* when tastes, income, other goods, or expectations change.

		Quantity Demanded (hours per semester)	
	Price (per hour)	Initial Demand	After Increase in Income
A	$50	1	8
B	45	2	9
C	40	3	10
D	35	5	12
E	30	7	14
F	25	9	16
G	20	12	19
H	15	15	22
I	10	20	27

FIGURE 2.3
Shifts vs. Movements

A demand curve shows how a consumer responds to price changes. If the determinants of demand stay constant, the response is a *movement* along the curve to a new quantity demanded. In this case, the quantity demanded increases from 5 (point d_1), to 12 (point g_1), when price falls from $35 to $20 per hour.

If the determinants of demand change, the entire demand curve *shifts*. In this case, an increase in income increases demand. With more income, Tom is willing to buy 12 hours at the initial price of $35 (point d_2), not just the 5 hours he demanded before the lottery win.

Key terms are defined in the margin when they first appear. Web site references are directly tied to the book's content, not hung on like ornaments. End-of-chapter discussion questions use tables, graphs, and boxed news stories from the text, reinforcing key concepts.

Reinforced Key Concepts

In addition to the real-world applications that run through the body of the text, *The Micro Economy Today* intersperses boxed domestic (Applications) and global (World View) case studies. Although nearly every text on the market now offers boxed applications, *The Micro Economy Today's* presentation is distinctive. First, the sheer number of Applications (75) and World View (26) boxes is unique. Second, and more important, *every* boxed application is referenced in the body of the text. Third, *every* Applications and World View comes with a brief, self-contained explanation. Fourth, the Applications and World View boxes are the subject of the end-of-chapter Discussion Questions and Student Problem Set exercises. In combination, these distinctive features assure that students will actually read the boxed applications and discern their economic content. The *Test Bank* also provides subsets of questions tied to the Applications and World View boxes so that instructors can confirm student use of this feature.

Boxed and Annotated Applications

A mini Web site directory is provided in each chapter's marginal Web Notes. These URLs aren't random picks; they were selected because they let students extend and update adjacent in-text discussions.

Web Notes

Photos and Cartoons

The text presentation is also enlivened with occasional photos and cartoons that reflect basic concepts. The "Boxing Day Madness" photograph (Applications, p. 44) is a vivid testimony to how goods are often allocated when demand exceeds supply. The CanJet aircraft parked outside a hanger at the Halifax International Airport (Applications, p. 210) in rather neglected surroundings provides a striking visual image of the demise of CanJet. The cartoon on this page reminds students that not all economists are of the same mind. Every photo and cartoon is annotated and referenced in the body of the text. These visual features are an integral part of the presentation, not diversions.

Photo from CBC News, http://www.cbc.ca/money/story/2006/12/26/shopping-boxing.html

Readability

The one adjective invariably used to describe *The Micro Economy Today* is "readable." Professors often express a bit of shock when they realize that students actually enjoy reading the book. (Well, not as much as a Stephen King novel, but a whole lot better than most textbooks they've had to plow through.) The writing style is lively and issue-focused. Unlike any other textbook on the market, every boxed feature, every graph, every table, and every cartoon is explained and analyzed. Every feature is also referenced in the text, so students actually learn the material rather than skipping over it. Because readability is ultimately in the eye of the beholder, you might ask a couple of students to read and compare an analogous chapter in *The Micro Economy Today* and in another text. This is a test *The Micro Economy Today* usually wins.

Student Problem Set

WHICH ECONOMIST SHOULD WE LISTEN TO TODAY?

By MAL, Associated Features, Inc. Reprinted with permission.

Analysis: There are different theories about when and how the government should "fix" the economy. Policymakers must decide which advice to follow in specific situations.

We firmly believe that students must *work* with key concepts in order to really learn them. Homework assignments are *de rigueur* in our own classes. To facilitate homework assignments, we have prepared the *Student Problem Set,* which includes built-in numerical and graphing problems that build on the tables, graphs, and boxed material in each chapter. Grids for drawing graphs are also provided. The Student Problem Set is located at the end of this book. (Answers are available in the *Instructor's Resource Manual,* in downloadable form on the book's Web site).

All of these pedagogical features add up to an unusually supportive learning context for students. With this support, students will learn and retain more economic concepts—and maybe even enjoy the educational process.

DISTINCTIVE MICRO

The Micro Economy Today focuses on the performance of specific companies and government programs to showcase the principles of market structure, labour-market functioning, redistribution, and regulation.

Competitive Market Dynamics

The real power of the market originates in competitive forces that breed innovation in products and technology. Other texts treat the competitive firm as a lifeless agent buffeted by larger market forces, but this book provides a very different perspective. *The Micro Economy Today* has two chapters on perfect competition: Chapter 6 on firm behaviour and Chapter 7 on industry behaviour. Chapter 7 traces the actual evolution of the computer industry from the 1976 Apple I to the iMac. It gives students a real-world sense of how market structure changes over time and lets them see how dynamic, even revolutionary, competitive markets can be. The rise and fall of "dot.coms" and the ongoing plunge in MP3 player (iPod) prices reinforce the notion that competitive markets move with lightning speed to satisfy consumer demand.

As mentioned earlier, Chapter 11 focuses on the (de)regulation of private industry. The chapter first examines the qualities of natural monopoly and the rationale for regulating its behaviour. The trade-offs inherent in any regulatory strategy are highlighted in the review of the railroad, cable TV, airline, telephone, and electricity industries. As in so many areas, the choice between imperfect markets and imperfect regulation is emphasized.

(De)Regulation

One of the most important economic (and political) issues of the day is the environment. While most principles texts incorporate environmental externalities simply as an example, *The Micro Economy Today* is the only text to allocate a complete chapter to environmental protection. The discussion includes an outline of the different types of pollution as well as their different forms (e.g., smog, greenhouse gases, organic, thermal, etc.). Students will appreciate the detailed analysis of the market incentives and the regulatory options available to protect the environment. The wealth of case studies, reports, and recent policies at both the national level (e.g., Quebec's new carbon tax, Toronto's landfill woes) and international level (the Stern Report) help link theory with reality.

Environmental Protection

The Micro Economy Today offers parallel chapters on taxes and transfers. Chapters 15 and 16 emphasize the central trade-offs between equity and efficiency that plague tax and transfer policies. The varying distributional effects of specific taxes and transfers are highlighted. Examples include data measuring the progressiveness of the federal tax system, as well as data examining the proportion of government spending allocated to social insurance versus social spending. Taken together, the two chapters underscore the government's role in reshaping the market's answer to the FOR WHOM question.

Taxes and Transfers

Chapter 14 emphasizes the *economic* rather than the institutional role of financial markets, a topic rarely found in competing texts. The stock and bond markets are viewed as arbiters of risk and mechanisms of resource allocation. The mechanisms of present value discounting are also covered. The chapter starts with the financing of Columbus's New World expedition and ends with a look at the role today's venture capitalists play in promoting growth and technology.

Financial Markets

Although real-world content is a general attribute of *The Micro Economy Today*, the level of detail in the micro section is truly exceptional. Figure 9.1 (p. 195) offers concentration ratios in significantly greater detail compared to other texts. No other text provides such specific data, though this is the kind of detail that students can relate to. The oligopoly chapter (9) examines specific price and non-price behaviour of competing Canadian firms (Mountain Crest beer vs. Molson/Labatt, Air Canada vs. CanJet), reviews a slew of national and international price-fixing cases (paper companies, auction houses, laser eye surgery, airlines), identifies recent mergers in Canadian industries (beer, banking, oil and gas), and discusses the effect of government regulation in the Canadian taxi industry. The chapter on monopolistic competition (10) starts with an examination of Tim Hortons and ends with a look at the most valuable brand names in Canada and the world. Students will recognize these names and absorb the principles of market structure. After reading the chapter on labour markets (13) and examining the recent multi-million dollar contracts of Vernon Wells of the Toronto Blue Jays and David Beckham of the Los Angeles Galaxy, baseball and soccer fans will gain a greater appreciation of labour-demand principles.

Real Companies, Real Products

APPLICATIONS

Mountain Crest Brewing Feud

WINNIPEG, August 22, 2005—Manjit and Ravinder Minhas set out with the goal of selling low-cost suds and ended up in the crosshairs of Canada's largest beer producers.

The Calgary-based siblings incorporated Mountain Crest Brewing Co. three-and-a-half years ago in response to what they and their university buddies considered to be excessively high prices set by the country's virtual duopoly in the beer market, Labatt Breweries of Canada and Molson Inc. (now Molson Coors Brewing Co.).

Mountain Crest first burst on to the beer scene with a cans-only offering; Labatt and Molson paid little attention. But as it carved out a significant niche with price-conscious beer drinkers (said to be about ten percent of the Alberta market), it quickly got the attention of the two national breweries.

When Mountain Crest moved two provinces east into Manitoba late last year with a subsidiary called Minhas Creek Brewing Co., Labatt and Molson were lying in wait. Just as Minhas Creek Classic Lager received the licensing green light

to list for $6.95 per six-pack (three dollars cheaper than the industry norm) Labatt Lucky Lager, Molson Dry, and Molson Black Label Ice were immediately discounted to $6.90 for six-packs of cans only, not bottles.

Arguably the biggest controversy surrounding Mountain Crest/Minhas Creek involves where its beer is produced. The company makes no secret that it contracts out the brewing of its recipes to two Wisconsin-based breweries, City Brewery in Lacrosse and Joseph Huber Brewery in Monroe.

Labatt went so far as to take out a full-page ad in four Manitoba daily newspapers in June preying on local patriotism by accusing Minhas Creek of producing an American beer masquerading as a Canadian one. This is a serious insult in a country that prides itself on its high quality beer and where one of the national pastimes is mocking watered-down American brew.

Source: Renée Alexander, brandchannel.com, August 22, 2005, http://www.brandchannel.com/features_profile.asp?pr_id=246, accessed October 11, 2006.

Analysis: Incumbent firms in an oligopoly market structure can respond to new competition by lowering their prices and/or increasing their marketing efforts.

DISTINCTIVE INTERNATIONAL

The global economy runs through every chapter of *The Micro Economy Today*.

World Views

The most visible evidence of this globalism is in the 26 World View boxes that are distributed throughout the text. As noted earlier, these boxed illustrations offer specific global illustrations of basic principles. To facilitate their use, every World View has a brief caption that highlights the theoretical relevance of the example. The *Test Bank* and Student Problem Set also offer questions based on the World Views.

Vested Interests

Consistent with the reality-based content of the entire text, the discussion of international trade goes beyond basic principles to policy trade-offs and constraints. It's impossible to make sense of trade debates and trade policy without recognizing the vested interests that battle trade principles. Chapter 17 emphasizes that there are both winners and losers associated with every change in trade flows. While DaimlerChrysler works on an agreement to import sub-compact cars from China to benefit Canadian consumers, (see Application on page 369), the Canadian Auto Workers raise concerns about potential job losses in Ontario. Because vested interests are typically highly concentrated and well organized (a single industry group or trade union), they can often bend trade rules and promote policies to their advantage. Trade disputes over appliances "dumped" into Canada, softwood lumber exports to the United States and import restrictions on a key ingredient used to produce cheese help illustrate the realities of trade policy. The ongoing protests against the World Trade Organization (WTO) and the North American Free Trade Agreement (NAFTA) are also assessed in terms of competing interests.

Free trade is also not just about Canada and other countries. British Columbia and Alberta recently enacted a Trade, Investment, and Labour Mobility Agreement (TILMA) that "aims to slash trade barriers [between the provinces] and red tape and increase labour mobility in a bid to create the country's second largest economic trade zone behind Ontario."[1] However, this free trade initiative within Canada is also controversial and so far no other provinces have joined.

TECHNOLOGY SOLUTIONS

Lyryx Assessment for Economics is a leading edge online assessment program designed to support both students and instructors. The assessment takes the form of a homework assignment called a Lab. The assessments are algorithmically generated and automatically graded so that students get instant grades and detailed feedback. New Labs are randomly generated each time, providing the student with unlimited opportunities to try a question. After they submit a Lab for marking, students receive extensive feedback on their work, thus enhancing their learning experience.

For the Student: Lyryx Assessment for Economics offers algorithmically generated and automatically graded assignments. Students get instant grades and instant feedback—no need to wait until the next class to find out how well they did! Grades are instantly recorded in a grade book that the student can view.

Students are motivated to do their labs for two reasons: first because it can be tied to assessment, and second, because they can try the lab as many times as they wish prior to the due date with only their best grade being recorded.

Instructors know from experience that if students are doing their economics homework, they will be successful in the course. Recent research regarding the use of Lyryx has shown that when labs are tied to assessment, even if worth only a small percentage of the total grade of the course, students WILL do their homework—and MORE THAN ONCE!

For the Instructor: The goal of Lyryx Assessment for Economics is for instructors to use the labs for course marks instead of creating and marking their own assignments, saving instructors and teaching assistants valuable time which they can use to help students directly. After registering their courses with Lyryx, instructors can create labs of their choice by selecting problems from our bank of questions, and set a deadline for each one of these labs. The content, marking, and feedback of the problems has been developed and implemented with the help of experienced instructors in economics. Instructors have access to all their students' marks and can view their labs. At any time, the instructors can download the class grades for their own programs.

Please contact your *i*Learning Sales Specialist for additional information on the Lyryx Assessment Economics system.

Visit http://lyryx.com

Available 24/7. *i*Study provides instant feedback so you can study when you want, how you want and where you want.

This exciting and innovative online study guide provides students with a completely new way to learn. The motivating interactive exercises are not only enjoyable, but ensure the students' active involvement in the learning process, boosting their ability to retain and apply key concepts. Each chapter of *i*Study includes a chapter quick review, learning objectives, a puzzle using key terms, true and false questions, multiple choice questions, problems and applications with instant feedback, and a glossary available as downloadable MP3 audio files.

To see a sample chapter, go to the Online Learning Centre at **www.mcgrawhill.ca/ olc/schiller.** Full access to *i*Study can be purchased at the website or by purchasing a pin code card through your campus bookstore.

Instructors: Contact your *i*Learning Sales Specialist for additional information regarding packaging access to *i*Study with the student text.

---

[1]See the Application on page 377 "B.C. Premier shines spotlight on free trade".

Student Online Learning Centre (OLC)

The Online Learning Centre (OLC) offers learning aids such as access to Σ-Stat and the CANSIM II database, self-grading multiple-choice and true-or-false questions. *The Micro Economy Today* OLC is located at **www.mcgrawhill.ca/olc/schiller.**

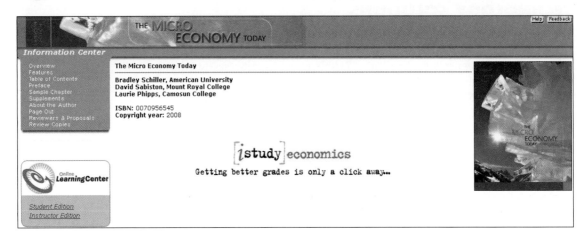

Σ-STAT

Σ-STAT is Statistics Canada's education resource that allows you to view socio-economic and demographic data in charts, graphs, and maps. Access to Σ-STAT and the CANSIM II database is made available from this website by special agreement between McGraw-Hill Ryerson and Statistics Canada to purchasers of the Schiller textbook. Please visit the Online Learning Centre for additional information.

SUPPORT FOR THE INSTRUCTOR

Service takes on a whole new meaning with McGraw-Hill Ryerson and *The Micro Economy Today*. More than just bringing you the textbook, we have consistently raised the bar in terms of innovation and educational research—both in economics and in education in general. These investments in learning and the education community have helped us to understand the needs of students and educators across the country, and allowed us to foster the growth of truly innovative, integrated learning.

Instructor's Online Learning Centre (OLC)

The OLC includes a password-protected Web site for Instructors; visit us at **www.mcgrawhill.ca/olc/schiller.** The site offers downloadable supplements and PageOut, the McGraw-Hill Ryerson course Web site development centre.

News Flashes. The U.S. author, Brad Schiller, writes two-page News Flashes that discuss major economic events as they occur. Many of these deal with international events and provide excellent lecture material that can be copied for student use. They will be posted to the Instructors portion of the OLC as they become available so check back often.

New Chapter on Global Poverty

Available on the Online Learning Centre
U.S. author, Brad Schiller, is a leading authority in Global Poverty and introduces it to the principles course with this new chapter. An array of global data, theory, and policy combine to make an engaging and eye-opening study of this world-wide issue.

Instructor's CD-ROM

Instructor's Resource Manual. The Canadian authors have prepared the *Instructor's Resource Manual.*

The *Instructor's Resource Manual* is also available online, and it includes chapter summaries, "lecture launchers" to stimulate class discussion, and media exercises to extend the analysis. Other features include a section that details common misconceptions regarding the material in a particular chapter; learning outcomes of the chapter; and answers to the Questions for Discussion and the Student Problem Sets. Also, there are debate projects found in the *Instructor's Resource Manual.* In addition, there is a photocopy-ready Print Media Exercise for each chapter.

Computerized Test Bank. Author David Sabiston adapted the *Test Bank* for the Canadian edition. He assures a high level of quality and consistency of the test questions and the greatest possible correlation with the content of the text as well as the *i*Study. All questions are coded according to level of difficulty and have a text-page reference where the student will find a discussion of the concept on which the question is based. The computerized *Test Bank* is available in EZ Test, a flexible and easy-to-use electronic testing program. EZ Test can produce high-quality graphs from the test banks and feature the ability to generate multiple tests, with versions "scrambled" to be distinctive. This software will meet the various needs of the widest spectrum of computer users. The computerized test bank is offered in micro and macro versions, each of which contains nearly 4,000 questions including over 200 essay questions.

PowerPoint Presentations. Angela Chow, Centennial College, prepared presentation slides using Microsoft PowerPoint software. These slides are a step-by-step review of the key points in each chapter, and use animation to show students how graphs build and shift.

Image Bank. All figures and tables are available in digital format in the Instructor's CD and the Online Learning Centre.

COURSE MANAGEMENT

PageOut. McGraw-Hill Ryerson's course management system, PageOut, is the easiest way to create a Web site for your economics course. There is no need for HTML coding, graphic design, or a thick how-to book. Just fill in a series of boxes in plain English and click on one of our professional designs. In no time, your course is online!

For the integrated instructor, we offer *Microeconomics* content for complete online courses. Whatever your needs, you can customize the *Microeconomics* Online Learning Centre content and author your own online course materials. It is entirely up to you. You can offer online discussion and message boards that will complement your office hours and reduce the lines outside your door. Content cartridges are also available for course management systems, such as **WebCT** and **Blackboard.** Ask your *i*Learning Sales Specialist for details.

SUPERIOR SERVICE

Service takes on a whole new meaning with McGraw-Hill Ryerson and economics. More that just bringing you the textbook, we have consistently raised the bar in terms of innovation and educational research—both in economics and in educational in general. These investments in learning and the education community have helped us to understand the needs of students and educators across the country and allowed us to foster the growth of truly innovative, integrated learning.

Integrated Learning. Your Integrated Learning Sales Specialist is a McGraw-Hill Ryerson representative who has the experience, product knowledge, training, and support to help you assess and integrate any of your products, technology, and services into your course for optimum teaching and learning performance. Whether it's helping your students improve their grades or putting your entire course online, your *i*Learning Sales

Specialist is there to help you do it. Contact your *i*Learning Sales Specialist today to learn how to maximize all of McGraw-Hill Ryerson's resources!

***i*Learning Services.** McGraw-Hill Ryerson offers a unique *i*Service package designed for Canadian faculty. Our mission is to equip providers of higher education with superior tools and resources required for excellence in teaching. For additional information, visit **www. mcgrawhill.ca/highereducation/iservices** or contact your local *i*Learning Sales Specialist.

Teaching, Learning & Technology Conference Series. The educational environment has changed tremendously in recent years, and McGraw-Hill Ryerson continues to be committed to helping you acquire the skills you need to succeed in this new milieu. Our innovative Teaching, Learning & Technology Conference Series brings faculty together from across Canada with 3M Teaching Excellence award winners to share teaching and learning best practices in a collaborative and stimulating environment. Preconference workshops on general topics, such as teaching large classes and technology integration, will also be offered. We will also work with you at your own institution to customize workshops that best suit the needs of your faculty.

ACKNOWLEDGMENTS

The birth of this first Canadian edition of *The Micro Economy Today* has been made far easier through the patience, expertise, support, and professionalism of the McGraw-Hill Ryerson team: Bruce McIntosh, Sponsoring Editor; Maria Chu, Senior Developmental Editor; Joanne Limebeer, Supervising Editor; and Cat Haggert, freelance Copy Editor. Many thanks to Bruce for sharing his passion for motorcycles and introducing David to Peter Egan's book, *Leanings*. On countless occasions both Maria and Joanne answered our queries and concerns, no matter how trivial, in their typical efficient and calming manner. And just as we started to tire of the whole process, Cat's probing questions and delightful sense of humour provided the required impetus to finish the task at hand.

The quality of the presentation and readability has been improved by a number of reviewers who were generous enough to tell us what we had done right and helped us to see many areas where we could do better, often providing suggestions that led us to do just that. They include:

Worku Aberra,
Dawson College

Aphy Artopoulo,
Seneca College

Michael Bozzo,
Mohawk College

James Butko,
Niagara College

David Desjardins,
John Abbott College

Livio Di Matteo,
Lakehead University

Bruno Fullone,
George Brown College

Pierre-Pascal Gendron,
Humber College Institute of
Technology & Advanced
Learning

Abdelkrim Hammi,
Vanier College

Susan Kamp,
University of Alberta

George Kennedy,
College of New Caledonia

Borys Kruk,
University College of the
North

Tomi Ovaska,
University of Regina

Kevin Richter,
Douglas College

Jean Louis Rosmy,
Malaspina College

Herbert Schuetze,
University of Victoria

Lance Shandler,
Kwantlen College

Peter Sinclair,
Wilfrid Laurier University

Panagiotis (Peter) Tsigaris,
Thompson Rivers University

Brian Van Blarcom,
Acadia University

Carl Weston,
Mohawk College

A special thank you goes to Joan McEachern, Kwantlen University College, who provided the technical review of the text.

Bradley R. Schiller
David R. Sabiston
Laurie C. Phipps

PART 1

Basic Concepts

The image on the cover depicts beautiful new ice crystals growing on the ancient Canadian Rockies. The heat from the brilliant sun in the background alters their shapes on a daily basis. In some respects, this geographical snapshot captures the basic microeconomic concepts outlined in Chapters 1 to 3.

Economists' viewpoints on how we decide to allocate our current scarce resources (the growing ice crystals) are frequently based on the foundations created by the perceptive insights of our ancestors (the Canadian Rockies). As an individual trying to find the right amount of labour to supply in a hot Alberta market, or as a consumer deciding on how much New Brunswick lobster to purchase, or as a producer in the Saguenay deciding whether to shut down an aluminum pot line, we can turn to the great economists from the eighteenth and nineteenth century such as Adam Smith, David Ricardo, and Alfred Marshall.

Their research into the decision-making process leads us to the basic concept of opportunity costs (Chapter 1) and the classical demand and supply model (Chapter 2). In the background, influencing our decisions is the ever-present government (the sun). Governments, as both referees and players, continuously define the institutional framework within which consumers and producers operate, and their important role is discussed in detail in Chapter 3.

Economics: The Core Issues

In February 2004, Intel Corporation announced a research breakthrough that stunned the high-tech industry. The company's engineers had created a new processor with 125 million transistors—the tiny parts that regulate the flow of electricity on a silicon chip. The new transistors were so small (90 nanometres, or less than one thousandth the width of a human hair) that 1 billion of them could be packed onto a single chip. That was a gargantuan leap from the 42-million-transistor Pentium 4 chip that dominated the market: and light-years away from the 2,300-transistor chip that powered IBM computers in 1972. What does all this have to do with you? For starters, it means that every time Intel innovates in this way all electronic goods and services will be able to operate faster and with more options. In other words, the extraordinary array of goods we now confront in the marketplace will continue to expand and improve.

Maybe more isn't always better, but the history of humankind reveals a relentless quest for more and better output. To a large extent, the quest for more output has been driven by necessity. The world's population keeps growing, but the amount of land doesn't. That's why the English economist Thomas Malthus predicted in 1778 that the world would run out of food long before the nineteenth century ended. He didn't know that a few years later someone would invent the iron plow (1808), the reaper (1826), or the milking machine (1878). And Malthus had no conception of what biotechnology's "green revolution" might become and no clues at all about electronic circuits. So his prediction of global starvation turned out to be unduly pessimistic.

Although we've managed to increase global food output faster than the population has grown, we can't be complacent. The United Nations predicts that the world's population, now at 6.4 billion, will increase by another billion every 10 years. Even if we find ways for food output to keep pace, we can't be satisfied. Our future goals are much more ambitious. We want an ever higher standard of living, not just enough food on the table. No matter how fast our incomes grow, we always want more. The living standards earlier generations dreamed of we now take for granted. Today's luxuries—plasma TVs, camera phones, satellite radio—will most likely be viewed as necessities in a few years, but only if we keep squeezing more and more output out of available resources.

LEARNING OBJECTIVES

By the end of this chapter, you should be able to:

1.1 Identify the three core economic questions that all nations must answer

1.2 Explain the importance of scarcity

1.3 Understand how opportunity costs influence decision-making

1.4 Explain the relationship between opportunity costs and production possibilities curves

1.5 Understand the roles of markets and governments in the allocation of resources

1.6 Identify the difference between micro and macro economics

1.7 Recognize the difference between economic theory and reality

WORLD VIEW

Cloudy Days in Tomorrowland

We'd like to think all *our* predictions will prove right. But the highways of history are littered with wrong calls, false insights and bad guesses. Here's a sampler of twentieth-century futurology that flopped.

I confess that in 1901, I said to my brother Orville that man would not fly for 50 years . . . Ever since, I have distrusted myself and avoided all predictions.

—Wilbur Wright, *U.S. aviation pioneer, 1908*

I must confess that my imagination . . . refuses to see any sort of submarine doing anything but suffocating its crew and floundering at sea.

—H. G. Wells, *British novelist, 1901*

Airplanes are interesting toys but of no military value.

—Marshal Ferdinand Foch, *French military strategist and future World War I commander, 1911*

The horse is here to stay, but the automobile is only a novelty—a fad.

—*A president of the Michigan Savings Bank advising* Horace Rackham *(Henry Ford's lawyer) not to invest in the Ford Motor Co., 1903. Rackham ignored the advice, bought $5,000 worth of stock and sold it several years later for $12.5 million.*

Radio has no future.

—Lord Kelvin, *Scottish mathematician and physicist, former president of the Royal Society, 1897*

Everything that can be invented has been invented.

—Charles H. Duell, *U.S. commissioner of patents, 1899*

Who the hell wants to hear actors talk?

—Harry M. Warner, *Warner Brothers, 1927*

There is no reason for any individual to have a computer in their home.

—Kenneth Olsen, *president and founder of Digital Equipment Corp., 1977*

[Man will never reach the moon] regardless of all future scientific advances.

—Dr. Lee De Forest, *inventor of the Audion tube and a father of radio, February 25, 1967*

We don't like their sound. Groups of guitars are on the way out.

—Decca Records, *rejecting the Beatles, 1962*

What use could this company make of an electrical toy?

—*Western Union president* William Orton, *rejecting Alexander Graham Bell's offer to sell his struggling telephone company to Western Union for $100,000*

Computers in the future may . . . perhaps only weigh 1.5 tons.

—Popular Mechanics, *forecasting the development of computer technology, 1949*

Stocks have reached what looks like a permanently high plateau.

—Irving Fisher, *professor of economics, Yale University, October 17, 1929*

The Olympics can no more lose money than a man can have a baby.

—Jean Drapeau, *mayor of Montreal, 1973*

Analysis: No one predicts the future well. But the economic choices we make today about the use of scarce resources will determine the kind of future we have.

Ironically, some people fear we will do exactly that—and end up destroying the environment in the process. They foresee a doomsday in which greenhouse gases generated by ever-rising production levels will overheat the earth, melt the polar icecaps, flood coastal areas, and destroy crops.

As the quotes in the World View illustrate, no one really knows how the future will unfold. Even some of history's greatest minds have made predictions that turned out to be ludicrous. In gazing into the future, however, we can be certain of some fundamental principles. The first principle is that resources will always be scarce, relative to our desires. Second, how we use those scarce resources will shape our future. If we use resources today to miniaturize electronic circuits, we'll be able to produce more and better products in the future. Likewise, if we build more factories and cyber networks today, we'll be able to produce more output tomorrow. If we install more pollution controls in cars, power plants, and factories today, we'll even have cleaner air tomorrow.

WEB NOTE

Intel Corporation showcases its latest technology at www.intel.com/technology/ architecture-silicon/index.htm.

© CP/Richard Buchan

© CP/Action Press

Analysis: Each car manufacturer must decide how to allocate its scarce resources across product lines. More resources allocated to one brand imply fewer resources available for other brands.

> **economics:** The study of how best to allocate scarce resources among competing uses.

The science of economics helps us frame these choices. In a nutshell, **economics** is the study of how people use scarce resources. All decision-makers (individuals, private firms, and public organizations) make choices subject to their particular constraints. How do you decide how much time to spend studying for your economics midterm exam? Would your decision change if your political science midterm was scheduled for the same day? How does Chrysler decide whether to use its factories to produce sport utility vehicles (e.g., Dodge Nitro) or subcompact automobiles (e.g., the Smart Car)? How much do you think their decision is influenced by Canadian demographics, the expected price of oil, or the interest rate policy of the Bank of Canada? How does the provincial government of Ontario decide to allocate its annual budget between health care, education, and social services? Would its decision change if the federal government reduced transfer payments to the provinces?

In each case, alternative ways of using scarce labour, land, and building resources are available, and we have to choose one use over another. The decision-making process, therefore, involves *trade-offs.* Choosing one option necessarily implies giving up another. An hour watching the last period of a hockey game, for example, means that hour cannot be used to study for your economics midterm.

In this first chapter we explore the nature of scarcity and the kinds of choices it forces us to make. As we'll see, *three core issues must be resolved:*

- *WHAT to produce with our limited resources.*
- *HOW to produce the goods and services we select.*
- *FOR WHOM goods and services are produced;* that is, who should get them.

We also have to decide who should answer these questions. Should the marketplace decide what gets produced and how and for whom? Or should the government dictate output choices, regulate production processes, and redistribute incomes? Should Microsoft decide what features get included in a computer's operating system, or should the government make that decision? Should private companies provide airport security or should the government assume that responsibility? Should interest rates be set by financial institutions alone, or should the government try to control interest rates? The battle over *who* should answer the core questions is often as contentious as the questions themselves.

1.1 THE ECONOMY IS US

To learn how the economy works, let's start with a simple truth: *The economy is us.* "The economy" is simply an abstraction referring to the grand sum of all our production and consumption activities. What we collectively produce is what the economy

*"Meaningless statistics were up one-point-five per cent
this month over last month."*

Analysis: Many people think of economics as dull statistics. But economics
is really about human behaviour—how people decide to use scarce resources
and how those decisions affect market outcomes.

produces; what we collectively consume is what the economy consumes. In this sense,
the concept of "the economy" is no more difficult than the concept of "the family." If
someone tells you that the Jones family has an annual income of $42,000, you know
that the reference is to the collective earnings of all the Joneses. Likewise, when someone reports that the nation's income is $1.5 trillion per year—as it now is—we should
recognize that the reference is to the grand total of everyone's income. If we work
fewer hours or get paid less, both family income *and* national income decline. The
"meaningless statistics" (see accompanying cartoon) often cited in the news are just
a summary of our collective market behaviour.

The same relationship between individual behaviour and aggregate behaviour applies
to specific output. If we as individuals insist on driving cars rather than taking public
transportation, the economy will produce millions of cars each year and consume vast
quantities of oil. In a slightly different way, the federal government spends billions
of dollars on the protection of persons and property to satisfy our desire for law and
order. In each case, the output of the economy reflects the collective behaviour of the
individuals who participate in the economy.

We may not always be happy with the output of the economy. But we can't ignore
the link between individual action and collective outcomes. If the highways are
clogged and the air is polluted, we can't blame someone else for the transportation
choices we made. If we're disturbed by the size of our military spending, we must still
accept responsibility for our choices. In either case, we continue to have the option
of reallocating our resources. We can create a different outcome the next day, month,
or year.

1.2 SCARCITY: THE CORE PROBLEM

Although we can change economic outcomes, we can't have everything we want. If
you go to the mall with $20 in your pocket, you can only buy so much. The money
in your pocket sets a *limit* to your spending.

The output of the entire economy is also limited. The limits in this case are set not
by money but by the resources available for producing goods and services. Everyone
wants more housing, new schools, better transit systems, and a new car. But even a
country as rich as Canada can't produce everything people want. So, like every other
nation, we have to grapple with the core problem of **scarcity**—the fact that there aren't
enough resources available to satisfy all our desires.

scarcity: Lack of enough resources
to satisfy all desired uses of those
resources.

Factors of Production

The resources used to produce goods and services are called **factors of production.** *The four basic factors of production are*

- *Land*
- *Labour*
- *Capital*
- *Entrepreneurship*

These are the *inputs* needed to produce desired *outputs*. To produce this textbook, for example, we needed paper, printing presses, a building, and lots of labour. We also needed people with good ideas who could put it together. To produce the education you're getting in this class, we need not only a textbook but a classroom, a teacher, and a blackboard as well. Without factors of production, we simply can't produce anything.

Land. The first factor of production, land, refers not just to the ground but to all natural resources. Crude oil, water, air, and minerals are all included in our concept of "land."

Labour. Labour too has several dimensions. It's not simply a question of how many bodies there are. When we speak of labour as a factor of production, we refer to the skills and abilities to produce goods and services. Hence, both the quantity and the quality of human resources are included in the "labour" factor.

Capital. The third factor of production is capital. In economics the term **capital** refers to final goods produced for use in further production. The residents of fishing villages in southern Thailand, for example, braid huge fishing nets. The sole purpose of these nets is to catch more fish. The nets themselves become a factor of production in obtaining the final goods (fish) that people desire. Thus, they're regarded as *capital*. Blast furnaces used to make steel and desks used to equip offices are also capital inputs.

Entrepreneurship. The more land, labour, and capital available, the greater the amount of potential output. A farmer with 10,000 acres, 12 employees, and six tractors can grow more crops than a farmer with half those resources. But there's no guarantee that he will. The farmer with fewer resources may have better ideas about what to plant, when to irrigate, or how to harvest the crops. *It's not just a matter of what resources you have but also of how well you use them.* This is where the fourth factor of production—**entrepreneurship**—comes in. The entrepreneur is the person who sees the opportunity for new or better products and brings together the resources needed for producing them. If it weren't for entrepreneurs, Thai fishermen would still be using sticks to catch fish. Without entrepreneurship, farmers would still be milking their cows by hand. If someone hadn't thought of a way to miniaturize electronic circuits, you wouldn't have a cell phone.

The role of entrepreneurs in economic progress is a key issue in the market-versus-government debate. The Austrian economist Joseph Schumpeter argued that free markets unleash the "animal spirits" of entrepreneurs, propelling innovation, technology, and growth. Critics of government regulation argue that government interference in the marketplace, however well intentioned, tends to stifle those very same animal spirits.

Limits to Output

No matter how an economy is organized, there's a limit to how fast it can grow. The most evident limit is the amount of resources available for producing goods and services. These resource limits imply that we can't produce everything we want. One of Prime Minister Stephen Harper's key priorities for his Conservative minority government in 2006 was making "our streets and communities safer by cracking down on crime." While many individuals and organizations applauded the decision to tackle crime issues, a number of Canadians wondered how they would pay for the various, newly-proposed programs (e.g., National Victims' Ombudsman Office, Missing Persons Registry, etc.). In *dollar* terms, the money would have to come from other programs. In *economic* terms, the resources devoted to the creation of these programs would be unavailable for producing other government goods and services such as education, health care, and highways.

"There's no such thing as a free lunch."

Analysis: All goods and services have an opportunity cost. Even the resources used to produce a "free lunch" could have been used to produce something else.

WEB NOTE

To see how wait times for health services vary across provinces, go to the Canadian Institute for Health Information's (CIHI) Web site at www.cihi.ca/ and look under the "Research and Reports" tab.

Opportunity Costs

Every time we use scarce resources in one way, we give up the opportunity to use them in other ways. If more resources are devoted to fighting crime, fewer resources are available to reduce the wait times for health care services. Lengthier wait times represent an **opportunity cost** of fighting crime. *Opportunity cost is what is given up to get something else.* Even a so-called free lunch has an opportunity cost (see cartoon). The resources used to produce the lunch could have been used to produce something else.

opportunity cost: The most desired goods or services that are forgone to obtain something else.

Your economics class also has an opportunity cost. The building space used for your economics class can't be used to show movies at the same time. Your professor can't lecture (produce education) and repair motorcycles simultaneously. The decision to use these scarce resources (capital, labour) for an economics class implies producing less of other goods.

Even reading this book is costly. That cost is not measured in dollars and cents. The true (economic) cost is, instead, measured in terms of some alternative activity. What would you like to be doing right now? The more time you spend reading this book, the less time you have available for that alternative use of your time. The opportunity cost of reading this text is the best alternative use of your scarce time. If you are missing your favourite TV show, we'd say that show is the opportunity cost of reading this book. It is what you gave up to do this assignment. Hopefully, the benefits you get from studying will outweigh that cost. Otherwise this wouldn't be the best way to use your scarce time.

1.3 PRODUCTION POSSIBILITIES

The opportunity costs implied by our every choice can be illustrated easily. Suppose a nation can only produce two goods, wheat and softwood lumber. In addition, assume that both goods use all four basic factors of production (land, labour, capital, and entrepreneurship). Our initial problem is to determine the limits of output. How many metric tonnes of wheat or millions of board-feet[1] of softwood lumber can be produced in one year with all available resources?

Before going any further, notice how opportunity costs affect the answer. If we devote all of our available resources to softwood lumber, no resources are available for the production of wheat. In this case, total wheat forgone is the opportunity cost of a decision to employ all of our resources in softwood lumber production. In a similar fashion, each and every time we decide to produce more of one good, the opportunity cost can be measured by the amount of the other good forgone.

---

[1]A board-foot (1 foot × 1 foot × 1 inch) is the unit of measurement for lumber in North America.

Production of Wheat (Metric tonnes/year)		Production of Softwood Lumber (Millions of board-feet/year)
A	0	10.0
B	1	9.0
C	2	7.5
D	3	5.5
E	4	3.0
F	5	0.0

TABLE 1.1
Production Possibilities Schedule

As long as resources are limited their use entails an opportunity cost. In this case, resources used to produce softwood lumber cannot simultaneously be used to produce wheat. Hence, the forgone tonnes of wheat are the opportunity cost of producing softwood lumber. If, for example, all of our resources were used to produce softwood lumber (row *A*), the opportunity cost of this decision is 5 metric tonnes of wheat—that is, the maximum amount of wheat forgone if all the resources were used to produce wheat instead (row *F*). Similarly, the opportunity cost of producing wheat can be measured in the forgone amount of softwood lumber.

The Production Possibilities Curve

production possibilities: The alternative combinations of final goods and services that could be produced in a given time period with all available resources and technology.

To calculate these opportunity costs we need more details about the production processes involved—specifically, how many resources are required to produce wheat or softwood lumber. Table 1.1 summarizes the hypothetical choices, or **production possibilities,** that are obtainable for this nation given all available resources as well as the current state of technology. Row *A* of the table shows the consequence of a decision to produce only softwood lumber. With all of our resources allocated to softwood lumber, we can produce a maximum of 10 million board-feet per year. If we want to produce any wheat, we must cut back on softwood lumber production and move those resources into the wheat production; this is the essential choice (or trade-off) that we must make.

The remainder of Table 1.1 identifies the full range of production choices. For the production of the first metric tonne of wheat, for example, we see that the required resources amount to the equivalent of one million board-feet of softwood lumber (Row *B*) since production has fallen from 10 to 9. Therefore, the opportunity cost for production of the first metric tonne of wheat is one million board-feet of softwood lumber.

As we proceed down the rows of Table 1.1, the nature of opportunity costs becomes apparent. Each additional tonne of wheat implies the loss (opportunity cost) of softwood lumber production. Similarly, if we start from the bottom of the table and work our way up, additional softwood lumber production necessarily implies the loss of some wheat output.

These trade-offs between wheat and softwood lumber production are illustrated in the production possibilities curve (PPC) of Figure 1.1. *Each point on the production possibilities curve depicts an alternative mix of output* that could be produced in a year, given total available resources and current technology.

Notice in particular how points *A* through *F* in Figure 1.1 represent the choices described in each row of Table 1.1. A production possibilities curve, then, is simply a graphic summary of production possibilities, as described in Table 1.1. It illustrates the alternative goods and services we could produce and the implied opportunity costs of each choice. In other words, *the production possibilities curve illustrates two essential principles:*

- *Scarce resources.* There's a limit to the amount we can produce in a given time period with available resources and technology.
- *Opportunity costs.* We can obtain additional quantities of any desired good only by reducing the potential production of another good.

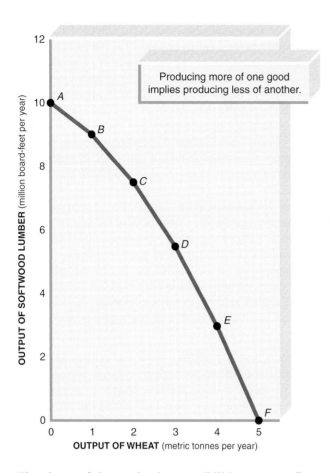

Producing more of one good implies producing less of another.

FIGURE 1.1
A Production Possibilities
Curve (PPC)

A production possibilities curve describes the various output combinations that can be produced in a given time period with available resources and technology. It represents a menu of output choices an economy confronts. Point *B*, for example, indicates that we could produce a combination of one metric tonne of wheat and nine million board-feet of softwood lumber in one year. A move to point *C*, and an increase total output of wheat from one to two metric tonnes, requires reducing production of softwood lumber by one and one-half million board-feet (from nine to seven and one-half million board-feet). This curve is a graphical illustration of the production possibilities schedule in Table 1.1.

The shape of the production possibilities curve reflects another limitation on our choices. Notice how opportunity costs increase as we move along the production possibilities curve. Recall that our opportunity cost for the first metric tonne of wheat is one million board-feet of softwood lumber (moving from point *A* to point *B*). What is the opportunity cost for the second metric tonne of wheat? As we move from point *B* to point *C*, total production of softwood lumber has fallen from nine million board-feet to seven and one-half million board-feet. Therefore, the opportunity cost of producing the second metric tonne of wheat is one and one-half million board-feet of softwood lumber. Notice that as we continue in a similar manner along the PPC, each production of an additional metric tonne of wheat implies a *greater opportunity cost* as measured in millions of board-feet of softwood lumber. These increases in opportunity cost are reflected in the outward bend of the production possibilities curve.

Why do opportunity costs increase? Mostly because it's difficult to move resources from one industry to another. **Resources tend to be specialized**—that is, they are better suited to the production of one good rather than another good. Consider our example where we start at point *A* with all resources devoted to the production of softwood lumber. If we wanted to produce our first metric tonne of wheat and move to point *B*, what can we say about the resources that we would shift out of the softwood lumber industry and into wheat production? Well, there must be some type of land, for example, currently used in the production of softwood lumber that is better suited for the production of wheat. Imagine trying to grow softwood lumber on the hot, dry, windswept prairies of Saskatchewan! Similarly, there are workers whose skills are better suited to farming as well as capital that could easily be converted to the production of wheat. So, that initial one metric tonne of wheat comes at a relatively low opportunity cost. But what happens if we want to produce another metric tonne of wheat? Since we have

Increasing Opportunity Costs

already chosen the land best suited for wheat, the subsequent tracts of land will not be as productive and we require more land to produce the same amount of wheat. This statement can also be generalized to the other factors of production. Consider what would happen if we wanted to produce that last metric tonne of wheat (move from point *E* to point *F*). We have now reached the stage where we are using land most suited for softwood lumber. Imagine trying to grow wheat in the temperate, rainy, climate of British Columbia! Similarly, the workers moving into wheat production possess skills more suited to softwood lumber and the remaining softwood lumber capital would be extremely difficult to convert to wheat production. Therefore, the opportunity cost of producing that last metric tonne of wheat is extremely high.

The difficulties entailed in transferring labour skills, capital, and entrepreneurship from one industry to another are so universal that we often speak of the *law of increasing opportunity cost*. This law says that we must give up ever-increasing quantities of other goods and services in order to get more of a particular good. The law isn't based solely on the specialization of resources. The *mix* of factor inputs makes a difference as well. Some industries, such as the automobile industry, are capital-intensive—that is, they use much more physical capital relative to other industries. As we move resources away from other industries into the automobile sector, available capital may restrict our output capabilities.[2]

Efficiency

efficiency: Maximum output of a good from the resources used in production.

Not all of the choices on the production possibilities curve are equally desirable. They are, however, all *efficient*. Efficiency means squeezing *maximum* output out of available resources. Every point of the production possibilities curve satisfies this condition. Although the *mix* of output changes as we move around the production possibilities curve, at every point we are getting as much *total* output as physically possible. Since **efficiency** in production means simply "getting the most from what you've got," every point on the production possibilities curve is efficient. At any point on the curve we are using all available resources in the best way we know how.

Inefficiency

There's no guarantee, of course, that we'll always use resources so efficiently. *A production possibilities curve shows* **potential** *output, not necessarily* **actual** *output.* If we're inefficient, actual output will be less than that potential. This happens. In the real world, workers sometimes loaf on the job. Or they call in sick and go to a baseball game instead of working. Managers don't always give the clearest directions or stay in touch with advancing technology. Even students sometimes fail to put forth their best effort on homework assignments. This kind of slippage can prevent us from achieving maximum production. When that happens, we end up *inside* the production possibilities curve rather than *on* it.

Point *Y* in Figure 1.2 illustrates the consequence of inefficient production. At point *Y*, we are producing only three million board-feet of softwood lumber and two metric tonnes of wheat. This is less than our potential. We could produce four million board-feet of softwood lumber without cutting back wheat production (point *B*). Or we could get an extra metric tonne of wheat without sacrificing any softwood lumber production (point *C*). Instead, we're producing *inside* the production possibilities curve at point *Y*. Such inefficiencies plagued centrally planned economies. Government-run factories guaranteed everyone a job regardless of how much output he or she produced. They became bloated bureaucracies; as many as 40 percent of the workers were superfluous. When communism collapsed, many of these factories were "privatized," that is, sold to private investors. The privatized companies were able to fire thousands of workers and *increase* output. Governments in Europe and Latin America have also sold off many of their state-owned

---

[2]Note that the more specialized our resources are, and the greater the difference in the mix of factors of production between products, the greater the "bend" in the PPC. At the other extreme, if resources are perfectly substitutable between goods and the mix of factor inputs is identical, the PPC becomes a linear relationship and we experience *"constant"* opportunity costs.

WORLD VIEW

India's Economy Gets a New Jolt From Mr. Shourie

NEW DELHI—In March 2001, strikers opposed to the Indian government's sale of an aluminum company threatened to fast until they died, an act of civil disobedience made famous by the nation's founding father, Mahatma Gandhi. India's privatization czar, Arun Shourie, was unmoved. "I said you can do what you want," recalls Mr. Shourie, photos of Mr. Gandhi hanging on the office wall in front of him. "But we're still not going to talk to you." The strike folded weeks later.

The sale of Bharat Aluminum Co. was a big test of Mr. Shourie's three-year campaign to sell off the almost 250 companies owned by India's central government. . . .

Since becoming Minister of Disinvestment in 2000, Mr. Shourie has taken state-owned companies once thought sacrosanct, such as India's long-distance telephone company and its biggest auto maker, and placed them in private hands. . . .

In India, state-owned companies provide a vast patronage system to ministers, party officials, and even petty bureaucrats.

For that system's beneficiaries, privatization represents a "loss of control, prestige, and money," says a banker who has advised the government on privatizations. . . .

What Mr. Shourie learned about the condition of many state-owned companies shocked him. On one fact-finding trip, he toured a state-owned airport hotel in New Delhi that had only a 3% occupancy rate and inoperable toilets. A state-owned tourist hotel in the south of the country had a crematorium and two burial grounds on its land. And a fertilizer company in West Bengal hadn't produced an ounce of product in 14 years. "The employees just sat around all day playing carrom," says Mr. Shourie, referring to an Indian board game.

—Jay Solomon and Joanna Slater

Analysis: When resources are used inefficiently, a nation's output lies *inside* its production possibilities. By privatizing inefficient state enterprises, India hopes to increase total output and reach its production possibilities.

enterprises in the hopes of increasing efficiency and reaching the production possibilities curve. India's "Minister of Disinvestment" has been pursuing the same strategy, as the World View attests.

Countries may also end up inside their production possibilities curve if all available resources aren't used. In 1993, for example, as many as 1.64 million Canadians (or 11.4% of the labour force) were officially looking for work each week, but no one hired them. As a result, we were stuck inside the production possibilities curve, producing less output than we could have. A basic challenge for policymakers is to eliminate unemployment and keep the economy on its production possibilities curve. By May 2006, Canada was much closer to this goal with unemployment at 1.07 million people (or 6.4% of the labour force—the lowest value in over 30 years).

Unemployment

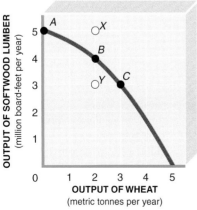

FIGURE 1.2
Points Inside and Outside the Curve

Points outside the production possibilities curve (point X) are unattainable with available resources and technology. Points inside the curve (point Y) represent the incomplete use of available resources. Only points on the production possibilities curve (A, B, C) represent maximum use of our production capabilities.

FIGURE 1.3
Growth: Increasing Production Possibilities

A production possibilities curve is based on *available* resources and technology. If more resources or better technology becomes available, production possibilities will increase. This economic growth is illustrated by the *shift* from PP_1 to PP_2.

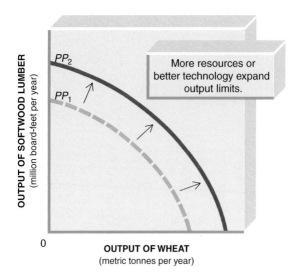

OUTPUT OF SOFTWOOD LUMBER
(million board-feet per year)

PP_2

PP_1

More resources or better technology expand output limits.

0

OUTPUT OF WHEAT
(metric tonnes per year)

Economic Growth

Figure 1.2 also illustrates an output mix that everyone would welcome. Point X lies *outside* the production possibilities curve. It suggests that we could get *more* goods than we're capable of producing! Unfortunately, point X is only a mirage: All output combinations that lie outside the production possibilities curve are unattainable with available resources and technology.

Things change, however. Every year, population growth and immigration increase our supply of labour. As we continue building factories and machinery, the stock of available capital also increases. The *quality* of labour and capital also increases when we train workers and pursue new technologies. Entrepreneurs may discover new products or better ways of producing old ones (e.g., Intel's latest chips). All these changes increase potential output. This is illustrated in Figure 1.3 by the outward *shift* of the production possibilities curve. Before the appearance of new resources or better technology, our production possibilities were limited by the curve PP_1. **With more resources or better technology, our production possibilities increase.** This greater capacity to produce is represented by curve PP_2. This outward shift of the production possibilities curve is the essence of **economic growth.** With economic growth, countries can have more of *all* goods and services. Without economic growth, living standards decline as the population grows. This is the problem that plagues some of the world's poorest nations, where population increases every year but output often doesn't.

economic growth: An increase in output (real GDP); an expansion of production possibilities.

1.4 BASIC DECISIONS

Production possibilities define the output choices that a nation confronts. From these choices every nation must make some basic decisions. As we noted at the beginning of this chapter, the three core economic questions are

- *WHAT to produce*
- *HOW to produce*
- *FOR WHOM to produce*

WHAT

There are millions of points along a production possibilities curve, and each one represents a different mix of output. We can choose only *one* of these points at any time. The point we choose determines what mix of output gets produced.

The production possibilities curve doesn't tell us which mix of output is best; it just lays out a menu of available choices. It's up to us to pick out the one and only mix of output that will be produced at a given time. This WHAT decision is a basic decision every nation must make.

Decisions must also be made about HOW to produce. Should we generate electricity by burning coal, smashing atoms, or transforming solar power? Should we harvest ancient forests even if that destroys endangered owls or other animal species? Should we dump municipal and industrial waste into nearby rivers, or should we dispose of it in some other way? There are lots of different ways of producing goods and services, and someone has to make a decision about which production methods to use. The HOW decision is a question not just of efficiency but of social values as well.

HOW

After we've decided what to produce and how, we must address a third basic question: FOR WHOM? Who is going to get the output produced? Should everyone get an equal share? Should everyone wear the same clothes and drive identical cars? Should some people get to enjoy seven-course banquets while others forage in garbage cans for food scraps? How should the goods and services an economy produces be distributed? Are we satisfied with the way output is now distributed?

FOR WHOM

1.5 THE MECHANISMS OF CHOICE

Answers to the questions of WHAT, HOW, and FOR WHOM largely define an economy. But who formulates the answers? Who actually decides which goods are produced, what technologies are used, or how incomes are distributed?

Adam Smith had an answer back in 1776. In his classic work *The Wealth of Nations,* Smith said the "invisible hand" determines what gets produced, how, and for whom. The invisible hand he referred to wasn't a creature from a science fiction movie but, instead, a characterization of the way markets work.

The Invisible Hand of a Market Economy

Consider the decision about how many cars to produce in Canada. There's no "auto czar" who dictates production. Not even General Motors can make such a decision. Instead, the *market* decides how many cars to produce. Millions of consumers signal their desire to have a car by browsing the Internet, visiting showrooms, and buying cars. Their purchases flash a green light to producers, who see the potential to earn more profits. To do so, they'll increase auto output. If consumers stop buying cars, profits will disappear. Producers will respond by reducing output, laying off workers, and even closing factories. These interactions between consumers and producers determine how many cars are produced.

Notice how the invisible hand moves us along the production possibilities curve. If consumers demand more cars, the mix of output will include more cars and less of other goods. If auto production is scaled back, the displaced autoworkers will end up producing other goods and services, which will change the mix of output in the opposite direction.

Adam Smith's invisible hand is now called the **market mechanism.** Notice that it doesn't require any direct contact between consumers and producers. Communication is indirect, transmitted by market prices and sales. Indeed, *the essential feature of the market mechanism is the price signal.* If you want something and have sufficient income, you can buy it. If enough people do the same thing, the total sales of that product will rise, and perhaps its price will as well. Producers, seeing sales and prices rise, will want to exploit this profit potential. To do so, they'll attempt to acquire a larger share of available resources and use it to produce the goods we desire. That's how the "invisible hand" works.

market mechanism: The use of market prices and sales to signal desired outputs (or resource allocations).

The market mechanism can also answer the HOW question. To maximize their profits, producers will seek to use the lowest-cost method of producing a good. By observing prices in the marketplace, they can determine if their current production method is the most profitable. If not, they can search for a lower-cost method and adopt it.

The market mechanism can also resolve the FOR WHOM question. A market distributes goods to the highest bidder. In a pure market economy, individuals who are willing and able to pay the most for a good tend to get it.

laissez faire: The doctrine of "leave it alone," of nonintervention by government in the market mechanism.

Government Intervention and Command Economies

WEB NOTE

For more information on Smith, Malthus, Keynes, and Marx, visit McMaster University's Department of Economics link to the "History of Economic Thought" at http://socserv. mcmaster.ca/econ/ugcm/3ll3/.

Continuing Debates

Adam Smith was so impressed with the ability of the market mechanism to answer the basic WHAT, HOW, and FOR WHOM questions that he urged government to "leave it alone" (**laissez faire**). In his view, the price signals and responses of the marketplace were likely to do a better job of allocating resources than any government could.

The laissez-faire policy Adam Smith favoured has always had its share of critics. Karl Marx emphasized how free markets tend to concentrate wealth and power in the hands of the few, at the expense of the many. As he saw it, unfettered markets permit the capitalists (those who own the machinery and factories) to enrich themselves while the proletariat (the workers) toil long hours for subsistence wages. Marx argued that the government not only had to intervene but had to *own* all the means of production—the factories, the machinery, the land—to avoid savage inequalities. In *Das Kapital* (1867) and the *Communist Manifesto* (1848), he laid the foundation for a communist state in which the government would be the master of economic outcomes.

The British economist John Maynard Keynes seemed to offer a less drastic solution. The market, he conceded, was pretty efficient in organizing production and building better mousetraps. However, individual producers and workers had no control over the broader economy. The cumulative actions of so many economic agents could easily tip the economy in the wrong direction. A completely unregulated market might veer off in one direction and then another as producers all rushed to increase output at the same time or throttled back production in a herdlike manner. The government, Keynes reasoned, could act like a pressure gauge, letting off excess steam or building it up as the economy needed. With the government maintaining overall balance in the economy, the market could live up to its performance expectations. While assuring a stable, full-employment environment, the government might also be able to redress excessive inequalities. In Keynes's view, government should play an active but not all-inclusive role in managing the economy.

These historical views shed perspective on today's political debates. The core of most debates is some variation of the WHAT, HOW, or FOR WHOM questions. Much of the debate is how these questions should be answered. Generally speaking, politicians whose ideologies are considered right-of-centre on the political spectrum favour Adam Smith's laissez-faire approach, whereas left-of-centre politicians tend to think government intervention is likely to improve the answers. Similarly, right-leaning politicians often resist workplace regulation, affirmative action, and tax increases on the grounds that such interventions impair market efficiency. Their left-leaning opponents, on the other hand, frequently argue that such interventions help temper excesses of the market and promote both equity and efficiency.

The debate over how best to manage the economy is not unique to Canada. Countries around the world confront the same choice, between reliance on the market and reliance on the government. Few countries have ever relied exclusively on either one or the other to manage their economy. Even the former Soviet Union, where the government owned all the means of production and central planners dictated how they were to be used, made limited use of free markets. In Cuba, the government still manages the economy's resources but encourages farmers' markets and some private trade and investment. As a previous World View indicated, India is now letting the market play a larger role in deciding what is produced, how it is produced, and who gets the resulting output.

The World View on the next page categorizes nations by the extent of their market reliance. Hong Kong scores high on this "Index of Economic Freedom" because its tax rates are relatively low, the public sector is comparatively small, and there are few restrictions on private investment or trade. By contrast, North Korea scores extremely low because the government owns all property, directly allocates resources, sets wages, and limits trade.

The rankings shown in the World View are neither definitive nor stable. In 1989, Russia began a massive transformation from a state-controlled economy to a more

WORLD VIEW

Index of Economic Freedom

Hong Kong ranks number one among the world's nations in economic freedom. It achieves that status with low tax rates, free-trade policies, minimal government regulation, and secure property rights. These and other economic indicators place Hong Kong at the top of the Heritage Foundation's 2006 country rankings by the degree of "economic freedom." The "most free" and the "least free" (repressed) economies on the list of 157 countries are as follows.

Greatest Economic Freedom	Least Economic Freedom
Hong Kong	Nigeria
Singapore	Haiti
Ireland	Turkmenistan
Luxembourg	Laos
United Kingdom	Cuba
Iceland	Belarus
Estonia	Venezuela
Denmark	Libya
United States	Zimbabwe
Australia	Burma
New Zealand	Iran
Canada	Korea, North

Source: Heritage Foundation, *2006 Index of Economic Freedom,* Washington, DC, 2006. www.heritage.org

Analysis: All nations must decide whether to rely on market signals or government directives to determine economic outcomes. Nations that rely the least on government intervention score highest on this Index of Economic Freedom.

market-oriented economy. Some of the former republics (e.g., Estonia) became relatively free, while others (e.g., Turkmenistan) still rely on extensive government control of the economy. China has greatly expanded the role of private markets and Cuba is moving in the same direction in fits and starts. Even Libya—one of the "least-free" nations on the Heritage list—is just now experimenting with some market reforms.

In Canada, the changes have been less dramatic. Over the past few decades, the overall tendency of federal governments—both Conservative and Liberal—has been towards promoting the allocation of resources through the market economy. This does not necessarily reduce the importance of the role of the government.

The recent concern about environmental issues is a good example. Many Canadians believe that without some sort of government intervention, producers (and consumers) will continue to pollute the environment. They argue that there are few market incentives to reduce pollution and that we cannot simply rely on moral convictions to tackle the problem. In an effort to address the pollution associated with automobiles, the 2007 federal budget presented by the Harper government included a Vehicle Efficiency Incentive which provided a rebate of up to $2,000 to people who bought more fuel efficient vehicles and penalized those who purchased gas-guzzlers with new taxes of up to $4,000. Rather than impose specific gas consumption limits, the government is relying on the market mechanism to reduce emissions. The Applications on the next page illustrate some of the problems created with this new legislation.

WEB NOTE

To learn how the Heritage Foundation defines economic freedom, visit its Web site at www.heritage.org.

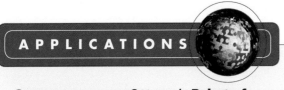

Controversy over Ottawa's Rebate for Fuel-Efficient Cars

Unhappy auto companies that sell subcompact cars are revising marketing plans and sales forecasts now that Ottawa has provided a competitive advantage to Toyota Canada Inc. with environmental provisions in the new federal budget.

Buyers of cars that use less than 6.5 litres of gas to go 100 kilometres will receive a rebate of at least $1,000. The Toyota Yaris, rated by Natural Resources Canada at 6.4 litres per 100 kilometres, qualifies for the $1,000. The Honda

Fit, which has a rating of 6.6 litres for every 100 kilometres doesn't make the grade. A rebate of $1,000 is a major advantage in segment of the market where the vehicles sell in the $12,000 to $14,000 range. "What we're concerned about is letting one [model] in a very price-sensitive segment of the market receive the rebate when all the vehicles in that segment of the market are fuel efficient," Hyundai Auto Canada president Steve Kelleher said yesterday.

Source: Greg Keenan, *The Globe and Mail*, March 22, 2007, page B1.

	Fuel economy (litres per 100 kilometres)	Rebate
Toyota Yaris: $14,605 (four door)	6.4	$1,000
Honda Fit: $14,980 (five-speed manual)	6.6	$0
Hyundai Accent: $12,995 (five-speed manual)	6.9	$0
Nissan Versa: $14,498	7.2	$0
Chevrolet Aveo: $12,995	7.55	$0

Analysis: Governments' attempts to influence resource allocation through the market mechanism are often controversial since they can create "winners" and "losers."

A Mixed Economy

mixed economy: An economy that uses both market signals and government directives to allocate goods and resources.

No one wants to rely exclusively on Adam Smith's invisible hand. Nor is anyone willing to have the economy steered exclusively by the highly visible hand of the government. *Canada, like most nations, uses a combination of market signals and government directives to select economic outcomes.* The resulting compromises are called **mixed economies.**

The reluctance of countries around the world to rely exclusively on either market signals or government directives is due to the recognition that both mechanisms can and do fail on occasion. As we've seen, market signals are capable of answering the three core questions of WHAT, HOW, and FOR WHOM. But the answers may not be the best possible ones.

Market Failure

market failure: An imperfection in the market mechanism that prevents optimal outcomes.

When market signals don't give the best possible answers to the WHAT, HOW, and FOR WHOM questions, we say that the market mechanism has *failed*. Specifically, **market failure** means that the invisible hand has failed to achieve the best possible outcomes. If the market fails, we end up with the wrong (*sub*optimal) mix of output, too much unemployment, polluted air, or an inequitable distribution of income.

In a market-driven economy, for example, producers will select production methods based on cost. Cost-driven production decisions, however, may lead a factory to spew pollution into the environment rather than to use cleaner but more expensive methods of production. The resulting pollution may be so bad that society ends up worse off as a result of the extra production. In such a case we may need government intervention to force better answers to the WHAT and HOW questions.

We could also let the market decide who gets to consume cigarettes. Anyone who had enough money to buy a pack of cigarettes would then be entitled to smoke. What if, however, children aren't experienced enough to balance the risks of smoking against the pleasures? What if nonsmokers are harmed by secondhand smoke? In this case as well, the market's answer to the FOR WHOM question might not be optimal.

Government intervention may move us closer to our economic goals. If so, the resulting mix of market signals and government directives would be an improvement over a purely market-driven economy. But government intervention may fail as well. **Government failure** occurs when government intervention fails to improve market outcomes or actually makes them worse.

The collapse of communism revealed how badly government directives can fail. But government failure also occurs in less spectacular ways. For example, the government may intervene to force an industry to clean up its pollution. The government's directives may impose such high costs that the industry closes factories and lays off workers. Some cutbacks in output might be appropriate, but they could also prove excessive. The government might also mandate pollution control technologies that are too expensive or even obsolete. None of this has to happen, but it might. If it does, government failure will have worsened economic outcomes.

The government might also fail if it interferes with the market's answer to the FOR WHOM question. For 50 years, communist China distributed goods by government directive, not market performance. Incomes were more equal, but uniformly low. To increase output and living standards, China has turned to market incentives (see the World View on the next page). As entrepreneurs respond to these incentives, everyone may become better off—even while inequality increases.

The current practice of raising taxes to fund transfer payments may also worsen economic outcomes. If the government raises taxes on the rich to pay welfare benefits for the poor, neither the rich nor the poor may see much purpose in working. In that case, the attempt to give everybody a "fair" share of the pie might end up shrinking the size of the pie. If that happened, society could end up worse off.

None of these failures has to occur, but each might. The challenge for society is to minimize failures by selecting the appropriate balance of market signals and government directives. This isn't an easy task. It requires that we know how markets work and why they sometimes fail. We also need to know what policy options the government has and how and when they might work.

Government Failure

> **government failure:** Government intervention that fails to improve economic outcomes.

Seeking Balance

1.6 WHAT ECONOMICS IS ALL ABOUT

Understanding how economies function is the basic purpose of studying economics. We seek to know how an economy is organized, how it behaves, and how successfully it achieves its basic objectives. Then, if we're lucky, we can discover better ways of attaining those same objectives.

Economists don't formulate an economy's objectives. Instead, they focus on the *means* available for achieving given *goals*. Under the preamble of the Bank of Canada Act, for example, the Bank's mandate is "generally to promote the economic and financial welfare of Canada." The economist's job is to help design policies that will best achieve these goals. One of the Bank's responsibilities is for monetary policy; how much money circulates in the economy, and what that money is worth. To that extent, the current cornerstone of the Bank's monetary policy framework is its inflation-control system, the goal of which is to keep the persistent rise over time in the average price of goods and services near 2 percent—the midpoint of a 1 to 3 percent target range. The means by which the Bank attains this end is by influencing short-term interest rates.

End vs. Means

Analysis: Government-directed production, prices, and incomes may increase equalities but blunt incentives. Private property and market-based incomes motivate higher productivity and growth.

Macro vs. Micro

The study of economics is typically divided into two parts: macroeconomics and microeconomics. Macroeconomics focuses on the behaviour of an entire economy—the "big picture." In macroeconomics we worry about such national goals as full employment, control of inflation, and economic growth, without worrying about the well-being or behaviour of specific individuals or groups. The essential concern of **macroeconomics** is to understand and improve the performance of the economy as a whole.

Microeconomics is concerned with the details of this big picture. In microeconomics we focus on the individuals, firms, and government agencies that actually compose the larger economy. Our interest here is in the behaviour of individual economic actors. What are their goals? How can they best achieve these goals with their limited resources? How will they respond to various incentives and opportunities?

> **macroeconomics:** The study of aggregate economic behaviour, of the economy as a whole.

> **microeconomics:** The study of individual behaviour in the economy, of the components of the larger economy.

A primary concern of macroeconomics, for example, is to determine how much money, *in total,* consumers will spend on goods and services. In microeconomics, the focus is much narrower. In micro, attention is paid to purchases of *specific* goods and services rather than just aggregated totals. Macro likewise concerns itself with the level of *total* business investment, while micro examines how *individual* businesses make their investment decisions.

Although they operate at different levels of abstraction, macro and micro are intrinsically related. Macro (aggregate) outcomes depend on micro behaviour, and micro (individual) behaviour is affected by macro outcomes. One can't fully understand how an economy works until one understands how all the participants behave and why they behave as they do. But just as you can drive a car without knowing how its engine is constructed, you can observe how an economy runs without completely disassembling it. In macroeconomics we observe that the car goes faster when the accelerator is depressed and that it slows when the brake is applied. That's all we need to know in most situations. At times, however, the car breaks down. When it does, we have to know something more about how the pedals work. This leads us into micro studies. How does each part work? Which ones can or should be fixed?

Our interest in microeconomics is motivated by more than our need to understand how the larger economy works. The "parts" of the economic engine are people. To the extent that we care about the welfare of individuals in society, we have a fundamental interest in microeconomic behaviour and outcomes. In this regard, we examine how individual consumers and business firms seek to achieve specific goals in the marketplace. The goals aren't always related to output. Gary Becker won the 1992 Nobel Prize in economics for demonstrating how economic principles also affect decisions to marry, to have children, or to engage in criminal activities.

Theory vs. Reality

The distinction between macroeconomics and microeconomics is one of many simplifications we make in studying economic behaviour. The economy is much too vast and complex to describe and explain in one course (or one lifetime). Accordingly, we focus on basic relationships, ignoring annoying detail. In so doing, we isolate basic principles of economic behaviour and then use those principles to predict economic events and develop economic policies. This means that we formulate theories, or *models,* of economic behaviour and then use those theories to evaluate and design economic policy.

These models of economic behaviour and subsequent policies rely primarily on data and empirical observation to justify their accuracy. Economists use the term *positive statements* to identify the questions or the relationships of interest. By definition, positive statements can be verified with empirical data. "An increase in the minimum wage will lead to an increase in the unemployment rate for teenagers" or "giving each Albertan a $400 prosperity cheque will lead to higher inflation in the province" are examples of positive statements; the accuracy of each statement can be empirically verified. But statements such as "we should increase minimum wages" or "the province of Alberta should invest more money in health care and not give out prosperity cheques" are examples of *normative statements.* Such statements are based on an individual's principles or value judgments and cannot be deemed true or false through any formal empirical analysis.

Economics—both theory and policy—focuses on positive statements. But these statements frequently need to be set in the proper context. Our model of consumer behaviour assumes, for example, that people buy less of a good when its price rises. In reality, however, people *may* buy *more* of a good at increased prices, especially if those high prices create a certain snob appeal or if prices are expected to increase still further. In predicting consumer responses to price increases, we typically ignore such possibilities by *assuming* that the price of the good in question is the *only* thing that changes. This assumption of "other things remaining equal" (unchanged) (in Latin, **ceteris paribus**) allows us to make straightforward predictions. If instead we described consumer responses to increased prices in any and all circumstances (allowing everything to change at once), every prediction would be accompanied by a book full of exceptions and qualifications. We'd look more like lawyers than economists.

ceteris paribus: The assumption of nothing else changing.

Although the assumption of *ceteris paribus* makes it easier to formulate economic theory and policy, it also increases the risk of error. If other things do change in significant ways, our predictions (and policies) may fail. But, like weather forecasters, we continue to make predictions, knowing that occasional failure is inevitable. In so doing, we're motivated by the conviction that it's better to be approximately right than to be dead wrong.

Politics. Politicians can't afford to be quite so complacent about economic predictions. Policy decisions must be made every day. And a politician's continued survival in office frequently depends on his or her government's choices. During his tenure (1984–1993), Prime Minister Brian Mulroney introduced free trade agreements with the United States and Mexico, replaced the Manufacturers' Sales Tax with the Goods and Services Tax (GST) and attempted to end Quebec's constitutional grievances with the Meech Lake Accord. Were these the right choices? Did they influence the 1993 elections results? Probably, but economic theory alone can't completely answer these questions. Political decisions are not only derived by examining economic trade-offs (opportunity costs), but also social values. By all accounts, Paul Martin was a well-respected and competent politician. As the Minister of Finance (1993–2003) under the Chrétien government, he successfully turned a $42 billion federal deficit into annual surpluses. Yet, his tenure as Prime Minister (2003–2006) was overshadowed by a major government sponsorship scandal left over from the Chrétien years. While the subsequent investigation by the Gomery Commission cleared Martin of any personal wrongdoing, the damage was done and his party fell to defeat in January 2006.

"Politics"—the balancing of competing interests—is an inevitable ingredient of economic policy. On occasion, political expediency of a policy takes precedence over economic implications. Prime Minister Stephen Harper's decision to reduce the GST from 7 percent to 6 percent in July 2006 received plenty of political support, but many economists argued that *income* tax reform rather than *consumption* tax changes would be a more efficient manner to reduce the tax burden.

WEB NOTE

Comparative data on the percentage of goods and services the various national governments provide is available from the Penn World Tables at www.pwt.econ.upenn.edu.

Imperfect Knowledge. One last word of warning before you read further. Economics claims to be a science, in pursuit of basic truths. We want to understand and explain how the economy works without getting tangled up in subjective value judgments. This may be an impossible task. First, it's not clear where the truth lies. For more than 200 years economists have been arguing about what makes the economy tick. None of the competing theories has performed spectacularly well. Indeed, few economists have successfully predicted major economic events with any consistency. Even annual forecasts of inflation, unemployment, and output are regularly in error. Worse still, never-ending arguments about what caused a major economic event continue long after it occurs. In fact, economists are still arguing over the primary causes of the Great Depression of the 1930s!

In part, this enduring controversy reflects diverse sociopolitical views on the appropriate role of government. Some people think a big public sector is undesirable, even if it improves economic performance. But the controversy has even deeper roots. Major gaps in our understanding of the economy persist. We know how much of the economy works, but not all of it. We're adept at identifying all the forces at work, but not always successful in gauging their relative importance. In point of fact, we may *never* find an absolute truth, because the inner workings of the economy change over time. When economic behaviour changes, our theories must be adapted.

In view of all these debates and uncertainties, don't expect to learn everything there is to know about the economy today in this text or course. Our goals are more modest. We want to develop a reasonable perspective on economic behaviour, an understanding of basic principles. With this foundation, you should acquire a better view of how the economy works. Daily news reports on economic events should make more sense. Debates on tax and budget policies should take on more meaning. You may even develop some insights that you can apply toward running a business or planning a career, or—if the Nobel prize-winning economist Gary Becker is right—developing a lasting marriage.

SUMMARY

- Scarcity is a basic fact of economic life. Factors of production (land, labour, capital, and entrepreneurship) are scarce in relation to our desires for goods and services.
- All economic activity entails opportunity costs. Factors of production (resources) used to produce one output cannot simultaneously be used to produce something else. When we choose to produce one thing, we forsake the opportunity to produce some other good or service.
- A production possibilities curve illustrates the limits to production and the opportunity costs associated with different output combinations. It shows the alternative combinations of final goods and services that could be produced in a given period if all available resources and technology are used efficiently.
- The bent shape of the production possibilities curve reflects the law of increasing opportunity costs. This law states that increasing quantities of any good can be obtained only by sacrificing ever-increasing quantities of other goods.
- Inefficient or incomplete use of resources will fail to attain production possibilities. Additional resources or better technologies will expand them. This is the essence of economic growth.
- Every country must decide WHAT to produce, HOW to produce, and FOR WHOM to produce with its limited resources.
- The choices of WHAT, HOW, and FOR WHOM can be made by the market mechanism or by government directives. Most nations are mixed economies, using a combination of these two choice mechanisms.
- Market failure exists when market signals generate suboptimal outcomes. Government failure occurs when government intervention worsens economic outcomes. The challenge for economic theory and policy is to find the mix of market signals and government directives that best fulfills our social and economic goals.
- The study of economics focuses on the broad question of resource allocation. Macroeconomics is concerned with allocating the resources of an entire economy to achieve aggregate economic goals (e.g., full employment). Microeconomics focuses on the behaviour and goals of individual market participants.

Key Terms

economics 4	production possibilities 8	market failure 16
scarcity 5	efficiency 10	government failure 17
factors of production 6	economic growth 12	macroeconomics 18
capital 6	market mechanism 13	microeconomics 18
entrepreneurship 6	laissez faire 14	*ceteris paribus* 19
opportunity cost 7	mixed economy 16	

Questions for Discussion

1. What opportunity costs did you incur in reading this chapter? If you read four more chapters of this book today, would your opportunity cost (per chapter) increase? Explain.
2. How much time could you spend on homework in a day? How much do you spend? How do you decide?
3. What's the real cost of the food in the free lunch cartoon?
4. What economic benefits might India get from privatizing state enterprises (World View, p. 11)?
5. How might a nation's production possibilities be affected by the following?
   a. A decrease in taxes.
   b. An increase in government regulation.
   c. An increase in military spending.
   d. An increase in college tuition.
   e. Faster, more powerful electronic chips.
6. Markets reward individuals according to their output; communism rewards people according to their needs. How might these different systems affect work effort?
7. How does government intervention affect post-secondary admissions? Who would go to college in a completely private (market) post-secondary system?
8. How will the Chinese economy benefit from private property? (See World View, page 18.) Is there any downside to greater entrepreneurial freedom?
9. How many resources should we allocate to reducing automobile pollution? How will we make this decision?

PROBLEMS   The Student Problem Set to accompany this chapter can be found at the end of the book.

WEB ACTIVITIES   Web Activities to accompany this chapter can be found on the Online Learning Centre at **http://www.mcgrawhill.ca/olc/schiller**.

A P P E N D I X

USING GRAPHS

Economists like to draw graphs. In fact, we didn't even make it through the first chapter without a few graphs. This appendix looks more closely at the way graphs are drawn and used. The basic purpose of a graph is to illustrate a relationship between two *variables*. Consider, for example, the relationship between grades and studying. In general, we expect that additional hours of study time will lead to higher grades. Hence, we should be able to see a distinct relationship between hours of study time and grade-point average.

Suppose that we actually surveyed all the students taking this course with regard to their study time and grade-point averages. The resulting information can be compiled in a table such as Table 1A.1.

According to the table, students who don't study at all can expect an F in this course. To get a C, the average student apparently spends 8 hours a week studying. All those who study 16 hours a week end up with an A in the course.

These relationships between grades and studying can also be illustrated on a graph. Indeed, the whole purpose of a graph is to summarize numerical relationships.

We begin to construct a graph by drawing horizontal and vertical boundaries, as in Figure 1A.1. These boundaries are called the *axes* of the graph. On the vertical axis (often called the *y*-axis) we measure one of the variables; the other variable is measured on the horizontal axis (the *x*-axis).

In this case, we shall measure the grade-point average on the vertical axis. We start at the *origin* (the intersection of the two axes) and count upward, letting the distance between horizontal lines represent half (0.5) a grade point. Each horizontal line is numbered, up to the maximum grade-point average of 4.0.

TABLE 1A.1
Hypothetical Relationship of Grades to Study Time

Study Time (hours per week)	Grade-Point Average
16	4.0 (A)
14	3.5 (B+)
12	3.0 (B)
10	2.5 (C+)
8	2.0 (C)
6	1.5 (D+)
4	1.0 (D)
2	0.5 (F+)
0	0.0 (F)

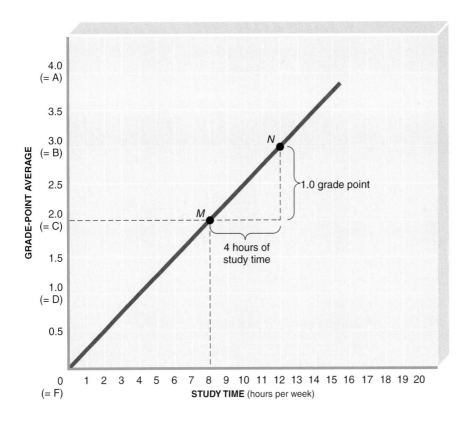

The Relationship of Grades to Study Time

The upward (positive) slope of the curve indicates that additional studying is associated with higher grades. The average student (2.0, or C grade) studies 8 hours per week. This is indicated by point *M* on the graph.

The number of hours each week spent doing homework is measured on the horizontal axis. We begin at the origin again, and count to the right. The *scale* (numbering) proceeds in increments of 1 hour, up to 20 hours per week.

When both axes have been labelled and measured, we can begin illustrating the relationship between study time and grades. Consider the typical student who does eight hours of homework per week and has a 2.0 (C) grade-point average. We illustrate this relationship by first locating eight hours on the horizontal axis. We then move up from that point a distance of 2.0 grade points, to point *M*. Point *M* tells us that eight hours of study time per week is typically associated with a 2.0 grade-point average.

The rest of the information in Table 1A.1 is drawn (or *plotted*) on the graph the same way. To illustrate the average grade for people who study 12 hours per week, we move upward from the number 12 on the horizontal axis until we reach the height of 3.0 on the vertical axis. At that intersection, we draw another point (point *N*).

Once we've plotted the various points describing the relationship of study time to grades, we may connect them with a line or curve. This line (curve) is our summary. In this case, the line slopes upward to the right—that is, it has a *positive* slope. This slope indicates that more hours of study time are associated with *higher* grades. Were higher grades associated with *less* study time, the curve in Figure 1A.1 would have a *negative* slope (downward from left to right).

Slopes

The upward slope of Figure 1A.1 tells us that higher grades are associated with increased amounts of study time. That same curve also tells us *by how much* grades tend to rise with study time. According to point *M* in Figure 1A.1, the average student studies 8 hours per week and earns a C (2.0 grade-point average). To earn a B (3.0 average), students apparently need to study an average of 12 hours per week (point *N*). Hence an increase of four hours of study time per week is associated with a one-point increase in grade-point average. This relationship between *changes* in study time and *changes* in grade-point average is expressed by the steepness, or *slope,* of the graph.

The slope of any graph is calculated as

$$\text{Slope} = \frac{\text{vertical distance between two points}}{\text{horizontal distance between two points}}$$

In our example, the vertical distance between *M* and *N* represents a change in grade-point average. The horizontal distance between these two points represents the change in study time. Hence the slope of the graph between points *M* and *N* is equal to

$$\text{Slope} = \frac{3.0 \text{ grade} - 2.0 \text{ grade}}{12 \text{ hours} - 8 \text{ hours}} = \frac{1 \text{ grade point}}{4 \text{ hours}}$$

In other words, a four-hour increase in study time (from 8 to 12 hours) is associated with a one-point increase in grade-point average (see Figure 1A.1).

Shifts   The relationship between grades and studying illustrated in Figure 1A.1 isn't inevitable. It's simply a graphical illustration of student experiences, as revealed in our hypothetical survey. The relationship between study time and grades could be quite different.

Suppose that the university decided to raise grading standards, making it more difficult to achieve every grade other than an F. To achieve a C, a student now would need to study 12 hours per week, not just 8 (as in Figure 1A.1). Whereas students could previously expect to get a B by studying 12 hours per week, now they'd have to study 16 hours to get that grade.

Figure 1A.2 illustrates the new grading standards. Notice that the new curve lies to the right of the earlier curve. We say that the curve has *shifted* to reflect a change in the relationship between study time and grades. Point *R* indicates that 12 hours of study time now "produces" a C, not a B (point *N* on the old curve). Students who now study only four hours per week (point *S*) will fail. Under the old grading policy,

FIGURE 1A.2
A Shift

When a relationship between two variables changes, the entire curve *shifts*. In this case a tougher grading policy alters the relationship between study time and grades. To get a C, one must now study 12 hours per week (point *R*), not just 8 hours (point *M*).

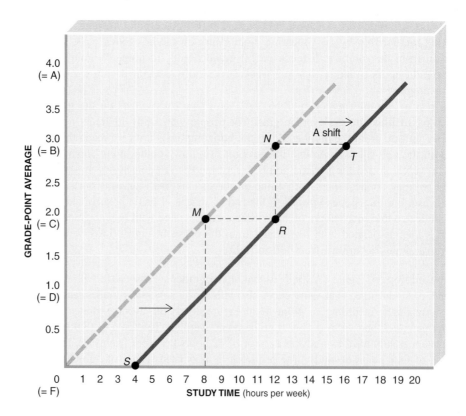

they could have at least gotten a D. ***When a curve shifts, the underlying relationship between the two variables has changed.***

A shift may also change the slope of the curve. In Figure 1A.2, the new grading curve is parallel to the old one; it therefore has the same slope. Under either the new grading policy or the old one, a four-hour increase in study time leads to a one-point increase in grades. Therefore, the slope of both curves in Figure 1A.2 is

$$\text{Slope} = \frac{\text{vertical change}}{\text{horizontal change}} = \frac{1}{4}$$

This too may change, however. Figure 1A.3 illustrates such a possibility. In this case, zero study time still results in an F. But now the payoff for additional studying is reduced. Now it takes six hours of study time to get a D (1.0 grade point), not four hours as before. Likewise, another 4 hours of study time (to a total of 10) raises the grade by only two-thirds of a point. It takes six hours to raise the grade a full point. The slope of the new line is therefore

$$\text{Slope} = \frac{\text{vertical change}}{\text{horizontal change}} = \frac{1}{6}$$

The new curve in Figure 1A.3 has a smaller slope than the original curve and so lies below it. What all this means is that it now takes a greater effort to *improve* your grade.

In Figures 1A.1–1A.3 the relationship between grades and studying is represented by a straight line—that is, a *linear curve.* A distinguishing feature of linear curves is that they have the same (constant) slope throughout. In Figure 1A.1, it appears that *every* four-hour increase in study time is associated with a one-point increase in average grades. In Figure 1A.3, it appears that every six-hour increase in study time leads to a one-point increase in grades. But the relationship between studying and grades may not be linear. Higher grades may be more difficult to attain. You may be able to raise a C to a B by studying four hours more per week. But it may

Linear vs. Nonlinear Curves

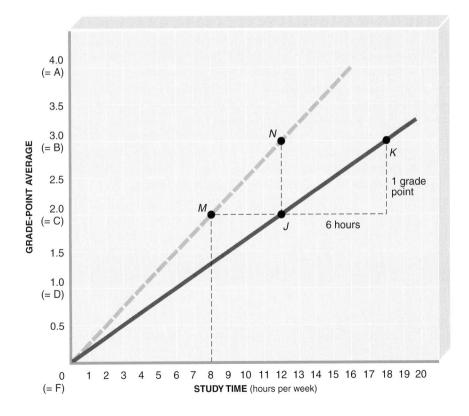

FIGURE 1A.3
A Change in Slope

When a curve shifts, it may change its slope as well. In this case, a new grading policy makes each higher grade more difficult to reach. To raise a C to a B, for example, one must study six additional hours (compare points *J* and *K*). Earlier it took only four hours to move the grade scale up a full point. The slope of the line has declined from 0.25(= 1 ÷ 4) to 0.17(= 1 ÷ 6).

FIGURE 1A.4
A Nonlinear Relationship

Straight lines have a constant slope, implying a constant relationship between the two variables. But the relationship (and slope) may vary. In this case, it takes six extra hours of study to raise a C (point *W*) to a B (point *X*) but eight extra hours to raise a B to an A (point *Y*). The slope decreases as we move up the curve.

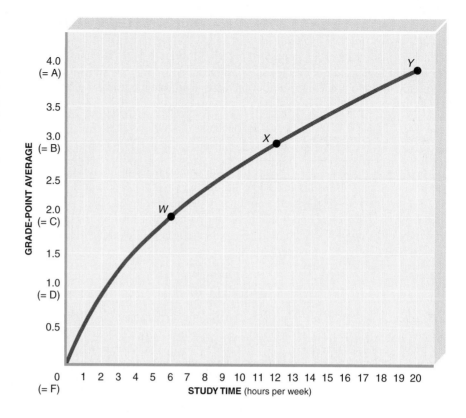

be harder to raise a B to an A. According to Figure 1A.4, it takes an additional eight hours of studying to raise a B to an A. Thus the relationship between study time and grades is *nonlinear* in Figure 1A.4; the slope of the curve changes as study time increases. In this case, the slope decreases as study time increases. Grades continue to improve, but not so fast, as more and more time is devoted to homework. You may know the feeling.

Causation

Figure 1A.4 doesn't by itself guarantee that your grade-point average will rise if you study four more hours per week. In fact, the graph drawn in Figure 1A.4 doesn't prove that additional study ever results in higher grades. The graph is only a summary of empirical observations. It says nothing about cause and effect. It could be that students who study a lot are smarter to begin with. If so, then less-able students might not get higher grades if they studied harder. In other words, the *cause* of higher grades is debatable. At best, the empirical relationship summarized in the graph may be used to support a particular theory (e.g., that it pays to study more). Graphs, like tables, charts, and other statistical media, rarely tell their own story; rather, they must be *interpreted* in terms of some underlying theory or expectation.

CHAPTER 2

Introduction to Supply and Demand

LEARNING OBJECTIVES

By the end of this chapter, you should be able to:

2.1 Identify the categories and goals of market participants

2.2 Understand the circular flow concept dealing with product and factor markets

2.3 Explain and graphically illustrate demand curves

2.4 Identify the determinants of demand

2.5 Explain and graphically illustrate supply curves

2.6 Identify the determinants of supply

2.7 Graphically illustrate effects of changes in demand and/or changes in supply on equilibrium prices and quantities

2.8 Explain how the market mechanism works and resolves the WHAT, HOW, and FOR WHOM questions

The lights went out in California in January 2001. With only minutes of warning, sections of high-tech Silicon Valley, San Francisco, the state capital of Sacramento, and a host of smaller cities went dark. Schools closed early, traffic signals malfunctioned, ATM machines shut down, and elevators abruptly stopped. "It's like we're living in Bosnia," said Michael Mischer, an Oakland, California baker. "How could this happen?"[1]

The California electricity crisis of 2000–2001—where average prices for wholesale electricity skyrocketed from $30 ($US) per megawatt-hour (MWh) in January 2000 to $300 ($US) per MWh in January 2001—occurred shortly after California moved away from regulated market prices toward unregulated market prices. California's Governor, Grey Davis, argued that out-of-state power company "pirates" were gouging Californian residents with exorbitant prices and suggested price controls, state purchase of transmission lines, and customer refunds from "profiteering" power companies. Critics of the governor's explanation suggested that government intervention, not the market, was the cause of the electricity crisis. The decision to let markets dictate wholesale prices, but still retain caps on retail prices ($100 ($US) per MWh) did not provide consumers with the proper incentives to conserve energy when demand increased. In addition, the previous regulated market did not provide adequate incentives for power producers to expand capacity and now, with California enjoying a boom, the sudden increase in demand for electricity could only result in short-term higher prices. They urged the state to rely more on the market than on state legislators to avoid future blackouts.

As the crises continued, it was clear that both sides had valid arguments. The independent agency regulating transmission of wholesale energy prices, the Federal Energy Regulatory Commission (FERC), testified that the ". . . major factors contributing to the electricity crisis in California were insufficient infrastructure, dysfunctional market rules, and inadequate market oversight and enforcement. These and other factors caused wholesale prices for spot power during the crisis to be unjust and unreasonable . . . the Commission Staff found evidence of significant market manipulation in Western energy markets during 2000 and 2001."[2]

[1] Rene Sanchez and William Booth, "California Forced to Turn the Lights Off," *Washington Post*, January 18, 2001, p. 1.
[2] Summary of Testimony of Pat Wood III, Chairman, Federal Energy Regulatory Commission to US House of Representatives, April 8, 2003. (http://www.ferc.gov/press-room/cong-test/2003/04-08-03-wood.pdf)

California's 2000 to 2001 energy crisis is a classic illustration of why the choice between market reliance and government intervention is so critical and often so controversial. Moreover, the U.S. experience can also help guide Canadian provincial policy-makers as both Alberta and Ontario have started the process of deregulation in electricity markets. The goal of this chapter is to examine that choice in a more coherent framework by focusing on how *unregulated* markets work. How does the market mechanism decide WHAT to produce, HOW to produce, and FOR WHOM to produce? Specifically,

- **What determines the price of a good or service?**
- **How does the price of a product affect its production and consumption?**
- **Why do prices and production levels often change?**

Once we've seen how unregulated markets work, in the next chapter, we'll observe how government intervention may alter market outcomes—for better or worse.

2.1 MARKET PARTICIPANTS

Maximizing Behaviour

A good way to start figuring out how markets work is to see who participates in them. The answer is simple: just about every person and institution on the planet. All these market participants come into the marketplace to satisfy specific goals. Consumers, for example, come with a limited amount of income to spend. Their objective is to buy the most desirable goods and services that their limited budgets will permit. We can't afford *everything* we want, so we must make *choices* about how to spend our scarce dollars. Our goal is to *maximize* the utility (satisfaction) we get from our available incomes.

Businesses also try to maximize in the marketplace. In their case, the quest is for maximum *profits*. Business profits are the difference between sales receipts and total costs. To maximize profits, business firms try to use resources efficiently in producing products that consumers desire.

The public sector also has maximizing goals. The economic purpose of government is to use available resources to serve public needs. The resources available for this purpose are limited too. Hence, local, provincial, and federal governments must use scarce resources carefully, striving to maximize the general welfare of society. International consumers and producers pursue these same goals when participating in our markets.

Market participants sometimes lose sight of their respective goals. Consumers sometimes buy impulsively and later wish they'd used their income more wisely. Likewise, a producer may take a two-hour lunch, even at the sacrifice of maximum profits. And elected officials sometimes put their personal interests ahead of the public's interest. In all sectors of the economy, however, ***the basic goals of utility maximization, profit maximization, and welfare maximization explain most market activity.***

Specialization and Exchange

The notion that buying and selling goods and services in the market might maximize our well-being originates in two simple observations. First, most of us are incapable of producing everything we desire to consume. Second, even if we *could* produce all our own goods and services, it would still make sense to specialize, producing only one product and trading it for other desired goods and services.

Suppose you were capable of growing your own food, stitching your own clothes, building your own shelter, and even writing your own economics text. Even in this little utopia, it would still make sense to decide how *best* to expend your limited time and energy and to rely on others to fill in the gaps. If you were *most* proficient at growing food, you would be best off spending your time farming. You could then exchange some of your food output for the clothes, shelter, and books you wanted. In the end, you'd be able to consume *more* goods than if you'd tried to make everything yourself.

Our economic interactions with others are thus necessitated by two constraints:

1. Our absolute inability as individuals to produce all the things we need or desire.
2. The limited amount of time, energy, and resources we have for producing those things we could make for ourselves.

Together, these constraints lead us to specialize and interact. Most of the interactions that result take place in the market.

2.2 THE CIRCULAR FLOW

Figure 2.1 summarizes the kinds of interactions that occur among market participants. Note first that the figure identifies four separate groups of participants. Domestically, the rectangle labelled "Consumers" includes all 30 million consumers in Canada. Grouped in the "Business firms" box are all the domestic business enterprises that buy and sell goods and services. The third participant, "Governments," includes the many separate agencies of the federal government, as well as provincial and local governments. Figure 2.1 also illustrates the role of global actors.

The easiest way to keep track of all this market activity is to distinguish two basic markets. Figure 2.1 makes this distinction by portraying separate circles for product markets and factor markets. In **factor markets,** factors of production are exchanged. Market participants buy or sell land, labour, or capital that can be used in the production process. When you go looking for work, for example, you're making a factor of production—your labour—available to producers. The producers will hire you—purchase

The Two Markets

factor market: Any place where factors of production (e.g., land, labour, capital) are bought and sold.

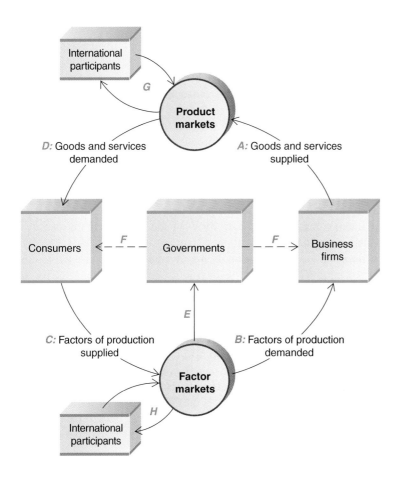

FIGURE 2.1
The Circular Flow

Business firms supply goods and services to product markets (point *A*) and purchase factors of production in factor markets (*B*). Individual consumers supply factors of production such as their own labour (*C*) and purchase final goods and services (*D*). Federal, provincial, and local governments acquire resources in factor markets (*E*) and provide services to both consumers and businesses (*F*). International participants also take part by supplying imports, purchasing exports (*G*), and buying and selling factors of production (*H*).

your services in the factor market—if you're offering the skills they need at a price they're willing to pay. The same kind of interaction occurs in factor markets when the government enlists workers into the armed services or when the Japanese buy pulp and paper mills in British Columbia.

Interactions within factor markets are only half the story. At the end of a hard day's work, consumers go to the grocery store (or to a virtual store online) to buy desired goods and services—that is, to buy *products*. In this context, consumers again interact with business firms, this time purchasing goods and services those firms have produced. These interactions occur in **product markets.** Foreigners also participate in the product market by supplying goods and services (imports) to Canada and buying some of our output (exports).

The government sector also supplies services. (e.g., education, national defence, health service, highways.) In California, Governor Davis even wanted the state to supply electricity to households and businesses. Most government services aren't explicitly sold in product markets, however. Typically, they're delivered "free," without an explicit price (e.g., public elementary schools, highways). This doesn't mean government services are truly free, though. There's still an opportunity cost associated with every service the government provides. Consumers and businesses pay that cost indirectly through taxes rather than directly through market prices.

In Figure 2.1, the arrow connecting product markets to consumers (point *D*) emphasizes the fact that consumers, by definition, don't supply products. When individuals produce goods and services, they do so within the government or business sector. For instance, a doctor, a dentist, or an economic consultant functions in two sectors. When selling services in the market, this person is regarded as a "business"; when away from the office, he or she is regarded as a "consumer." This distinction is helpful in emphasizing that *the consumer is the final recipient of all goods and services produced.*

Locating Markets. Although we refer repeatedly to two kinds of markets in this book, it would be a little foolish to go off in search of the product and factor markets. Neither market is a single, identifiable structure. The term *market* simply refers to a place or situation where an economic exchange occurs—where a buyer and seller interact. The exchange may take place on the street, in a taxicab, over the phone, by mail, or in cyberspace. In some cases, the market used may in fact be quite distinguishable, as in the case of a retail store, the Toronto Stock Exchange, or a federal employment office. But whatever it looks like, *a market exists wherever and whenever an exchange takes place.*

Dollars and Exchange

Figure 2.1 provides a useful summary of market activities, but it neglects one critical element of market interactions: dollars. Each arrow in the figure actually has two dimensions. Consider again the arrow linking consumers to product markets: It's drawn in only one direction because consumers, by definition, don't provide goods and services directly to product markets. But they do provide something: dollars. If you want to obtain something from a product market, you must offer to pay for it (typically, with cash, cheque, or credit card). Consumers exchange dollars for goods and services in product markets.

The same kinds of exchange occur in factor markets. When you go to work, you exchange a factor of production (your labour) for income, typically a paycheque. Here again, the path connecting consumers to factor markets really goes in two directions: one of real resources, the other of dollars. Consumers receive wages, rent, and interest for the labour, land, and capital they bring to the factor markets. Indeed, nearly *every market transaction involves an exchange of dollars for goods (in product markets) or resources (in factor markets).* Money is thus critical in facilitating market exchanges and the specialization the exchanges permit.

product market: Any place where finished goods and services (products) are bought and sold.

In every market transaction there must be a buyer and a seller. The seller is on the **supply** side of the market; the buyer is on the **demand** side. As noted earlier, we *supply* resources to the market when we look for a job—that is, when we offer our labour in exchange for income. We *demand* goods when we shop in a supermarket—that is, when we're prepared to offer dollars in exchange for something to eat. Business firms may *supply* goods and services in product markets at the same time they're *demanding* factors of production in factor markets. Whether one is on the supply side or the demand side of any particular market transaction depends on the nature of the exchange, not on the people or institutions involved.

2.3 DEMAND

To get a sense of how the demand side of market transactions work, we'll focus first on a single consumer. Then we'll aggregate to illustrate *market* demand.

We can begin to understand how market forces work by looking more closely at the behaviour of a single market participant. Let us start with Tom, who is in his fourth year at Maritime University. Tom has majored in everything from art history to government in his three years at Maritime University. He didn't connect to any of those fields and is on the brink of academic dismissal. To make matters worse, his parents have threatened to cut him off financially unless he gets serious about his course work. By that, they mean he should enroll in courses that will lead to a job after graduation. Tom thinks he has found the perfect solution: Web design. Everything associated with the Internet pays big bucks. Plus, the girls seem to think Webbies are "cool." Or at least so Tom thinks. And his parents would definitely approve. So Tom has enrolled in Web-design courses.

Unfortunately for Tom, he never developed computer skills. Until he got to Maritime University, he thought mastering Sony's latest alien-attack video game was the pinnacle of electronic wizardry. His parents gave him a Wi-Fi laptop, but he used it only for surfing hot video sites. The concept of using his computer for course work, much less developing some Web content, was completely foreign to him. To compound his problems, Tom didn't have a clue about "streaming," "interfacing," "animation," or the other concepts the Web-design instructor outlined in the first lecture.

Given his circumstances, Tom was desperate to find someone who could tutor him in Web design. But desperation is not enough to secure the services of a Web architect. In a market-based economy, you must also be willing to *pay* for the things you want. Specifically, ***a demand exists only if someone is willing and able to pay for the good***—that is, exchange dollars for a good or service in the marketplace. Is Tom willing and able to *pay* for the Web-design tutoring he so obviously needs?

Let us assume that Tom has some income and is willing to spend some of it to get a tutor. Under these assumptions, we can claim that Tom is a participant in the *market* for Web-design services.

But how much is Tom willing to pay? Surely, Tom is not prepared to exchange *all* his income for help in mastering Web design. After all, Tom could use his income to buy more desirable goods and services. If he spent all his income on a Web tutor, that help would have an extremely high *opportunity cost.* He would be giving up the opportunity to spend that income on other goods and services. He'd pass his Web-design class but have little else. It doesn't sound like a good idea to Tom. Even though Tom says he would be willing to pay *anything* to pass the Web-design course, he probably has lower prices in mind. Indeed, it would be more reasonable to assume that there are *limits* to the amount Tom is willing to pay for any given quantity of Web-design tutoring. These limits will be determined by how much income Tom has to spend and how many other goods and services he must forsake to pay for a tutor.

Tom also knows that his grade in Web design will depend in part on how much tutoring service he buys. He can pass the course with only a few hours of design help. If he wants a better grade, however, the cost is going to escalate quickly.

Supply and Demand

supply: The ability and willingness to sell (produce) specific quantities of a good at alternative prices in a given time period, *ceteris paribus.*

demand: The ability and willingness to buy specific quantities of a good at alternative prices in a given time period, *ceteris paribus.*

Individual Demand

Naturally, Tom wants it all: an A in Web design and a ticket to higher-paying jobs. But here again the distinction between *desire* and *demand* is relevant. He may *desire* to master Web design, but his actual proficiency will depend on how many hours of tutoring he is willing to *pay* for.

We assume, then, that when Tom starts looking for a Web-design tutor he has in mind some sort of **demand schedule,** like that described in Figure 2.2. According to row *A* of this schedule, Tom is willing and able to buy only one hour of tutoring service per semester if he must pay $50 an hour. At such an outrageous price he will learn minimal skills and pass the course. Just the bare minimum is all Tom is willing to buy at that price.

At lower prices, Tom would behave differently. According to Figure 2.2, Tom would purchase more tutoring services if the price per hour were less. At lower prices, he would not have to give up so many other goods and services for each hour of techni-

demand schedule: A table showing the quantities of a good a consumer is willing and able to buy at alternative prices in a given time period, *ceteris paribus.*

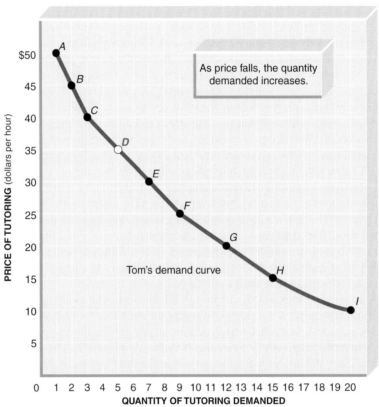

As price falls, the quantity demanded increases.

Tom's demand curve

PRICE OF TUTORING (dollars per hour)

QUANTITY OF TUTORING DEMANDED
(hours per semester)

FIGURE 2.2

A Demand Schedule and Curve

A demand schedule indicates the quantities of a good a consumer is able and willing to buy at alternative prices (*ceteris paribus*). The demand schedule below indicates that Tom would buy five hours of Web tutoring per semester if the price were $35 per hour (row *D*). If Web tutoring were less expensive (rows *E–I*), Tom would purchase a larger quantity.

A demand curve is a graphical illustration of a demand schedule. Each point on the curve refers to a specific quantity that will be demanded at a given price. If, for example, the price of Web tutoring were $35 per hour, this curve tells us the consumer would purchase five hours per semester (point *D*). If Web tutoring cost $30 per hour, seven hours per semester would be demanded (point *E*). Each point on the curve corresponds to a row in the schedule.

	Tom's Demand Schedule	
	Price of Tutoring (per hour)	**Quantity of Tutoring Demanded (hours per semester)**
A	$50	1
B	45	2
C	40	3
D	35	5
E	30	7
F	25	9
G	20	12
H	15	15
I	10	20

cal help. The reduced opportunity costs implied by lower service prices increase the attractiveness of professional help. Indeed, we see from row *I* of the demand schedule that Tom is willing to purchase 20 hours per semester—the whole bag of design tricks—if the price of tutoring is as low as $10 per hour.

Notice that the demand schedule doesn't tell us anything about *why* this consumer is willing to pay specific prices for various amounts of tutoring. Tom's expressed willingness to pay for Web-design tutoring may reflect a desperate need to finish a Web-design course, a lot of income to spend, or a relatively small desire for other goods and services. All the demand schedule tells us is what the consumer is *willing and able* to buy, for whatever reasons.

Also observe that the demand schedule doesn't tell us how many hours of design help the consumer will *actually* buy. Figure 2.2 simply states that Tom is *willing and able* to pay for one hour of tutoring per semester at $50 per hour, for two hours at $45 each, and so on. How much tutoring he purchases will depend on the actual price of such services in the market. Until we know that price, we cannot tell how much service will be purchased. Hence *"demand" is an expression of consumer buying intentions, of a willingness to buy, not a statement of actual purchases.*

A convenient summary of buying intentions is the **demand curve,** a graphical illustration of the demand schedule. The demand curve in Figure 2.2 tells us again that this consumer is willing to pay for only one hour of tutoring per semester if the price is $50 per hour (point *A*), for two if the price is $45 (point *B*), for three at $40 an hour (point *C*), and so on. Once we know what the market price of tutoring actually is, a glance at the demand curve tells us how much service this consumer will buy.

What the notion of *demand* emphasizes is that the amount we buy of a good depends on its price. We seldom, if ever, decide to buy only a certain quantity of a good at whatever price is charged. Instead, we enter markets with a set of desires and a limited amount of money to spend. How much we actually buy of any good will depend on its price.

A common feature of demand curves is their downward slope. As the price of a good falls, people purchase more of it. In Figure 2.2 the quantity of Web-tutorial services demanded increases (moves rightward along the horizontal axis) as the price per hour decreases (moves down the vertical axis). This inverse relationship between price and quantity is so common we refer to it as the **law of demand.**

demand curve: A curve describing the quantities of a good a consumer is willing and able to buy at alternative prices in a given time period, *ceteris paribus.*

law of demand: The quantity of a good demanded in a given time period increases as its price falls, *ceteris paribus.*

Determinants of Demand

The demand curve in Figure 2.2 has only two dimensions—quantity demanded (on the horizontal axis) and price (on the vertical axis). This seems to imply that the amount of tutoring demanded depends only on the price of that service. This is surely not the case. A consumer's willingness and ability to buy a product at various prices depend on a variety of forces. *The determinants of market demand include*

- *Tastes* (desire for this and other goods).
- *Income* (of the consumer).
- *Other goods* (their availability and price).
- *Expectations* (for income, prices, tastes).
- *Number of buyers.*

Tom's "taste" for tutoring has nothing to do with taste buds. *Taste* is just another word for desire. In this case Tom's taste for Web-design services is clearly acquired. If he didn't have to pass a Web-design course, he would have no desire for related services, and thus no demand. If he had no income, he couldn't *demand* any Web-design tutoring either, no matter how much he might *desire* it. If his current income doubled in value, however, Tom would undoubtedly, demand more Web-design tutoring at each and every price (see the Applications box).

Other goods also affect the demand for tutoring services. Their effect depends on whether they're *substitute* goods or *complementary* goods. A **substitute good** is one that might be purchased instead of tutoring services. In Tom's simple world, pizza is a substitute for tutoring. If the price of pizza fell, Tom would use his limited income

substitute goods: Goods that substitute for each other; when the price of good *x* rises, the demand for good *y* increases, *ceteris paribus.*

Millions of Albertans Receive Prosperity Cheques

In 2006, the provincial government of Alberta decided to share the wealth associated with high energy prices by giving a tax-free cheque of $400 to each man, woman, and child residing in the province.

These prosperity cheques, fondly known as "Ralph bucks" in honour of the premier, Ralph Klein, amounted to roughly $1.4 billion dollars of additional spending income into the hands of Albertans. Not surprisingly, there were some innovative attempts on the behalf of suppliers of goods and services to get consumers to part with their newly acquired cheques. Resorts in the Rocky Mountains, for example, offered weekend accommodation for exactly $400, and a popular Scandinavian furniture store also offered packages equal to $400.

While there was considerable public debate on the merits of the prosperity cheques, most Albertans took advantage of the one-time offer and spent the money on goods and services.

Analysis: One of the determinants of demand is income—for most goods and services, an increase in income leads to an increase in demand.

complementary goods: Goods frequently consumed in combination; when the price of good *x* rises, the demand for good *y* falls, *ceteris paribus*.

to buy more pizzas and cut back on his purchases of Web tutoring. When the price of a substitute good falls, the demand for tutoring services declines.

A **complementary good** is one that's typically consumed with, rather than instead of, tutoring. If textbook prices or tuition increases, Tom might take fewer classes and demand *less* Web-design assistance. In this case, a price increase for a complementary good causes the demand for tutoring to decline.

Expectations also play a role in consumer decisions. If Tom expected to flunk his Web-design course anyway, he probably wouldn't waste any money getting tutorial help; his demand for such services would disappear. On the other hand, if he expects a Web tutor to determine his college fate, he might be more willing to buy such services.

Ceteris Paribus

If demand is in fact such a multidimensional decision, how can we reduce it to only the two dimensions of price and quantity? In Chapter 1 we first encountered this *ceteris paribus* trick. To simplify their models of the world, economists focus on only one or two forces at a time and *assume* nothing else changes. We know a consumer's tastes, income, other goods, and expectations all affect the decision to hire a tutor. But we want to focus on the relationship between quantity demanded and price. That is, we want to know what *independent* influence price has on consumption decisions. To find out, we must isolate that one influence, price, and assume that the determinants of demand remain unchanged.

The *ceteris paribus* assumption is not as far-fetched as it may seem. People's tastes, income, and expectations do not change quickly. Also, the prices and availability of other goods don't change all that fast. Hence, a change in the *price* of a product may be the only factor that prompts a change in quantity demanded.

The ability to predict consumer responses to a price change is important. What would happen, for example, to enrollment at your school if tuition doubled? Must we guess? Or can we use demand curves to predict how the quantity of applications will change as the price of college goes up? *Demand curves show us how changes in market prices alter consumer behaviour.* We used the demand curve in Figure 2.2 to predict how Tom's Web-design ability would change at different tutorial prices.

Although demand curves are useful in predicting consumer responses to market signals, they aren't infallible. The problem is that *the determinants of demand can and do change.* When they do, a specific demand curve may become obsolete. A *demand curve (schedule) is valid only so long as the underlying determinants of demand remain constant.* If the *ceteris paribus* assumption is violated—if tastes, income, other goods, or expectations change—the ability or willingness to buy will change.When this happens, the demand curve will **shift** to a new position.

Suppose, for example, that Tom won $1,000 in a lottery. This increase in his income would greatly increase his ability to pay for tutoring services. Figure 2.3 shows the effect of this windfall on Tom's demand. The old demand curve, D_1, is no longer relevant. Tom's lottery winnings enable him to buy more tutoring at any price, as illustrated by the new demand curve, D_2. According to this new curve, lucky Tom is now willing and able to buy 12 hours per semester at the price of $35 per hour (point d_2). This is a large increase in demand; previously (before winning the lottery) he demanded only five hours at that price (point d_1).

Shifts in Demand

> **shift in demand:** A change in the quantity demanded at any (every) given price.

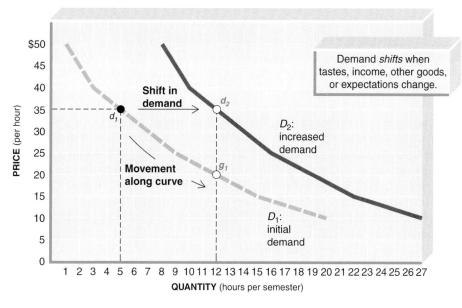

| | Price (per hour) | Quantity Demanded (hours per semester) | |
		Initial Demand	After Increase in Income
A	$50	1	8
B	45	2	9
C	40	3	10
D	35	5	12
E	30	7	14
F	25	9	16
G	20	12	19
H	15	15	22
I	10	20	27

FIGURE 2.3
Shifts vs. Movements

A demand curve shows how a consumer responds to price changes. If the determinants of demand stay constant, the response is a *movement* along the curve to a new quantity demanded. In this case, the quantity demanded increases from 5 (point d_1), to 12 (point g_1), when price falls from $35 to $20 per hour.

If the determinants of demand change, the entire demand curve *shifts*. In this case, an increase in income increases demand. With more income, Tom is willing to buy 12 hours at the initial price of $35 (point d_2), not just the 5 hours he demanded before the lottery win.

With his higher income, Tom can buy more tutoring services at every price. Thus, *the entire demand curve shifts to the right when income goes up.* Figure 2.3 illustrates both the old (prelottery) and the new (postlottery) demand curves.

Income is only one of the basic determinants of demand. Changes in any of the other determinants of demand would also cause the demand curve to shift. Tom's taste for Web tutoring might increase dramatically, for example, if his parents promised to buy him a new car for passing Web design. In that case, he might be willing to forgo other goods and spend more of his income on tutors. *An increase in taste (desire) also shifts the demand curve to the right.*

Movements vs. Shifts

It's important to distinguish shifts of the demand curve from movements along the demand curve. *Movements along a demand curve are a response to price changes for that good.* Such movements assume that determinants of demand are unchanged. By contrast, *shifts of the demand curve occur when the determinants of demand change.* When tastes, income, other goods, or expectations are altered, the basic relationship between price and quantity demanded is changed (shifts).

For convenience, movements along a demand curve and shifts of the demand curve have their own labels. Specifically, take care to distinguish

- *Changes in quantity demanded:* movements along a given demand curve, in response to price changes of that good.
- *Changes in demand:* shifts of the demand curve due to changes in tastes, income, other goods, or expectations.

Tom's behaviour in the Web-tutoring market will change if either the price of tutoring changes (a movement) or the underlying determinants of his demand are altered (a shift). Notice in Figure 2.3 that he ends up buying 12 hours of Web tutoring if either the price of tutoring falls or his income increases. Demand curves help us predict those market responses.

Market Demand

market demand: The total quantities of a good or service people are willing and able to buy at alternative prices in a given time period; the sum of individual demands.

Whatever we say about demand for Web-design tutoring on the part of one wannabe Web master, we can also say about every student at Maritime University (or, for that matter, about all consumers). Some students have no interest in Web design and aren't willing to pay for related services: They don't participate in the Web-tutoring market. Other students want such services but don't have enough income to pay for them: They too are excluded from the Web-tutoring market. A large number of students, however, not only have a need (or desire) for Web tutoring but also are willing and able to purchase such services.

What we start with in product markets, then, is many individual demand curves. Fortunately, it's possible to combine all the individual demand curves into a single **market demand.** The aggregation process is no more difficult than simple arithmetic. Suppose you would be willing to buy one hour of tutoring per semester at a price of $80 per hour. George, who is also desperate to learn Web design, would buy two at that price; and I would buy none, since my publisher (McGraw-Hill) creates a Web page for me (try www.mcgrawhill.ca/olc/schiller). What would our combined (market) demand for hours of tutoring be at that price? Clearly, our individual inclinations indicate that we would be willing to buy a total of three hours of tutoring per semester if the price were $80 per hour. Our combined willingness to buy—our collective market demand— is nothing more than the sum of our individual demands. The same kind of aggregation can be performed for all consumers, leading to a summary of the total market demand for a specific good or service. This *market demand is determined by the number of potential buyers and their respective tastes, incomes, other goods, and expectations.*

The Market Demand Curve

Figure 2.4 provides the basic market demand schedule for a situation in which only three consumers participate in the market. It illustrates the same market situation with demand curves. The three individuals who participate in the market demand for

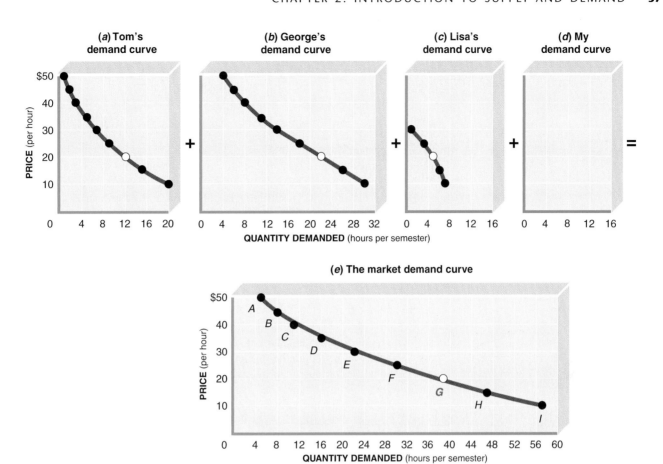

FIGURE 2.4
Construction of the Market Demand Curve

Market demand represents the combined demands of all market participants. To determine the total quantity of Web tutoring demanded at any given price, we add the separate demands of the individual consumers. Row *G* of this schedule indicates that a *total* quantity of 39 hours per semester will be demanded at a price of $20 per hour. This same conclusion is reached by adding the individual demand curves, leading to point *G* on the market demand curve (see above).

	Price (per hour)	Tom	+	George	+	Lisa	+	Me	=	Market Demand
A	$50	1		4		0		0		5
B	45	2		6		0		0		8
C	40	3		8		0		0		11
D	35	5		11		0		0		16
E	30	7		14		1		0		22
F	25	9		18		3		0		30
G	20	12		22		5		0		39
H	15	15		26		6		0		47
I	10	20		30		7		0		57

Quantity of Tutoring Demanded (hours per semester)

Web tutoring at Maritime University obviously differ greatly, as suggested by their respective demand schedules. Tom *has* to pass his Web-design classes or confront college and parental rejection. He also has a nice allowance (income), so can afford to buy a lot of tutorial help. His demand schedule is portrayed in the first column of the table (and is identical to the one we examined in Figure 2.2). George is also desperate to acquire some job skills and is willing to pay relatively high prices for Web-design tutoring. His demand is summarized in the second column under Quantity of tutoring Demanded in the table.

The third consumer in this market is Lisa. Lisa already knows the nuts and bolts of Web design, so she isn't so desperate for tutorial services. She would like to upgrade her skills, however, especially in animation and e-commerce applications. But her limited budget precludes paying a lot for help. She will buy some technical support only if the price falls to $30 per hour. Should tutors cost less, she'd even buy quite a few hours of Web-design services. Finally, there is my demand schedule (column 4 under Quantity of tutoring Demanded), which confirms that I really don't participate in the Web-tutoring market.

The differing personalities and consumption habits of Tom, George, Lisa, and me are expressed in our individual demand schedules and associated curves in Figure 2.4. To determine the *market* demand for tutoring from this information, we simply add these four separate demands. The end result of this aggregation is, first, a *market* demand schedule and, second, the resultant *market* demand curve. These market summaries describe the various quantities of tutoring that Maritime University students are *willing and able* to purchase each semester at various prices.

How much Web tutoring will be purchased each semester? Knowing how much help Tom, George, Lisa, and I are willing to buy at various prices doesn't tell you how much we're actually going to purchase. To determine the actual consumption of Web tutoring, we have to know something about prices and supplies. Which of the many different prices illustrated in Figures 2.3 and 2.4 will actually prevail? How will that price be determined?

2.4 SUPPLY

market supply: The total quantities of a good that sellers are willing and able to sell at alternative prices in a given time period, *ceteris paribus.*

To understand how the price of Web tutoring is established, we must also look at the other side of the market: the supply side. We need to know how many hours of tutoring services people are willing and able to *sell* at various prices, that is, the **market supply.** As on the demand side, the *market supply* depends on the behaviour of all the individuals willing and able to supply Web tutoring at some price.

Determinants of Supply

Let's return to the Maritime University campus for a moment. What we need to know now is how much tutorial Web service people are willing and able to provide. Generally speaking, Web-page design can be fun, but it can also be drudge work, especially when you're doing it for someone else. Software programs like PhotoShop, Flash, and Fireworks have made Web-page design easier and more creative. And Wi-Fi laptops have made Web tutoring more convenient. But teaching someone else to design Web pages is still work. So few people offer to supply tutoring services just for the fun of it. Web designers do it for money. Specifically, they do it to earn income that they, in turn, can spend on goods and services they desire.

How much income must be offered to induce Web designers to do a job depends on a variety of things. The ***determinants of market supply include***

* ***Technology***
* ***Factor costs***
* ***Prices of other goods***
* ***Taxes and subsidies***
* ***Expectations***
* ***Number of sellers***

The technology of Web design, for example, is always getting easier and more creative. With a program like PageOut, for example, it's very easy to create a bread-and-butter Web page. A continuous stream of new software programs (e.g., Fireworks,

DreamWeaver) keeps stretching the possibilities for graphics, animation, interactivity, and content. These technological advances mean that Web-design services can be supplied more quickly and cheaply. They also make *teaching* Web design easier. As a result, they induce people to supply more tutoring services at every price.

How much Web-design service is offered at any given price also depends on the cost of factors of production. If the software programs needed to create Web pages are cheap (or, better yet, free), Web designers can afford to charge lower prices. If the required software inputs are expensive, however, they will have to charge more money per hour for their services.

Prices of other goods can also affect the willingness to supply Web-design services. If you can make more income waiting tables than you can tutoring lazy students, why would you even boot up the computer? As the prices paid for other goods and services change, they will influence people's decision about whether to offer Web services.

In the real world, the decision to supply goods and services is also influenced by government tax and subsidy policies. Federal, provincial, and local governments impose taxes on income earned in the marketplace. When tax rates are high, people get to keep less of the income they earn. Once taxes start biting into paycheques, some people may conclude that tutoring is no longer worth the hassle and withdraw from the market. Conversely, if governments subsidize certain productive activities, this lowers the costs of production and existing firms have an incentive to produce more at any given price. In addition, subsidies tend to attract new suppliers, since the opportunity costs of allocating resources into the industry are now lower.

Expectations are also important on the supply side of the market. If Web designers expect higher prices, lower costs, or reduced taxes, they may be more willing to learn new software programs. On the other hand, if they have poor expectations about the future, they may just sell their computers and find something else to do.

Finally, we note that the number of available tutors will affect the quantity of service offered for sale at various prices. If there are lots of willing tutors on campus, a large quantity of tutorial service will be available.

All these considerations—factor costs, technology, expectations—affect the decision to offer Web services and at what price. In general, we assume that Web architects will be willing to provide more tutoring if the per-hour price is high and less if the price is low. In other words, there is a **law of supply** that parallels the law of demand. On the supply side the law says that *larger quantities will be offered for sale at higher prices.* Here again, the laws rest on the *ceteris paribus* assumption: The quantity supplied increases at higher prices *if* the determinants of supply are constant. ***Supply curves are upward-sloping to the right,*** as in Figure 2.5. Note how the *quantity supplied* jumps from 39 hours (point *d*) to 130 hours (point *h*) when the price of Web service doubles (from $20 to $40 per hour).

Figure 2.5 also illustrates how market supply is constructed from the supply decisions of individual sellers. In this case, only three Web masters are available. Ann is willing to provide a lot of tutoring at low prices, whereas Bob requires at least $20 an hour. Cory won't talk to students for less than $40 an hour.

By adding the quantity each Webhead is willing to offer at every price, we can construct the market supply curve. Notice in Figure 2.5, for example, how the quantity supplied to the market at $45 (point *i*) comes from the individual efforts of Ann (93 hours), Bob (33 hours), and Cory (14 hours). ***The market supply curve is just a summary of the supply intentions of all producers.***

None of the points on the market supply curve (Figure 2.5) tells us how much Web tutoring is actually being sold on the Maritime University campus. ***Market supply is an expression of sellers' intentions—an offer to sell—not a statement of actual sales.*** My next door neighbour may be willing to sell his 1994 Honda Civic for $8,000, but most likely he'll never find a buyer at that price. Nevertheless, his *willingness* to sell his car at that price is part of the *market supply* of used cars.

WEB NOTE

Sellers of books and cars post asking prices for their products on the Internet. With the help of search engines such as autoweb.com and www.bookfinder.com, consumers can locate the seller who's offering the lowest price. By examining a lot of offers, you could also construct a supply curve showing how the quantity supplied increases at higher prices.

law of supply: The quantity of a good supplied in a given time period increases as its price increases, *ceteris paribus.*

Market Supply

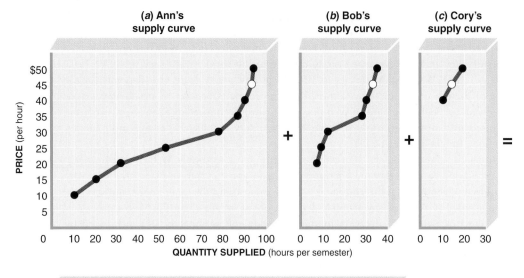

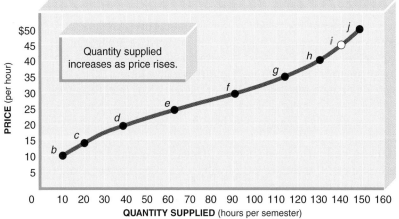

FIGURE 2.5
Market Supply

The market supply curve indicates the *combined* sales intentions of all market participants. If the price of tutoring were $45 per hour (point *i*), the *total* quantity of services supplied would be 140 hours per semester. This quantity is determined by adding the supply decisions of all individual producers. In this case, Ann supplies 93 hours, Bob supplies 33, and Cory supplies the rest.

	Price (per hour)	Quantity of Tutoring Supplied by				
		Ann	+ Bob	+ Cory	=	Market
j	$50	94	35	19		148
i	45	93	33	14		140
h	40	90	30	10		130
g	35	86	28	0		114
f	30	78	12	0		90
e	25	53	9	0		62
d	20	32	7	0		39
c	15	20	0	0		20
b	10	10	0	0		10

Shifts of Supply

As with demand, there's nothing sacred about any given set of supply intentions. Supply curves *shift* when the underlying determinants of supply change. Thus, we again distinguish

*   *Changes in quantity supplied:* movements along a given supply curve.
*   *Changes in supply:* shifts of the supply curve.

Our Latin friend *ceteris paribus* is once again the decisive factor. If the price of a product is the only variable changing, then we can **track changes in quantity supplied**

APPLICATIONS

Wheat Prices Increase as Disaster Hits Prairies

In their annual crop season report, Alberta's Department of Agriculture, Food and Rural Development wrote "The 2002 crop season will be remembered as one of the worst in Alberta's farming history. The season was full of challenges for producers from beginning to end. Major challenges included a cool and dry spring, persistent dryness in much of Alberta, flooding in the Southern Region in June, heat in July, cool and wet conditions in August, early frosts, damp, cool weather conditions during the harvest season and severe insect problems."

The unique weather patterns and insect challenges of 2002, combined with a prolonged drought in the prairies, reduced the overall production of wheat in Alberta to 3.5 million (metric) tonnes, down from 5.8 million tonnes in 2001 and 8.2 million tonnes in 1999. Over this time period, September prices increased from $137/(metric) tonne in 1999 to $170/tonne in 2001 and $204 in 2002. As the graph indicates, for a relatively constant market demand, this considerable reduction in the supply of wheat (leftward shift) substantially increased prices.

Sources: "Wheat Prices Increase as Disaster Hits Prairies," Ministry of Agriculture, Food and Rural Development, Government of Alberta, "Alberta 2002 Crop Season in Review with Feed and Harvest Summary Report" (http://www.agric.gov.ab.ca/economic/stats.crpsum02.html. Reproduced with the permission of the Minister of Public Works and Government Services Canada, 2007.); and Statistics Canada: Farm Product Prices, Crops and Livestock—Table 002–0043.

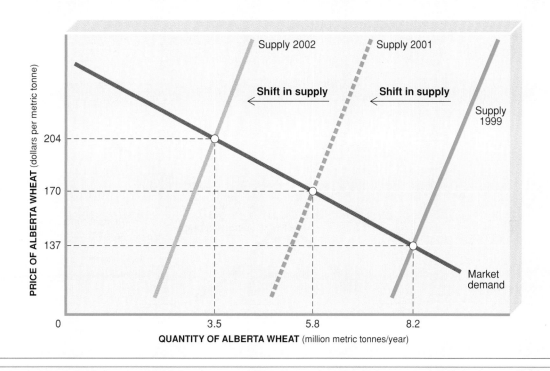

Analysis: When factor costs or availability worsen, the supply curve shifts to the left. Such leftward supply-curve shifts push prices up the market demand curve.

along the supply curve. But if *ceteris paribus* is violated—if technology, factor costs, the profitability of producing other goods, tax rates, expectations, or the number of sellers change—then *changes in supply are illustrated by shifts of the supply curve.*

The Applications box above illustrates how a supply shift sent wheat prices soaring in 2002. When poor weather and insect problems reduced harvests, the wheat supply curve shifted leftward and prices increased substantially.

2.5 EQUILIBRIUM

The abrupt spike in wheat prices offers some clues as to how the forces of supply and demand set, and change, market prices. To get a more detailed sense of how those forces work, we'll return to the mythical Maritime University Web tutoring market for a moment. How did supply and demand resolve the WHAT, HOW, and FOR WHOM questions in that market?

Figure 2.6 helps answer that question by bringing together the market supply and demand curves we've already examined (Figures 2.4 and 2.5). When we put the two curves together, we see that *only one price and quantity are compatible with the existing intentions of both buyers and sellers.* This equilibrium occurs at the intersection of the two curves in Figure 2.6. Once it's established, Web tutoring will cost $20 per hour. At that **equilibrium price,** campus Webheads will sell a total of 39 hours of tutoring per semester—the same amount that students wish to buy at that price. Those 39 hours of tutoring service will be part of WHAT is produced.

> **equilibrium price:** The price at which the quantity of a good demanded in a given time period equals the quantity supplied.

Market Clearing

An equilibrium doesn't imply that everyone is happy with the prevailing price or quantity. Notice in Figure 2.6, for example, that some students who want to buy Web-design assistance services don't get any. These would-be buyers are arrayed along the demand curve *below* the equilibrium. Because the price they're *willing* to pay is less than the

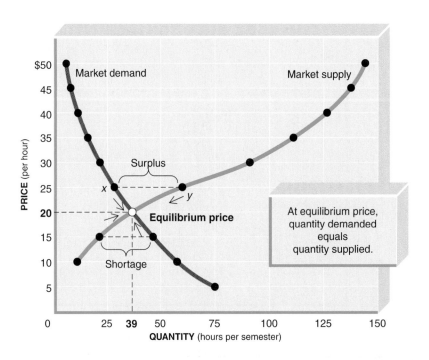

FIGURE 2.6
Equilibrium Price

Only at equilibrium is the quantity demanded equal to the quantity supplied. In this case, the equilibrium price is $20 per hour, and 39 hours is the equilibrium quantity. At higher prices, a market surplus exists—the quantity supplied exceeds the quantity demanded. At prices below equilibrium, a market shortage exists.

The intersection of the demand and supply curves in the graph represents equilibrium price and output in this market.

Price (per hour)	Quantity Supplied (hours per semester)		Quantity Demanded (hours per semester)
$50	148		5
45	140		8
40	130	market	11
35	114	surplus	16
30	90		22
25	62		30
20	39	equilibrium	39
15	20	market	47
10	10	shortage	57

equilibrium price, they don't get any Web-design help. The market's FOR WHOM answer includes only those students willing and able to pay the equilibrium price.

Likewise, some would-be sellers in the market don't sell as much service as they might like. These people are arrayed along the supply curve *above* the equilibrium. Because they insist on being paid a price higher than the equilibrium price, they don't actually sell anything.

Although not everyone gets full satisfaction from the market equilibrium, that unique outcome is efficient. The equilibrium price and quantity reflect a compromise between buyers and sellers. No other compromise yields a quantity demanded that's exactly equal to the quantity supplied.

The Invisible Hand. The equilibrium price isn't determined by any single individual. Rather, it's determined by the collective behaviour of many buyers and sellers, each acting out his or her own demand or supply schedule. It's this kind of impersonal price determination that gave rise to Adam Smith's characterization of the market mechanism as "the invisible hand." In attempting to explain how the *market mechanism* works, the famed eighteenth-century economist noted a certain feature of market prices. The market behaves as if some unseen force (the invisible hand) were examining each individual's supply or demand schedule and then selecting a price that assured an equilibrium. In practice, the process of price determination isn't so mysterious: It's a simple process of trial and error.

An Initial Surplus. To appreciate the power of the market mechanism, consider what occurs if the price of Web-design assistance services differs from the equilibrium price. Suppose, for example, that campus Webheads band together and agree to charge a price of $25 per hour. Figure 2.6 illustrates the consequences of this *dis*equilibrium pricing. At $25 per hour, campus Webheads would be offering more tutoring services (point *y*) than Tom, George, and Lisa were willing to buy (point *x*) at that price. A **market surplus** of Web services would exist in the sense that more tutoring was being offered for sale (supplied) than students cared to purchase at the available price.

As Figure 2.6 indicates, at a price of $25 per hour, a market surplus of 32 hours per semester exists. Under these circumstances, campus Webheads would be spending many idle hours at their keyboards waiting for customers to appear. Their waiting will be in vain because the quantity of Web tutoring demanded will not increase until the price of tutoring falls. That is the clear message of the demand curve. As would-be tutors get this message, they'll reduce their prices. This is the response the market mechanism signals.

As sellers' asking prices decline, the quantity demanded will increase. This concept is illustrated in Figure 2.6 by the movement along the demand curve from point *x* to lower prices and greater quantity demanded. As we move down the market demand curve, the *desire* for Web-design help doesn't change, but the quantity people are *able and willing to buy* increases. When the price falls to $20 per hour, the quantity demanded will finally equal the quantity supplied. This is the *equilibrium* illustrated in Figure 2.6.

An Initial Shortage. A very different sequence of events would occur if a market shortage existed. Suppose someone were to spread the word that Web-tutoring services were available at only $15 per hour. Tom, George, and Lisa would be standing in line to get tutorial help, but campus Web designers wouldn't be willing to supply the quantity desired at that price. As Figure 2.6 confirms, at $15 per hour, the quantity demanded (47 hours per semester) would greatly exceed the quantity supplied (20 hours per semester). In this situation, we may speak of a **market shortage,** that is, an excess of quantity demanded over quantity supplied. At a price of $15 an hour, the shortage amounts to 27 hours of tutoring services.

Surplus and Shortage

market surplus: The amount by which the quantity supplied exceeds the quantity demanded at a given price; excess supply.

market shortage: The amount by which the quantity demanded exceeds the quantity supplied at a given price; excess demand.

APPLICATIONS

Boxing Day Madness

Toronto (CP)—Millions of bargain-hunters across Canada were out in full force Monday on one of the biggest shopping days of the year looking for Boxing Day deals.

A Future Shop on Montreal's busy Ste. Catherine Street hired extra security and erected metal barricades to maintain control of about 1,500 people who lined up well around a

city block. Extra police cars were also parked along the street. "It's a bit nuts," said Barry McGarr, 23, one of the store's employees who was trying to ensure people stayed in line. "They start pushing each other. I've seen someone fall and people just walking over them just to save a few bucks. I find it's madness."

In Alberta, thousands of shoppers jammed West Edmonton Mall. Many of the stores had security guards posted at the doors to prevent too many people from entering at one time. Cathy Williams said she and her daughter circled the mall in their car for more than half an hour searching for a parking space. In desperation, they convinced a man on his way out to allow them to follow him as he walked to his vehicle so they could take his spot. "It's warfare; you have to do that," Williams explained.

In Vancouver, massive lineups formed outside most of the upscale clothing stores on the city's downtown trendy Robson Street. Some of the queues, like the ones outside designer shops Salvatore Ferragamo and Armani, had three or four dozen people waiting for them to open. "Some of these clothes are 70 percent off," said Lina Sun, 20, an English student.

Source: Tara Brautigam, "Boxing Day Madness," December 26, 2005. Used with permission of The Canadian Press.

Analysis: When prices fall below equilibrium, the quantity demanded exceeds the quantity supplied. For this shortage, initial allocation of these goods goes to those people willing and able to stand in line.

When a market shortage exists, not all consumer demands can be satisfied. Some people who are *willing* to buy Web help at the going price ($15) won't be able to do so. To assure themselves of sufficient help, Tom, George, Lisa, or some other consumer may offer to pay a *higher* price, thus initiating a move up the demand curve in Figure 2.6. The higher prices offered will in turn induce other enterprising Web-heads to tutor more, thus ensuring an upward movement along the market supply curve. Thus, a higher price tends to evoke a greater quantity supplied, as reflected in the upward-sloping supply curve. Notice, again, that the *desire* to tutor Web design hasn't changed; only the quantity supplied has responded to a change in price.

Self-Adjusting Prices. What we observe, then, is that *whenever the market price is set above or below the equilibrium price, either a market surplus or a market shortage will emerge.* To overcome a surplus or shortage, buyers and sellers will change their behaviour. Webheads will have to compete for customers by reducing prices when a market surplus exists. If a shortage exists, buyers will compete for service by offering to pay higher prices. Only at the *equilibrium* price will no further adjustments be required.

Sometimes the market price is slow to adjust, and a disequilibrium persists. This is often the case with tickets to rock concerts, football games, and other one-time events (see the Applications box). People initially adjust their behaviour by standing in ticket lines for hours, hoping to buy a ticket at the below-equilibrium price. The tickets are typically resold ("scalped"), however, at prices closer to equilibrium.

Business firms can discover equilibrium prices by trial and error. If they find that consumer purchases aren't keeping up with production, they may conclude that their price is above the equilibrium price. They'll have to get rid of their accumulated inventory. To do so they'll have to lower their price (by a Grand End-of-Year Sale, perhaps). In the happy situation where consumer purchases are outpacing production, a firm might conclude that its price was a trifle too low and give it a nudge upward. In any case, the equilibrium price can be established after a few trials in the marketplace.

No equilibrium price is permanent. The equilibrium price established in the Maritime University tutoring market, for example, was the unique outcome of specific demand and supply schedules. Those schedules themselves were based on our assumption of *ceteris paribus*. We assumed that the "taste" (desire) for Web-design assistance was given, as were consumers' incomes, the price and availability of other goods, and expectations. Any of these determinants of demand could change. When one does, the demand curve has to be redrawn. Such a shift of the demand curve will lead to a new equilibrium price and quantity. Indeed, *the equilibrium price will change whenever the supply or demand curve shifts.*

Changes in Equilibrium

A Demand Shift. We can illustrate how equilibrium prices change by taking another look at the Maritime University tutoring market. Our original supply and demand curves, together with the resulting equilibrium (point E_1), are depicted in Figure 2.7. Now suppose that all the professors at Maritime University begin requiring class-specific Web pages from each student. The increased need (desire) for Web-design ability will affect market demand. Tom, George, and Lisa are suddenly willing to buy more Web tutoring at every price than they were before. That is, the *demand* for Web services has increased. We can represent this increased demand by a rightward *shift* of the market demand curve, as illustrated in Figure 2.7*a*.

Note that the new demand curve intersects the (unchanged) market supply curve at a new price (point E_2), the equilibrium price is now $30 per hour. This new equilibrium price will persist until either the demand curve or the supply curve shifts again.

A Supply Shift. Figure 2.7*b* illustrates a *supply* shift. The decrease (leftward shift) in supply might occur if some on-campus Webheads got sick. Or approaching exams might convince would-be tutors that they have no time to spare. ***Whenever supply decreases (shifts left), price tends to rise,*** as in Figure 2.7*b*.

Market outcomes shifted even more dramatically after eastern Canada's "ice storm of the century" in January 1998. The prolonged freezing rain downed telephone cables and power lines through the area and hundreds of thousands of people were without electricity for up to three weeks. Environmental catastrophes of this magnitude can have serious economic consequences. The demand for generators, for example, increased significantly. As the graphical analysis in the Applications box on page 48 indicates, the initial increase in demand gave rise to shortages and eventually the equilibrium price for generators increased.

The World View on page 49 shows how rapid price adjustments can alleviate market shortages and surpluses. In this unusual case, a restaurant continuously adjusts its prices to ensure that everything on the menu is ordered.

Simultaneous Shifts. Up to now, we have discussed how *single* shifts in either the demand or the supply curve can influence equilibrium prices and quantities. But what happens if we observe *simultaneous* shifts? That is, what would happen if both the demand curve and the supply curve changed over the time period under consideration? We can use our knowledge about how single shifts affect equilibrium to derive an answer, but as we shall see, there are *three possible outcomes* for each combination of simultaneous shifts. In the final analysis, the important factor is the relative magnitudes of the shifts.

FIGURE 2.7

Changes in Equilibrium

If demand or supply change (shift), market equilibrium will change as well.

Demand shift. In (*a*), the rightward shift of the demand curve illustrates an increase in demand. When demand increases, the equilibrium price rises (from E_1 to E_2).

Supply shift. In (*b*), the leftward shift of the supply curve illustrates a decrease in supply. This raises the equilibrium price to E_3.

Demand and supply curves shift only when their underlying determinants change, that is, when *ceteris paribus* is violated.

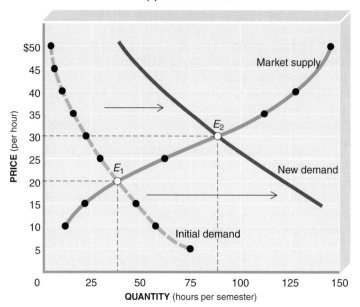

(*a*) A demand shift

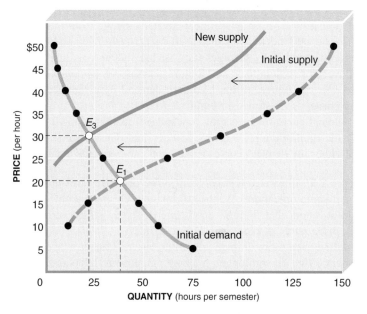

(*b*) A supply shift

In Figure 2.7, we illustrated how equilibrium prices and quantities in Web-tutoring services were affected individually by (a) an increase in demand and (b) a decrease in supply. Now, suppose that over the semester we observed both of these shifts simultaneously. Figure 2.8 illustrates the three potential new equilibrium outcomes. In panel (*a*), we see that the increase in demand is quite large while the decrease in supply is relatively small. Combined, both the new equilibrium price and quantity of Web-tutoring hours has increased. In panel (*b*), however, the increase in demand is relatively small while the decrease in supply is quite large. This combination leads to a higher equilibrium price, but a lower equilibrium in the quantity of Web-tutoring hours. Finally, in panel (*c*), we see that, once again, the equilibrium price has increased. But in this case, the equilibrium quantity of Web-tutoring hours has not changed from its original position.

In each of the three cases, we see that the equilibrium price has increased. What is different, however, is the equilibrium quantity; it can increase, decrease, or remain

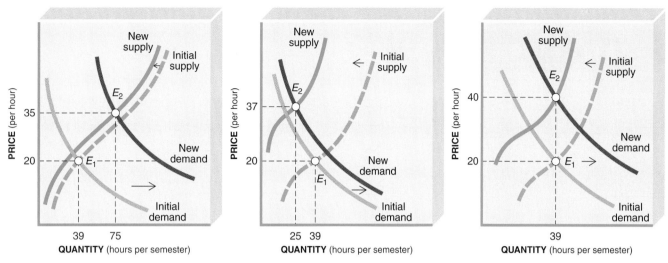

FIGURE 2.8
Simultaneous Shifts and Changes in Equilibrium

Whenever demand and supply curves shift simultaneously, there are three possible outcomes. The actual outcome depends on the relative magnitudes of the shifts. One equilibrium variable (either price or quantity) will move in one direction while the other is

indeterminate—that is, it may increase, decrease, or remain constant. In this example, where demand for Web-tutoring services increases and the supply decreases, we see that the equilibrium price always increases, but the equilibrium quantity is indeterminate.

constant. The magnitude of the demand shift relative to the supply shift determines which of these three cases prevails.

This case captures the basics of simultaneous shifts.[3] Whenever we encounter simultaneous shifts in demand and supply curves, one of the equilibrium variables (either price or quantity) will definitely move in one direction whereas the other variable is indeterminate—it may increase, decrease or remain constant.

2.6 MARKET OUTCOMES

Notice how the market mechanism resolves the basic economic questions of WHAT, HOW, and FOR WHOM.

WHAT

The WHAT question refers to the amount of Web tutorial services to include in society's mix of output. The answer at Maritime University was 39 hours of tutoring per semester. This decision wasn't reached in a referendum, but instead in the market equilibrium (Figure 2.6). In the same way but on a larger scale, millions of consumers and a handful of auto producers decide to include 2.6 million or so cars and trucks in each year's mix of output. Auto prices and quantities adjust until consumers buy the same quantity that auto manufacturers produce.

HOW

The market mechanism also determines HOW goods are produced. Profit-seeking producers will strive to produce Web designs and automobiles in the most efficient way. They'll use market prices to decide not only WHAT to produce but also what resources to use in the production process. If new software simplifies Web design—and is priced low enough—Webheads will use it. Likewise, auto manufacturers will use robots rather than humans on the assembly line if robots reduce costs and increase profits.

FOR WHOM

Finally, the invisible hand of the market will determine who gets the goods produced. At Maritime University, who got Web tutoring? Only those students who were willing and able to pay $20 per hour for that service. FOR WHOM are all those automobiles

---

[3]Note that there are four possible simultaneous shift examples: (1) both demand and supply increase, (2) both demand and supply decrease, (3) demand increases and supply decreases, and (4) demand decreases and supply increases. Each of these examples has three possible outcomes—can you illustrate these twelve graphs?

APPLICATIONS

Canada's 1998 Ice Storm

For six days in January 1998, freezing rain and ice pellets fell over a vast area of eastern Ontario, western Quebec, New Brunswick, and Nova Scotia. The weight of the ice—up to 10 cm thick in places—downed utility poles, transmission towers, and hydro wires creating massive power outages for many weeks. The prolonged loss of electricity created a sudden surge in demand for generators. Within days, all businesses selling generators in the affected area had sold out and individuals were driving hundreds of kilometres in search of the nearest available source. For those fortunate enough to find a generator, life became somewhat manageable during this crisis. For those unable to secure a generator, life was challenging during those hectic weeks. For example, Canada's largest aluminum producer, Alcan Aluminum Ltd., had to shut down their Beaurnhois smelting operations for six weeks, since the aluminum metal froze in the pots. It required costly and time-consuming jack hammering to return to normal operations.

Farmers were hit especially hard. Dairy and hog farmers were left without power, frantically sharing generators to run milking machines and to care for new-born piglets. The damage in eastern Ontario and southern Quebec was so severe that major rebuilding, not repairing, of the electrical grid had to be undertaken. What it took human beings a half century to construct took nature a matter of hours to knock down.

Source: Meteorological Services, Environment Canada, "The Worst Storm in Canadian History?" (http://www.msc-smc.ec.gc.ca/media/icestorm98/icestorm98_the_worst_e.cfm).

© CP/Jacques Boissinot

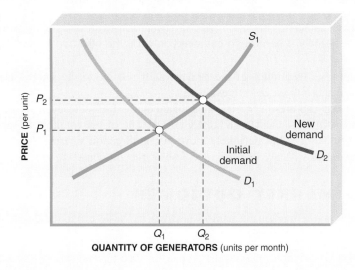

Analysis: When a determinant of demand (e.g., tastes, expectations) changes, the demand curve shifts. When this happens, the equilibrium price will change.

produced each year? The answer is the same: those consumers who are willing and able to pay the market price for a new car.

Optimal, Not Perfect

Not everyone is happy with these answers, of course. Tom would like to pay only $10 an hour for a tutor. And some of the Maritime University students don't have enough income to buy any tutoring. They think it's unfair that they have to design their own Web pages while richer students can have someone else do their design work for them. Students who can't afford cars are even less happy with the market's answer to the FOR WHOM question.

Although the outcomes of the marketplace aren't perfect, they're often optimal. Optimal outcomes are the best possible *given* our incomes and scarce resources. In other words, we expect the choices made in the marketplace to be the best possible choices for each participant. Why do we draw such a conclusion? Because Tom and George and everybody in our little Maritime University drama had (and continue to

WORLD VIEW

Dining on the Downtick

Canadians aren't the only consumers who fall for packaging. Since late January, Parisians (not to mention TV crews from around the world) have been drawn to 6 rue Feydeau to try La Connivence, a restaurant with a new gimmick. The name means "collusion," and yes, of course, La Connivence is a block away from the Bourse, the French stock exchange.

What's the gimmick? Just that the restaurant's prices fluctuate according to supply and demand. The more a dish is ordered, the higher its price. A dish that's ignored gets cheaper.

Customers tune in to the day's menu (couched in trading terms) on computer screens. Among a typical day's options: *forte baisse du haddock* ("precipitous drop in haddock"), *vif recul de la côte de boeuf* ("rapid decline in beef ribs"), *la brochette de lotte au plus bas* ("fish kabob hits bottom"). Then comes the major decision—whether to opt for the price that's listed when you order or to gamble that the price will have gone down by the time you finish your meal.

So far, only main dishes are open to speculation, but co-owners Pierre Guette, an ex-professor at a top French business school, and Jean-Paul Trastour, an ex-journalist at *Le Nouvel Observateur*, are adding wine to the risk list.

La Connivence is open for dinner, but the midday "session" (as the owners call it) is the one to catch. That's when the traders of Paris leave the floor to push their luck *à table*. But here, at least, the return on their $15 investment (the average price of a meal) is immediate—and usually good.

—Christina de Liagre

Analysis: A market surplus signals that price is too high; a market shortage suggests that price is too low. This restaurant adjusts price until the quantity supplied equals the quantity demanded.

have) absolute freedom to make their own purchase and consumption decisions. And also because we assume that sooner or later they'll make the choices they find most satisfying. The results are *optimal* in the sense that everyone has done as well as she or he could, given their income and talents.

SUMMARY

- Individual consumers, business firms, government agencies, and foreigners participate in the marketplace by offering to buy or sell goods and services, or factors of production. Participation is motivated by the desire to maximize utility (consumers), profits (business firms), or the general welfare (government agencies) from the limited resources each participant has.

- All market transactions involve the exchange of either factors of production or finished products. Although the actual exchanges can occur anywhere, they take place in product markets or factor markets, depending on what is being exchanged.

- People willing and able to buy a particular good at some price are part of the market demand for that product. All those willing and able to sell that good at some price are part of the market supply. Total market demand or supply is the sum of individual demands or supplies.

- Supply and demand curves illustrate how the quantity demanded or supplied changes in response to a change in the price of that good, if nothing else changes (*ceteris paribus*). Demand curves slope downward; supply curves slope upward.

- Determinants of market demand include the number of potential buyers and their respective tastes (desires), incomes, other goods, and expectations. If any of these determinants change, the demand curve shifts. Movements along a demand curve are induced only by a change in the price of that good.

- Determinants of market supply include factor costs, technology, profitability of other goods, expectations, tax rates, and number of sellers. Supply shifts when these underlying determinants change.

- The quantity of goods or resources actually exchanged in each market depends on the behaviour of all buyers and sellers, as summarized in market supply and demand curves. At the point where the two curves intersect, an equilibrium price—the price at which the quantity demanded equals the quantity supplied—is established.

- A distinctive feature of the equilibrium price and quantity is that it's the only price-quantity combination acceptable to buyers and sellers alike. At higher prices, sellers supply more than buyers are willing to purchase (a market surplus); at lower prices, the amount demanded exceeds the quantity supplied (a market shortage). Only the equilibrium price clears the market.

- Shifts in the demand curve or the supply curve or both curves (i.e., simultaneous shifts) lead to either market surpluses or market shortages at current prices. Adjustments occur in the market and a new equilibrium price and quantity emerges.

Key Terms

factor market 29	law of demand 33	law of supply 39
product market 30	substitute goods 33	equilibrium price 42
supply 31	complementary goods 34	market surplus 43
demand 31	shift in demand 35	market shortage 43
demand schedule 32	market demand 36	
demand curve 33	market supply 38	

Questions for Discussion

1. In our story of Tom, the student confronted with a Web-design assignment, we emphasized the great urgency of his desire for Web tutoring. Many people would say that Tom had an "absolute need" for Web help and therefore was ready to "pay anything" to get it. If this were true, what shape would his demand curve have? Why isn't this realistic?

2. With respect to the demand for college enrollment, which of the following would cause (1) a movement along the demand curve or (2) a shift of the demand curve?
   a. An increase in incomes.
   b. Lower tuition.
   c. More student loans.
   d. An increase in textbook prices.

3. One of the determinants of demand is income. For most goods, an increase in income leads to increases in demand—these are called *normal goods*. Some goods and services, however, are *inferior*—an increase in income leads to a decrease in demand. List three goods/services that you consider inferior. Illustrate the new equilibrium prices and quantities for one of these goods when there is an increase in income.

4. Which determinants of demand for generators changed when Eastern Canada was ravaged by the ice storm (pages 45 and 48)?

5. Can you explain the practice of scalping tickets for major sporting events in terms of market shortages? How else might tickets be distributed?

6. How else besides higher prices could the 2001 market shortage in California's electricity market have been alleviated? Consider both demand- and supply-side options.

7. Graphically illustrate what happens to the equilibrium price and quantity of Web-design tutoring if both demand and supply *simultaneously increase*. (Hint: There are three possible outcomes—each depends on the relative magnitude of the shifts.)

8. The World View on page 49 describes the use of prices to achieve an equilibrium in the kitchen. What happens to the food at more traditional restaurants?

9. Is there a shortage of on-campus parking at your school? If so, how would a market system resolve the shortage?

10. Do Internet price information services tend to raise or lower the price consumers pay for a product?

EXERCISES

PROBLEMS The Student Problem Set to accompany this chapter can be found at the end of the book.

WEB ACTIVITIES Web Activities to accompany this chapter can be found on the Online Learning Centre at **http://www.mcgrawhill.ca/olc/schiller**.

CHAPTER 3

The Public Sector

The market has a keen ear for private wants, but a deaf ear for public needs.
—Robert Heilbroner

LEARNING OBJECTIVES

By the end of this chapter, you should be able to:

3.1 Define the concept of market failure

3.2 Explain how the four sources of market failure (public goods, externalities, market power, and equity) provide a justification for government intervention

3.3 Define price controls and compare price ceilings and price floors

3.4 Explain how the public sector makes decisions

3.5 Understand how government intervention may fail to achieve our economic goals

Markets do work: The interaction of supply and demand in product markets *does* generate goods and services. Likewise, the interaction of supply and demand in labour markets *does* yield jobs, wages, and a distribution of income. As we've observed, the market is capable of determining WHAT goods to produce, HOW, and FOR WHOM.

But are the market's answers good enough? Is the mix of output produced by unregulated markets the best possible mix? Will producers choose the production process that strikes a desirable balance between production and the environment? Will the market-generated distribution of income be fair enough? Will there be enough jobs for everyone who wants one?

In reality, markets don't always give us the best-possible outcomes. Markets dominated by a few powerful corporations may charge excessive prices, limit output, provide poor service, or even retard technological advance. In the quest for profits, producers may sacrifice the environment for cost savings. In unfettered markets, some people may not get life-saving health care, basic education, or even adequate nutrition. When markets generate such outcomes, government intervention may be needed to ensure better answers to the WHAT, HOW, and FOR WHOM questions.

This chapter identifies the circumstances under which government intervention is desirable. To this end, we answer the following questions:

* **Under what circumstances do markets fail?**
* **How can government intervention help?**
* **How much government intervention is desirable?**

As we'll see, there's substantial agreement about how and when markets fail to give us the best WHAT, HOW, and FOR WHOM answers. But there's much less agreement about whether government intervention improves the situation. Indeed, many Canadians are ambivalent about government intervention. They want the government to "fix" the mix of output, protect the environment, and ensure an adequate level of income for everyone. But voters are equally quick to blame government meddling for many of our economic woes.

3.1 MARKET FAILURE

We can visualize the potential for government intervention by focusing on the WHAT question. Our goal here is to produce the best-possible mix of output with existing resources. We illustrated this goal earlier with production possibilities curves. Figure 3.1 assumes that of all the possible combinations of output we could produce, the unique combination at point *X* represents the most desirable one. In other words, it's the **optimal mix of output,** the one that maximizes our collective social utility. We haven't yet figured out how to pinpoint that optimal mix; we're simply using the arbitrary point *X* in Figure 3.1 to represent that best-possible outcome.

Ideally, the *market mechanism* would lead us to point *X*. Price signals in the marketplace are supposed to move factors of production from one industry to another in response to consumer demands. If we demand more computers—offer to buy more at a given price—more resources (labour) will be allocated to computer manufacturing. Similarly, a fall in demand will encourage producers to stop making computers and offer their services in another industry. ***Changes in market prices direct resources from one industry to another,*** moving us along the perimeter of the production possibilities curve.

Where will the market mechanism take us? Will it move resources around until we end up at the optimal point *X*? Or will it leave us at another point on the production possibilities curve, with a *sub*optimal mix of output? (If point *X* is the *optimal,* or best-possible, mix, all other output mixes must be *sub*optimal.)

We use the term *market failure* to refer to situations where the market generates less than perfect (suboptimal) outcomes. If the invisible hand of the marketplace produces a mix of output that's different from the one society most desires, then it has failed. ***Market failure implies that the forces of supply and demand haven't led us to the best point on the production possibilities curve.*** Such a failure is illustrated by point *M* in Figure 3.1. Point *M* is assumed to be the mix of output generated by market forces. Notice that the market mix (*M*) doesn't represent the optimal mix, which is assumed to be at point *X*. The market in this case *fails;* we get the wrong answer to the WHAT question.

Market failure opens the door for government intervention. If the market can't do the job, we need some form of *nonmarket* force to get the right answers. In terms of Figure 3.1, we need something to change the mix of output—to move us from point *M* (the market mix of output) to point *X* (the optimal mix of output). Accordingly, ***market failure establishes a basis for government intervention.*** We look to the government to push market outcomes closer to the ideal.

optimal mix of output: The most desirable combination of output attainable with existing resources, technology, and social values.

FIGURE 3.1
Market Failure

We can produce any mix of output on the production possibilities curve. Our goal is to produce the optimal (best-possible) mix of output, as represented by point *X*. Market forces, however, might produce another combination, like point *M*. In that case, the market fails—it produces a suboptimal mix of output.

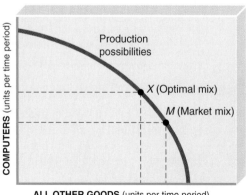

Causes of Market Failure. Because market failure is the justification for government intervention, we need to know how and when market failure occurs. ***The four specific sources of market failure are***

- ***Public goods***
- ***Externalities***
- ***Market power***
- ***Equity***

We will first examine the nature of these problems, then see why government intervention is called for in each case.

The market mechanism has the unique capability to signal consumer demands for various goods and services. By offering to pay higher or lower prices for some goods, we express our preferences about WHAT to produce. However, this mode of communication works efficiently only if the benefits of consuming a particular good are available only to the individuals who purchase that product.

Consider doughnuts, for example. When you eat a doughnut, you alone get the satisfaction from its sweet, greasy taste—that is, you derive a private benefit. No one else benefits from your consumption of a doughnut: The doughnut you purchase in the market is yours alone to consume; it's a **private good.** Accordingly, your decision to purchase the doughnut will be determined only by your anticipated satisfaction, your income, and your opportunity costs.

No Exclusion. Many goods and services, however, are different from doughnuts. When you buy a doughnut, you exclude others from consumption of that product. If Tim Hortons sells you a particular pastry, it can't supply the same pastry to someone else. If you devour it, no one else can. In this sense, the transaction and product are completely private.

The same exclusiveness is not characteristic of some of the services provided by your community such as fire protection and police protection. If you reside in a townhouse complex and your neighbour's house catches fire, both you and your neighbour simultaneously benefit from the firefighters' services. A police officer patrolling the streets of downtown Montreal is effectively providing protection to residents, merchants, as well as tourists who may be in the neighbourhood during his or her shift. These are not divisible services; the consumption of fire and police protection is a communal feat, no matter who pays for their services. Accordingly, these services are regarded as a **public good** in the sense that ***consumption of a public good by one person doesn't preclude consumption of the same good by another person.*** By contrast, a doughnut is a private good because if I eat it, no one else can consume it.

The Free-Rider Dilemma. The communal nature of public goods creates a dilemma. If you and I both benefit from police protection, for example, which one of us should hire the police officer? I'd prefer that you hire the officer, thereby giving me protection at no direct cost. As a result, I may publicly profess no desire for police services ("I have a karate black belt so I can take care of myself."), secretly hoping to take a **free ride** on your market purchase. Unfortunately, you too have an incentive to conceal your desire for police protection. Consequently, neither one of us may step forward to demand police protection. We'll both end up without the service.

Flood control is also a public good. No one in the valley wants to be flooded out. But each landowner knows that a flood-control dam will protect *all* the landowners, regardless of who pays. Either the entire valley is protected or no one is. Accordingly, individual farmers and landowners may say they don't *want* a dam and aren't willing to *pay* for it. Everyone is waiting and hoping that someone else will pay for flood control. In other words, everyone wants a *free ride*. Thus, if we leave it to market forces, no one will *demand* flood control and all the property in the valley will be washed away.

Public Goods

private good: A good or service whose consumption by one person excludes consumption by others.

public good: A good or service whose consumption by one person does not exclude consumption by others.

free rider: An individual who reaps direct benefits from someone else's purchase (consumption) of a public good.

Napster Gets Napped

Shawn Fanning had a brilliant idea for getting more music: download it from friends' computers to the Internet. So he wrote software in 1999 that enabled online file-sharing of audio files. This peer-to-peer (P2P) online distribution system became an overnight sensation: in 2000–01 nearly 60 million consumers were using Napster's software to acquire recorded music.

At first blush, Napster's service looked like a classic "public good." The service was free, and one person's consumption did not impede another person from consuming the same service. Moreover, the distribution system was configured in such a way that nonpayers could not be excluded from the service.

The definition of "*public good*" relies, however, on whether nonpayers *can* be excluded, not whether they *are* excluded.

In other words, technology is critical in classifying goods as "public" or "private." In Napster's case, encryption technology that could exclude nonpayers was available, but the company had *chosen* not to use it. After being sued by major recording companies for copyright infringement, Napster changed its tune. In July 2001, it shut down its free download service. Two years later it re-opened with a *fee-based* service that could exclude nonpayers. Although free downloads are still available (e.g., Kazaa, LiveWire), fee-based services have sprung up all over (e.g., Apple's iTunes Music Store, Wal-Mart). For most consumers, music downloads are now a private good.

Source: "Napster is Back!" *NewsFlash,* October 2003.

Analysis: A product is a "public good" only if nonpayers *cannot* be excluded from its consumption. Napster had the technical ability to exclude nonpayers but initially chose not to do so. Fee-based music downloads are a private good.

The difference between public goods and private goods often rests on *technical considerations* not political philosophy; do we have the technical capability to exclude nonpayers? In the case of flood control, we simply don't have that capability. Even city streets have the characteristics of public goods. Although theoretically we could restrict the use of streets to those who paid to use them, a tollgate on every corner would be exceedingly expensive and impractical. Here again, joint or public consumption appears to be the only feasible alternative. As the accompanying Applications box on Napster emphasizes, the technical capability to exclude nonpayers is the key factor in identifying "public goods."

Note that radio transmissions from AM and FM radio stations—often provided by private firms—are public goods. Once a station sets up a radio transmitter and sends out its signal, anyone with a radio can listen to the channel without excluding others and without having to pay the radio station. We now have "satellite" radio where subscribers can listen to all music or all sports or all news without commercial interruption. Clearly one subscriber's usage does not prevent another subscriber from enjoying the same channel, but companies producing these satellite signals (Sirius, XM, and WorldSpace) are able to use technology to prevent the free-rider problem by charging monthly fees to access the signal. Satellite radio is a private good.

To the list of public goods we could add snow removal, the administration of justice (including prisons), the regulation of commerce, the conduct of foreign relations, airport traffic control, and even Canada Day fireworks. These services—which cost *billions* of dollars and employ thousands of workers—provide benefits to everyone, no matter who pays for them. In each instance it's technically impossible or prohibitively expensive to exclude nonpayers from the services provided.

Underproduction of Public Goods. The free riders associated with public goods upset the customary practice of paying for what you get. If I can get all the protection, flood control, and laws I want without paying for them, I'm not about to complain. I'm perfectly happy to let you pay for the services while we all consume them. Of course, you may feel the same way. Why should you pay for these services if you can consume

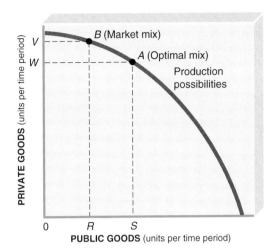

FIGURE 3.2
Underproduction of Public Goods

Suppose point *A* represents the optimal mix of output, that is, the mix of private and public goods that maximizes society's welfare. Because consumers won't demand purely public goods in the marketplace, the price mechanism won't allocate so many resources to their production. Instead, the market will tend to produce a mix of output like point *B*, which includes fewer public goods (O*R*) than is optimal (O*S*).

just as much of them when your neighbours foot the whole bill? It might seem selfish not to pay your share of the cost of providing public goods. But you'd be better off in a material sense if you spent your income on doughnuts, letting others pick up the tab for public services.

Because the familiar link between paying and consuming is broken, public goods can't be peddled in the supermarket. People are reluctant to buy what they can get free, a perfectly rational response for consumers who have limited incomes to spend. Hence, *if public goods were marketed like private goods, everyone would wait for someone else to pay.* The end result might be a total lack of public services. This is the kind of dilemma Robert Heilbroner had in mind when he spoke of the market's "deaf ear" (see quote at the beginning of this chapter).

The production possibilities curve in Figure 3.2 illustrates the dilemma created by public goods. Suppose that point *A* represents the optimal mix of private and public goods. It's the mix of goods and services we'd select if everyone's preferences were known and reflected in production decisions. The market mechanism won't lead us to point *A*, however, because the *demand* for public goods will be hidden. If we rely on the market, nearly everyone will withhold demand for public goods, waiting for a free ride to point *A*. As a result, we'll get a smaller quantity of public goods than we really want. The market mechanism will leave us at a mix of output like that at point *B*, with few, if any, public goods. Since point *A* is assumed to be optimal, point *B* must be *suboptimal* (inferior to point *A*). The market fails: We can't rely on the market mechanism to allocate enough resources to the production of public goods, no matter how much they might be desired.

Note that we're using the term "public good" in a way different from how most people use it. To most people, "public good" refers to any good or service the government produces. In economics, however, the meaning is much more restrictive. The term "public good" refers only to those nonexcludable goods and services that must be consumed jointly, both by those who pay for them and by those who don't. Public goods can be produced by either the government or the private sector. Private goods can be produced in either sector as well. The problem is that *the market tends to underproduce public goods and overproduce private goods.* If we want more public goods, we need a *nonmarket* force—government intervention—to get them. The government will have to force people to pay taxes, then use the tax revenues to pay for the production of fire/police protection, flood control, snow removal, and other public goods.

The free-rider problem associated with public goods is one justification for government intervention. It's not the only justification, however. Further grounds for intervention arise from the tendency of costs or benefits of some market activities to "spill over" onto third parties.

Externalities

APPLICATIONS

Second-hand Smoke Hurts Others

Second-hand smoke can harm babies before and after they are born. Several chemicals in second-hand smoke can pass into a baby's blood, affecting how an unborn baby develops. Babies exposed to second-hand smoke before they were born are more likely to be small and less healthy. They are also at a higher risk of dying during childbirth or dying of SIDS (sudden infant death syndrome).

Second-hand smoke hurts older children too. Children are more at risk of getting sick than adults when they breathe in second-hand smoke because their bodies are still growing. They breathe faster than adults, so they absorb more harmful chemicals. Children's immune systems, which protect them from getting sick, are not yet fully developed. Children who regularly breathe in second-hand smoke are more likely to suffer from coughing and wheezing, painful ear infections, asthma, bronchitis, and pneumonia. They are also more likely to have a higher risk of heart disease and to take up smoking themselves.

Source: *Clear the Air.* Canadian Cancer Society 2007.

Analysis: The health risks imposed on nonsmokers via "passive smoke" represent external costs. The market price of cigarettes doesn't reflect these costs borne by third parties.

Your demand for a good reflects the amount of satisfaction you expect from its consumption. The price you're willing to pay acts as a market signal to producers of your preferences. Often, however, your *consumption* may affect others. The purchase of cigarettes, for example, expresses a smoker's demand for that good. But others may suffer from that consumption. In this case, smoke literally spills over onto other consumers, causing them discomfort and possibly even ill health (see the Applications box above). Yet their loss isn't reflected in the market: The harm caused to nonsmokers is *external* to the market price of cigarettes.

externalities: Costs (or benefits) of a market activity borne by a third party; the difference between the social and private costs (benefits) of a market activity.

The term **externalities** refers to all costs or benefits of a market activity borne by a third party, that is, by someone other than the immediate producer or consumer. ***Whenever externalities are present, market prices aren't a valid measure of a good's value to society.*** As a consequence, the market will fail to produce the right mix of output. Specifically, ***the market will underproduce goods that yield external benefits and overproduce those that generate external costs.***

External Costs. Figure 3.3 shows how external costs cause the market to overproduce cigarettes. The market demand curve includes only the wishes of smokers, that is, people who are willing and able to purchase cigarettes. The forces of market demand and supply result in a market equilibrium at E_M in which q_M cigarettes are produced and consumed. The market price P_M reflects the value of cigarettes to smokers.

The well-being of *non*smokers isn't reflected in the market equilibrium at E_M. To take the *non*smoker's interests into account, we must subtract the external costs imposed on *them* from the value that *smokers* put on cigarettes. In general,

$$\text{Social demand} = \text{market demand} + \text{externalities}$$

In this case, the externality is a *cost*, so we must *subtract* the external cost from market demand to get a full accounting of social demand. The "social demand" curve in Figure 3.3 reflects this computation. To find this curve, we subtract the amount of external cost from every price on the market demand curve. What the *social* demand curve tells us is how much society would be willing and able to pay for cigarettes if the preferences of both smokers and nonsmokers were taken into account.

The social demand curve in Figure 3.3 creates a new equilibrium at q_O. This is the *optimal* quantity of cigarettes to produce (and consume). Yet the market alone would

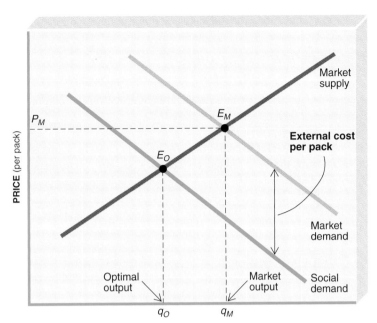

FIGURE 3.3
Externalities

The market responds to consumer demands, not externalities. Smokers demand q_M cigarettes. But external costs on nonsmokers imply that the *social* demand for cigarettes is less than (below) *market* demand. The socially optimal level of output is q_O, less than the market output q_M.

produce more than that (q_M). Government intervention may be needed to move the mix of output closer to society's optimal point.

The externalities associated with cigarette consumption have prompted many forms of government intervention, including mandatory health warnings on cigarette packaging, bans on advertising, and restrictions on locales where people may smoke. Courts have even determined that child custody decisions may be influenced by the smoking habits of the divorcing parents. All these interventions restrict the ability of individuals to maximize their personal utility in the marketplace. They're motivated by the recognition that the market mechanism responds only to the market demands of smokers and is unable to respond to nonmarketed externalities.

Externalities also exist in *production*. A power plant that burns high-sulphur coal damages the surrounding environment. Yet the damage inflicted on neighbouring people, vegetation, and buildings is external to the cost calculations of the firm. Because the cost of such pollution is not reflected in the price of electricity, the firm will tend to produce more electricity (and pollution) than is socially desirable. To reduce this imbalance, the government has to step in and change market outcomes.

External Benefits. Externalities can also be beneficial. A product may generate external *benefits* rather than external *costs*. Your college is an example. The students who attend your school benefit directly from the education they receive. That's why they (and you) are willing to *pay* for tuition, books, and other services. The students in attendance aren't the only beneficiaries of this educational service, however. The research that a university conducts may yield benefits for a much broader community. The values and knowledge students acquire may also be shared with family, friends, and co-workers. These benefits would all be *external* to the market transaction between a paying student and the school. Positive externalities also arise from immunizations against infectious diseases.

If a product yields external benefits, the social demand is greater than the market demand. In this case, the social value of the good *exceeds* the market price (by the amount of external benefit). Accordingly, society wants *more* of the product than the market mechanism alone will produce at any given price. To get that additional output, the government may have to intervene with subsidies or other policies. We conclude then that *the market fails by*

- *Overproducing goods that have external costs.*
- *Underproducing goods that have external benefits.*

If externalities are present, the market won't produce the optimal mix of output. To get that optimal mix, we need government intervention.

Market Power

In the case of both public goods and externalities, the market fails to achieve the optimal mix of output because the price signal is flawed. The price consumers are willing and able to pay for a specific good doesn't reflect all the benefits or costs of producing that good.

The market may fail, however, even when the price signals are accurate. The *response* to price signals, rather than the signals themselves, may be flawed.

monopoly: A firm that produces the entire market supply of a particular good or service.

Restricted Supply. Market power is often the cause of a flawed response. Suppose there were only one airline company in the world. This single seller of airline travel would be a **monopoly**—that is, the only producer in that industry. As a monopolist, the airline could charge extremely high prices without worrying that travellers would flock to a competing airline. At the same time, the high prices paid by consumers would express the importance of that service to society. Ideally, such prices would act as a signal to producers to build and fly more planes—to change the mix of output. But a monopolist doesn't have to cater to every consumer's whim. It can limit airline travel and obstruct our efforts to achieve an optimal mix of output.

market power: The ability to alter the market price of a good or a service.

Monopoly is the most severe form of **market power.** More generally, market power refers to any situation in which a single producer or consumer has the ability to alter the market price of a specific product. If the publisher (McGraw-Hill) charges a high price for this book, you'll have to pay the tab. McGraw-Hill has market power because there are relatively few economics textbooks and your professor has required you to use this one. You don't have power in the textbook market because your decision to buy or not won't alter the market price of this text. You're only one of the million students who are taking an introductory economics course this year.

The market power McGraw-Hill possesses is derived from the copyright on this text. No matter how profitable textbook sales might be, no one else is permitted to produce or sell this particular book. Patents are another common source of market power because they also preclude others from making or selling a specific product. Market power may also result from control of resources, restrictive production agreements, or efficiencies of large-scale production.

Whatever the source of market power, the direct consequence is that one or more producers attain discretionary power over the market's response to price signals. They may use that discretion to enrich themselves rather than to move the economy toward the optimal mix of output. In this case, the market will again fail to deliver the most desired goods and services.

competition policy: Government policies and laws identifying and regulating the competitive process.

The mandate for government intervention in this case is to prevent or dismantle concentrations of market power. That's the basic purpose of antitrust or **competition policy.** In Canada, the Competition Bureau administers and enforces the laws. The Bureau's mandate is to "promote and maintain fair competition so that Canadians can benefit from competitive prices, product choice and quality services."

natural monopoly: An industry in which one firm can achieve economies of scale over the entire range of market supply.

In some cases, it may be economically efficient to have one large firm supply an entire market. Such a situation arises in **natural monopoly,** where a single firm can achieve economies of scale over the entire range of market output. Utility companies, land-based telephone service, subway systems, and cable all exhibit such scale (size) efficiencies. In these cases, a monopoly *structure* may be economically desirable. The government may have to regulate the *behaviour* of a natural monopoly, however, to ensure that consumers get the benefits of that greater efficiency.

APPLICATIONS

Labatt Pleads Guilty—Pays $250,000 Fine

In 2004, the Competition Bureau launched an inquiry into the pricing practices of the Labatt Brewing Company in Quebec. There was evidence suggesting that Labatt encouraged price increases and/or discouraged price decreases in discount beer sold in convenience and grocery retailers. In one instance, it

© CP/Aaron Harris

was alleged that a Labatt sales representative offered $2,000 to a retailer to increase the price of a competitor's product. On other occasions, sales representatives offered free cases of beer to certain retailers.

"Labatt's actions, through some of its sales representatives, resulted in some discount beer consumers in Sherbrooke and elsewhere in the province being offered discount beer at a higher price, while Labatt's competitors were unable to provide independent retailers and consumers with better prices," said Senior Deputy Commissioner Denyse MacKenzie. "In order to safeguard the competitive process and ensure that consumers benefit from the lowest possible prices for goods and services, the Competition Bureau will continue to fully enforce the price maintenance provision of the Competition Act."

In November 2005, Labatt pleaded guilty to the charges and was fined $250,000.

Source: Labatt Pleads Guilty and Pays $250,000 Fine Following a Competiton Bureau Investigation, OTTAWA, November 23, 2005. Competition Bureau Canada. Reproduced with the permission of the Minister of Public Works and Government Services Canada, 2007.

Analysis: Firms with considerable market power, such as Labatt Brewing Company, can engage in pricing activity that violates the Competition Act. As Canada's watchdog, the Competition Bureau adjudicates all cases of price maintenance.

Public goods, externalities, and market power all cause resource misallocations. Where these phenomena exist, the market mechanism will fail to produce the optimal mix of output in the best-possible way.

Beyond the questions of WHAT and HOW to produce, we're also concerned about FOR WHOM output is produced. The market answers this question by distributing a larger share of total output to those with the most income. Although this result may be efficient, it's not necessarily equitable. If such outcomes violate our vision of equity, we may want the government to change the market-generated distribution of income or the distribution of output, or both.

Taxes and Transfers. The tax-and-transfer system is the principal mechanism for redistributing incomes. The idea here is to take some of the income away from those who have "too much" and give it to those whom the market has left with "too little." Taxes are levied to take back some of the income received from the market. Those tax revenues are then redistributed via transfer payments to those deemed needy, such as the poor, the aged, and the unemployed. **Transfer payments** are income payments for which no goods or services are exchanged. They're used to bolster the incomes of those for whom the market itself provides too little.

Some people argue that we don't need the government to help the poor—that private charity alone will suffice. Unfortunately, private charity alone has never been adequate. One reason private charity doesn't suffice is the "free-rider" problem. If I contribute heavily to the poor, you benefit from safer streets (fewer muggers), a better environment (fewer slums and homeless people), and a clearer conscience (knowing fewer people are starving). In this sense, the relief of misery is a *public* good. Were I the only taxpayer to benefit substantially from the reduction of poverty, then charity

Inequity

transfer payments: Payments to individuals for which no current goods or services are exchanged, like Employment Insurance (EI), welfare, and unemployment benefits.

would be a private affair. As long as income support substantially benefits the public at large, then income redistribution is a *public* good, for which public funding is appropriate. This is the *economic* rationale for public income-redistribution activities. To this rationale one can add such moral arguments as seem appropriate.

Minimum Wage. Government intervention in the market-generated distribution of income also comes in the form of minimum wage laws. In an effort to provide workers with a minimum level of income, provincial governments in Canada have instituted minimum wage laws that effectively prevent employers from paying workers less than a specific hourly wage. Without these laws, a number of jobs—particularly those which require minimum skills, education, and experience—would pay less than this government-legislated rate. Minimum wages are a specific form of government price controls known as **price floors.** Price floors set a lower limit on the price of a good or service. In this case, the services of labour are set at a particular rate per hour. Guaranteed minimum prices for agriculture products are another example of price floors.

Given the demand and supply of labour in Figure 3.4, an unfettered market for labour would provide q_M hours of labour per month at a market wage rate of $5. With a minimum wage set at $8, this higher wage rate reduces the quantity demand for labour to q^d_{min} and provides the monetary incentive for workers to increase the quantity supplied of labour to q^s_{min}. Since the employers cannot be forced into offering the amount of hours that workers are willing to work at the minimum wage of $8 ($q^s_{min}$), the number of actual hours worked will be limited to q^d_{min}. The difference between the quantity supplied and the quantity demanded ($q^s_{min} - q^d_{min}$) represents the excess supply of labour (i.e., unemployment) created as a result of the minimum wage.

Figure 3.4 indicates how minimum wages laws are a double-edged sword. Those who are successful in finding a job will benefit from higher wages, but the minimum wage will also reduce employment and increase the unemployment rate for those people it was intended to help, namely the younger, less-skilled, less-educated workers.

Inequities in Market Output. We have examined how governments intervene when inequities exist with the market-generated distribution of income. But what about

price floor: Lower limit imposed on the price of a good or service.

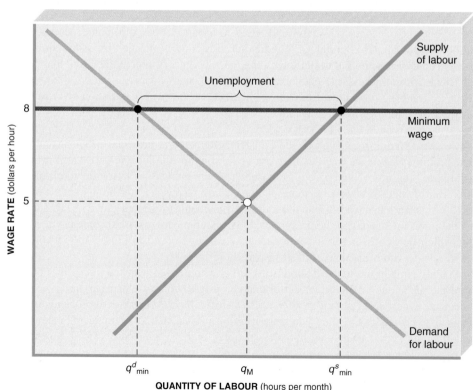

FIGURE 3.4
Price Floors Create Surpluses

A minimum wage of $8 reduces the quantity demand for labour to q^d_{min} and increases the quantity supplied to q^s_{min}. The amount of labour exchanged under minimum wage is q^d_{min}, creating unemployment (i.e., a surplus of labour) equal to $q^s_{min} - q^d_{min}$.

inequities associated with the market-generated levels of output? There is a widespread consensus in Canada that everyone is entitled to some minimum level of shelter, food, health, and education. How can governments ensure that citizens receive a minimum amount of a good/service or that citizens have the ability to "afford" a certain level of output? Often they come through *government provision* of subsidized goods and services. In the case of education (primary and secondary) and to a certain degree, health services, the provincial governments provide these services and pay for them through the collection of taxes. Taxpayers who consume these services are being subsidized by those who do not consume them. In other cases, governments subsidize the *private provision* of goods and services. In Alberta, for example, the provincial government has created a natural gas rebate program. When natural gas prices are above the trigger price of $5.50/gigajoule (GJ), consumers receive a minimum rebate of $1.50/GJ.

Price Ceilings. Similar to the minimum wage analysis above, government can use price controls to ensure that certain goods and services are "affordable" to those with the lowest levels of income. In this case, governments set an upper limit on the price of the good or service—this is called a **price ceiling.** We can return to our example of the California electricity crisis of 2000–01 (discussed in Chapter 2) to analyze the effects of a price ceiling. In 1996, the state of California set a price ceiling of 10¢/kilowatt hour (kWh) or, alternatively, $100/megawatt-hour (MWh). As Figure 3.5

price ceiling: Upper limit imposed on the price of a good or service.

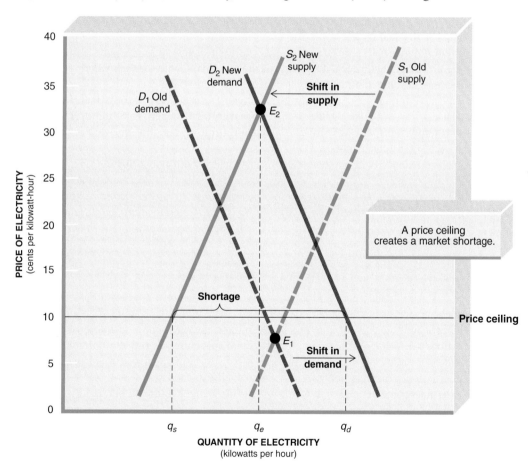

FIGURE 3.5
Price Ceilings Create Shortages

In 1996, the state of California set a price ceiling of 10 cents per kilowatt-hour. Initially, this price was above the market equilibrium (E_1) and had no impact. By 2001, however, demand had increased (to D_2) and supply had decreased (to S_2). At the ceiling price the quantity demanded (q_d) exceeded the quantity supplied (q_s), causing a market shortage and rolling blackouts. At the higher equilibrium (E_2) price there are no blackouts. Consumers reduce their energy consumption (to q_e from q_d) and power companies increase electricity deliveries (to q_e from q_s).

illustrates, in 1996 the price ceiling had no impact on equilibrium prices and quantities since it was set well above market equilibrium. But by 2001, the combination of an increase in demand (due to a growing economy) and a decrease in supply (due to maintenance problems and market manipulation), the quantity of electricity demanded (q_d in Figure 3.5) far exceeded the quantity supplied (q_s). This is a classic case of market shortage.

Initially, most of the state's residents welcomed Governor Gray Davis's January 2001 promises to keep cheap electricity flowing to the state's homes and businesses. But as wholesale price increased 10-fold from \$30/MWh to \$300/MWh, wholesalers were unwilling to sell as much as consumers demanded at the retail price ceiling. Because of the shortage, not everyone who was willing and able to pay the ceiling price (10¢/kWh) could get the electricity they demanded. That's when the state had to resort to rolling blackouts. The blackouts left everyone with less electricity than they demanded and that experience helped convince Californians that a price ceiling set at 10¢/kWh wasn't as good as it appeared. In April 2001 the 1996 price ceiling was raised 26 percent, reflecting the market events of the past year.

Macro Instability

unemployment: The inability of labour-force participants to find jobs.

inflation: An increase in the average level of prices of goods and services.

The micro failures of the marketplace imply that we're at the wrong point on the production possibilities curve or inequitably distributing the output produced. There's another basic question we've swept under the rug, however. How do we get to the production possibilities curve in the first place? To reach the curve, we must utilize all available resources and technology. Can we be confident that the invisible hand of the marketplace will use all available resources? Or will some people face **unemployment**—that is, be willing to work but unable to find a job?

And what about prices? Price signals are a critical feature of the market mechanism. But the validity of those signals depends on some stable measure of value. What good is a doubling of salary when the price of everything you buy doubles as well? Generally, rising prices will enrich people who own property and impoverish people who rent. That's why we strive to avoid **inflation**—a situation in which the *average* price level is increasing.

Historically, the marketplace has been wracked with bouts of both unemployment and inflation. These experiences have prompted calls for government intervention at the macro level. *The goal of macro intervention is to foster economic growth—to get us on the production possibilities curve (full employment), maintain a stable price level (price stability), and increase our capacity to produce (growth).*

3.2 GOVERNMENT FAILURE

Some government intervention in the marketplace is clearly desirable. The market mechanism can fail for a variety of reasons, leaving a laissez-faire economy short of its economic goals. But how much government intervention is desirable? Communist nations once thought that complete government control of production, consumption, and distribution decisions was the surest path to utopia. They learned the hard way that not only markets but governments as well can fail.

In this context, *government failure* means that government intervention fails to move us closer to our economic goals.

In Figure 3.6, the goal of government intervention is to move the mix of output from point M (failed market outcome) to point X (the social optimum). But government intervention might unwittingly move us to point G_1, making matters worse. Or the government might overreact, sending us to point G_2. Red tape and onerous regulation might even force us to point G_3, *inside* the production possibilities curve (with less total output than at point M). All those possibilities (G_1, G_2, G_3) represent government failure. Government intervention is desirable only to the extent that it *improves* market outcomes (e.g., G_4). Government intervention in the FOR WHOM question is desirable only if the distribution of income and output gets better, not worse, as a result

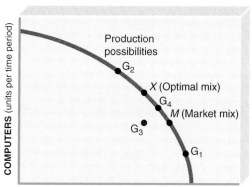

FIGURE 3.6
Government Failure

When the market produces a subopti-mal mix of output (point *M*), the goal of government is to move output to the social optimum (point *X*). A move to G_4 would be an improvement in the mix of output. But government intervention *may* move the economy to points G_1, G_2, or G_3—all reflecting government failure.

of taxes and transfers. Even when outcomes improve, government failure may occur if the costs of government intervention exceeded the benefits of an improved output mix, cleaner production methods, or a fairer distribution of income and output.

Many taxpayers identify the source of government failure as the "waste" of tax dollars by politicians and public servants. Recent examples, they argue, include the federal sponsorship scandal discussed in Chapter 1 and the Canadian gun registry, where the initial cost of the registry was projected to be $119 *million* dollars but massive cost overruns have pegged the cost to be closer to $2 *billion* (see Applications).

Perceptions of Waste

Government "waste" implies that the public sector isn't producing as many services as it could with the sources at its disposal. Such inefficiency implies that we're producing somewhere *inside* our production possibilities curve rather than on it (e.g., point G_3 in Figure 3.6). If the government is wasting resources this way, we can't possibly be producing the optimal mix of output.

Even if the government weren't wasting resources, it might still be guilty of govern-ment failure. As important as efficiency in government may be, it begs the larger

Opportunity Cost

APPLICATIONS

Auditor General "Blasts" Gun Registry

In 1995, the Liberal government of Jean Chrétien passed Bill C-68 calling for harsher sentences for crimes committed using firearms as well as the creation of a gun registry requiring all gun owners to be licensed and registered. The registry was projected to cost about $119 million, but with revenues gen-erated by registration fees, taxpayers would only have to pay $2 million.

Six year later, in December 2002, the Office of the Audi-tor General in Canada, which holds the government account-able for its stewardship of public funds, "blasted the federal government for exceeding its estimated budget, saying that, by the time the smoke cleared and all gun owners and their guns were registered, the program would have cost taxpayers

more than $1 billion." And in May 2006, "Auditor General Sheila Fraser reports that the former Liberal government twice misinformed Parliament about tens of millions of dollars of overspending at the Canada Firearms Centre. Fraser finds that the planned computerized gun registry system is three years overdue and so far has cost $90 million, three times more than expected."

While the debate continues about whether or not the im-plementation of a gun registry will help save lives and deter crimes committed with firearms, most Canadians feel that the cost overruns associated with the registry are excessive.

Source: Based on *InDepth: Gun Control.* "Implementing the Firearms Act—The Rising Cost," CBC News Online. Updated June 19, 2006.

Analysis: Market failure justifies government intervention. If the government wastes resources, however, it too may fail to satisfy our economic goals.

question of how many government services we really want. In reality, ***the issue of government waste encompasses two distinct questions:***

- ***Efficiency:*** Are we getting as much service as we could from the resources we allocate to government?
- ***Opportunity cost:*** Are we giving up too many private-sector goods to get those services?

If the government is producing goods inefficiently, we end up *inside* the production possibilities curve, with less output than attainable. Even if the government is efficient, however, the *mix* of output may not be optimal, as points G_1 and G_2 in Figure 3.6 illustrate. ***Everything the government does entails an opportunity cost.*** The more police officers or schoolteachers employed by the public sector, the fewer workers available to private producers and consumers. Similarly, the more computers, pencils, and paper consumed by government agencies, the fewer accessible to individuals and private companies.

When assessing government's role in the economy, ***we must consider not only what governments do but also what we give up to allow them to do it.*** The theory of public goods tells us only what activities are appropriate for government, not the proper *level* of such activity. National defence is clearly a proper function of the public sector. Not so clear, however, is how much the government should spend on tanks, aircraft carriers, and missile shields. The same is true of environmental protection or law enforcement.

The concept of opportunity costs puts a new perspective on the whole question of government size. Before we can decide how big is "too big," we must decide what we're willing to give up to support the public sector. A military force of 100,000 men and women is "too big" from an economic perspective only if we value the forgone private production and consumption more highly than we value the added strength of our defenses. The government has gone "too far" if the highway it builds is less desired than the park and homes it implicitly replaced. In these and all cases, the assessment of bigness must come back to a comparison of what is given up with what is received. The assessment of government failure thus comes back to points on the production possibilities curve. Has the government moved us closer to the optimal mix of output (e.g., point G_4 in Figure 3.6) or not?

WEB NOTE

For a brief history of the gun registry, visit the Canadian Broadcasting Corporation's (CBC) Web site at http://www.cbc.ca/news/background/guncontrol/.

Cost-Benefit Analysis

This is a tough question to answer in the abstract. We can, however, use the concept of opportunity cost to assess the effectiveness of specific government interventions. From this perspective, ***additional public-sector activity is desirable only if the benefits from that activity exceed its opportunity costs.*** In other words, we compare the benefits of a public project to the value of the private goods given up to produce it. By performing this calculation repeatedly along the perimeter of the production possibilities curve, we could locate the optimal mix of output—the point at which no further increase in public-sector spending activity is desirable.

This same principle can be used to decide *which* goods to produce within the public sector. A public project is desirable only to the extent that it promises to yield some benefits (or utility). But all public projects involve opportunity costs. Hence, a project should be pursued only if its anticipated benefits exceeded the value of alternative resource uses. In this sense, the public sector confronts the same kind of dilemma we consumers have. There are hundreds of goods and services we'd *like* to have, but scarce resources require us to select only the best possible ones. That implies getting the highest possible ratio of benefits to costs.

Valuation Problems. Although the principles of cost-benefit analysis are simple enough, they're deceptive. How are we to measure the potential benefits of improved police services, for example? Should we estimate the number of robberies and murders prevented, calculate the worth of each, and add up the benefits? And how are we supposed to calculate the worth of a saved life? By a person's earnings? value of assets? number of friends? And what about the increased sense of security people have when they know the police are patrolling in their neighbourhood? Should this be included in the benefit calculation? Some people will attach great value to this service; others will attach little. Whose values should be the standard?

When we're dealing with (private) market goods and services, we can gauge the benefits of a product by the amount of money consumers are willing to pay for it. This price signal isn't available for most public services, however, because of externalities and the nonexclusive nature of pure public goods (the free-rider problem). Hence, *the value (benefits) of public services must be estimated because they don't have (reliable) market prices.* This opens the door to endless political squabbles about how beneficial any particular government activity is.

The same problems arise in evaluating the government's efforts to redistribute incomes. Government transfer payments now go to retired workers, disabled people, veterans, farmers, sick people, students, pregnant women, unemployed people, poor people, and a long list of other recipients. To pay for all these transfers, the government must raise tax revenues. With so many people paying taxes and receiving transfer payments, the net effects on the distribution of income aren't easy to figure out. Yet we can't determine whether this government intervention is worth it until we know how the FOR WHOM answer was changed and what the tax-and-transfer effort cost us. Here again, there's at least a possibility of government failure.

In practice, we rely on political mechanisms, not cost-benefit calculations, to decide what to produce in the public sector and how to redistribute incomes. *Voting mechanisms substitute for the market mechanism in allocating resources to the public sector and deciding how to use them.* Some people have even suggested that the variety and volume of public goods are determined by the most votes, just as the variety and volume of private goods are determined by the most dollars. Thus, governments choose that level and mix of output (and related taxation) that seem to command the most votes.

Ballot Box Economics

In the midst of all this complexity and uncertainty, another factor may be decisive—namely, self-interest. In principle, government officials are supposed to serve the people. It doesn't take long, however, before officials realize that the public is indecisive about what it wants and takes very little interest in government's day-to-day activities. With such latitude, government officials can set their own agendas. Those agendas may give higher priority to personal advancement than to the needs of the public. Agency directors may foster new programs that enlarge their mandate, enhance their visibility, and increase their prestige or income. Members of Parliament may likewise pursue legislative favours like tax breaks for supporters more diligently than they pursue the general public interest. In such cases, the probability of attaining the optimal mix of output declines.

Public-Choice Theory

The theory of **public choice** emphasizes the role of self-interest in public decision making. Public-choice theory essentially extends the analysis of market behaviour to political behaviour. Public officials are assumed to have specific personal goals (for example, power, recognition, wealth) that they'll pursue in office. *A central tenet of public-choice theory is that bureaucrats are just as selfish (utility maximizing) as everyone else.*

public choice: Theory of public-sector behaviour emphasizing rational self-interest of decision makers and voters.

Public-choice theory provides a neat and simple explanation for public-sector decision making. But critics argue that the theory provides a woefully narrow view of public servants. Some people do selflessly pursue larger, public goals, such critics argue, and ideas can overwhelm self-interest. Steven Kelman of Harvard, for example, argues that narrow self-interest can't explain the deregulation movement of the 1980s, or, in the United States, the War on Poverty of the 1960s, or the tax revolt of the 1970s. These tidal changes in public policy reflect the power of ideas, not simple self-interest.

Although self-interest can't provide a complete explanation of public decision making, it adds important perspectives on the policy process. James Buchanan of George Mason University (Virginia) won the 1986 Nobel Prize in economics for helping develop this public-choice perspective. It adds a personal dimension to the faceless mechanics of ballot box economics, cost-benefit analysis, and other "objective" mechanisms of public-sector decision making.

SUMMARY

- Government intervention in the marketplace is justified by market failure, that is, suboptimal market outcomes.
- The micro failures of the market originate in public goods, externalities, market power, and an inequitable distribution of income. These flaws deter the market from achieving the optimal mix of output or distribution of income.
- Public goods are those that can't be consumed exclusively; they're jointly consumed regardless of who pays. Because everyone seeks a free ride, no one demands public goods in the marketplace. Hence, the market underproduces public goods.
- Externalities are costs (or benefits) of a market transaction borne by a third party. Externalities create a divergence between social and private costs or benefits, causing suboptimal market outcomes. The market overproduces goods with external costs and underproduces goods with external benefits.
- Market power enables a producer to thwart market signals and maintain a suboptimal mix of output. Competition policy seeks to prevent or restrict market power. The government may also regulate the behaviour of powerful firms.
- The market-generated distribution of income may be unfair. This inequity may prompt the government to intervene with taxes and transfer payments that redistribute incomes.

- Government intervention in the market-generated distribution of income and output can also take the form of price controls. Price floors impose a lower limit on the price of a good or service while price ceilings impose an upper limit. Such price controls create an imbalance between quantities demanded and quantities supplied resulting in market shortages.
- The macro failures of the marketplace are reflected in unemployment and inflation. Government intervention is intended to achieve full employment and price stability.
- Government failure occurs when intervention moves us away from rather than toward the optimal mix of output (or income). Failure may result from outright waste (operational inefficiency) or from a misallocation of resources.
- All government activity must be evaluated in terms of its opportunity cost, that is, the *private* goods and services forgone to make resources available to the public sector.
- Allocation decisions within the public sector may be based on cost-benefit analysis or votes. The self-interests of government agents may also affect decisions of when and how to intervene.

Key Terms

optimal mix of output 52	monopoly 58	price floor 60
private good 53	market power 58	price ceiling 61
public good 53	competition policy 58	unemployment 62
free rider 53	natural monopoly 58	inflation 62
externalities 56	transfer payments 59	public choice 65

Questions for Discussion

1. Why should taxpayers subsidize public colleges and universities? What external benefits are generated by higher education?
2. If everyone seeks a free ride, what mix of output will be produced in Figure 3.2? Why would anyone voluntarily contribute to the purchase of public goods like flood control or snow removal?
3. Could local fire departments be privately operated, with their services sold directly to customers? What problems would be involved in such a system?

4. Why might Canada Day fireworks be considered a public good? Who should pay for them? What about airport security?

5. What is the specific market-failure justification for government spending on (*a*) public universities, (*b*) health care, (*c*) trash pickup, (*d*) highways, (*e*) police? Would a purely private economy produce any of these services?

6. Why should the well-being of nonsmokers affect the price and quantity of cigarettes produced?

7. The government now spends over $55 billion a year on pension benefits. Why don't we leave it to individuals to save for their own retirement?

8. What government actions might cause failures like points G_1, G_2, and G_3 in Figure 3.6? Can you give examples?

9. Consider a power plant that burns high-sulphur coal and damages the surrounding environment, but is not responsible for the costs of these damages. Graphically illustrate both the unfettered market outcome and the socially desirable outcome.

10. Suppose, as the result of a booming economy, that the rental rates for one-bedroom apartments have doubled in the past year from $1,000/month to $2,000/month. In an effort to make apartments more affordable to the lower income individuals, the city has decided to place a price ceiling of $1,200 on all one-bedroom apartments. Graphically illustrate the initial equilibrium price and quantity. Now, show how the boom affects the equilibrium values. Finally, indicate how the price ceiling influences the quantity exchanged in the market. What do you think might happen in the market for one-bedroom apartments as a consequence of this policy?

EXERCISES

PROBLEMS   The Student Problem Set to accompany this chapter can be found at the end of the book.

WEB ACTIVITIES   Web Activities to accompany this chapter can be found on the Online Learning Centre at **http://www.mcgrawhill.ca/olc/schiller**.

PART 2

Product Markets: The Basics

The prices and products we see every day emerge from decisions made by millions of individual consumers and firms. A primary objective of microeconomic theory is to explain how those decisions are made. How do consumers decide which products to buy and in what quantities? What does it cost business firms to produce the goods and services consumers demand? Chapters 4 and 5 address these issues.

The Demand for Goods

After the September 2001 terrorist attacks on the World Trade Centre and the Pentagon, few Americans wanted to board an airplane. When U.S. airports reopened a week later, hardly any passengers showed up. Most planes departed with very light loads. Despite pleas from political and business leaders, consumers refused to fly. Then the airlines reduced airfares—to *really* low levels. Two weeks after the terrorist attacks, roundtrip cross-country fares got as low as $118, with no advance purchase or minimum-stay requirements. Suddenly, air travel regained popularity. Within days after the fare cuts, travellers started filling up the planes again.

The experience of the airlines underscores the importance of *prices* in determining consumer behaviour. Consumers "want," "need," and "just have to have" a vast array of goods and services. When decision time comes, however, product *prices* often dictate what consumers will actually buy. As we observed in Chapter 2, the quantity of a product *demanded* depends on its price. When the airlines cut airfares in late September 2001, consumers purchased a *lot* more tickets.

This chapter takes a closer look at how product prices affect consumer decisions. We focus on three related questions:

- **How do we decide how much of any good to buy?**
- **How does a change in a product's price affect the quantity we purchase or the amount of money we spend on it?**
- **Why do we buy certain products but not others?**

The law of demand (first encountered in Chapter 2) gives us some clues for answering these questions. But we need to look beyond that law to fashion more complete answers. We need to know what forces give demand curves their downward-sloping shape. We also need to know more about how to *use* demand curves to predict consumer behaviour.

LEARNING OBJECTIVES

By the end of this chapter, you should be able to:

4.1 Define the concept of utility

4.2 Explain the law of diminishing marginal utility

4.3 Explain how the utility-maximizing rule leads to the creation of a demand curve

4.4 Identify and explain the four determinants of demand

4.5 Define and compute price elasticity of demand, income elasticity, and cross-price elasticity

4.6 Identify the four determinants of price elasticity of demand

4.7 Define total revenue and explain the relationship to price elasticity of demand

4.1 DETERMINANTS OF DEMAND

In seeking explanations for consumer behaviour, we have to recognize that the field of economics doesn't have all the answers. But it does offer a unique perspective that sets it apart from other fields of study.

Consider first the explanations of consumer behaviour offered by other fields of study. Psychiatrists and psychologists have had a virtual field day formulating such explanations. Freud was among the first to describe us humans as bundles of subconscious (and unconscious) fears, complexes, and anxieties. From a Freudian perspective, we strive for ever higher levels of consumption to satisfy basic drives for security, sex, and ego gratifications. Like the most primitive of people, we clothe and adorn ourselves in ways that assert our identity and worth. We eat and smoke too much because we need the oral gratifications and security associated with mother's breast. Oversized homes and cars give us a source of warmth and security remembered from the womb. On the other hand, we often buy and consume some things we expressly don't desire, just to assert our rebellious feelings against our parents (or parent substitutes). In Freud's view, it's the constant interplay of these id, ego, and superego drives that motivates us to buy, buy, buy.

Sociologists offer additional explanations for our consumption behaviour. Lloyd Warner and David Riesman, for example, noted our yearning to stand above the crowd, to receive recognition from the masses. For people with exceptional talents, such recognition may come easily. But for the ordinary person, recognition may depend on conspicuous consumption. A sleek car, a newer fashion, a more exotic vacation become expressions of identity that provoke recognition, even social acceptance. We strive for ever higher levels of consumption—not just to keep up with the Joneses but to surpass them.

Not *all* consumption is motivated by ego or status concerns, of course. Some food is consumed for the sake of self-preservation, some clothing worn for warmth, and some housing built for shelter. The typical Canadian consumer has more than enough income to satisfy these basic needs. In today's economy, most consumers also have *discretionary* income that can be used to satisfy psychological or sociological longings.

The Sociopsychiatric Explanation

WEB NOTE

For the most recent data on Statistics Canada's annual survey of Canadian households, visit http://www.statcan.ca/start.html and type "Survey of household spending" in the search box.

APPLICATIONS

Canada's Consumption Patterns

Each year, Statistics Canada surveys over 21,000 households across the country in an effort to capture Canadians' spending habits. Not only are the data used by government departments to formulate policy, but various organizations such as social agencies and consumer advocates also use the data to support their positions and lobby governments. From the most recent survey, here are some dollar values as measured by the annual median expenditure per household:

Men vs. Women

- On average, Canadian women spend 15% more on clothing than Canadian men, but almost 40% more on clothing accessories.
- Both men and women spend an equal amount on footwear ($200) and on jewellery and watches ($100).

East vs. West

- Households from Prince Edward Island spend twice as much ($400) on bingos—net of winnings—than households in Alberta ($200). But Albertans spend significantly more ($200) on casinos than households from Prince Edward Island ($60).
- Households in Newfoundland and Labrador spend 29% less on cigarettes than Manitobans ($1,400 vs. $1,800).
- Ontario and Alberta consume the highest amount of alcoholic beverages served on licensed premises ($240).

Source: "Canada's Consumption Patterns," adapted from Statistics Canada CANSIM database, http://cansim2.statcan.ca. Survey of household spending, tables 203-0006, 203-0013, and 203-0014.

Analysis: Consumer patterns vary by gender, geographic location, and other characteristics. Economists try to isolate the common influences on consumer behaviour.

As the Applications box below indicates, Canadians spend some of this discretionary income on games of chance, jewellery, clothing accessories, cigarettes, and alcohol.

The Economic Explanation

Although psychiatrists and sociologists offer intriguing explanations for our consumption patterns, their explanations fall a bit short. Sociopsychiatric theories tell us why teenagers, men, and women *desire* certain goods and services. But they don't explain which goods will actually be *purchased*. Desire is only the first step in the consumption process. To acquire goods and services, one must be willing and able to *pay* for one's wants. Producers won't give you their goods just to satisfy your Freudian desires. They want money in exchange for their goods. Hence, ***prices and income are just as relevant to consumption decisions as are more basic desires and preferences.***

In explaining consumer behaviour, economists focus on the *demand* for goods and services. As we observed in Chapter 2, *demand* entails the *willingness and ability to pay* for goods and services. To say that someone *demands* a particular good means that he or she will offer to *buy* it at some price(s). ***An individual's demand for a specific product is determined by these four factors:***

- *Tastes* (desire for this and other goods).
- *Income* (of the consumer).
- *Expectations* (for income, prices, tastes).
- *Other goods* (their availability and prices).

Note again that desire (tastes) is only one determinant of demand. Other determinants of demand (income, expectations, and other goods) also influence whether a person will be willing and able to buy a certain good at a specific price.

The remainder of this chapter examines these determinants of demand. The objective is not only to explain consumer behaviour but also to predict how consumption patterns change in response to *changes* in the price of a good or to *changes* in underlying tastes, income, prices or availability of other goods, or expectations.

4.2 UTILITY THEORY AND THE DEMAND CURVE

Utility Theory

The starting point for an economic analysis of demand is quite simple. Economists accept consumer tastes as the outcome of sociopsychiatric and cultural influences. They don't look beneath the surface to see how those tastes originated. Economists simply note the existence of certain tastes (desires) and then look to see how those tastes affect consumption decisions. The first observation is that the more pleasure a product gives us, the higher the price we'd be willing to pay for it. If the oral sensation of buttered popcorn at the movies really turns you on, you're likely to be willing to pay dearly for it. If, on the other hand, you have no great taste or desire for popcorn, the theatre might have to give it away before you'd eat it. Economists use the term **utility** to refer to the expected pleasure or satisfaction obtained from goods and services.

utility: The pleasure or satisfaction obtained from a good or service.

Measuring Utility. Measuring the level of satisfaction can be quite challenging; after all, how would we compare the level of satisfaction that different individuals might have for the same amount of a particular good? As it turns out, it is not critical whether we call the unit of measurement "utils" or some other term. The unit of measurement must simply measure "ordinal" utility by capturing the ranking and not the strengths of preferences. For example, if one box of popcorn provides Jean with 100 utils and the second box provides 50 utils, we do not say that the first box provides twice the satisfaction of the second, but simply that the first box of popcorn gives Jean greater satisfaction than the second. Another individual such as Jack may value the first box of popcorn at 8 utils and the second box at 2 utils. Here again, we simply say that Jack receives greater satisfaction for the first box, not that he receives four times as much pleasure as the second box. Once we select a unit of measurement that captures the ordinal ranking for any individual, we are ready to proceed with our analysis.

Total vs. Marginal Utility. We also make an important distinction between total utility and marginal utility. **Total utility** refers to amount of satisfaction obtained from your *entire* consumption of a good or service. By contrast, **marginal utility** refers to the amount of satisfaction that you get from consuming an *additional* (i.e., "marginal") unit of a good or service. We can make the link between total and marginal utility by recognizing that marginal utility simple measures the *change in total utility* that results from the consumption of one more unit. Specifically,

$$\text{Marginal utility} = \frac{\text{change in total utility}}{\text{change in quantity consumed}}$$

total utility: The amount of satisfaction obtained from entire consumption of a product.

marginal utility: The change in total utility obtained by consuming one additional (marginal) unit of a good or service.

Diminishing Marginal Utility. The concepts of total and marginal utility explain not only why we buy popcorn at the movies but also why we stop eating it at some point. Even people who love popcorn (i.e., derive great *total* utility from it) don't eat endless quantities of it. Why not? Presumably because the thrill diminishes with each mouthful. The first box of popcorn may bring sensual gratification, but the second or third box is likely to bring a stomachache. We express this change in perceptions by noting that the *marginal* utility of the first box of popcorn is higher than the additional or *marginal* utility derived from the second box.

The behaviour of popcorn connoisseurs isn't abnormal. As a rule, the amount of additional utility we obtain from a product declines as we continue to consume it. The third slice of pizza isn't as desirable as the first, the sixth beer not as satisfying as the fifth, and so forth. Indeed, this phenomenon of diminishing marginal utility is so nearly universal that economists have fashioned a law around it. This **law of diminishing marginal utility** states that each successive unit of a good consumed yields less *additional* utility.

The law of diminishing marginal utility does *not* say that we won't like the second box of popcorn, the third pizza slice, or the sixth beer; it just says we won't like them as much as the ones we've already consumed. Time is also important here: If the first box of popcorn was eaten last year, the second box may now taste just as good. The law of diminishing marginal utility applies to short time periods.

Figure 4.1 illustrates how Jean's utility changes with the level of consumption. Notice that total utility continues to rise as we consume the first four boxes (ugh!) of popcorn. But total utility increases by smaller and smaller increments. Each successive step of the total utility curve in Figure 4.1 is a little smaller.

Note that the marginal utility curve (*b*) is plotted at the *midpoints* between the quantities of popcorn. This is due to fact that marginal utility measures the *changes* in total utility associated with changes in consumption. This is an important graphing technique that will be used throughout the text for plotting all marginal measurements.

The height of each step of the total utility curve in Figure 4.1 represents *marginal* utility—the increments to total utility. *Marginal* utility is clearly diminishing. Nevertheless, because marginal utility is still *positive*, total utility is increasing. **As long as marginal utility is positive, total utility must be increasing** (note that the total utility curve is still rising for the fourth box of popcorn).

The situation changes with the fifth box of popcorn. According to Figure 4.1, the good sensations associated with popcorn consumption are completely forgotten by the time the fifth box arrives. Nausea and stomach cramps take over. Indeed, the fifth box is absolutely *distasteful*, as reflected in the downturn of *total* utility and the *negative* value for marginal utility. We were happier—in possession of more total utility—with only four boxes of popcorn. The fifth box—yielding *negative* marginal utility—reduces

law of diminishing marginal utility: The marginal utility of a good declines as more of it is consumed in a given time period.

WEB NOTE

Jeremy Bentham (1748–1832) introduced the term "utility" and is considered the founder of British "Utilitarianism." For a brief biography go to http://www.ucl.ac.uk/Bentham-Project/info/jb.htm. Beware of the Auto-Icon!

FIGURE 4.1

Total vs. Marginal Utility

The table shows that Jean's total utility increases for the first four boxes of popcorn that she eats during a show, whereas the fifth box starts to reduce her total utility. Looking at the marginal utility portion of the table, we see that while each of the first 4 boxes has a positive value (100, 50, 20, and 10), these values are decreasing in size—this simply reflects law of diminishing marginal utility. The *shape* or *slope*, of the total utility curve (*a*) illustrates the general idea of diminishing marginal utility. Total utility increases with the first four boxes, but at a diminishing rate (i.e., the slope is always positive but becoming smaller and smaller). Consumption of the fifth box leads to a negative marginal utility, hence the reason that the total utility curve starts to fall (i.e., slope is negative) when Jean buys the fifth box.

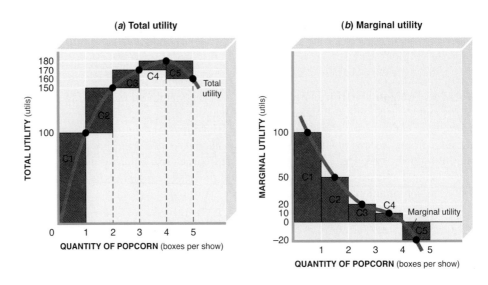

Quantity (Boxes of Popcorn)	Total Utility		Marginal Utility
0	0		
1	100	>	100
2	150	>	50
3	170	>	20
4	180	>	10
5	160	>	−20

total satisfaction. This is the kind of sensation you'd probably experience if you ate six hamburgers (see the cartoon on the next page).

Not every good ultimately reaches negative marginal utility. Yet the more general principle of diminishing marginal utility is experienced daily. That is, ***eventually additional quantities of a good yield increasingly smaller increments of satisfaction.***

Price and Quantity

Marginal utility is essentially a measure of how much we desire particular goods, our *taste*. But which ones will we buy? Clearly, we don't always buy the products we most desire. *Price* is often a problem. All too often we have to settle for goods that yield less marginal utility simply because they are available at a lower price. This explains why most people don't drive Porsches. Our desire ("taste") for a Porsche may be great, but its price is even greater. The challenge for most of us is to somehow reconcile our tastes with our bank balances.

In deciding whether to buy something, our immediate focus is typically on a single variable, namely *price*. Assume for the moment that a person's tastes, incomes, and expectations are set in stone, and that the prices of other goods are set as well. This is the *ceteris paribus* assumption we first encountered in Chapter 1. It doesn't mean that other influences on consumer behaviour are unimportant. Rather, *ceteris paribus* simply allows us to focus on one variable at a time. In this case, we are focusing on price. What we want to know is how high a price a consumer is willing to pay for another unit of a product.

The concepts of marginal utility and *ceteris paribus* enable us to answer this question. The more marginal utility a product delivers, the more a consumer will be willing to pay for it. We also noted that marginal utility *diminishes* as increasing quantities of a product are consumed, suggesting that consumers are willing to pay progressively *less* for additional quantities of a product. The moviegoer willing to pay 50 cents for that first mouth-watering ounce of buttered popcorn may not be willing to pay so much for a

From James Eggert, *Invitation to Economics*, 2nd ed. p. 160. © 1991 by Bristlecone Books. Reprinted with permission of The McGraw-Hill Companies, Inc.

Analysis: No matter how much we like a product, marginal utility is likely to diminish as we consume more of it. If marginal utility becomes *negative* (as here), total satisfaction will decrease.

second or third ounce. The same is true for a second pizza, the sixth beer, and so forth. *With given income, tastes, expectations, and prices of other goods and services, people are willing to buy additional quantities of a good only if its price falls.* In other words, as the marginal utility of a good diminishes, so does our willingness to pay.

This is simply a restatement of the *law of demand* and the resulting *demand curve* definition that we saw in Chapter 2. For a single good, therefore, our demand curve captures the relationship between price, marginal utility, and quantity demanded. Specifically, for any given unit increase in quantity demanded, the price that we are willing to pay must equal the marginal utility associated with that extra unit (P = MU). This would require finding a dollar-value measurement for utility (see Figure 4.2) and we would expect these values to vary from individual to individual.

Utility Theory and Multiple Goods. So far our analysis of utility theory and demand curves has focused on the decision to buy a single good. In what manner can we use utility theory to derive demand curves when a consumer decides to buy many goods? After all, when we go shopping, our concern isn't always limited to how much of one good to purchase. Rather, we must decide which of many available goods to buy at their respective prices.

The presence of so many goods complicates consumption decisions. Our basic objective remains the same, however: We want to get as much satisfaction as possible from our available income. In striving for that objective, we have to recognize that the purchase of any single good means giving up the opportunity to buy more of other goods. In other words, consuming popcorn (or any other good) entails distinct *opportunity costs*.

The economic explanation for consumer choice builds on the theory of marginal utility and the law of demand. Suppose you have a choice between buying a Coke and playing a video game. The first proposition of consumer choice simply states that if you think a Coke will be more satisfying than playing a video game, you'll prefer to buy the Coke. Hardly a revolutionary proposition.

Marginal Utility vs. Price

FIGURE 4.2
Marginal Utility and Individual's Demand Curve for One Good

Once we convert Jean's marginal utility values (see table in Figure 4.2) into a dollar-value equivalent, we can derive her demand curve for boxes of popcorn per show. Note that we did not include the fifth box of popcorn since we assume Jean is intelligent enough to know when to stop before nausea and stomach cramps take over!

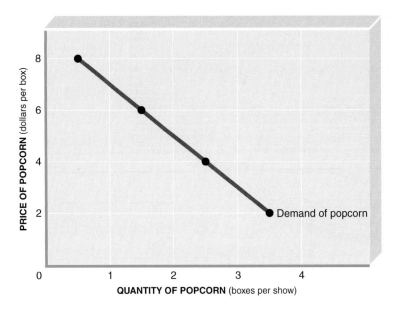

Quantity (Boxes of Popcorn)	Total Utility		Marginal Utility	Dollar Values of Marginal Utility ($/box)
0	0			
1	100	>	100	$8
2	150	>	50	6
3	170	>	20	4
4	180	>	10	2

The second postulate of consumer-choice theory takes into account market prices. Although you may *prefer* to drink a Coke rather than play a video game, one play of a video game is cheaper than a Coke. Under these circumstances, your budget may win out over your desires. There's nothing irrational about playing a video game instead of buying a more desirable Coke when you have a limited amount of income to spend. On the contrary, **rational behaviour requires one to compare the anticipated utility of each expenditure with its price.** The smart thing to do then is to choose those products that promise to provide the most pleasure for the amount of income available.

Suppose your desire for a Coke is greater than your desire to play a video game. Then using our utility theory, we know that the marginal utility of the first Coke (say 15 utils) must be greater than the marginal utility of the first video game (say 10 utils). Which one should you consume? Before reaching for the Coke, you'd better look at prices. What if a Coke costs $2, whereas a video game costs $1? Which one gives you the most satisfaction per dollar spent? You should see that you get more utility per dollar by playing that first video game (10 utils/$1) rather than drinking that first Coke (15 utils/$2 = 7.5 utils/$1).

The same principle explains why some rich people drive a Ford rather than a shiny new Mercedes. Clearly, the marginal utility (MU) of driving a Mercedes is substantially higher than the MU of driving a Ford. But a new Mercedes is also considerably more expensive than a Ford. So when a rich person drives a Ford, it must be the case that the Ford yields more marginal utility per dollar spent (MU/P) than the Mercedes.

	Cokes (Utility)			Video Games (Utility)		
Quantity	Total Utility	Marginal Utility	$\dfrac{MU_{Coke}}{P_{Coke}=\$2}$	Total Utility	Marginal Utility	$\dfrac{MU_{Video\ Game}}{P_{Video\ Game}=\$1}$
0	0			0		
		> 15	7.5		> 10	10
1	15			10		
		> 8	4		> 9	9
2	23			19		
		> 2	1		> 7	7
3	25			26		
		> 0	0		> 5	5
4	25			31		
		> −3	−1.5		> 3	3
5	22			34		
		> −10	−5		> 1	1
6	12			35		

TABLE 4.1
Maximizing Utility

Q: How can you get the most satisfaction (utility) from $6 if you must choose between buying Cokes that cost $2 each and video games that cost $1 each?

A: By drinking one Coke and playing four video games. See text for explanation.

The key to utility maximization, then, isn't simply to buy the things you like best. Instead, you must compare goods on the basis of their marginal utility *and* price. ***To maximize utility, the consumer should choose that good which delivers the most marginal utility per dollar.***

Utility Maximization

This basic principle of consumer choice is easily illustrated. Suppose you have $6.00 to spend on a combination of Cokes and video games, the only consumer goods available. Your objective, as always, is to get the greatest satisfaction possible from this limited income. That is, you want to maximize the *total* utility attainable from the expenditure of your income. The question is how to do it. What combination of Cokes and games will maximize the utility you get from $6?

Table 4.1 indicates how marginal utility diminishes with increasing consumption of a product. Look at what happens to the good taste of Coke. The marginal utility of the first Coke is 15; but the MU of the second Coke is only 8 utils. Once you've quenched your initial thirst, a second Coke still tastes good but isn't nearly so satisfying as the first one. A third Coke yields even less marginal utility, and a fourth one none at all (MU = 0). A fifth or sixth Coke would make your teeth rattle and cause other discomforts—its marginal utilities are actually negative.

The final, and most important, column under the Coke heading is the marginal utility per dollar spent on Coke (MU$_{Coke}$/P$_{Coke}$), and it represents the satisfaction per dollar spent on Cokes for all levels of consumption. Since this column simply divides the marginal utilities by the price of Coke ($2), these values also decrease as the amount of Coke consumed increases.

Video games also conform to the law of diminishing marginal utility. However, marginal utility doesn't decline quite so rapidly in the consumption of video games. The second game is almost as much fun (MU = 9) as the first (MU = 10). Not until you've played several games do you begin to feel the tension and enjoy the game less. By the sixth game, marginal utility is fast approaching zero. Again, the final column under the Video Games heading refers to the marginal utility per dollar spent on video games (MU$_{Video\ Game}$/P$_{Video\ Game}$) and the descending values reflect the diminishing marginal utility of video games.

With these psychological insights to guide us, we can now determine how best to spend $6. What we're looking for is that combination of Cokes and video games that *maximizes* the total utility attainable from an expenditure of $6. We call this combination **optimal consumption**—that is, the mix of goods that yields the most utility for the available income.

optimal consumption: The mix of consumer purchases that maximizes the utility attainable from available income.

We can start looking for the optimal mix of consumer purchases by assessing the utility of spending the entire $6 on video games. At $1 per play, we could buy six games. This would give us *total* utility of 35 utils (see Table 4.1).

Alternatively, you could also spend all your income on Cokes. With $6 to spend, you could buy three Cokes. However, this would generate only 25 utils of total utility.

Hence, if you were forced to choose between *only* drinking Cokes or *only* playing video games, you'd pick the games.

Fortunately, we don't have to make such extreme choices. In reality, we can buy a *combination* of Cokes and video games. This complicates our decision making (with more choices) but permits us to attain higher levels of total satisfaction.

Finding Optimal Consumption. The basic approach to utility maximization is to purchase that good next that delivers the most *marginal utility per dollar*. We saw earlier that you would chose to consume the first video game before the first Coke because the satisfaction you received per dollar spent on the video game was greater than the satisfaction per dollar spent on the Coke (See Table 4.1).

$$\left[\frac{MU_{\text{Video Game}}}{P_{\text{Video Game}=\$1}} = 10 \right] > \left[\frac{MU_{\text{Coke}}}{P_{\text{Coke}=\$2}} = 7.5 \right]$$

As a rational consumer, therefore, you would spend $1 on the video game. After purchasing the video game, you have $5 left to spend on Cokes and video games. How do you proceed? Well, ask yourself the following question. Should I purchase a second video or should I purchase my first Coke? Again, you would look at the marginal utility that you receive per dollar spent. And since,

$$\left[\frac{MU_{\text{Video Game}}}{P_{\text{Video Game}=\$1}} = 9 \right] > \left[\frac{MU_{\text{Coke}}}{P_{\text{Coke}=\$2}} = 7.5 \right]$$

you would purchase the second video game rather than the first Coke and have $4 remaining. Proceeding in this fashion, you should see that after spending the $6, you end up drinking one Coke and playing four video games. Was it worth it? Do you end up with more total utility than you would have received from any other combination? The answer is yes. The *total* utility of one Coke (15 utils) and four video games (31 utils) is 46 utils. This is significantly better than the alternatives of spending your $6 on Cokes alone (total utility = 25) or games alone (total utility = 35). In fact, the combination of one Coke and four video games is the best one you can find. Because this combination maximizes the total utility of your income ($6), it represents *optimal consumption*.

Utility-Maximizing Rule

Optimal consumption implies that the utility-maximizing combination of goods has been found. If this is true, you can't increase your total utility by trading one good for another. All goods included in the optimal consumption mix yield the *same* marginal utility per dollar. In theory, we know we've reached maximum utility when we've satisfied the following rule:

$$\text{Utility-maximizing rule: } \frac{MU_x}{P_x} = \frac{MU_y}{P_y}$$

where x and y represent any two goods included in our consumption.

Rational consumer choice thus depends on comparisons of marginal utilities and prices. If a dollar spent on product X yields more marginal utility than a dollar spent on product Y, we should buy product X. To use this principle, of course, we have to know the amounts of utility obtainable from various goods and be able to perform a little arithmetic. By doing so, however, we can get the greatest satisfaction from our limited income.

You may be wondering why the utility-maximizing rule does not hold for our simple example of Cokes and video games. Our optimum consumption bundle of one Coke and four video games is indeed the best combination but at these values, we see that.

$$\left[\frac{MU_{\text{Video Game}}}{P_{\text{Video Game}=\$1}} = 5 \right] < \left[\frac{MU_{\text{Coke}}}{P_{\text{Coke}=\$2}} = 7.5 \right]$$

This inequality would suggest that we give up video games in favour of another Coke—remember, all our income has been spent, so buying more of one good implies less of the other. But if we did this we would have to give up two video games (at $1 each) since we need $2 for a Coke. If we now settled for two Cokes and two video games, however, not only would the inequality still exist (you should verify that it is reversed!), but the total utility would also be lower than 46 utils (you should also verify this). The problem lies in the fact that we have discrete values of these goods. That is, we have to purchase a complete unit—either a full Coke or a full video game. If we could purchase half a can of Coke or half a video game, perhaps even ⅓ of each good, we could eventually find some combination of these two goods where the utility-maximizing rule holds.

Utility Theory, Multiple Goods, and Demand Curves. We are now in a position to use our utility theory along with multiple goods to derive demand curves. Recall that the demand curve is a relationship between the quantity of a good a consumer is willing and able to buy at alternative prices, *ceteris paribus*. What would happen to your optimum consumption bundle if the price of Cokes fell from $2 to $1 whereas the price of video games remained at $1 and the amount that you had to spend on these two goods also remained constant at $6? Well, you would simply go through the same procedure as you did for deriving our original optimal consumption bundle. That is, you would compare the marginal utility per dollar spent on the first Coke with the marginal utility spent on the first video game and decide which gives you the greatest satisfaction. Table 4.2 has the new values associated with the price of Coke set at $1. You would select a Coke first since

$$\left[\frac{MU_{Coke}}{P_{Coke=\$1}} = 15\right] > \left[\frac{MU_{Video\ Game}}{P_{Video\ Game=\$1}} = 10\right]$$

Once your first purchase is made, you continue in the same manner until the remaining $5 of our income is spent (i.e., does the second Coke give you more satisfaction than the first video game?). You should be able to confirm that your new optimal consumption bundle is two Cokes and four video games.

This basic approach to utility maximization creates your demand curve for Cokes. At a price of $2 per Coke, your optimum consumption was one Coke. When the price of Coke decreased to $1, *ceteris paribus*, your optimum consumption was two Cokes. We could continue in this manner, selecting many different prices for Coke, and derive your complete demand curve for Cokes!

All these tables and equations make consumer choice look dull and mechanical. Economic theory seems to suggest that consumers walk through shopping malls with marginal-utility tables and hand-held computers. In reality, no one does this—not even

Equilibrium Outcomes

Quantity	Cokes (Utility)			Video Games (Utility)		
	Total Utility	Marginal Utility	$\frac{MU_{Coke}}{P_{Coke=\$1}}$	Total Utility	Marginal Utility	$\frac{MU_{Video\ Game}}{P_{Video\ Game=\$1}}$
0	0			0		
		> 15	15		> 10	10
1	15			10		
		> 8	8		> 9	9
2	23			19		
		> 2	2		> 7	7
3	25			26		
		> 0	0		> 5	5
4	25			31		
		> −3	−3		> 3	3
5	22			34		
		> −10	−10		> 1	1
6	12			35		

TABLE 4.2
Maximizing Utility with New Prices

If the price of Cokes decreases from $2 to $1, *ceteris paribus*, the marginal utility per dollar spent on Cokes changes for each quantity purchased. With the price of video games remaining at $1 and income also constant at $6, the new optimal consumption is two Cokes and four video games.

your economics instructor. Yet, economic theory is pretty successful in predicting consumer decisions. Consumers don't always buy the optimal mix of goods and services with their limited income. But after some trial and error, consumers adjust their behaviour. What economic theory predicts is that the final choices—the *equilibrium* outcomes—will be the predicted optimal ones.

4.3 PRICE ELASTICITY

The theory of demand helps explain consumer behaviour. But it's not terribly helpful to the theatre owner who's actually worried about popcorn sales. The general observation that popcorn sales decline when prices increase would be of little use. What the theatre owner wants to know is *by how much* the quantity demanded would fall if the price were raised.

This is the same problem the airlines confronted after the September 2001 terrorist attacks. They knew more people would fly if airfares were reduced. But by *how much* did they have to cut fares to fill their planes again?

The central question in all these decisions is the response of quantity demanded to a change in price. ***The response of consumers to a change in price is measured by the price elasticity of demand.*** Specifically, the **price elasticity of demand** refers to the percentage change in quantity demanded divided by the percentage change in price—that is,

> **price elasticity of demand:** The percentage change in quantity demanded divided by the percentage change in price.

$$\text{Price elasticity}\ (E) = \frac{\%\ \text{change in quantity demanded}}{\%\ \text{change in price}}$$

What would the value of price elasticity be if air travel didn't change at all when price decreased by 5 percent? In that case the price elasticity of demand would be

$$E = \frac{\%\ \text{change in quantity demanded}}{\%\ \text{change in price}}$$

$$= \frac{0}{5} = 0$$

But is this realistic? According to the law of demand, the quantity demanded goes up when price goes down. So we'd expect *somebody* to buy more airline tickets if fares fell by 5 percent. In a large market like air travel, we don't expect *everybody* to jump on a plane when airfares are reduced. But if *some* consumers fly more, the percentage change in quantity demanded will be larger than zero. Indeed, ***the law of demand implies that the price elasticity of demand will always be greater than zero.*** Technically, the price elasticity of demand (E) would be a *negative* number since quantity demanded and price always move in opposite directions. For simplicity, however, E is typically expressed in absolute terms (without the minus sign). ***The key question, then, is how much greater than zero E actually is.***

Computing Price Elasticity

To get a feel for the dimensions of elasticity, consider the example of an individual's demand curve (see Figure 4.3). At a price of 45 cents an ounce (point B in Figure 4.3), the average moviegoer demands two ounces of popcorn per show. At the lower price of 40 cents per ounce (point C), the quantity demanded jumps to four ounces per show.

We can summarize this response with the price elasticity of demand. To do so, we have to calculate the *percentage* changes in quantity and price. Consider the percentage change in quantity first. In this case, the change in quantity demanded

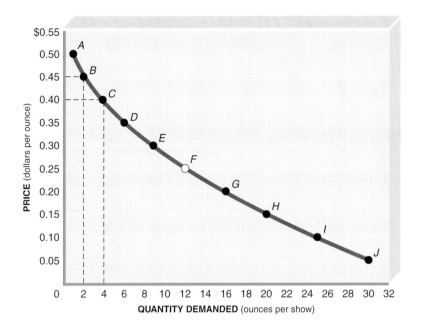

FIGURE 4.3
An Individual's Demand Curve

This demand curve illustrates the specific quantities demanded at alternative prices. If popcorn sold for 25 cents per ounce, this consumer would buy 12 ounces per show (point *F*). At higher prices, less popcorn would be purchased.

is 4 ounces − 2 ounces = 2 ounces. The *percentage* change in quantity demanded is therefore

$$\% \text{ change in quantity demanded} = \frac{2}{q}$$

The problem is to transform the denominator q into a number. Should we use the quantity of popcorn purchased *before* the price reduction, that is, $q_1 = 2$? Or should we use the quantity purchased *after* the price reduction, that is, $q_2 = 4$? The choice of denominator will have a big impact on the computed percentage change. To ensure consistency, economists prefer to use the *average* quantity in the denominator.[1] The average quantity is simply

$$\text{Average quantity} = \frac{q_1 + q_2}{2} = \frac{2 + 4}{2} = 3 \text{ ounces}$$

We can now complete the calculation of the percentage change in quantity demanded. It is

$$\begin{array}{l} \% \text{ change in} \\ \text{quantity demanded} \end{array} = \frac{\begin{array}{c}\text{change in}\\\text{quantity}\end{array}}{\begin{array}{c}\text{average}\\\text{quantity}\end{array}} = \frac{q_2 - q_1}{\dfrac{q_1 + q_2}{2}} = \frac{2}{3} = 0.667$$

Popcorn sales increased by an average of 67 percent when the price of popcorn was reduced from 45 cents to 40 cents per ounce.

The computation of the percentage change in price is similar. We first note that the price of popcorn fell by 5 cents (45¢ − 40¢) when we move from point *B* to point *C* on the demand curve (Figure 4.3). We then compute the *average* price of popcorn in this range of the demand curve as

$$\begin{array}{l}\text{Average price}\\\text{of popcorn}\end{array} = \frac{p_1 + p_2}{2} = \frac{45 + 40}{2} = 42.5 \text{ cents}$$

---

[1]This procedure is referred to as the *arc* (midpoint) elasticity of demand. If a single quantity (price) is used in the denominator, we refer to the *point* elasticity of demand.

This average is our denominator in calculating the percentage price change. Using these numbers, we see that the absolute value of the percentage change is

$$\% \text{ change in price} = \frac{\text{change in price}}{\text{average price}} = \frac{p_2 - p_1}{\dfrac{p_1 + p_2}{2}} = \frac{5}{42.5} = 0.118$$

The price of popcorn fell by 11.8 percent.

Now we have all the information required to compute the price elasticity of demand. In this case,

$$E = \frac{\% \text{ change in quantity demanded}}{\% \text{ change in price}} = \frac{0.667}{0.118} = 5.65$$

What we get from all these calculations is a very useful number. It says that the consumer response to a price reduction will be extremely large. Specifically, the quantity of popcorn consumed will increase 5.65 times as fast as price falls. A 1 percent reduction in price brings about a 5.65 percent increase in purchases. The theatre manager can therefore boost popcorn sales greatly by lowering price a little.

Elastic vs. Inelastic Demand. We characterize the demand for various goods in one of three ways: *elastic, inelastic,* or *unitary elastic*. If **E is larger than 1, demand is elastic.** Consumer response is large relative to the change in price.

If E is less than 1, we say demand is inelastic. **If demand is inelastic, consumers aren't very responsive to price changes.**

If E is equal to 1, demand is unitary elastic. In this case, the percentage change in quantity demanded is exactly equal to the percentage change in price.

Consider the case of smoking. Many smokers claim they'd "pay anything" for a cigarette after they've run out. But would they? Would they continue to smoke just as many cigarettes if prices doubled or tripled? If so, the demand curve would be vertical (as in Figure 4.4*b*) rather than downward-sloping. Research suggests this is

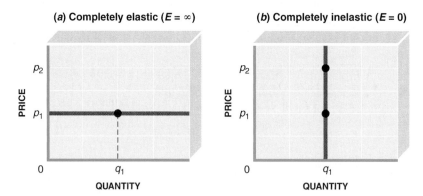

FIGURE 4.4
Extremes of Elasticity

If demand were perfectly elastic ($E = \infty$), the demand curve would be *horizontal*. In that case, any increase in price (e.g., p_1 to p_2) would cause quantity demanded to fall to zero.

A *vertical* demand curve implies that an increase in price won't affect the quantity demanded. In this situation of completely *in*elastic ($E = 0$) demand, consumers are willing to pay *any* price to get the quantity q_1.

In reality, elasticities of demand for goods and services lie between these two extremes (obeying the law of demand).

Product	Price Elasticity
Relatively elastic (E > 1)	
Airline travel, long run	2.4
Restaurant meals	2.3
Fresh fish	2.2
New cars, short run	1.2–1.5
Unitary elastic (E = 1)	
Private education	1.1
Radios and televisions	1.2
Shoes	0.9
Movies	0.9
Relatively inelastic (E < 1)	
Cigarettes	0.4
Coffee	0.3
Gasoline, short run	0.2
Electricity (in homes)	0.1
Long-distance phone calls	0.1

Sources: Compiled from Hendrick S. Houthakker and Lester D. Taylor, *Consumer Demand in the United States, 1929–1970* (Cambridge: Harvard University Press, 1966); F. W. Bell, "The Pope and Price of Fish," *American Economic Review*, December 1968; Herbert Scarf and John Shoven, *Applied General Equilibrium Analysis* (New York: Cambridge University Press, 1984); and Michael Ward, "Product Substitutability and Competition in Long-Distance Telecommunications," *Economic Inquiry*, October 1999.

TABLE 4.3
Elasticity Estimates

Price elasticities vary greatly. When the price of gasoline increases, consumers reduce their consumption only slightly. When the price of fish increases, however, consumers cut back their consumption substantially. These differences reflect the availability of immediate substitutes, the prices of the goods, and the amount of time available for changing behaviour.

not the case: Higher cigarette prices *do* curb smoking. There is at least *some* elasticity in the demand for cigarettes. But the elasticity of demand is low; Table 4.3 indicates that the elasticity of cigarette demand is only 0.4.

Although the average adult smoker is not very responsive to changes in cigarette prices, teen smokers apparently are. As the accompanying Applications box indicates, teen smoking dropped about 4 percent from 2001–2002. Notice the difficulty in calculating the price elasticity of teenage cigarette consumption. Higher taxes did lead to price increases of "regular" cigarettes, but other factors such as advertising, smoking bans, and prices of "discount" cigarettes also changed. Unless we can find a way to remove the effects of these other factors on the teenage demand for cigarettes, our required *ceteris paribus* condition is no longer valid.

According to Table 4.3, the demand for airline travel is even more price-elastic. Whenever a fare cut is announced, the airlines get swamped with telephone inquiries. If fares are discounted by 25 percent, the number of passengers may increase by as much as 60 percent. As Table 4.3 shows, the elasticity of airline demand is 2.4, meaning that the percentage change in quantity demanded (60 percent) will be 2.4 times larger than the price cut (25 percent).

Why are consumers price-sensitive (*E* > 1) with some goods and not (*E* < 1) with others? To answer that, we must go back to the demand curve itself. The elasticity of demand is computed between points on a given demand curve. Hence, *the price elasticity of demand is influenced by all the determinants of demand.* Four factors are particularly worth noting.

Necessities vs. Luxuries. Some goods are so critical to our everyday life that we regard them as "necessities." A hair brush, toothpaste, and perhaps textbooks might fall into this category. Our "taste" for such goods is so strong that we can't imagine getting along without them. As a result, we don't change our consumption of "necessities" very much when the price increases; *demand for necessities is relatively inelastic.*

WEB NOTE

The Canadian Cancer Society (http://www.cancer.ca) encourages smokers to take advantage of the National Non-Smoking Week each January and to take the first steps to becoming a non-smoker. For the latest statistics on smoking trends, click on the "Publications" box after you select your province.

Determinants of Elasticity

APPLICATIONS

Teen Smoking Rate Drops Below that of General Population: StatsCan

OTTAWA (CP)—Fewer teens lit up last year, as their smoking rate fell below that of the general population for the first time in almost a decade, Statistics Canada reported Monday.

The twice-yearly tobacco use monitoring survey found that 18 percent of teens aged 15 to 19 smoked last year, down from 22 percent in 2002. Girls were more likely (20 percent) to light up than boys (17 percent), but drops in smoking among Quebec boys and Ontario girls accounted for much of the overall decrease.

The Canadian Cancer Society welcomed the news, but said more needs to be done to get at those still on the weed. "The results of this survey are encouraging," said Rob Cunningham, a senior policy analyst for the society.

Cunningham said the drop in teen smoking was likely the result of a number of things, including higher taxes, graphic visual warnings on packages, advertising and promotion restrictions, and bans on smoking in the workplace and in public places.

Cunningham said a new threat to the anti-smoking movement has arisen in the form of discount cigarettes. The cut-rate smokes, which sell for at least a dollar a pack less than regular brands, have traditionally held only 1 or 2 percent of the market, but that has changed in recent months, he said.

In the second quarter of the year, discount cigarettes made up 28 percent of the market and one major tobacco company has predicted they'll soon account for 40 percent.

"Our recommended response to this . . . is to increase tobacco taxes," Cunningham said. "There's new room for governments to increase tobacco taxes."

Source: John Ward, Canadian Press, August 9, 2004. Used with the permission of the Canadian Press.

Analysis: The effectiveness of higher cigarette prices in curbing teen smoking depends on the price elasticity of demand.

A "luxury" good, by contrast, is something we'd *like* to have but aren't likely to buy unless our income jumps or the price declines sharply, such as vacation travel, new cars, and camera phones. We want them but can get by without them. That is, *demand for luxury goods is relatively elastic.*

Availability of Substitutes. Our notion of which goods are necessities is also influenced by the availability of substitute goods. The high elasticity of demand for fish (Table 4.3) reflects the fact that consumers can always eat chicken, beef, or pork if fish prices rise. On the other hand, most coffee drinkers can't imagine any other product that could substitute for a cup of coffee. As a consequence, when coffee prices rise, consumers don't reduce their purchases very much at all. Likewise, the low elasticity of demand for gasoline reflects the fact that most cars can't run on alternative fuels. In general, *the greater the availability of substitutes, the higher the price elasticity of demand.* This is a principle that New York City learned when it raised the price of cigarettes in 2002. As the Applications box explains, smugglers quickly supplied a substitute good and legal sales of cigarettes declined drastically in New York City.

Relative Price (to income). Another important determinant of elasticity is the price of the good in relation to a consumer's income. Airline travel and new cars are quite expensive, so even a small percentage change in their prices can have a big impact on a consumer's budget (and consumption decisions). The demand for such "big-ticket" items tends to be elastic. By contrast, coffee is so cheap for most people that even a large *percentage* change in price doesn't affect consumer behaviour very much.

Because the relative price of a good affects price elasticity, the value of *E changes* along a given demand curve. At current prices the elasticity of demand for coffee is low. How would consumers behave, however, if coffee cost $5 a cup? Some people would still consume coffee. At such higher prices, however, the quantity demanded would be much more sensitive to price changes. Accordingly, when we observe, as in Table 4.3, that the demand for coffee is price-inelastic, that observation applies only

APPLICATIONS

New York City's Costly Smokes

New York City has the nation's costliest smokes. NYC Mayor Michael Bloomberg raised the city's excise tax from 8 cents a pack to $1.50 effective July 2002. Together with state and federal taxes, that raised the retail price of smokes in NYC to nearly $8 a pack.

Mayor Bloomberg expected the city to reap a tax bonanza from the 350 million packs of cigarettes sold annually in NYC. What he got instead was a lesson in elasticity. NYC smokers can buy cigarettes for a lot less money outside the city limits.

Or they can stay home and buy cigarettes on the Internet from (untaxed) Indian reservations, delivered by UPS. They can also buy cigarettes smuggled in from low-tax states like Kentucky, Virginia, and North Carolina. What matters isn't the price elasticity of demand for cigarettes in general (around 0.4), but the elasticity of demand for *NYC-taxed* cigarettes. That turned out to be quite high. Unit sales of NYC cigarettes plummeted by 44 percent after the "Bloomberg tax" was imposed.

Source: *"NewsFlash," Economy Today,* October 2002.

Analysis: If demand is price-elastic, a price increase will lead to a disproportionate drop in unit sales. In this case, the ready availability of substitutes (cigarettes from other jurisdictions) made demand highly price-elastic.

to the current range of prices. Were coffee prices dramatically higher, the price elasticity of demand would be higher as well. As a rule, *the price elasticity of demand declines as price moves down the demand curve.*

Time. Finally, time affects the price elasticity of demand. Car owners can't switch to electric autos every time the price of gasoline goes up. In the short run, the elasticity of demand for gasoline is quite low. With more time to adjust, however, consumers can buy more fuel-efficient cars, relocate their homes or jobs, and even switch fuels. As a consequence, *the long-run price elasticity of demand is higher than the short-run elasticity.* Nobel Prize-winning economist Gary Becker used the distinction between long-run and short-run elasticities to explain why a proposed increase in cigarette excise taxes wouldn't generate nearly as much revenue as President Clinton expected (see the Applications box).

APPLICATIONS

Professor Becker Corrects President's Math

President Clinton has seized upon the cigarette excise tax as an expedient and politically correct means of increasing federal revenue. In 1994, the federal government took in $12 billion from the present 24-cents-per-pack tax. If the tax were quadrupled to $1 a pack, Clinton figures tax revenues would increase by more than $50 billion over three years. Those added revenues would help finance the health-care reforms the President so dearly wants.

Professor Gary Becker, a Nobel Prize–winning economist at the University of Chicago, says Clinton's math is wrong. The

White House assumed that cigarette sales would drop by 4 percent for every 10 percent increase in price. Professor Becker says that reflects only the first-year response to higher prices, not the full adjustment of smokers' behaviour. Over a three-year period, cigarette consumption is likely to decline by 8 percent for every 10 percent increase in price—twice as much as Clinton assumed. As a result, the $1-a-pack tax will bring in much less revenue than President Clinton projected.

Source: *BusinessWeek,* August 15, 1994. © 1994 The McGraw-Hill Companies, Inc. Reprinted with permission. www.businessweek.com

Analysis: It takes time for people to adjust their behaviour to changed prices. Hence, the short-run price elasticity of demand is lower than the long-run elasticity.

4.4 PRICE ELASTICITY AND TOTAL REVENUE

The concept of price elasticity refutes the popular misconception that producers charge the "highest price possible." Except in the very rare case of completely inelastic demand, this notion makes no sense. Indeed, higher prices may actually *lower* total sales revenue.

The **total revenue** of a seller is the amount of money received from product sales and is determined by the quantity of the product sold and the price at which it is sold:

> **total revenue:** The price of a product multiplied by the quantity sold in a given time period.

$$\text{Total revenue} = \text{price} \times \text{quantity sold}$$

In the price elasticity example, if the price of popcorn is 40 cents per ounce and only four ounces are sold, total revenue equals $1.60 per show. This revenue is illustrated by the shaded rectangle in Figure 4.5. (The area of a rectangle is equal to its height [p] times its width [q].)

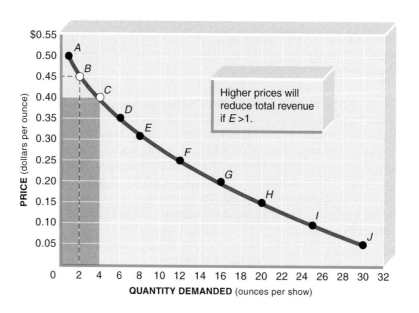

FIGURE 4.5

Elasticity and Total Revenue

Total revenue is equal to the price of the product times the quantity sold. It is illustrated by the area of the rectangle formed by $p \times q$. The shaded rectangle illustrates total revenue ($1.60) at a price of 40 cents and a quantity demanded of four ounces. When price is increased to 45 cents, the rectangle and total revenue shrink (see dashed lines) because demand is relatively elastic in that price range. Price hikes increase total revenue only if demand is inelastic.

	Price	×	Quantity Demanded	=	Total Revenue
A	50¢		1		$0.50
B	45		2		0.90
C	40		4		1.60
D	35		6		2.10
E	30		8		2.40
F	25		12		3.00
G	20		16		3.20
H	15		20		3.00
I	10		25		2.50
J	5		30		1.50

If Demand is	Effect on Total Revenue of	
	Price Increase	Price Reduction
Elastic ($E > 1$)	Decrease	Increase
Inelastic ($E < 1$)	Increase	Decrease
Unitary elastic ($E = 1$)	No change	No change

TABLE 4.4
Price Elasticity of Demand and Total Revenue

The impact of higher prices on total revenue depends on the price elasticity of demand. Higher prices result in higher total revenue only if demand is inelastic. If demand is elastic, *lower* prices result in *higher* revenues.

Now consider what happens to total revenue when the price of popcorn is increased. From the law of demand, we know that an increase in price will lead to a decrease in quantity demanded. But what about total revenue? The change in total revenue depends on *how much* quantity demanded falls when price goes up.

Suppose we raise popcorn prices again, from 40 cents back to 45 cents. What happens to total revenue? At 40 cents per box, four ounces are sold (see Figure 4.5) and total revenue equals $1.60. If we increase the price to 45 cents, only two ounces are sold and total revenue drops to 90 cents. In this case, an *increase* in price leads to a *decrease* in total revenue. This new and smaller total revenue is illustrated by the dashed rectangle in Figure 4.5.

Price increases don't always lower total revenue. If consumer demand was relatively *inelastic* ($E < 1$), a price increase would lead to *higher* total revenue. Thus, we conclude that

- *A price hike increases total revenue only if demand is inelastic ($E < 1$).*
- *A price hike reduces total revenue if demand is elastic ($E > 1$).*
- *A price hike does not change total revenue if demand is unitary-elastic $E = 1$.*

Table 4.4 summarizes these and other responses to price changes.

Changing Value of E. Once we know the price elasticity of demand, we can predict how consumers will respond to changing prices. We can also predict what will happen to the total revenue of the seller when price is raised or reduced. Figure 4.6 shows how elasticity and total revenue change along a given demand curve. Demand for cigarettes is *elastic* ($E > 1$) at prices above $6 per pack but *inelastic* ($E < 1$) at lower prices.

The bottom half of Figure 4.6 shows how total revenue changes along the demand curve. At very high prices (e.g., $14 a pack), few cigarettes are sold and total revenue is low. As the price is reduced, however, the quantity demanded increases so much that total revenue *increases,* despite the lower price. With each price reduction from $14 down to $6 total revenue increases.

Price cuts below $6 a pack continue to increase the quantity demanded (the law of demand). The increase in unit sales is no longer large enough, however, to offset the price reductions. Total revenue starts falling after price drops below $6 per pack. The lesson to remember here is that ***the impact of a price change on total revenue depends on the (changing) price elasticity of demand.***

FIGURE 4.6

Price Elasticity Changes along a Demand Curve

The concept of price elasticity can be used to determine whether people will spend more money on cigarettes when price rises. The answer to this question is yes and no, depending on how high the price goes.

Notice in the table and the graphs that total revenue rises when the price of cigarettes increases from $2 to $4 a pack and again to $6. At low prices, the demand for cigarettes appears relatively inelastic: Price and total revenue move in the same direction.

As the price of cigarettes continues to increase, however, total revenue starts to fall. As the price is increased from $6 to $8 a pack, total revenue drops. At higher prices, the demand for cigarettes is relatively elastic: Price and total revenue move in *opposite* directions. Hence, the price elasticity of demand depends on where one is on the demand curve.

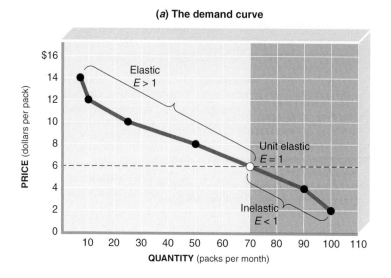

(*a*) The demand curve

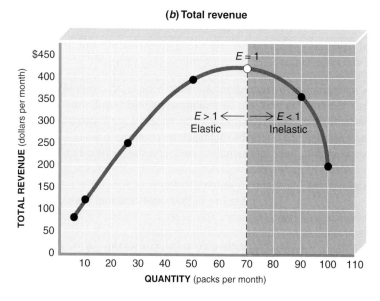

(*b*) Total revenue

Price of Cigarettes	×	Quantity Demanded	=	Total Revenue	
$2		100		$200 ⎫	Low elasticity
4		90		360 ⎬	(total revenue rising
6		70		420 ⎭	as price increases)
8		50		400 ⎫	High elasticity
10		25		250 ⎪	(total revenue falling
12		10		120 ⎬	as price increases)
14		6		84 ⎭	

4.5 OTHER ELASTICITIES

The price elasticity of demand tells us how consumers will respond to a change in the price of a good under the assumption of *ceteris paribus*. But other factors do change, and consumption behaviour may respond to those changes as well.

We recognized this problem in Chapter 2 when we first distinguished *movements* along a demand curve from *shifts* of the demand curve. A movement along an unchanged demand curve represents consumer response to a change in the *price* of that specific good. The magnitude of that movement is expressed in the price elasticity of demand.

When the underlying determinants of demand change, the entire demand curve shifts. These shifts also alter consumer behaviour. The *price* elasticity of demand is of no use in gauging these behavioural responses, since it refers to price changes (movements along a constant demand curve) for that good only.

A change in any determinant of demand will shift the demand curve. Suppose consumer incomes were to increase. How would popcorn consumption be affected? Figure 4.7 provides an answer. Before the change in income, consumers demanded 12 ounces of popcorn at a price of 25 cents per ounce. With more income to spend, the new demand curve (D_2) suggests that consumers will now purchase a greater quantity of popcorn at every price. The increase in income has caused a rightward *shift in demand*. If popcorn continues to sell for 25 cents per ounce, consumers will now buy 16 ounces per show (point N) rather than only 12 ounces (point F).

It appears that changes in income have a substantial impact on consumer demand for popcorn. The graph in Figure 4.7 doesn't tell us, however, how large the change in income was. Will a *small* increase in income cause such a shift, or does popcorn demand increase only when moviegoers have a *lot* more money to spend?

Figure 4.7 doesn't answer these questions. But a little math will. Specifically, the **income elasticity of demand** relates the *percentage* change in quantity demanded to the *percentage* change in income—that is,

$$\text{Income elasticity of demand} = \frac{\begin{array}{c}\% \text{ change in} \\ \text{quantity demanded} \\ \text{(at given price)}\end{array}}{\begin{array}{c}\% \text{ change in} \\ \text{income}\end{array}}$$

The similarity to the price elasticity of demand is apparent. In this case, however, the denominator is *income* (a determinant of demand), not *price*.

Computing Income Elasticity. As was the case with price elasticity, we compute income elasticity with *average* values for the changes in quantity and income. Suppose

Shifts vs. Movements

Income Elasticity

income elasticity of demand: Percentage change in quantity demanded divided by percentage change in income.

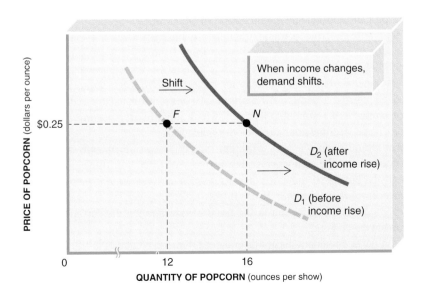

FIGURE 4.7
Income Elasticity

If income changes, the demand curve *shifts*. In this case, an increase in income enables consumers to buy more popcorn at every price. At a price of 25 cents, the quantity demanded increases from 12 ounces (point *F*) to 16 ounces (point *N*). The *income elasticity of demand* measures this response of demand to a change in income.

that the shift in popcorn demand illustrated in Figure 4.7 occurred when income increased from $110 per week to $120 per week. We would then compute

$$\text{Income elasticity} = \frac{\dfrac{\text{change in quantity demanded}}{\text{average quantity}}}{\dfrac{\text{change in income}}{\text{average income}}}$$

$$= \frac{\dfrac{16 \text{ ounces} - 12 \text{ ounces}}{14 \text{ ounces}}}{\dfrac{\$120 - \$110}{\$115}}$$

$$= \frac{4}{14} \div \frac{10}{115}$$

$$= \frac{0.286}{0.087} = 3.29$$

Popcorn purchases are very sensitive to changes in income. When incomes rise by 8.7 percent, popcorn sales increase by a whopping 28.6 percent (that is, 8.7% × 3.29). The computed elasticity of 3.29 summarizes this relationship.

Normal vs. Inferior Goods. Demand and income don't always move in the same direction. Popcorn is a **normal good** because consumers buy more of it when their incomes rise. People actually buy *less* of some goods, however, when they have more income. With low incomes, people buy discount clothes, used textbooks, and cheap beer, and they eat at home. With more money to spend, they switch to designer clothes, new books, premium beers, and restaurant meals. The former items are called **inferior goods** because the quantity demanded falls when income rises. Similarly, when incomes *decline,* people demand *more* spaghetti and the services of credit agencies and pawnbrokers. *For inferior goods, the income elasticity of demand is negative: for normal goods, it is positive.*

normal good: Good for which demand increases when income rises.

inferior good: Good for which demand decreases when income rises.

Cross-Price Elasticity

Changes in income are only one of the forces that shift demand curves. If popcorn were the only snack offered in movie theatres, people would undoubtedly eat more of it. In reality, people have other choices: candy, soft drinks, ice cream, and more. Thus, the decision to buy popcorn depends not only on its price but also on the price and availability of other goods.

Suppose for the moment that the prices of these other goods were to fall. Imagine that candy bars were put on sale for a quarter, rather than the usual dollar. Would this price reduction on candy affect the consumption of popcorn?

According to Figure 4.8, the demand for popcorn might *decrease* if the price of candy fell. The leftward shift of the demand curve from D_1 to D_2 tells us that consumers now demand less popcorn at every price. At 25 cents per ounce, consumers now demand only 8 ounces of popcorn (point R) rather than the previous 12 ounces (point F). In other words, a decline in the price of *candy* has caused a reduction in the demand for *popcorn*. We conclude that candy and popcorn are *substitute goods*— when the price of one declines, demand for the other falls.

Popcorn sales would follow a very different path if the price of soft drink fell. People like to wash down their popcorn with a soft drink. When soft drink prices fall, moviegoers actually buy *more* popcorn. Here again, *a change in the price of one good affects the demand for another good.* In this case, however, we're dealing with *complementary goods,* since a decline in the price of one good causes an increase in the demand for the other good.

The distinction between substitute goods and complementary goods is illustrated in Figure 4.8. Note that *in the case of substitute goods the price of one good and the demand for the other move in the same direction.* (A *decrease* in candy prices causes a *decrease* in popcorn demand.) Likewise, as the price of music downloads *declined,*

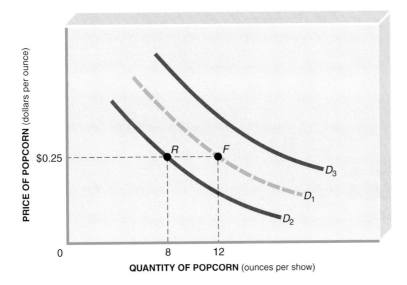

FIGURE 4.8
Substitutes and Complements

The curve D_1 represents the initial demand for popcorn, given the prices of other goods. Other prices may change, however. If a reduction in the price of another good (candy) causes a *reduction* in the demand for this good (popcorn), the two goods are *substitutes*. Popcorn demand shifts to the left (to D_2) when the price of a substitute good falls.

If a reduction in the price of another good (e.g., Pepsi) leads to an *increase* in the demand for this good (popcorn), the two goods are *complements*. Popcorn demand shifts to the right (to D_3) when the price of a complementary good falls.

the demand for CD burners (a complementary good) *increased* but the demand for pre-recorded music CDs (substitute goods) *declined.*

In the case of complementary goods (e.g., Pepsi and popcorn, cream and coffee), the price of one good and the demand for the other move in opposite directions. This helps explain why North American consumers bought more cars in 1998–99 when gasoline prices were falling and fewer SUVs in 2004 when gasoline prices were rising. The concept of complementary goods also explains why the demand for computer software increases when the price of computer hardware drops.

Calculating Cross-Price Elasticity. The mathematical relationship between the price of one good and demand for another is summarized in yet another elasticity concept. The **cross-price elasticity of demand** is the *percentage* change in the quantity demanded on one good divided by the *percentage* change in the price of *another* good—that is,

$$\text{Cross-price elasticity of demand} = \frac{\%\text{ change in quantity demanded of good } X \text{ (at given price)}}{\%\text{ change in price of good } Y}$$

cross-price elasticity of demand: Percentage change in the quantity demanded of X divided by percentage change in price of Y.

Influencing Demand. Sidney Crosby, the youngest player in history to win the National Hockey League's scoring title, signed a multi-million dollar, five-year deal with Reebok before he even played his first professional hockey game. Just a few weeks after signing his Reebok contract, he signed another multi-million dollar contract with Gatorade. These endorsement deals are designed to help persuade us to purchase Reebok Hockey gear and to drink Gatorade sports beverages. Do his sponsors know something economic theory doesn't? Economists *assume* consumers know what they want and will act rationally to get the most satisfaction they can. The companies that sponsored hockey star Sidney Crosby don't accept that assumption. They think your tastes will follow Crosby's lead.

Advertisers now spend over $200 *billion* ($US) per year to change our tastes. This spending works out to over $400 ($US) per consumer in the United States, one of the highest per capita advertising rates in the world (see World View box on the next page). In Canada advertisers spend over $150 ($US) per consumer. Some of this advertising (including product labelling) is intended to provide information about existing products or to bring new products to our attention. A great deal of advertising, however, is also designed to exploit our senses and lack of knowledge. Recognizing that we're guilt-ridden, insecure, and sex-hungry, advertisers promise exoneration, recognition, and love; all we have to do is buy the right product.

Where the Pitch Is Loudest

AD SPENDING PER CAPITA

TOTAL SPENDING

U.S.	$438
Japan	$263
United Kingdom	$249
Germany	$238
France	$167
Canada	$157
Spain	$122
Italy	$121
Brazil	$52

$79
World average per person

Source: *Ad Age Global,* February 2001. Reprinted with permission. Copyright Crain Communications, Inc. 2001.

Analysis: Producers advertise to change consumer tastes (preferences). At higher levels of income, advertising is likely to play a greater role in consumption decisions.

A favourite target of advertisers is our sense of insecurity. Thousands of products are marketed in ways that appeal to our need for identity. Thousands of brand images are designed to help the consumer answer the nagging question, Who am I? The answers, of course, vary. Molson Canadian beer says, "I am Canadian" and Miller High Life says that it is "the champagne of beers"; if you eat at Taco Bell, you are someone who thinks "outside the bun"; Camel cigarettes must be healthier because "more doctors smoke Camels than any other cigarette"; Gatorade says that "it's inside Sidney" so if it's inside you, shouldn't you be able to stickhandle the puck like Sid the Kid?

Are Wants Created?

Advertising can't be blamed for all of our foolish consumption. Even members of the most primitive tribes, uncontaminated by the seductions of advertising, adorned themselves with rings, bracelets, and pendants. Furthermore, advertising has grown to massive proportions only in the past 50 years, but consumption spending has been increasing throughout recorded history. Finally, a lot of advertising simply fails to change buying decisions. Accordingly, it's a mistake to attribute the growth or content of consumption entirely to the persuasions of advertisers.

This isn't to say that advertising has necessarily made us happier. The objective of all advertising is to alter the choices we make. Just as product images are used to attract us to particular products, so are pictures of hungry, ill-clothed children used to persuade us to give money to charity. In the same way, public relations gimmicks are employed to sway our votes for public servants. In the case of consumer products, advertising seeks to increase tastes for particular goods and services and therewith our willingness to pay. *A successful advertising campaign is one that shifts the demand curve for a specific product to the right,* inducing consumers to increase their purchases of a product at every price (see Figure 4.9). Advertising may also increase brand loyalty, making the demand curve less elastic (reducing consumer responses to price increases). By influencing our choices in this way, advertising will

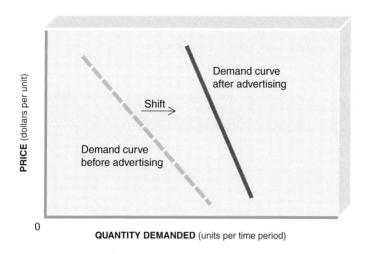

The Impact of Advertising on a Demand Curve

Advertising seeks to increase our taste for a particular product. If our taste (the product's perceived utility) increases, so will our willingness to buy. The resulting change in demand is reflected in a rightward shift of the demand curve, often accompanied by diminished elasticity.

affect the consumption choices we make in the economy tomorrow. Advertising alone is unlikely to affect the total *level* of consumption, however.

SUMMARY

- Our desires for goods and services originate in the structure of personality and social dynamics and aren't explained by economic theory. Economic theory focuses on *demand*—that is, our ability and willingness to buy specific quantities of a good at various prices.
- Marginal utility measures the additional satisfaction obtained from consuming one more unit of a good. The law of diminishing marginal utility says that the more of a product we consume, the smaller the increments of pleasure we tend to derive from additional units of it. This is a basis for the law of demand.
- In choosing among alternative goods and services, a consumer compares the prices and anticipated satisfactions that they offer. To maximize utility with one's available income—to achieve an optimal mix of goods and services—one has to get the most utility for every dollar spent. To do so, one must compare the relative prices and pleasures and choose those goods which offer the most marginal utility per dollar.
- The price elasticity of demand is a numerical measure of consumer response to a change in price, *ceteris paribus*. It equals the percentage change in quantity demanded divided by the

percentage change in price. Elasticity depends on the relative price of a good, the availability of substitutes, and time.

- The effect of a price change on total revenue depends on price elasticity. Total revenue and price move in the same direction only if demand is price-inelastic ($E < 1$).
- The shape and position of any particular demand curve depend on a consumer's income, tastes, expectations, and the price and availability of other goods. Should any of these factors change, the assumption of *ceteris paribus* will no longer hold, and the demand curve will *shift*.
- The income elasticity of demand measures the response of demand to a change in income. If demand increases with income, the product is a normal good. If demand declines (shifts left) when income rises, it's an inferior good.
- Cross-price elasticity measures the response of demand for one good to a change in the price of another. The cross-price elasticity of demand is positive for substitute goods and negative for complementary goods.
- Advertising seeks to change consumer tastes and thus the willingness to buy. If tastes do change, the demand curve for that product will shift.

Key Terms*

utility 72
total utility 73
marginal utility 73
law of diminishing marginal utility 73
optimal consumption 77

price elasticity of demand 80
total revenue 86
income elasticity of demand 89
normal good 90
inferior good 90

cross-price elasticity of demand 91
indifference curve (A) 96
indifference map (A) 97
budget constraint (A) 97
marginal rate of substitution (A) 99

*(**A**) indicates the key term is found in the Appendix.

Questions for Discussion

1. What does the demand for enrollments in your college look like? What is on the axes? Is the demand price-elastic? Income-elastic? How could you find out?
2. If the marginal utility of pizza never diminished, how many pizzas would you eat?
3. How does total and marginal utility change as you spend more time surfing the net?
4. If the price of gasoline doubled, how would consumption of (a) gasoline, (b) cars, (c) public transportation be affected? How quickly would these adjustments be made?
5. Identify two goods each whose demand exhibits (a) high income elasticity, (b) low income elasticity, (c) high price elasticity, (d) low price elasticity. What accounts for the differences in elasticity?
6. Why is the demand for New York City cigarettes so much more elastic than the overall market demand for cigarettes? (See the Applications box, page 85.)

7. Why are per capita advertising expenditures so high in the United States and so low in Brazil? (See World View box, page 92.)
8. According to the Applications box on page 84, what factors contributed to the decline in Canadian teenage smoking rates? Explain whether each contributing factor resulted in a shift of, or a movement along the demand curve for cigarettes.
9. If you owned a movie theatre, would you want the demand for movies to be elastic or inelastic?
10. How has the Internet affected the price elasticity of demand for air travel?
11. If the elasticity of demand for coffee is so low (Table 4.3), why doesn't Starbucks raise the price of coffee to $10 a cup?
12. What would happen to unit sales and total revenue for this textbook if the bookstore reduced its price?

EXERCISES

PROBLEMS   The Student Problem Set to accompany this chapter can be found at the end of the book.

WEB ACTIVITIES   Web Activities to accompany this chapter can be found on the Online Learning Centre at **http://www.mcgrawhill.ca/olc/schiller**.

APPENDIX

INDIFFERENCE CURVES

A consumer's demand for any specific product is an expression of many forces. As we've observed, the actual quantity of a product demanded by a consumer varies inversely with its price. The price-quantity relationship is determined by

- *Tastes* (desire for this and other goods).
- *Income* (of the consumer).
- *Expectations* (for income, prices, tastes).
- *Other goods* (their availability and price).

Economic theory attempts to show how each of these forces affects consumer demand. Thus far, we've used two-dimensional demand curves to illustrate the basic principles of demand. We saw that, in general, a change in the price of a good causes a movement along the demand curve, while a change in tastes, income, expectations, or other goods shifts the entire demand curve to a new position.

We haven't looked closely at the origins of demand curves, however. We assumed that a demand curve could be developed from observations of consumer behaviour, such as the number of boxes of popcorn that were purchased at various prices (Figure 4.3).

Combination	Cokes	Video Games
A	1	8
B	2	5
C	3	4

TABLE 4A.1
Equally Satisfying Combinations

Different combinations of two goods may be equally satisfying. In this case we assume that the combinations A, B, and C all yield equal total utility. Hence, the consumer will be indifferent about which of the three combinations he or she receives.

Likewise, we observed how the demand curve shifts in response to changes in tastes, income, expectations, or other goods (Figures 4.7 and 4.8).

It's possible, however, to derive a demand curve without actually observing consumer behaviour. In theory we can identify consumer *preferences* (tastes), then use those preferences to construct a demand curve. In this case, the demand curve is developed explicitly from known preferences rather than on the basis of market observations. The end result—the demand curve—is the same, at least so long as consumers' behaviour in product markets is consistent with their preferences.

Indifference curves are a mechanism for illustrating consumer tastes. We examine their construction and use in this appendix. As suggested above, indifference curves provide an explicit basis for constructing a demand curve. In addition, they are another way of viewing how consumption is affected by price, tastes, and income. Indifference curves are also a useful tool for illustrating explicitly consumer *choice*—that is, the decision to purchase one good rather than another.

Recall the dilemma that arises when you want Coke and video games but don't have enough money to buy enough of each. The income constraint compels you to make hard decisions. You have to consider the *marginal utility* per dollar each additional Coke or video game will provide, then make a selection. With careful introspection and good arithmetic you can select the optimal mix of Cokes and video games—that is, the combination that yields the most satisfaction (utility) for the income available. This process of identifying your *optimal consumption* was illustrated in Table 4.1.

Finding your optimal consumption is difficult because you must assess the marginal utility of each prospective purchase. In Table 4.1 we assumed that the marginal utility of the first Coke was 15 utils, while the first video game had a marginal utility of 10. Then we had to specify the marginal utility of every additional Coke and video game. Can we really be so specific about our tastes?

Indifference curves require a bit less arithmetic. ***Instead of trying to measure the marginal utility of each prospective purchase, we now look for combinations of goods that yield equal satisfaction.*** All we need do is determine that one particular combination of Cokes and video games is as satisfying as another. We don't have to say how many "units of pleasure" both combinations provide—it's sufficient that they're both equally satisfying.

The initial combination of one Coke and eight video games is designated as a combination A in Table 4A.1. This combination of goods yields a certain, but unspecified, level of total utility. What we want to do now is to find another combination of Cokes and games that's just as satisfying as combination A. Finding other combinations of equal satisfaction isn't easy, but it's at least possible. After a lot of soul searching, we decide that two Cokes and five video games would be just as satisfying as one Coke and eight games.[1] This combination is designated as B in Table 4A.1.

Table 4A.1 also depicts a third combination of Cokes and video games that's as satisfying as the first. Combination C includes three Cokes and four games, a mix of consumption assumed to yield the same total utility as one Coke and eight games (combination A).

Notice that we haven't said anything about how much pleasure combinations A, B, and C provide. We're simply asserting that these three combinations are *equally* satisfying.

Constructing an Indifference Curve

[1]The utility computations used here aren't based on Table 4.1; a different set of tastes is assumed.

FIGURE 4A.1

An Indifference Curve

An indifference curve illustrates the various combinations of two goods that would provide equal satisfaction. The consumer is assumed to be indifferent to a choice between combinations *A, B,* and *C* (and all other points on the curve), as they all yield the same total utility.

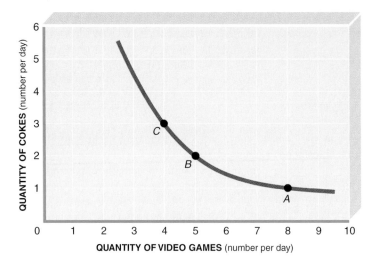

indifference curve: A curve depicting alternative combinations of goods that yield equal satisfaction.

Figure 4A.1 illustrates the information about tastes that we've assembled. Points *A, B,* and *C* represent the three equally satisfying combinations of Cokes and video games we've identified. By connecting these points we create an **indifference curve.** The indifference curve illustrates all combinations of two goods that are equally satisfying. A consumer would be just as happy with any combination represented on the curve, so a choice among them would be a matter of indifference.

An Indifference Map. Not all combinations of Cokes and video games are as satisfying as combination *A,* of course. Surely, two Cokes and eight games would be preferred to only one Coke and eight games. Indeed, *any combination that provided more of one good and no less of the other would be preferred.* Point *D* in Figure 4A.2 illustrates just one such combination. Combination *D* must yield more total utility than combination *A* because it includes one more Coke and no fewer games. A consumer wouldn't be indifferent to a choice between *A* and *D;* on the contrary, combination *D* would be preferred.

Combination *D* is also preferred to combinations *B* and *C.* How do we know? Recall that combinations *A, B,* and *C* are all equally satisfying. Hence, if combination *D* is better than *A,* it must also be better than *B* and *C.* Given a choice, a consumer would select combination *D* (two Cokes, eight games) in preference to *any* combination depicted on indifference curve I_1.

There are also combinations that are as satisfying as *D,* of course. These possibilities are illustrated on indifference curve I_2. All these combinations are equally satisfying and must therefore be preferred to any points on indifference curve I_1. In general, *the farther the indifference curve is from the origin, the more total utility it yields.*

FIGURE 4A.2

An Indifference Map

All combinations of goods depicted on any given indifference curve (e.g., I_1) are equally satisfying. Other combinations, not on I_1, are more *or* less satisfying, however, and thus lie on higher (I_2) or lower (I_3) indifference curves. An indifference map shows all possible levels of total utility (e.g., $I_1, I_2, I_3, \ldots, I_n$) and their respective consumption combinations.

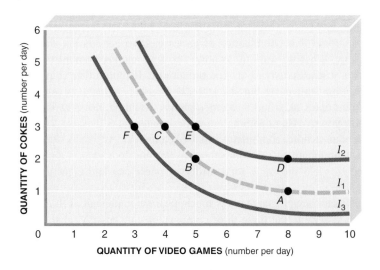

The curve I_3 illustrates various combinations that are less satisfying. Combination F, for example, includes three Cokes and three games. This is one game less than the number available in combination C. Therefore, F yields less total utility than C and isn't preferred: A consumer would rather have combination C than F. By the same logic we used above, all points on indifference curve I_3 are less satisfying than combinations on curve I_2 or I_1.

Curves 1, 2, and 3 in Figure 4A.2 are the beginnings of an **indifference map.** An indifference map depicts all the combinations of goods that would yield various levels of satisfaction. A single indifference curve, in contrast, illustrates all combinations that provide a single (equal) level of total utility.

indifference map: The set of indifference curves that depicts all possible levels of utility attainable from various combinations of goods.

We assume that all consumers strive to maximize their utility. They want as much satisfaction as they can get. In the terminology of indifference curves, this means getting to the indifference curve that's farthest from the origin. The farther one is from the origin, the greater the total utility.

Utility Maximization

Although the goal of consumers is evident, the means of achieving it isn't so clear. Higher indifference curves aren't only more satisfying, they're also more expensive. We're confronted again with the basic conflict between preferences and prices. With a limited amount of income to spend, we can't attain infinite satisfaction (the farthest indifference curve). We have to settle for less (an indifference curve closer to the origin). The question is: How do we maximize the utility attainable with our limited income?

The Budget Constraint. For starters, we have to determine how much we have to spend. Suppose for the moment that we can spend $2 per day and that Cokes and video games are still the only objects of our consumption desires. The price of a Coke is 50 cents; the price of a game is 25 cents. Accordingly, the maximum number of Cokes we could buy is four per day if we didn't play any video games. On the other hand, we could play as many as eight games if we were to forsake Coke.

Figure 4A.3 depicts the limitations placed on our consumption possibilities by a finite income. The **budget constraint** illustrates all combinations of goods affordable with a given income. In this case, the outermost budget line illustrates the combinations of Cokes and video games that can be purchased with $2.

The budget line is easily drawn. The end points of the budget constraint are found by dividing one's income by the price of the good on the corresponding axis. Thus, the outermost curve begins at four Cokes ($2 ÷ 50 cents) and ends at eight games ($2 ÷ 25 cents). All the other points on the budget constraint represent other combinations of Cokes and video games that could be purchased with $2.

A smaller income is also illustrated in Figure 4A.3. If we had only $1 to spend, we could afford fewer Cokes and fewer games. Hence, a smaller income is represented by a budget constraint that lies closer to the origin.

budget constraint: A line depicting all combinations of goods that are affordable with a given income and given prices.

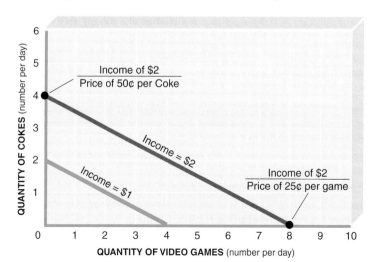

FIGURE 4A.3
The Budget Constraint

Consumption possibilities are limited by available income. The budget constraint illustrates this limitation. The end points of the budget constraint are equal to income divided by the price of each good. All points on the budget constraint represent affordable combinations of goods.

FIGURE 4A.4
Optimal Consumption

The optimal consumption combination—the one that maximizes the utility
of spendable income—lies at the point
where the budget line is tangent to (just
touches) an indifference curve. In this
case, point *M* represents the optimal
mix of Cokes and video games, since no
other affordable combination lies on a
higher indifference curve than I_c.

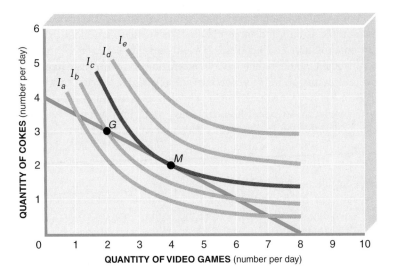

Optimal Consumption. With a budget constraint looming before us, the limitation
on utility maximization is evident. We want to reach the highest indifference curve
possible. Our limited income, however, restricts our grasp. We can go only as far as
our budget constraint allows. In this context, *the objective is to reach the highest
indifference curve that is compatible with our budget constraint.*

Figure 4A.4 illustrates the process of achieving optimal consumption. We start with
an indifference map depicting all utility levels and product combinations. Then we impose
a budget line that reflects our income. In this case, we continue to assume that Coke
costs 50 cents, video games cost 25 cents, and we have $2 to spend. Hence, *we can
afford only those consumption combinations that are on or inside the budget line.*

Which particular combination of Cokes and video games maximizes the utility of
our $2? It must be two Cokes and four video games, as reflected in point *M*. Notice
that point *M* isn't only on the budget line but also touches indifference curve I_c. No
other point on the budget line touches I_c or any higher indifference curve. Accordingly,
I_c represents the most utility we can get for $2 and is attainable only if we consume
two Cokes and four video games. Any other affordable combination yields less total
utility—that is, falls on a lower indifference curve. Point *G*, for example, which offers
three Cokes and two video games for $2, lies on the indifference curve I_b. Because
I_b lies closer to the origin than I_c, point *G* must be less satisfying than point *M*. We
conclude, then, that *the point of tangency between the budget constraint and an
indifference curve represents optimal consumption.* It's the combination we should
buy if we want to maximize the utility of our limited income.

Marginal Utility and Price: A Digression. We earlier illustrated the utility-
maximizing rule, which required a comparison of the ratios of marginal utilities to
prices. Specifically, optimal consumption was represented as that combination of
Cokes and video games that yielded

$$\frac{MU \text{ Coke}}{P \text{ Coke}} = \frac{MU \text{ games}}{P \text{ games}}$$

Does point *M* in Figure 4A.4 conform to this rule?

To answer this question, first rearrange the preceding equation as follows:

$$\frac{MU \text{ Coke}}{MU \text{ games}} = \frac{P \text{ Coke}}{P \text{ games}}$$

In this form, the equation says that the relative marginal utilities of Cokes and video
games should equal their relative prices when consumption is optimal. In other words,
if a Coke costs twice as much as a video game, then it must yield twice as much

marginal utility if the consumer is to be in an optimal state. Otherwise, some substitution of Cokes for video games, or vice versa, would be desirable.

With this foundation, we can show that point M conforms to our earlier rule. Consider first the slope of the budget constraint, which is determined by the relative prices of Cokes and video games. In fact, ***the (absolute) slope of the budget constraint equals the relative price of the two goods.*** In Figure 4A.4 the slope equals the price of video games divided by the price of Cokes (25 cents ÷ 50 cents = ½). It tells us the rate at which video games can be exchanged for Cokes in the market. In this case, one video game is "worth" half a Coke.

The relative marginal utilities of the two goods are reflected in the slope of the indifference curve. Recall that the curve tells at what rate a consumer is willing to substitute one good for another, with no change in total utility. In fact, the slope of the indifference curve is called the **marginal rate of substitution.** It's equal to the relative marginal utilities of the two goods. Presumably one would be indifferent to a choice between two Cokes + five games and three Cokes + four games—as suggested in Table 4A.1—only if the third Coke were as satisfying as the fifth video game.

> **marginal rate of substitution:** The rate at which a consumer is willing to exchange one good for another; the relative marginal utilities of two goods.

At the point of optimal consumption (M) in Figure 4A.4 the budget constraint is tangent to the indifference curve I_c, which means that the two curves must have the same slope at the point. In other words,

$$\frac{P \text{ games}}{P \text{ Cokes}} = \frac{MU \text{ games}}{MU \text{ Cokes}}$$

or alternatively,

$$\frac{\text{Rate of}}{\text{market exchange}} = \frac{\text{marginal rate}}{\text{of substitution}}$$

Both indifference curves and marginal utility comparisons lead us to the same optimal mix of consumption.

We noted at the beginning of this appendix that indifference curves not only give us an alternative path to optimal consumption but also can be used to derive a demand curve. To do this, we need to consider how the optimal consumption combination changes when the price of one good is altered. We can see what happens in Figure 4A.5.

Figure 4A.5 starts with the optimal consumption attained at point M, with income of $2 and prices of 50 cents for a Coke and 25 cents for a video game. Now we're going to change the price of video games and observe how consumption changes.

Suppose that the price of a video game doubles, from 25 cents to 50 cents. This change will shift the budget constraint inward: Our income of $2 now buys a maximum of four games rather than eight. Hence, the lower end point of the budget

Deriving the Demand Curve

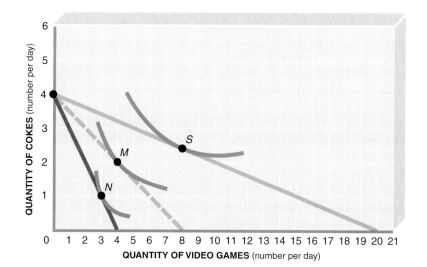

FIGURE 4A.5
Changing Prices

When the price of a good changes, the budget constraint shifts, and a new consumption combination must be sought. In this case, the price of video games is changing. When the price of games increases from 25 cents to 50 cents, the budget constraint shifts inward and optimal consumption moves from point M to point N.

FIGURE 4A.6

The Demand for Video Games

Figure 4A.5 shows how optimal consumption is altered when the price of video games changes. From that figure we can determine the quantity of video games demanded at alternative prices, *ceteris paribus.* That information is summarized here in the demand schedule (below) and the demand curve (above).

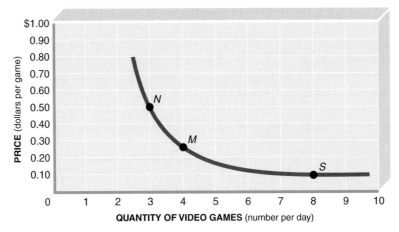

Point	Price (per game)	Quantity Demanded (games per day)
N	50 cents	3
M	25	4
S	10	8

constraint moves from eight games to four games. ***Whenever the price of a good changes, the budget constraint shifts.***

Only one end of the budget constraint is changed in Figure 4A.5. The budget line still begins at four Cokes because the price of Coke is unchanged. If only one price is changed, then only one end of the budget constraint is shifted.

Because the budget constraint has shifted inward, the combination *M* is no longer attainable. Two Cokes (at 50 cents each) and four games (at 50 cents each) now cost more than $2. We're now forced to accept a lower level of total utility. According to Figure 4A.5, optimal consumption is now located at point *N.* This is the point of tangency between the new budget constraint and a lower indifference curve. At point *N* we consume one Coke and three video games.

Consider what has happened here. The price of video games has increased (from 25 cents to 50 cents), and the quantity of games demanded has decreased. This is the kind of relationship that demand curves describe. *Demand curves* indicate how the quantity demanded of a good changes in response to a change in its price, given a fixed income and all other things held constant. Not only does Figure 4A.5 provide the same information, it also conforms to the *law of demand:* As the price of games increases, the quantity demanded falls.

Suppose the price of video games were to fall rather than increase. Specifically, assume that the price of a game fell to 10 cents. This price reduction would shift the budget constraint farther out on the horizontal axis, since as many as 20 games could then be purchased with $2. As a result of the price reduction, we can now buy more goods and thus attain a higher level of satisfaction.

Point *S* in Figure 4A.5 indicates the optimal combination of Cokes and video games at the new video game price. At these prices, we consume 8 video games and 2.4 Cokes (we may have to share with a friend). The law of demand is again evident: When the price of video games declines, the quantity demanded increases.

The Demand Schedule and Curve. Figure 4A.6 summarizes the information we've acquired about the demand for video games. The demand schedule depicts the price-quantity relationships prevailing at optimal consumption points *N*, *M*, and *S* (from Figure 4A.5). The demand curve generalizes these observations to encompass other prices. What we end up with is a demand curve explicitly derived from our (assumed) knowledge of consumer tastes.

CHAPTER 5

The Costs of Production

LEARNING OBJECTIVES

By the end of this chapter, you should be able to:

5.1 Define the production function

5.2 Define the short run and explain how it leads to the law of diminishing marginal returns

5.3 Define and graph the relationship between marginal and average physical productivity

5.4 Define, calculate, and graph all cost functions

5.5 Explain and graph the relationship between marginal cost and marginal physical productivity

5.6 Explain and graph the relationship between marginal costs and average costs

5.7 Define the long run and explain how cost functions differ across time frames

5.8 Define economies of scale, diseconomies of scale, and constant returns to scale

5.9 Explain how productivity and wage rates influence unit labour costs

Last year Canadian consumers bought more than $400 *billion* worth of imported goods, including Japanese cars, Italian shoes, and toys from China. As you might expect, this angers domestic producers, who frequently end up with unsold goods, half-empty factories, and unemployed workers. They rage against the "unfair" competition from abroad, asserting that producers in Korea, Brazil, and China can undersell Canadian producers because workers in these countries are paid dirt-poor wages.

But lower wages don't necessarily imply lower costs. You could pay me $2 per hour to type and still end up paying a lot for typing. Truth is, I type only about 10 words a minute, with lots of misteaks. The cost of producing goods depends not only on the price of inputs (e.g., labour) but also on how much they produce.

In this chapter we begin looking at the costs of producing the goods and services that market participants demand. We confront the following questions:

- **How much output *can* a firm produce?**
- **How do the *costs* of production vary with the rate of output?**
- **Do larger firms have a cost advantage over smaller firms?**

The answers to these questions are important not only to producers faced with foreign competition but to consumers as well. The costs of producing a good have a direct impact on the prices consumers pay.

5.1 THE PRODUCTION FUNCTION

No matter how large a business is or who owns it, all businesses confront one central fact: It costs something to produce goods. To produce corn, a farmer needs land, water, seed, equipment, and labour. To produce fillings, a dentist needs a chair, a drill, some space, and labour. Even the "production" of educational services such as this economics class requires the use of labour (your teacher), land (on which the school is built), and capital (the building, blackboard, computers). In short, unless you're producing unrefined, unpackaged air, you need *factors of production*—that is, resources that can be used to produce a good or service. The factors of production used in production provide the basic measure of economic cost. The costs of your economics class, for example, are measured by the amounts of land, labour, and capital it requires. These are *resource* costs of production.

To assess the costs of production, we must first determine how many resources are actually needed to produce a given product. You could use a lot of resources to produce a product or use just a few. What we really want to know is how *best* to produce. What's the *smallest* amount of resources needed to produce a specific product? Or we could ask the same question from a different perspective: What's the *maximum* amount of output attainable from a given quantity of resources?

> **production function:** A technological relationship expressing the maximum quantity of a good attainable from different combinations of factor inputs.

The answers to these questions are reflected in the **production function,** which tells us the maximum amount of good X producible from various combinations of factor inputs. With one chair and one drill, a dentist can fill a *maximum* of 32 cavities per day. With two chairs, a drill, and an assistant, a dentist can fill up to 55 cavities per day.

A production function is a technological summary of our ability to produce a particular good.[1] Table 5.1 provides a partial glimpse of one such function. In this case, the output is designer jeans, as produced by Low-Rider Jeans Corporation. The essential inputs in the production of jeans are land, labour (garment workers), and capital (a factory and sewing machines). With these inputs, Low-Rider Jeans Corporation can produce and sell hip-hugging jeans to style-conscious consumers.

Varying Input Levels

As in all production endeavours, we want to know how much output we can produce with available resources. To make things easy, we'll assume that the factory is already built, with fixed space dimensions. The only inputs we can vary are labour (the number of garment workers per day) and additional capital (the number of sewing machines we lease per day).

Capital Input (sewing machines per day)	Labour Input (workers per day)								
	0	1	2	3	4	5	6	7	8
	Jeans Output (pairs per day)								
0	0	0	0	0	0	0	0	0	0
1	0	15	34	44	48	50	51	51	47
2	0	20	46	64	72	78	81	82	80
3	0	21	50	73	83	92	99	103	103

TABLE 5.1
A Production Function

A production function tells us the maximum amount of output attainable from alternative combinations of factor inputs. This particular function tells us how many pairs of jeans we can produce in a day with a given factory and varying quantities of capital and labour. With one sewing machine, and one operator, we can produce a maximum of 15 pairs of jeans per day, as indicated in the second column of the second row. To produce more jeans, we need more labour or more capital.

[1] By contrast, the production possibilities curve discussed in Chapter 1 expresses our ability to produce various *combinations* of goods, given the use of *all* our resources. The production possibilities curve summarizes the output capacity of the entire economy. A production function describes the capacity of a single firm.

In these circumstances, the quantity of jeans we can produce depends on the amount of labour and capital we employ. ***The purpose of a production function is to tell us just how much output we can produce with varying amounts of factor inputs.*** Table 5.1 provides such information for jeans production.

Consider the simplest option, that of employing no labour or capital (the upper-left corner in Table 5.1). An empty factory can't produce any jeans; maximum output is zero per day. Even though land, capital (an empty factory), and even denim are available, some essential labour and capital inputs are missing, and jeans production is impossible.

Suppose now we employ some labour (a machine operator) but don't lease any sewing machines. Will output increase? Not according to the production function. The first row in Table 5.1 illustrates the consequences of employing labour without any capital equipment. Without sewing machines (or even needles, another form of capital), the operators can't make jeans. Maximum output remains at zero, no matter how much labour is employed in this case.

The dilemma of machine operators without sewing machines illustrates a general principle of production: ***The productivity of any factor of production depends on the amount of other resources available to it.*** Industrious, hardworking machine operators can't make designer jeans without sewing machines.

> **productivity:** Output per unit of input, for example, output per labour-hour.

We can increase the productivity of garment workers by providing them with machines. The production function again tells us by *how much* jeans output could increase. Suppose we leased just one machine per day. Now the second row in Table 5.1 is the relevant one. It says jeans output will remain at zero if we lease one machine but employ no labour. If we employ one machine *and* one worker, however, the jeans will start rolling out the front door. Maximum output under these circumstances (row 2, column 2) is 15 pairs of jeans per day. Now we're in business!

The remaining columns in row 2 tell us how many additional jeans we can produce if we hire more workers, still leasing only one sewing machine. With one machine and two workers, maximum output rises to 34 pairs per day. If a third worker is hired, output could increase to 44 pairs.

Table 5.1 also indicates how production would increase with additional sewing machines (capital). By reading down any column of the table, you can see how more machines increase potential jeans soutput.

Efficiency

The production function summarized in Table 5.1 underscores the essential relationship between resource *inputs* and product *outputs*. It's also a basic introduction to economic costs. To produce 15 pairs of jeans per day, we need one sewing machine, an operator, a factory, and some denim. All these inputs comprise the *resource cost* of producing jeans.

Another feature of Table 5.1 is that it conveys the *maximum* output of jeans producible from particular input combinations. The standard garment worker and sewing machine, when brought together at Low-Rider Jeans Corporation, can produce *at most* 15 pairs of jeans per day. They could also produce a lot less. Indeed, a careless cutter can waste a lot of denim. A lazy or inattentive one won't keep the sewing machines humming. As many a producer has learned, actual output can fall far short of the limits described in the production function. Indeed, jeans output will reach the levels in Table 5.1 only if the jeans factory operates with relative *efficiency*. This requires getting maximum output from the resources used in the production process. ***The production function represents maximum technical efficiency—that is, the most output attainable from any given level of factor inputs.***

We can always be inefficient, of course. This merely means getting less output than possible for the inputs we use. But this isn't a desirable situation. To a factory manager, it means less output for a given amount of input (cost). To society as a whole, inefficiency implies a waste of resources. If Low-Rider Jeans isn't producing efficiently, we're being denied some potential output. It's not only a question of having fewer jeans. We could also use the labour and capital now employed by Low-Rider Jeans to produce something else. Specifically, the *opportunity cost* of a product is measured by the most desired goods and services that could have been produced with the same resources. Hence, if jeans production isn't up to par, society is either (1) getting fewer jeans than it should for the resources devoted to jeans production or (2) giving up too many other goods and services to get a desired quantity of jeans.

Although we can always do worse than the production function suggests, we can't do better, at least in the short run. The production function represents the *best* we can do with our current technological know-how. For the moment, at least, there's no better way to produce a specific good. As our technological and managerial capabilities increase, however, we'll attain higher levels of future productivity. These advances in our productive capability will be represented by new production functions.

Short-Run Constraints

Let's step back from the threshold of scientific advance for a moment and return to Low-Rider Jeans. Forget about possible technological breakthroughs in jeans production (e.g., electronic sewing machines or robot operators) and concentrate on the economic realities of our modest endeavour. For the present we're stuck with existing technology. In fact, all the output figures in Table 5.1 are based on the use of a specific factory. Once we've purchased or leased that factory, we've set a limit to current jeans production. When such commitments to fixed inputs (e.g., the factory) exist, we're dealing with a **short-run** production problem. If no land or capital were in place—if we could build or lease any size factory—we'd be dealing with a *long-run* decision.

short run: The period in which the quantity (and quality) of some inputs can't be changed.

Our short-run objective is to make the best possible use of the factory we've acquired. This entails selecting the right combination of labour and capital inputs to produce jeans. To simplify the decision, we'll limit the number of sewing machines in use. If we lease only one sewing machine, then the second row in Table 5.1 is the only one we have to consider. In this case, the single sewing machine (capital) becomes another short-run constraint on the production of jeans. With a given factory and one sewing machine, the short-run rate of output depends entirely on how many workers are hired.

Figure 5.1 illustrates the short-run production function applicable to the factory with one sewing machine. As noted before, a factory with a sewing machine but no machine operators produces no jeans. This was observed in Table 5.1 (row 1, column 0) and is now illustrated by point *A* in Figure 5.1. To get any jeans output, we need to hire some labour. In this simplified example, **labour is the variable input that determines how much output we get from our fixed inputs (land and capital)**. By placing one worker in the factory, we can produce 15 pairs of jeans per day. This possibility is represented by point *B*. The remainder of the production function shows how jeans output changes as we employ more workers in our single-machine factory.

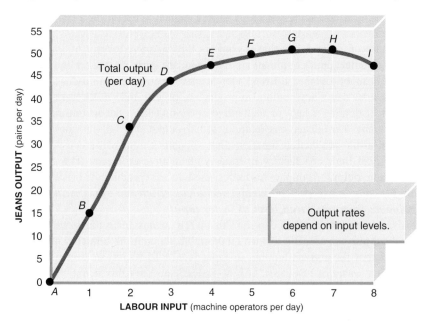

FIGURE 5.1
Short-Run Production Function

In the short run some inputs (e.g., land, capital) are fixed in quantity. Output then depends on how much of a variable input (e.g., labour) is used. The short-run production function shows how output changes when more labour is used. This figure is based on the second (one-machine) row in Table 5.1.

5.2 MARGINAL AND AVERAGE PRODUCTIVITY

The short-run production function not only defines the *limit* to output but also shows how much each worker contributes to that limit. Notice again that jeans output increases from zero (point *A* in Figure 5.2) to 15 pairs (point *B*) when the first machine operator is hired. In other words, total output *increases* by 15 pairs when we employ the first worker. This increase is called the **marginal physical product (MPP)** of that first worker—that is, the *change* in total output that results from employment of one more unit of (labour) input, or

marginal physical product (MPP): The change in total output associated with one additional unit of input.

$$\text{Marginal physical} \atop \text{product (MPP)} = \frac{\text{change in total output}}{\text{change in input quantity}}$$

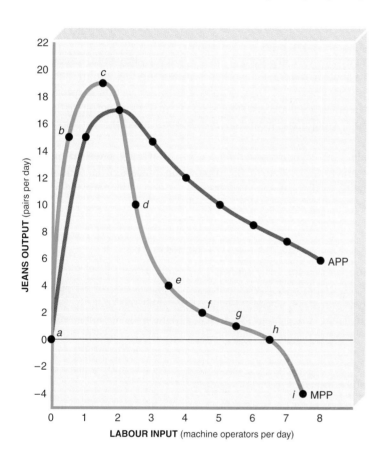

	Number of Workers	Total Output	Marginal Physical Product	Average Physical Product
a	0	0		
b	1	15	> 15	15.00
c	2	34	> 19	17.00
d	3	44	> 10	14.67
e	4	48	> 4	12.00
g	5	50	> 2	10.00
g	6	51	> 1	8.50
h	7	51	> 0	7.29
i	8	47	> −4	5.88

FIGURE 5.2

Marginal Physical Product (MPP) and Average Physical Product (APP)

Marginal physical product is the *change in total output* that results from employing one more unit of input. Average physical product measures the *average output* per unit of input at each level of input. Notice that MPP intersects the APP at its maximum point—why is this always true?

With zero workers, total output was zero. With the first worker, total output increases to 15 pairs of jeans per day. The MPP of the first worker is 15 pairs of jeans.

If we employ a second operator, jeans output more than doubles, to 34 pairs per day (point *C*). The 19-pair *increase* in output represents the marginal physical product of the *second* worker.

The higher MPP of the second worker raises a question about the first. Why was the first's MPP lower? Laziness? Is the second worker faster, less distracted, or harder working?

The second worker's higher MPP isn't explained by superior talents or effort. We assume, in fact, that all "units of labour" are equal—that is, one worker is just as good as another.[2] Their different marginal products are explained by the structure of the production process, not by their respective abilities. The first garment worker not only had to sew jeans but also to unfold bolts of denim, measure the jeans, sketch out the patterns, and cut them to approximate size. A lot of time was spent going from one task to another. Despite the worker's best efforts, this person simply couldn't do everything at once.

A second worker alleviates this situation. With two workers, less time is spent running from one task to another. While one worker is measuring and cutting, the other can continue sewing. This improved *ratio* of labour to other factors of production results in the large jump in total output. The second worker's superior MPP isn't unique to this person: It would have occurred even if we'd hired the workers in the reverse order.

average physical product (APP): The average productivity of a factor of production—calculated by dividing total output by total units of input.

We can also consider how *average output per worker* or **average physical product (APP)** changes as workers are added to the production process. The APP simply identifies how productive workers are on average—that is, we divide the total amount of output produced by the total amount of units used, or

$$\frac{\text{Average physical}}{\text{product (APP)}} = \frac{\text{total output}}{\text{total input quantity}}$$

In the case of the first worker, the MPP and APP are both equal to 15. The second worker, with a MPP of 19 pairs of jeans, boosts total production to 34 pairs and increases the APP to 17 pairs per worker (34/2). As we shall see later, the relationship between marginal and average productivity will help us to understand the relationship between marginal and average costs—important concepts for profit-maximizing firms. In the meantime, we focus our attention on the graph and table in Figure 5.2. Notice that the values for the MPP are placed midway between the labour inputs to capture the *change* in total output.

Diminishing Marginal Returns

Unfortunately, total output won't keep rising so sharply if still more workers are hired. Look what happens when a third worker is hired. Total jeans production increases from 34 to 44 pairs of jeans per day. But the increase is only 10 pairs per day. Hence, the third worker's MPP (10 pairs) is *less* than that of the second (19 pairs). Marginal physical product is *diminishing*. This concept is illustrated by point *d* in Figure 5.2.

What accounts for this decline in MPP? The answer lies in the ratio of labour to other factors of production. A third worker begins to crowd our facilities. We still have only one sewing machine. Two people can't sew at the same time. As a result, some time is wasted as the operators wait for their turns at the machine. Even if they split up the various jobs, there will still be some "downtime," since measuring and cutting aren't as time-consuming as sewing. Consequently, we can't make full use of a third worker. The relative scarcity of other inputs (capital and land) constrains the third worker's marginal physical product.

---

[2] In reality, garment workers do differ greatly in energy, talent, and diligence. These differences can be eliminated by measuring units of labour in *constant-quality* units. A person who works twice as hard as everyone else would count as two *quality-adjusted* units of labour.

Resource constraints are even more evident when a fourth worker is hired. Total output increases again, but the increase this time is very small. With three workers, we got 44 pairs of jeans per day; with four workers, we get a maximum of 48 pairs. Thus the fourth worker's MPP is only 4 pairs of jeans. There simply aren't enough machines to make productive use of so much labour.

If a seventh worker is hired, the operators get in one another's way, argue, and waste denim. From the table in Figure 5.2, notice that total output doesn't increase at all when a seventh worker is hired. The MPP of the seventh worker is zero (point *h*). Were an eighth worker hired, total output would actually *decline,* from 51 pairs to 47 pairs. The eighth worker has a *negative* MPP (point *i*).

Law of Diminishing Returns. The problems of crowded facilities apply to most production processes. In the short run, a production process is characterized by a fixed amount of available land and capital. Typically, the only factor that can be varied in the short run is labour. Yet, *as more labour is hired, each unit of labour has less capital and land to work with.* This is simple division: The available facilities are being shared by more and more workers. At some point, this constraint begins to pinch. When it does, marginal physical product declines. This situation is so common that it's the basis for the **law of diminishing returns,** which says that the marginal physical product of any factor of production, such as labour, will diminish at some point, as more of it is used in a given production setting. Notice in Figure 5.2 how diminishing returns set in when the third worker was hired.

> **law of diminishing returns:** The marginal physical product of a variable input declines as more of it is employed with a given quantity of other (fixed) inputs.

Marginal vs. Average Productivity. How do diminishing *marginal* returns affect *average* returns? If you said that average returns should also diminish, you would be correct. Similarly, when we had increasing marginal returns (*b* to *c*), we also had increasing average returns. In fact, you can see from the graph in Figure 5.2 that the average physical product curve has roughly the same "inverted-U" shape as the marginal physical product; it increases, reaches a peak, and then falls. This is not a coincidence. Whenever the marginal product is greater than the average product, the average must be increasing and conversely, whenever the marginal product is lower than the average product, the average must be decreasing. A good example of this relationship is your grade in this course. Suppose your instructor has five quizzes, equally weighted, throughout the semester. If your average grade after the third quiz is 75 percent, what would a mark of 80 percent on your next quiz (marginal mark) do to your average? Since your marginal mark is greater than your average, your average will rise. The same principle applies for the productivity of inputs. From a graphical point of view, you should see that this relationship implies that the MPP curve must *always* intersect the APP at its peak.

5.3 RESOURCE COSTS

A production function tells us how much output a firm *can* produce with its existing plant and equipment. It doesn't tell us how much the firm will *want* to produce. A firm *might* want to produce at capacity if the profit picture were bright enough. On the other hand, a firm might not produce *any* output if costs always exceeded sales revenue. The most desirable rate of output is the one that maximizes total **profit**—the difference between total revenue and total costs.

> **profit:** The difference between total revenue and total cost.

The production function therefore is just a starting point for supply decisions. To decide how much output to produce with that function, a firm must next examine the costs of production. How fast do costs rise when output increases?

The law of diminishing returns provides a clue to how fast costs rise. *The economic cost of a product is measured by the value of the resources needed to produce it.*

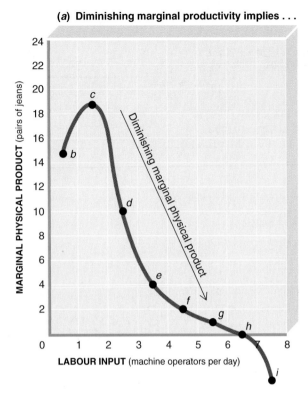

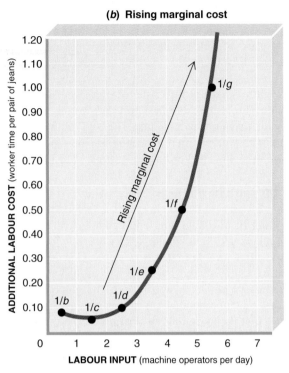

FIGURE 5.3
Falling MPP Implies Rising Marginal Cost

Marginal physical product (MPP) is the additional output obtained by employing one more unit of input. If MPP is falling, each additional unit of input is producing less additional output, which means that the input cost of each unit of output is rising. The third

worker's MPP is 10 pairs (point *d* in part *a*). Therefore, the labour cost of these additional jeans is approximately 1/10 unit of labour per pair (point 1/*d* in part *b*).

What we've seen here is that those resource requirements eventually increase. Each additional sewing machine operator produces fewer and fewer jeans. In effect, then, each additional pair of jeans produced uses more and more labour.

Suppose we employ one sewing machine and one operator again, for a total output of 15 pairs of jeans per day; see point *b* in Figure 5.3*a*. Now look at production from another perspective, that of *costs*. How much labour cost are we using at point *b* to produce one pair of jeans? The answer is simple. Since one worker is producing 15 pairs of jeans, the labour input per pair of jeans must be one-fifteenth of a worker's day, that is, 0.067 unit of labour; see point 1/*b* in Figure 5.3*b*. All we're doing here is translating *output* data into related *input* (cost) data.

Marginal Resource Cost

The next question is, How do input costs change when output increases? As point *c* in Figure 5.3*a* reminds us, total output increases by 19 pairs when we hire a second worker. What's the implied labour cost of those *additional* 19 pairs? By dividing one worker by 19 pairs of jeans, we observe that the labour cost of that extra output is one-nineteenth, or 0.053 of a worker's day; see point 1/*c* in Figure 5.3*b*.

When we focus on the *additional* costs incurred from increasing production, we're talking about *marginal* costs. Specifically, **marginal cost (MC)** refers to the *increase* in total costs required to get one additional unit of output. More generally,

marginal cost (MC): The increase in total cost associated with a one-unit increase in production.

$$\text{Marginal cost (MC)} = \frac{\text{change in total cost}}{\text{change in output}} = \frac{\Delta TC}{\Delta q}$$

In our simple case where labour is the only variable input, the marginal cost of the added jeans is

$$\text{Marginal cost} = \frac{1 \text{ additional worker}}{19 \text{ additional pairs}} = \frac{1}{\text{MPP}}$$

$$= 0.053 \text{ workers per pair}$$

The amount 0.053 of labour represents the *change* in total resource cost when we produce one *additional* pair of jeans.

Notice in Figure 5.3*b* that the marginal labour cost of jeans production declines when the second worker is hired. Marginal cost falls from 0.067 unit of labour (plus denim) per pair (point 1/*b* in Figure 5.3*b*) to only 0.053 unit of labour per pair (point 1/*c*). It costs less labour *per pair* to use two workers rather than only one. This is a reflection of the second worker's increased MPP. ***Whenever MPP is increasing, the marginal cost of producing a good must be falling.*** This is illustrated in Figure 5.3 by the move from *b* to *c* in part *a* and the corresponding move from 1/*b* to 1/*c* in part *b*.

Unfortunately, marginal physical product typically declines at some point. As it does, the marginal costs of production rise. In this sense, each additional pair of jeans becomes more expensive—it uses more and more labour per pair. Figure 5.3 illustrates this inverse relationship between MPP and marginal cost. The third worker has an MPP of 10 pairs, as illustrated by point *d*. The marginal labour input of these extra 10 pairs is thus 1 ÷ 10, or 0.10 unit of labour. In other words, one-tenth of a third worker's daily effort goes into each pair of jeans. This additional labour cost *per unit* is illustrated by 1/*d* in part *b* of the figure.

Note in Figure 5.3 how marginal physical product declines after point *c* and how marginal costs rise after point 1/*c*. This is no accident. ***If marginal physical product declines, marginal cost increases.*** Thus, increasing marginal cost is as common as—and the direct result of—diminishing returns. These increasing marginal costs aren't the fault of any person or factor, simply a reflection of the resource constraints found in any established production setting (i.e., existing and limited plant and equipment). In the short run, the quantity and quality of land and capital are fixed, and we can vary only their intensity of use, such as with more or fewer workers. It's in this short-run context that we keep running into diminishing marginal returns and rising marginal costs.

Average Physical Product and Average Resource Cost. Now that we understand this inverse relationship between marginal physical productivity and marginal resource costs, we can briefly extend the analysis to *average* physical productivity and *average* resource costs. Suppose we had included the APP in Figure 5.3*a*. What would its cost counterpart, call it average resource cost, look like? Your intuition should tell you that it probably has the same u-shape as the marginal cost curve. Where would the marginal resource cost curve intersect the average resource cost curve? The relationship between APP and MPP should give you a hint—see question number 10 at the end of the chapter.

5.4 DOLLAR COSTS

This entire discussion of diminishing returns and marginal costs may seem a bit alien. After all, we're interested in the costs of production, and costs are typically measured in *dollars,* not such technical notions as MPP. Jeans producers need to know how many dollars it costs to keep jeans flowing; they don't want a lecture on marginal physical product.

Jeans manufacturers don't have to study marginal physical products, or even the production function. They can confine their attention to dollar costs. The dollar costs observed, however, are directly related to the underlying production function. To

TABLE 5.2
The Total Costs of Production (total cost of producing 15 pairs of jeans per day)

The total cost of producing a good equals the market value of all the resources used in its production. In this case, the production of 15 pairs of jeans per day requires resources worth $245.

Resource Input	×	Unit Price	=	Total Cost
1 factory		$100 per day		$100
1 sewing machine		20 per day		20
1 operator		80 per day		80
1.5 bolts of denim		30 per bolt		45
Total cost				$245

understand *why* costs rise—and how they might be reduced—some understanding of the production function is necessary. In this section we translate production functions into dollar costs.

Total Cost

total cost: The market value of all resources used to produce a good or service.

The **total cost** of producing a product includes the market value of all the resources used in its production. To determine this cost we simply identify all the resources used in production, determine their value, and then add up everything.

In the production of jeans, these resources included land, labour, and capital. Table 5.2 identifies these resources, their unit values, and the total dollar cost associated with their use. This table is based on an assumed output of 15 pairs of jeans per day, with the use of one worker and one sewing machine (point *B* in Figure 5.1). The rent on the factory is $100 per day, a sewing machine rents for $20 per day, the wages of a garment worker are $80 per day. We'll assume Low-Rider Jeans Corporation can purchase bolts of denim for $30 apiece, with each bolt providing enough denim for 10 pairs of jeans. In other words, one-tenth of a bolt ($3 worth of material) is required for one pair of jeans. We'll ignore any other potential expenses. With these assumptions, the total cost of producing 15 pairs of jeans per day amounts to $245, as shown in Table 5.2.

Fixed Costs. Total costs will change of course as we alter the rate of production. But not all costs increase. In the short run, some costs don't increase at all when output is increased. These are **fixed costs,** in the sense that they don't vary with the rate of output. The factory lease is an example. Once you lease a factory, you're obligated to pay for it, whether or not you use it. The person who owns the factory wants $100 per day. Even if you produce no jeans, you still have to pay that rent. That's the essence of fixed costs.

fixed costs: Costs of production that don't change when the rate of output is altered (e.g., the cost of basic plant and equipment).

The leased sewing machine is another fixed cost. When you rent a sewing machine, you must pay the rental charge. It doesn't matter whether you use it for a few minutes or all day long—the rental charge is fixed at $20 per day.

Variable Costs. Labour costs are another story altogether. The amount of labour employed in jeans production can be varied easily. If we decide not to open the factory tomorrow, we can just tell our only worker to take the day off without pay. We'll still have to pay rent, but we can cut back on wages. On the other hand, if we want to increase daily output, we can also get additional workers easily and quickly. Labour is regarded as a **variable cost** in this line of work—that is, a cost that *varies* with the rate of output.

variable costs: Costs of production that change when the rate of output is altered (e.g., labour and material costs).

The denim itself is another variable cost. Denim not used today can be saved for tomorrow. Hence, how much we "spend" on denim today is directly related to how many jeans we produce. In this sense, the cost of denim input varies with the rate of jeans output.

Figure 5.4 illustrates how these various costs are affected by the rate of production. On the vertical axis are the costs of production, in dollars per day. Notice that the

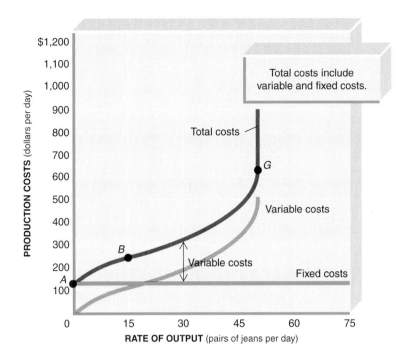

FIGURE 5.4
The Cost of Jeans Production

Total cost includes both fixed and variable costs. Fixed costs must be paid even if no output is produced (point *A*). Variable costs start at zero and increase with the rate of output. The total cost of producing 15 pairs of jeans (point *B*) includes $120 in fixed costs (rent on the factory and sewing machines) and $125 in variable costs (denim and wages). Total cost rises as output increases, because additional variable costs must be incurred.

In this example, the short-run capacity is equal to 51 pairs (point *G*). If still more inputs are employed, costs will rise but not total output.

total cost of producing 15 pairs per day is still $245, as indicated by point *B*. This cost figure consists of

Dollar Cost of Producing 15 Pairs

Fixed costs:		
Factory rent	$100	
Sewing machine rent	20	
Subtotal		$120
Variable costs:		
Wages to labour	$80	
Denim	45	
Subtotal		$125
Total costs		$245

If we increase the rate of output, total costs will rise. ***How fast total costs rise depends on variable costs only,*** however, since fixed costs remain at $120 per day. (Notice the horizontal fixed-cost curve in Figure 5.4.)

With one sewing machine and one factory, there's an absolute limit to daily jeans production. According to the production function in Figure 5.1, the capacity of a factory with one machine is roughly 51 pairs of jeans per day. If we try to produce more jeans than this by hiring additional workers, our total costs will rise, but our output won't. Recall that the seventh worker had a *zero* marginal physical product (Figure 5.2). In fact, we could fill the factory with garment workers and drive total costs sky-high. But the limits of space and one sewing machine don't permit output in excess of 51 pairs per day. This limit to productive capacity is represented by point *G* on the total cost curve. Further expenditure on inputs will increase production *costs* but not *output*.

Although there's no upper limit to costs, there is a lower limit. If output is reduced to zero, total costs fall only to $120 per day, the level of fixed costs, as illustrated by point *A* in Figure 5.4. As before, ***there's no way to avoid fixed costs in the short run.*** Indeed, those fixed costs define the short run.

Average Costs

average total cost (ATC): Total cost divided by the quantity produced in a given time period.

While Figure 5.4 illustrates *total* costs of production, other measures of cost are often desired. One of the most common measures of cost is average, or per-unit, cost. **Average total cost (ATC)** is simply total cost divided by the rate of output:

$$\text{Average total cost (ATC)} = \frac{\text{total cost}}{\text{total output}} = \frac{TC}{q}$$

At an output of 15 pairs of jeans per day, total costs are $245. The average cost of production is thus $16.33 per pair (= 245 ÷ 15) at this rate of output.

Figure 5.5 shows how average costs change as the rate of output varies. Row *J* of the cost schedule, for example, again indicates the fixed, variable, and total costs of producing 15 pairs of jeans per day. Fixed costs are still $120; variable costs are $125. Thus the total cost of producing 15 pairs per day is $245, as we saw earlier.

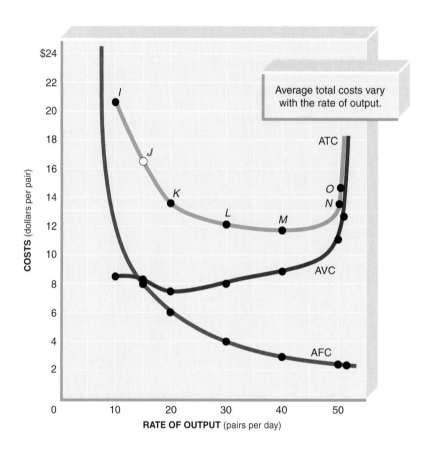

Average total costs vary with the rate of output.

FIGURE 5.5
Average Costs

Average total cost (ATC) in column 7 equals total cost (column 4) divided by the rate of output (column 1). Since total cost includes both fixed (column 2) and variable (column 3) costs, ATC also equals AFC (column 5) plus AVC (column 6). This relationship is illustrated in the graph. The ATC of producing 15 pairs per day (point *J*) equals $16.33; the sum of AFC ($8) and AVC ($8.33).

	(1) Rate of Output	(2) Fixed Costs	+	(3) Variable Costs	=	(4) Total Costs	(5) Average Fixed Costs	+	(6) Average Variable Costs	=	(7) Average Total Costs
H	0	$120		$ 0		$120	—		—		—
I	10	120		85		205	$12.00		$ 8.50		$20.50
J	15	120		125		245	8.00		8.33		16.33
K	20	120		150		270	6.00		7.50		13.50
L	30	120		240		360	4.00		8.00		12.00
M	40	120		350		470	3.00		8.75		11.75
N	50	120		550		670	2.40		11.00		13.40
O	51	120		633		753	2.35		12.41		14.76

The rest of row *J* shows the average costs of jeans production. These figures are obtained by dividing each dollar total (columns 2, 3, and 4) by the rate of physical output (column 1). At an output rate of 15 pairs per day, **average fixed cost (AFC)** is $8 per pair, **average variable cost (AVC)** is $8.33, and *average total cost (ATC)* is $16.33. ATC, then, is simply the sum of AFC and AVC:

average fixed cost (AFC): Total fixed cost divided by the quantity produced in a given time period.

average variable cost (AVC): Total variable cost divided by the quantity produced in a given time period.

$$ATC = AFC + AVC$$

Falling AFC. At this relatively low rate of output, fixed costs are a large portion of total costs. The rent paid for the factory and sewing machines works out to $8 per pair ($120 ÷ 15). This high average fixed cost accounts for nearly one-half of total average costs. This suggests that it's quite expensive to lease a factory and sewing machine to produce only 15 pairs of jeans per day. To reduce average costs, we must make fuller use of our leased plant and equipment.

Notice what happens to average costs when the rate of output is increased to 20 pairs per day (row *K* in Figure 5.5). Average fixed costs go down, to only $6 per pair. This sharp decline in AFC results from the fact that total fixed costs ($120) are now spread over more output. Even though our rent hasn't dropped, the *average* fixed cost of producing jeans has.

If we produce more than 20 pairs of jeans per day, AFC will continue to fall. Recall that

$$AFC = \frac{\text{total fixed cost}}{\text{total output}} = \frac{TFC}{q}$$

The numerator is fixed (at $120 in this case). But the denominator increases as output expands. Hence, *any increase in output will lower average fixed cost.* This is reflected in Figure 5.5 by the constantly declining AFC curve.

As jeans output increases from 15 to 20 pairs per day, AVC falls as well. AVC includes the price of denim purchased and labour costs. The price of denim is unchanged, at $3 per pair ($30 per bolt). But per-unit *labour* costs have fallen, from $5.33 to $4.50 per pair. Thus, the reduction in AVC is completely due to the greater productivity of a second worker. To get 20 pairs of jeans, we had to employ a second worker part-time. In the process, the marginal physical product of labour rose and AVC fell.

With both AFC and AVC falling, ATC must decline as well. In this case, *average total cost* falls from $16.33 per pair to $13.50. This is reflected in row *K* in the table as well as in point *K* on the ATC curve in Figure 5.5.

Rising AVC. Although AFC continues to decline as output expands, AVC doesn't keep dropping. On the contrary, AVC tends to start rising quite early in the expansion process. Look at column 6 of the table in Figure 5.5. After an initial decline, AVC starts to increase. At an output of 20 pairs, AVC is $7.50. At 30 pairs, AVC is $8.00. By the time the rate of output reaches 51 pairs per day, AVC is $12.41.

Average variable cost rises because of diminishing returns in the production process. We discussed this concept before. As output expands, each unit of labour has less land and capital to work with. Marginal physical product falls. As it does, labour costs *per pair of jeans* rise, pushing up AVC.

U-Shaped ATC. The steady decline of AFC, when combined with the typical increase in AVC, results in a U-shaped pattern for average total costs. In the early stages of output expansion, the large declines in AFC outweigh any increases in AVC. As a result, ATC tends to fall. Notice that ATC declines from $20.50 to $11.75 as output increases from 10 to 40 pairs per day. This is also illustrated in Figure 5.5 with the downward move from point *I* to point *M*.

The battle between falling AFC and rising AVC takes an irreversible turn soon thereafter. When output is increased from 40 to 50 pairs of jeans per day, AFC continues to fall (row N in the table). But the decline in AFC (-60 cents) is overshadowed by the increase in AVC ($+\$2.25$). Once rising AVC dominates, ATC starts to increase as well. ATC increases from $11.75 to $13.40 when jeans production expands from 40 to 50 pairs per day.

This and further increases in average total costs cause the ATC curve in Figure 5.5 to start rising. ***The initial dominance of falling AFC, combined with the later resurgence of rising AVC, is what gives the ATC curve its characteristic U shape.***

Minimum Average Cost. It's easy to get lost in this thicket of intertwined graphs and jumble of equations. A couple of landmarks will help guide us out, however. One of those is located at the very bottom of the U-shaped average total cost curve. Point *M* in Figure 5.5 represents *minimum* average total costs. By producing exactly 40 pairs per day, we minimize the amount of land, labour, and capital used per pair of jeans. For Low-Rider Jeans Corporation, point *M* represents least-cost production—the lowest-cost jeans. For society as a whole, point *M* also represents the lowest possible opportunity cost: At point *M*, we're minimizing the amount of resources used to produce a pair of jeans and therefore maximizing the amount of resources left over for the production of other goods and services.

As attractive as point *M* is, you shouldn't conclude that it's everyone's dream. The primary objective of producers is to maximize *profits*. This is not necessarily the same thing as minimizing average *costs*.

Marginal Cost

One final cost concept is important. Indeed, this last concept is probably the most important one for production. It's *marginal cost*. We encountered this concept in our discussion of resource costs, where we noted that marginal cost refers to the value of the resources needed to produce one more unit of a good. To produce *one* more pair of jeans, we need the denim itself and a very small amount of additional labour. These are the extra or added costs of increasing output by one pair of jeans per day. To compute the *dollar* value of these marginal costs, we could determine the market price of denim and labour and then add them up.

However, there's a much easier way to compute marginal cost. ***Marginal cost refers to the change in total costs associated with one more unit of output.*** Accordingly, we can simply observe *total* dollar costs before and after the rate of output is increased. The difference between the two totals equals the *marginal cost* of increasing the rate of output. This technique is much easier for jeans manufacturers who don't know much about marginal resource utilization but have a sharp eye for dollar costs. It's also a lot easier for economics students, of course. But they have an obligation to understand the resource origins of marginal costs and what causes marginal costs to rise or fall. As we noted before, ***diminishing returns in production cause marginal costs to increase as the rate of output is expanded.***

Figure 5.6 shows what the marginal costs of producing jeans looks like. At each output rate, marginal cost is computed as the *change* in total cost divided by the *change* in output. Once again, note that the values for the *marginal* costs are plotted at the *midpoints* of the rates of output to reflect the *change* in total costs. When output increases from 20 jeans to 30 jeans, total cost rises by $90. Dividing this change in costs by 10 (the change in output) gives us a marginal cost of $9, as illustrated by point *s*.

Notice in Figure 5.6 how the marginal cost curve slopes up after point *r*. This rise in marginal costs reflects the law of diminishing returns. As increases in output become more difficult to achieve, they also become more expensive. Each additional pair of jeans beyond point *r* requires a bit more labour than the preceding pair and thus entails rising marginal cost.

A Cost Summary

All these cost calculations can give you a real headache. They can also give you second thoughts about jumping into Low-Rider Jeans or any other business. There are tough choices to be made. A given firm can produce many different rates of output,

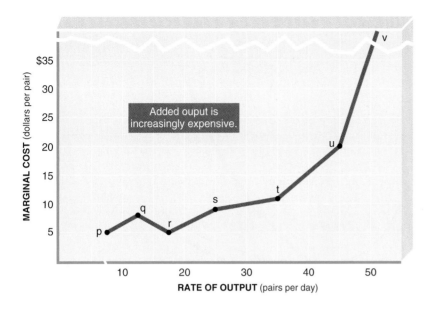

FIGURE 5.6
Marginal Costs

Marginal cost is the change in total cost that occurs when more output is produced. MC equals $\Delta TC/\Delta q$. When diminishing returns set in, MC begins rising, as it does here after the output rate of 20 pairs per day is exceeded.

		Rate of Output	Total Cost		$\dfrac{\Delta TC}{\Delta q} = MC$
p	<	0	$120	>	$85/10 = $8.5
q	<	10	205	>	$40/5 = $8.0
r	<	15	245	>	$25/5 = $5.0
s	<	20	270	>	$90/10 = $9.0
t	<	30	360	>	$110/10 = $11.0
u	<	40	470	>	$200/10 = $20.0
v	<	50	670	>	$83/1 = $83.0
		51	753		

each of which entails a distinct level of costs. ***The output decision has to be based not only on the* capacity *to produce (the production function) but also on the* costs *of production (the cost functions).*** Only those who make the right decisions will succeed in business.

The decision-making process is made a bit easier with the glossary in Table 5.3 and the generalized cost curves in Figure 5.7. As before, we're concentrating on a short-run production process, with fixed quantities of land and capital. In this case,

---

Total costs of production are comprised of **fixed costs** and **variable costs:**

$$TC = FC + VC$$

Dividing total costs by the quantity of output yields the **average total cost:**

$$ATC = \frac{TC}{q}$$

which also equals the sum of **average fixed cost** and **average variable cost:**

$$ATC = AFC + AVC$$

The most important measure of changes in cost is **marginal cost,** which equals the increase in total costs when an additional unit of output is produced:

$$MC = \frac{\text{change in total cost}}{\text{change in output}} = \frac{\Delta TC}{\Delta q}$$

TABLE 5.3
A Guide to Costs

A quick reference to key measures of cost.

FIGURE 5.7
Basic Cost Curves

With total cost and the rate of output, all other cost concepts can be computed. The resulting cost curves have several distinct features. The AFC curve always slopes downward. The MC curve typically rises, sometimes after a brief decline. The ATC curve has a U shape. And the MC curve will always intersect both the ATC and AVC curves at their lowest points (*m* and *n*, respectively).

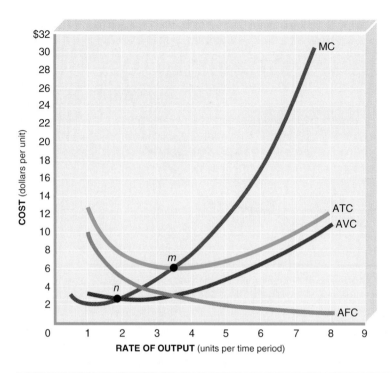

Rate of Output	TC	MC	ATC	AFC	AVC
0	$10.00	—	—	—	—
1	13.00	$ 3.00	$13.00	$10.00	$ 3.00
2	15.00	2.00	7.50	5.00	2.50
3	19.00	4.00	6.33	3.33	3.00
4	25.00	6.00	6.25	2.50	3.75
5	34.00	9.00	6.80	2.00	4.80
6	48.00	14.00	8.00	1.67	6.33
7	68.00	20.00	9.71	1.43	8.28
8	98.00	30.00	12.25	1.25	11.00

however, we've abandoned the Low-Rider Jeans Corporation and provided hypothetical costs for an idealized production process. The purpose of these figures is to provide a more general view of how the various cost concepts relate to each other. Note that MC, ATC, AFC, and AVC can all be computed from total costs. All we need, then, are the first two columns of the table in Figure 5.7, and we can compute and graph all the rest of the cost figures.

Average Total Cost vs. Marginal Cost. The centrepiece of Figure 5.7 is the U-shaped ATC curve. Of special significance is its relationship to marginal costs. Notice that *the MC curve intersects the ATC curve at its lowest point* (point *m*). This will always be the case. So long as the marginal cost of producing one more unit is less than the previous average cost, average costs must fall. ***Thus, average total costs decline as long as the marginal cost curve lies below the average cost curve,*** as to the left of point *m* in Figure 5.7.

We already observed, however, that marginal costs rise as output expands, largely because additional workers reduce the amount of land and capital available to each worker (in the short run, the size of plant and equipment is fixed). Consequently, at some point (*m* in Figure 5.7) marginal costs will rise to the level of average costs.

As marginal costs continue to rise beyond point *m*, they begin to pull average costs up, giving the average cost curve its U shape. ***Average total costs increase*** *whenever marginal costs exceed average costs.* This is the case to the right of point *m*, since the marginal cost curve always lies above the average cost curve in that part of Figure 5.7.

This relationship between average total cost and marginal cost should sound familiar. It follows the same logic as the relationship between average physical product (APP) and marginal physical product (MPP) discussed earlier. Now, that we understand the basic relationship between marginal and average values, we can proceed with the final link between changes in productivity and changes in costs. Before we make that link, however, we need to talk briefly about the differences in productivity and costs when our time frame extends beyond the short run.

5.5 LONG-RUN COSTS

We've confined our discussion thus far to short-run production costs. *The short run is characterized by fixed costs*—a commitment to specific plant and equipment. A factory, an office building, or some other plant and equipment have been leased or purchased: We're stuck with *fixed costs*. In the short run, our objective is to make the best use of those fixed costs by choosing the appropriate rate of production.

The long run opens up a whole new range of options. In the **long run,** we have no lease or purchase commitments. We're free to start all over again, with whatever scale of plant and equipment we desire and whatever technology is available. Quite simply, *there are no fixed costs in the long run.* Nor are there any commitments to existing technology.

long run: A period of time long enough for all inputs to be varied (no fixed costs).

In 2006, Alcan—Canada's largest producer of primary aluminum—and its partners could have built an aluminum smelter of any size in the Middle East. But they decided to build one with a capacity of 320 kilotonnes per year with the possibility of constructing a second smelter of similar size in the future (see the Applications box). In addition, they could also have used any available technology but chose the "proven AP35 Technology"; the first time this particular technology was incorporated into a new smelter. In building the plant, Alcan and its partners incur substantial fixed costs, and once completed will focus on the *short-run* production decision of how many kilotonnes of aluminum to produce each year.

APPLICATIONS

Alcan and Partners Build US$1.7 Billion Aluminum Smelter in Middle East

Sharm el-Sheikh, Egypt—In April 2006, a senior Vice President of Alcan, Cynthia Carroll, announced that "Alcan's leadership in proven smelting technology, based on full economic cost, environmental impact, and potential for smelter expansion, is a strength which will yield sustainable business opportunities here in the Middle East." This statement was based on Alcan's commitment, along with its partners, Oman Oil Company S.A.O.C. (OOC) and the Abu Dhabi Water and Electricity Authority (ADWEA), to proceed with construction of a $1.7 billion ($US) primary aluminum smelter in Sohar, Oman. Alcan has a 20 percent stake in the 350 kilotonne per year smelter, marking the first time that proven AP35 technology will be used in a new smelter. To date, 17 percent of the world's primary aluminum capacity, excluding China, employs AP technology, including 30 percent of the capacity in the Middle East. The smelter will be in the lowest quartile of the industry cash cost curve and add approximately two percent to Alcan's global smelting base. A second potline of similar capacity could be established in the future.

Source: Based on "Alcan and Partners build US$1.7 billion aluminum smelter in middle east." Distributed by PRNewswire, April 6, 2004, on behalf of Alcan Inc. http://www.prnewswire.co.uk/cgi/news/release?id=167778.

Analysis: In the long run, a firm has no fixed costs and can select any desired plant size. Once a plant is built, leased, or purchased, a firm has fixed costs and focuses on short-run output decisions.

FIGURE 5.8
Long-Run Costs with Three Plant Size Options

Long-run cost possibilities are determined by all possible short-run options. In this case, there are three options of varying size (ATC₁, ATC₂, and ATC₃). In the long run, we'd choose the plant that yielded the lowest average cost for any desired rate of output. The solid portion of the curves (LATC) represents these choices. The smallest factory (ATC₁) is best for output levels below *a*; the largest (ATC₃) is best for output rates in excess of *b*.

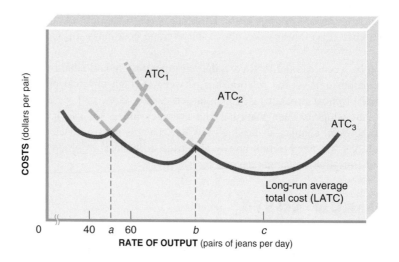

Long-Run Average Costs

The opportunities available in the long run include building a plant of any desired size. Suppose we still wanted to go into the jeans business. In the long run, we could build or lease any size factory we wanted and could lease as many sewing machines as we desired. Figure 5.8 illustrates three choices: a small factory (ATC₁), a medium-sized factory (ATC₂) and a large factory (ATC₃). As we observed earlier, it's very expensive to produce lots of jeans with a small factory. The ATC curve for a small factory (ATC₁) starts to head straight up at relatively low rates of output. In the long run, we'd lease or build such a factory only if we anticipated a continuing low rate of output.

The ATC₂ curve illustrates how costs might fall if we leased or built a medium-sized factory. With a small-sized factory, ATC becomes prohibitive at an output of 50 to 60 pairs of jeans per day. A medium-sized factory can produce these quantities at lower cost. Moreover, ATC continues to drop as jeans production increases in the medium-sized factory—at least for a while. Even a medium-sized factory must contend with resource constraints and therefore rising average costs: Its ATC curve is U-shaped also.

If we expected to sell really large quantities of jeans, we'd want to build or lease a large factory. Beyond the rate of output *b*, the largest factory offers the lowest average total cost. There's a risk in leasing such a large factory, of course. If our sales don't live up to our high expectations, we'll end up with very high fixed costs and thus very expensive jeans. Look at the high average cost of producing only 60 pairs of jeans per day with the large factory (ATC₃).

In choosing an appropriate factory, then, we must decide how many jeans we expect to sell. Once we know our expected output, we can easily pick the right-sized factory. It will be the one that offers the lowest ATC for that rate of output. If we expect to sell fewer jeans than *a*, we'll choose the small factory in Figure 5.8. If we expect to sell jeans at a rate between *a* and *b*, we'll select a medium-sized factory. Beyond rate *b*, we'll want the largest factory. These choices are reflected in the solid part of the three ATC curves. The composite "curve" created by these three segments constitutes our long-run cost possibilities. ***The long-run cost curve is just a summary of our best short-run cost possibilities, using existing technology and facilities.***

We might confront more than three choices, of course. There's really no reason we couldn't build a factory to any desired size. In the long run, we face an infinite number of scale choices, not just three. The effect of all these choices is to smooth out the long-run cost curve. Figure 5.9 depicts the long-run curve that results. Each rate of output is most efficiently produced by some size (scale) of plant. That sized plant indicates the minimum cost of producing a particular rate of output. Its corresponding short-run ATC curve provides one point on the long-run ATC curve.

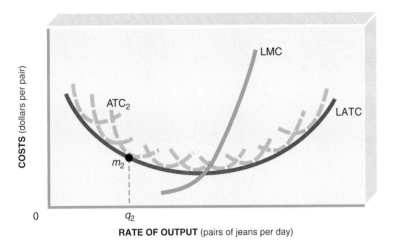

FIGURE 5.9
Long-Run Costs with Unlimited Options

If plants of all sizes can be built, short-run options are infinite. In this case, the LATC curve becomes a smooth U-shaped curve. Each point on the curve represents lowest-cost production for a plant size best suited to one rate of output. The long-run ATC curve has its own MC curve, LMC.

Like all average cost curves, the long-run (LATC) curve has its own marginal cost curve. The long-run marginal cost (LMC) curve isn't a composite of short-run marginal cost curves. Rather, it's computed on the basis of the costs reflected in the long-run ATC curve itself. We won't bother to compute those costs here. Note, however, that the long-run MC curve—like all MC curves—intersects its associated average cost curve at its lowest point.

Long-Run Marginal Costs

5.6 ECONOMIES OF SCALE

Figure 5.8 seems to imply that a producer must choose either a small plant or a larger one. That isn't completely true. The choice is often between one large plant or *several* small ones. Suppose the desired level of output was relatively large, as at point c in Figure 5.8. A single small plant (ATC$_1$) is clearly not up to the task. But what about using several small plants rather than one large one (ATC$_3$)? How would costs be affected?

Notice what happens to *minimum ATC* in Figure 5.8 when the size (scale) of the factory changes. When a medium-sized factory (ATC$_2$) replaces a small factory (ATC$_1$), minimum average cost drops (the bottom of ATC$_2$ is below the bottom of ATC$_1$). This implies that a jeans producer who wants to minimize costs should build one medium-sized factory rather than try to produce the same quantity with two small ones. **Economies of scale** exist in this situation: Larger facilities reduce minimum average costs. Such economies of scale help explain why the average size of crop farms in Saskatchewan has doubled over the past twenty-five years (see the Applications box on the next page).

Larger production facilities don't always result in cost reductions. Suppose a firm has the choice of producing the quantity Q_m from several small factories or from one large, centralized facility. Centralization may have three different impacts on costs; these are illustrated in Figure 5.10. In each illustration, we see the average total cost (ATC) curve for a typical small firm or plant and the ATC curve for a much larger plant producing the same product.

Figure 5.10*a* depicts a situation in which there's no economic advantage to centralization of manufacturing operations, because a large plant is no more efficient than a lot of small plants. The critical focus here is on the *minimum* average costs attainable for a given rate of output. Note that the lowest point on the smaller plant's ATC curve (point c) is no higher or lower than the lowest point on the larger firm's ATC curve (point m_1). Hence, it would be just as cheap to produce the quantity Q_m from a multitude of small plants as it would be to produce Q_m from one large plant. Thus increasing the size (or *scale*) of individual plants won't reduce minimum average costs: This is a situation of **constant returns to scale.**

economies of scale: Reductions in minimum average costs that come about through increases in the size (scale) of plant and equipment.

Constant Returns

constant returns to scale: Increases in plant size do not affect minimum average cost: minimum per-unit costs are identical for small plants and large plants.

Farm Size in Saskatchewan

Saskatchewan has roughly 40 percent of the agricultural land in Canada and, on average, has the largest farms. As the latest Statistics Canada Census on Agriculture indicates, there has been a downward trend in the *number* of farms in Saskatchewan (as in all the other provinces). As the number of farms fell, however, over the past 25 years the average size of crop farms in Saskatchewan has doubled—from 180 hectares to 364 hectares. Decreasing grain prices along with the elimination of transportation subsidies (Western Grain Transportation Act) in 1995 effectively reduced the ability of small, high-cost farms in Saskatchewan to survive under these conditions.

Source: "Farm Size in Saskatchewan," adapted from Statistics Canada publication, *Farm Data and Farm Operator Data (Full release) for the 2001 Census of Agriculture Plus Selected Historical Data,* Catalogue 95F0302XIE. Released on December 4, 2002, http://www.statcan.ca/bsolc/english/bsolc?catno=95F0302X.

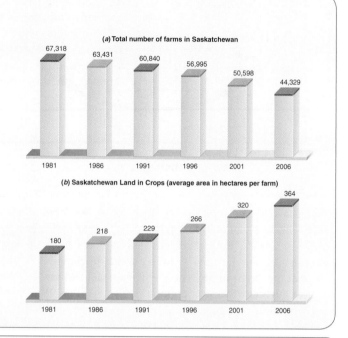

Analysis: As the size of a farm increases, it may be able to reduce the costs of doing business. Economies of scale give a large farm a competitive advantage over smaller farms.

Economies of Scale

Figure 5.10*b* illustrates the situation in which a larger plant can attain a lower minimum average cost than a smaller plant. That is, economies of scale (or *increasing returns to scale*) exist. This is evident from the fact that the larger firm's ATC curve falls *below* the dashed line in the graph (m_2 is less than c). The greater efficiency of the large factory might come from any of several sources.

This is the situation of the average Saskatchewan farm size depicted in the Applications box above. Combining two or three small, 180 hectare farms, for example,

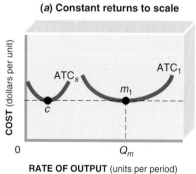

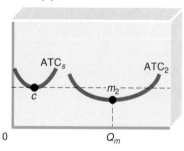

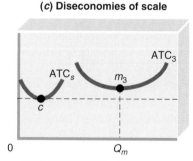

FIGURE 5.10
Economies of Scale

A lot of output (Q_m) can be produced from one large plant or many small ones. Here we contrast the average total costs associated with one small plant (ATC_s) and three large plants (ATC_1, ATC_2, and ATC_3). If a large plant attains the same *minimum* average costs (point m_1 in part *a*) as a smaller plant (point *c*), there's no advantage to large size (scale). Many small plants can produce the same output just as cheaply. However, either economies (part *b*) or diseconomies (part *c*) of scale may exist.

can reduce some of the administrative costs of farming if they are centralized under the management of one farm. It may also be the case that one tractor is sufficient to harvest the crop. Some kinds of machinery may be economical only if they're used to produce massive volumes,[3] an opportunity only large farms have. Larger farms can also take advantage of *specialization* and *division of labour* by having workers develop expertise in a particular skill. By contrast, a smaller farm might have to use the same individual(s) to perform several functions, thereby reducing productivity at each task. Finally, from an organizational standpoint, a larger farm might acquire a persistent cost advantage through the process of learning-by-doing. That is, its longer experience and greater volume of output may translate into improved organization and efficiency.

Even though large plants may be able to achieve greater efficiencies than smaller plants, there's no assurance that they actually will. In fact, increasing the size (scale) of a plant may actually *reduce* operating efficiency, as depicted in Figure 5.10c. Workers may feel alienated in a plant of massive proportions and feel little commitment to productivity. Creativity may be stifled by rigid corporate structures and off-site management. A large plant may also foster a sense of anonymity that induces workers to underperform. When these things happen, *diseconomies of scale* result. Microsoft tries to avoid such diseconomies of scale by creating autonomous cells of no more than 35 employees ("small plants") within its larger corporate structure.

Diseconomies of Scale

In evaluating long-run options, then, we must be careful to recognize that *efficiency and size don't necessarily go hand in hand.* Some firms and industries may be subject to economies of scale, but others may not. Bigger isn't always better.

We started this chapter by discussing one of the classical arguments presented by trade protectionists: we need to protect our home industries because we cannot compete with cheap (and unfair, of course!) foreign labour. If cheap labour is the foundation for trade, why aren't countries such as Haiti and Vietnam trading powerhouses? Why is it the case that those countries which are large trading nations (Germany, Japan, the United States, and Canada) also have the highest wage rates? Clearly, there must be more to trade than cheap labour.

Productivity and Costs Revisited

Cheap Foreign Labour? Cheap labour keeps costs down in many countries. The average wage in Mexico, for example, ranges from $2 to $3 an hour, compared to over $18 an hour in Canada. Low wages are *not,* however, a reliable measure of global competitiveness. To compete in global markets, one must produce more *output* for a given quantity of *inputs.* In other words, labour is "cheap" only if it produces a lot of output in return for the wages paid.

A worker's contribution to output is measured by *marginal physical product (MPP).* What we saw in this chapter was that *a worker's productivity (MPP) depends on the quantity and quality of other resources in the production process.* In this regard, Canadian workers have a tremendous advantage: They work with vast quantities of capital and state-of-the-art technology. They also come to the workplace with more education. Their high wages reflect this greater productivity.

Unit Labour Costs. A true measure of global competitiveness must take into account both factor costs (e.g., wages) and productivity. One such measure is **unit labour costs,** which indicates the labour cost of producing one unit of output. It's computed as

unit labour cost: Hourly wage rate divided by output per labour-hour.

$$\text{Unit labour cost} = \frac{\text{wage rate}}{\text{MPP}}$$

---

[3]In other words, the machinery itself may be subject to economies of scale.

Suppose the MPP of Canadian worker is 9 units per hour and the wage is $18 an hour. The unit labour cost would be

$$\frac{\text{Unit labour cost}}{\text{(Canada)}} = \frac{\$18/\text{hour}}{9 \text{ units/hour}} = \frac{\$2/\text{unit}}{\text{of output}}$$

By contrast, assume the average worker in Mexico has an MPP of 1 unit per hour and a wage of $3 an hour. In this case, the unit labour cost would be

$$\frac{\text{Unit labour cost}}{\text{(Mexico)}} = \frac{\$3}{1} = \frac{\$3/\text{unit}}{\text{of output}}$$

According to these hypothetical examples, "cheap" Mexican labour is no bargain. Mexican labour is actually *more* costly in production, despite the lower wage rate.

WEB NOTE

For current data on international comparisons of manufacturing productivity and unit labour cost trends, visit the U.S. Bureau of Labor Statistics at http://www.bls.gov/fls/prodsupptabletoc.htm.

Productivity Advance. What these calculations illustrate is how important productivity is for global competitiveness. If we want Canada to stay competitive in global markets, Canadian productivity must increase as fast as that in other nations.

The production function introduced in this chapter helps illustrate the essence of global competitiveness in the economy tomorrow. Until now, we've regarded a firm's production function as a technological fact of life—the *best* we could do, given our state of technological and managerial knowledge. In the real world, however, the best is always getting better. Science and technology are continuously advancing. So is our knowledge of how to organize and manage our resources. These advances keep *shifting* production functions upward: More can be produced with any given quantity of inputs. In the process, the costs of production shift downward, as illustrated in Figure 5.11 by the downward shifts of the MC and ATC curves. These downward shifts imply that we can get more of the goods and services we desire with available resources. We can also compete more effectively in global markets.

B2B Solutions. The Internet has been an important source of productivity gains in the last 10 years. Although the Internet originated over 30 years ago, its commercial potential emerged with the creation of the World Wide Web around 1990. As recently as 1995 there were only 10,000 Web sites. Now there are over 80 *million* sites. This vastly expanded spectrum of information has helped businesses cut costs in many ways. The cost of gathering information about markets and inputs has been reduced. With the reach of the Internet, firms can engage in greater specialization. Firms can also manage their inventories and supply chains much more efficiently. Transaction and communications costs are reduced as well. For those companies that take advantage

FIGURE 5.11

Improvements in Productivity Reduce Costs

Advances in technological or managerial knowledge increase our productive capability. This is reflected in upward shifts of the production function (part *a*) and downward shifts of production cost curves (part *b*).

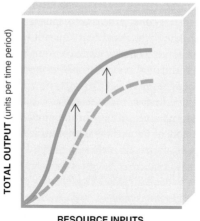

(a) When the production function shifts up . . .

TOTAL OUTPUT (units per time period)

RESOURCE INPUTS
(units per time period)

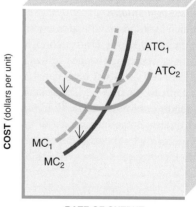

(b) Cost curves shift down

COST (dollars per unit)

ATC₁
ATC₂
MC₁
MC₂

RATE OF OUTPUT
(units per time period)

of the Internet, all of these productivity improvements can reduce production costs and unit labour costs. A firm's ability to maintain or increase its global competitiveness is contingent on finding these new sources of productivity—whether they come from within the firm or outside (such as the Internet).

SUMMARY

- A production function indicates the maximum amount of output that can be produced with different combinations of inputs. It's a technological relationship and changes (shifts) when new technology or management techniques are discovered.
- In the short run, some inputs (e.g., land and capital) are fixed in quantity. Increases in (short-run) output result from more use of variable inputs (e.g., labour).
- The contribution of a variable input to total output is measured by its marginal physical product (MPP). This is the amount by which *total* output increases when one more unit of the input is employed.
- The MPP of a factor tends to decline as more of it is used in a given production facility. Diminishing marginal returns result from crowding more of a variable input into a production process, reducing the amount of fixed inputs *per unit* of variable input.
- Marginal cost is the increase in total cost that results when output is increased by one unit. Marginal cost increases whenever marginal physical product diminishes.

- Not all costs go up when the rate of output is increased. Fixed costs such as space and equipment leases don't vary with the rate of output. Only variable costs such as labour and materials go up when output is increased.
- Average total cost (ATC) equals total cost divided by the quantity of output produced. ATC declines whenever marginal cost (MC) is less than average cost and rises when MC exceeds it. The MC and ATC curves intersect at minimum ATC (the bottom of the U). That intersection represents least-cost production.
- In the long run there are no fixed costs; the size (scale) of production can be varied. The long-run ATC curve indicates the lowest cost of producing output with facilities of appropriate size.
- Economies of scale refer to reductions in minimum average cost attained with larger plant size (scale). If minimum ATC rises with plant size, diseconomies of scale exist.
- Global competitiveness and domestic living standards depend on productivity advances. Improvements in productivity shift production functions up and push cost curves down.

Key Terms

production function 102
productivity 103
short run 104
marginal physical product (MPP) 105
average physical product (APP) 106
law of diminishing returns 107

profit 107
marginal cost (MC) 108
total cost 110
fixed costs 110
variable costs 110
average total cost (ATC) 112

average fixed cost (AFC) 113
average variable cost (AVC) 113
long run 117
economies of scale 119
constant returns to scale 119
unit labour cost 121

Questions for Discussion

1. What are the production costs of your economics class? What are the fixed costs? The variable costs? What's the marginal cost of enrolling more students?
2. Suppose all your friends offered to help wash your car. Would marginal physical product decline as more friends helped? Why or why not?
3. Every spring, thousands of university and college students seek help from friends and acquaintances to move their belongings from one place of residence to another. In return for their services, students typically offer the moving crew pizza and beer. As a student, would you provide your workers with the "refreshments" before or after the move has been completed? Explain your reasoning using the concepts discussed in this chapter.
4. Corporate funeral giants have replaced small family-run funeral homes in many areas, in large part because of the lower costs they achieve. What kind of economies of scale exist in the funeral business? Why doesn't someone build one colossal funeral home and drive costs down further?

5. Are colleges subject to economies of scale or dis-economies?

6. Why don't more Canadian firms move to Mexico to take advantage of low wages there? Would an *identical* plant in Mexico be as productive as its Canadian counterpart?

7. How would your productivity in completing course work be measured? Has your productivity changed since you began your post-secondary studies? What caused the productivity changes? How could you increase productivity further?

8. What is the economic cost of doing this homework?

9. Graphically illustrate the relationship between marginal physical product and average physical product when we have increasing marginal returns followed by diminishing marginal returns. On a second graph, show how the MPP and APP influence the relationship between marginal cost and average (variable) cost.

E X E R C I S E S

PROBLEMS

The Student Problem Set to accompany this chapter can be found at the end of the book.

WEB ACTIVITIES

Web Activities to accompany this chapter can be found on the Online Learning Centre at **http://www.mcgrawhill.ca/olc/schiller**.

A P P E N D I X

PRODUCTIVITY, UNIT COSTS, AND EXCHANGE RATES

In our discussion on productivity and costs on pages 108–119, we omitted a variable that can play an important role when comparing unit labour costs across nations—namely, the exchange rate. By definition, the exchange rate is simply the price of another nation's currency. For example, it costs about $1.15 Canadian to purchase $1.00 U.S. and about $2.50 to buy one British pound (£). Changes in the value of a country's exchange rate (appreciations and depreciations) can have a considerable impact on unit labour costs.

Returning to our example, you will notice that when comparing the unit labour costs between Canada and Mexico, the Mexican wage rate is converted from their national currency (peso) to Canadian dollars. This is important, of course, since we require a common base from which we can measure and compare unit labour costs. Suppose the Mexican wage rate is 27 pesos/hour and the initial exchange rate is $1 = 9 pesos, this gives us our Mexican wage in Canadian dollars

$$\text{Mexican wage} = \frac{\$1}{9 \text{ pesos}} \times \frac{27 \text{ pesos}}{1 \text{ hour}} = \frac{\$3}{1 \text{ hour}}$$

But, what would happen if the Mexican peso depreciated, *ceteris paribus,* with respect to the Canadian dollar? If the exchange rate is now $1 = 12 pesos, then the new Mexican wage in Canadian dollars is:

$$\text{Mexican wage} = \frac{\$1}{12 \text{ pesos}} \times \frac{27 \text{ pesos}}{1 \text{ hour}} = \frac{\$2.25}{1 \text{ hour}}$$

APPLICATIONS

Bombardier Calls on Feds to Stabilize High Loonie

MONTREAL (CP)—The head of Bombardier Inc. has called on the federal government and the central bank to put the brakes on the ascending loonie or risk losing jobs to offshore production.

"If the Canadian dollar continues to gain ground, manufacturing companies that export will have almost no other choice but to increase the U.S. content of their business or move production to countries where costs will allow them to be more competitive," Laurent Beaudoin said Tuesday.

Beaudoin also told the annual meeting of shareholders that the Bank of Canada should step in to regulate the Canadian dollar.

"While I understand the Bank of Canada's role is to control inflation by varying interest rates, I have a hard time understanding why it only steps in when there is a loss of confidence in the Canadian dollar, and not in the opposite case when there is excess confidence that leads to an overly rapid appreciation of our currency."

Beaudoin echoed a call already made by the CEO of newsprint giant Abitibi-Consolidated Inc. Abitibi's John Weaver recently called for the Canadian government to stabilize the high-flying loonie, which he said has battered forestry companies. Weaver told his annual shareholders' meeting earlier this month that Canada's monetary policy should take into account currency fluctuations.

Canadian Unit Labour Costs		
Years	% Change in Canadian Unit Labour Costs	% Change in Canadian Unit Labour Costs in $US
1990 vs. 1995	3.5	−12
1995 vs. 2000	6.8	−1.3
2000 vs. 2005	8.9	33.5

Source: "Canadian Unit Labour Costs," adapted from Statistics Canada website, http://www40.statcan.ca/101/cst01/econ78a.htm and also available from Statistics Canada CANSIM database Table 383-0008.

—Karine Fortin

Source: Used with permission of the Canadian Press.

Analysis: Global competitiveness depends on unit labour costs. Wages, productivity, and exchange rates determine the value of unit labour costs when measured in different currencies. Canadian unit labour costs show a distinctive upward trend over the past 15 years.

Given that the marginal productivity in Mexico has not changed (i.e., 1 unit per hour), this depreciation of the Mexican peso reduces the unit labour cost to $2.25/unit of output. Consequently, the unit labour cost gap between Mexico and Canada is substantially reduced. So, we have three distinct concerns when looking at international comparisons of unit labour costs; wage rates, productivity, and exchange rates.

As the Applications box above discusses, Canadian manufacturers suffered significantly higher unit labour costs when the Canadian dollar appreciated from $1 US = $1.62 Cdn in January 2002 to $1 US = $1.09 Cdn in May 2006. The associated table compares Canadian unit labour costs in both Canadian and U.S. dollars over 5-year intervals starting in 1990. In the 1990s, increases in Canadian unit labour costs were offset by the depreciation of the Canadian dollar and therefore when converted to U.S. dollars, the unit labour costs decreased. However, increases in the Canadian unit labour costs over the 2000–2005 period were exacerbated by the appreciation of the Canadian dollar.

Market Structure

Although market demand and production functions set limits to output choices, not all firms respond the same way to these limits. The number and size of the firms in a market—industry structure—also affect production and pricing decisions. Chapters 6 through 10 examine how different market structures affect the supply of goods and services—the quantity, quality, and prices of goods and services in specific product markets.

The Competitive Firm

America Online would love to raise the price of accessing its archive of information and Internet services. It isn't likely to do so, however, because too many other firms also offer online services and Net access. If America Online raises its prices, customers might sign up with another company.

Your campus bookstore may be in a better position to raise prices. On most university and college campuses there's only one bookstore. If the campus store increases the price of books or supplies, most of its customers (you) will have little choice but to pay the higher tab.

As we discover in this and the next few chapters, the degree of competition in product markets is a major determinant of product prices, quality, and availability. Although all firms are in business to make a profit, their profit opportunities are limited by the amount of competition they face.

This chapter begins an examination of how businesses make price and production decisions. We first explore the nature of profits and how they're computed. We then observe how one type of firm—a perfectly competitive one—can *maximize* its profits by selecting the right rate of output. The following questions are at the centre of this discussion:

• **What are *profits?***
• **What are the unique characteristics of competitive firms?**
• **How much output will a competitive firm produce?**

The answers to these questions will shed more light on how the *supply* of goods and services is determined in a market economy.

6.1 THE PROFIT MOTIVE

The basic incentive for producing goods and services is the expectation of profit. *Owning* plant and equipment isn't enough. To generate a current flow of income, one must *use* that plant and equipment to produce and sell goods.

Profit is the difference between a firm's sales revenues and its total costs. It's the residual that the owners of a business receive. The recipient of the residual may be the sole owner of a corner grocery store, or it may be the group of stockholders who collectively own a large corporation. In either case, it's the quest for profit that motivates people to own and operate a business.

Profit isn't the only thing that motivates producers. Like the rest of us, producers also worry about social status and crave recognition. People who need to feel important, to control others, or to demonstrate achievement are likely candidates for running a business. Many small businesses are maintained by people who gave up 40-hour weeks, $50,000 incomes, and a sense of alienation in exchange for 80-hour weeks, $45,000 incomes, and a sense of identity and control.

In large corporations, the profit motive may lie even deeper below the surface. Stockholders of large corporations rarely visit corporate headquarters. The people who manage the corporation's day-to-day business may have little or no stock in the company. Such nonowner-managers may be more interested in their own jobs, salaries, and self-preservation than in the profits that accrue to the stockholding owners. If profits suffer, however, the corporation may start looking for new managers. The accompanying cartoon notwithstanding, the "bottom line" for virtually all businesses is the level of profits.

Other Motivations

If it weren't possible to make a profit, few people would choose to supply goods and services. Yet the general public remains suspicious of the profit motive. As the Applications box indicates, one out of four people thinks the profit motive is bad. An even higher percentage believes the profit motive results in *inferior* products at inflated prices.

As we'll see, the profit motive *can* induce business firms to pollute the environment, restrict competition, or maintain unsafe working conditions. However, ***the profit motive also encourages businesses to produce the goods and services consumers desire, at prices they're willing to pay.*** The profit motive, in fact, moves the "invisible hand" that Adam Smith said orchestrates market outcomes.

Is the Profit Motive Bad?

"You know what I think, folks? Improving technology isn't important. Increased profits aren't important. What's important is to be warm, decent human beings."

Analysis: The principal motivation for producing goods and services is to earn a profit. Although other goals may seem desirable, businesses that fail to earn a profit won't survive.

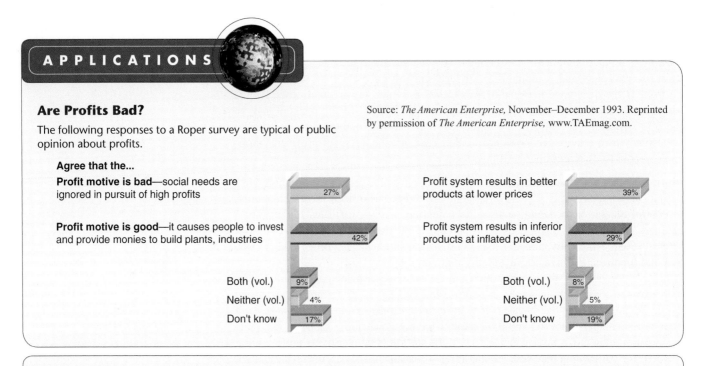

Are Profits Bad?

The following responses to a Roper survey are typical of public opinion about profits.

Source: *The American Enterprise*, November–December 1993. Reprinted by permission of *The American Enterprise*, www.TAEmag.com.

Agree that the...

Profit motive is bad—social needs are ignored in pursuit of high profits 27%

Profit motive is good—it causes people to invest and provide monies to build plants, industries 42%

Both (vol.) 9%
Neither (vol.) 4%
Don't know 17%

Profit system results in better products at lower prices 39%

Profit system results in inferior products at inflated prices 29%

Both (vol.) 8%
Neither (vol.) 5%
Don't know 19%

Analysis: The profit motive is the primary incentive for supplying goods and services. Many consumers are distrustful of that motive, however.

6.2 COSTS AND PROFITS: ECONOMIC VS. ACCOUNTING

Economic Profits

economic cost: The value of all resources used to produce a good or service; opportunity cost.

explicit costs: A payment made for the use of a resource.

implicit cost: The value of resources used, even when no direct payment is made.

Everyone agrees that profit represents the difference between total revenues and total costs. Where people part ways is over the decision of what to include in total costs. **Economic cost** refers to the value of *all* resources used in production, whether or not they receive an explicit payment. By contrast, most businesses count only **explicit costs**—that is, those they actually write cheques for. They typically don't take into account the **implicit costs** of the labour or land and buildings they might own. As a result, they understate costs.

Consider the Low-Rider Jeans example from Chapter 5 for a moment to see the difference. When we computed the dollar cost of producing 15 pairs of jeans per day, we noted the following resource inputs:

INPUTS	COST PER DAY
1 factory rent	$100
1 machine rent	20
1 machine operator	80
1.5 bolts of denim	45
Total cost	$245

The total value of the resources used in the production of 15 pairs of jeans was thus $245 per day. But this figure needn't conform to *actual* dollar costs. Suppose the owners of Low-Rider Jeans decided to sew jeans. Then they wouldn't have to hire a worker or pay $80 per day in wages. *Explicit costs*—the *dollar* payments—would drop to $165 per day. The producers and their accountant would consider this a remarkable achievement. They might assert that the cost of producing jeans had fallen.

Economic Cost

An economist would draw no such conclusions. ***The essential economic question is how many resources are used in production.*** This hasn't changed. One unit of labour is still being employed at the factory; now it's simply the owner, not a hired worker.

In either case, one unit of labour is not available for the production of other goods and services. Hence, society is still paying $245 for jeans, whether the owners of Low-Rider Jeans write cheques in that amount or not. The only difference is that we now have an *implicit cost* rather than an explicit one. We really don't care who sews jeans—the essential point is that someone (i.e., a unit of labour) does.

The same would be true if Low-Rider Jeans owned its own factory rather than rented it. If the factory were owned rather than rented, the owners probably wouldn't write any rent cheques. Hence, accounting costs would drop by $100 per day. But the factory would still be in use for jeans production and therefore unavailable for the production of other goods and services. The economic (resource) cost of producing 15 pairs of jeans would still be $245.

The distinction between an economic cost and an accounting cost is essentially one between resource and dollar costs. *Dollar cost* refers to the explicit dollar outlays made by a producer; it's the lifeblood of accountants. *Economic cost,* in contrast, refers to the *value* of *all* resources used in the production process; it's the lifeblood of economists. In other words, economists count costs as

$$\text{Economic cost} = \text{explicit costs} + \text{implicit costs}$$

As this formula suggests, *economic and accounting costs will diverge whenever any factor of production is not paid an explicit wage (or rent, etc.).*

If businesses (and their accountants) understate true costs, they'll overstate true profits. Part of the accounting "profit" will really be compensation to unpaid land, labour, or capital used in the production process. *Whenever economic costs exceed explicit costs, observed (accounting) profits will exceed true (economic) profits.* Indeed, what appears to be an accounting profit may actually disguise an economic loss, as illustrated by Mr. Fujishige's strawberry farm, once located right next to Disneyland (see the Applications box). To determine the **economic profit** of a business, we must subtract all implicit factor costs from observed accounting profits:

economic profit: The difference between total revenues and total economic costs.

$$\text{Economic profit} = \text{total revenue} - \text{total economic costs}$$
$$= \text{total revenue} - (\text{explicit costs} + \text{implicit costs})$$
$$= (\text{total revenue} - \text{explicit costs}) - \text{implicit costs}$$
$$= \text{accounting profit} - \text{implicit costs}$$

APPLICATIONS

Strawberry Fields Forever?

ANAHEIM, CALIFORNIA—Hiroshi Fujishige is a successful strawberry farmer. For over 40 years he has been earning a profit growing and selling strawberries and other produce from his 58-acre farm. Mr. Fujishige could make even more money if he stopped growing strawberries. His 58-acre strawberry patch is located across the street from Disneyland. The people from Disney have offered him $32 million just to *lease* the farm; developers have offered as much as $2 million per acre to *buy* the land. But Mr. Fujishige, who lives in a tiny house on the farm he bought 45 years ago (for $2500!) isn't selling. "I'm a farmer, and I've been farming since I got out of high school in 1941," he says. As long as he can make a profit from strawberries, he says, he'll keep growing them.

Source: *Washington Post*, March 9, 1994. © 1994, The Washington Post. Reprinted with permission. www.washingtonpost.com

Analysis: Accounting profits may overrate the profitability of an enterprise by failing to consider the opportunity cost of all resources used in production. If the opportunity cost of the land were deducted, this farm would show an economic loss. In 1998 Mr. Fujishige died and his family sold all but 3.5 acres of his farm to Disneyland for its new California Adventure theme park.

TABLE 6.1
The Computation of Economic Profit

To calculate economic profit, we must take account of *all* costs of production. The economic costs of production include the implicit (opportunity) costs of the labour and capital a producer contributes to the production process. The accounting profits of a business take into account only explicit costs paid by the owner. Reported (accounting) profits will exceed economic profits whenever implicit costs are ignored.

Total (gross) revenues per month	$27,000
less explicit costs:	
Cost of merchandise sold	$17,000
Wages to cashier, stock, and delivery help	2,500
Rent and utilities	800
Taxes	700
Total explicit costs	$21,000
Accounting profit (revenue minus explicit costs)	$ 6,000
less implicit costs:	
Wages of owner-manager, 300 hours @ $10 per hour	$ 3,000
Return on inventory investment, 10% per year on $120,000	1,000
Total implicit costs	$ 4,000
Economic profit (revenue minus *all* costs)	$ 2,000

Suppose, for example, that Table 6.1 accurately summarizes the revenues and costs associated with a local drugstore. Monthly sales revenues amount to $27,000. Explicit costs paid by the owner-manager include the cost of merchandise bought from producers for resale to consumers ($17,000), wages to the employees of the drugstore, rent and utilities paid to the landlord, and local sales and business taxes. When all these explicit costs are subtracted from total revenue, we're left with an *accounting profit* of $6,000 per month.

The owner-manager of the drugstore may be quite pleased with an accounting profit of $6,000 per month. He's working hard for this income, however. To keep his store running, the owner-manager is working 10 hours per day, seven days a week. This adds up to 300 hours of labour per month. Were he to work this hard for someone else, his labour would be compensated explicitly—with a paycheque. Although he doesn't choose to pay himself this way, his labour still represents a real resource cost. To compute *economic* profit, we must subtract this implicit cost from the drugstore's accounting profits. Suppose the owner could earn $10 per hour in the best alternative job. Multiplying this wage rate ($10) by the number of hours he works in the drugstore (300), we see that the implicit cost of his labour is $3,000 per month.

The owner has also used his savings to purchase inventory for the store. He purchased the goods on his shelves for $120,000. If he had invested his savings in some other business, he could have earned a return of 10 percent per year. This forgone return represents a real cost. In this case, the implicit return (opportunity cost) on his capital investment amounts to $12,000 per year (10 percent × $120,000), or $1,000 per month.

To calculate the *economic* profit this drugstore generates, we count both explicit and implicit costs. Hence, we must subtract all implicit factor payments (costs) from reported profits. The residual in this case amounts to $2,000 per month. That's the drugstore's *economic* profit.

Note that when we compute the drugstore's economic profit, we deduct the opportunity cost of the owner's capital. Specifically, we assumed that his funds would have reaped a 10 percent return somewhere else. In effect, we've assumed that a "normal" rate of return is 10 percent. This **normal profit** (the opportunity cost of capital) is an economic cost. Rather than investing in a drugstore, the owner could have earned a 10 percent return on his funds by investing in a fast-food franchise, a music store, a steel plant, or some other production activity. By choosing to invest in a drugstore instead, the owner was seeking a *higher* return on his funds—more than he could have obtained elsewhere. In other words, *economic profits represent something over and above "normal profits."*

Our treatment of "normal" returns as an economic cost leads to a startling conclusion: On average, economic profits are zero. Only firms that reap *above-average* returns can claim economic profits. This seemingly strange perspective on profits emphasizes the opportunity costs of all economic activities. *A productive activity reaps an economic profit only if it earns more than its opportunity cost.*

normal profit: The opportunity cost of capital; zero economic profit.

Naturally, everyone in business wants to earn an economic profit. But relatively few people can stay ahead of the pack. To earn economic profits, a business must see opportunities that others have missed, discover new products, find new and better methods of production, or take above-average risks. In fact, economic profits are often regarded as a reward to entrepreneurship, the ability and willingness to take risks, to organize factors of production, and to produce something society desires.

Entrepreneurship

Consider the local drugstore again. People in the neighbourhood clearly want such a drugstore, as evidenced by its substantial sales revenue. But why should anyone go to the trouble and risk of starting and maintaining one? We noted that the owner-manager *could* earn $3,000 in wages by accepting a regular job plus $1,000 per month in returns on capital by investing in an "average" business. Why should he take on the added responsibilities and risk of owning and operating his own drugstore?

The inducement to take on the added responsibilities of owning and operating a business is the potential for economic profit, the extra income over and above normal factor payments. In the case of the drugstore owner, this extra income is the economic profit of $2,000 (Table 6.1). In the absence of such additional compensation, few people would want to make the extra effort required.

Don't forget, however, that the *potential* for profit is not a *guarantee* of profit. Quite the contrary. Substantial risks are attached to starting and operating a business. Tens of thousands of businesses fail every year, and still more suffer economic losses. From this perspective, profit also represents compensation for the risks incurred in owning or operating a business.

Risk

6.3 MARKET STRUCTURE

Not all businesses have an equal opportunity to earn an economic profit. The opportunity for profit may be limited by the *structure* of the industry in which the firm is engaged. One of the reasons Microsoft is such a profitable company is that it has long held a *near-monopoly* on computer operating systems. As the supplier of virtually all operating systems, Microsoft could raise software prices without losing many customers. T-shirt shops, by contrast, have to worry about all the other stores that sell similar products in the area (see the Applications box). Faced with so much

APPLICATIONS

T-Shirt Shop Owner's Lament: Too Many T-Shirt Shops

The small Texas beach resort of South Padre Island boasts white sand, blue skies (much of the time), the buoyant waters of the Gulf of Mexico and, at last count, more than 40 T-shirt shops.

And that's a problem for Shy Oogav, who owns one of those shops. "Every day you have to compete with other shops," he says. "And if you invent something new, they will copy you."

Padre Island illustrates a common condition in the T-shirt industry—unbridled, ill-advised growth. Many people believe T-shirts are the ticket to a permanent vacation—far too many people. "In the past years, everything that closed opened up again as a T-shirt shop," says Maria C. Hall, executive director of the South Padre Island Chamber of Commerce.

Mr. Oogav, a 29-year-old immigrant from Israel, came to South Padre Island on vacation six years ago, thought he had found paradise and stayed on. He subsequently got a job with one of the town's T-shirt shops, which then numbered fewer than a dozen. Now that he owns his own shop, and the competition has quadrupled, his paradise is lost. "I don't sleep at night," he says, morosely.

—Mark Pawlosky

Source: *The Wall Street Journal*, July 31, 1995. Reprinted by permission of The Wall Street Journal. © 1995 Dow Jones & Company, Inc. All rights reserved worldwide. www.wsj.com

Analysis: The ability to earn a profit depends on how many other firms offer similar products. A perfectly competitive firm, facing numerous rivals, has difficulty maintaining prices or profits.

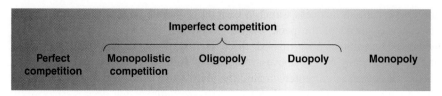

FIGURE 6.1
Market Structures

The number and relative size of firms producing a good vary across industries. Market structures range from perfect competition (a great many firms producing the same good) to monopoly (only one firm). Most real-world firms are along the continuum of *imperfect* competition. Included in that range are duopoly (two firms), oligopoly (a few firms), and monopolistic competition (many firms).

market structure: The number and relative size of firms in an industry.

perfect competition: A market in which no buyer or seller has market power.

competition, the owner of a T-shirt shop doesn't have the power to raise prices, or accumulate economic profits.

Figure 6.1 illustrates various **market structures.** At one extreme is the monopoly structure in which only one firm produces the entire supply of the good. At the other extreme is **perfect competition.** In perfect competition a great many firms supply the same good.

There are relatively few monopolies or perfectly competitive firms in the real world. Most of the businesses in Canada fall between these extremes. They're more accurately characterized by gradations of *imperfect* competition—markets in which competition exists, but individual firms still retain some discretionary power over prices. In a *duopoly,* two firms supply the entire market. In an *oligopoly,* like credit-card services, a handful of firms (Visa, MasterCard, American Express) dominate. In *monopolistic competition,* like fast-food restaurants, there are enough firms to ensure some competition, but not so many as to preclude some limited monopoly-type power. We examine all these market structures in later chapters, after we establish the nature of perfect competition.

6.4 THE NATURE OF PERFECT COMPETITION

Structure

A perfectly competitive industry has several distinguishing characteristics, including

- *Many firms*—Lots of firms are competing for consumer purchases.
- *Identical products*—The products of the different firms are identical, or nearly so.
- *Low-entry barriers*—It's relatively easy to get into the business.

The T-shirt business has all these traits, which is why storeowners have a hard time maintaining profits (see previous Applications box).

Price Takers

Because they always have to contend with a lot of competition, T-shirt shops can't increase profits by raising T-shirt prices. Millions of T-shirts are sold in Canada each year, by thousands of retail outlets. In such a competitive industry the many individual firms that make up the industry are all *price takers:* They take the price the market sets. A competitive firm can sell all its output at the prevailing market price. If it boosts its price above that level, consumers will shop elsewhere. In this sense, a perfectly competitive firm has no *market power*—no ability to control the market price for the good it sells.

At first glance, it might appear that all firms have market power. After all, who's to stop a T-shirt shop from raising prices? The important concept here, however, is *market* price, that is, the price at which goods are actually sold. If one shop raises its price to $15 and 40 other shops sell the same T-shirts for $10, it won't sell many shirts, and maybe none at all.

You may confront the same problem if you try to sell this book at the end of the semester. You might want to resell this textbook for $50. But you'll discover that the bookstore won't buy it at that price. With many other students offering to sell their books, the bookstore knows it doesn't have to pay the $50 you're asking. Because you don't have any market power, you have to accept the going price if you want to sell this book.

The same kind of powerlessness is characteristic of the small wheat farmer. Like any producer, the lone wheat farmer can increase or reduce his rate of output by making alternative production decisions. But his decision won't affect the market price of wheat.

Even a Canadian wheat farmer with a large 1,000 hectare farm can't change the price of wheat. At an above-average yield of 2.5 metric tonnes per hectare, this farm would produce 2,500 metric tonnes per year. But roughly *25 million* metric tonnes are brought to the Canadian market each year (and over *100 million* on the international market), so another 2,500 metric tonnes simply won't be noticed. In other words, *the output of the lone farmer is so small relative to the market supply that it has no significant effect on the total quantity or price in the market.*

A distinguishing characteristic of *powerless* firms is that, individually, they can sell all the output they produce at the prevailing market price. We call all such producers **competitive firms;** they have no independent influence on market prices. *A perfectly competitive firm is one whose output is so small in relation to market volume that its output decisions have no perceptible impact on price.*

It's important to distinguish between the market demand curve and the demand curve confronting a particular firm. T-shirt shops don't contradict the law of demand. The quantity of T-shirts purchased in the market still depends on T-shirt prices. That is, the *market* demand curve for T-shirts is still downward-sloping. A single T-shirt shop faces a horizontal demand curve only because its share of the market is so small that changes in its output don't disturb market equilibrium.

Collectively, though, individual firms do count. If all 40 of the T-shirt shops on South Padre Island (see the previous Applications box) were to increase shirt production at the same time, the market equilibrium would be disturbed. That is, a competitive market composed of individually powerless producers still sees a lot of action. The power here resides in the collective action of all the producers, however, not in the individual action of any one. Were T-shirt production to increase so abruptly, the shirts could be sold only at lower prices, in accordance with the downward-sloping nature of the *market* demand curve. Figure 6.2 illustrates the distinction between the actions of a single producer and those of the market. Notice that

- *The market demand curve for a product is always downward-sloping (law of demand).*
- *The demand curve confronting a perfectly competitive firm is horizontal.*

> **competitive firm:** A firm without market power, with no ability to alter the market price of the goods it produces.

Market Demand Curves vs. Firm Demand Curves

FIGURE 6.2
Market vs. Firm Demand

Consumer demand for any product is downward-sloping, as in the T-shirt market. The equilibrium price (p_e) of T-shirts is established by the intersection of *market* demand and *market* supply. This market-established price is the only one at which an individual shop can sell T-shirts. If the shop owner asks a higher price (e.g., p_i), no one will buy his shirts, since they can buy identical T-shirts from other shops at p_e. But he can sell all his shirts at the equilibrium price. The shop owner thus confronts a horizontal demand curve for his own output. (Notice the difference in market and individual shop quantities on the horizontal axes of the two graphs.)

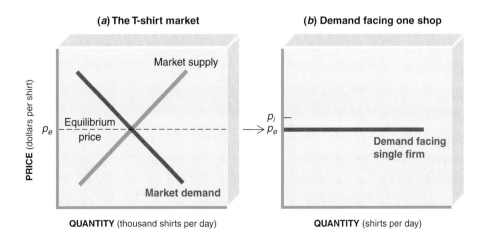

(a) The T-shirt market

Market supply

Equilibrium price p_e

Market demand

PRICE (dollars per shirt)

QUANTITY (thousand shirts per day)

(b) Demand facing one shop

p_i
p_e

Demand facing single firm

QUANTITY (shirts per day)

production decision: The selection of the short-run rate of output (with existing plant and equipment).

6.5 THE PRODUCTION DECISION

Since a competitive firm can sell all its output at the market price, it has only one decision to make: how much to produce. Choosing a rate of output is a firm's **production decision.** Should it produce all the output it can? Or should it produce at less than capacity?

Output and Revenues

In searching for the most desirable rate of output, focus on the distinction between total *revenue* and total *profit. Total revenue* is simply the price of the good multiplied by the quantity sold:

$$\text{Total revenue} = \text{price} \times \text{quantity}$$

Since a competitive firm can sell all its output at the market price (p_e), total revenue is a simple multiple of p_e. The total revenue of a T-shirt shop, for example, is the price of shirts (p_e) multiplied by the quantity sold. Figure 6.3 shows the total revenue curve that results from this multiplication. Note that *the total revenue curve of a perfectly competitive firm is an upward-sloping straight line, with a slope equal to* p_e.

If a competitive firm wanted to maximize its total *revenue,* its production decision would be simple: It would always produce at capacity. Life isn't that simple, however; *the objective is to maximize profits, not revenues.*

Output and Costs

To maximize profits, a firm must consider how increased production will affect *costs* as well as *revenues.* How do costs vary with the rate of output?

As we observed in Chapter 5, producers are saddled with certain costs in the *short run.* A T-shirt shop has to pay the rent every month no matter how few shirts it sells. The Low-Rider Jeans Corporation in Chapter 5 had to pay the rent on its factory and lease payments on its sewing machine. These *fixed costs* are incurred even if no output is produced. Once a firm starts producing output it incurs *variable costs* as well.

Since profits depend on the *difference* between revenues and costs, the costs of added output will determine how much profit a producer can make. Figure 6.4 illustrates a typical total cost curve. Total costs increase as output expands. But the rate of cost increase varies. At first total costs rise slowly (notice the gradually declining slope until point z), then they increase more quickly (the rising slope after point z). This S-shaped curve reflects the *law of diminishing returns.* As we first observed in Chapter 5, *marginal costs (MC)* often decline in the early stages of production and then increase as the available plant and equipment are used more intensively. These changes in marginal cost cause *total* costs to rise slowly at first, then to pick up speed as output increases.

FIGURE 6.3
Total Revenue

Because a competitive firm can sell all its output at the prevailing price, its total revenue curve is linear. In this case, the market (equilibrium) price of T-shirts is assumed to be $8. Hence, a shop's total revenue is equal to $8 multiplied by quantity sold.

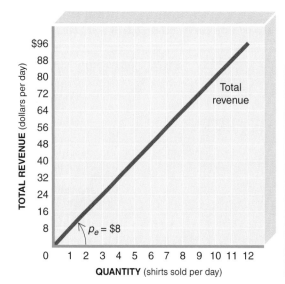

Price × (per shirt)	Quantity = (shirts per day)	Total revenue
$8	1	$ 8
8	2	16
8	3	24
8	4	32
8	5	40
8	6	48
8	7	56
8	8	64
8	9	72

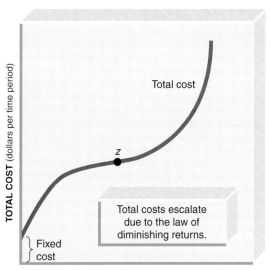

FIGURE 6.4
Total Cost

Total cost increases with output. The rate of increase isn't steady, however. Typically, the rate of cost increase slows initially, then speeds up. After point z, diminishing returns (rising marginal costs) cause accelerating costs. These accelerating costs limit the profit potential of increased output.

You may suspect by now that the road to profits is not an easy one. It entails comparing ever-changing revenues with ever-changing costs. Figure 6.5 helps simplify the problem by bringing together typical total revenue and total cost curves. Notice how total costs exceed total revenues at high rates of output (beyond point *g*). As production capacity is approached, costs tend to skyrocket, offsetting any gain in sales revenue.

Total profit in Figure 6.5 is represented by the vertical distance between the two curves. Total costs in this case exceed total revenue at low rates of output as well as at very high rates. The firm is profitable only at output rates between *f* and *g*.

Although all rates of output between *f* and *g* are profitable, they aren't *equally* profitable. A quick glance at Figure 6.5 confirms that the vertical distance between total revenue and total cost varies considerably within that range. ***The primary objective of the producer is to find that one particular rate of output that maximizes total profits.*** With a ruler, one could find it in Figure 6.5 by measuring the distance between the revenue and cost curves at all rates of output. In the real world, most producers need more practical guides to profit maximization.

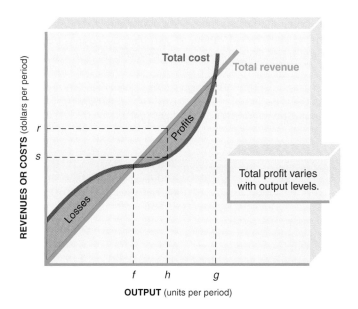

FIGURE 6.5
Total Profit

Profit is the *difference* between total revenue and total cost. It is represented as the vertical distance between the total revenue curve and the total cost curve. At output *h*, profit equals *r* minus *s*. The objective is to find that rate of output that *maximizes* profit.

6.6 PROFIT-MAXIMIZING RULE

The best single rule for maximizing profits in the short run is straightforward: Never produce a unit of output that costs more than it brings in. By following this simple rule, a producer is likely to make the right production decision. We see how this rule works by looking first at the revenue side of production ("what it brings in"), then at the cost side ("what it costs").

Marginal Revenue = Price

marginal revenue (MR): The change in total revenue that results from a one-unit increase in the quantity sold.

In searching for the most profitable rate of output, we need to know what an additional unit of output will bring in—that is, how much it adds to the total revenue of the firm. In general, the contribution to total revenue of an additional unit of output is called **marginal revenue (MR).** Marginal revenue is the *change* in total revenue that occurs when output is increased by one unit; that is,

$$\text{Marginal revenue} = \frac{\text{change in total revenue}}{\text{change in output}} = \frac{\Delta \text{TR}}{\Delta q}$$

To calculate marginal revenue, we compare the total revenues received before and after a one-unit increase in the rate of production; the *difference* between the two totals equals marginal revenue.

When the price of a product is constant, it's easy to compute marginal revenue. Suppose we're operating a catfish farm. Our product is catfish, sold at wholesale at the prevailing price of $13 per bushel. In this case, a one-unit increase in sales (one more bushel) increases total revenue by $13. As illustrated in Table 6.2, as long as the price of a product is constant, price and marginal revenue are one and the same thing. Hence, *for perfectly competitive firms, price equals marginal revenue.*

Marginal Cost

Keep in mind why we're breeding and selling catfish. It's not to maximize *revenues* but to maximize *profits.* To gauge profits, we need to know not only the price of fish but also how much each bushel costs to produce. As we saw in Chapter 5, the added cost of producing one more unit of a good is its *marginal cost.* Figure 6.6 summarizes the marginal costs associated with the production of catfish.

The production process for catfish farming is wonderfully simple. The factory is a pond; the rate of production is the number of fish harvested from the pond per day. A farmer can alter the rate of production at will, up to the breeding capacity of the pond.

Assume that the *fixed* cost of the pond is $10 per day. The fixed costs include the rental value of the pond and the cost of electricity for keeping the pond oxygenated so the fish can breathe. These fixed costs must be paid no matter how many fish the farmer harvests.

To harvest catfish from the pond, the farmer must incur additional costs. Labour is needed to net and sort the fish. The cost of labour is *variable,* depending on how much output the farmer decides to produce. If no fish are harvested, no variable costs are incurred.

The *marginal costs* of harvesting are the additional costs incurred to harvest *one* more bushel of fish. Generally, we expect marginal costs to rise as the rate of production increases. The law of diminishing returns we encountered in Chapter 5 applies

Analysis: Fish farmers want to maximize profits.

TABLE 6.2
Total and Marginal Revenue

Marginal revenue (MR) is the *change* in total revenue associated with the sale of one more unit of output. A third bushel increases total revenue from $26 to $39; MR equals $13. If the price is constant (at $13 here), marginal revenue equals price.

Quantity Sold (bushels per day)	×	Price (per bushel)	=	Total Revenue (per day)	Marginal Revenue (per bushel)
0	×	$13	=	$ 0>	
1	×	13	=	13>	$13
2	×	13	=	26>	13
3	×	13	=	39>	13
4	×	13	=	52>	13

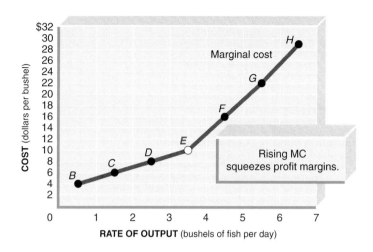

FIGURE 6.6
The Costs of Catfish Production

Marginal cost is the increase in total cost associated with a one-unit increase in production. When production expands from two to three units per day, total costs increase by $8 (from $20 to $28 per day). The marginal cost of the third bushel is therefore $8, as illustrated by point *D* in the graph. Recall that our *marginal* values are plotted at the midpoints.

	Rate of Output (bushels per day)	Total Cost (per day)	Marginal Cost (per unit)	Average Total Cost (per unit)
A	0	$ 10		—
B	1	14	> 4	14
C	2	20	> 6	10
D	3	28	> 8	9.33
E	4	38	> 10	9.5
F	5	54	> 16	10.8
G	6	76	> 22	12.67
H	7	105	> 29	15

to catfish farming as well. As more labour is hired, each worker has less space (pond area) and capital (access to nets, sorting trays) to work with. Accordingly, it takes a little more labour time (marginal cost) to harvest each additional fish.

Figure 6.6 illustrates these marginal costs. Notice how the MC rises as the rate of output increases. As the rate of output increases from three to four bushels per day, the marginal cost is $10. Hence the fourth bushel increases total costs by $10.[1] The fifth bushel is even more expensive, with a marginal cost of $16.

We're now in a position to make a production decision. The rule about never producing anything that adds more to cost than it brings in can now be stated in more technical terms. Since price equals marginal revenue for competitive firms, we can base the production decision on a comparison of *price* and marginal cost.

MC > p. We don't want to produce an additional unit of output if its MC exceeds its price. If MC exceeds price, we're spending more to produce that extra unit than we're getting back: total profits will decline if we produce it.

p > MC. The opposite is true when price exceeds MC. If an extra unit brings in more revenue than it costs to produce, it is adding to total profit. Total profits must increase in this case. Hence, a competitive firm wants to expand the rate of production whenever price exceeds MC.

Profit-Maximizing Rate of Output

[1]Note that we place the value of MC = $10 at the mid-point in Figure 6.6 (i.e., at a rate of output = 3.5 bushels of fish per day). If we want to find the marginal cost at *exactly* four bushels of fish per day, take the two rates of output that place four bushels at the midpoint, namely five and three bushels. The increase in the total cost is $26 ($54 − $28) while the increase in output is 2 (5 − 3). Therefore the marginal cost of each of these two units is $13; this is the value at exactly four bushels of fish per day.

Price Level	Production Decision
price > MC	increase output
price = MC	maintain output (profits maximized)
price < MC	decrease output

TABLE 6.3
Short-Run Profit-Maximization Rules for Competitive Firm

The relationship between price and marginal cost dictates short-run production decisions. For competitive firms, profits are maximized at that rate of output where price = MC. (See Table 7.2 for long-run rules.)

p = MC. Since we want to expand output when price exceeds MC and contract output if price is less than MC, the profit-maximizing rate of output is easily found. *For perfectly competitive firms, profits are maximized at the rate of output where price equals marginal cost.* The implications of this **profit-maximization rule** are summarized in Table 6.3.

Figure 6.7 illustrates the application of our profit-maximization rule in catfish farming. The prevailing wholesale price of catfish is $13 a bushel. At this price we can sell all the catfish we can produce, up to our short-run capacity. The catfish can't be

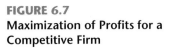

profit-maximization rule: Produce at that rate of output where marginal revenue equals marginal cost.

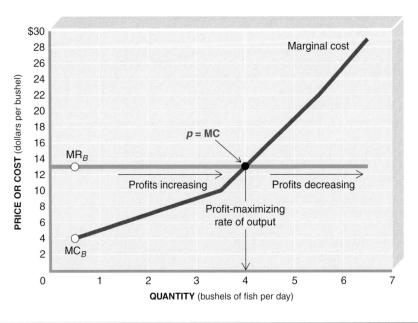

FIGURE 6.7
Maximization of Profits for a Competitive Firm

A competitive firm maximizes total profit at the output rate where MC = *p*. If MC is less than price, the firm can increase profits by producing more. If MC exceeds price, the firm should reduce output. In this case, profit maximization occurs at an output of four bushels per day.

	(1) Number of Bushels (per day)	(2) Price	(3) Total Revenue	−	(4) Total Cost	=	(5) Total Profit	(6) Marginal Revenue	(7) Marginal Cost
A	0	$13	$ 0		$ 10		−$10		
								$13	$ 4
B	1	13	13		14		−1		
								13	6
C	2	13	26		20		6		
								13	8
D	3	13	39		28		11		
								13	10
E	4	13	52		38		14		
								13	16
F	5	13	65		54		11		
								13	22
G	6	13	78		76		2		
								13	29
H	7	13	91		105		−14		

APPLICATIONS

Southern Farmers Hooked on New Cash Crop

Catfish are replacing crops and dairy farming as a cash industry in much of the South, particularly in Mississippi's Delta region, where 80 percent of farm-bred catfish are grown.

Production has skyrocketed in the USA from 16 million pounds in 1975 to an expected 340 million pounds this year.

The business is growing among farmers in Alabama, Arkansas and Louisiana.

Catfish farming is similar to other agriculture, experts say. One thing is the same: It takes money to get started.

"If you have a good row-crop farmer, you have a good catfish farmer," says James Hoffman of Farm Fresh Catfish Co. in Hollandale, Miss. "But you can't take a poor row-crop farmer and make him a good catfish farmer."

Greensboro, Ala., catfish farmer Steve Hollingsworth says he spends $18,000 a week on feed for the 1 million catfish in his ponds.

"Each of the ponds has about 100,000 fish," he says. "You get about 60 cents per fish, so that's about $60,000."

The investment can be lost very quickly "if something's wrong in that pond," like an inadequate oxygen level, Hollingsworth says.

"You can be 15 minutes too late getting here, and all your fish are gone," he says.

—Mark Mayfield

Source: *USA Today,* December 5, 1989. Copyright 1989 USA TODAY. Reprinted with permission. www.usatoday.com

Analysis: People go into a competitive business like catfish farming to earn a profit. Once in business, they try to maximize total profits by equating price and marginal cost.

---

sold at a higher price because lots of farmers raise catfish and sell them for $13 (see the Applications box). If we try to charge a higher price, consumers will buy their fish from other vendors. Hence, we confront a horizontal demand curve at the price of $13.

The costs of producing catfish were examined in Figure 6.6. The key concept illustrated here is marginal cost. The MC curve slopes upward, in conventional fashion.

Figure 6.7 also depicts the total revenues, costs, and profits of alternative production rates. Study the table first. Notice that the firm loses $10 per day if it produces no fish (row *A*). At zero output, total revenue is zero ($p \times q = 0$). However, the firm must still contend with fixed costs of $10 per day. Total profit—total revenue minus total cost—is therefore *minus* $10; the firm incurs a loss.

The table shows how this loss is reduced when one bushel of fish is harvested per day. The production and sale of one bushel per day bring in $13 of total revenue (column 3). The total cost of producing one bushel per day is $14 (column 4). Hence, the total loss at an output rate of one bushel per day is $1 (column 5). This may not be what we hoped for, but it's certainly better than the $10 loss incurred at zero output.

The superiority of harvesting one bushel per day rather than none is also evident in columns 6 and 7. The first bushel produced has a *marginal revenue* of $13. Its *marginal cost* is only $4. Hence, it brings in more added revenue than it adds to costs. Under these circumstances—whenever price exceeds MC—output should definitely be expanded. That is one of the decision rules summarized in Table 6.3.

The excess of price over MC for the first unit of output is also illustrated by the graph in Figure 6.7. Point MR$_B$ ($13) lies above MC$_B$ ($4); the *difference* between these two points measures the contribution that the first bushel makes to the total profits of the firm. In this case, that contribution equals $13 − $4 = $9, and production losses are reduced by that amount when the rate of output is increased from zero to one bushel per day.

As long as price exceeds MC, further increases in the rate of output increase total profit. Notice what happens to profits when the rate of output is increased from one to two bushels per day (row *C*). The price (MR) of the second bushel is $13, its

WEB NOTE

Check out the real world of catfish farming at www.aces.edu/pubs/docs/A/ANR-0273/.

MC is $6. Therefore it *adds* $7 to total profits. Instead of losing $1 per day, the firm is now making a profit of $6 per day.

The firm can make even more profits by expanding the rate of output further. You should be able to confirm that the third bushel makes a $5 contribution to profits whereas the fourth bushel adds an extra $3 to profits.

But what happens if we expand output beyond four bushels per day? The marginal revenue of the fifth bushel remains constant at $13 but the marginal cost is $16. Since production of the fifth bushel adds more to costs than to revenues, profits *decline* (by $3). ***Output should not be increased if MC exceeds price.*** Note that in Figure 6.7 the marginal cost curve lies above the price line at all output levels in excess of four bushels per day. Consequently, given this price of $13, the fourth unit of output represents the highest rate of output that the firm desires.

The correct production decision—the profit-maximizing decision—is shown in Figure 6.7 by the intersection of the price and MC curves. At this intersection, price equals MC and profits are maximized. If we produced less, we'd be giving up potential profits. If we produced more, total profits would also fall (review Table 6.3).

Adding Up Profits

To reach the right production decision, we've relied on *marginal* revenues and costs. Having found the desired rate of output, however, we may want to take a closer look at the profits we are accumulating. Figure 6.8 provides pictures of our success.

Total profits are represented in Figure 6.8*a* by the vertical distance between the total revenue and total cost curves. This is a straightforward interpretation of our definition of total profits—that is,

$$\text{Total profits} = \text{TR} - \text{TC}$$

The vertical distance between the TR and TC curves is maximized at the output of four bushels per day.

Our success in catfish farming can also be illustrated by examining the *per unit* revenues and *per unit* costs (i.e., the *per unit* profits) in Figure 6.8*b*. Total profit is

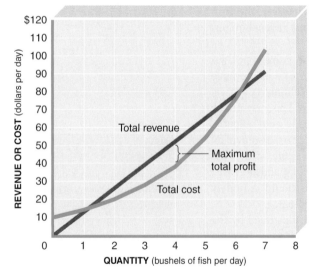

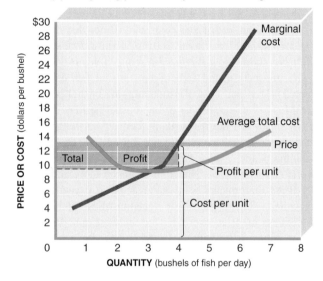

FIGURE 6.8
Alternative Views of Total Profit

Total profit can be computed as TR − TC, as in part *a*. Or it can be computed as profit *per unit* (*p* − ATC) multiplied by the quantity sold. This is illustrated in part *b* by the shaded rectangle. To find the profit-maximizing output, we could use either of these graphs or just the price and MC curves in Figure 6.7.

equal to the *profit per unit* multiplied by the number of units produced and sold. Profit per unit, in turn, is equal to the price minus average total costs—that is,[2]

$$\text{Profit per unit} = p - \text{ATC}$$

The price of catfish is illustrated in Figure 6.8*b* by the horizontal price line at $13. The average total cost of producing catfish is shown by the ATC curve. Like the ATC curve we encountered in Chapter 5, this one has a U shape. The *difference* between price and average cost—profit per unit—is illustrated by the vertical distance between the price and ATC curves. At four bushels per day, for example, profit per unit equals $13 − $9.50 = $3.50.

To compute *total* profits, we note that

$$\text{Total profits} = \text{profit per unit} \times \text{quantity}$$

$$= (p - \text{ATC}) \times q$$

In this case, the four bushels generate a profit of $3.50 each, for a *total* profit of $14 per day. *Total* profits are illustrated in Figure 6.8*b* by the shaded rectangle. (Recall that the area of a rectangle is equal to its height, the profit per unit, multiplied by its width, the quantity sold.)

Profit per unit is not only used to compute total profits but is often also of interest in its own right. Businesspeople like to cite statistics on "markups," which are a crude index to per-unit profits. However, **the profit-maximizing producer never seeks to maximize per-unit profits. What counts is total profits, not the amount of profit per unit.** This is the old $5 ice cream problem again. You might be able to maximize profit per unit if you could sell 1 cone for $5, but you would make a lot more money if you sold 100 cones at a per-unit profit of only 50 cents each.

Similarly, **the profit-maximizing producer has no desire to produce at that rate of output where ATC is at a minimum.** Minimum ATC does represent least-cost production. But additional units of output, even though they raise average costs, will increase total profits. This is evident in Figure 6.8; price exceeds MC for some output to the right of minimum ATC (the bottom of the U). Therefore, total profits are increasing as we increase the rate of output beyond the point of minimum average costs.

6.7 THE SHUTDOWN DECISION

The rule established for short-run profit maximization doesn't guarantee any profits. By equating price and marginal cost, the competitive producer is only assured of achieving the *optimal* output. This is the best possible rate of output for the firm, given the existing market price and the (short-run) costs of production.

But what if the best possible rate of output generates a loss? What should the producer do in this case? Keep producing output? Or shut down the factory and find something else to do?

The first instinct may be to shut down the factory to stop the flow of red ink. But this isn't necessarily the wisest course of action. It may be smarter to keep operating a money-losing operation than to shut it down.

The rationale for this seemingly ill-advised course of action resides in the fixed costs of production. **Fixed costs must be paid even if all output ceases.** The firm

---

[2]To see this relationship, recall that Total profits = TR − TC

$$= (p \times q) - \text{TC}$$

And since, by definition, profit per unit = Total profits/q

$$= (p \times q)/q - \text{TC}/q$$

$$= p - \text{ATC}$$

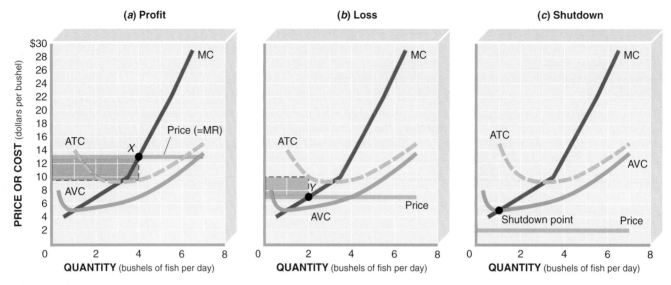

FIGURE 6.9
The Firm's Shutdown Point

A firm should cease production only if total revenue is lower than total *variable* cost. The shutdown decision may be based on a comparison of price and AVC. If the price of catfish per bushel was $13, a firm would earn a profit at point X in part a. At a price of $7, (point Y in part b), the firm is losing money (p is less than ATC) but is more than covering all variable costs (p is greater than AVC). If the price falls to $2 per bushel, as in part c, output should cease (p is less than AVC).

must still pay rent on the factory and equipment even if it doesn't use these inputs. That's why we call such costs "fixed."

The persistence of fixed costs casts an entirely different light on the shutdown decision. Since fixed costs will have to be paid in any case, the question becomes: Which option creates greater losses? Does the firm lose more money by continuing to operate (and incurring a loss) or by shutting down (and incurring a loss equal to fixed costs)? In these terms, the answer becomes clear: *A firm should shut down only if the losses from continuing production exceed fixed costs.* This happens when total revenue is less than total *variable* cost.

Price vs. AVC   The shutdown decision can be made without explicit reference to fixed costs. Figure 6.9 shows how. The relationship to focus on is between the price of a good and its average *variable* cost.

The curves in Figure 6.9 represent the short-run costs and potential demand curves for catfish. As long as the price of catfish is $13 per bushel, the typical firm will produce four a day, as determined by the intersection of the MC and MR (= price) curves (point X, in part a). In this case, price ($13) exceeds average *total* cost ($9.50) and catfish farming is profitable.

The situation wouldn't look so good, however, if the market price of catfish fell to $7. Following the rule for profit maximization, the firm would be led to point Y in part b, where MC intersects the new demand (price) curve. At this intersection, the firm would produce two bushels per day. But total revenues would no longer cover total costs, as can be seen from the fact that the ATC curve now lies *above* the price line. The ATC of producing two bushels is $10.00 (Figure 6.6); price is $7. Hence, the firm is incurring a loss of $6 per day (two bushels at a loss of $3 each).

Should the firm stay in business under the circumstances? The answer is yes. Recall that the catfish farmer has already dug the pond and installed equipment at a (fixed) cost of $10 per day. The producer will have to pay these fixed costs whether or not the machinery is used. Stopping production would result in a loss amounting to $10 per day. Staying in business, even when catfish prices fall to $7 each, generates a loss of only $6 a day. In this case, *where price exceeds average variable cost but not average total cost, the profit-maximization rule minimizes losses.*

If the price of catfish falls far enough, the producer may be better off ceasing production altogether. Suppose the price of catfish fell to $2 per bushel (Figure 6.9c). A price this low doesn't even cover the variable cost of producing one bushel per day ($4). Continued production of even one bushel per day would imply a total loss of $12 per day ($10 of fixed costs plus $2 of variable costs). Higher rates of output would lead to still greater losses. Hence, the firm should shut down production, even though that action implies a loss of $10 per day. In all cases *where price doesn't cover average variable costs at any rate of output, production should cease.* Thus, the **shutdown point** occurs where price is equal to minimum average *variable* cost. Any lower price will result in losses larger than fixed costs. In Figure 6.9, the shutdown point occurs at a price of $5, where the MC and AVC curves intersect.

The Shutdown Point

shutdown point: That rate of output where price equals minimum AVC.

6.8 THE INVESTMENT DECISION

When a firm shuts down, it doesn't necessarily leave (exit) the industry. General Motors still produces automobiles, for example, even though it idled 14 plants in 2001 (see the Applications box). *The shutdown decision is a* **short-run** *response.* It's based on the fixed costs of an established plant and the variable costs of operating it.

Ideally, a producer would never get into a money-losing business in the first place. Entry was based on an **investment decision** that the producer now regrets. *Investment decisions are long-run decisions,* however, and the firm now must pay for its bad luck or poor judgment. The investment decision entails the assumption of fixed costs (e.g., the lease of the factory); once the investment is made, the short-run production decision is designed to make the best possible use of those fixed inputs. The short-run profit-maximizing rule we've discussed applies only to this second decision; it assumes that a production unit exists. The accompanying Applications box shows the contrast between production and investment decisions.

investment decision: The decision to build, buy, or lease plant and equipment; to enter or exit an industry.

APPLICATIONS

GM Plans Temporary Shutdown

In early 2001, General Motors Corp. (GM) decided to temporarily shut down 14 North American plants in an effort to reduce the high levels of automobile inventories. Three of these fourteen plants were Canadian; two in Oshawa, Ontario and one in Sainte-Thérèse, Quebec.

The surge in North American automobile inventories was attributed to the significant reduction in U.S. vehicle sales. GM believed that a three-month shutdown would be sufficient to reduce inventory to "normal" levels.

During this three-month shutdown, however, both Canadian and American workers still received a portion of their salary. In Canada, plant workers received 65 percent of their regular pay cheque while American workers received 95 percent.

Source: Based on "GM Plans Brief Shutdown." From CBC News, January 26, 2001. http://cbc.ca/.

Wal-Mart's German Retreat

Want to know how not to do business in Germany? Just ask Wal-Mart. After nine years of trying to make a go of it, the Bentonville (Ark.)-based retailer said July 28 that it will sell its 85 stores to German rival Metro.

The retreat is hardly surprising given Wal-Mart's numerous missteps in Germany. Perhaps its most glaring was misjudging the German consumer and business culture. For instance, German Wal-Marts adopted the U.S. custom of bagging groceries, which many German consumers find distasteful because they tend not to like strangers handling their food.

It also imported its U.S.-style company ethic, which includes strongly discouraging interoffice romances. Many employees found the code intrusive. The company also had repeated clashes with unions.

Source: Based on "Wal-Mart German Retreat." From Kate Normal, *Business Week,* (July 28, 2006), http://www.businessweek.com/.

Analysis: GM's decision to idle 14 plants was a short-run *shutdown* decision; they are still in business. Wal-Mart, by contrast, made a long-run decision to cease operations and *exit* the industry.

The investment decision is of enormous importance to producers. The fixed costs that we've ignored in the production decision represent the producers' (or the stockholders') investment in the business. If they're going to avoid an economic loss, they have to generate at least enough revenue to recoup their investment—that is, the cost of (fixed) plant and equipment. Failure to do so will result in a net loss, despite allegiance to our profit-maximizing rule.

Whether fixed costs count, then, depends on the decision being made. For producers trying to decide how best to utilize the resources they've purchased or leased, fixed costs no longer enter the decision-making process. For producers deciding whether to enter business, sign a lease, or replace existing machinery and plant, fixed costs count very much. Businesspeople will proceed with an investment only if the *anticipated* profits are large enough to compensate for the effort and risk undertaken.

Long-Run Costs

When businesspeople make an investment decision, they confront not one set of cost figures but many. A plant not yet built can be designed for various rates of production and alternative technologies. In making long-run decisions, a producer isn't bound to one size of plant or to a particular mix of tools and machinery. In the long run, one can be flexible. In general, ***a producer will want to build, buy, or lease a plant that's the most efficient for the anticipated rate of output.*** This is the (dis)economy of scale phenomenon we discussed in the previous chapter. Once the right plant size is selected, the producer may proceed with the problem of short-run profit maximization. Once production is started, he can only hope that the investment decision was a good one and that a shutdown can be avoided.

6.9 DETERMINANTS OF SUPPLY

Whether the time frame is the short run or the long run, the one central force in production decisions is the quest for profits. Producers will go into production—incur fixed costs—only if they see the potential for economic profits. Once in business, they'll expand the rate of output so long as profits are increasing. They'll shut down—cease production—when revenues don't at least cover variable costs (loss exceeds fixed costs).

Nearly anyone could make money with these principles if given complete information on costs and revenues. What renders the road to fortune less congested is the general absence of such complete information. In the real world, production decisions involve considerably more risk. People often don't know how much profit or loss they'll incur until it's too late to alter production decisions. Consequently, businesspeople are compelled to make a reasoned guess about prices and costs, then proceed. By way of summary, we can identify the major influences that will shape their short- and long-run decisions on how much output to supply to the market.

Short-Run Determinants

A competitive firm's short-run production decisions are dominated by marginal costs. Hence, the quantity of a good supplied will be affected by all forces that alter MC. Specifically, ***the determinants of a firm's supply include***

- ***The price of factor inputs.***
- ***Technology*** (the available production function).
- ***Expectations*** (for costs, sales, technology).
- ***Taxes and subsidies.***

Each determinant affects a producer's ability and willingness to supply output at any particular price.

The price of factor inputs determines how much the producer must pay for resources used in production. Technology determines how much output the producer will get from each unit of input. Expectations are critical because they express producers' perceptions of what future costs, prices, sales, and profits are likely to be. And finally, taxes and subsidies may alter costs or the amount of profit a firm gets to keep.

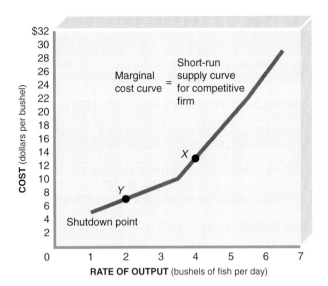

FIGURE 6.10
A Competitive Firm's Short-Run Supply Curve

For competitive firms, marginal cost defines the lowest price a firm will accept for a given quantity of output. In this sense, the marginal cost curve is the supply curve; it tells us how quantity supplied will respond to price. At $p = \$13$, the quantity supplied is four; at $p = \$7$, the quantity supplied is two.

Recall, however, that the firm will shut down if price falls below minimum average variable cost. The supply curve does not exist below minimum AVC ($5 in this case).

The Short-Run Supply Curve. By using the familiar *ceteris paribus* assumption, we can isolate the effect of price on supply decisions. In other words, we can draw a short-run **supply curve** the same way we earlier constructed consumer demand curves. In this case, the forces we assume constant are input prices, technology, expectations, and taxes. The only variable we allow to change is the price of the product itself.

Figure 6.10 illustrates the response of quantity supplied to a change in price. Notice the critical role of marginal costs: ***The marginal cost curve is the short-run supply curve for a competitive firm.*** Recall our basic profit-maximization rule. A competitive producer wants to supply a good only if its price exceeds its marginal cost. Hence, marginal cost defines the lower limit for an "acceptable" price. A catfish farmer is willing and able to produce four bushels per day only if the price of a bushel is $13 (point X). If the price of catfish dropped to $7, the *quantity* supplied would fall to two (point Y). The marginal cost curve tells us what the quantity supplied would be at all other prices as well. As long as price exceeds minimum AVC (the shutdown point), the MC curve summarizes the response of a producer to price changes: It *is* the short-run supply curve of a perfectly competitive firm.

The shape of the marginal cost curve provides a basic foundation for the *law of supply*. Because marginal costs tend to rise as output expands, an increase in output makes sense only if the price of that output rises. If the price does rise, it's profitable to increase the quantity supplied.

> **supply curve:** A curve describing the quantities of a good a producer is willing and able to sell (produce) at alternative prices in a given time period, *ceteris paribus*.

All the forces that shape the short-run supply curve are subject to change. Factor prices change; technology changes; expectations change; and tax laws get revised. ***If any determinant of supply changes, the supply curve shifts.***

A reduction in wage rates, for example, would reduce the marginal cost of producing catfish. This would shift the supply curve downward, making it possible for producers to supply larger quantities at any given price.

An improvement in technology would have the same effect. By increasing productivity, new technology would lower the marginal cost of producing a good. The supply curve would shift downward.

Supply Shifts

Changes in taxes will also alter supply behaviour. But not all taxes have the same effect; some alter short-run supply behaviour, others affect only long-run supply decisions.

Tax Effects

Property Taxes. Property taxes are levied by local governments on land and buildings. The tax rate is typically some small fraction (e.g., 1 percent) of total value. Hence, the owner of a $10 million factory might have to pay $100,000 per year in property taxes.

(a) Property taxes affect fixed costs

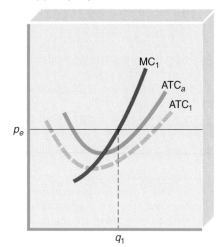

(b) Payroll taxes alter marginal costs

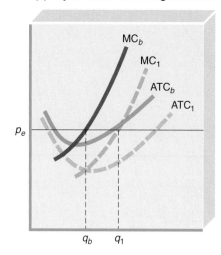

(c) Profits taxes don't change costs

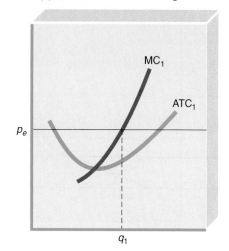

FIGURE 6.11
Impact of Taxes on Business Decisions

(a) Property taxes are a fixed cost for the firm. Since they don't affect marginal costs, they leave the optimal rate of output (q_1) unchanged. Property taxes raise average costs, however, and so reduce profits. Lower profits may alter investment decisions.

(b) Payroll taxes add directly to marginal costs and so reduce the optimal rate of output (to q_b). Payroll taxes also increase average costs and lower total and per-unit profits.

(c) Taxes on profits are neither a fixed cost nor a variable cost since they depend on the existence of profits. They don't affect marginal costs or price and so leave the optimal rate of output (q_1) unchanged. By reducing after-tax profits, however, such taxes lessen incentives to invest.

Property taxes have to be paid regardless of whether the factory is used. Hence, ***property taxes are a fixed cost*** for the firm. These additional fixed cost increase total costs and thus shift the average total cost (ATC) upward, as in Figure 6.11a.

Notice that the MC curve doesn't move when property taxes are imposed. Property taxes aren't based on the quantity of output produced. Accordingly, the production decision of the firm isn't affected by property taxes. The quantity q_1 in Figure 6.11a remains the optimal rate of output even after a property tax is introduced.

Although the optimal output remains at q_1, the profitability of the firm is reduced by the property tax. Profit per unit has been reduced by the upward shift of the ATC curve. If property taxes reduce profits too much, firms may move to a low-tax jurisdiction or another industry (investment decisions).

WEB NOTE

For a more detailed look at the Employment Insurance program, visit http://www. hrsdc.gc.ca/en/employment/ei/ index.shtml.

Payroll Taxes. Payroll taxes have very different effects on business decisions. Payroll taxes are levied on the wages paid by the firm. In 2006, for example, employers in Canada paid the federal government $2.62 per $100 of insurable earnings—up to a maximum of $39,000 insurable earnings—for each employee hired. These premiums—collected under the Employment Insurance Act—are designed to cover the annual employment insurance payments to all officially unemployed workers. Similar forms of payroll taxes are levied by federal and provincial governments to finance pension and health benefits.

All payroll taxes add to the cost of hiring labour. In the absence of a tax, a worker might cost the firm $8 per hour. Once Employment Insurance (EI) and other taxes are levied, the cost of labour increases to $8 plus the amount of tax. Hence, $8-per-hour labour might end up costing the firm $12 or more. In other words, ***payroll taxes increase marginal costs.*** This is illustrated in Figure 6.11b by the upward shift of the MC curve.

Notice how payroll taxes change the production decision. The new MC curve (MC_b) intersects the price line at a lower rate of output (q_b). Thus payroll taxes tend to reduce output and employment.

APPLICATIONS

E-Commerce Increasing Competition

Ten years ago the T-shirt shop owners on South Padre Island (see the Applications box, page 133) had to worry only about the other 40 shops at that beach resort. They worried that other shops might offer T-shirts at lower prices, forcing all the shops to cut prices. Now the level of competition is much higher. Beachgoers can now buy T-shirts at virtual shops on the Internet. Indeed, consumers can click on the Internet to find out the price of almost anything. There are even electronic shopping services that will find the lowest price for a product. Want a better deal on a car? You don't have to visit a dozen dealerships. With a few clicks, you can find the lowest price for the car you want and get directions to the appropriate dealer. In fact, you don't have to go anywhere: More and more producers will sell you their products directly over the Internet.

E-commerce intensifies competition in many ways. By allowing a consumer to shop worldwide, the Net vastly increases the number of firms in a virtual market. Even your campus bookstore now has to worry about textbook prices available at Amazon.com, Barnes and Noble, and other online booksellers.

Electronic commerce also reduces transaction costs. Retailers don't need stores or catalogues to display their products, and they can greatly reduce inventories by producing to order. This is how Dell computer supplies the $20 million of computers it sells per day online.

The evident advantages of e-commerce have made it the virtual market of choice for many consumers, businesses, and government agencies. In 2005, Canadian private sector firms increased their online sales to $36 billion. While this value of e-commerce accounts for only about 1 percent of total revenues for private firms, the trend is what counts. With online sales increasing by at least 37 percent in the past four consecutive years, e-commerce is certain to intensify competition in the economy tomorrow.

Source: Adapted from Statistics Canada publication *The Daily,* Catalogue 11-001. "Value of Internet Sales," April 20, 2006, http://www.statcan.ca/Daily/English/060420/d060420b.htm.

	Internet Sales With or Without Online Payment ($ millions)				
	2001	**2002**	**2003**	**2004**	**2005**
Private sector	6,336.6	10,815.3	18,164.4	26,438.0	36,267.7
Public sector	180.3	263.6	756.5	1,881.5	2,924.7
Total	6,516.9	11,078.9	18,920.9	28,319.5	39,192.4

TABLE 6.4
Value of Internet Sales

Profit Taxes. Taxes are also levied on the profits of a business. Such taxes are very different from either property or payroll taxes since profit taxes are paid only when profits are made. Thus they are neither a fixed cost nor a variable cost! As Figure 6.11c indicates, neither the MC nor the ATC curve moves when a profits tax is imposed. The only difference is that the firm now gets to keep less of its profits, instead "sharing" its profits with the government.

Although a profits tax has no direct effect on marginal or average costs, it does reduce the take-home (after-tax) profits of a business. This may reduce investments in new businesses. For this reason, many people urge the government to *reduce* corporate tax rates and so encourage increased investment.

WEB NOTE

If you want to shop for T-shirts at a cybermall, check out www.tshirtmall.com.

SUMMARY

- Economic profit is the difference between total revenue and total cost. Total economic cost includes the value (opportunity cost) of *all* inputs used in the production, not just those inputs for which an explicit payment is made.

- Because it must contend with many competitors, a competitive firm has no control over the price of its output. It effectively confronts a horizontal demand for its output (even though the *market* demand for the product is downward-sloping).

- The short-run objective of a firm is to maximize profits from the operation of its existing facilities (fixed costs). For a competitive firm, the profit-maximizing output occurs at the point where marginal cost equals price (marginal revenue).
- A firm may incur a loss even at the optimal rate of output. It shouldn't shut down, however, so long as price exceeds average *variable* cost. If revenues at least cover variable costs, the firm's loss from production is less than fixed cost.
- In the long run a producer can be flexible. There are no fixed costs and the firm may choose any-sized plant it wants. The decision to incur fixed costs (i.e., build, buy, or lease a plant) or to enter or exit an industry is an investment decision.

- A competitive firm's supply curve is identical to its marginal cost curve (above the shutdown point at minimum average variable cost). In the short run, the quantity supplied will rise or fall with price.
- The determinants of supply include the price of inputs, technology, taxes, and expectations. Should any of these determinants change, the firm's supply curve will shift.
- Business taxes alter business behaviour. Property taxes raise fixed costs; payroll taxes increase marginal costs. Profit taxes raise neither fixed costs nor marginal costs but diminish the take-home (after-tax) profits of a business.
- The Internet has created virtual stores that intensify price competition.

Key Terms

economic cost 130
explicit cost 130
implicit cost 130
economic profit 131
normal profit 132

market structure 134
perfect competition 134
competitive firm 135
production decision 136
marginal revenue (MR) 138

profit-maximization rule 140
shutdown point 145
investment decision 145
supply curve 147

Questions for Discussion

1. What economic costs will a large corporation likely overlook when computing its "profits"? How about the owner of a family-run business or farm?
2. How can the demand curve facing a firm be horizontal if the market demand curve is downward-sloping?
3. How many fish should a commercial fisherman try to catch in a day? Should he catch as many as possible or return to dock before filling the boat with fish? Under what economic circumstances should he not even take the boat out?
4. If a firm is incurring an economic loss, would society be better off if the firm shut down? Would the firm want to shut down? Explain.
5. Why wouldn't a profit-maximizing firm want to produce at the rate of output that minimizes average total cost?
6. What rate of output is appropriate for a "nonprofit" corporation (such as a hospital)?
7. Why did GM only temporarily shut down its production facilities while Wal-Mart permanently got out of its business in several markets (see the Applications box, p. 145)? Explain in terms of fixed and variable costs.
8. What was the opportunity cost of Mr. Fujishige's farm? (See the Applications box, page 131.) Is society better off with another Disney theme park? Explain.
9. Is America Online a perfectly competitive firm? Explain your answer.
10. If a perfectly competitive firm raises its price above the prevailing market rate, how much of its sales might it lose? Why? Can a competitive firm ever raise its prices? If so, when? Would a competitive firm ever *lower* its prices? Why or why not?

EXERCISES

PROBLEMS The Student Problem Set to accompany this chapter can be found at the end of the book.

WEB ACTIVITIES Web Activities to accompany this chapter can be found on the Online Learning Centre at **http://www.mcgrawhill.ca/olc/schiller**.

CHAPTER 7

Competitive Markets

By the end of this chapter, you should be able to:

7.1 Explain how the market supply curve is derived from firm supply curves

7.2 Identify and explain six general observations about structure, behaviour, and outcomes of a competitive market

7.3 Identify the process whereby all firms' economic profits are reduced to zero in the long run

7.4 Compare allocative vs. production efficiency

7.5 Explain how the market mechanism, combined with competition, leads to both allocative efficiency and production efficiency

Catfish farmers in the southern United States are very upset. During the past two decades they've invested millions of dollars in converting cotton farms into breeding ponds for catfish. They now have over 150,000 acres of ponds and supply 80 percent of the United States' catfish consumption. But unfortunately, catfish prices have been dropping. In 2003 alone catfish prices fell 15 percent, to a low of 55 cents per pound. With production costs averaging 65 cents a pound, most catfish farmers are now losing money. Indeed, many farmers in Arkansas, Mississippi, and Louisiana have simply stopped feeding their fish. A lot of farmers are expected to refill their ponds with dirt and start planting cotton again.

It wasn't supposed to happen this way. Ten years ago, catfish looked like a sure thing. But so many Southern farmers got into the business that catfish prices started falling. Then Vietnam started exporting catfish to the United States, putting still further pressure on prices (see the World View box on the next page).

The dilemma catfish farmers find themselves in is a familiar occurrence in competitive markets. When profits look good, everybody wants to get in on the act. As more and more firms start producing the good, prices and profits tumble. This helps explain why thousands of new firms are formed each year and why thousands of others fail.

This chapter focuses on the behaviour of competitive markets. We have three principal questions:

- **How are prices determined in competitive markets?**
- **How does competition affect the profits of a firm or industry?**
- **What does society gain from market competition?**

The answers to these questions will reveal how markets work when all producers are relatively small and lack market power. In subsequent chapters we emphasize how market outcomes change when markets are less competitive.

Whiskered Catfish Stir a New Trade Controversy

LAKE VILLAGE, ARK.—Alleamer Tyler works in quality control at Farm Fresh Catfish, a processing plant in this small Delta town on the edge of the Mississippi River. Her days are sometimes slower than in the past, because she doesn't test as many fish as she once did.

"The imports have made a huge impact," says Ms. Tyler, one of Farm Fresh's 100 employees.

Because of Vietnamese fish imports, the U.S. catfish production has plunged in the past year. At Farm Fresh, 95,000 pounds a day were processed last year. This year, it's down to 65,000.

Mississippi leads the nation in catfish production, followed by Arkansas and Louisiana. Most U.S. catfish are raised in the Delta, one of the most poverty-stricken areas in the country. It's a place where the loss of even a few jobs that pay $8 an hour leaves a void in the local economy.

Catfish producers say imports from Vietnam have soared from 575,000 pounds in 1998 to as much as 20 million pounds this year.

—Suzi Parker

Source: *Suzi Parker*, October 3, 2001. © 2001 Suzi Parker. www.csmonitor.com

Analysis: When economic profits exist in an industry, more producers try to enter. As they do, prices and economic profits decline. When losses are incurred, firms begin to exit the industry.

7.1 THE MARKET SUPPLY CURVE

In the previous chapter we examined the supply behaviour of a perfectly competitive firm. The perfectly competitive firm is a price taker. It *responds* to the market price by producing that rate of output where marginal cost equals price.

But what about the *market* supply of catfish? We need a market supply curve to determine the *equilibrium price* the individual farmer will confront. In the previous chapter we simply drew a market supply curve arbitrarily to establish a market price. Now, our objective is to find out where that *market supply* curve comes from.

Like the market supply curves we first encountered in Chapter 2, we can calculate the market supply of catfish by simple addition. All we have to do is add up the quantities each of America's 2,000 catfish farmers stands ready to supply at each price. Then we'll know the total quantity of fish to be supplied to the market at that price. Figure 7.1

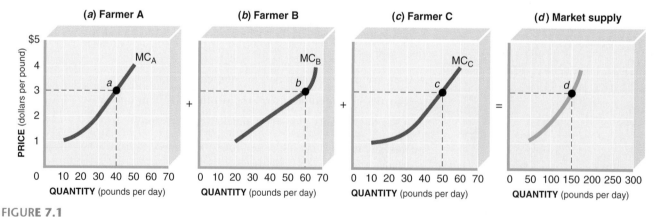

FIGURE 7.1

Competitive Market Supply

The portion of the MC curve that lies above AVC is a competitive firm's short-run supply curve. The curve MC_A tells us that Farmer A will produce 40 pounds of catfish per day if the market price is $3 per pound.

To determine the *market* supply, we add up the quantities supplied at each price by every farmer. The total quantity supplied to the market at the price of $3 is 150 pounds per day ($a + b + c$). Market supply depends on the number of firms and their respective marginal costs.

(*a*) Market entry pushes price down and . . .

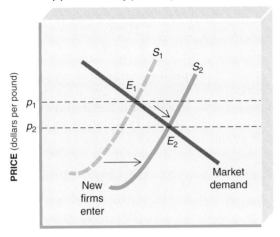

(*b*) Reduces profits of competitive firm

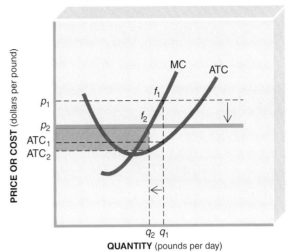

FIGURE 7.2
Market Entry

If economic profits exist in an industry, more firms will want to enter it. As they do, the market supply curve will shift to the right and cause the market price to drop from p_1 to p_2 (part *a*). The lower market price, in turn, will reduce the output and profits of the typical firm. In part *b*, the firm's output falls from q_1 to q_2.

illustrates this summation. Notice that *the market supply curve is the sum of the marginal cost curves of all the firms.* Hence, whatever determines the marginal cost of a typical firm will also affect industry supply. Specifically, *the market supply of a competitive industry is determined by*

- *The price of factor inputs.*
- *Technology.*
- *Expectations.*
- *Taxes and subsidies.*
- *The number of firms in the industry.*

Entry and Exit

If more firms enter an industry, the market supply curve will shift to the right. This is the problem confronting the catfish farmers in Mississippi. It's fairly inexpensive to get into the catfish business: You can start with a pond, some breeding stock, and relatively little capital equipment. These *investment decisions* shift the market supply curve to the right and drive down catfish prices. This process is illustrated in Figure 7.2.

If prices fall too far, entry will cease and some catfish farmers will drain their ponds and plant cotton again. As they leave (exit) the industry, the market supply curve will shift to the left.

Tendency toward Zero Profits

The profit motive drives these entry and exit decisions. Ten years ago catfish farming looked a whole lot more profitable than cotton farming. Farmers responded by flooding their cotton fields to create fish ponds.

The resulting shift of market supply caused the *economic profits* in catfish farming to disappear. Eventually the returns in catfish farming were no better than those in cotton farming. When that happened, cotton farmers stopped building fish ponds and resumed planting cotton. *When economic profits disappear, entry ceases, and the market stabilizes.* At that new equilibrium, catfish farmers earn only a normal (average) rate of return.

Catfish farmers would be happier, of course, if the price of catfish didn't decline to the point where economic profits disappear. But how are they going to prevent it?

competitive market: A market in which no buyer or seller has market power.

WEB NOTE

You can track catfish output and prices and even get recipes at the Catfish Institute's Web site: www.catfishinstitute.com.

Low Barriers to Entry

barriers to entry: Obstacles, such as patents, that make it difficult or impossible for would-be producers to enter a particular market.

Market Characteristics of Perfect Competition

Alleamer Tyler evidently knows all about the laws of supply and demand (see the previous World View). She would dearly like to keep all those Vietnamese catfish out of her country. She also wishes those farmers in Maine would keep cranberries in their ponds rather than catfish. She would also like to get other farmers in the southern United States to slow production a little before all the profits disappear. But Ms. Tyler is powerless to stop the forces of a **competitive market.** She can't even afford to reduce her *own* catfish production. Even though she has 200 acres of ponds, nobody would notice the resulting drop in market supplies, and catfish prices would continue to slide. The only one affected would be Ms. Tyler, who'd be denying herself the opportunity to share in the (dwindling) fortunes of the catfish market while they lasted.

Ms. Tyler's dilemma goes a long way toward explaining why catfish farming isn't highly profitable. Whenever the profit picture looks good, everybody tries to get in on the action. This kind of pressure on prices and profits is a fundamental characteristic of competitive markets. *As long as it's easy for existing producers to expand production or for new firms to enter an industry, economic profits won't last long.* As we'll see shortly, this is a lesson Steve Jobs and Apple Computer have learned repeatedly.

New producers will be able to enter a profitable industry and help drive down prices and profits as long as they don't encounter significant barriers. Such **barriers to entry** may include patents, control of essential factors of production, control of distribution outlets, well-established brand loyalty, or even governmental regulation. All such barriers make it expensive, risky, or impossible for new firms to enter an industry. In the absence of such barriers, new firms can enter an industry more readily and at less risk. Not surprisingly, firms already entrenched in a profitable industry do their best to keep out newcomers by erecting barriers to entry. Unfortunately for Ms. Tyler, there are few barriers to entering the catfish business; all you need to get started is a pond and a few fish.

7.2 COMPETITION AT WORK: MICROCOMPUTERS

The catfish economics example illustrates a few general observations about the structure, behaviour, and outcomes of a competitive market:

- *Many firms.* A competitive market includes a great many firms, none of which has a significant share of total output.
- *Perfect information.* All buyers and sellers have complete information on available supply, demand, and prices.
- *Identical products.* Products are homogeneous. One firm's product is the same as any other firm's product.
- *MC = p.* All competitive firms will seek to expand output until marginal cost equals price, in as much as price and marginal revenue are identical for such firms.
- *Low barriers.* Barriers to enter the industry are low. If economic profits are available, more firms will enter the industry.
- *Zero economic profit.* The tendency of production and market supplies to expand when profit is high puts heavy pressures on prices and profits in competitive industries. Economic profit will approach zero in the long run as prices are driven down to the level of average production costs.

Few markets have all the characteristics listed above. That is, *few, if any, product markets are perfectly competitive.* However, many industries function much like the competitive model we sketched out. In addition to catfish farming, most other agricultural product markets are characterized by highly competitive market structures, with hundreds or even thousands of producers supplying the market. Other highly

APPLICATIONS

Competition Helps Drop Laptop Prices Worldwide Sales Jump 40%

Laptop bargains abound this holiday season, partly because of stiff competition between tech heavy-weights Dell and Hewlett-Packard.

Laptops likely will sell for an average $1,300 this month—a new low, says researcher NPD Group. In 2003's first 10 months, 15% of laptops sold for less than $1,000 vs. 6% last year.

Entry-level laptops have seen the steepest drops. This is the first year it's easy to find quality ones for less than $1,000, says NPD computer analyst Stephen Baker.

Savvy shoppers find even better deals. Best Buy recently sold an entry-level Toshiba laptop with Windows XP and a DVD player for $499, after rebates.

Makers and retailers are dropping prices to compete in the fast-growing laptop market

—Michelle Kessler

Source: *USA Today*, December 8, 2003. USA TODAY Copyright 2003. Reprinted with permission.

Analysis: Competitive pressures compel laptop producers to keep improving the product and reducing prices. The lure of profits encourages firms to enter this expanding market even as prices drop.

---

competitive, and hence not very profitable, businesses are T-shirt shops, retail food, printing, clothing manufacturing and retailing, dry-cleaning establishments, beauty salons, and furniture. Online stockbroker services have also become highly competitive. In these markets, prices and profits are always under the threat of expanded supplies brought to market by existing or new producers.

The electronics industry offers numerous examples of how competition reduces prices and profits. Between 1972 and 1983, the price of small, hand-held calculators fell from $200 to under $10. The price of digital watches fell even more dramatically, from roughly $2,000 in 1975 to under $7 in 1990. Videocassette recorders (VCRs) that sold for $2,000 in 1979 now sell for less than $70. DVD players that cost $1,500 in 1997 now sell for under $80. Cell phones that sold for $1,000 ten years ago are now given away. The same kind of competitive pressures have reduced the price of laptop computers. New entrants keep bringing better laptops to market, while driving prices down (see the Applications box).

The driving force behind all these price reductions and quality improvements is *competition*. Do you really believe the price of accessing the Net would be falling if only one firm controlled access to the Internet? Do you think thousands of software writers would be toiling away right now if popular programs didn't generate enormous profits? Would America Online and Dell Computer keep rolling out new products and services if other companies weren't always snapping at their heels?

To appreciate how the process of competition works, we will examine the development of the personal computer industry. *As in other industries, the market structure of the computer industry has evolved over time. It was never a monopoly, nor was it ever perfect competition.* In its first couple of years it was dominated by only a few companies (like Apple) that were enormously successful. The high profits the early microcomputer producers obtained attracted swarms of imitators. Over 250 firms entered the microcomputer industry between 1976 and 1983 in search of high profits. The entry of so many firms transformed the industry's market structure: The industry became *more* competitive, even though not *perfectly* competitive. The increased competition pushed prices downward and improved the product. When prices and profits tumbled, scores of companies went bankrupt. They left a legacy, however, of a vastly larger market, much improved computers, and sharply lower prices.

Market Evolution

We'll use the early experiences of the microcomputer industry to illustrate the key behavioural features of a competitive market. As we'll see, many of these competitive features are still at work in the PC market, even though the current market structure is more oligopolistic in nature: in North America, about a half-dozen firms (Dell, Hewlett-Packard, IBM-Levano, Acer, Toshiba, and Apple) account for the vast majority of sales. In the markets for Internet services, content software, and digital music players, the competitive features are even more visible.

Initial Conditions: The Apple I

The microcomputer industry really got started in 1977. Prior to that time, microcomputers were essentially a hobby item for engineers and programmers, who bought circuits, keyboards, monitors, and tape recorders and then assembled their own basic computers. Steve Jobs, then working at Atari, and Steven Wozniak, then working at Hewlett-Packard, were among these early computer enthusiasts. They spent their days working on large systems and their nights and weekends trying to put together small computers from mail-order parts.

Eventually, Jobs and Wozniak decided they had the capability to build commercially attractive small computers. They ordered the parts necessary for building 100 computers and set up shop in the garage of Jobs's parents. Their finished product—the Apple I (see photo)—was nothing more than a circuit board with a simple, built-in operating system. This first microcomputer was packaged in a wooden box. Despite primitive characteristics, the first 100 Apple I computers sold out immediately. This quick success convinced Jobs and Wozniak to package their computers more fully—which they did by enclosing them in plastic housing—and to offer more of them for sale. Shortly thereafter, in January 1977, Apple Computer, Inc. was established.

Apple revolutionized the market by offering a preassembled desktop computer with attractive features and an accessible price. The impact on the marketplace was much like that of Henry Ford's early Model T: Suddenly a newfangled piece of technology came into reach of the average U.S. household, and everybody, it seemed, wanted one. The first mass-produced Apple computer—called the Apple II—was just a basic keyboard with an operating system that permitted users to write their own programs. The computer had no disk drive, no monitor, and only 4K of random access memory (RAM). Consumers had to use their TV sets as screens and audiocassettes for data storage. This primitive Apple II was priced at just under $1,300 when it debuted in June 1977. Apple was producing computers at the rate of 500 per month.

WEB NOTE

Apple Computer, Inc.'s Web site details the development of their computer, including photos. Visit Apple at www.apple-history.com.

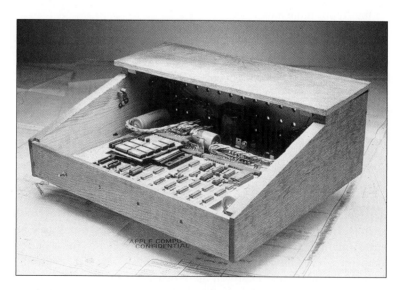

Analysis: The Apple I launched the personal computer industry in 1976. Hundreds of firms entered the industry to improve on this first preassembled microcomputer.

(a) The computer industry

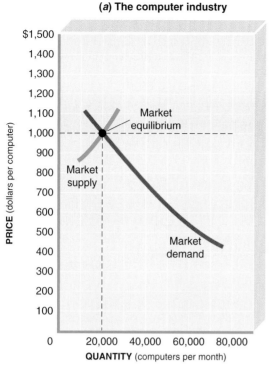

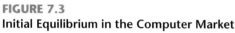

(b) The typical firm

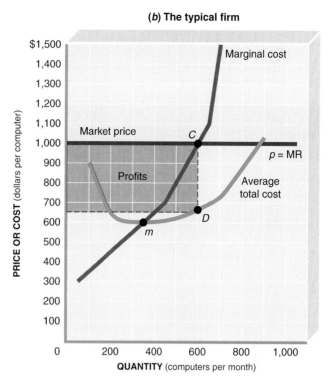

FIGURE 7.3
Initial Equilibrium in the Computer Market

(a) **The Industry**   In 1978, the market price of microcomputers was $1,000. This price was established by the intersection of the market supply and demand curves.

(b) **A Firm**   Each competitive producer in the market sought to produce computers at that rate (600 per month) where marginal cost equaled price (point C). Profit per computer was equal to price (point C) minus average total cost (point D). Total profits for the typical firm are indicated by the shaded rectangle.

Apple didn't engineer or manufacture chips or semiconductor components. Instead, it simply packaged existing components purchased from outside suppliers. Hence, it was easy for other companies to follow Apple's lead. Within a very brief time, other firms, such as Tandy (Radio Shack), also started to assemble computers. By the middle of 1978, the basic small computer was selling for $1,000, and industry sales were about 20,000 a month. Figure 7.3 depicts the initial (1978) equilibrium in the computer market and the approximate costs of production for the typical computer manufacturer at that time.

The short-run goal of every producer is to find the rate of output that maximizes profits. Finding this rate entails making the best possible *production decision*. In this short-run context, ***each competitive firm seeks the rate of output at which marginal cost equals price.***

Figure 7.3b illustrates the cost and price curves the typical computer producer confronted in 1978. As in most lines of production, the marginal costs of computer production increased with the rate of output. Marginal costs rose in part because output could be increased in the short-run (with existing plant and equipment) only by crowding additional workers onto the assembly line. In 1978, Apple had only 10,000 square feet of manufacturing space. As more workers were hired, each worker had less capital and land to work with, and marginal physical product fell. The law of diminishing returns pushed marginal costs up.

The upward-sloping marginal cost curve intersected the price line at an output level of 600 computers per month (point C in Figure 7.3b).[1] That was the profit-maximizing

The Production Decision

---

[1]The marginal cost curves depicted here rise more steeply than they did in reality, but the general shape of the curves is our primary concern at this point.

TABLE 7.1
Computer Revenues, Costs, and Profits

Producers seek that rate of output where total profit is maximized. This table illustrates the alternatives the typical computer producer faced in 1978. The profit-maximizing rate of output occurred at 600 computers per month. At that rate of output, marginal cost was equal to price ($1,000), and profits were $200,000 per month.

Output per Month	Price	Total Revenue	Total Cost	Total Profit	Marginal Revenue*	Marginal Cost*	Average Total Cost	Profit/Unit (p – ATC)
0	—		$ 60,000	–$60,000			—	—
					$1,000	$300		
100	$1,000	$100,000	90,000	10,000	1,000	400	$ 900.00	$100.00
200	1,000	200,000	130,000	70,000	1,000	500	650.00	350.00
300	1,000	300,000	180,000	120,000	1,000	600	600.00	400.00
400	1,000	400,000	240,000	160,000	1,000	700	600.00	400.00
500	1,000	500,000	310,000	190,000	1,000	900	620.00	380.00
600	1,000	600,000	400,000	200,000			666.67	333.33
					1,000	1,100		
700	1,000	700,000	510,000	190,000	1,000	1,900	728.57	271.43
800	1,000	800,000	700,000	100,000	1,000	2,200	875.00	125.00
900	1,000	900,000	920,000	–20,000			1,022.22	–22.22

*Note that output levels are calibrated in hundreds in this example; that's why we must have divided the *change* in total costs and revenues from one output level to another by 100 to calculate marginal revenue and marginal cost. Very few manufacturers deal in units of 1.

rate of output (MC = p) for the typical manufacturer. To manufacture any more than 600 computers per month would raise marginal costs over price and reduce total profits. To manufacture any less would be to pass up an opportunity to make another buck.

Profit Calculations

Table 7.1 shows how much *profit* a typical computer manufacturer was making in 1978. As the profit column indicates, the typical computer manufacturer could make a real killing in the computer market, reaping a monthly profit of $200,000 by producing and selling 600 microcomputers.

We could also calculate the computer manufacturers' profits by asking how much the manufacturers make on *each* computer and then multiplying that figure by total output since

Total profit = profit per unit × quantity sold

We can compute these profits by studying the first and last columns in Table 7.1 or by using a little geometry in Figure 7.3*b*. In the figure, average costs (total costs divided by the rate of output) are portrayed by the *average total cost (ATC)* curve. At the output rate of 600 (the row in white in Table 7.1), the distance between the price line ($1,000 at point *C*) and the ATC curve ($666.67 at point *D*) is $333.33, which represents the average **profit per unit.** Multiplying this figure by the number of units sold (600 per month) will give us *total* profit per month. Total profits are represented by the shaded rectangle in Figure 7.3*b* and are equal to our earlier profit figure of $200,000 per month.

profit per unit: Total profit divided by the quantity produced in a given time period; price minus average total cost.

The Lure of Profits

While gaping at the computer manufacturer's enormous profits, we should remind ourselves that those profits might not last long. Indeed, the more quick-witted among us already will have seen and heard enough to know they've discovered a good thing. And in fact, the kind of profits the early microcomputer manufacturers attained attracted a lot of entrepreneurial interest. ***In competitive markets, economic profits attract new entrants.*** This is what happened in the catfish industry and also in the computer industry. Within a very short time, a whole crowd of profit maximizers entered the microcomputer industry in hot pursuit of its fabulous profits. By the end of 1980, Apple had a lot of competition, including new entrants from IBM, Xerox, Digital Equipment, Casio, Sharp, and others.

Low Entry Barriers

A critical feature of the microcomputer market was its lack of entry barriers. A microcomputer is little more than a box containing a microprocessor "brain," which connects to a keyboard (to enter data), a memory (to store data), and a screen (to display data). Although the microprocessors that guide the computer are extremely sophisticated, they can be purchased on the open market. Thus, to enter the computer industry, all one needs is some space, some money to buy components, and some dexterity in putting parts together. Such *low entry barriers permit new firms to enter competitive markets.* According to Table 7.1, the typical producer needed only $60,000 of plant and equipment (fixed costs) to get started in the microcomputer market. Jobs and Wozniak had even less when they started making Apples in their garage.

A Shift of Market Supply

Figure 7.4 shows what happened to the computer market and the profits of the typical firm once the word got out. As more and more entrepreneurs heard how profitable computer manufacturing could be, they quickly got hold of a book on electronic circuitry, rushed to the bank, got a little financing, and set up shop. Before many months had passed, scores of new firms had started producing small computers. *The entry of new firms shifts the market supply curve to the right.* In Figure 7.4a, the supply curve shifted from S_1 to S_2. Almost as fast as a computer can calculate a profit (loss) statement, the willingness to supply increased abruptly.

But the new computer companies were in for a bit of disappointment. With so many new firms hawking microcomputers, it became increasingly difficult to make a fast buck. The downward-sloping market demand curve confirms that a greater quantity of microcomputers could be sold only if the price of computers dropped. And drop it did. The price slide began as computer manufacturers found their inventories growing

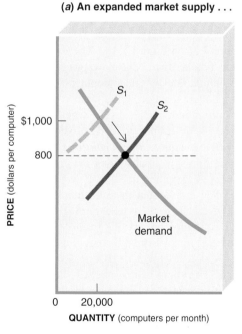

(a) An expanded market supply . . .

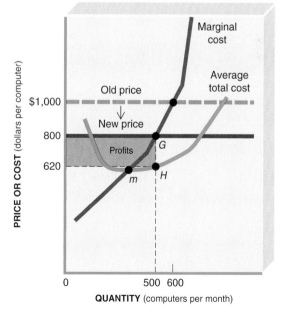

(b) Lowers price and profits for the typical firm

FIGURE 7.4
The Competitive Price and Profit Squeeze

(*a*) **The Industry** The economic profits in the computer industry encouraged new firms to enter the industry. As they did, the market supply curve shifted from S_1 to S_2. This rightward shift of the supply curve lowered the equilibrium price of computers.

(*b*) **A Firm** The lower market price, in turn, forced the typical producer to reduce output to the point where MC and price were equal again (point *G*). At this reduced rate of output, the typical firm earned less total profit than it had earned before.

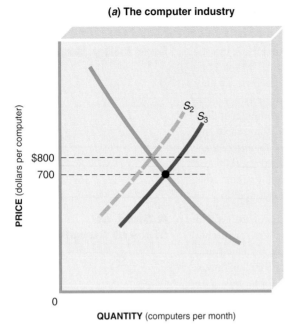

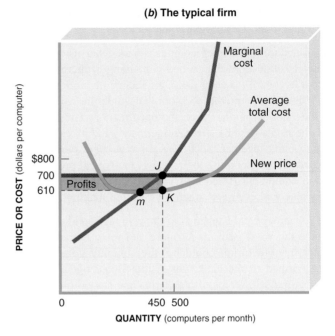

(a) The computer industry

(b) The typical firm

FIGURE 7.5
The Competitive Squeeze Approaching Its Limit

(a) The Industry Even at a price of $800 per computer, economic profits attracted still more entrepreneurs, shifting the market supply curve further (S_3). The next short-term equilibrium occurred at a price of $700 per computer.

(b) A Firm At this reduced market price, the typical manufacturer wanted to supply only 450 computers per month (point *J*). Total profits were much lower than they had been earlier, with fewer producers and higher prices.

and so offered price discounts to maintain sales volume. The price fell rapidly, from $1,000 in mid-1978 to $800 in early 1980.

The sliding market price squeezed the profits of each firm, causing the profit rectangle to shrink (compare Figure 7.3*b* to Figure 7.4*b*). The lower price also changed the production decision of the typical firm. The new price ($800) intersected the unchanged MC curve at the output rate of 500 computers per month (point *G* in Figure 7.4*b*). With average production costs of $620 (Table 7.1), the firm's total profits in 1980 were only $90,000 per month [$(P - ATC) \times 500$]. Not a paltry sum, to be sure, but nothing like the fantastic fortunes pocketed earlier.

As long as an economic profit is available, it will continue to attract new entrants. Those entrepreneurs who were a little slow in absorbing the implications of Figure 7.3 eventually woke up to what was going on and tried to get in on the action, too. Even though they were a little late, they didn't want to miss the chance to cash in on the $90,000 in monthly profits still available to the typical firm. Hence, the market supply curve continued to shift, and computer prices slid further, as in Figure 7.5. This process squeezed the profits of the typical firm still more, further shrinking the profit rectangle.

short-run competitive equilibrium: p = MC.

As long as economic profits exist in **short-run competitive equilibrium**, that equilibrium won't last. If the rate of profit obtainable in computer production is higher than that available in other industries, new firms will enter the industry. Conversely, if the short-run equilibrium is unprofitable, firms will exit the industry. Profit-maximizing entrepreneurs have a special place in their hearts for economic profits, not computers.

long-run competitive equilibrium: p = MC = minimum ATC.

Price and profit declines will cease when the price of computers equals the minimum average cost of production. At that price (point *m* in Figure 7.5*b*), there's no more economic profit to be squeezed out. Firms no longer have an incentive to enter the industry, and the supply curve stops shifting. This situation represents the **long-run competitive equilibrium** for the firm and for the industry. *In long-run equilibrium,*

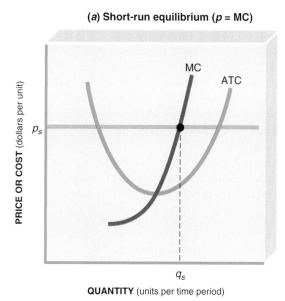

(a) Short-run equilibrium (p = MC)

(b) Long-run equilibrium (p = MC = ATC)

FIGURE 7.6
Short- vs. Long-run Equilibrium for the Competitive Firm

(*a*) **Short-Run**   Competitive firms strive for the rate of output at which marginal cost (MC) equals price. When they achieve that rate of output, they are in *short-run equilibrium*. They have no incentive to alter the rate of output produced with existing (fixed) plant and equipment.

(*b*) **Long-Run**   If the short-run equilibrium (q_S) is profitable ($p >$ ATC), other firms will want to enter the industry. As they do, market price will fall until it reaches the level of minimum ATC. In this *long-run equilibrium* (q_L), economic profits are zero and nobody wants to enter or exit the industry.

entry and exit cease, and zero economic profit (that is, normal profit) prevails (see Figure 7.6). Table 7.2 summarizes the profit-maximizing rules that bring about this long-run equilibrium.

Once a long-run equilibrium is established, it will continue until market demand shifts or technological progress reduces the cost of computer production. In fact, that's just what happened in the computer market.

Home Computers vs. Personal Computers

As profit margins narrowed to the levels shown in Figure 7.5, quick-thinking entrepreneurs realized that future profits would have to come from product improvements or cost reductions. By adding features to the basic microcomputer, firms could expect to increase the demand for microcomputers and fetch higher prices. On the other hand, cost reductions would permit firms to widen their profit margins at existing prices or to reduce prices and increase sales. This second strategy wouldn't require assembling more complex computers or risking consumer rejection of an upgraded product.

In late 1979 and early 1980, both product-development strategies were pursued. In the process, two distinct markets were created. Microcomputers upgraded with new features came to be known as *personal* computers, or PCs. The basic unadorned

Price Level	Result for a Typical Firm	Market Response
$p >$ ATC	Profits	Enter industry (or expand capacity)
$p <$ ATC	Loss	Exit industry (or reduce capacity)
$p =$ ATC	Break even	Maintain existing capacity (no entry or exit)

TABLE 7.2
Long-Run Rules for Entry and Exit

Firms will enter an industry if economic profits exist ($p >$ ATC). They will exit if economic losses prevail ($p <$ ATC). Entry and exit cease in long-run equilibrium ($p =$ ATC). (See Table 6.3 for short-run profit-maximization rules.)

computer first introduced by Apple came to be known as a *home* computer. The limited capabilities of that basic home computer greatly restricted its usefulness to simple household record keeping, games, and elementary programming.

Apple chose the personal computer route. It started enlarging the memory of the Apple II in late 1978 (from 4K to as much as 48K). It offered a monitor (produced by Sanyo) for the first time in May 1979. Shortly thereafter, Apple ceased making the basic Apple II and instead produced only upgraded versions (the Apple IIe, the IIc, and the III). Hundreds of other companies followed Apple's lead, touting increasingly sophisticated personal computers.

While one pack of entrepreneurs was chasing PC profits, another pack was going after the profits still available in home computers. This group chose to continue producing the basic Apple II look-alike, hoping to profit from greater efficiency, lower costs, and increasing sales.

Price Competition in Home Computers

The home computer market confronted the fiercest form of price competition. With prices continually sliding, the only way to make an extra buck was to push down the cost curve.

To reduce costs, firms sought to reduce the number of microprocessor chips installed in the computer's "brain." Fewer chips not only reduce direct materials costs, but more importantly, they decrease the amount of labour required for computer assembly. The key to lower manufacturing costs was more powerful chips. More powerful chips appeared when Intel, Motorola, and Texas Instruments developed 16-bit chips, doubling the computer's "brain" capabilities.

Further Supply Shifts

WEB NOTE

Visit Government of Canada information services for entrepreneurs at http://www.cbsc.org/.

The impact of the improved chips on computer production costs and profits is illustrated in Figure 7.7, which takes over where Figure 7.5 left off. Recall that the market price of computers had been driven down to $700 by the beginning of 1980. At this price the typical firm maximized profits by producing 450 computers per month, as determined by the intersection of the prevailing price and MC curves (point *J* in Figure 7.7).

The only way for the firm to improve profitability at this point was to reduce costs. The new chips made such cost reductions easy. Such *technological improvements are illustrated by a downward shift of the ATC and MC curves.* Notice, for example, that

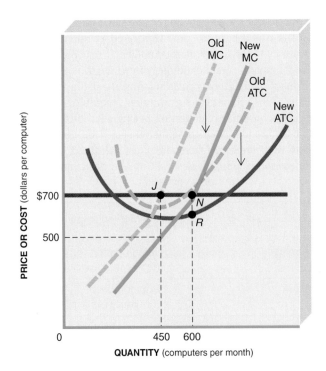

FIGURE 7.7

A Downward Shift of Costs Improves Profits and Stimulates Output

The quest for profits encouraged producers to discover cheaper ways to manufacture computers. The resulting improvements lowered costs and encouraged further increases in the rate of output. The typical computer producer increased output from point *J* (where *p* = old MC) to point *N* (where *p* = new MC).

Date		Price of Texas Instruments Model 99/4A
December	1979	$950
February	1980	700
June	1980	650
April	1981	525
December	1981	400
April	1982	249
September	1982	199
January	1983	149
September	1983	99
November	1983	49

TABLE 7.3
Plummeting Prices

Improved technology and fierce competition forced home computer prices down. In the span of only a few years, the price of a basic home computer fell from just under $1,000 to only $49. In the process, price fell below average variable cost, and many firms were forced to shut down.

the new technology permits 450 home computers to be produced for a lower marginal cost ($500) than previously (point *J*).

The lower cost structure increases the profitability of computer production and stimulates a further increase in production. Note in particular that the "new MC" curve intersects the price ($700) line at an output of 600 computers per month (point *N*). By contrast, the old, higher MC curve dictated a production rate of only 450 computers per month for the typical firm (point *J*) at that price. Thus, existing producers suddenly had an incentive to *expand* production, and new firms had a greater incentive to *enter* the industry. The great rush into computer production was on again.

The market implications of another entrepreneurial stampede should now be obvious. As more and more firms tried to get in on the action, the market supply curve again shifted to the right. As output increased, computer prices slid further down the market demand curve.

Table 7.3 illustrates how steeply home computer prices fell after 1980. Texas Instruments (TI) was one of the largest firms producing home computers in 1980. The lower costs made possible by improved microprocessors enabled TI to sell its basic home computer for $650 in 1980. Despite modest improvements in the TI machine, TI had to reduce its price to $525 in early 1981 to maintain unit sales. Shortly thereafter, the additional output of new entrants and existing companies pushed market prices down still further, to around $400.

Even at $400, TI and other home computer manufacturers were making handsome profits. In the fourth quarter of 1981, total industry sales were in excess of 200,000 per month—10 times the volume sold just three years earlier. Profits were good, too. A single company, Atari, recorded total profits of $137 million in the fourth quarter of 1981, far more profit than Apple Computer, Inc. had made during its first five *years* of production. The profits of the home computer market appeared boundless.

The remainder of Table 7.3 shows the consequences of the continued competition for those "boundless" profits. Between December 1981 and January 1983, the retail price of home computers fell from $400 to $149. Profit margins became razor-thin. Fourth-quarter profits at Atari, for example, fell from $137 million in 1981 to only $1.2 million in 1983.

That didn't stop the competitive process, however. At Texas Instruments, minimum *variable* costs were roughly $100 per computer, so TI and other manufacturers could afford to keep producing even at lower prices. And they had little choice but to do so, since if they didn't, other companies would quickly take up the slack. Industry output kept increasing, despite shrinking profit margins. The increased quantity supplied pushed computer prices ever lower.

By the time computer prices reached $99, TI was losing $300 million per year. In September 1983, the company recognized that the price would no longer even

Shutdowns

cover average variable costs. ***Once a firm is no longer able to cover variable costs, it should shut down production.*** When the price of home computers dipped below minimum average variable costs, TI had reached the *shutdown point,* and the company ceased production. At the time TI made the shutdown decision, the company had an inventory of nearly 500,000 unsold computers. To unload them, TI reduced its price to $49, forcing lower prices and losses on other computer firms.

Exits

Shortly after Texas Instruments shut down its production, it got out of the home computer business altogether. Mattel, Atari, and scores of smaller companies also withdrew from the home computer market. The exit rate between 1983 and 1985 matched the entry rate of the period 1979 to 1982.

The Personal Computer Market

The same kind of price competition that characterized the home computer market eventually hit the personal computer market too. As noted earlier, the microcomputer industry split into two segments around 1980, with most firms pursuing the upgraded personal computer market.

At first, competition in the PC market was largely confined to product improvements. Firms added more memory, faster microprocessors, better monitors, expanded operating systems, new applications software, and other features. New entrants into the market—Compaq in 1982; then Dell, AST, Gateway, and more—were the source of most product innovations.

The stampede of new firms and products into the PC market soon led to outright price competition too. As firms discovered that they couldn't sell all the PCs they were producing at prevailing prices, they were forced to offer price discounts. These discounts soon spread, and the slide down the demand curve accelerated.

Firms that couldn't keep up with the dual pace of improving technology and falling prices soon fell by the wayside. Scores of firms ceased production and withdrew from the industry once prices fell below minimum average variable cost. Even Apple, which had taken the "high road" to avoid price competition in home computers, was slowed by price competition. And IBM, which had entered the industry late, was forced to shut down its PC division after realizing that steep price cuts would be required to sell its small PCs (the "PCjr") to household users (Applications box).

APPLICATIONS

IBM to Halt PCjr Output Next Month

Computer's Sales Dried Up After Steep Price Cuts Ended Earlier This Year

NEW YORK—International Business Machines Corp. ended its up-and-down struggle to revive its PCjr home computer by announcing it would stop making the product next month.

The surprise move marks IBM's most visible product failure since its enormously successful entry into the personal-computer business four years ago. IBM announced the PCjr in late 1983 and began selling it early last year with an advertising campaign believed to exceed $40 million. IBM's efforts to make junior a hit ranged from technical changes to steep price cuts. But while aggressive IBM price cuts before Christmas increased PCjr sales substantially, sales dried up after the promotions ended in January. . . .

At the time of its introduction, the PCjr had a list of $699 or $1,269, depending on the model. The prices later were cut to $599 and $999, and the more powerful model's price dropped below the $800 level during the Christmas promotion.

—Dennis Kneale

Analysis: Competition forces firms to improve products and reduce prices. Those firms that can't keep up are forced to shut down and perhaps exit the industry.

7.3 THE COMPETITIVE PROCESS

It is now evident that consumers reaped substantial benefits from competition in the computer market. Millions of home and personal computers have been sold. Along the way, technology has made personal computers 200 times faster than the first Apple IIs, with 300 times more memory. The current iMac computer (2.16 GHz Intel Core 2 Duo processor and 1 GB of memory) makes the 1976 Apple I (1.023 *MHz* processor and 4*K* [expandable to 8*K*!] memory) look positively prehistoric. Many consumers have found that computers are great for doing accounting chores, keeping records, writing papers, playing games, and accessing the Internet. Perhaps it's true that an abundance of inexpensive computers would have been produced in other market (or nonmarket) situations as well. But we can't ignore the fact that *competitive market pressures are a driving force behind the growth of the computer industry.* And they continue to alter firm behaviour, as the accompanying Applications box confirms.

The squeeze on prices and profits that we've observed in the computer market is a fundamental characteristic of the competitive process. Indeed, the *market mechanism* works best under such circumstances. The existence of economic profits is an indication that consumers place a high value on a particular product and are willing to pay a comparatively high price to get it. The high price and profits signal this information to profit-hungry entrepreneurs, who come forward to satisfy consumer demands. Thus, *high profits in a particular industry indicate that consumers want a different mix of output* (more of that industry's goods). The competitive squeeze on those same profits indicates that resources are being reallocated to produce that desired mix. In a competitive market, consumers get more of the goods they desire—and at a lower price.

    The ability of competitive markets to allocate resources efficiently across industries originates in the way competitive prices are set. To attain the optimal mix of output, we must know the *opportunity cost* of producing different goods. A competitive market gives us the information necessary for making such choices. Why? Because

Allocative Efficiency: The Right Output Mix

APPLICATIONS

Dell's Move to Embrace Retail Is a Sign of Changing Marketplace

When Michael Dell's upstart computer-building company began doing business in 1984, it was able to carve out a niche in the computer industry by shunning retailers and resellers, and selling directly to the consumer. Twenty-three years later and now a giant company with sales of close to $60 billion, Dell Inc. is altering its strategy by embracing partners in areas it had previously avoided.

The most prominent of these changes was the company's announcement a week ago that it would begin selling models of its Dimension series desktops at 3,500 Wal-Marts in the United States, Canada and Puerto Rico in June. If the move seems unusual, these are unusual circumstances for the company. After years as the top PC seller in North America, Dell has lost its place as market leader to Hewlett Packard, and seen its earnings flatten.

Dell has also attempted to reach out to previously ignored consumer bases, such as its decision earlier this year to start offering the Linux-based Ubuntu operating system, to give customers an alternative to Microsoft's ubiquitous Windows OS.

Eddie Chan, a consumer technology analyst with IDC, said Dell's access to Wal-Mart's customer data could help the company learn more about the kinds of choices customers are making, and that could prove invaluable when marketing future models.

In at least one area—the look of its computers—Dell has fallen behind companies like Apple, said Chan. And Dell himself acknowledged that cheaper prices have made design an increasingly important differentiator for notebook and desktop manufacturers, as clunky, faceless PCs give way to sleeker designs.

"It's a hyper-competitive market," said Chan. "And it's always evolving. Dell's move to retail is a good signal of the company's openness to change."

Source: "Dell's move to embrace retail is a sign of changing marketplace," June 1, 2007. By Paul Jay, www.cbc.ca.

Analysis: Competitive pressures force companies to improve products, cut prices, and adjust to changes in customers' preferences.

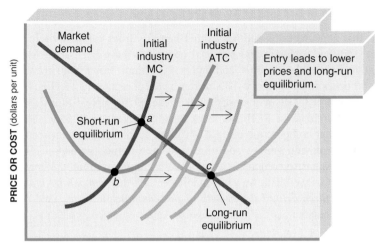

FIGURE 7.8
Summary of Competitive Process

All competitive firms seek to produce at that output where MC = *p*. Hence, a competitive *industry* will produce at that rate of output where *industry* MC (the sum of all firms' MC curves) intersects market demand (point *a*).

If economic profits exist in the industry (as they do here), more firms will enter the industry. As they do, the *industry* MC (supply) curve will shift to the right. The shifting MC curve will pull the *industry* ATC curve along with it. As the *industry* MC curve continues to shift rightward, the intersection of MC and ATC (point *b*) eventually will reach the demand curve at point *c*. At point *c*, MC still equals price, but no economic profits exist and entry (shifts) will cease. Point *c* will be the *long-term* equilibrium of the industry.

If competitive pressures reduce costs (i.e., improve technology), the supply (MC) curve will shift further to the right and *down,* reducing long-term prices even more.

Note that MC = *p* in both short- and long-run equilibrium. Notice also that equilibrium must occur on the market demand curve.

competitive firms always strive to produce at the rate of output at which price equals marginal cost. Hence, ***the price signal the consumer gets in a competitive market is an accurate reflection of opportunity cost.*** As such, it offers a reliable basis for making choices about the mix of output and attendant allocation of resources. In this sense, the **marginal cost pricing** characteristic of competitive markets permits society to answer the WHAT-to-produce question efficiently. The amount consumers are willing to pay for a good (its price) equals its opportunity cost (marginal cost).

marginal cost pricing: The offer (supply) of goods at prices equal to their marginal cost.

Production Efficiency: Minimum Average Cost

When the competitive pressure on prices is carried to the limit, we also get the right answer to the HOW-to-produce question. Competition drives costs down to their bare minimum—the hallmark of economic *efficiency.* This was illustrated by the tendency of computer prices to be driven down to the level of *minimum* average costs. Figure 7.8 summarizes this competitive process, showing how the industry moves from short-run to long-run equilibrium. Once the long-run equilibrium has been established, society is getting the most it can from its available (scarce) resources.

Zero Economic Profit

Competitive pressures also affect the FOR WHOM question. At the limit of long-run equilibrium, all economic profit is eliminated. This doesn't mean that producers are left empty-handed, however. First, the zero-profit limit is rarely, if ever, reached, because new products are continually being introduced, consumer demands change, and more efficient production processes are discovered. In fact, the competitive process creates strong pressures to pursue product and technological innovation. In a competitive market, the adage about the early bird getting the worm is particularly apt. As we observed in the computer market, the first ones to perceive and respond to the potential profitability of computer production were the ones who made the greatest profits.

The sequence of events common to competitive markets evolves as follows:

- High prices and profits signal consumers' demand for more output.
- Economic profit attracts new suppliers.
- The market supply curve shifts to the right.
- Prices slide down the market demand curve.
- A new equilibrium is reached at which increased quantities of the desired product are produced and its price is lower. Average costs of production are at or near a minimum, much more of the product is supplied and consumed, and economic profit approaches zero.
- Throughout the process, producers experience great pressure to keep ahead of the profit squeeze by reducing costs, a pressure that frequently results in product and technological innovation.

What is essential to remember about the competitive process is that the *potential threat of other firms expanding production or of new firms entering the industry keeps existing firms on their toes.* Even the most successful firm can't rest on its laurels for long. To stay in the game, competitive firms must continually update technology, improve their product, and reduce costs. It is the same lesson a lot of entrepreneurs learned in the unusually fast rise and quick death of "dot.com" companies (1998–2001).

Competition didn't end with computers or dot.com companies. Just ask Steve Jobs, the guy who started the personal computer business back in 1977. He introduced another hot consumer product in November 2001—the iPod. The iPod was the first mass-produced portable digital music player. It allowed consumers to download, store, and retrieve up to 1,000 songs. Its compact size, sleek design, and simple functionality made it an instant success: Apple was selling iPods as fast as they could be produced, piling up huge profits in the process.

So what happened? Other entrepreneurs quickly got the scent of iPod's profits. Within a matter of months, competitors were designing their own digital music players. By 2003, the "attack of the iPod clones" (see the Applications box) was in full force. Major players like Sony (MusicBox), Dell (JukeBox), Samsung (Yepp), and Creative Technology (Muvo Slim) were all bringing MP3 players to the market. Competitors were adding new features, shrinking the size, and reducing prices.

Relentless Profit Squeeze

$49 iPods

APPLICATIONS

Attack of the iPod Clones
New Players Give Apple a Run For Its Money in Portable Music; Recording Songs From the Radio

APPLE COMPUTER'S iPod portable music player is one of the best digital products of any kind ever invented. Its design is simply brilliant, and, since its debut two years ago next month, it has become an icon. Nearly 1.5 million iPods have been sold, and the slender white gadget has become the best-selling portable music player on the market, even though it is also the most expensive.

There have been other high-capacity digital music players, both before and since the iPod appeared. Most have been cheaper, but all have been inferior to the iPod, mainly because

they were too big, and too clumsy to use. Meanwhile, Apple has kept improving the iPod, making it smaller and more capable.

Now, however, a new generation of would-be iPod killers is hitting the market. And, after two years of studying Apple's work, the makers of these new players are finally giving the iPod a run for its money. These products are nearly as small as the iPod, and have aped its widely admired user interface. Some have more features, and are less expensive.

—Walter S. Mossberg

Source: *The Wall Street Journal,* October 29, 2003. Reprinted by permission of The Wall Street Journal, © 2003 Dow Jones & Company. All rights reserved worldwide. www.wsj.com.

Analysis: Economic profits attract entrepreneurs. As competition intensifies, products improve and prices fall.

Analysis: Competition forces Apple to make better and cheaper iPods.

Under these circumstances, Apple could not afford to sit back and admire its profits. Steve Jobs knew he'd have to keep running to stay ahead of the MP3-player pack. He kept improving the iPod. Within two years, Apple had three generations of iPods, each substantially better than the last. Memory capacity increased tenfold (to 10,000 songs), features were added, and the size shrank further. In January 2004, Apple brought out the iPodMini, a credit card-sized MP3 player that is 40 percent smaller than the original iPod but has the same 1,000-song capacity. Its initial price was $249, 40 percent less than the original iPod. Hence, in less than two and a half years, the price fell by 40 percent even while quality improved dramatically.

Is that the end of the story? No way. By mid-2004 there were at least 60 iPod clones in the market, with more entrants in sight. Rivals were using flash memory chips rather than hard disks (even though this reduces memory capacity) to cut costs and prices. Microsoft was working on a new MP3 player to interface with its Media Player software and huge music library. Sony was promising to bring a $60 digital music player to the market.

With this kind of unrelenting pressure, Apple will have to keep improving the iPod and reducing its price. By the time you graduate, iPods will surely be selling for $49 or less. If that sounds preposterous, look back at the price/quality history of personal computers. The unrelenting pressure of competition is what forces producers to keep delivering better products at lower prices. Competition is not *perfect* in the MP3-player market (as we'll see), but it is still a *powerful* force.

SUMMARY

- A perfectly competitive firm has no power to alter the market price of the product it sells. The perfectly competitive firm confronts a horizontal demand curve for its own output even though the relevant *market* demand curve is negatively sloped.
- Profit maximization induces the competitive firm to produce at that rate of output where marginal costs equal price. This represents the short-run equilibrium of the firm.
- If short-run profits exist in a competitive industry, new firms will enter the market. The resulting shift of supply will drive market prices down the market demand curve. As prices fall, the profit of the industry and its constituent firms will be squeezed.
- The limit to the competitive price and profit squeeze is reached when price is driven down to the level of minimum

average total cost. At this point (long-run equilibrium) additional output and profit will be attained only if technology is improved (lowering costs) or if market demand increases.
- Firms will shut down production if price falls below average variable cost. Firms will exit the industry if they foresee continued economic losses.
- The most distinctive thing about competitive markets is the persistent pressure they exert on prices and profits. The threat of competition is a tremendous incentive for producers to respond quickly to consumer demands and to seek more efficient means of production. In this sense, competitive markets do best what markets are supposed to do—efficiently allocate resources.

Key Terms

competitive market   154
barriers to entry   154

profit per unit   158
short-run competitive equilibrium   160

long-run competitive equilibrium   160
marginal cost pricing   166

Questions for Discussion

1. Why would anyone want to enter a profitable industry knowing that profits would eventually be eliminated by competition?

2. Why wouldn't producers necessarily want to produce output at the lowest average cost? Under what conditions would they end up doing so?

3. What industries do you regard as being highly competitive? Can you identify any barriers to entry in those industries?
4. How does Dell plan on regaining its position as top PC seller in North America (See Applications box, page 165)? What reasons can you provide for Dell's latest decisions? How does Dell's new business practices mirror the theoretical behaviour of a competitive firm discussed in this chapter?
5. What might cause catfish prices to rise far enough to eliminate losses in the industry? (See the Applications box, page 152.)

6. As the price of computers fell, what happened to their quality? How is this possible?
7. Why is the price of laptop computers declining? (See the Applications box, page 155.)
8. Is "long-run" equilibrium permanent? What forces might dislodge it?
9. What would happen to iPod sales and profits if Apple kept price and profit margins high?
10. Identify two products that have either (*a*) fallen sharply in price or (*b*) gotten significantly better without price increases. How did these changes come about?

E X E R C I S E S

PROBLEMS The Student Problem Set to accompany this chapter can be found at the end of the book.

WEB ACTIVITIES Web Activities to accompany this chapter can be found on the Online Learning Centre at **http://www.mcgrawhill.ca/olc/schiller**.

8 CHAPTER

Monopoly

In Canada, the sale of wine, spirits, and beer falls under provincial jurisdiction, with each province instituting its own rules and regulations. The degree of government intervention, however, varies significantly from province to province. In Ontario, for example, the Liquor Control Board of Ontario (LCBO) owns and operates all the retail outlets selling liquor. They decide where to build their stores as well as the brands (and quantities) of liquor to be offered for sale. Moreover, the LCBO sets the prices for each brand of liquor sold. Since the LCBO does not face any competition, we say that this government agency has *market power;* that is, they can raise the prices of their products without fear of losing many customers. In fact, the LCBO can vary the brands offered and open/close stores without any significant change in overall sales. Such power is alien to competitive firms. Competitive firms are always under pressure to reduce costs, improve quality, and cater to consumer preferences.

With respect to liquor, the Quebec agency, the Société des alcools du Québec (SAQ) operates in a similar manner to the LCBO. At the other end of the spectrum, Alberta has complete privatization of liquor at the retail level. While the Alberta government still regulates import, wholesale, and distribution aspects, the retail sector has over 1,000 private liquor store outlets.

In this chapter we examine how market structure influences market outcomes. Specifically, we examine how a market controlled by a single producer—a monopoly—behaves. We're particularly interested in the following questions:

- **What price will a monopolist charge?**
- **How much output will the monopolist produce?**
- **Are consumers better or worse off when only one firm controls an entire market?**

LEARNING OBJECTIVES

By the end of this chapter, you should be able to:

8.1 Define market power and monopoly

8.2 Identify six barriers to entry

8.3 Explain and illustrate how a monopolist maximizes profits

8.4 Explain the differences between competitive and monopoly equilibrium during the short-run and the long-run

8.5 Discuss limits to exercise of market power and role of price elasticity of demand

8.6 Identify and critically explain the four cases where monopolies might benefit society.

8.1 MARKET POWER

The essence of market power is the ability to alter the price of a product. The catfish farmers in Chapter 7 had no such power. Because 2,000 farms were producing and selling the same good, each catfish producer had to act as a *price taker*. Each producer could sell all it wanted at the prevailing price but would lose all its customers if it tried to charge a higher price.

Firms that have market power *can* alter the price of their output without losing all their customers. Sales volume may drop when price is increased, but the quantity demanded won't drop to zero. In other words, ***firms with market power confront downward-sloping demand curves for their own output.***

The distinction between perfectly competitive (powerless) and imperfectly competitive (powerful) firms is illustrated again in Figure 8.1. Figure 8.1*a* re-creates the market situation that confronts a single catfish farmer. In Chapter 6, we assumed that the prevailing price of catfish was $13 a bushel and that a small, competitive firm could sell its entire output at this price. Hence, each individual firm effectively confronted a horizontal demand curve.

We also noted earlier that catfish don't violate the law of demand. As good as catfish taste, people aren't willing to buy unlimited quantities of them at $13 a bushel. To induce consumers to buy more catfish, the market price of catfish must be reduced.

This seeming contradiction between the law of demand and the situation of the competitive firm is resolved in Figure 8.1. There are *two* relevant demand curves. The one on the left, which appears to contradict the law of demand, refers to a single competitive producer. The one on the right refers to the entire *industry*, of which the competitive producer is one very tiny part. The industry or market demand curve *does* slope downward, even though individual competitive firms are able to sell their own output at the going price.

An industry needn't be composed of many small firms. The entire output of catfish could be produced by a single large producer. Such a firm would be a *monopoly*—a single firm that produces the entire market supply of a good.

The emergence of a monopoly obliterates the distinction between industry demand and the demand curve facing the firm. A monopolistic firm *is* the industry. Hence, there's only *one* demand curve to worry about, and that's the market (industry) demand curve, as illustrated in Figure 8.1*b*. This simplifies things: ***In monopoly situations, the demand curve facing the firm is identical to the market demand curve for the product.***

Although monopolies simplify the geometry, they complicate the arithmetic of *profit maximization.* The basic rule for maximizing profits is unchanged—that is, produce the rate of output where marginal revenue equals marginal cost. This rule applies to *all* firms. In a competitive industry, however, this general rule was simplified. For competitive

The Downward-Sloping Demand Curve

Monopoly

Price and Marginal Revenue

(a) The competitive firm

PRICE (dollars per bushel)

$13

Demand facing competitive firm

0

QUANTITY
(bushels of fish per day)

(b) The industry

PRICE (dollars per bushel)

Market demand

$13

0

QUANTITY
(thousands of bushels of fish per day)

FIGURE 8.1
Firm vs. Industry Demand

A competitive firm can sell its entire output at the prevailing market price. In this sense, the firm confronts a horizontal demand curve, as in part *a.* Nevertheless, market demand for the product still slopes downward. The demand curve confronting the industry is illustrated in part *b.* Note the difference in the units of measurement (single bushels vs. thousands).

FIGURE 8.2
Price Exceeds Marginal Revenue in Monopoly

If a firm must lower its price to sell additional output, marginal revenue is less than price. If this firm wants to increase its sales from 1 to 2 bushels per day, for example, price must be reduced from $13 to $12. The marginal revenue of the second bushel is therefore only $11. This is indicated in row C of the table and by point *c* on the graph.

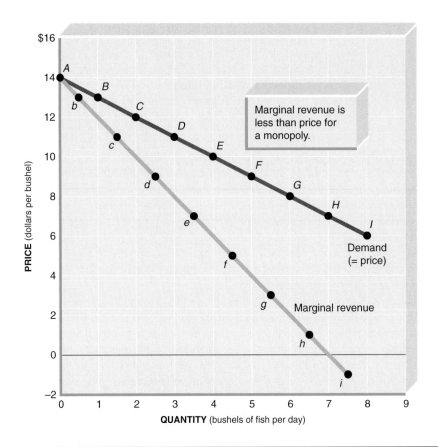

	(1) Quantity	×	(2) Price	=	(3) Total Revenue	(4) Marginal Revenue (= ΔTR ÷ Δq)
A	0		$14		$ 0	
B	1		13		13	$13
C	2		12		24	11
D	3		11		33	9
E	4		10		40	7
F	5		9		45	5
G	6		8		48	3
H	7		7		49	1
I	8		6		48	−1

firms, marginal revenue is equal to price. Hence, a competitive firm can maximize profits by producing at that rate of output where marginal cost equals *price*.

This special adaptation of the profit-maximizing rule doesn't work for a monopolist. The demand curve facing a monopolist is downward-sloping. Because of this, ***marginal revenue isn't equal to price for a monopolist.*** On the contrary, marginal revenue is always *less* than price in a monopoly, which makes it just a bit more difficult to find the profit-maximizing rate of output.

Figure 8.2 is a simple illustration of the relationship between price and marginal revenue. The monopolist can sell one bushel of fish per day at a price of $13. If he wants to sell a larger quantity of fish, however, he has to reduce his price. According to the demand curve shown here, the price must be lowered to $12 to sell two bushels per day. This reduction in price is shown by a movement along the demand curve from point *B* to point *C*.

How much additional revenue does the second bushel bring in? It's tempting to say that it brings in $12, since that's its price. *Marginal revenue (MR),* however, refers to the *change* in *total* revenue that results from a one-unit increase in output. More generally, we use the formula

$$\frac{\text{Marginal}}{\text{revenue}} = \frac{\text{change in total revenue}}{\text{change in quantity sold}} = \frac{\Delta \text{TR}}{\Delta q}$$

where the delta symbol Δ denotes "change in." According to this formula, the marginal revenue of the second bushel is only $11, not the $12 price for which it was sold.

Figure 8.2 summarizes the calculations necessary for computing MR. Row *B* of the table indicates that the total revenue resulting from one sale per day is $13. To increase sales, price must be reduced. Row *C* indicates that total revenue rises to $24 per day when fish sales double. The *increase* in total revenue resulting from the added sales is thus $11. This concept is illustrated in the last column of the table and by point *c* on the marginal revenue curve.

Notice that the MR of the second bushel ($11) is *less* than its price ($12) because both bushels are being sold for $12 apiece. In effect, the firm is giving up the opportunity to sell only one bushel per day at $13 in order to sell a larger quantity at a lower price. In this sense, the firm is sacrificing $1 of potential revenue on the first bushel to increase *total* revenue. Marginal revenue measures the change in total revenue that results.

So long as the demand curve is downward-sloping, MR will always be less than price. Compare columns 2 and 4 of the table in Figure 8.2. At each rate of output, marginal revenue is less than price. This is also evident in the graph: ***The MR curve lies below the demand (price) curve at every point where output is positive.***

Although the presence of market power adds a new wrinkle, the rules of profit maximization remain the same. Now instead of looking for an intersection of marginal cost and price, we look for the intersection of marginal cost and marginal revenue. This is illustrated in Figure 8.3 by the intersection of the MR and MC curves (point *d*). Looking

Profit Maximization

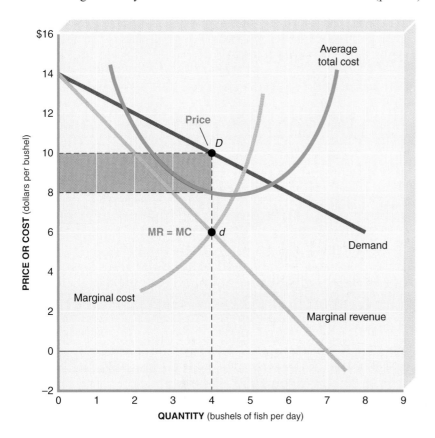

FIGURE 8.3
Profit Maximization

The most profitable rate of output is indicated by the intersection of marginal revenue and marginal cost (point *d*). This intersection (MC = MR) establishes four bushels as the profit maximizing rate of output. Point *D* indicates that consumers will pay $10 per bushel for this much output. Total profits equal price ($10) minus average total cost ($8), multiplied by the quantity sold (4).

down from that intersection, we see that the associated rate of output is four bushels per day. Thus four bushels is the profit-maximizing rate of output.

How much should the monopolist charge for these four bushels? Naturally, the monopolist would like to charge a very high price. But the ability to charge a high price is limited by the demand curve. If the monopolist charges $13, consumers will buy only one bushel, leaving three unsold bushels of rotting fish. Not a pretty picture. As the monopolist will soon learn, *only one price is compatible with the profit-maximizing rate of output.* In this case, the price is $10. This price is found in Figure 8.3 by moving up from the quantity four until reaching the demand curve at point *D*. Point *D* tells us that consumers are able and willing to buy four bushels of fish per day only at the price of $10 each. A monopolist who tries to charge more than $10 won't be able to sell all four bushels.

Figure 8.3 also illustrates the total profits of the catfish monopoly. To compute total profits we can first calculate profit per unit, that is, price minus *average* total cost. In this case, profit per unit is $2. Multiplying profit per unit by the quantity sold (4) gives us total profits of $8 per day, as illustrated by the shaded rectangle.

8.2 MARKET POWER AT WORK: THE COMPUTER MARKET REVISITED

To develop a keener appreciation for the nature of market power, we can return to the computer market of Chapter 7. This time we make some different assumptions about market structure. In particular, assume that a single firm, Universal Electronics, acquires an exclusive patent on the production of the microprocessors that function as the computer's "brain." This one firm is now in a position to deny potential competitors access to the basic ingredient of computers. The patent thus functions as a *barrier to entry,* to be erected or set aside at the will of Universal Electronics.

Universal's management is familiar enough with the principles of economics (including W. C. Fields's advice about never giving a sucker an even break) to know when it's on to a good thing. It's not about to let anyone have a slice of the profit pie. Even the Russians understood this strategy during the heyday of communism. They made sure no one else could produce sable furs that could compete with their monopoly (see the World View box). Let's assume that Universal Electronics

WORLD VIEW

Foxy Soviets Pelt the West

Sable Monopoly Traps Hard Currency, Coats, Capitalists

LENINGRAD—Crown sable from the eastern Siberian region of Barguzin, star of the Soviet fur collection, went on sale just as a deep freeze gripped this former imperial city. . . .

Fur is one of the Soviet Union's best known consumer goods exports. It is also bait for a country eager to trap hard currency: last year, the Soviet Union earned $100 million in fur sales.

In the case of sable, the Soviet Union has something no one else has—in capitalist lingo, a monopoly.

Ivan the Terrible is said to have made the sale of live sables abroad a crime punishable by death. Peter the Great on his travels in the West is said to have carried along trunks of sable skins to use as currency.

In the best-selling novel *Gorky Park,* popular among fur traders, it was the Soviet sable monopoly that was the key to the tangled tale of murderous intrigue.

There is another story, origin and veracity unknown, that an American once traded a rare North American species to the Soviets in exchange for two live Russian sables—only to find when he got home that they had been sterilized.

—Celestine Bohlen

Source: *The Washington Post,* February 5, 1985. © 1985 The Washington Post. Reprinted with permission. www.washingtonpost.com

Analysis: To ward off potential competition, a monopoly must erect barriers to entry. By not letting live sables leave the country, Russia maintained a monopoly on sable furs.

is equally protective of its turf and will refuse to sell or give away any rights to its patent or the chips it produces. That is, Universal Electronics sets itself up as a computer monopoly.

Let's also assume that Universal has a multitude of manufacturing plants, each of which is identical to the typical competitive firm in Chapter 7. This is an unlikely situation because a monopolist would probably achieve *economies of scale* by closing at least a few plants and consolidating production in larger plants. Universal would maintain a multitude of small plants only if constant returns to scale or actual diseconomies of scale were rampant. Nevertheless, by assuming that multiple plants are maintained, we can compare monopoly behaviour with competitive behaviour on the basis of identical cost structures. In particular, if Universal continues to operate the many plants that once comprised the competitive home computer industry, it will confront the same short-run marginal and average cost curves already encountered in Chapter 7. Later in this chapter we relax this assumption of multiplant operations to determine whether, in the long run, a monopolist may actually lower production costs below those of a competitive industry.

Figure 8.4*a* re-creates the marginal costs the typical competitive firm faced in the early stages of the microcomputer boom (from Figure 7.3 and Table 7.1). We now assume that this MC curve also expresses the costs of operating one of Universal's many (identical) plants. Thus, the extension of monopoly control is assumed to have no immediate effect on production costs.

The market demand for computers is also assumed to be unchanged. There's no reason why people should be less willing to buy computers now than they were

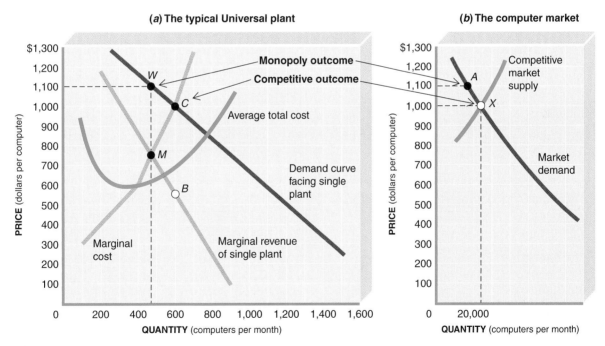

FIGURE 8.4
Initial Conditions in the Monopolized Computer Market

We assume that a monopoly firm (Universal Electronics) would confront the same costs (MC and ATC) and demand as would the competitive industry in Chapter 7. In the initial short-run equilibrium, the competitive price was $1,000 (point C). However, the monopolist isn't bound by the competitive market price. Instead, the monopolist must contend with downward-sloping demand and marginal revenue curves. If each monopoly plant produced

where MC = $1,000 (point C in part *a*), marginal cost (point C) would exceed marginal revenue (point B). To maximize profits, the monopolist must find that rate of output where MC = MR (point M in part *a*). That rate of output can be sold at the monopoly price of $1,100 (point W in part *a*). Part *b* illustrates the market implications of the monopolist's production decision: A reduced quantity is sold at a higher price (point A).

when the market was competitive. Most consumers have no notion of how many firms produce a product. Even if they knew, there's no reason why their demand for the product would change. Thus, Figure 8.4b expresses an unchanged demand for computers.

Our immediate concern is to determine how Universal Electronics, as a monopolist, will respond to these unchanged demand and cost curves. Will it produce exactly as many computers as the competitive industry did? Will it sell the computers at the same price that the competitive industry did? Will it improve the product as much or as fast?

The Production Decision

Like any producer, Universal Electronics will strive to produce its output at the rate that maximizes total profits. But unlike competitive firms, Universal will explicitly take account of the fact that an increase in output will put downward pressure on computer prices. This may threaten corporate profits.

The implications of Universal's market position for the *production decision* of its many plants can be seen in the new price and marginal revenue curves imposed on each of its manufacturing plants. Universal can't afford to let each of its plants compete with the others, expanding output and driving down prices; that's the kind of folly reserved for truly competitive firms. Instead, Universal will seek to *coordinate* the production decisions of its plants, instructing all plant managers to expand or contract output simultaneously, to achieve the corporate goal of profit maximization.

A simultaneous reduction of output by each Universal plant will lead to a significant reduction in the quantity of computers supplied to the market. This reduced supply will cause a move up the market demand curve to higher prices. By the same token, an expansion of output by all Universal plants will lead to an increase in the quantity supplied to the market and a slide down the market demand curve. As a consequence, each of the monopolist's plants effectively confronts a downward-sloping demand curve. These downward-sloping demand curves are illustrated in Figure 8.4a.[1]

Notice that in Figure 8.4b the *market* demand for computers is unchanged; only the demand curve confronting each plant (firm) has changed. A competitive *industry,* like a monopoly, must obey the law of demand. But the individual firms that comprise a competitive industry all act independently, *as if* they could sell unlimited quantities at the prevailing price. That is, they all act as if they confronted a horizontal demand curve at the market price of $1,000. A competitive firm that doesn't behave in this fashion will simply lose sales to other firms. In contrast, *a monopolist not only foresees the impact of increased production on market price but can also prevent such production increases by its separate plants.*

Marginal Revenue. The downward-sloping demand curve now confronting each Universal plant implies that marginal revenue no longer equals price. Notice that the marginal revenue curve in Figure 8.4a lies *below* the demand curve at every rate of output. Because marginal revenue is less than price for a monopoly, Universal's plants would no longer wish to produce up to the point where marginal cost equals price. *Only firms that confront a horizontal demand curve (perfect competitors) equate marginal cost and price.* Universal's plants must stick to the generic profit-maximizing rule about equating marginal revenue and marginal cost. Should the individual plant managers forget this rule, Universal's central management will fire them.

The output and price implications of Universal's monopoly position become apparent as we examine the new revenue and cost relationships. Recall that the equilibrium price of computers in the early stages of the home computer boom was

---

[1]The demand and marginal revenue curves in Figure 8.4a are illustrative; they're not derived from earlier tables. As discussed above, we're assuming that the central management of Universal determines the profit-maximizing rate of output and then instructs all individual plants to produce equal shares of that output.

$1,000. This equilibrium price is indicated in Figure 8.4*b* by the intersection of the competitive market supply curve with the market demand curve (point *X*). Each competitive *firm* produced up to the point where marginal cost (MC) equaled that price (point *C* in Figure 8.4*a*). At that point, each competitive firm was producing 600 computers a month.

Reduced Output. The emergence of Universal as a monopolist alters these production decisions. Now each Universal plant *does* have an impact on market price because its behaviour is imitated simultaneously by all Universal plants. In fact, the marginal revenue associated with the 600th computer is only $575, as indicated by point *B* in Figure 8.4*a*. At this rate of output, the typical Universal plant would be operating with marginal costs ($1,000) far in excess of marginal revenues ($575). Such behaviour is inconsistent with profit maximization.

The enlightened Universal plant manager will soon discover that the profit-maximizing rate of output is less than 600 computers per month. In Figure 8.4*a* we see that the marginal revenue and marginal cost curves intersect at point *M*. This MR = MC intersection occurs at an output level of only 475 computers per month. Accordingly, the typical Universal plant will want to produce *fewer* computers than were produced by the typical competitive firm in the early stages of the home computer boom. Recall that individual competitive firms had no incentive to engage in such production cutbacks. They couldn't alter the market supply curve or price on their own and weren't coordinated by a central management. Thus, the first consequence of Universal's monopoly position is a reduction in the rate of industry output.

The reduction in output at each Universal plant translates automatically into a decrease in the *quantity supplied* to the market. As consumers compete for this reduced market supply, they'll bid computer prices up. We can observe the increased prices in Figure 8.4 by looking at either the typical Universal plant or the computer market. Notice that in Figure 8.4*a* the price is determined by moving directly up from point *M* to the demand curve confronting the typical Universal plant. The demand curve always tells how much consumers are willing to pay for any given quantity. Hence, once we've determined the quantity that's going to be supplied (475 computers per month), we can look at the demand curve to determine the price ($1,100 at point *W*) that consumers will pay for these computers. That is,

The Monopoly Price

- *The intersection of the marginal revenue and marginal cost curves establishes the profit-maximizing rate of output.*
- *The demand curve tells us how much consumers are willing to pay for that specific quantity of output.*

Figure 8.4*a* shows how Universal's monopoly position results in both reduced output and increased prices. This result is also evident in Figure 8.4*b*, where we see that a smaller quantity supplied to the market will force a move up the demand curve to the higher price of $1,100 per computer (point *A*).

Universal's objective was and remains the maximization of profits. That it has succeeded in its effort can be confirmed by scrutinizing Figure 8.5. As you can see, the typical Universal plant ends up selling 475 computers a month at a price of $1,100 each (point *W*). The *average total cost (ATC)* of production at this rate of output is approximately $620 (point *K*), as was detailed in Table 7.1.

Monopoly Profits

As always, we can compute total profit as

$$\text{Total profit} = \text{profit per unit} \times \text{quantity sold}$$

In this case, we see that

$$\text{Total profit} = (\$1,100 - \$620) \times 475$$

$$= \$228,000$$

FIGURE 8.5

Monopoly Profits: The Typical Universal Plant

The profit-maximizing rate of output occurs where the marginal cost and marginal revenue curves intersect (point *M*). The demand curve indicates the price (point *W*) that consumers will pay for this output. Total profit equals price (*W*) minus average total cost (*K*) multiplied by the quantity sold (475). Total profits are represented by the shaded rectangle.

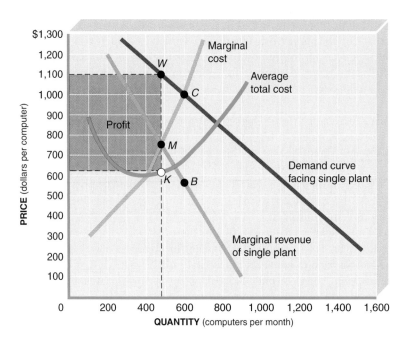

This figure may be compared with the monthly profit of $190,000 earned by the typical competitive firm in the early stages of the computer boom (see Table 7.1).

It's apparent from these profit figures that Universal management has learned its economic principles well. By reducing the output of each plant and raising prices a little, it has managed to enlarge the size of the profit pie while keeping it all to itself, of course. This can be seen again in Figure 8.6, which is an enlarged illustration of the *market* situation for the home computer industry. The figure translates the economics of our single-plant and competitive-firm comparison into the dimensions of the whole industry.

Figure 8.6 reaffirms that the competitive industry in Chapter 7 initially produces the quantity q_c and sells it at a price of $1,000 each. Its profits are denoted by the rectangle formed by the points *R, X, U, T*. The monopolist, on the other hand, produces the

FIGURE 8.6

Monopoly Profit: The Entire Company

Total profits of the monopolist (including all plants) are illustrated by the shaded rectangle. The monopolist's total output q_m is determined by the intersection of the (industry) MR and MC curves. The price of this output is determined by the market demand curve (point *A*). In contrast, a competitive industry would produce q_c computers in the short run and sell them at a lower price (*X*) and profit per unit (*X* − *U*). Those profits would attract new entrants until long-run equilibrium (point *V*) was reached. (See Figure 7.8 for a summary of competitive market equilibrium.)

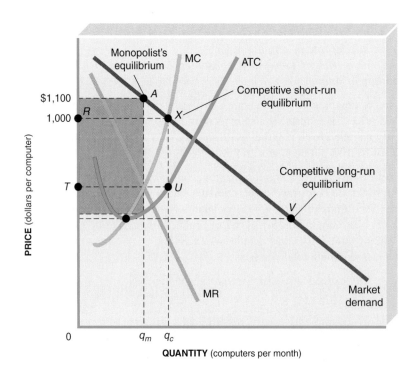

smaller q_m and charges a higher price, $1,100. The monopoly firm's profits are indicated by the larger profit rectangle shaded in the figure. We see that *a monopoly receives larger profits than a comparable competitive industry by reducing the quantity supplied and pushing prices up.* The larger profits make Universal very happy and make consumers a little sadder and wiser. Consumers are now paying more and getting less.

The higher profits Universal Electronics attained as a result of its monopoly position aren't the end of the story. The existence of economic profit tends to bring profit-hungry entrepreneurs swarming like locusts. In the competitive home computer industry in Chapter 7, the lure of high profits brought about an enormous expansion of home computer output and a steep decline in home computer prices. In Figure 8.6 the long-run equilibrium of a competitive industry is indicated by point V. What then can we expect to happen in the home computer market now that Universal has a monopoly position and is enjoying huge profits?

Remember that Universal is now assumed to have an exclusive patent on microprocessor chips and can use this patent as an impassable barrier to entry. Consequently, would-be competitors can swarm around Universal's profits until their wings drop off; Universal isn't about to let them in on the spoils. By locking out the potential competition, Universal can prevent the surge in computer output that pushed prices down the market demand curve. As long as Universal is able to keep out the competition, only the more affluent consumers will be able to use computers. The same phenomenon explains why ticket prices for live concerts are so high. Because Clear Channel Entertainment controls most concert venues and Ticketmaster is the exclusive ticket distributor, fans have to pay monopoly prices to see Godsmack, Bare Naked Ladies, Pearl Jam, or other live concerts (see the Applications box). A monopoly has no incentive to move from point A in Figure 8.6, and there's no competitive pressure to force such a move. Universal may discover ways to reduce the costs of production and thus lower prices, but there's no *pressure* on it to do so, as there was in the competitive situation.

Barriers to Entry

APPLICATIONS

Concerts Becoming a Pricier Affair; Music Industry Consolidation Has Brought Higher Ticket Fees. Some Cry Foul.

Members of the popular heavy-rock band Godsmack say they want to make tickets affordable for their current U.S. tour. But the economics of the concert industry may jar fans harder than the mosh pit at the band's show.

The face value of a general admission ticket to Godsmack's concert Wednesday at Verizon Wireless Amphitheatre is $20. But no one attending the band's performance gets to pay that amount.

Instead, fans who purchase tickets on the phone or online are socked with a series of surcharges that boost the price to $35.60. These added costs, tacked on by distribution giant Ticketmaster and concert promotion conglomerate Clear Channel Entertainment, include a convenience fee, a facility fee and a handling charge.

Moreover, a hidden $3.50 parking fee is buried in the price of each ticket by Clear Channel, owner of the Verizon Amphitheatre in Irvine. All told, the fees add a 116% markup to the cost of a $16.50 ticket. . . .

In recent years, Clear Channel has emerged as the dominant force in the $1.6-billion concert industry. . . .

"They can pretty much dictate the costs, ad rates and ticket prices," said Jon Stoll, president of Fantasma Productions, a competing promoter in West Palm Beach, Fla. "If one company controls the live-music industry, there's nobody that can really bring ticket prices down."

—Jeff Leeds

Source: *Los Angeles Times*, July 17, 2001. © 2001 Tribune Media Services, Inc. All rights reserved. Reprinted with permission.

Analysis: Control of concert sites and ticket distribution allow Clear Channel Entertainment and Ticketmaster to charge monopoly prices for live concerts.

8.3 A COMPARATIVE PERSPECTIVE OF MARKET POWER

The different outcomes of the computer industry under competitive and monopoly conditions illustrate basic features of market structures. We may summarize the sequence of events that occurs in each type of market structure as follows:

COMPETITIVE INDUSTRY	MONOPOLY INDUSTRY
• High prices and profits signal consumers' demand for more output.	• High prices and profits signal consumers' demand for more output.
• The high profits attract new suppliers.	• Barriers to entry are erected to exclude potential competition.
• Production and supplies expand.	• Production and supplies are constrained.
• Prices slide down the market demand curve.	• Prices don't move down the market demand curve.
• A new equilibrium is established wherein more of the desired product is produced, its price falls, average costs of production approach their minimum, and economic profits approach zero.	• No new equilibrium is established; average costs aren't necessarily at or near a minimum, and economic profits are at a maximum.
• Price equals marginal cost throughout the process.	• Price exceeds marginal cost at all times.
• Throughout the process, there's great pressure to keep ahead of the profit squeeze by reducing costs or improving product quality.	• There's no squeeze on profits and thus no pressure to reduce costs or improve product quality.

In our discussion, we assumed that the competitive industry and the monopoly both started from the same position—an initial equilibrium in which the price of computers is $1,000. In reality, an industry may manifest concentrations of market power *before* such an equilibrium is established. That is, the sequence of events we've depicted may be altered (with step 3 occurring first, for example). Nevertheless, the basic distinctions between competitive and monopolistic behaviour are evident.

Productivity Advances. To the extent that monopolies behave as we've discussed, they affect not just the price and output of a specific product but broader economic outcomes as well. Remember that competitive industries tend, in the long run, to produce at minimum average costs. Competitive industries also pursue cost reductions and product improvements relentlessly. These pressures tend to expand our production possibilities. No such forces are at work in the monopoly we've discussed here. Hence, there's a basic tendency for monopolies to inhibit productivity advances and economic growth.

The Mix of Output. Another important feature of competitive markets is their observed tendency toward *marginal cost pricing*. Marginal cost pricing is important to consumers because it permits rational choices among alternative goods and services. In particular, it informs consumers of the true opportunity costs of various goods, thereby allowing them to choose the mix of output that delivers the most utility with available resources. In our monopoly example, however, consumers end up getting fewer computers than they'd like, while the economy continues to produce other, less desired goods. Thus, the mix of output shifted away from computers when Universal took over the industry.

The power to influence prices and product flows may have far-reaching consequences for our economic welfare. Changes in prices and product flows directly influence the level and composition of output, employment and resource allocation, the level and distribution of income, and, of course, the level and structure of prices. Hence, firms that wield significant market power affect all dimensions of economic welfare.

Political Power. Market power isn't the only kind of power wielded in society, of course. Political power, for example, is a different kind of power and important in its own right. Indeed, the power to influence an election or to sway a parliamentary vote may ultimately be more important than the power to increase the price of laundry soap. Nevertheless, market power is a force that influences the way we live, the incomes we earn, and our relationships with other countries. Moreover, market power may be the basis for political power: The individual or firm with considerable market power is likely to have the necessary resources to influence an election or sway a vote on a parliamentary committee.

The Limits to Power

Even though market power enables a producer to manipulate market outcomes, there's a clear limit to the exercise of power. Even a monopolist can't get everything it wants. Universal, for example, would really like to sell q_m computers at a price of $1,500 each because that kind of price would bring it even greater profits. Yet, despite its monopoly position, Universal is constrained to sell that quantity of computers at the lower price of $1,100 each. Even monopolists have their little disappointments.

The ultimate limit to a monopolist's power is evident in Figure 8.6. Universal's attainment of a monopoly position allows it only one prerogative: the ability to alter the quantity of output *supplied* to the market. This is no small prerogative, but it's far from absolute power. Universal, and every other monopolist, must still contend with the market *demand* curve. Note again that the new equilibrium in Figure 8.6 occurs at a point on the *unchanged* demand curve. In effect, ***a monopolist has the opportunity to pick any point on the market demand curve and designate it as the new market equilibrium.*** The point it selects will depend on its own perceptions of effort, profit, and risk (in this case point A, determined by the intersection of marginal revenue and marginal cost).

The ultimate constraint on the exercise of market power, then, resides in the market demand curve. How great a constraint the demand curve imposes depends largely on the **price elasticity of demand.** The greater the price elasticity of demand, the more a monopolist will be frustrated in attempts to establish both high prices and high volume. Consumers will simply reduce their purchases if price is increased. If, however, consumer demand is highly inelastic—if consumers need or want that product badly and few viable substitutes are available—the monopolist can reap tremendous profits from market power.

Notice, however, that a monopolist will always operate on the elastic portion of a linear demand curve. How do we know this? Well, recall that the profit-maximizing rule implies that monopolists choose production where MR = MC. We can assume that the production of an additional unit of a good will lead to positive marginal costs—that is, each time a firm produces a good, they will incur additional costs. At best, their marginal cost is zero. Therefore, given that marginal costs are positive (or zero), a monopolist's profit-maximizing level of output can only occur where the marginal revenue is also positive (or zero).

Now, if we look closely at the relationship between a linear demand curve and its associated marginal revenue curve, we see that the marginal revenue curve has the same price-intercept (*y*-axis) as the demand curve, but is twice as steep as the demand curve. As a consequence, it intersects the quantity axis (MR = 0) at a level of output that is equal to the midpoint of the demand curve. By definition of a linear demand curve, this point is also associated with the midpoint of the demand curve's price axis.[2] Remember from our earlier discussions on elasticity (see Chapter 4), that the elasticity of demand at the midpoint of a linear demand curve is equal to one (i.e., it is unit elastic). Beyond this point, all subsequent levels of output are associated with negative MR values and elasticities of demand less than one (i.e., inelastic portion of the demand curve). Therefore, the positive values of MR are only associated with the elastic portion of the demand curve.

Price Discrimination

> price discrimination: The sale of an identical good at different prices to different consumers by a single seller.

Even in situations where the *market* demand is relatively elastic, a monopolist may be able to extract high prices. A monopolist has the power not only to raise the market price of a good (by reducing the quantity supplied) but also to charge various prices for the same good. Recall that the market demand curve reflects the combined willingness of many individuals to buy. Some of those individuals are willing to buy the good at prices higher than the market price, just as other individuals will buy only at lower prices. A monopolist may be able to increase total profits by selling each unit of the good separately, at a price each *individual* consumer is willing to pay. This practice is called **price discrimination.**

The airline industry has practiced price discrimination for many years. Basically, there are two distinct groups of travellers: business and nonbusiness travellers. Business executives must fly from one city to another on a certain day and at a particular time. They typically make flight arrangements on short notice and may have no other way to get to their destination. Nonbusiness travellers, such as people on vacation and students going home during semester break, usually have more flexible schedules. They may plan their trips weeks or months in advance and often have the option of travelling by car, bus, or train.

The different travel needs of business and vacation travellers are reflected in their respective demand curves. Business demand for air travel tends to be less price-elastic than the demand of nonbusiness travellers. Few business executives would stop flying if airfares increased. Higher airfares would, however, discourage air travel by nonbusiness travellers.

What should airlines do in this case? Should they *raise* airfares to take advantage of the relative price inelasticity of business demand, or should they *lower* airfares to attract more nonbusiness travellers?

They should do both. In fact, they *have* done both. The airlines offer a full-fare ride, available at any time, and a discount-fare ride, available only by purchasing a ticket in advance and agreeing to some restrictions on time of departure. The advance purchase and other restrictions on discount fares effectively exclude most business travellers, who end up paying full fare. The higher full fare doesn't, however, discourage most nonbusiness travellers, who can fly at a discount. Consequently, the airlines are able to sell essentially identical units of the same good (an airplane ride) at substantially different prices to different customers. Indeed, by experimenting with various discount fares and travel restrictions, airlines can discriminate even more thoroughly among passengers, thereby reaping the highest possible *average* price for the quantity supplied. Plumbers, lawyers, and car dealers commonly practice the same type of price discrimination. In all these cases, the seller may "adjust" the price to the income and taste of each individual consumer. In effect, the seller is able to "divide and conquer" the individual consumers who are positioned along the length of the market demand curve. A monopolist is best positioned to engage in price discrimination, since consumers have no competitive alternatives.

Entry Barriers

It's the lack of competitors that gives monopolists such pricing power. Accordingly, ***the preservation of monopoly power depends on keeping potential competitors out of the market.*** A monopolist doesn't want anyone else to produce an *identical* product

---

[2]In Figure 8.3, for example, the marginal revenue curve intersects the quantity axis at a value of seven bushels of fish per day. The price corresponding to this quantity ($7) lies at the midpoint of the demand curve since the price intercept is $14.

APPLICATIONS

Privatization of Alcohol Trade in Ontario and Quebec: Consumers Would Come out Ahead in an Alberta-style System, Says the MEI

MONTREAL, October 05, 2005—A new study from the Montreal Economic Institute concludes that privatizing the Liquor Control Board of Ontario (LCBO) and the Société des alcools du Québec (SAQ) would not only benefit consumers from these provinces but could also result in higher liquor sale revenues for both the Ontario and Quebec governments.

Strongly backed by figures, the Research Paper published today compares the performances of the LCBO and SAQ, which enjoy a similar monopoly, with the retail liquor market in Alberta, which was largely liberalized in the early 1990s. Data shows that this system provides a number of advantages to consumers:

Number of Stores:

The number of stores per 100,000 inhabitants is five times higher in Alberta (42.1) than in Ontario (7.7) and three times higher than Quebec (12.8). Even in absolute numbers, Alberta (1,087 stores) beats out Ontario (779) and Quebec (801).

Availability of Products:

Examining the number of products available on the provincial market, Quebec (7,148 products) does better than Ontario

(3,449) but Alberta, with its liberalized market, offers consumers many more products (11,575) than the SAQ or LCBO.

Product Prices:

Various price surveys lead to the conclusion that Alberta consumers pay amounts that are similar to those in other provinces, though prices may differ according to individual products or product groups.

Government Revenues:

The fear that privatization of the LCBO and SAQ would cause the Ontario and Quebec governments to lose a stable source of income is not justified. In 2002–03, Alberta's flat markup on alcoholic beverages brought in more for the provincial government ($24.27 per litre of absolute alcohol sold) than the Ontario ($23.42) or Quebec ($23.43) governments collected in dividends from their respective publicly owned monopolies.

Source: "Privatization of Alcohol Trade in Ontario and Quebec: Consumers Would Come out Ahead in an Alberta-style System, Says the MEI," Montreal Economic Institute, Media News, October 5, 2005, http://www.iedm.org. Used with the permission of Montreal Economic Institute.

Analysis: Competition can lead to a greater choice and access of products.

or even a *close substitute*. To do that, a monopoly must erect and maintain barriers to market entry. It was the absence of significant entry barriers that permitted iPod clones to attack Apple's profits (Applications box, p. 167). Some of the entry barriers used to repel such attacks include:

Patents. This was the critical barrier in the mythical Universal Electronics case. A government-awarded patent gives a producer 20 years of exclusive rights to produce a particular product. The Polaroid Corporation used its patents to keep Eastman Kodak and other potential rivals out of the market for instant development cameras.

Monopoly Franchises. The government also creates and maintains monopolies by giving a single firm the exclusive right to supply a particular good or service, even though other firms can produce it. The Liquor Control Board of Ontario (LCBO), for example, is granted exclusive right to retail wine and liquor in Ontario. Private companies may legally purchase the right to "monopoly" power. For an acceptable price, your campus cafeteria may grant an exclusive right to a private company to supply all your food and beverage requirements. Or perhaps the Bank of Nova Scotia may purchase the right to be the sole supplier of banking services on your campus. Ticketmaster has the exclusive right to sell concert tickets to events promoted by Clear Channel Entertainment (now Live Nation Inc.) until its contract expires at the end of 2008.

Control of Key Inputs. A company may lock out competition by securing exclusive access to key inputs. Airlines need landing rights and terminal gates to compete. Oil

Pepsi Takes Coke to Court

Rival Presses for Monopoly of Fountain Sales, Suit Says

NEW YORK, May 7—Pepsi accused Coke today of monopolizing the sales of fountain soft drinks at restaurant chains and movie theatres by threatening to take away Coke from distributors that carried Pepsi as well.

The lawsuit filed in U.S. District Court did not pertain to sales of bottles or cans of the soft drinks, only to fountain-dispensed drinks handled by large food service distributors who control deliveries to chains of restaurants and theatres.

The lawsuit, filed by Pepsi-Cola's parent, PepsiCo Inc., asked the court to restrain Coca-Cola from entering into agreements with its distributors to exclude Pepsi and to award Pepsi undetermined damages.

"Coca-Cola's message to food service distributors is clear: If a distributor carries Pepsi at a customer's request, the distributor will be terminated by Coke," the lawsuit said.

Source: *The Washington Post*, May 8, 1998. © 1998 The Washington Post. Reprinted with permission. www.washingtonpost.com

Analysis: A firm can acquire a monopoly by attaining exclusive access to key inputs or distribution systems.

and gas producers need pipelines to supply their product. Utility companies need transmission networks to supply consumers with electricity. Pepsi says it needs access to Coke-dominated restaurants (see the Applications box above). Software vendors need to know the features of computer operating systems. If a single company controls these critical inputs, it can lock out potential competition. That's alleged to be a prime source of Microsoft's monopoly power.

Lawsuits. In the event that competitors actually surmount other entry barriers, a monopoly may sue it out of existence. Typically, start-up firms are rich in ideas but cash poor. They need to get their products to the market quickly to generate some cash. A timely lawsuit alleging patent or copyright infringement can derail such a company by absorbing critical management, cash, and time. Long before the merits of the lawsuit are adjudicated, the company may be forced to withdraw from the market.

Acquisition. When all else fails, a monopolist may simply purchase a potential competitor. As the cartoon on the next page suggests, mergers tend to raise consumer prices.

Economies of Scale. Last but far from least, a monopoly may persist because of economies of scale. If large firms have a substantial cost advantage over smaller firms, the smaller firms may not be able to compete. We look at this entry barrier again in a moment.

8.4 PROS AND CONS OF MARKET POWER

Despite the strong case against market power, it's conceivable that monopolies could also benefit society. One argument made for concentrations of market power is that monopolies have greater ability to pursue research and development. Another argument is that the lure of market power creates a tremendous incentive for invention and innovation. A third argument in defense of monopoly is that large companies can produce goods more efficiently than smaller firms. Finally, it's argued that even monopolies have to worry about *potential* competition and will behave accordingly.

Research and Development

In principle, monopolies are well positioned to undertake valuable research and development. First, such firms are sheltered from the constant pressure of competition. Second, they have the resources (monopoly profits) with which to carry out expensive

Analysis: Mergers and acquisitions reduce competition in an industry. The increased industry concentration may lead to higher prices.

R&D functions. The manager of a perfectly competitive firm, by contrast, has to worry about day-to-day production decisions and profit margins. As a result, she is unable to take the longer view necessary for significant research and development and couldn't afford to purchase such a view even if she could see it.

The basic problem with the R&D argument is that it says nothing about *incentives*. Although monopolists have a clear financial advantage in pursuing research and development activities, they have no clear incentive to do so. Research and development aren't necessarily required for profitable survival. In fact, research and development that make existing plant and equipment technologically obsolete run counter to a monopolist's vested interest and so may actually be suppressed (see the Applications box). In contrast,

APPLICATIONS

Jury Rules Magnetek Unit Is Liable for Keeping Technology off Market

SAN FRANCISCO—Is a company liable if it deliberately keeps a technology off the market? Apparently so, judging from an unusual ruling by a California jury.

A county superior court jury in Oakland ordered a unit of Magnetek Inc. to pay $25.8 million to two California entrepreneurs and their companies. They charged that the unit had failed to bring the pair's energy-saving fluorescent-light technology to market in a profitable manner, suppressing it in favor of an outmoded technology.

The lawsuit reads like familiar legends of big business quashing inventions that threaten its interests. . . .

In 1984, the two entrepreneurs, C. R. Stevens and William R. Alling, charged that Universal Manufacturing Corp., now a unit of Los Angeles–based Magnetek, buried a technology through which fluorescent lights use 70 percent less energy. The two said they sold Universal the technology, called a solid-state ballast, in 1981 after the company promised to market it aggressively.

Instead, they charged, Universal suppressed the technology to protect its less-efficient existing ballast models. "They told us they were going to be first on the market with our tech, yet they planned otherwise," said Mr. Alling.

—Stephen Kreider Yoder

Source: *The Wall Street Journal,* January 10, 1990. Reprinted by permission of The Wall Street Journal. © 1990 Dow Jones & Company, Inc. All rights reserved worldwide. www.wsj.com

Analysis: A monopoly has little incentive (no competitive pressure) to pursue R&D. In fact, R&D that threatens established products or processes may be suppressed.

a perfectly competitive firm can't continue to make significant profits unless it stays ahead of the competition. This pressure constitutes a significant incentive to discover new products or new and cheaper ways of producing existing products.

Entrepreneurial Incentives

The second defense of market power uses a novel incentive argument. Every business is out to make a buck, and it's the quest for profits that keeps industries running. Thus, it's argued, even greater profit prizes will stimulate more entrepreneurial activity. Small, creature firms will work harder and longer if they can dream of one day possessing a whole monopoly.

The incentive argument for market power is enticing but not entirely convincing. After all, an innovator can make substantial profits in a competitive market before the competition catches up. Recall that the early birds did get the worm in the competitive computer industry (see Chapter 7), even though profit margins were later squeezed. It's not evident that the profit incentives available in a competitive industry are at all inadequate.

We must also recall the arguments about research and development efforts. A monopolist has little incentive to pursue R&D. Furthermore, entrepreneurs who might pursue product innovation or technological improvements may be dissuaded by their inability to penetrate a monopolized market. The barriers to entry that surround market power may not only keep out potential competitors but also lock out promising ideas.

Economies of Scale

A third defense of market power is the most convincing. A large firm, it's argued, can produce goods at a lower unit (average) cost than a small firm. If such *economies of scale* exist, we could attain greater efficiency (higher productivity) by permitting firms to grow to market-dominating size.

We sidestepped this argument in our story about the Universal Electronics monopoly. We explicitly assumed that Universal confronted the same production costs as the competitive industry. We simply converted each typical competitive firm into a separate plant owned and operated by Universal. Universal wasn't able to produce computers any more cheaply than the competitive counterpart, and we concerned ourselves only with the different production decisions made by competitive and monopolistic firms.

A monopoly *could,* however, attain greater cost savings. By centralizing various functions it might be able to eliminate some duplicative efforts. It might also shut down some plants and concentrate production in fewer facilities. If these kinds of efficiencies are attained, a monopoly would offer attractive resource savings. This is why the Canadian Competition Tribunal—and subsequently the Federal Court of Appeal—approved a merger between two major companies involved in the retailing and wholesaling of propane and related equipment in Canada (see the Applications box on the next page).

There's no guarantee, however, of such economies of scale. As we observed in Chapter 5, increasing the size (scale) of a plant may actually *reduce* operating efficiency (see Figure 5.10). In evaluating the economies-of-scale argument for market power, then, we must recognize that ***efficiency and size don't necessarily go hand in hand. Some firms and industries may be subject to economies of scale, but others won't.***

Natural Monopolies. Industries that exhibit economies of scale over the entire range of market output are called *natural monopolies.* In these cases, one single firm can produce the entire market supply more efficiently than any large number of (smaller) firms. As the size (scale) of the one firm increases, its minimum average costs continue to fall. These economies of scale give the one large producer a decided advantage over would-be rivals. Hence, ***economies of scale act as a "natural" barrier to entry.***

Local cable and utility services are classic examples of natural monopoly. A single cable or utility company can supply the market more efficiently than a large number of competing firms.

APPLICATIONS

Competition Bureau Appeals Decision in Superior Propane Case

OTTAWA, September 6, 2000—The Competition Bureau announced today that it has filed a notice of appeal with the Federal Court regarding the Competition Tribunal's recent decision to allow the Superior Propane/ICG Propane merger to proceed on the basis of efficiencies. The Bureau has requested that its appeal, which focuses on the efficiency defence, be dealt with expeditiously.

On August 30, 2000, the Competition Tribunal rendered its decision regarding the merger of Superior Propane and ICG Propane. The Tribunal found that the merger was likely to prevent competition in Atlantic Canada and lessen competition substantially in many local markets across Canada, as well as for national account customers. It recognized that, as a result of the merger, Superior and ICG would have a combined market share of 70 percent on a national basis and a monopoly in a number of markets. The Tribunal also acknowledged the high level of concentration, high barriers to entry, lack of effective remaining competition, and the absence of foreign competition in the propane industry in Canada.

Nevertheless, the majority of the Tribunal concluded that the two companies should be allowed to merge (with partial divestiture of ICG) because it was satisfied that the efficiencies presented by Superior would be greater than, and would offset the effects of, any prevention or lessening of competition. However, in a strongly worded dissent, one of the three panel members concluded that Superior had not established an efficiencies defence and that the Tribunal should make the order for total divestiture of ICG.

Source: Competition Bureau Canada, "What is the Competition Bureau?" Competition Bureau, 2007. Reproduced with the permission of the Minister of Public Works and Government Services Canada, 2007.

Analysis: While mergers can lead to monopolies, the efficiency benefits associated with economies of scale can outweigh the costs of reduced competition.

Although natural monopolies are economically desirable, they may be abused. We must ask whether and to what extent consumers are reaping some benefit from the efficiency a natural monopoly makes possible. Do consumers end up with lower prices, expanded output, and better service? Or does the monopoly keep most of the benefits for itself, in the form of higher prices and profits? Multiplex movie theatres, for example, achieve economies of scale by sharing operating and concession facilities among as many as 30 screens. But do moviegoers get lower prices for movies or popcorn? Not often. Because megamultiplex theatres tend to drive out competition, they don't have to reduce prices when costs drop. Under such circumstances, we may need government "trustbusters" to ensure that the benefits of increased efficiency are shared with consumers. (The potential and pitfalls of government regulation are examined in Chapter 11.)

Governmental regulators aren't necessarily the only force keeping monopolists in line. Even though a firm may produce the entire supply of a particular product at present, it may face *potential* competition from other firms. Potential rivals may be sitting on the sidelines, watching how well the monopoly fares. If it does too well, these rivals may enter the industry, undermining the monopoly structure and profits. In such **contestable markets,** monopoly behaviour may be restrained by potential competition.

How "contestable" a market is depends not so much on its structure as on entry barriers. If entry barriers are insurmountable, would-be competitors are locked out of the market. But if entry barriers are modest, they'll be surmounted when the lure of monopoly profits is irresistible. When Cable News Network's (CNN) profits reached irresistible proportions, both domestic and foreign companies decided to invade CNN's monopoly market (see the World View on the next page). Since then, CNN hasn't been nearly as profitable.

From the perspective of contestable markets, the whole case against monopoly is misconceived. Market *structure* per se isn't a problem; what counts is market *behaviour*.

Contestable Markets

contestable market: An imperfectly competitive industry subject to potential entry if prices or profits increase.

New Competition May Mean Bad News for CNN

A growing crowd of media giants wants to make sure that most people don't get their news from Cable News Network. They're all gunning for the lucrative Turner Broadcasting System unit with a host of rival 24-hour news networks, spurred by new technologies for delivering TV programs and shifting alliances in the cable business. . . .

Last year, with the market to itself, CNN and its related news businesses, including a Headline News channel, generated about $227 million in operating profit for Turner Broadcasting System Inc.

But CNN may not keep its monopoly for long. If the proposed services can overcome huge distribution hurdles caused by lack of space on crowded cable systems, their strong brand names and well-known correspondents and anchors may be enough to lure viewers away from CNN.

Capital Cities/ABC Inc., for example, said yesterday that it will launch a 24-hour news service in the U.S. in 1997, using ABC News's star talent and rerunning some of its popular shows. . . .

Other companies have similar ideas. General Electric Co.'s NBC for the past year has been putting together a detailed plan for launching its own national news network with a strong local component. . . .

Meanwhile, Britain's BBC is also trying to start a global news channel. And News Corp. Chairman Rupert Murdoch, whose British BSkyB service already offers a 24-hour news channel, said last week that he wants to launch a U.S. competitor to CNN. . . .

Behind all the expansion plans is a straightforward economic calculation: Companies already in the news business think they can squeeze out more profits with relatively little new cost by expanding to 24 hours of TV news.

—Elizabeth Jensen and John Lippman

Analysis: As a monopolist's profits grow, would-be competitors will try to overcome barriers to entry. If entry is possible, a monopolized market may be contestable.

If potential rivals force a monopolist to behave like a competitive firm, then monopoly imposes no cost on consumers or on society at large.

Potential competitors will always look for ways to enter a profitable market. Eventually they'll surmount entry barriers or develop substitute goods that supplant a monopolist's products.

Consumer advocates assert that we shouldn't have to wait for the invisible hand to dismantle a monopoly. They say the government should intervene to dismantle a monopoly or at least force it to change its behaviour. Then consumers would get lower prices and better products a whole lot sooner.

Microsoft's dominant position in the computer industry highlights this issue. Microsoft produces the operating system (Windows) that powers 9 out of 10 personal computers. It also produces a huge share of applications software, including Internet browsers. Critics fear that this kind of monopoly power is a threat to consumers. They say Microsoft charges too much for its systems software, suppresses substitute technologies, and pushes potential competitors around. In short, Microsoft is a bully. Applying the current U.S. **antitrust** legislation, the Department of Justice filed an antitrust action against Microsoft.

Microsoft: Bully or Genius?

antitrust: Government intervention to alter market structure or prevent abuse of market power.

The Microsoft Case. The first accusation levelled against Microsoft was that it thwarted competitors in operating systems by erecting entry barriers such as exclusive purchase agreements with computer manufacturers. These agreements either forbade manufacturers from installing a rival operating system or made it prohibitively expensive. The second accusation against Microsoft was that it used its monopoly position in *operating* systems to gain an unfair advantage in the *applications* market. It did this by not disclosing operating features that make applications run more efficiently or by bundling software, thereby forcing consumers to accept Microsoft applications along with the operating system. When the latter occurs, consumers have little incentive to buy a competing product. Microsoft also prohibited computer manufacturers from displaying rival product icons on the Windows desktop. Finally, Microsoft was accused of thwarting competition by simply buying out promising rivals.

Microsoft's Defense. Bill Gates, Microsoft's chairman, scoffed at the government's charges. He contends that Microsoft dominates the computer industry only because it continues to produce the best products at attractive prices. Microsoft doesn't need to lock out potential competitors, he argues, because it can and does beat the competition with superior products. Furthermore, Gates argues, the software industry is a highly *contestable* market even if not a perfectly competitive one. So Microsoft has to behave like a competitive firm even though it supplies most of the industry's output. In short, Microsoft is a genius, not a bully. Therefore, the government should leave Microsoft alone and let the market decide who best serves consumers.

The Verdict. After nine years of litigation, a federal court determined that Microsoft was more of a bully than a genius (see the Applications box). The court concluded that Microsoft not only held a monopoly position in operating systems but that it had abused that position in a variety of anticompetitive ways. As a result, consumers were harmed. **The real economic issue, the court asserted, was not whether Microsoft was improving its products (it was) or reducing prices (it was) but instead how much *faster* products would have improved and prices fallen in a more competitive**

APPLICATIONS

Judge Says Microsoft Broke Antitrust Law

A federal judge yesterday found Microsoft Corp. guilty of violating antitrust law by waging a campaign to crush threats to its Windows monopoly, a severe verdict that opens the door for the government to seek a breakup of one of the most successful companies in history.

Saying that Microsoft put an "oppressive thumb on the scale of competitive fortune," U.S. District Judge Thomas Penfield Jackson gave the Justice Department and 19 states near-total victory in their lawsuit. His ruling puts a black mark on the reputation of a software giant that has been the starter engine of the "new economy."

"Microsoft mounted a deliberate assault upon entrepreneurial efforts that, left to rise or fall on their own merits, could well have enabled the introduction of competition into the market for Intel-compatible PC operating systems," Jackson said.

The sweeping guilty verdict—coming two days after out-of-court settlement talks collapsed—harkens back to the monumental monopolization cases against Standard Oil and AT&T and validates the government's power to enforce antitrust law in the information age. It comes at a time when Microsoft faces substantial business obstacles to expanding its software dominance from the desktop to the Internet.

In blunt language, Jackson depicted a powerful and predatory company that employed a wide array of tactics to destroy any innovation that posed a danger to the dominance of Windows. Among the victims were corporate stars of the multibillion-dollar computer industry: Intel Corp., Apple Computer Inc., International Business Machines Corp. and RealNetworks Inc.

To crush the competitive threat posed by the Internet browser, Jackson ruled, Microsoft integrated its own Internet browser into its Windows operating system "to quell incipient competition," bullied computer makers into carrying Microsoft's browser by threatening to withhold price discounts and demanded that computer makers not feature rival Netscape's browser in the PC desktop as a condition of licensing the Windows operating system.

Only when the separate categories of conduct are viewed, as they should be, as a single, well-coordinated course of action does the full extent of the violence that Microsoft has done to the competitive process reveal itself," Jackson wrote in the 43-page ruling.

—James V. Grimaldi

Source: *The Washington Post*, April 4, 2000. © 2000 The Washington Post. Reprinted with permission. www.washingtonpost.com

Analysis: A federal court concluded that Microsoft followed the textbook script of monopoly: erecting entry barriers, suppressing innovation, and charging high prices.

Europeans Come Down Hard on Microsoft

BERLIN, March 24—Microsoft Corp. is abusing a "near monopoly" in crucial computer software to squeeze out competitors, the European Union ruled Wednesday after a contentious five-year investigation. It ordered the company to pay a fine of more than $600 million, and to offer two versions of its Windows operating system in Europe, one without software for playing digital music and videos.

The order effectively puts Microsoft on notice that future attempts to add features to Windows could be challenged in Europe if the additions put rival products at a competitive disadvantage. The ruling is intended to ensure that "anyone who develops new software has a fair opportunity to compete in the marketplace," EU competition commissioner Mario Monti said in Brussels. . . .

EU officials, in defense of their action, said they sought to establish what has eluded Microsoft competitors in the United States: legal precedent to limit the company's 20-year-old practice of constantly incorporating new applications such as the Windows Media Player into the operating system, then capitalizing on Windows' nearly universal distribution to overwhelm rival products.

—John Burgess

Source: *The Washington Post,* March 24, 2004. © 2004 The Washington Post. Reprinted with permission.

Analysis: EU regulators are seeking to lower entry barriers for firms that want to compete for software applications.

market. By limiting consumer choices and stifling competition, Microsoft had denied consumers better and cheaper information technology.

The Remedy. The trial judge suggested that Microsoft might have to be broken into two companies—an operating software company and an applications software company—to ensure enough competition. In November 2001, however, the U.S. Department of Justice decided to seek *behavioural* remedies only. With Windows XP about to be launched, the Justice Department only required Microsoft to lower entry barriers for competing software applications (e.g., disclose middleware specifications, refrain from exclusive contracts, open desktops to competition). Although Microsoft reluctantly agreed to change its conduct in many ways, rivals complained that they still didn't have a fair chance of competing against the Microsoft monopoly. European regulators agreed, imposing still greater restrictions on Microsoft's business practices in 2004 (see the World View box). Critics contend, however, that market *structure* is still the critical factor in determining market outcomes.

> **WEB NOTE**
>
> You can track the antitrust case against Microsoft on several Web sites. See www.antitrustinstitute.org, a source for news and research, and www.usdoj.gov/atr/pubdocs.html for DOJ documents.

SUMMARY

- Market power is the ability to influence the market price of goods and services. The extreme case of market power is monopoly, a situation in which only one firm produces the entire supply of a particular product.
- The distinguishing feature of any firm with market power is the fact that the demand curve it faces is downward-sloping. In the case of monopoly, the demand curve facing the firm and the market demand curve are identical.
- The downward-sloping demand curve facing a monopolist creates a divergence between marginal revenue and price. To sell larger quantities of output, the monopolist must lower product prices. A firm without market power has no such problem.
- Like other producers, a monopolist will produce at the rate of output at which marginal revenue equals marginal cost. Because marginal revenue is always less than price in monopoly, the monopolist will produce less output than a competitive industry confronting the same market demand and costs. That reduced rate of output will be sold at higher prices, in accordance with the (downward-sloping) market demand curve.
- A monopoly will attain a higher level of profit than a competitive industry because of its ability to equate

industry (that is, its own) marginal revenues and costs. By contrast, a competitive industry ends up equating marginal costs and price, because its individual firms have no control over market supply.

- Because the higher profits attained by a monopoly will attract envious entrepreneurs, barriers to entry are needed to prohibit other firms from expanding market supplies. Patents are one such barrier to entry.
- The defense of market power rests on (1) the alleged ability of large firms to pursue long-term research and development, (2) the incentives implicit in the chance to attain market power, (3) the efficiency that larger firms may attain, and (4) the contestability of even monopolized markets. The first two arguments are weakened by

the fact that competitive firms are under much greater pressure to innovate and can stay ahead of the profit game only if they do so. The contestability defense at best concedes some amount of monopoly exploitation.

- A natural monopoly exists when one firm can produce the output of the entire industry more efficiently than can a number of small firms. This advantage is attained from economies of scale. Large firms aren't necessarily more efficient, however, because either constant returns to scale or diseconomies of scale may prevail.
- Antitrust laws restrain the acquisition and abuse of monopoly power. Where barriers to entry aren't insurmountable, market forces may ultimately overcome a monopoly as well.

Key Terms

price discrimination 182   contestable market 187   antitrust 188

Questions for Discussion

1. The objective in the game of Monopoly is to get all the property and then raise the rents. Can this power be explained with market supply and demand curves?
2. Is single ownership of a whole industry necessary to exercise monopoly power? How might an industry with many firms achieve the same result? Can you think of any examples?
3. Why don't monopolists try to establish "the highest price possible," as many people allege? What would happen to sales? To profits?
4. In 1990, a federal court decided that Eastman Kodak had infringed on Polaroid's patent when it produced similar instant-photo cameras. The court then had to award Polaroid compensation for damages. What was the nature of the damages to Polaroid? How could you compute them? (The court awarded Polaroid a record $900 million!)
5. What would have happened to iPod prices and features if Apple had not faced competition from iPod clones (Chapter 7)?

6. What entry barriers helped protect the following?
   (a) The Russian sable monopoly (see World View box, page 174).
   (b) The Ticketmaster monopoly (see the Applications box, page 179).
   (c) The CNN monopoly (see the World View box, page 188).
7. Assuming that a monopoly firm faces the same costs (MC and ATC) and demand as does the competitive industry, graphically compare the short-run equilibrium under the two market structures (i.e., indicate the profit-maximizing prices, outputs, and profits).
8. Why did the Competition Tribunal permit the merger between two propane companies even though the merger would lead to a "combined market share of 70 percent on a national basis and a monopoly in a number of markets"?
9. Do price reductions and quality enhancements on Microsoft products prove that Microsoft is a perfectly competitive firm? What should be the test of competitiveness?

EXERCISES

PROBLEMS   The Student Problem Set to accompany this chapter can be found at the end of the book.

WEB ACTIVITIES   Web Activities to accompany this chapter can be found on the Online Learning Centre at **http://www.mcgrawhill.ca/olc/schiller**.

Oligopoly

People of the same trade seldom meet together, but the conversation ends in a conspiracy against the public, or in some diversion to raise prices.
—Adam Smith, *The Wealth of Nations*, 1776

Although it's convenient to think of the economy as composed of the powerful and the powerless, market realities don't always provide such clear distinctions. There are very few perfectly competitive markets in the world, and few monopolies. Market power is an important phenomenon nonetheless; it's just that it's typically shared by several firms rather than monopolized by one. In the soft drink industry, for example, Coca-Cola and Pepsi share tremendous market power, even though neither company qualifies as a pure monopoly. The same kind of power is shared by Molson's and Labatt's in the Canadian beer market and by Sony, Nintendo, and Microsoft in the video game console market. Apple Computer, Inc., too, now has power in the digital music player market, which it shares with Sony, Dell, and other firms.

These market structures fall between the extremes of perfect competition and pure monopoly; they represent *imperfect competition*. They contain some elements of competitive rivalry but also exhibit traces of monopoly. In many cases, imperfect competitors behave much like a monopoly, restricting output, charging higher prices, and reaping greater profits than firms in a competitive market. But behaviour in imperfectly competitive markets is more complicated than in a monopoly because it involves a number of decision makers (firms) rather than only one.

This chapter focuses on one form of imperfect competition: *oligopoly*. We examine the nature of decision making in this market structure and the likely impacts on prices, production, and profits. What we want to know is:

- **What determines how much market power a firm has?**
- **How do firms in an oligopoly set prices and output?**
- **What problems does an oligopoly have in maintaining price and profit?**

LEARNING OBJECTIVES

By the end of this chapter, you should be able to:

9.1 Define the characteristics of an oligopoly market structure

9.2 Identify the determinants of market power in oligopolies

9.3 Explain the interdependency between firms operating under oligopoly

9.4 Understand why oligopolists often pursue non-price rather than price competition

9.5 Explain how the kinked demand curve captures some of the features of oligopoly

9.6 Identify the forms of coordination among oligopolists and explain how oligopolists can maximize industry profits

9.7 Discuss the rationale for government intervention

9.1 MARKET STRUCTURE

As we saw in Chapter 8, Microsoft is virtually the sole supplier of computer operating systems; as a monopoly, it has tremendous market power. The corner grocery store, on the other hand, must compete with other stores and has less control over prices. But even the corner grocery isn't completely powerless. If it's the only grocery within walking distance, or the only one open on Sunday—it too exerts *some* influence on prices and product flows. The amount of power it possesses depends on the availability of *substitute goods,* that is, the proximity and convenience of alternative retail outlets.

Degrees of Power

Between the extremes of monopoly and perfect competition are many gradations of market power (see Figure 6.1). To sort them out, we classify firms into five specific *market structures,* based on the number and relative size of firms in an industry.

Table 9.1 summarizes the characteristics of the five major market structures. At one extreme is the structure of *perfect competition,* the subject of Chapters 6 and 7. At the other extreme of the power spectrum is perfect *monopoly.* A perfect monopoly exists when only one firm is the exclusive supplier of a particular product. Our illustration of Universal Electronics (the imaginary computer monopolist in Chapter 8) exemplifies such a firm.

Between the two extremes of perfect competition and perfect monopoly lies most of the real world, which we call *imperfectly competitive.* **In imperfect competition, individual firms have some power in a particular product market.** *Oligopoly* refers to one of these imperfectly competitive market structures. **Oligopoly** is a situation in which only a *few* firms have a great deal of power in a product market. An oligopoly may exist because only a few firms produce a particular product or because a few firms account for most, although not all, of a product's output.

oligopoly: A market in which a few firms produce all or most of the market supply of a particular good or service.

The number of firms in an industry is a key characteristic of market structure. The amount of market power the firms possess, however, depends on several factors. *The determinants of market power include*

Determinants of Market Power

- *Number of producers.*
- *Size of each firm.*
- *Barriers to entry.*
- *Availability of substitute goods.*

When only one or a few producers or suppliers exist, market power is automatically conferred. In addition to the number of producers, however, the size of each firm is

Characteristic	Market Structure				
	Perfect Competition	Monopolistic Competition	Oligopoly	Duopoly	Monopoly
Number of firms	Very large number	Many	Few	Two	One
Barriers to entry	None	Low	High	High	High
Market power (control over price)	None	Some	Substantial	Substantial	Substantial
Type of product	Standardized	Differentiated	Standardized or differentiated	Standardized or differentiated	Unique

TABLE 9.1

Characteristics of Market Structures

Market structure varies, depending on the number of producers, their size, barriers to entry, and the availability of substitute goods.

An oligopoly is an imperfectly competitive structure in which a few firms dominate the market.

also important. Although over 70 Canadian brewers and microbrewers supply beer in Canada, the two largest brewers, Molson and Labatt, account for roughly 80 percent of total sales. Hence, it wouldn't make sense to categorize that industry on the basis of only the number of firms; relative size is also important.

A third and critical determinant of market power is the extent of barriers to entry. A highly successful monopoly or oligopoly arouses the envy of other profit maximizers. If it's a *contestable market,* potential rivals will seek to enter the market and share in the spoils. Should they succeed, the power of the former monopolist or oligopolists would be reduced. Accordingly, ease of entry into an industry limits the ability of a powerful firm to dictate prices and product flows. In Chapter 8 we saw how monopolies erect barriers to entry (e.g., patents) to maintain their power.

A fourth determinant of market power is the availability of substitute goods. If a monopolist or other power baron sets the price of a product too high, consumers may decide to switch to close substitutes. Thus, the price of Molson Canadian is kept in check by the price of Labatt Blue, and the price of sirloin steak is restrained by the price of chicken and pork. By the same token, a lack of available substitute products keeps the prices of insulin and antiretroviral drugs (for AIDS/HIV infection) high.

Measuring Market Power

Although there are many determinants of market power, most observers use just one yardstick to measure the extent of power in an industry.

> concentration ratio (CR): The proportion of total industry output produced by the largest firms (usually the four largest).

Concentration Ratio. The standard measure of market power is the **concentration ratio (CR).** This ratio tells the share of output (or combined market share) accounted for by the largest firms in an industry. The CR4, for example, measures the market share (i.e., the proportion of an industry's total sales) of the four largest firms, whereas the CR8 measures the market share of the eight largest firms. Figure 9.1 gives these two concentration ratios for selected industries in the Canadian manufacturing sector.[1] Using these ratios, one can readily distinguish between an industry composed of hundreds of small, relatively powerless firms and another industry dominated by a few large and powerful firms. Thus, the concentration ratio is a measure of market power that relates the size of firms to the size of the product market.

As we can see from Figure 9.1, the metal door/window industry has the lowest concentration ratios in the Canadian manufacturing sector and consequently, on a national scale, none of these firms has market power. At the other end of the spectrum, we notice that the tobacco industry is the most concentrated manufacturing sector from this selected group. In particular, the cigarette market is dominated by three large firms: Imperial Tobacco Canada; Rothmans, Benson & Hedges Incorporated; and JTI-Macdonald. While there are a few other cigarette manufacturers (Grand River Enterprises, Bastos of Canada Ltd., and Tabac ADL), their combined sales represent an extremely small portion of the total market.

Firm Size. We noted before that market power isn't necessarily associated with firm size—in other words, a small firm could possess a lot of power in a relatively small market. Within the framework of an oligopoly market structure, however, we examine and analyze cases where market power and firms size go hand in hand. In fact, some of these firms are so large that the dollar value of their

---

[1]The industries are classified according to the North American Industry Classification Structure (NAICS) and the data is categorized at the *4-digit* level. For example, the "Manufacturing" sector is a 2-digit level (31–33). Within this sector, the "Beverage and Tobacco Manufacturing" industry is a 3-digit level (312), and drilling down to a 4-digit level gives us the "Beverage Manufacturing" category (3121) illustrated in Figure 9.1. We can go even further—to a 5-digit level—and find, for example, the concentration ratios in the "Wineries" sector (31213).

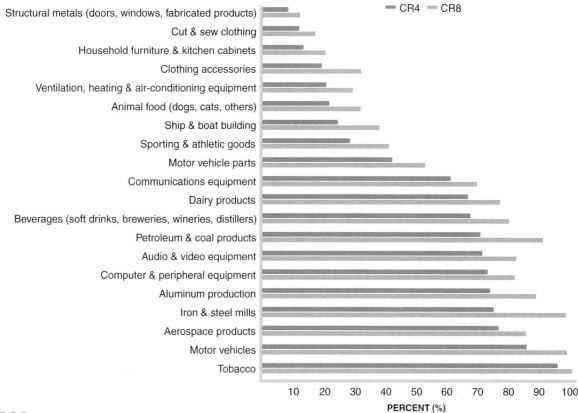

FIGURE 9.1
Power in Canadian Manufacturing Markets

The domestic production of many familiar products is concentrated among a few firms. These firms have substantial control over the quantity supplied to the market and thus over market price. The concentration ratio measures the share of

total output produced by the largest producers in a given market.

Source: Concentration ratios in Canadian Manufacturing Sector (2003). Manufacturing, Construction and Energy Division, Statistics Canada, 2003.

sales volumes exceeds the entire output of most *countries* in the world (see the World View box on the next page)!

A high concentration ratio or large firm size isn't the only way to achieve market power. The supply and price of a product can be altered by many firms acting in unison. Even 1,000 small producers can band together to change the quantity supplied to the market, thus exercising market power. Recall how our mythical Universal Electronics (Chapter 8) exercised market power by coordinating the production decisions of its many separate plants. Those plants could have attempted such coordination on their own even if they hadn't all been owned by the same corporation.

Finally, all the figures and corporations cited here refer to *national* markets. They don't convey the extent to which market power may be concentrated in a *local* market. In fact, many industries with low concentration ratios nationally are represented by just one or a few firms locally. Prime examples include milk, newspapers, and transportation (both public and private). For example, few Canadian cities have two or more independently owned daily newspapers, and nearly all those newspapers rely on only two news services (Associated Press and Canadian Press). The only metal window and door manufacturer in a small community such as Wawa, Ontario, for example, possesses a certain amount of market power (within a given geographic area) even though its output only represents a minuscule fraction of total Canadian sales. Perhaps you've also noticed that most college campuses have only one bookstore. It may not be a *national* powerhouse, but it does have the power to influence what goods are available on campus and how much they cost.

Measurement Problems

WORLD VIEW

Putting Size in Global Perspective

The largest firms in the United States Europe, and Japan, are also dominant forces in global markets. They export products to foreign markets and produce goods abroad for sale there or to import back into the United States. In terms of size alone, these business giants rival most of the world's nations. GM's gross sales, for example, would make it the twenty-fifth largest "country" in terms of national GDP.

American corporations aren't the only giants in the global markets. Toyota (Japan) and Royal Dutch Shell (Netherlands) are among the foreign giants that contest global markets.

Rank	Country or Corporation	Sales or GDP ($US)	Rank	Country or Corporation	Sales or GDP ($US)
1	United States	$10,383	21	**British Petroleum**	$233
2	Japan	3,993	22	**ExxonMobil**	223
3	Germany	1,984	23	Austria	204
4	United Kingdom	1,566	24	**Royal Dutch/Shell**	202
5	France	1,431	25	**General Motors**	195
6	China	1,266	26	Norway	190
7	Italy	1,184	27	Poland	189
8	Canada	714	28	Saudi Arabia	188
9	Spain	653	29	Turkey	183
10	Mexico	637	30	Denmark	173
11	India	510	31	Indonesia	173
12	South Korea	477	32	**Ford Motor**	164
13	Brazil	452	33	Hong Kong	162
14	The Netherlands	418	34	**Daimler/Chrysler**	158
15	Australia	409	35	**Toyota**	153
16	Russia	347	36	**General Electric**	134
17	Switzerland	267	37	Greece	133
18	**Wal-Mart Stores**	263	38	Finland	131
19	Belgium	245	39	Thailand	127
20	Sweden	240	40	**Total**	118

Sources: World Bank and *Fortune* magazine (2002–2003 data in billions).

Analysis: Firm size is a determinant of market power. The size of the largest firms, as measured by total revenue, exceeds the value of total output in most of the world's 200-plus countries.

9.2 OLIGOPOLY BEHAVIOUR

With so much market power concentrated in so few hands, it's unrealistic to expect market outcomes to resemble those of perfect competition. As we observed in Chapter 8, *market structure affects market behaviour and outcomes.* In that chapter we focused on the contrast between monopoly and perfect competition. Now we focus on the behaviour of a more common market structure: oligopoly.

To isolate the unique character of oligopoly, we'll return to the computer market. In Chapter 7 we observed that the computer market was highly competitive in its early stages, when entry barriers were low and hundreds of firms were producing similar products. In Chapter 8 we created an impassable barrier to entry (a patent on the electronic brain of the computer) that transformed the computer industry into a monopoly of Universal Electronics. Now we'll transform the industry again. This time we'll create an oligopoly by assuming that three separate firms (Universal, World, and

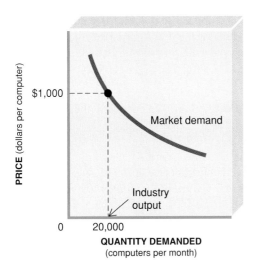

FIGURE 9.2
Initial Conditions in the Computer Market

As in Chapters 7 and 8, we assume that the initial equilibrium in the home computer market occurs at a price of $1,000 and a quantity of 20,000 per month. How will an oligopoly alter these outcomes?

International) all possess patent rights. The patent rights permit each firm to produce and sell all the computers it wants and to exclude all other would-be producers from the market. With these assumptions, we create three **oligopolists,** the firms that share an *oligopoly.* Our objective is to see how market outcomes would change in such a market structure.

As before, we'll assume that the initial conditions in the computer market are represented by a market price of $1,000 and market sales of 20,000 computers per month, as illustrated in Figure 9.2.

We'll also assume that the **market share** of each producer is accurately depicted in Table 9.2. Thus, Universal Electronics is assumed to be producing 8,000 computers per month, or 40 percent of total market supply. World Computers has a market share of 32.5 percent, while International Semiconductor has only a 27.5 percent share.

The first thing to note about the computer oligopoly is that it's likely to exhibit great internal tension. Neither World Computers nor International Semiconductor is really happy playing second or third fiddle to Universal Electronics. Each company would like to be number one in this market. On the other hand, Universal too would like a larger market share, particularly in view of the huge profits being made on computers. As we observed in Chapter 7, the initial equilibrium in the computer industry yielded an *average* profit of $333.33 per computer, and total *industry* profits of $6.67 million per month (20,000 × $333.33). Universal would love to acquire the market shares of its rivals, thereby grabbing all this industry profit for itself.

But how does an oligopolist acquire a larger market share? In a truly competitive market, a single producer could expand production at will, with no discernible impact on market supply. But *in an oligopoly, increased sales on the part of one firm will be noticed immediately by the other firms.*

oligopolist: One of the dominant firms in an oligopoly.

The Initial Equilibrium

market share: The percentage of total market output produced by a single firm.

The Battle for Market Shares

Producer	Output (computers per month)	Market Share (%)
Universal Electronics	8,000	40.0%
World Computers	6,500	32.5
International Semiconductor	5,500	27.5
Total industry output	20,000	100.0%

TABLE 9.2
Initial Market Shares of Microcomputer Producers

The market share of a firm is the percentage of total market output it produces. These are hypothetical market shares of three fictional oligopolists.

How do we know that increased sales will be noticed so quickly? Because increased sales by one firm will have to take place either at the existing market price ($1,000) or at a lower price. Either of these two events will ring an alarm at the corporate headquarters of the other two firms.

Increased Sales at the Prevailing Market Price. Consider first the possibility of Universal Electronics increasing its sales at the going price of $1,000 per computer. We know from the demand curve in Figure 9.2 that consumers are willing to buy *only* 20,000 microcomputers per month at that price. Hence, any increase in computer sales by Universal must be immediately reflected in *lower* sales by World or International. That is, ***increases in the market share of one oligopolist necessarily reduce the shares of the remaining oligopolists.*** If Universal were to increase its sales from 8,000 to 9,000 computers per month, the combined monthly sales of World and International would have to fall from 12,000 to 11,000 (see Table 9.2). The *quantity demanded* at $1,000 remains 20,000 computers per month (see Figure 9.2). Thus, any increased sales at that price by Universal must be offset by reduced sales by its rivals.

This interaction among the market shares of the three oligopolists ensures that Universal's sales success will be noticed. It won't be necessary for World Computers or International Semiconductor to engage in industrial espionage. These firms can quickly figure out what Universal is doing simply by looking at their own (declining) sales figures.

Increased Sales at Reduced Prices. Universal could pursue a different strategy. Specifically, Universal could attempt to increase its sales by lowering the price of its computers. Reduced prices would expand total market sales, possibly enabling Universal to increase its sales without directly reducing the sales of either World or International.

But this outcome is most unlikely. If Universal lowered its price from $1,000 to, say, $900, consumers would flock to Universal Computers, and the sales of World and International would plummet. After all, we've always assumed that consumers are rational enough to want to pay the lowest possible price for any particular good. It's unlikely that consumers would continue to pay $1,000 for a World or International machine when they could get basically the same computer from Universal for only $900. If there were no difference, either perceived or real, among the computers of the three firms, a *pure* oligopoly would exist. In that case, Universal would capture the *entire* market if it lowered its price below that of its rivals.

More often, consumers perceive differences in the products of rival oligopolists, even when the products are essentially identical. These perceptions (or any real differences that may exist) create a *differentiated* oligopoly. In this case, Universal would gain many but not all customers if it reduced the price of its computers. That's the outcome we'll assume here. In either case, there simply isn't any way that Universal can increase its sales at reduced prices without causing all the alarms to go off at World and International.

Retaliation

So what if all the alarms do go off at World Computers and International Semiconductor? As long as Universal Electronics is able to enlarge its share of the market and grab more profits, why should it care if World and International find out? Indeed, Universal might even get some added satisfaction knowing that World and International are upset by its marketing success.

Universal *does* have something to worry about, though. World and International may not be content to stand by and watch their market shares and profits diminish. On the contrary, World and International are likely to take some action of their own once they discover what's going on.

There are two things World and International can do once they decide to act. In the first case, where Universal is expanding its market share at prevailing prices ($1,000), World and International can retaliate by

- Stepping up their own marketing efforts.
- Cutting prices on their computers.

To step up their marketing efforts, World and International might increase their advertising expenditures, repackage their computers, put more sales representatives on the street, or sponsor a college homecoming week. Such attempts at **product differentiation** are designed to make one firm's products appear different and superior to those produced by other firms. If successful, such marketing efforts will increase sales and market share or at least stop its rivals from grabbing larger shares.

An even quicker way to stop Universal from enlarging its market share is for World and International to lower the price of *their* computers. Such price reductions will destroy Universal's hopes of increasing its market share at the old price. In fact, this is the other side of a story we've already told. If the price of World and International computers drops to, say, $900, it's preposterous to assume that Universal will be able to expand its market share at a price of $1,000. Universal's market share will shrink if it maintains a price of $1,000 per computer after World and International drop their prices to $900. Hence, the threat to Universal's market share grab is that the other two oligopolists will retaliate by reducing *their* prices. Should they carry out this threat, Universal would be forced to cut computer prices too, or accept a greatly reduced market share.

The same kind of threat exists in the second case, where we assumed that Universal Electronics expands its sales by initiating a price reduction. World and International aren't going to just sit by and applaud Universal's marketing success. They'll have to respond with price cuts of their own. Universal would then have the highest price on the market, and computer buyers would flock to cheaper substitutes. Accordingly, it's safe to conclude that *an attempt by one oligopolist to increase its market share by cutting prices will lead to a general reduction in the market price.* The three oligopolists will end up using price reductions as weapons in the battle for market shares, the kind of behaviour normally associated with competitive firms. Should this behaviour continue, not only will oligopoly become less fun, but it will also become less profitable as prices slide down the market demand curve (Figure 9.3). This is why *oligopolists avoid price competition and instead pursue nonprice competition* (e.g., advertising, product differentiation). With a new entrant into the market, however, incumbent firms may initially try both price and nonprice competition (see the Applications box) in an effort to retain market share.

product differentiation: Features that make one product appear different from competing products in the same market.

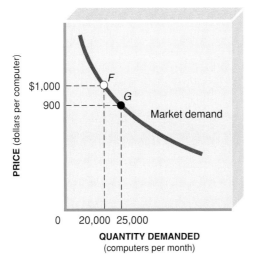

FIGURE 9.3
Rivalry for Market Shares Threatens an Oligopoly

If oligopolists start cutting prices to capture larger market shares, they'll be behaving much like truly competitive firms. The result will be a slide down the market demand curve to lower prices, increased output, and smaller profits. In this case, the market price and quantity would move from point *F* to point *G* if rival oligopolists cut prices to gain market shares.

Mountain Crest Brewing Feud

WINNIPEG, August 22, 2005—Manjit and Ravinder Minhas set out with the goal of selling low-cost suds and ended up in the crosshairs of Canada's largest beer producers.

The Calgary-based siblings incorporated Mountain Crest Brewing Co. three-and-a-half years ago in response to what they and their university buddies considered to be excessively high prices set by the country's virtual duopoly in the beer market, Labatt Breweries of Canada and Molson Inc. (now Molson Coors Brewing Co.).

Mountain Crest first burst on to the beer scene with a cans-only offering; Labatt and Molson paid little attention. But as it carved out a significant niche with price-conscious beer drinkers (said to be about ten percent of the Alberta market), it quickly got the attention of the two national breweries.

When Mountain Crest moved two provinces east into Manitoba late last year with a subsidiary called Minhas Creek Brewing Co., Labatt and Molson were lying in wait. Just as Minhas Creek Classic Lager received the licensing green light

to list for $6.95 per six-pack (three dollars cheaper than the industry norm) Labatt Lucky Lager, Molson Dry, and Molson Black Label Ice were immediately discounted to $6.90 for six-packs of cans only, not bottles.

Arguably the biggest controversy surrounding Mountain Crest/Minhas Creek involves where its beer is produced. The company makes no secret that it contracts out the brewing of its recipes to two Wisconsin-based breweries, City Brewery in Lacrosse and Joseph Huber Brewery in Monroe.

Labatt went so far as to take out a full-page ad in four Manitoba daily newspapers in June preying on local patriotism by accusing Minhas Creek of producing an American beer masquerading as a Canadian one. This is a serious insult in a country that prides itself on its high quality beer and where one of the national pastimes is mocking watered-down American brew.

Source: Renée Alexander, "Mountain Crest Brewing Feud," brandchannel.com, August 22, 2005. Reprinted with permission from brandchannel.com, produced by Interbrand.

Analysis: Incumbent firms in an oligopoly market structure can respond to new competition by lowering their prices and/or increasing their marketing efforts.

9.3 THE KINKED DEMAND CURVE

The close interdependence of oligopolists—and the limitations it imposes on individual price and output decisions—is the principal moral of this story about Universal Electronics, World Computers, and International Semiconductor. We can summarize this story with the aid of the kinked demand curve in Figure 9.4.

FIGURE 9.4
The Kinked Demand Curve Confronting an Oligopolist

The shape of the demand curve facing an oligopolist depends on the responses of its rivals to its price and output decisions. If rival oligopolists match price reductions but not price increases, the demand curve will be kinked.

Initially, the oligopolist is at point *A*. If it raises its price to $1,100 and its rivals don't raise their prices, it will be driven to point *B*. If its rivals match a price reduction (to $900), the oligopolist will end up at point *C*.

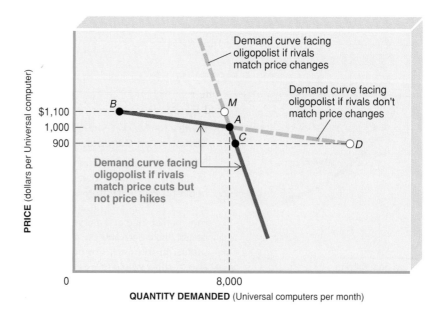

Recall that at the beginning of this oligopoly story Universal Electronics had a market share of 40 percent and was selling 8,000 computers per month at a price of $1,000 each. This output is represented by point *A* in Figure 9.4. The rest of the demand curve illustrates what would happen to Universal's unit sales if it changed its selling price. What we have to figure out is why this particular demand curve has such a strange "kinked" shape.

Consider first what would happen to Universal's sales if it lowered the price of its computers to $900. In general, we expect a price reduction to increase sales. However, *the degree to which an oligopolist's sales increase when its price is reduced depends on the response of rival oligopolists.* Suppose World and International didn't match Universal's price reduction. In this case, Universal would have the only low-priced computer in the market. Consumers would flock to Universal, and sales would increase dramatically, to point *D*. But point *D* is little more than a dream, as we've observed. World and International are sure to cut their prices to $900 too, to maintain their market shares. As a consequence, Universal's sales will expand only slightly, to point *C* rather than to point *D*. Universal's increased sales at point *C* reflect the fact that the total quantity demanded in the market has risen as the market price has fallen to $900 (see Figure 9.3). Thus, although Universal's *market share* may not have increased, its monthly sales have.

The section of the demand curve that runs from point *A* to point *D* is unlikely to exist in an oligopolistic market. Instead, *we expect rival oligopolists to match any price reductions* that Universal initiates, forcing Universal to accept the demand curve that runs from point *A* through point *C*. The Applications box illustrates such behaviour in the airline industry, where rivals were forced to match price cuts introduced by Delta.

Rivals' Response to Price Reductions

What about price increases? How will World and International respond if Universal raises the price of its computers to $1,100?

Recall that the demand for computers is assumed to be price-elastic in the neighborhood of $1,000 and that all computers are basically similar. Accordingly, if Universal raises its price and neither World nor International follows suit, Universal will be out there alone with a higher price and reduced sales. *Rival oligopolists may choose not to match price increases.* In terms of Figure 9.4, a price increase that isn't matched by rival oligopolists will drive Universal from point *A* to point *B*. At point *B*, Universal is selling very few computers at its price of $1,100 each.[2]

Is this a likely outcome? Suffice it to say that World Computers and International Semiconductor wouldn't be unhappy about enlarging their own market shares. Unless they see the desirability of an industrywide price increase, they're not likely to come to Universal's rescue with price increases of their own. This is why Northwest Airlines decided not to match the fare hikes announced by its rivals (see the Applications box).

Anything is possible, however, and World and International might match Universal's price increase. In this case, the *market price* would rise to $1,100 and the total quantity of computers demanded would diminish. Under such circumstances Universal's sales would diminish, too, in accordance with its (constant) share of a smaller market. This would lead us to point *M* in Figure 9.4. This is how WestJet responded to Air Canada's increases in fare prices—note that oligopoly firms frequently match competitors' price increases when the initiating factor is a common cost increase (see the Applications box).

Rivals' Response to Price Increases

---

[2]Notice again that we're assuming that Universal is able to sell some computers at a higher price (point *B*) than its rivals. The kinked demand curve applies primarily to differentiated oligopolies. As we'll discuss later, such differentiation may result from slight product variations, advertising, customer habits, location, friendly service, or any number of other factors. Most oligopolies exhibit some differentiation.

Airlines Drop Fare Hikes

Major airlines abandoned fare increases of as much as $20 on one-way tickets after all carriers failed to match the increases. . . .

Continental Airlines and AMR Corp.'s American Airlines yesterday became the last of the major airlines to roll back increases that were put in place last Tuesday and were matched initially by most airlines except Northwest Airlines.

—Gary McWilliams

WestJet, Air Canada Raise Fares Due to Rising Fuel Prices

WestJet, Canada's second biggest airline, has matched fare increases announced Monday by Air Canada to help offset record prices for aviation fuel.

Both airlines are raising domestic fares by $8 to $15 each way.

Delta Cuts Fares 25 Percent; Rival Lines Follow Suit

Major airlines slashed fares about 25 percent yesterday in the hope that leisure summer passengers will make up for the sharp decline in business travel that has pushed airline revenue down dramatically.

Delta Air Lines cut fares in the United States, Latin America and Asia. Other airlines such as United, American, Continental, Northwest and US Airways immediately said they would match Delta's 25 percent fare reductions in markets where they compete.

—Keith L. Alexander

Analysis: If rivals match price cuts but not price increases, the demand curve confronting an oligopolist will be kinked. Prices will increase only when all firms agree to raise them at the same time.

We may draw two conclusions from Figure 9.4:

- *The shape of the demand curve an oligopolist faces depends on the responses of its rivals to a change in the price of its own output.*
- *That demand curve will be kinked if rival oligopolists match price reductions but not price increases.*

9.4 GAME THEORY

One implication of the kinked demand curve is that oligopolists can't make truly independent price or output decisions. Because only a few producers participate in the market, *each oligopolist has to consider the potential responses of rivals when formulating price or output strategies.* This *strategic interaction* is the inevitable consequence of their oligopolistic position.

What makes oligopoly particularly interesting is the *uncertainty* of rivals' behaviour. For example, Universal *would* want to lower its prices *if* it thought its rivals wouldn't retaliate with similar price cuts. But it can't be sure of that response. Universal must instead consider the odds of its rivals matching a price cut. If the odds are high, Universal might decide *not* to initiate a price cut. Or maybe Universal might offer price discounts to just a few select customers, hoping World and International might not notice or react to small changes in market share.

The Payoff Matrix. Table 9.3 summarizes the strategic options each oligopolist confronts. In this case, let's assume that Universal is contemplating a price cut. The "payoff matrix" in the table summarizes the various profit consequences of such a move. One thing should be immediately clear: ***The payoff to an oligopolist's price cut depends on how its rivals respond.*** Indeed, the only scenario that increases Universal's profit is one in which Universal reduces its price and its rivals don't. We visualized this outcome earlier as a move from point *A* to point *D* in Figure 9.4. Note again that this scenario implies losses for Universal's two rival oligopolists.

The remaining cells in the payoff matrix show how profits change with other action/response scenarios. One thing is evident: If Universal *doesn't* reduce prices, it can't increase profits. In fact, it might end up as the Big Loser if its rivals reduce *their* prices while Universal stands pat.

The option of reducing price doesn't guarantee a profit, but at least it won't decimate Universal's market share or profits. If rivals match a Universal price cut, all three oligopolists will suffer small losses.

So what should Universal do? The *collective* interests of the oligopoly are protected if no one cuts the market price. But an individual oligopolist could lose big time if it holds the line on price when rivals reduce price. Hence each oligopolist might decide to play it safe by *initiating* a price cut.

Expected Gain (Loss). The decision to initiate a price cut boils down to an assessment of *risk*. If you thought the risk of a "first strike" was high, you'd be more inclined to reduce price. This kind of risk assessment is the foundation of game theory. You could in fact make that decision by *quantifying* the risks involved. Consider again the option of reducing price. As the first row of Table 9.3 shows, rivals can respond in one of only two ways. If they follow suit, a small loss is incurred by Universal. If they don't, there's a huge gain for Universal. To quantify the risk assessment, we need two pieces of information: (1) the size of each "payoff" and (2) the probability of its occurrence.

Suppose the "huge gain" is $1 million and the "small loss" is $20,000. What should Universal do? The huge gain looks enticing, but we now know it's not likely to happen. But *how* unlikely is it? What if there's only a 1 percent chance of rivals not matching a price reduction? In that case, the *expected* payoff to a Universal price cut is

$$\text{Expected value} = \left[\begin{array}{c}\text{Probability of}\\\text{rivals matching}\end{array} \times \begin{array}{c}\text{Size of}\\\text{loss from}\\\text{price cuts}\end{array}\right] + \left[\begin{array}{c}\text{Probability}\\\text{of rivals}\\\text{not matching}\end{array} \times \begin{array}{c}\text{Gain}\\\text{from lone}\\\text{price cut}\end{array}\right]$$

$$= [(0.99) \times (-\$20,000)] + [(0.01) \times (\$1 \text{ million})]$$

$$= -\$19,800 + \$10,000$$

$$= -\$9,800$$

Hence, it's not a good idea. Once potential payoffs and probabilities are taken into account, a unilateral price cut doesn't look promising.

WEB NOTE

The "Prisoner's Dilemma" (who should confess) is a classic game theory problem. Try solving this and other games at www.gametheory.net/web/PDilemma.

	Rivals' Actions	
Universal's Options	**Reduce Price**	**Don't Reduce Price**
Reduce price	Small loss for everyone	Huge gain for Universal; rivals lose
Don't reduce price	Huge loss for Universal; rivals gain	No change

TABLE 9.3
Oligopoly Payoff Matrix

The payoff to an oligopolist's price cut depends on its rivals' responses. Each oligopolist must assess the risks and rewards of each scenario before initiating a price change. Which option would you choose?

Coke and Pepsi May Call Off Pricing Battle

ATLANTA—A brief but bitter pricing war within the soft-drink industry might be drawing to a close—all because no one wants to be blamed for having fired the first shot.

Coca-Cola Enterprises Inc., Coca-Cola Co.'s biggest bottler, said in a recent memorandum to executives that it will "attempt to increase prices" after July 4 amid concern that heavy price discounting in most of the industry is squeezing profit margins.

The memo is a response to statements made to analysts last week by top PepsiCo Inc. executives. Pepsi, of Purchase, N.Y., said "irrational" pricing in much of the soft-drink industry might temporarily squeeze domestic profits, and it laid the blame for the price cuts at Coke's door.

That clearly incensed executives at Coca-Cola and Coca-Cola Enterprises, which had no desire to be criticized for threatening profit margins for the entire industry. Indeed, industry analysts in the wake of Pepsi's statements expressed concern that profit margins for Pepsi and Coke bottlers may erode as a result of cutthroat pricing. . . .

In the June 5 memo, Summerfield K. Johnston Jr. and Henry A. Schimberg, the chief executive and the president of Coca-Cola Enterprises, respectively, said the bottler's plan is to "succeed based on superior marketing programs and execution rather than the short-term approach of buying share through price discounting. . . . We have absolutely no motivation to decrease prices except in response to a competitive initiative."

—Nikhil Deogun

Source: *The Wall Street Journal*, June 12, 1997. Reprinted by permission of *The Wall Street Journal*. © 1998 Dow Jones & Company, Inc. All rights reserved worldwide. www.wsj.com

Analysis: Price discounting can destroy oligopoly profits. When it occurs, rival oligopolists seek to end it as quickly as possible.

These kinds of computations underlay the Cold War games that the world's one-time superpowers played. Neither side was certain of the enemy's next move but knew it could bring total destruction. As a consequence, the United States and the former Soviet Union continually probed each other's responses but were quick to retreat from the brink whenever all-out retaliation was threatened. Oligopolists play the same kind of game on a much smaller scale, using price discounts and advertising rather than nuclear warheads as their principal weapons. The reward they receive for coexistence is the oligopoly profits that they continue to share. This reward, together with the threat of mutual destruction, leads oligopolists to limit their price rivalry. This explains why Coke and Pepsi quickly ended their brief 1997 price war (see the Applications box). After finger-pointing about who started the war, the companies pulled back from the brink of mutual profit destruction.

This isn't to say oligopolists won't ever cut prices or use other means to gain market share. They might, given the right circumstances and certain expectations of how rivals will behave. Indeed, there are a host of different price, output, and marketing strategies an oligopolist might want to pursue. The field of **game theory** is dedicated to the study of how decisions are made when such strategic interaction exists, for example, when the outcome of a business strategy depends on the decisions rival firms make. Just as there are dozens of different moves and countermoves in a chess game, so too are there numerous strategies oligopolists might use to gain market share.

game theory: The study of decision making in situations where strategic interaction (moves and counter-moves) between rivals occurs.

9.5 OLIGOPOLY VS. COMPETITION

While contemplating alternative strategies for maximizing their *individual* profits, oligopolists are also mindful of their common interest in maximizing *joint* (industry) profits. They want to avoid behaviour that destroys the very profits that they're vying for. Indeed, they might want to coordinate their behaviour in a way that maximizes *industry* profits. If they do, how will market outcomes be affected?

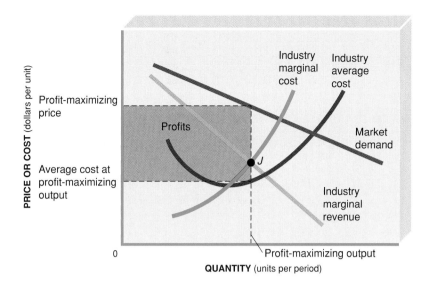

FIGURE 9.5
Maximizing Oligopoly Profits

An oligopoly strives to behave like a monopoly. Industry profits are maximized at the rate of output at which the industry's marginal cost equals the marginal revenue (point *J*). In a monopoly, this profit all goes to one firm; in an oligopoly, it must be shared among a few firms.

In an oligopoly, the MC and ATC curves represent the combined production capabilities of several firms, rather than only one. The industry MC curve is derived by horizontally summing the MC curves of the individual firms.

Price and Output

Thus far we've focused on a single oligopolist's decision about whether to *change* the price of its output. But how was the initial (market) price determined? In this example, we assumed that the initial price was $1,000 per computer, the price that prevailed initially in a *competitive* market. But the market is no longer competitive. As we saw in the previous chapter, a change in industry structure will affect market outcomes. A monopolist, for example, would try to maximize *industry* profits, all of which it would keep. To do this, it would select that one rate of output where marginal revenue equals marginal cost, and it would charge whatever price consumers were willing and able to pay for that rate of output (see Figure 9.5).

An oligopoly would seek similar profits. An oligopoly is really just a *shared* monopoly. Hence, ***an oligopoly will want to behave like a monopoly, choosing a rate of industry output that maximizes total industry profit.***

The challenge for an oligopoly is to replicate monopoly outcomes. To do so, the firms in an oligopoly must find the monopoly price and maintain it. This is what the members of OPEC are trying to do when they meet to establish a common price for the oil they sell (see the World View box). To reach agreement requires a common view of the industry demand curve, satisfaction with respective market shares, and precise coordination.

Competitive industries would also like to reap monopoly-like profits. But competitive industries experience relentless pressure on profits, as individual firms expand output, reduce costs, and lower prices. To maximize industry profits, competitive firms would have to band together and agree to restrict output and raise prices. If they did, though, the industry would no longer be competitive. The potential for maximizing industry profits is clearly greater in an oligopoly because fewer firms are involved and each is aware of its dependence on the behaviour of the others.

WEB NOTE

To find more about OPEC's mission statement and publications visit http://www.opec.org/.

Sticky Prices

An oligopoly may not be coordinated enough to set the price that maximizes industry profits. Whatever price is established, however, will tend to be stable. This price stability is partly a reflection of the strategic interdependence that characterizes oligopoly. As the kinked demand curve illustrates, unilateral price changes can be self-destructive. So price competition is generally avoided.

Price stability is also facilitated by the "cost cushion" that surrounds an oligopolist's production decision. Like all producers, an oligopolist wants to produce where MR = MC. This *profit-maximization rule* implies that a *change* in marginal cost will alter the production decision. This isn't necessarily the case for an oligopolist, however. An oligopolist has a gap in its MR curve that serves as a cushion against small changes in MC. This cushion results from the kink in the oligopolist's demand curve.

OPEC Cuts Oil Production by 1.2M Barrels

DOHA, Qatar—Oil cartel OPEC decided to cut production by a greater-than-expected 1.2 million barrels a day on Friday, and some members indicated it was open to further cuts.

United Arab Emirates oil minister Mohammed bin Dhaen al-Hamili made the announcement at a news conference after OPEC's oil ministers held an emergency meeting in the capital of Qatar.

Support for the move by the de facto leader of the cartel, Saudi Arabia oil minister Ali Naimi, shows the group's unity on the issue of price. OPEC price hawks such as Nigeria and Venezuela have strongly advocated a cartel-wide production cut since the start of the month. But without public support from Saudi Arabia, the market took with a grain of salt the likelihood of any cuts.

"This was a surprise, and gave the market an impression they are serious," said Ken Hasegawa, a broker at Himawari CX in Tokyo.

Crude oil prices have declined more than 25 percent since mid-July. After the announcement, a barrel of light sweet crude rose 47 cents to $58.97 in electronic trading on the New York Mercantile Exchange, up from its close Thursday at $58.50.

"If the market doesn't stabilize, they are going to continue to cut production," said Phil Flynn, an analyst at Alaron Trading Corp. in Chicago. "Prices from $57 to $60 is an area they are willing to defend."

Source: Tarek Al-Issawi, The Associated Press (October 20, 2006). Used with permission of The Associated Press.

Analysis: An oligopoly tries to act like a shared monopoly. To maximize industry profit, the firms in an oligopoly must concur on what the monopoly price is and agree to maintain it by limiting output and allocating market shares.

The kinked demand curve is really a composite of two separate demand curves (Figure 9.6). One curve is predicated on the assumption that rival oligopolists don't respond to price increases (d_1). The other curve is predicated on the assumption that rivals do respond to price cuts (d_2). Each demand curve has its own marginal revenue curve, as shown in Figure 9.6. The demand curve d_1 has *marginal revenue (MR)* curve mr_1, for example, while demand curve d_2 has marginal revenue curve mr_2.

If the kinked demand curve dictates an oligopolist's behaviour, each firm confronts the possibility of starting down the demand curve d_1 and switching to d_2 at point A.

FIGURE 9.6
An Oligopolist's Marginal Revenue Curve

A kinked demand curve incorporates portions of two different demand curves (d_1 and d_2). Hence a kinked demand curve also has portions of two distinct marginal revenue curves (mr_1 and mr_2). Below the kink in the demand curve (point A), a gap exists between the two marginal revenue curves. The segment SF comes from marginal revenue curve mr_1; the segment GH comes from mr_2.

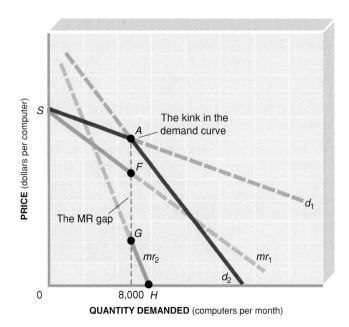

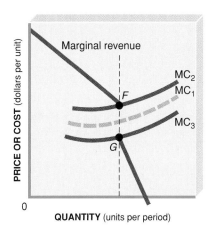

FIGURE 9.7
The Cost Cushion

The gap in an oligopolist's marginal revenue curve creates a "cost cushion." If marginal cost rises (MC_2) or falls (MC_3) within that gap ($F - G$), the profit-maximizing rate of output (MC = MR) is unchanged.

Hence, from point S to point A the curve mr_1 depicts the relevant marginal revenues. At point A (the quantity of 8,000 computers per month), however, we suddenly switch demand curves (to d_2). Therefore, we must seek out a new marginal revenue curve corresponding to d_2. To the right of point A, the marginal revenue curve mr_2 is operational.

The oligopolist's marginal revenue curve thus contains two distinct segments. In Figure 9.6, the first segment runs from point S to point F. The second segment runs from point G down to point H (below the horizontal axis MR is negative and so of no interest here).

Between points F and G *there's a gap in the oligopolist's marginal revenue curve.* Notice that *this gap occurs just below the kink in the demand curve.* This gap creates a cost cushion. Look at the marginal cost curves in Figure 9.7. If the marginal cost curve passes through the gap in the marginal revenue curve, *modest shifts of the marginal cost curve will have no impact on the production decision of an oligopolist.* That is, an oligopolist need not reduce its rate of output when marginal costs rise somewhat or increase its rate of output when marginal costs fall. As a consequence, an oligopolist's output doesn't fluctuate as much as either a competitive firm's or a profit-maximizing monopolist's. The cost cushion implied by the gap in its MR curve allows the oligopolist to maintain a given price for longer periods and to incur higher marketing costs (such as advertising) if the need arises. In other words, the kinked demand curve results in "sticky" prices. Given the uncertain consequences of any unilateral price change, this cost cushion reinforces the aversion of oligopolists to price competition.

9.6 COORDINATION PROBLEMS

A successful oligopoly will achieve monopoly-level profits by restricting industry output. As we've observed, however, this outcome depends on mutual agreement and coordination among the oligopolists. This may not come easily. *There's an inherent conflict in the joint and individual interests of oligopolists.* Their joint, or collective, interest is in maximizing industry profit. The individual interest of each oligopolist, however, is to maximize its own share of sales and profit. This conflict creates great internal tension within an oligopoly. Recall that each firm wants as large a market share as possible, at prevailing prices. But encroachments in the market shares of rival oligopolists threaten to bring retaliation, price reductions, and reduced industry profits. To avoid such self-destructive behaviour, oligopolists must coordinate their production decisions so that

- *Industry* output and price are maintained at profit-maximizing levels.
- Each oligopolistic *firm* is content with its market share.

APPLICATIONS

Competition Bureau Investigation Leads to Record Fine in Domestic Conspiracy

Fine Paper Merchants Sentenced to Pay $37.5 Million; Key Personnel to Be Removed

OTTAWA—The Competition Bureau announced today that Cascades Fine Papers Group Inc., Domtar Inc. and Unisource Canada, Inc. each pleaded guilty in the Superior Court of Justice in Toronto to two counts of conspiring to lessen competition unduly contrary to section 45 of the Competition Act.

Each company was sentenced to record fines of $12.5 million for their part in the domestic conspiracy of carbonless sheets. A prohibition order was issued against the companies and key personnel involved in the conspiracy will be removed from their positions in the paper merchant business.

The Bureau's investigation, which began in 2002, revealed that the convicted companies conspired to avoid competing with one another in the carbonless sheet markets in Ontario from October 1999 to September 2000, and during 2000 in Quebec, contrary to section 45 of the Competition Act. Carbonless sheets are used by commercial printers in the manufacture of forms and receipts.

The accused corporations admitted that the illegal agreements extended to:

- respecting each other's market share to stabilize prices
- coordinating a response to a new market entrant
- implementing a common discount program
- maintaining price discipline to avoid a price war, and
- sharing sales and pricing data

Source: "Competition Bureau Investigation Leads to Record Fine in Domestic Conspiracy." Competition Bureau of Canada, January 9, 2006, accessed October 14, 2006, http://www.competitionbureau.gc.ca/internet/index.cfm?itemID=2018&lg=e. Reproduced with the permission of the Minister of Public Works and Government Services Canada, 2007.

Analysis: In addition to price-fixing, oligopolies can also engage in other forms of coordination that contravene antitrust laws in Canada.

Price-Fixing

price-fixing: Explicit agreements among producers regarding the price(s) at which a good is to be sold.

To bring about this happy outcome, rival oligopolists could discuss their common interests and attempt to iron out an agreement on both issues. Identifying the profit-maximizing rate of industry output would be comparatively simple, as Figure 9.5 illustrated. Once the optimal rate of output was found, the associated profit-maximizing price would be evident. The only remaining issue would be the division of industry output among the oligopolists, that is, the assignment of market shares.

The most explicit form of coordination among oligopolists is called **price-fixing.** In this case, the firms in an oligopoly explicitly agree to charge a uniform (monopoly) price. This is what OPEC members do when they get together to set oil prices (see the World View, p. 206). In addition to price-fixing, three paper companies in Canada engaged in several other illegal forms of coordination (see Applications). Some other examples of price-fixing include the following:

Vitamins. Seven firms from four nations were accused of fixing global prices on bulk vitamins from 1990 to 1998. They also allocated market shares for vitamins A, B2, C, and E. In 1999, the companies paid a record $1.05 billion fine.

Baby Formula. Two makers of baby formula (Bristol-Myers Squibb and American Home Products) agreed to pay $5 million in 1992 to settle Florida charges that they had fixed prices on baby formula. Three companies control 95 percent of this $1.3 billion national market.

Auction Commissions. Sotheby's and Christie's, who together control 90 percent of the world's art auction business, admitted in 2000 to fixing commission rates throughout the 1990s. They paid a $512 million fine when they got caught.

Laser Eye Surgery. The U.S. Federal Trade Commission charged the two companies that sell the lasers used for corrective eye surgery (VISX and Summit Technology) with price-fixing that inflated the retail price of surgery by $500 per eye.

Memory Chips. In 2004, prosecutors claimed that the world's largest memory-chip (DRAM) manufacturers (Samsung, Micron, Infineon) fixed prices in the $16 billion-a-year DRAM market. By 2006 all three companies had pleaded guilty and paid punitive fines—in addition to jail terms for some executives.

Airline Flights. In 2006, British and American regulators started an investigation of several major airlines, including British Airways, on the suspicion of illegally conspiring to fix the amount of fuel surcharges imposed on long-distance passenger flights to and from the UK.

Although price-fixing agreements are still a reality in many product markets, oligopolies have discovered that they don't need *explicit* agreements to arrive at uniform prices; they can achieve the same outcome in more subtle ways. **Price leadership** rather than price-fixing will suffice. If all oligopolists in a particular product market follow the lead of one firm in raising prices, the result is the same as if they had all agreed to raise prices simultaneously. Instead of conspiring in motel rooms, the firms can achieve their objective simply by reading *The Wall Street Journal* or industry publications and responding appropriately. This is apparently how Coke and Pepsi communicated their desire to end their 1997 price war (see the Applications box on page 204).

Whenever oligopolists successfully raise the price of a product, the law of demand tells us that unit sales will decline. Even in markets with highly inelastic demand, *some* decrease in sales always accompanies an increase in price. When this happens in a monopolistic industry, the monopolist simply cuts back his rate of output. In an oligopoly, however, no single firm will wish to incur the whole weight of that cutback. Some form of accommodation is required by all the oligopolists.

The adjustment to the reduced sales volume can take many forms. Members of OPEC, for example, assign explicit quotas for the oil output of each member country (see the World View box on page 206). Such open and explicit production-sharing agreements transform an oligopoly into a **cartel.**

Because cartels openly violate Canada's Competition Act, oligopolies have to be more circumspect in divvying up shared markets.

More often the oligopolists let the sales and output reduction be divided up according to consumer demands, intervening only when market shares are thrown markedly out of balance. At such times an oligopolist may take drastic action, such as **predatory pricing.** Predatory price cuts are temporary price reductions intended to drive out new competition or reestablish market shares. The sophisticated use of price cutting can also function as a significant barrier to entry, inhibiting potential competitors from trying to gain a foothold in the price cutter's market. Once again, this type of behaviour contravenes Canada's Competition Act. But is matching a new entrant's lower price the result of "competitive forces" or a deliberate intent to drive out the new competitor? From the Competition Bureau's perspective, the abuse of dominance provisions of the Competition Act (section 79) imply that firms cover their "avoidable costs"—costs that would be avoidable if the service/product was not provided (see the Applications box).

Price Leadership

price leadership: An oligopolistic pricing pattern that allows one firm to establish the (market) price for all firms in the industry.

Allocation of Market Shares

cartel: A group of firms with an explicit, formal agreement to fix prices and output shares in a particular market.

predatory pricing: Temporary price reductions designed to alter market shares or drive out competition.

APPLICATIONS

Air Canada Using Predatory Pricing: CanJet

TORONTO—Upstart discount air carrier CanJet Airlines is once again accusing Air Canada of predatory pricing. The latest allegations came after Air Canada announced a new round of fare reductions in CanJet's territory in eastern Canada.

CanJet said Air Canada is offering cheap flights on popular routes where it has competition, such as $99 to fly St. John's

CP/Andrew Vaughan

to Halifax or Halifax to Ottawa. On routes where Air Canada does not face competition, fares have not been lowered, CanJet charges. The discount carrier said Air Canada is charging $379 for a one-way unrestricted flight between Deer Lake and Halifax, and $359 for a seat on the Saint John to Ottawa route.

"We refuse to bend under the most recent pricing attack by Air Canada," Mark Winders, CanJet's chief operating officer, said in a press release. "We believe that Air Canada's actions are not in the best interest of the traveling public but are intended to eliminate competition in the Canadian domestic market," Winders said.

A previous Competition Bureau investigation ordered Air Canada to eliminate cut-rate fares on five routes. The Bureau said that these routes did not cover their "avoidable costs" and, as such, the prices were predatory. Avoidable costs are the necessary costs incurred to provide airline services-fuel, aircraft costs, pilots, crews, tickets and meals, etc.—that could be avoided if the service was not provided.

On September 10, 2006, CanJet ceased all regularly scheduled passenger flights and moved into charter service, citing "rising business risks."

Source: "Air Canada Using Predatory Pricing: CanJet," February 15, 2001, www.cbc.ca.

Analysis: Predatory pricing entails the use of temporary price cuts to weaken the financial condition of rival companies. It can be used to enforce higher prices or otherwise reduce competition.

9.7 BARRIERS TO ENTRY

If oligopolies succeed in establishing monopoly prices and profits, they'll attract the envy of would-be entrants. To keep potential competitors out of their industry, oligopolists must maintain *barriers to entry*. ***Above-normal profits can't be maintained over the long run unless barriers to entry exist.*** The entry barriers erected include those monopolists use (Chapter 8).

Patents

Patents are a very effective barrier to entry. Potential competitors can't set up shop until they either develop an alternative method for producing a product or receive permission from the patent holder to use the patented process. Such permission, when given, costs something, of course.

Distribution Control

Another way of controlling the supply of a product is to take control of distribution outlets. If a firm can persuade retail outlets not to peddle anyone else's competitive wares, it will increase its market power. This control of distribution outlets can be accomplished through selective discounts, long-term supply contracts, or expensive gifts at Christmas. Recall from Chapter 8 (see the Applications box, page 179) how Clear Channel and Ticketmaster locked up concert arenas. Frito-Lay elbows out competing snack companies by paying high fees to "rent" shelf space in grocery stores (see the Applications box on the next page). Such up-front costs create an entry barrier for potential rivals. Even if a potential rival can come up with the money, the owner of an arena or grocery store chain may not wish to anger the firm that dominates the market.

APPLICATIONS

Frito-Lay Devours Snack-Food Business

Once again, Frito-Lay is chewing up the competition.

The announcement Wednesday that Anheuser-Busch Cos. is selling off its Eagle Snacks business highlights the danger of trying to compete against Frito-Lay in the salty-snacks game. The company owns half of the $15 billion salty-snacks market.

"Frito's a fortress," says Michael Branca, an analyst at NatWest Securities. "And it continues to expand its realm. I'd tell anyone else trying to get into the business, don't try to expand, don't try to impinge on Frito's territory or you'll get crushed."

In fact, competitors say that it is Frito-Lay's tactics with retailers that make it an invincible foe. Because many retailers are charging more and more for shelf space—$40,000 a foot annually in some instances—many regional companies say Frito-Lay is paying retailers to squeeze out competing brands.

"Frito can afford it," says a regional snack company executive. "But we can't. It's become a real-estate business."

Frito-Lay can also afford to out-promote its competitors. In 1993, the company spent more than $60 million on advertising, while Eagle spent less than $2 million.

—Robert Frank

Snack-Food Giant

Frito-Lay's market share in various snack-food categories.

	Salty Snacks		Potato Chips		Tortilla Chips	
	1990	1995	1990	1995	1990	1995
Market share	43%	52%	45%	52%	63%	72%

Source: *The Wall Street Journal*, October 27, 1995. Reprinted by permission of The Wall Street Journal. © 1995 Dow Jones & Company. All rights reserved worldwide. www.wsj.com

Analysis: Barriers to entry such as self-space rental and advertising enable a firm to maintain market dominance. Acquisitions also reduce competition.

New car warranties also serve as an entry barrier. The warranties typically require regular maintenance at authorized dealerships and the exclusive use of authorized parts. These provisions limit the ability of would-be competitors to provide cheaper auto parts and service. Frequent-flier programs have similar effects in the airline industry.

Large and powerful firms can also limit competition by outright *acquisition.* A *merger* between two firms amounts to the same thing, although mergers often entail the creation of new corporate identities.

In Canada, mergers and acquisitions have occurred across a wide spectrum of industries. In the beer industry, Sleeman's—Canada's third-largest beer producer—agreed to a $400-million takeover by Japan's Sapporo breweries while Molson and U.S.-based Adolph Coors Co. merged to form the world's fifth largest brewer. In the banking industry, the Toronto-Dominion Bank and Canada Trust merged to form the TD Canada Trust Bank. In the oil industry, Alberta Energy merged in an $8.9-billion share swap deal with PanCanadian Energy to form energy giant EnCana and, subsequent to this merger, the U.S. subsidiaries of EnCana sold their offshore oil and gas interests in the Gulf of Mexico to Norwegian oil producer Statoil.

Although the Competition Bureau acts as a watchdog to ensure that mergers and acquisitions do not "unduly lessen competition," the government often helps companies or industries acquire and maintain control of market supply. Patents are issued by and enforced by the federal government and so represent one form of supply-restricting regulation. By imposing tariff-rate quotas[3] on imports of butter, cheese, and ice cream, for example, the federal government reduces potential competition in these Canadian product markets. Government regulation also limits domestic competition in many industries. The Canadian Dairy Commission's mandate is to coordinate federal

Mergers and Acquisition

WEB NOTE

For a list of recent Canadian merges visit http//www.cbc.ca/news/background/mergers.

Government Regulation

---

[3]Tariff Rate Quotas (TRQ) allow a specific physical amount of goods to be imported at one tariff rate (within-quota rate) and any imports above this specified amount to be imported at a higher tariff rate (over-quota rate).

and provincial dairy policies through the use of supply management practices such as support prices and market share quotas.

City and provincial controls frequently govern entry into the taxi industry. In addition to the basic set of licensing standards (valid license/insurance, background checks, and vehicle inspection), cities such as Ottawa, Toronto, Calgary, and Vancouver also limit the number of taxi licenses. The rationale for this "plate" system (medallion system in the United States) is typically two-fold: firstly, to ensure standards and avoid unsafe vehicles and/or poor driver quality, and secondly, to minimize the potential for market power through possible economies of scale and scope. While the debate continues whether or not to remove these entry control restrictions, one salient feature of this market is the increasing value of the plates. With a restricted supply of taxis and the ability to transfer the existing plates, they are a highly valued commodity—particularly in growing communities such as Calgary.[4]

Nonprice Competition

Producers who control market supply can enhance their power even further by establishing some influence over market demand. The primary mechanism of control is *advertising*. To the extent that a firm can convince you that its product is essential to your well-being and happiness, it has effectively shifted your demand curve. ***Advertising not only strengthens brand loyalty but also makes it expensive for new producers to enter the market.*** A new entrant must buy both production facilities and advertising outlets.

The cigarette industry is a classic case of high concentration and product differentiation. As Figure 9.1 shows, the top four cigarette companies produce 95 percent of all domestic output; small, generic firms produce the rest. Yet you would never guess that such high concentration exists in the industry if you glanced at the cigarette shelves at the local supermarket. Together, the top four cigarette companies produce dozens of brands. To solidify brand loyalties, the cigarette industry spends millions of dollars annually on advertising and promotion.

Another highly-concentrated industry that advertises heavily is the automobile industry. Each year, North American, European, and East Asian car manufacturers spend millions of advertising dollars in Canada trying to persuade Canadian consumers to purchase their products. Over the past decade, the form of advertising has expanded from identification of desirable characteristics (greater safety, more "standard" features, and excellence in service) towards monetary incentives ("employee pricing" and zero purchase financing).

Training

In today's technology-driven markets, early market entry can create an important barrier to later competition. Customers of computer hardware and software, for example, often become familiar with a particular system or computer package. To switch to a new product may entail significant cost, including the retraining of user staff. As a consequence, would-be competitors will find it difficult to sell their products even if they offer better quality and lower prices.

The popular Lotus 1-2-3 spreadsheet program illustrates this market barrier. Lotus Development Corporation introduced Lotus 1-2-3 in 1982 as one of the first spreadsheets for the IBM personal computer. By 1988, Lotus had 3.5 million copies of its program in use—82 percent of all spreadsheet sales. Although other software firms offered comparable (and even better) products at much lower prices, users were reluctant to try new software that would require retraining. (IBM bought Lotus in 1995, further raising the entry barrier.) Microsoft gained a similar advantage by bundling Net-access and applications software with Windows. Once consumers become accustomed to Microsoft features, they're less inclined to purchase potential substitutes.

Network Economies

The widespread use of a particular product may also heighten its value to consumers, thereby making potential substitutes less viable. The utility of instant messaging—or even a telephone—depends on how many of your friends have computers or telephones. If no one else had a phone or computer, there'd be no reason to own one. In other

---

[4]In June 2006, the Calgary Taxi Commission approved the issuance of six new regular Taxi Plate Licences (TPL) with a fee of $5,000 each—a far cry from a New York City's ongoing auctions of medallions at $500,000 ($US).

words, the larger the network of users, the greater the value of the product. Such network economies help explain why software developers prefer to write Windows-based programs than programs for rival operating systems. Network economics also explains why Microsoft doesn't want computer manufacturers to display icons for rival instant-messaging services on the Windows XP desktop. Whichever instant-messaging service expands the quickest may achieve a network entry barrier.

Examples of market power at work in product markets could be extended to the closing pages of this book. The few cases cited here, however, are testimony enough to the fact that market power has some influence on our lives. Market power *does* exist; market power *is* used. Although market power may result in economies of scale, the potential for abuse is evident. Market power contributes to *market failure* when it leads to resource misallocation (restricted output) or greater inequity (monopoly profits; higher prices).

What should we do about these abuses? Should we leave it to market forces to find ways of changing industry structure and behaviour? Or should the government step in to curb noncompetitive practices?

Industry Behaviour. Our primary concern is the *behaviour* of market participants. What ultimately counts is the quantity of goods supplied to the market, their quality, and their price. Few consumers care about the underlying *structure* of markets; what we seek are good market *outcomes*.

In principle, the government could change industry behaviour without changing industry structure. We could, for example, explicitly outlaw collusive agreements and cast a wary eye on industries that regularly exhibit price leadership. We could also dismantle barriers to entry and thereby promote contestable markets. We might also prohibit oligopolists from extending their market power via such mechanisms as acquisitions, excessive or deceptive advertising, and, alas, the financing of political campaigns. In fact, the existing *antitrust* law—the Competition Act—explicitly forbids most of these practices.

There are several problems with this behavioural approach. The first limitation is scarce resources. Policing markets and penalizing noncompetitive conduct require more resources than the public sector can muster. Indeed, the firms being investigated often have more resources than the public watchdogs.

The paucity of antitrust resources is partly a reflection of public apathy. Consumers generally are unaware of the relationship between market structure and their own economic welfare. They (and you) rarely think about the connection between market power and the price of the goods they buy, the wages they receive, or the way they live. As a result, there's little political pressure to regulate market behaviour.

The behavioural approach also suffers from the "burden-of-proof" requirement. How often will "trustbusters" catch colluding executives in the act? More often than not, the case for collusion rests on such circumstantial evidence as simultaneous price hikes, identical bids, or other market outcomes. The charge of explicit collusion is hard to prove. Even in the absence of explicit collusion, however, consumers suffer. If an oligopoly price is higher than what a competitive industry would charge, consumers get stuck with the bill whether or not the price was "rigged" by explicit collusions.

Industry Structure. The concept of tacit collusion directs attention to the *structure* of an industry. It essentially says that oligopolists and monopolists will act in their own best interest. To expect an oligopolist to disavow profit opportunities or to ignore its interdependence with fellow oligopolists is naive. It also violates the basic motivations imputed to a market economy. As long as markets are highly concentrated, we must expect to observe oligopolistic behaviour.

Public efforts to alter market structure have been less frequent than efforts to alter market behaviour. A prevalent feeling today, even among antitrust practitioners, is that the powerful firms are too big and too entrenched to make deconcentration a viable policy alternative.

Antitrust Enforcement

Objections to Antitrust. Some people think *less* antitrust activity is actually a wise policy. The companies challenged by the public "trustbusters" protest that they're being penalized for their success. The Aluminum Company of America (Alcoa) for example, attained a monopoly by investing heavily in a new product before anyone else recognized its value. Other firms too have captured dominant market shares by being first, best, or most efficient. Having "won" the game fairly, why should they have to give up their prize? They contend that noncompetitive *behaviour,* not industry *structure,* should be the only concern of antitrust.

Essentially the same argument is made for proposed mergers and acquisitions. The firms involved claim that the increased concentration will enhance productive efficiency (e.g., via economies of scale). They also argue that big firms are needed to maintain Canada's competitive position in international markets (which are themselves often dominated by foreign monopolies and oligopolies). Those same global markets, they contend, ensure that even highly concentrated domestic markets will be contested by international rivals.

Finally, critics of antitrust suggest that market forces themselves will ensure competitive behaviour. Foreign firms and domestic entrepreneurs will stalk a monopolist's preserve. People will always be looking for ways to enter a profitable market. Monopoly or oligopoly power may slow entry but is unlikely to stop it forever. Eventually, competitive forces will prevail.

Structural Guidelines. There are no easy answers. In theory, competition is valuable, but some mergers and acquisitions undoubtedly increase efficiency. Moreover, some domestic and international markets may require a minimum firm size not consistent with perfect competition. Finally, our regulatory resources are limited; not every acquisition or merger is worthy of public scrutiny.

Where would we draw the line? Can a firm hold a 22 percent market share, but not 30 percent? Are five firms too few, but six firms in an industry enough? Someone has to make those decisions. That is, ***the broad mandates of the antitrust laws must be transformed into specific guidelines for government intervention.***

The "Abuse of Dominance" provisions in sections 78 and 79 of the Competition Act address these issues. Possessing market power, per se, is not sufficient evidence to assume abuse of market power—a firm must also be engaging in anti-competitive behaviour that clearly demonstrates that there has been, or will likely be a significant impact on competition as a result of this behaviour. In the Abuse Guidelines, the Competition Bureau indicates that market shares of *less than 35 percent* do not normally give rise to concerns of market power, whereas the Competition Tribunal suggests that market shares of *less than 50 percent* would need to be tested to determine market power. The spirit of section 79 is to err on the side of non-intervention: currently, all cases brought to the Competition Tribunal have possessed market share in excess of 80 percent.

Contestability. Even when intervention is signalled, however, there are still decisions to make. Should a challenged merger be allowed? The same old questions arise. Will the proposed merger enhance efficiency in domestic and global markets? Or will it tend to constrain competitive forces, keeping consumer prices high?

The Competition Bureau's analysis begins with a definition of the relevant product market. They not only consider closely substitutable products but also the geographic market including foreign competition, imports, and transportation costs. Once dominance has been established, the Bureau must decide if the alleged practice by the dominant firm constitutes an anti-competitive act. This involves examining the degree to which this anti-competitive practice enhances or preserves the dominant firm's market power through the creation or the enhancement of barriers to entry (or barriers to expansion). In other words, contestability as well as structure now motivates antitrust decisions.

The Bureau uses the "but for" test to assess the impact of an anti-competitive practice on competition: but for the anti-competitive practice, would there be significantly more competition?

Under this standard, the question is not simply whether the relevant market would be competitive in the absence of the impugned practice, nor whether the level of competitiveness observed in the presence of the impugned practice is acceptable. Rather, the question is whether, absent the anti-competitive acts, the market would be characterized by, for example, materially lower prices, greater choice or better service.[5]

[5]Scott, Sheridan (Commissioner of Competition). Speaking Notes for Abuse of Dominance Under the Competition Act, delivered to the Federal Trade Commission/Department of Justice Hearings on Single-firm Conduct in Washington, D.C. on September 12, 2006.

SUMMARY

- Imperfect competition refers to markets in which individual suppliers (firms) have some independent influence on the price at which their output is sold. Examples of imperfectly competitive market structures are duopoly, oligopoly, and monopolistic competition.
- The extent of market power (control over price) depends on the number of firms in an industry, their size, barriers to entry, and the availability of substitutes.
- The concentration ratio is a measure of market power in a particular product market. It equals the share of total industry output accounted for by the largest firms, usually the top four.
- An oligopoly is a market structure in which a few firms produce all or most of a particular good or service; it's essentially a shared monopoly.
- Because oligopolies involve several firms rather than only one, each firm must consider the effect of its price and output decisions on the behaviour of rivals. Such firms are highly interdependent.
- Game theory attempts to identify different strategies a firm might use, taking into account the consequences of rivals' moves and countermoves.
- The kinked demand curve illustrates a pattern of strategic interaction in which rivals match a price cut but not a price hike. Such behaviour reinforces the oligopolistic aversion to price competition.

- A basic conflict exists between the desire of each individual oligopolist to expand its market share and the *mutual* interest of all the oligopolists in restricting total output so as to maximize industry profits. This conflict must be resolved in some way, via either collusion or some less explicit form of agreement (such as price leadership).
- Oligopolists may use price-fixing agreements or price leadership to establish the market price. To maintain that price, the oligopolists must also agree on their respective market shares.
- To maintain economic profits, an oligopoly must erect barriers to entry. Patents are one form of barrier. Other barriers include predatory price cutting (price wars), control of distribution outlets, government regulations, advertising (product differentiation), training, and network economies. Outright acquisition and merger may also eliminate competition.
- Market power may cause market failure. The symptoms of that failure include increased prices, reduced output, and a transfer of income from the consuming public to a relatively few powerful corporations and the people who own them.
- Government intervention may focus on either market structure or market behaviour. In either case, difficult decisions must be made about when and how to intervene.

Key Terms

oligopoly 193
concentration ratio 194
oligopolist 197
market share 197

product differentiation 199
game theory 204
price-fixing 208

price leadership 209
cartel 209
predatory pricing 209

Questions for Discussion

1. How many bookstores are on or near your campus? If there were more bookstores, how would the price of new and used books be affected?

2. What entry barriers exist in (a) the fast-food industry, (b) cable television, (c) the auto industry, (d) illegal drug trade, (e) beauty parlors?

3. How did Molson and Labatt respond to the introduction of a new competitor—Mountain Crest Brewing Co.— to their Manitoba market (see the Applications box, page 200)? Of all the possible responses available to Molson and Labatt, why do you think they chose these particular actions?
4. Why would OPEC members have a difficult time setting and maintaining a monopoly price? (See the World View box, page 206.)
5. If an oligopolist knows rivals will match a price cut, would he ever reduce his price?
6. How might the high concentration ratio in the aluminum production industry (Figure 9.1) affect the automobile industry?

7. Identify three products you purchase that aren't listed in Figure 9.1. What is the structure of those three markets?
8. What reasons might Northwest Airlines have for *not* matching its rivals' fare increases? (See the Applications box, page 202.)
9. What is another word for the "avoidable costs" discussed in the Air Canada vs. CanJet case (see the Applications box, page 210)? What do you think are an airline's "avoidable costs" associated with stand-by passengers?
10. Using the payoff matrix in Table 9.3, decide whether Universal should cut its price. What factors will influence the decision?
11. Dominos and Pizza Hut hold 66 percent of the delivered-pizza market. Should antitrust action be taken?

EXERCISES

PROBLEMS The Student Problem Set to accompany this chapter can be found at the end of the book.

WEB ACTIVITIES Web Activities to accompany this chapter can be found on the Online Learning Centre at **http://www.mcgrawhill.ca/olc/schiller**.

CHAPTER 10

Monopolistic Competition

LEARNING OBJECTIVES

By the end of this chapter, you should be able to:

10.1 Define monopolistic competition and identify the monopoly and perfect competition dimensions

10.2 Define product differentiation and explain the role of brand loyalty in pricing/output decisions

10.3 Illustrate the short-run and long-run profit-maximizing equilibrium output for a monopolistic competitor

10.4 Explain how monopolistic competition results in production inefficiency, allocative inefficiency, and excess capacity

With over 2,600 outlets in Canada and revenues of $1.48 billion in 2005, Tim Hortons is already the largest coffee franchise in the country. And the company is determined to keep growing by setting up business in airports, shopping malls, and just about anywhere consumers congregate, including some Esso retail gas stations. Even if Tim Hortons achieves such meteoric growth, however, it will never have great market power. There are hundreds of other coffee bars in Canada (e.g., Starbucks and Second Cup) and thousands of other places you can buy a cup of coffee (e.g., Dunkin Donuts and Sears).

With so many other close substitutes, the best Tim Hortons can hope for is a little brand loyalty. If enough consumers think of Tim Hortons when they get the caffeine urge, Tim Hortons will at least be able to charge more for coffee than a perfectly competitive firm. It won't enjoy *monopoly* profits, or even share the kind of monopoly profits *oligopolies* sometimes achieve. It may, however, be able to maintain an economic profit for many years.

Tim Hortons is an example of yet another market structure—*monopolistic competition*. In this chapter we focus on how such firms make price and output decisions and the market outcomes that result. Our objective is to determine

- **The unique features of monopolistic competition.**
- **How market outcomes are affected by this market structure.**
- **The long-run consequences of different market structures.**

In this chapter we'll also see why we can't escape the relentless advertising that bombards us from every angle.

monopolistic competition: A market in which many firms produce similar goods or services but each maintains some independent control of its own price.

10.1 STRUCTURE

As we first noted in Table 9.1, the distinguishing structural characteristic of **monopolistic competition** is that there are *many* firms in an industry. "Many" isn't an exact specification, of course. It's best understood as lying somewhere between the few that characterize oligopoly and the hordes that characterize perfect competition.

Low Concentration

A more precise way to distinguish monopolistic competition is to examine *concentration ratios*. Oligopolies have very high four-firm concentration ratios. As we saw in Chapter 9 (Figure 9.1), concentration ratios of 70 to 100 percent are common in oligopolies. By contrast, there's much less concentration in monopolistic competition. A few firms may stand above the rest, but the combined market share of the top four firms will typically be in the range of 20 to 40 percent. Hence, *low concentration ratios are common in monopolistic competition.*

According to the 2005 Canadian Coffee Drinking Study conducted by Maritz Research, roughly 70 percent of Canadian coffee consumption occurs at home, while the remaining 30 percent is divided between work and coffee-selling establishments such as Tim Hortons. In terms of concentration ratios, the combined market share of coffee consumption by Tim Hortons, Starbucks, Second Cup, and The Coffee Company is relatively small. Other examples of monopolistic competition include radio stations, health spas, apparel stores, convenience stores, and law firms. Even as large a firm as McDonald's might be regarded as a monopolistic competitor. Although "Mickey D's" has a huge share of the quickie *hamburger* market, its share of the much larger *fast-food* market is significantly smaller. The McDonald's outlets in Canada compete with thousands of fast-food outlets. If consumers regard pizzas, Chinese carry-outs, and delis as close substitutes for hamburgers, then the broader fast-food market is the appropriate basis for measuring market power and concentration.

Market Power

Although concentration rates are low in monopolistic competition, the individual firms aren't powerless. There is a *monopoly* aspect to monopolistic competition. Each producer in monopolistic competition is large enough to have some *market power*. If a perfectly competitive firm increases the price of its product, it will lose all its customers. Recall that a perfectly competitive firm confronts a horizontal demand curve for its output. Competition is less intense in monopolistic competition. *A monopolistically competitive firm confronts a downward-sloping demand curve for its output.* When Starbucks increases the price of coffee, it loses some customers, but nowhere close to all of them (see the Applications box, next page). Starbucks, like other monopolistically competitive firms, has some control over the price of its output. This is the *monopoly* dimension of monopolistic competition.

Independent Production Decisions

In an oligopoly, a firm that increased its price would have to worry about how rivals might respond. In monopolistic competition, however, there are many more firms. As a result, *modest changes in the output or price of any single firm will have no perceptible influence on the sales of any other firm.* This relative independence results from the fact that the effects of any one firm's behaviour will be spread over many other firms (rather than only two or three other firms, as in an oligopoly).

The relative independence of monopolistic competitors means that they don't have to worry about retaliatory responses to every price or output change. As a result, they confront more traditional demand curves, with no kinks. The kink in the oligopolist's curve results from the likelihood that rival oligopolists would match any price reduction (to preserve market shares) but not necessarily any price increase (to increase their shares). In monopolistic competition, the market shares of rival firms aren't perceptibly altered by one firm's price changes.

Low Entry Barriers

Another characteristic of monopolistic competition is the presence of *low barriers to entry*—it's relatively easy to get in and out of the industry. To become a coffee vendor, all you need is boiling water, some fresh beans, and cups. You can save on rent by

Latte Letdown: Starbucks Set to Raise Prices

THAT FRAPPUCCINO FIX is about to cost you more.

Starbucks Corp., the coffee giant that acclimated millions of Americans to paying unheard-of sums for a drink once largely made at home, is planning to raise its prices for the first time in four years. . . . Starbucks will bump up prices 4% to 5% this time, adding a dime or so to the average $2 to $2.50 drink. The increase affects the company's North American stores.

Demand for prepared coffee tends to be fairly resistant to price increases, and economics professors often use Starbucks as an example of a company whose product seems to have little price elasticity—that is, increases seem to have very little effect on consumer demand. By contrast, mass-market grocery brands such as Kraft Foods Inc.'s Folgers and Maxwell House coffees tend to be much more price-elastic, says Burt P. Flickinger III, managing director of Strategic Resource Group, a New York consulting firm that works with retailers and suppliers.

"In the end, Starbucks probably will be able to pass along a price increase without a very big falloff," says Frank Badillo, senior economist at Retail Forward Inc., a Columbus-based consulting firm.

—Steven Gray And Amy Merrick

Source: *The Wall Street Journal,* September 2, 2004. Reprinted by permission of The Wall Street Journal, © 2004 Dow Jones & Company. All rights reserved worldwide.

Analysis: A monopolistically-competitive firm has the power to increase price unilaterally. The greater the brand loyalty, the less unit sales will decline in response.

using a pushcart to dispense the brew. These unusually low entry barriers keep Starbucks and other coffee bars on their toes. Low entry barriers also tend to push economic profits toward zero. This is the *competitive* dimension of monopolistic competition.

10.2 BEHAVIOUR

Given the unique structural characteristics of monopolistic competition we should anticipate some distinctive behaviour.

One of the most notable features of monopolistically competitive behaviour is *product differentiation.* A monopolistically competitive firm is distinguished from a purely competitive firm by its downward-sloping demand curve. Individual firms in a perfectly competitive market confront horizontal demand curves because consumers view their respective products as interchangeable (homogeneous). As a result, an attempt by one firm to raise its price will drive its customers to other firms.

Product Differentiation

Brand Image. In monopolistic competition, each firm has a distinct identity—a *brand image.* Its output is perceived by consumers as being somewhat different from the output of all other firms in the industry. Nowhere is this more evident than in the fast-growing bottled water industry. Pepsi and Coke have become the leaders in the bottled water market as a result of effective marketing (see the Applications box on the next page). Although Aquafina (Pepsi) and Dasani (Coke) are just filtered municipal water, clever advertising campaigns have convinced consumers that these branded waters are different—and better—than hundreds of other bottled waters. As a result of such product differentiation, Pepsi and Coke can raise the price of their bottled waters without losing all their customers to rival firms. As this example illustrates, *perception* can be an important component in the ability to differentiate a product. Products can be identical, but as long as consumers perceive them as different, this is sufficient for firms to acquire a degree of market power.

APPLICATIONS

Water, Water Everywhere; Coke, Pepsi Unleash Flood of Ad Muscle

Water is water, at least until the marketers get hold of it.

Then a humble commodity that literally falls from the sky becomes something else. Something with "personality."

Not long ago, it would have been silly to think about branding water. But the big beverage companies are doing just that, and this summer marks the biggest-ever ad barrage for Dasani, Coke's water brand, and Aquafina, bottled by Pepsi-Cola Co.

Branding is an important issue in a category where sales grew by nearly 26 percent in 2000, to 807 million cases—the highest growth rate in the beverage industry. The challenge is getting attention in a highly fragmented market. There are hundreds of different water brands, and some are so small that they serve just a few towns.

"Consumers are trading up. They're willing to search for a brand," said Kellam Graitcer, Dasani brand manager at Coca-Cola. "We're trying to inject a little bit of personality into the category."

The two companies are likely to spend about $20 million each this year on ads.

—Scott Leith

Source: *Atlanta Journal–Constitution*, July 12, 2001. Copyright 2001 by The Atlanta Journal–Constitution. Reprinted with permission. www.accessatlanta.com/ajc

Analysis: By differentiating their products, monopolistic competitors establish brand loyalty. Brand loyalty gives producers greater control over the price of their products.

Brand Loyalty

At first blush, the demand curve facing a monopolistically competitive firm looks like the demand curve confronting a monopolist. There's a profound difference, however. In a monopoly, there are no other firms. In monopolistic competition, *each firm has a monopoly only on its brand image; it still competes with other firms offering close substitutes.* This implies that the extent of power a monopolistically competitive firm has depends on how successfully it can differentiate its product from that of other firms. The more brand loyalty a firm can establish, the less likely consumers are to switch brands when price is increased. In other words, *brand loyalty makes the demand curve facing the firm less price-elastic.*

Brand loyalty exists even when products are virtually identical. Gasoline of a given octane rating is a very standardized product. Nevertheless, most consumers regularly buy one particular brand. Because of that brand loyalty, Esso can raise the price of its gasoline by a penny or two a gallon without losing its customers to competing companies. According to the accompanying Applications feature, brand loyalty is particularly high for cigarettes, toothpaste, and even laxatives. Brand loyalty is less strong for paper towels and virtually nonexistent for tomatoes.

In the computer industry, product differentiation has been used to establish brand loyalty. Although virtually all computers use identical microprocessor "brains" and operating platforms, the particular mix of functions performed on any computer can be varied, as can its appearance (packaging). Effective advertising can convince consumers that one computer is "smarter," more efficient, or more versatile than another. Also, a single firm may differentiate itself by providing faster or more courteous customer service. If successful in any of these efforts, *each monopolistically competitive firm will establish some consumer loyalty.* With such loyalty a firm can alter its own price somewhat, without fear of great changes in unit sales (quantity demanded). In other words, the demand curve facing each firm will slope downward, as in Figure 10.1*a*.

One symptom of brand loyalty is consumers' tendency to repurchase the same brand. Nearly 9 out of 10 Apple Macintosh users stick with Apple products when they upgrade or replace computer components. Repurchase rates are 74 percent for Dell, 72 percent for Hewlett-Packard, and 66 percent for Gateway.

Who Can Be Loyal to a Trash Bag?

When generic products were coming on strong a few years ago, J. Walter Thompson, the New York–based ad agency, gauged consumers' loyalty to brands in 80 product categories. It found that the leader in market share was not necessarily the brand-loyalty leader. At that time, Bayer aspirin was the market share leader among headache remedies, but Tylenol had the most loyal following.

Thompson measured the degree of loyalty by asking people whether they'd switch for a 50 percent discount. Cigarette smokers most often said no, making them the most brand-loyal of consumers (see table). Film is the only one of the top five

products that the user doesn't put in his mouth—so why such loyalty? According to Edith Gilson, Thompson's senior president of research, 35-mm film is used by photography buffs, who are not your average snapshooter: "It's for long-lasting emotionally valued pictures, taken by someone who has invested a lot of money in his camera." Plenty of shoppers will try a different cola for 50 percent off, and most consumers think one plastic garbage bag or facial tissue is much like another.

—Anne B. Fisher

High-Loyalty Products	Medium-Loyalty Products	Low-Loyalty Products
Cigarettes	Cola drinks	Paper towels
Laxatives	Margarine	Crackers
Cold remedies	Shampoo	Scouring powder
35-mm film	Hand lotion	Plastic trash bags
Toothpaste	Furniture polish	Facial tissue

Brand names matter more in some products than in others, researchers find.

Analysis: Brand loyalty implies that consumers shun substitute goods even when they are cheaper. This renders the demand curve less price-elastic.

Another symptom of brand loyalty is the price differences between computer brands. Consumers are willing to pay more for an HP- or Dell-branded computer than a no-name computer with identical features. For the same reason, consumers are willing to pay more for Starbucks coffee or ice cream, even when identical products are available at lower prices.

Short-Run Price and Output

The monopolistically competitive firm's *production decision* is similar to that of a monopolist. Both types of firms confront downward-sloping demand and marginal revenue curves. To maximize profits, both seek the rate of output at which marginal revenue equals marginal cost. This short-run profit-maximizing outcome is illustrated by point K in Figure 10.1a. That MC = MR intersection establishes q_a as the profit-maximizing rate of output. The demand curve indicates (point F) that q_a of output can be sold at the price of p_a. Hence q_a, p_a illustrates the short-run equilibrium of the monopolistically competitive firm.

Entry and Exit

Figure 10.1a indicates that this monopolistically competitive firm is earning an **economic profit:** Price (p_a) exceeds average total cost (c_a) at the short-run rate of output. These profits are of course a welcome discovery for the firm. They also portend increased competition, however.

If firms in monopolistic competition are earning an economic profit, other firms will flock to the industry. Remember that **entry barriers are low in monopolistic competition so new entrants can't be kept out of the market.** If they get wind of the short-run profits depicted in Figure 10.1a, they'll come running.

As new firms enter the industry, supply increases and prices will be pushed down the market demand curve, just as in competitive markets. Figure 10.2a illustrates these

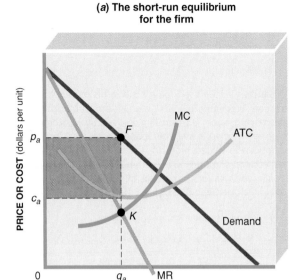

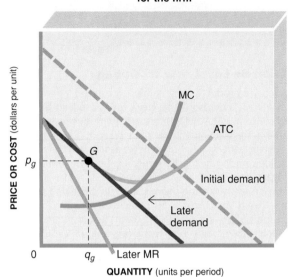

(a) The short-run equilibrium for the firm

(b) The long-run equilibrium for the firm

FIGURE 10.1
Equilibrium in Monopolistic Competition

(a) Short run   In the short run, a monopolistically competitive firm equates marginal revenue and marginal cost (point *K*). In this case, the firm sells the resulting output at a price (point *F*) above marginal cost. Total profits are represented by the shaded rectangle.

(b) Long run   In the long run, more firms enter the industry. As they do so, the demand curve facing each firm *shifts* to the left, as all market shares decline. Firms still equate MR and MC. Ultimately, however, the demand curve will be tangent to the ATC curve (point *G*), at which point price equals average total cost and no economic profits exist.

market changes. The initial price p_1 is set by the intersection of *industry* MC and MR. Because that price generates a profit, more firms enter. This entry shifts the *industry* cost structure to the right, creating a new equilibrium price, p_2.

The impact of this entry on the firms already in the market will be different from that in competitive markets, however. As new firms enter a monopolistically competitive industry, existing firms will lose customers. This is illustrated by the leftward shift of the demand curve facing each firm, as in Figure 10.2*b*. Accordingly, we conclude that *when firms enter a monopolistically competitive industry,*

- *The industry cost curves shift to the right, pushing down price* (Figure 10.2*a*).
- *The demand curves facing individual firms shift to the left* (Figure 10.2*b*).

As the demand curve it faces shifts leftward, the monopolistically competitive firm will have to make a new production decision. It need not charge the same price as its rivals, however, or coordinate its output with theirs. Each monopolistically competitive firm has some independent power over its (shrinking numbers of) captive customers.

No Long-Run Profits   Although each firm has some control over its own pricing decisions, continued leftward shifts of its demand curve will ultimately eliminate economic profits.

Long-run Equilibrium.   Notice in Figure 10.1*b* where the firm eventually ends up. In long-run equilibrium, marginal cost is again equal to marginal revenue. At that rate of output (q_g), however, there are no economic profits. At that output, price (p_g) is exactly equal to average total cost. The profit-maximizing equilibrium (point *G*) occurs where the demand curve is tangent to the ATC curve. If the demand curve shifted any farther left, price would always be less than ATC and the firm would incur losses. If the demand curve were positioned farther to the right, price would exceed

(a) Effect of entry on the industry

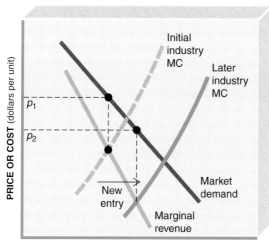

(b) Effect of entry on the monopolistically competitive firm

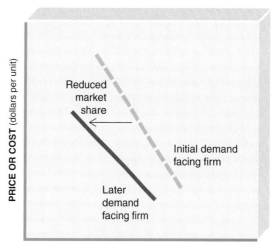

FIGURE 10.2
Market vs. Firm Effects of Entry

Barriers to entry are low in monopolistic competition. Hence, new firms will enter if economic profits are available.

(a) **The Market**   The entry of new firms will shift the *market* cost curves to the right, as in part *a*. This pushes the average price down the *market* demand curve.

(b) **The Firm**   The entry of new firms also affects the demand curve facing the typical firm. The *firm's* demand curve shifts to the left and becomes more elastic because more close substitutes (other firms) are available.

ATC at some rates of output. When the demand curve is *tangent* to the ATC curve, the firm's best possible outcome is to break even. At point *G* in Figure 10.1*b*, price equals ATC and economic profit is zero.

Will a monopolistically competitive firm end up at point *G*? As long as other firms can enter the industry, the disappearance of economic profits is inevitable. Firms will enter as long as the demand (price) line lies above ATC at some point. Firms will exit when the demand facing the firm lies to the left and below the ATC curve. Entry and exit cease when the firm's demand curve is *tangent* to the ATC curve. Once entry and exit cease, the long-run equilibrium has been established. *In the long run, there are no economic profits in monopolistic competition.*

Inefficiency

The zero-profit equilibrium of firms in monopolistic competition, as illustrated in Figure 10.1*b*, differs from the perfectly competitive equilibrium. In the long run, a competitive industry produces at the *lowest* point on the ATC curve and thus maximizes efficiency. In monopolistic competition, however, the demand curve facing each firm slopes downward. Hence, it can't be tangent to the ATC curve at its lowest point (the bottom of the U), as in perfect competition. Instead, the demand curve of a monopolistically competitive firm must touch the ATC curve on the *left* side of the U. Note in Figure 10.1*b* how point *G* lies above and to the left of the bottom of the ATC curve. This long-run equilibrium occurs at an output rate that is less than the minimum-cost rate of production. In long-run equilibrium, the monopolistically competitive industry isn't producing at minimum average co st. As a consequence, *monopolistic competition tends to be less efficient in the long run than a perfectly competitive industry.*

Excess Capacity. One symptom of the inefficiencies associated with monopolistic competition is industrywide excess capacity. Each firm tries to gain market share by building more outlets and advertising heavily. In equilibrium, however, the typical firm is producing at a rate of output that's less than its minimum-ATC output rate. This implies that the *same* level of *industry* output could be produced at lower cost with fewer firms. If that happened, the resources used to develop that excess capacity could be used for more desired purposes.

Flawed Price Signals. The misallocation of resources that occurs in monopolistic competition is a by-product of the flawed price signal that is transmitted in imperfectly competitive markets. Because the demand curve facing a firm in monopolistic competition slopes downward, such a firm will violate the principle of *marginal cost pricing*. Specifically, it will always price its output above the level of marginal costs, just like firms in an oligopoly or monopoly. Notice in Figure 10.1 that price lies above marginal cost in both the short- and long-run equilibrium. As a consequence, price always exceeds the opportunity cost. Consumers respond to these flawed signals by demanding fewer goods from monopolistically competitive industries than they would otherwise. We end up with the wrong (suboptimal) mix of output and misallocated resources.

Thus, *monopolistic competition results in both production inefficiency (above-minimum average cost) and allocative inefficiency (wrong mix of output).* This contrasts with the model of perfect competition, which delivers both minimum average total cost and efficient (MC-based) price signals. Figure 10.3 illustrates the long-run equilibrium for these two distinct market structures.

No Cease-Fire in Advertising Wars

Models of oligopoly and monopolistic competition show how industry structure affects market behaviour. Of particular interest is the way different kinds of firms "compete" for sales and profits. *In truly (perfectly) competitive industries, firms compete on the basis of price.* Competitive firms win by achieving greater efficiency and offering their products at the lowest possible price.

Firms in imperfectly competitive markets don't "compete" in the same way. In oligopolies, the kink commonly found in the demand curve facing each firm inhibits price reductions. In monopolistic competition, there's also a reluctance to engage in price competition. Because each firm has its own captive market—consumers who

FIGURE 10.3
Monopolistic Competition vs. Perfect Competition in the Long Run

In the long run, a perfectly competitive firm makes zero economic profits, takes the price as given (p_a), and produces at the minimum-cost rate of production (q_a). Even though a monopolistically competitive firm also makes zero economic profits in the long run, the fact that it has some market power ensures that the price is higher (p_b) and the rate of production (q_b) is less a perfectly competitive firm. The difference between the two levels of equilibrium output ($q_a - q_b$) represents the excess capacity associated with monopolistic competition. The long-run inefficiency of a monopolistically competitive firm is illustrated by the fact that at the equilibrium quantity, price is greater than marginal cost. ($p_b > c_b$).

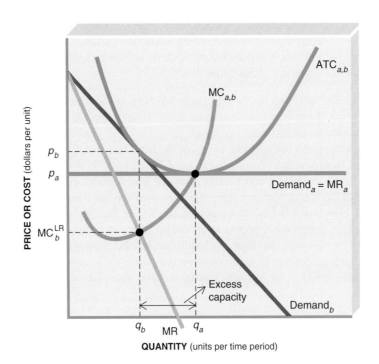

prefer its particular brand over competing brands—price reductions by one firm won't induce many consumers to switch brands. Thus, price reductions aren't a very effective way to increase sales or market share in monopolistic competition.

If imperfectly competitive firms don't compete on the basis of price, do they really compete at all? The answer is evident to anyone who listens to the radio, watches television, reads magazines or newspapers, or drives on the highway: ***Imperfectly competitive firms engage in nonprice competition.***

The most prominent form of *nonprice competition* is advertising. An imperfectly competitive firm typically uses advertising to enhance its own product's image, thereby increasing the size of its captive market (consumers who identify with a particular brand). The Coca-Cola Company hires rock stars to create the image that Coke is superior to other soft drinks, thereby creating brand loyalty. Procter & Gamble spends billions in the hope that these expenditures shift the demand for its products (e.g., Ivory Soap, Pampers, Jif peanut butter, Crest, Tide) to the right, while perhaps making it less price-elastic as well. America Online, Yahoo!, and Amazon.com spent hundreds of millions of dollars in the 1990s to establish brand loyalty in crowded dot.com markets. By contrast, perfectly competitive firms have no incentive to advertise because they can individually sell their entire output at the current market price.

A company that runs a successful advertising campaign can create enormous *goodwill* value. That value is reflected in stronger brand loyalty—as expressed in greater demand and smaller price elasticity. Often a successful brand image can be used to sell related products as well. According to the World View box on the next page, the most valuable brand name in Canada is the RBC Financial Group (Royal Bank of Canada), whose brand name value is $4 billion dollars. Four of the top 10 Canadian firms are in the banking/financial services. Contrast this to the world rankings, where the top firm is Coca-Cola and whose world-wide name recognition is worth nearly $70 billion ($US). Among the top ten global firms, the computer industry (Microsoft, IBM, and Intel) is the dominant sector.

Advertising isn't the only form of nonprice competition. Before the airline industry was deregulated (1984), individual airlines were compelled to charge the same price for any given trip; hence, price competition was prohibited. But airlines did compete—not only by advertising, but also by offering "special" meals, movies, more frequent or convenient departures, and faster ticketing and baggage services.

Is there anything wrong with nonprice competition? Surely airline passengers enjoyed their "special" meals, "extra" services, and "more convenient" departure times. But these services weren't free. As always, there were opportunity costs. From an air traveller's perspective, the "special" services stimulated by nonprice competition substituted for cheaper fares. With more price competition, customers could have chosen travel more cheaply *or* in greater comfort. From society's perspective, the resources used in advertising and other forms of nonprice competition could be used instead to produce larger quantities of desired goods and services (including airplane trips). Unless consumers are given the chance to *choose* between "more" service and lower prices, there's a presumption that nonprice competition leads to an undesirable use of our scarce resources. For example, marketing costs absorb over a third of the price of breakfast cereal. As a result of such behaviour, consumers end up with more advertising but less cereal than they would otherwise. They could, of course, save money by buying store brand or generic cereals. But they've never seen athletes or cartoon characters endorse such products. So consumers pay the higher price for branded cereals.

Models of imperfect competition imply that advertising wars between powerful corporations won't end anytime soon. As long as markets have the *structure* of oligopoly or monopolistic competition, we expect the *behaviour* of nonprice competition. Advertising jingles will be as pervasive in the economy tomorrow as they are today.

> **WEB NOTE**
>
> For the latest surveys and research on brands and brand loyalty, visit http://www.interbrand.com/surveys.asp.

The Best Canadian and Global Brands

A belief in the power of brands and brand management has spread far beyond the traditional consumer-goods marketers who invented the discipline. For companies in almost every industry, brands are important in a way they never were before. Why? For one thing, customers for everything from soda pop to software now have a staggering number of choices. And the Net can bring the full array to any computer screen with a click of the mouse. Without trusted brand names as touchstones, shopping for almost anything would be overwhelming. Meanwhile, in a global economy, corporations must reach customers in markets far from their home base. A strong brand acts as an ambassador when companies enter new markets or offer new products.

That's why companies that once measured their worth strictly in terms of tangibles such as factories, inventory, and cash have realized that a vibrant brand, with its implicit promise of quality, is an equally important asset. A brand has the power to command a premium price among customers and a premium stock price among investors. It can boost earnings and cushion cyclical downturns—and now, a brand's value can be measured.

Canada's and the World's 10 Most Valuable Brands

	Canada		World	
Rank	Brand	2006 Brand Value ($Cdn billions)	Brand	2006 Brand Value ($US billions)
1	RBC Financial Group	4.0	Coca-Cola	67.0
2	TD Canada Trust	3.2	Microsoft	56.9
3	Petro-Canada	3.1	IBM	56.2
4	Bell	2.9	GE	48.9
5	Shoppers Drug Mart	2.8	Intel	32.3
6	Tim Hortons	1.9	Nokia	30.1
7	BMO Financial Group	1.9	Toyota	27.9
8	Canadian Tire	1.6	Disney	27.8
9	Scotiabank	1.4	McDonald's	27.5
10	Telus	1.1	Mercedes	21.8

Source: Based on "Best Canadian Brands 2006: A Ranking by Brand Value," *Report on Business* Interbrand, July 24, 2006, http://www.ourfishbowl.com/images/surveys/Interbrand_BCB2006.pdf; and from the world: Interbrand press release "The BusinessWeek/Interbrand Annual Ranking of the 2006 Best Global Brands," July 26, 2006, http://www.ourfishbowl.com/images/press_releases/IB_Press_Release_BGB06.pdf.

Analysis: Brand names are valuable economic assets and assist a firm in maintaining a base of loyal customers. These brands have national and worldwide recognition as a result of heavy advertising.

SUMMARY

- There are many (rather than few) firms in monopolistic competition. The concentration ratio in such industries tends to be low (20–40 percent).
- Each monopolistically competitive firm enjoys some brand loyalty. This brand loyalty, together with its relatively small market share, gives each firm a high degree of independence in price and output decisions.

- The amount of market share and power a monopolistically competitive firm possesses depends on how successfully it differentiates its product from similar products. Accordingly, monopolistically competitive firms tend to devote more resources to advertising.

- Low entry barriers permit new firms to enter a monopolistically competitive industry whenever economic profits exist. Such entry eliminates long-run economic profit and reduces (shifts leftward) the demand for the output of existing firms.
- Monopolistic competition results in resource misallocations (due to flawed price signals) and inefficiency (above-minimum average cost).

- Monopolistic competition encourages nonprice competition instead of price competition. Because the resources used in nonprice competition (advertising, packaging, service, etc.) may have more desirable uses, these industry structures lead to resource misallocation.

Key Terms

monopolistic competition   218

Questions for Discussion

1. Why does Starbucks worry less about a potential "fall off" than does Maxwell House?
2. What are the entry barriers to the pizza business? Are they relatively high or low?
3. If auto firms eliminated their advertising, could they reduce car prices? What would happen to unit sales?
4. If one gas station reduces its prices, must other gas stations match the price reduction? Why or why not?
5. In a brand loyalty study, 70 percent of the people who swore loyalty to either Coke or Pepsi picked the wrong cola in a taste test! If consumers can't identify their favourite cola in blind taste tests, why then do people stick with one brand? What accounts for brand loyalty in bottled water (Applications box, p. 220)?

6. What kinds of resources are used in a TV advertising campaign? How else might those resources be used?
7. Why is the mix of output produced in competitive markets more desirable than that in monopolistically competitive markets?
8. How would our consumption of cereal change if cereal manufacturers stopped advertising? Would we be better or worse off?
9. Why are people willing to pay more for Dreyer's ice cream when it has a Starbucks brand on it?
10. According to the World View box on page 226, what gives brand names their value?

EXERCISES

PROBLEMS   The Student Problem Set to accompany this chapter can be found at the end of the book.

WEB ACTIVITIES   Web Activities to accompany this chapter can be found on the Online Learning Centre at **http://www.mcgrawhill.ca/olc/schiller**.

Regulatory Issues

Microeconomic theory provides insights into how prices and product flows are determined in unregulated markets. Sometimes those market outcomes are not optimal and the government intervenes to improve them. In this section we examine government regulation of natural monopolies (Chapter 11) and environmental protection (Chapter 12). The goal is to determine whether and how government regulation might improve market outcomes or worsen them.

(De)Regulation of Business

The lights went out in California in 2001—not just once but repeatedly. Offices went dark, air conditioners shut down, assembly lines stopped, and TV screens went blank. The state governor blamed power-company "profiteers" for the rolling blackouts. He charged the companies with curtailing power supplies and hiking prices. He wanted *more* regulation of the power industry. Industry representatives responded that government regulation was itself responsible for throwing California into a new Dark Age. *Less* regulation, not more, would keep the lights on, they claimed.

As a consequence of this crisis, the battle over government regulation of the power industry quickly spread to other U.S. states. Some states that were deregulating power suspended the process; others put (de)regulation plans on hold until they could better assess what went wrong in California. In Canada, the process for deregulation of the power sector continued in two provinces; Alberta and Ontario. And while both provinces have reached the stage of privatization at the retail access level, the process is far from complete.

Everyone agrees that markets sometime fail—that unregulated markets may produce the wrong mix of output, undesirable methods of production, or an unfair distribution of income. But government intervention can fail as well. Hence, we need to ask,

- **When is government regulation necessary?**
- **What form should that regulation take?**
- **When is it appropriate to deregulate an industry?**

In answering these questions we draw on economic principles as well as recent experience. This will permit us to contrast the theory of (de)regulation with reality.

LEARNING OBJECTIVES

By the end of this chapter, you should be able to:

11.1 Understand the justification for government intervention in a market

11.2 Explain the two government intervention methods for cases of market power leading to market failure

11.3 Define natural monopoly and identify the profit-maximizing equilibrium under this market structure

11.4 Discuss the methods used by governments to regulate natural monopolies and explain the potential problems associated with these methods

11.5 Identify and explain the costs associated with regulation

11.6 Explain the basic policy issue associated with the decision to (de)regulate

11.1 COMPETITION POLICY VS. REGULATION

A perfectly competitive market provides a model for economic efficiency. As we first observed in Chapter 2, the market mechanism can answer the basic economic questions of WHAT to produce, HOW to produce it, and FOR WHOM. Under ideal conditions, the market's answers may also be optimal—that is, they may represent the best possible mix of output. To achieve this *laissez-faire* ideal, all producers must be perfect competitors; people must have full information about tastes, costs and prices; all costs and benefits must be reflected in market prices; and pervasive economies of scale must be absent.

In reality, these conditions are rarely, if ever, fully attained. Markets may be dominated by large and powerful producers. In wielding their power, these producers may restrict output, raise prices, stifle competition, and inhibit innovation. In other words, market power may cause *market failure,* leaving us with suboptimal market outcomes.

As we observed in Chapter 9, the government has two options for intervention where market power prevails. It may focus on the *structure* of an industry or on its *behaviour.* In Canada, the **combine laws** or **competition policy** as defined by the Competition Act cover both options: they prohibit mergers and acquisitions that reduce potential competition (market structures) and forbid market practices (behaviour) that are anticompetitive.[1]

Government **regulation** has a different focus. Instead of worrying about industry structure, regulation focuses almost exclusively on *behaviour.* In general, regulation seeks to change market outcomes directly, by imposing specific limitations on price, output, or investment decisions.

Behavioural Focus

combine laws/competition policy: Government intervention to alter market structure or prevent abuse of market power.

regulation: Government intervention to alter the behaviour of firms, for example, in pricing, output, or advertising.

11.2 NATURAL MONOPOLY

When a natural monopoly exists, the choice between structural remedies and behavioural remedies is simplified. A *natural monopoly* is a *desirable* market structure, because it generates pervasive economies of scale. Because of these scale economies, a natural monopoly can produce the products consumers want at the lowest possible price. A single cable company is more efficient than a horde of cable firms developing a maze of cable networks. The same is true of local telephone service and many utilities. In all of these cases, a single company can deliver products at lower cost than a bunch of smaller firms. Dismantling such a natural monopoly would destroy that cost advantage. Hence, *regulation,* not antitrust, is the more sensible intervention.

Do we need to regulate natural monopolies? Even though a natural monopoly might enjoy economies of scale, it might not pass those savings along to consumers. In that case, the economies of scale don't do consumers any good, and the government might have to regulate the firm's behaviour.

To determine whether regulation is desirable, we first have to determine how an *unregulated* natural monopoly will behave.

Figure 11.1 illustrates the unique characteristics of a natural monopoly. ***The distinctive characteristic of a natural monopoly is its downward-sloping average total cost (ATC) curve.*** Because unit costs keep falling as the rate of production increases, a single large firm can underprice any smaller firm. Ultimately, it can produce all the market supply at the lowest attainable cost. In an unregulated market, such a firm will "naturally" come to dominate the industry.

Declining ATC Curve

[1] In the United States, the equivalent laws are called antitrust laws.

FIGURE 11.1

Natural Monopoly: Price Regulation

A natural monopoly confronts a downward-sloping ATC curve; MC is always less than ATC. If unregulated, a natural monopoly will produce q_A and charge p_A, as determined by the intersection of the marginal cost and marginal revenue curves (point A).

Regulation designed to achieve efficient prices will seek point B, where $p = $ MC. Still lower average costs (production efficiency) are attainable at higher rates of output, however. On the other hand, a zero-profit, zero-subsidy outcome exists only at point C.

Which price-output combination should be sought?

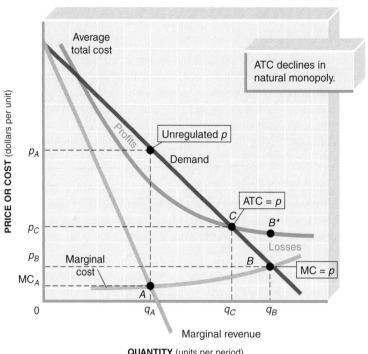

The force that pulls down the ATC curve in a natural monopoly is low marginal cost. Notice in Figure 11.1 that *the marginal cost (MC) curve lies below the ATC curve at all rates of output for a natural monopoly.* The ATC curve never rises into its conventional U shape because marginal costs never exceed average costs.

Subway systems, local telephone and utility companies, and cable TV operators are examples of natural monopoly. In all these cases, huge fixed costs are required to establish production facilities (such as subway tunnels and transmission cables). The marginal cost of producing another rider, call, or program is negligible, however. As a result, average total costs start high but continuously decline until capacity is reached.

The declining costs of a natural monopoly are of potential benefit to society. The *economies of scale* offered by a natural monopoly imply that no other market structure can supply the good as cheaply. Hence, **natural monopoly is a desirable market structure.** A competitive market structure—with many smaller firms—would have higher average cost.

Unregulated Behaviour

Although the **structure** *of a natural monopoly may be beneficial, its* **behaviour** *may leave something to be desired.* Natural monopolists have the same profit-maximizing motivations as other producers. Moreover, they have the monopoly power to achieve and maintain economic profits. Hence, there's no guarantee that consumers will reap the benefits of a natural monopoly. Critics charge that the monopolist tends to keep most of the benefits. This has been a recurrent criticism of cable TV operators: Consumers have complained about high prices, poor service, and a lack of programming choices from local cable monopolies.

Figure 11.1 illustrates the unregulated behaviour of a natural monopolist. Like all other producers, the natural monopolist will maximize profits by producing at that rate of output where marginal revenue equals marginal cost. Point *A* in Figure 11.1 indicates that an unregulated monopoly will end up producing the quantity q_A and charging the price p_A.

The natural monopolist's preferred outcome isn't the most desirable one for society. This price-output combination violates the competitive principle of *marginal cost pricing.* The monopoly price p_A greatly exceeds the marginal cost of producing q_A of output, as represented by MC$_A$ in Figure 11.1. As a result of this gap, consumers aren't getting accurate information about the *opportunity cost* of this product. This flawed price signal is the cause of market failure. We end up consuming less of this product (and more of other goods) than we would if charged its true opportunity cost. A suboptimal mix of output results.

The natural monopolist's profit-maximizing output (q_A) also fails to minimize average total cost. In a competitive industry, ATC is driven down to its minimum by relentless competition. In this case, however, reductions in ATC cease when the monopolist achieves the profit-maximizing rate of output (q_A). Were output to increase further, average total costs would fall.

Finally, notice that the higher price (p_A) associated with the monopolist's preferred output (q_A) ensures a fat profit. The *economic profit* may violate our visions of equity. In 2001, millions of Californians were convinced that this kind of "profiteering" was the root of their electricity woes.

11.3 REGULATORY OPTIONS

The suboptimal outcomes likely to emerge from a free-swinging natural monopoly prompt consumers to demand government intervention. The market alone can't overcome the natural advantage of pervasive economies of scale. But the government could compel different outcomes. The question is, which outcomes do we want? And how will we get them?

Price Regulation

For starters, we might consider price regulation. The natural monopolist's preferred price (p_A) is, after all, a basic cause of market failure. By regulating the firm, the government can compel a lower price. The California legislature did this in 1996 when it set a maximum retail price for electricity.

As is apparent from Figure 11.1 there are lots of choices in setting a regulated price. We start with the conviction that the unregulated price p_A is too high. But where on the demand curve below p_A do we want to be?

Price Efficiency. One possibility is to set the price at a level consistent with opportunity costs. As we saw earlier, a monopolist's unregulated price sends out a flawed price signal. By charging a price in excess of marginal cost, the monopolist causes a suboptimal allocation of resources. We could improve market outcomes, therefore, by compelling the monopolist to set the price equal to marginal cost. Such an efficient price would lead us to point B in Figure 11.1, where the demand curve and the marginal cost curve intersect. At that price (p_B), consumers would get optimal use of the good or service produced.

Subsidy. Although the price p_B will ensure allocative efficiency, it will also bankrupt the producer. In a natural monopoly, MC is always less than ATC. Hence, ***marginal cost pricing by a natural monopolist implies a loss on every unit of output produced.*** In this case, the loss per unit is equal to $B^* - B$. If confronted with the regulated price p_B, the firm will ultimately shut down and exit from the market. This was one of the many problems that plagued California. Unable to charge a price high enough to cover their costs, some of the state's utility companies were forced into bankruptcy.

If we want to require efficient pricing (p = MC), we must provide a subsidy to the natural monopoly. In Figure 11.1 the amount of the subsidy would have to equal the anticipated loss at q_B, that is, the quantity q_B multiplied by the per-unit loss ($B^* - B$). Such subsidies are provided to subway systems. With subsidies, local subway systems can charge fees below *average* cost and closer to *marginal* cost. These subsidized fares increase ridership, thus ensuring greater use of very expensive transportation systems.

Despite the advantages of this subsidized pricing strategy, taxpayers always complain about the cost of such subsidies. Taxpayers are particularly loath to provide them for private companies. Hence, political considerations typically preclude efficient (marginal cost) pricing, despite the economic benefits of this regulatory strategy.

Production Efficiency. Even if it were possible to impose marginal cost pricing, we still wouldn't achieve maximum production efficiency. Production efficiency is attained at the lowest possible average total cost. At q_B we're producing a lot of output but still have some unused capacity. Since ATC falls continuously, we could achieve still lower average costs if we increased output beyond q_B. *In a natural monopoly, production efficiency is achieved at capacity production, where ATC is at a minimum.*

Increasing output beyond q_B raises the same problems we encountered at that rate of output. At production rates in excess of q_B, ATC is always higher than price. Even MC is higher than price to the right of point *B*. Thus, *no regulated price can induce the monopolist to achieve minimum average cost. A subsidy would be required to offset the market losses.*

Profit Regulation

Instead of price regulation, we could try profit regulation. If we choose not to subsidize a natural monopolist, we must permit it to charge a price high enough to cover all its costs, including a normal profit. We can achieve the result by mandating a price equal to average total cost. In Figure 11.1 this regulatory objective is achieved at point *C*. In this case, the rate of output is q_C and the regulated price is p_C.

Profit regulation looks appealing for two reasons. First, it eliminates the need to subsidize the monopolist. Second, it allows us to focus on profits only, thus removing the need to develop demand and cost curves. In theory, all we have to do is check the firm's annual profit-and-loss statement to confirm that it's earning a normal (average) profit. If its profits are too high, we can force the firm to reduce its price; if profits are too low, we may permit a price increase.

Bloated Costs. While beautiful in principle, profit regulation can turn out ugly in practice. In particular, profit regulation can lead to bloated costs and dynamic inefficiency. *If a firm is permitted a specific profit rate (or rate of return), it has no incentive to limit costs.* On the contrary, higher costs imply higher profits. If permitted to charge 10 percent over unit costs, a monopolist may be better off with average costs of $6 rather than only $5. The higher costs translate into 60 cents of profit per unit rather than only 50 cents. Hence, there's an incentive to "pad costs." If those costs actually represent improvements in wages and salaries, fringe benefits, or the work environment, then cost increases are doubly attractive to the firm and its employees. Cost efficiency is as welcome as the plague under such circumstances.

Output Regulation

Given the difficulties in regulating prices and profits, regulators may choose to regulate output instead. The natural monopolist's preferred output rate is q_A, as illustrated again in Figure 11.2. We could compel this monopolist to provide a minimum level of service in excess of q_A. This regulated minimum is designated q_D in Figure 11.2. At q_D consumers get the benefit not only of more output but also of a lower price (p_D). At q_D total monopoly profit must also be less than at q_A, since q_A was the profit-maximizing rate of output.

It appears, then, that compelling any rate of output in excess of q_A can only benefit consumers. Moreover, output regulation is an easy rule to enforce.

Quality Deterioration. Unfortunately, minimum-service regulation can also cause problems. If forced to produce at the rate of q_D, the monopolist may seek to increase profits by cutting cost corners. This can be accomplished by deferring plant and equipment maintenance, reducing quality control, or otherwise lowering the quality of service. *Regulation of the quantity produced may induce a decline in quality.* Since a monopolist has no direct competition, consumers pretty much have to accept whatever quality the monopolist offers. This structural reality may explain why consumers complain so much about the services of local cable monopolies.

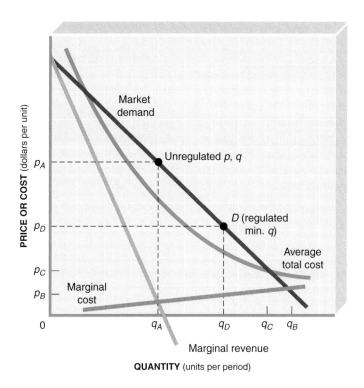

FIGURE 11.2
Minimum Service Regulation

Regulation may seek to ensure some minimal level of service. In this case, the required rate of output is arbitrarily set at q_D. Consumers are willing to pay p_D per unit for that output.

Regulated output q_D is preferable to the unregulated outcome (q_A, p_A) but may induce a decline in quality. Cost cutting is the only way to increase profits when the rate of output is fixed and price is on the demand curve.

In addition to encouraging quality deterioration, output regulation at q_D also violates the principle of marginal cost pricing. Because an economic profit exists at q_D, equity goals may be jeopardized as well. Hence, minimum service (output) regulation isn't a panacea for the regulatory dilemma. In fact, there is no panacea: *Goal conflicts are inescapable, and any regulatory rule may induce undesired producer responses.*

Imperfect Answers

The call for public regulation of natural monopolies is based on the recognition that the profit motive doesn't generate optimal outcomes in any monopoly environment. If unregulated, a natural monopolist will charge too much and produce too little. The regulatory remedy for these market failures isn't evident, however. Regulators can compel efficient prices or least-cost production only by offering a subsidy. Profit regulation is likely to induce cost-inflating responses. Output regulation is an incentive for quality deterioration. No matter which way we turn, regulatory problems result.

There's not much hope for transforming unregulated market failure into perfect regulated outcomes. In reality, regulators must choose a strategy that balances competing objectives (e.g., price efficiency and equity). A realistic goal for regulation is to *improve* market outcomes, not to *perfect* them. In the real world, *the choice isn't between imperfect markets and flawless government intervention but rather between imperfect markets and imperfect intervention.*

The argument for *deregulation* rests on the observation that government regulation sometimes worsens market outcomes. In some cases, *government failure* may be worse than market failure. Specifically, regulation may lead to price, cost, or production outcomes that are inferior to those of an unregulated market.

11.4 THE COSTS OF REGULATION

Improving outcomes in a particular market isn't adequate proof of regulatory success. We also have to consider the *costs* incurred to change market outcomes.

Administrative Costs

As we've observed, industry regulation entails various options and a host of trade-offs. Someone must sit down and assess these trade-offs. To make a sound decision, a regulatory administration must have access to lots of information. At a minimum, the regulator must have some clue as to the actual shape and position of the demand and cost curves depicted in Figures 11.1 and 11.2. Crude illustrations won't suffice when decisions about the prices, output, or costs of a multibillion-dollar industry are being made. The regulatory agency needs volumes of details about actual costs and demand and a platoon of experts to collect and analyze the needed data. All this labour represents a real cost to society, since the agency's lawyers, accountants, and economists could be employed elsewhere. In addition to federal regulatory agencies, thousands of other individuals are employed by provincial and municipal agencies. All of these regulators are part of our limited labour resources. By using them to regulate private industry, we are forgoing their use in the production of desired goods and services. This is a significant economic cost.

Compliance Costs

The administrative costs of regulation focus on resources used in the public sector. By its very nature, however, regulation also changes resource use in the private sector. Regulated industries must expend resources to educate themselves about the regulations, to change their production behaviour, and often to file reports with the regulatory authorities. The human and capital resources used for these purposes represent the *compliance* cost of regulation.

New rules on U.S. trucking, for example, illustrate how regulation can increase production costs. In 2003, the U.S. Department of Transportation reduced the amount of permitted driving time for interstate truckers (see the Applications box). This rule requires freight companies to use more trucks and more labour to transport goods, thereby raising economic costs. Although the resultant gain in safety is desired, the cost of achieving that gain is not inconsequential.

Efficiency Costs

Finally, we have to consider the potential costs of changes in output. Most regulation alters the mix of output, either directly or indirectly. Ideally, regulation will always improve the mix of output. But it's possible that bad decisions, incomplete information, or faulty implementation may actually *worsen* the mix of output. If this occurs,

APPLICATIONS

Costs of Trucking Seen Rising Under New Safety Rules

The first major changes in truck-driver work hours since 1939 are expected to reduce highway fatalities, but also contribute to the biggest increase in trucking rates in two decades. . . .

The new rules increase the time that truck drivers must set aside to rest in each 24-hour period to 10 hours from eight hours, and the total time a driver can be on duty will fall to 14 hours from 15 hours. . . .

The government estimates the new rules could cost trucking companies about $1.3 billion a year. . . .

Because trucks haul so much commerce, accounting for more than 81% of the nation's $571 billion freight-transportation bill last year, the effects could be far-reaching. Some users of truck transportation say higher trucking rates could lead to a broad-based increase in prices of goods from paper to chemicals, diapers to trash cans. . . .

Still, "there are about 410 fatalities a year attributed to fatigue-related truck crashes, and that's 410 very good reasons for changing the rule," says Annette Sandberg, administrator of the Transportation Department's Federal Motor Carrier Safety Administration. The agency expects the new rules to save up to 75 lives a year and prevent as many as 1,326 fatigue-related crashes a year.

—Daniel Machalaba

Analysis: Regulations designed to improve market outcomes typically impose higher costs. The challenge is to balance benefits and costs.

then the loss of utility associated with an inferior mix of output imposes a further cost on society, over and above administrative and compliance costs.

Efficiency costs may increase significantly over time. Consumer tastes change, demand and marginal revenue curves shift, costs change, and new technologies emerge. Can regulatory commissions respond to these changes as fast as the market mechanism does? If not, even optimal regulations may soon become obsolete and counterproductive. Worse still, the regulatory process itself may impede new technology, new marketing approaches, or improved production processes. These losses may be the most important. As Robert Hahn of the American Enterprise Institute observed:

> The measurable costs of regulation pale against the distortions that sap the economy's dynamism. The public never sees the factories that weren't built, the new products that didn't appear, or the entrepreneurial idea that drowned in a cumbersome regulatory process.[2]

These kinds of dynamic efficiency losses are a drag on economic growth, limiting outward shifts of the production possibilities curve while perpetuating an increasingly undesired mix of output.

Balancing Benefits and Costs

The economic costs of regulation are a reminder of the "no free lunch" maxim. Although regulatory intervention may improve market outcomes, that intervention isn't without cost. The real resources used in the regulatory process could be used for other purposes. Hence, even if we could achieve perfect outcomes with enough regulation, the cost of achieving perfection might outweigh the benefits. ***Regulatory intervention must balance the anticipated improvements in market outcomes against the economic cost of regulation.*** In principle, the marginal benefit of regulation must exceed its marginal cost. If this isn't the case, then additional regulation isn't desirable, even if it would improve short-run market outcomes.

11.5 DEREGULATION IN PRACTICE

The push to *de*regulate was prompted by two concerns. The first concern focused on the dynamic inefficiencies that regulation imposes. It appeared that these inefficiencies had accumulated over time, rendering regulated industries less productive than desired. The other push for deregulation came from advancing technology, which destroyed the basis for natural monopoly in some industries. A brief review of the resulting deregulation illustrates the impact of these forces.

Railroads

The railroad industry was the federal government's first broad regulatory target. Railroads are an example of natural monopoly, with high fixed costs and negligible marginal costs. Furthermore, there were no airports or interprovincial highways to compete with railroads in 1851 when Canada West and Canada East passed the Railway Act, setting the stage for the initial regulatory phase of the Canadian railway industry. The rationale for this act was based on the safety of railway builders and passengers; politicians of day were concerned about "fly-by-night" railway companies cutting corners on construction and maintenance. And while the government of Canada negotiated some regulated rail rates (see the Applications box) in the late 1800s, these were typically justified under the rubric of "nation-building." It was only with the establishment of the Board of Railway Commissioners in 1904 that the government of Canada had its first independent regulatory body with authority to regulate railways. This regulatory body was created with the intent of limiting monopolistic exploitation while assuring a fair profit to railroad owners.

With the advent of buses, trucks, subways, airplanes, and pipelines as alternative modes of transportation, railroad regulation became increasingly obsolete. Regulated cargoes, routes, and prices prevented railroads from adapting their prices or services to meet changing consumer demands. With regulation-protected routes, they also had

[2]Cited in *Fortune,* October 19, 1992, p. 94.

Crow's Nest Pass Agreement

During the 1890s, rich mineral deposits were discovered in the Kootenay region of southeastern British Columbia. Concerned about American developers extending their rail line northward as well as farmers complaining about high freight rates charged by the Canadian Pacific Railway (CPR), the Canadian government entered into an agreement with CPR on September 6, 1897. The Crow's Nest Pass Agreement provided the CPR with a cash subsidy of $3.3 million and title to extend a line through the Crow's Nest Pass to Nelson, British Columbia in exchange for reduced freight rates, in perpetuity, on eastbound grain and flour and westbound "settlers' effects."

Michael Rogers, 2004.

Over the years, the agreement was suspended, reinstated, and redefined, but the rates remained at the 1897 levels. As such, the "Crow rate" represented an increasingly smaller portion of the cost of grain transportation. For farmers, the rate was an important component of their cost structure—sufficient to attract and retain export markets. For CPR, it did not provide adequate revenues to undertake the required improvement and expansion of lines, nor the level of improved service demanded by farmers and other customers.

In 1983, the Western Grain Transportation Act permitted freight rates for grain to increase gradually—but never to exceed 10 percent of the world price for grain—and the government would pay the difference between the Crow rate and the current rate. In return, the railways agreed to spend $16.5 billion on new equipment and expansion of service by 1992.

By the 1990s, the subsidization of transportation costs on both grain and unprocessed grain products came under increased scrutiny by the United States and Mexico (Canada's NAFTA trading partners) as well as the World Trade Organization. Moreover, the federal government was facing serious budget deficits and under pressure to reduce subsidization programs. Finally, in 1993, after 97 years of debate and negotiated and legislative changes, the Crow's Nest Pass Agreement reached the end of the line.

Analysis: Changes in consumer demand, products, technology, and international commitments can erode the initial rationale for regulation and lead to the <u>de</u>regulation of an industry.

little incentive to invest in new technologies or equipment. As a result, railroad traffic and profits declined while other transportation industries flourished.

The National Transportation Act (NTA) of 1987 was a response to this crisis. It partially deregulated the railway industry in Canada and its major objective was to remove the red tape that railways experienced when attempting to abandon unprofitable lines. Critics of the NTA argued that railways violated the spirit of the legislation. The abandonment of existing lines was intended to be a last-resort option when potential buyers could not be found rather than the first and only choice. In 1996, one year after the federal government privatized Canadian National Railways, they addressed these NTA concerns with the passage of the Railway Abandonment Regulations under the new Canadian Transportation Act (CTA).[3]

Collectively, the railroad companies responded significantly to the increased deregulation of the industry. Table 11.1 presents some interesting 10-year comparisons using data from the Railway Association of Canada (RAC), an association representing some 60 freight, tourist, commuter, and intercity Canadian railway companies. There was a considerable increase in the volume of rail traffic as measured by revenue-tonne

[3]Through the consolidation and revision of both the National Transportation Act and the Railway Act, the Canadian Transportation Act further increased deregulation in the railway industry.

Category	1996	2005	Percent Change
Revenue tonne-kilometres (RTK)* (billions)	193.1	241.7	25.2%
Kilometres of road operated	51,530	48,893	−5.1
Freight cars ('000)	112	102	−8.9
Litres of fuel (millions)	2,043	2,209	8.1
RTK/litre of fuel consumed	138	168	21.7
Employees	47,556	35,389	−25.6
Annual wages per employee ($)	52,671	71,994	36.7
Freight revenue (¢) per tonne-kilometre**	2.30	2.49	8.3
Total operating revenue ($millions)	7,048	9,940	41
Total operating expenses ($millions)	6,659	7,776	16.8
RTK/employee[†] ('000)	5,929	11,210	189.1
Inflation index (CPI: 1996 = 100)	100.0	120.2	20.2

*Revenue tonne-kilometres (RTK) = Movement of one revenue producing tonne of freight the distance of one kilometre.

**Freight revenue (¢) per tonne-kilometre = Freight revenue/total tonnes

[†]Excludes companies not reporting both RTK and employees.

Source: The Railway Association of Canada (www.railcan.ca), accessed November 9, 2006.

TABLE 11.1
Ten-Year Comparison, Members of the Canadian Railway Association

kilometres (RTK) from 1996 to 2005—this in spite of a slight reduction in railway kilometres. Operating expenses measured in real terms (i.e., accounting for inflation) fell over this decade, and although employment in the industry dropped roughly 25 percent, wage remuneration increased in both nominal and real terms. This increase in wages is partly a reflection in the striking productivity gains. The traditional measure of productivity per worker in the railway industry (RTK/employee) shows gains of almost 200 percent over the decade! A portion of these gains is attributable, by definition, to the reduction of the labour force, but "better trained, higher paid and more flexible employees working with new, more productive processes and technology played an integral role in the industry's continuing success to achieve and build on these productivity gains."[4]

Railroad companies prospered by reconfiguring routes and services, lowering freight rates, and increasing investment in infrastructure. Similar effects have been seen with deregulation of railroads in the United States, where there have been concerns about mergers and acquisitions leading to increased concentration in the rail industry. In Canada, the deregulation process outlined in both legislative acts helped transfer thousands of kilometres of short-line routes from Canadian National Railways and Canadian Pacific Railways to short-line operators. More that 80 percent of these routes were originally destined for abandonment. These short-line and regional railways are important for regional economic development. Over the years, they have grown to approximately 40 companies covering over 15,000 kilometres.

The telephone industry has long been the classic example of a natural monopoly. Although enormous fixed costs are necessary to establish a telephone network, the marginal cost of an additional telephone call approaches zero. Hence, it made economic sense to have a single network of telephone lines and switches rather than a maze of competing ones. Recognizing these economies of scale, the government of Canada permitted legal local and regional monopolies on both long-distance and local telephone service. To assure that Canadian consumers would benefit from this natural monopoly, provincial regulators as well as the federal Canadian Radio-television and Telecommunications Commission (CRTC) regulated the industry. Although basic service was extremely reliable, there were

Telephone Service

[4]*Railway Trends 2006,* The Railway Association of Canada, p. 7.

cross-subsidization: Use of high prices and profits on one product to subsidize low prices on another product.

few value-added services and a "return-on-capital" regulatory approach resulted in over-investment in facilities but little investment in innovation. Moreover, the desire of Canadians to have the lowest possible local rates gave rise to the **cross-subsidization** of these rates at the expense of exorbitant long-distance rates.

Once again, technology outpaced regulation. Communications satellites made it much easier and less costly for new firms to provide long-distance telephone service. The advent of wireless technology (both digital and analog) removed the need for expensive underground, line-based telephone systems. Moreover, the populist demands for low local rates created an extremely profitable long-distance service sector of the industry. Accordingly, start-up firms clamoured to get into the industry, and consumers petitioned for lower rates.

Long Distance. In June 1992, Canada started the deregulation process in the long-distance telephone service with the CRTC approval of competition between business and residential public long-distance voice services in Quebec, Ontario, British Columbia, and the Maritime Provinces. In 1994, the 10 regional companies were required to provide equal access to their transmission networks. Over 200 new companies entered the industry and telephone rates fell by 40 percent. The quality of service also improved with fibre optic cable, advanced switching systems, cell phones, and myriad new phone-line services such as fax transmissions, remote access, and Voice over Internet Protocol (VoIP). All these changes have contributed to a substantial increase in long-distance telephone use in Canada. The same kinds of changes have occurred around the world as other telephone monopolies have crumbled (see the World View box).

Local Service. The deregulation of long-distance services was so spectacularly successful that observers wondered whether local telephone service might be deregulated as well. As competition in *long-distance* services increased, the monopoly nature of

WORLD   VIEW

Demise of Telephone Monopolies

The breakup of Canada's local and regional monopolies was spurred by new technology that undercut the basis for natural monopoly. The same technological advances have transformed the telecommunications industry around the world:

- *United States:* In 1982, the courts put an end to AT&T's monopoly. Over 800 firms have entered the industry and long-distance rates fell more than 40 percent.
- *Japan:* In 1984, the Japanese government ended the monopoly long held by Nippon Telegraph & Telephone (NTT). More than 500 companies have now entered the industry, chipping away at NTT's market share.
- *Great Britain:* The British government has privatized British Telecommunications and licensed another company to build a second, competing network.
- *France:* The French government has retained a single, state-owned network but opened the door to competition in equipment and services.

- *Germany:* The former state-owned monopoly was privatized in 1996. Competitive entry began in 1998.
- *Chile:* The long-established monopoly (Entel) was deregulated in 1994, and entry barriers dropped. Rates plunged and volume doubled. Within two years Entel's market share fell from 100 to 40 percent.
- *Brazil:* The state-owned monopoly (Telebras) was opened to competition in 1998.
- *Mexico:* In 1997, Mexico opened its telecommunications market to competition. New domestic and international fibre optic networks have been built, and phone rates have dropped dramatically.
- *European Union:* At the beginning of 1998, all local and long-distance markets were opened to competition.
- *China:* At the end of 2001, China split its fixed-line monopoly into two regional companies.

Analysis: The deregulation of telephone industries has spurred price competition and innovation, while greatly increasing the volume of telephone service.

local rates became painfully apparent: Local rates kept increasing after 1994 while long-distance rates were tumbling.

In September 1994, the CRTC established a new regulatory framework for Canada outlining the plans for gradual extension of competition into local telephone services. This plan allowed for competition between telephone companies, cable TV operators, wireless service providers, re-sellers, and special service providers across a range of voice, data, and video services. Competition in the local market evolved much more slowly than the long-distance sector. By 2005, however, competition had increased to the point where many Canadians could choose to buy their local service from cable companies, VoIP companies, and other telephone companies. In response to the growing competition, and based on a review of Canada's telecommunications framework by the Ministry of Industry, the CRTC set out the final two criteria for deregulation of local telephone services, namely that competitors must have at least 25 percent of the market and the incumbent must have provided competitors with well-functioning access to its network for a six-month period. After deregulation, the incumbents "will be required to ensure affordable basic residential service to vulnerable customers, such as those with no competitive alternative and those with disabilities, and to ensure that certain consumer rights and safeguards are maintained."

The telecommunications industry has changed dramatically since the inception of deregulation; it is perhaps the most affected sector of the Canadian economy. What is certain, however, is that the industry remains on the deregulatory path and often faces issues without previous precedent (see the Applications box).

WEB NOTE

For information on the Canadian Radio-television and Telecommunications Commission (CRTC), visit http://www.crtc.gc.ca/.

APPLICATIONS

Mergers and Mavericks in the Mobile Wireless Services

One of the anticipated outcomes of deregulation is a reduction in concentration leading to greater competition, improved services, and innovation. But what happens when new entrants merge with incumbents? Does the elimination of a competitor lead to a reversal of the deregulation process? In the case of the $1.4 billion acquisition of Microcell Telecommunications Inc. (Fido) by Rogers Wireless Communications Inc. in 2004, the Competition Bureau was not only concerned with the potential increase in market power, but also whether Microcell could be considered a "maverick"—a firm with a strong incentive to deviate from coordinated behaviour and consequently provide a strong stimulus to competition in the market. Fido had a history of innovative, competitive products such as per-second billing and flat-rate price plans. Elimination of a vigorous and effective competitor could potentially lessen competition.

In their decision regarding market power, the Competition Bureau argued that based on the history of vigorous competition in the wireless market and the anticipated rate of growth over the next six to seven years (from 44 percent to 70 percent of the population base), the post-merger competition from Telus and Bell would be sufficient to prevent Rogers from imposing and sustaining price increases. In fact, the Bureau argued that Rogers' rivals would likely respond in an effort to enhance their customer bases—a classical "kinked" demand curve response.

The Bureau identified and recognized Microcell's past history as a maverick but argued that its future role as a maverick would be drastically reduced. The company had recently emerged from court protection and, while not considered a "failing firm," it faced significant capital investments to support its current business network plans. Any capital expenditures on network infrastructure would necessarily increase pressure on its ability to support funding for the subsequent generation of products and service offerings. In the meantime, its competitors were moving forward with capital investment in newer technology and network improvements.

For these reasons and others, the Bureau's merger review concluded that the merger would not substantially lessen or prevent competition in the mobile wireless services market, and any application to the Bureau challenging the transaction was unwarranted.

Source: Competition Bureau Canada, Technical backgrounders, *Acquisitions of Microcell Telecommunications Inc. by Rogers Wireless Communications Inc.* April 12, 2005. Accessed November 11, 2006. http://www.competitionbureau.gc.ca/internet/index.cfm?itemID=257&lg=e. Reproduced with the permission of the Minister of Public Works and Government Services Canada, 2007.

Analysis: In deregulated industries, mergers will not necessarily "substantially lessen or prevent competition in the market."

Airlines   In the late 1920s and early 1930s, Canada's airline industry consisted mainly of regional "bush airlines" including Winnipeg-based Canadian Airways, which served local mining communities and transported mail. There was neither a national carrier nor air service linking the Atlantic and Pacific oceans.

In the mid-1930s, Prime Minister Mackenzie King recognized the growing importance of air transportation and created a Department of Transportation with C.D. Howe as its first minister. Howe initially envisioned a government-controlled airline with private collaboration between CP Rail, CN Rail, and Canadian Airways. The political manoeuvrings of the time, however, resulted in the 1937 legislated creation of a new government-owned airline called Trans-Canada Airlines; an independent subsidiary of Canadian National Railways.

With the passage of the Transportation Act of 1938 and the creation of the Board of Transport Commissioners, whose mandate included the control of routes and approval of rates, Canada entered into the regulation of the airline industry.

> The history of schedule airline regulation in Canada has been characterized by three major themes: an ongoing desire to ensure the safety of the flying public, a desire to ensure the financial health and stability of the firms developing domestic routes, and a desire to see that the flying public and the scheduled carriers have convenient access to a growing number of domestic and international destinations. These desires have sometimes been in harmony with each other, and on other occasions conflicts among them have complicated the regulation of air transportation.[5]

Early Regulation. Similar to the railroad industry, the initial rationale for the airline regulatory policies was based on a vision as well as an economic concern. The vision, of course, was "nation building," and this required the creation of a substantial infrastructure capable of accommodating both domestic and transcontinental routes. On the economic front, there was the recognition that in Canada—with its relatively small population and vast territory—the airline industry was a natural monopoly. Not surprisingly, therefore, many of the early regulatory airline polices duplicated those from the railway industry. These early days of the regulated industry saw Trans-Canada Airlines as the national carrier, transporting passengers across Canada and between nations, while Canadian Airways retained its north-south routes.

Later Regulation. By the late 1950s, the federal government had acquiesced to Canadian Airways lobbying and granted them both a domestic and transcontinental flight. Given that the two carriers could not compete via prices, each attempted to increase their load factors (the percentage of seats filled with passengers) by pursuing *product differentiation;* that is, by offering special meals, free drinks, and better service.

During the initial regulatory years, Canada and the United States had an "open skies policy," whereby each country granted reciprocal permission for air carriers to serve each other's territory. Over the years, however, the United States developed a system of government-subsidized monopoly routes. Combining these subsidies with the potential for economies of scale in the United States, Canadian regulators were concerned that U.S. airlines had an unfair advantage over Canadian airlines. Not willing to jeopardize the viability of two transcontinental airlines, Canada started to restrict access to their destinations served by U.S. airline carriers. Naturally, the U.S. reciprocated and these mutual restrictions continued until the 1960s.

Final Regulation. In 1978, the United States passed the Airline Deregulation Act, changing the structure and behaviour of the U.S. airline industry. Entry regulation was effectively abandoned and with the elimination of this *barrier to entry,* the number of U.S. carriers increased from 37 in 1978 to 174 in 1985. With the passing of the U.S.

---

[5]C.M. Fellows, G. Flanagan, and S. Shedd, *Economic Issues: A Canadian Perspective* (Toronto, Ontario: McGraw-Hill Ryerson Ltd., 1997).

deregulation legislation, the United States was anxious to renegotiate bilateral agreements with Canada to start increasing access to each other's territory. At this stage, Canada's two national airline carriers—Trans-Canada Airlines (now Air Canada) and Canadian Airlines—were facing the winds of deregulation.

Deregulation and Its Effects. In 1984, the "New Canadian Air Policy" deregulated the domestic airways, enabling airlines to set their own fares and choose their own destination routes. It also permitted charter companies to compete on the domestic transcontinental routes. The National Transportation Act in 1988 essentially completed the deregulation process.

In 1984, Wardair, a charter company, started to compete with Air Canada and Canadian. Over the years, there was consolidation of most of the other airline carriers by either Air Canada or Canadian. By the late 1980s, however, all three carriers were incurring losses and eventually Wardair was acquired by Canadian. The financial woes of both carriers continued into the early 1990s—exacerbated by the general recessionary conditions of the time. There was an attempt to merge in 1992, but each airline joined up with a U.S. partner. By 1999, Canadian's financial position had deteriorated to the point where the federal government permitted Air Canada to acquire Canadian. At this stage, Air Canada controlled approximately 80 percent of domestic traffic. There was renewed concern about a monopoly position and the government encouraged other domestic airlines to enter the market and compete. Many responded to the call, but most (e.g., CanJet, Roots Air, Royal) failed, merged, or moved on to the seasonal transcontinental charter routes. The one notable success was Calgary-based WestJet airlines. Following the business practices of the U.S. carrier Southwest, WestJet concentrated on highly travelled point-to-point routes rather than the hub-and-spoke route structures that emerged in the U.S. subsequent to deregulation. Moreover, they initially avoided larger airports in a metropolitan area (such as Toronto's Lester B. Pearson Airport) in favour of smaller airports (Hamilton) in order to reduce the airport landing fees.

While overall prices of domestic airfare have fallen, there has not been a noticeable decrease in the concentration ratio in the airline industry (See Table 11.2); the creation of WestJet in 1996 initially decreased concentration but the merger of Air Canada and Canadian in 2000 raised concentration levels back to those of 1989. Since this merger, however, competition for the busiest domestic routes has increased slightly with the addition of small airlines such as Harmony Airways. Survival of these small airlines is dependent on their ability to (1) provide services to the busiest North American commercial and vacation routes (e.g., Toronto, New York, San Francisco, Honolulu, and Las Vegas), and (2) differentiate their product from competitors (e.g., leather seats, no-charge advance seat selection, complimentary beverages, in-flight entertainment, etc.).

Percentage of Routes With	1989	1992	1996	2000
1 carrier	72.3	72.4	67.0[†]	75.9[††]
2 carriers	23.3	25.0	28.2	19.6
3 carriers	3.2	1.9	3.5	3.0
4 carriers	0.6	0.3	0.9	1.3
5 carriers	0.0	0.2	0.2	0.0
6 carriers	0.6	0.1	0.0	0.2
7 carriers	0.0	0.1	0.0	0.0
8 carriers	0.0	0.0	0.2	0.0

[†]Inception of WestJet Airlines.

[††]Merger of Air Canada and Canadian Airlines.

Source: Williams, George, *Airline Competition: Deregulation's Mixed Legacy,* Ashgate Publishing Company, Burlington, VT, p. 66. © 2000 used with permission of Ashgate Publishing Company.

TABLE 11.2
Level of Route Competition on Domestic Flights in Canada Between 1989 and 2000

After eleven years of deregulation, the concentration in the Canadian domestic airline industry has not changed significantly.

Electricity

The electric utility industry is the latest target for deregulation. Here again, the industry has long been regarded as a natural monopoly. The enormous fixed costs of a power plant and transmission network, combined with negligible marginal costs for delivering another kilowatt of electricity, gave electric utilities a downward-sloping average total cost curve. The focus of government intervention was therefore on rate regulation (behaviour) rather than promoting competition (structure).

Bloated Costs, High Prices. Critics of local utility monopolies complained that local rate regulation wasn't working well enough. To get higher (retail) prices, the utility companies allowed costs to rise. They also had no incentive to pursue new technologies that would reduce the costs of power generation or distribution. Big power users like steel companies complained that high electricity prices were crippling their competitive position. Other than moving their operations from a province with a high-cost power monopoly to a province with a low-cost power monopoly, the only other viable alternative would be to construct their own source of power generation. This is precisely what Alcan has done with their aluminum production facilities in Quebec and British Columbia.

Demise of Power Plant Monopolies. Advances in transmission technology gave consumers a new choice. High-voltage transmission lines can carry power thousands of miles with negligible power loss. Utility companies used these lines to link their power grids, thereby creating backup power sources in the event of regional blackouts. In doing so, however, they created a new entry point for potential competition. Now a Quebec power plant with surplus capacity can supply electricity to consumers in Ontario or Pennsylvania. There's no longer any need to rely on a regional utility monopoly.

Local Distribution Monopolies. Although technology destroyed the basis for natural monopolies in power *production,* local monopolies in power *distribution* remain. Electricity reaches consumers through the wires attached to every house and business. As with TV cables, there is a natural monopoly in electricity distribution; competing wire grids would be costly and inefficient.

To deliver the benefits of competition in power *production,* rival producers must be able to access these local distribution grids. This is the same problem that has plagued competition in local telephone service. The local power companies that own the local distribution grids aren't anxious to open the wires to new competition. The central problem for electricity deregulation has been to assure wider access to local distribution grids.

California's Mistakes. In the United States, the California legislature decided to resolve this problem by stripping local utility monopolies of their production capacity. By forcing utility companies to sell their power plants, California transformed its utilities into pure power *distributors.* This seemed to resolve the conflict between ownership and access to the distribution system. However, it also made California's utility companies totally dependent on third-party power producers, many of which were then out of state.

California also put a ceiling on the *retail* price its utilities could charge. But the state had no power to control the *wholesale* price of electricity in interstate markets. When wholesale prices rose sharply in 2000 (see the Applications box on the next page), California's utilities were trapped between rising costs and a fixed price ceiling. Fearful of a political backlash, the governor refused to raise the retail price ceiling. As a result, some of the utility companies were forced into bankruptcy and power supplies were interrupted. The state itself entered the utility business by buying power plants and more out-of-state power supplies. In the end, Californians ended up with very expensive electricity.

Financial Woes Heating Up

Pacific Gas and Electric is in financial trouble because the cost of power it purchases on the wholesale market is soaring higher than the fixed rate it charges its customers:

—Suzy Parker

Source: *USA Today*, January 10, 2001. Copyright 2001 USA Today. Reprinted with permission. www.usatoday.com

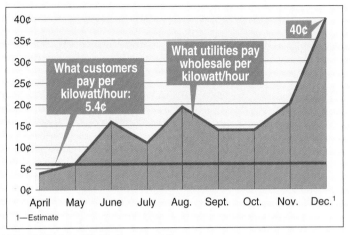

Source: Pacific Gas and Electric, (www.pge.com).

Analysis: When wholesale prices for electricity rose above the retail price ceiling established by the California legislature, the state's utility companies lost money on every kilowatt supplied. It was a recipe for financial disaster.

Canadian Strategies. Learning from California's policy mistakes, the two Canadian provinces leading the way in electricity deregulation (Alberta and Ontario) have not only deregulated power production, but have also moved towards deregulation at the wholesale and retail level.

In Ontario, for example, household and low-volume business customers can select a rate regulated by the Ontario Energy Board, the hourly wholesale rate determined by the Independent Electricity System Operator (IESO), or a rate provided by a licensed retailer. The latest innovation in the regulated rate plan (RRP) is the "Smart Meter" price; variable rates throughout the day depending on what time a kilowatt of electricity is consumed (see the Applications box). To take advantage of lower rates, a customer must have a meter installed in their house/business and consume the electricity at low-peak hours—mainly after midnight and on weekends.

What can we say about electricity prices under deregulation? In Canada, and in many other countries, deregulation has initially led to increases in prices. This short-term increase in prices is most often associated with cases where there is a shortage of capacity. *Uncertainty* surrounding how the new system (generation, transmission, wholesale and retail prices) will operate discourages investment in new generation facilities—at least until the "rules" are in place. Once the rules are in place and the new system is up and running, firms feel more confident about creating new generation capacity. We need to recognize, however, the significant time lags. Several years can pass from the time the decision is made to create a new power plant to the time it sends its first kilowatt of electricity into the transmission system. In Alberta, for example, over 4,000 megawatts (MW) of new power has come online during 1998–2005, raising the total existing generation capacity in 2006 to 11,500 MW. Yet, even with this substantial increase in capacity, Alberta remains a net importer of electricity; the booming energy sector has attracted thousands of new people to the province creating an increased demand for electricity. Once again, the province finds itself in a position of a short-term capacity shortage and the regulated rate option for consumers in Calgary has risen from 5.9 ¢/kWh in November 2005 to 8.8 ¢/kWh in November 2006.[6]

WEB NOTE

To view the latest electricity price options for Ontario households, see http://www.ieso.ca/imoweb/infoCentre/ic_index.asp.

APPLICATIONS

Electricity Price Options for Homeowners and Low-Volume Business Customers in Ontario

Regulated Price Plan †	Smart Meter †	Wholesale
Pay the regulated Price Plan (RPP) set by the Ontario Energy Board.	Pay smart meter RPP prices that change depending on when you use electricity.	Pay the hourly wholesale price of electricity. (Available to a limited number of consumers with interval meters)
Consumption of up to and including 1,000 kWh/month*: 5.5¢/kWh	**Weekdays**	
More than 1,000 kWh/month: 6.4¢/kWh	7 am to 11 am 9.7¢/kWh 11 am to 5 pm 7.1¢/kWh 5 pm to 8 pm 9.7¢/kWh 8 pm to 10 pm 7.1¢/kWh 10 pm to 7 am 3.4¢/kWh **Weekends** 3.4¢/kWh	Current hourly price: 4.76¢/kWh at 12:00 p.m. EST, November 21, 2006
* Threshold for business is 750 kWh/month		

†Rates valid from November 1, 2006 to April 30, 2007.

Source: Independent Electricity System Operator (IESO) of Ontario, http://www.ieso.ca/imoweb/infoCentre/ic_index.asp, accessed November 21, 2006.

Analysis: Electricity deregulation at the retail level has provided Ontario households and low-volume businesses with several options.

Other countries and U.S. states have demonstrated how deregulation can generate better results. Norway deregulated its electric industry in 1991, and prices soon declined by 20 percent. After the European Union started deregulating its electric industries in 1999, prices fell as well. In the United States all 50 states are at various stages of deregulation, amassing plenty of evidence on how best to use competition to reduce electricity costs and prices.

Deregulate Everything?

Deregulation of the railroad, telephone, airline, and electricity industries has yielded substantial benefits: more competition, lower prices, and improved services. Such experiences bolster the case for laissez faire. Nevertheless, we shouldn't jump to the conclusion that all regulation of business should be dismantled. All we know from experience is that the regulation of certain industries has become outmoded. Changing consumer demands, new technologies, and substitute goods had simply made existing regulations obsolete, even counterproductive. A combination of economic and political forces doomed them to extinction.

But were these regulations ever necessary? In the 1880s there were no viable alternatives to railroads for overland transportation. The forces of natural monopoly could easily have exploited consumers and retarded economic growth. The same was largely true for long-distance telephone service prior to the launching of communications satellites. One shouldn't conclude that regulatory intervention never made sense just because the regulations themselves later became obsolete.

WEB NOTE

The Institute of Public Administration of Canada (IPAC) has a Centre for Regulatory Innovation (called SmartTape™), which provides information on leading developments in regulatory practice. Visit http://www.smarttape.ca/.

[6]Alberta Government, The Office of the Utilities Consumer Advocate (UCA), *Historic Rate Summary,* http://www.ucahelps.gov.ab.ca/186.html.

Even today, most people recognize the need for regulation of many industries. The transmission networks for local telephone service and electricity delivery are still natural monopolies. The government can force owners to permit greater access, but an unregulated network owner could still extract monopoly profits through excessive prices. Hence, even a deregulated industry may still require some regulation at critical entry or supply junctures. Existing regulations may not be optimal, but they probably generate better outcomes than totally unregulated monopolies.

Likewise, few people seriously propose relying on competition and the good judgment of consumers to determine the variety or quality of drugs on the market. Regulations imposed by Health Canada restrain competition in the drug industry, raise production costs, and inhibit new technology. But they also make drugs safer. Here, as in other industries, there's a trade-off between the virtues of competition and those of regulation. The basic policy issue, as always, is whether the benefits of regulation exceed their administrative, compliance, and efficiency costs. The challenge for public policy in the economy tomorrow is to adapt regulations—or to discard them (that is, deregulate)—as market conditions, consumer demands, or technology changes.

SUMMARY

- Government intervention is justified when the market fails to generate the optimal (best possible) mix of output or distribution of income.
- Competition policy and regulation are alternative options for dealing with market power. Competition policy focuses on market structure and anticompetitive practices. Regulation stipulates specific market behaviour.
- Natural monopolies offer pervasive economies of scale. Because of this potential efficiency, a more competitive market *structure* may be inappropriate.
- Regulation of natural monopoly can focus on price, profit, or output *behaviour*. Price regulation may require subsidies; profit regulation may induce cost escalation; and output regulation may lead to quality deterioration. These problems compel compromises and acceptance of second-best solutions.

- The demand for deregulation rests on the argument that the costs of regulation exceed the benefits. These costs include the opportunity costs associated with regulatory administration and compliance as well as the (dynamic) efficiency losses that result from inflexible pricing and production rules.
- For the most part, deregulation of the railroad, telephone, and airline industries has been a success. In all these industries, regulation has been outmoded by changing consumer demands, products, and technology. As regulation was relaxed, these industries became more competitive, output increased, and prices typically fell.
- Recent experiences with deregulation don't imply that all regulation should end. Regulation is appropriate if market failure exists *and* if the benefits of regulation exceed the costs. As benefits and costs change, decisions about what and how to regulate must be reevaluated.

Key Terms

combine laws/competition policy 231 regulation 231 cross-subsidization 240

Questions for Discussion

1. Given the inevitable limit on airplane landings, how should available airport slots be allocated? How would market outcomes be altered?
2. Should the airline industry be reregulated?
3. Prior to deregulation, regional phone companies kept local phone rates low by subsidizing them from long-distance profits. Was such cross-subsidization in the public interest? Explain.
4. In most cities local taxi fares are regulated. Should such regulation end? Who would gain or lose?
5. In the Applications box on page 241, the "maverick" nature of Fido was considered in the Competition Bureau's analysis of its acquisition by Rogers Wireless Communications. What role does a maverick firm perform in an industry? Do you think the Competition

Bureau would have permitted the merger if Fido's maverick reputation was expected to continue?

6. How could a local phone or cable company reduce service quality if forced to accept price ceilings?

7. If cable TV were completely deregulated, would local monopolies ever confront effective competition? Does profit regulation inhibit or accelerate would-be competition?

8. Why is there resistance to (*a*) local phone companies providing video and data services and (*b*) mergers of local cable and telephone companies?

9. How do you think the installation of "Smart Meters" in Ontario will affect overall electricity consumption?

10. What should California have done to get better results from electricity deregulation?

EXERCISES

PROBLEMS   The Student Problem Set to accompany this chapter can be found at the end of the book.

WEB ACTIVITIES   Web Activities to accompany this chapter can be found on the Online Learning Centre at **http://www.mcgrawhill.ca/olc/schiller**.

CHAPTER 12

Environmental Protection

LEARNING OBJECTIVES

By the end of this chapter, you should be able to:

12.1 Identify three major types of pollution and explain how economists assess damage caused by pollution

12.2 Explain how market incentives encourage environmental damage

12.3 Define external costs, private costs, and social costs

12.4 Explain the role of market failures and externalities in both production and consumption arising from pollution

12.5 Discuss the regulatory options for correcting pollution externalities

12.6 Identify the opportunity costs of pollution-abatement investment

12.7 Discuss the effects of pollution-abatement investment on equilibrium prices, quantities, and incomes

A hole in the ozone layer is allowing increased ultraviolet radiation to reach the earth's surface. The hole is the result of excessive release of chlorine gases (chlorofluorocarbons, or CFCs) from air conditioners, plastic-foam manufacture, industrial solvents, and aerosol spray cans such as deodorants and insecticides. The resulting damage to the stratosphere is causing skin cancer, cataracts, and immune-system disorders.

Skin cancer may turn out to be one of our less serious problems. As carbon dioxide builds up in the atmosphere, it creates a gaseous blanket around the earth that traps radiation and heats the atmosphere. Scientists predict that this greenhouse effect will melt the polar ice caps, raise sea levels, flood coastal areas, and turn rich croplands into deserts within 60 years.

Everyone wants a cleaner and safer environment. So why don't we stop polluting the environment with CFCs, carbon dioxide, toxic chemicals, and other waste? If we don't do it ourselves, why doesn't the government force people to stop polluting?

Economics is part of the answer. To reduce pollution, we have to change our patterns of production and consumption. This entails economic costs, in terms of restricted consumption choices, more expensive ways of producing goods, and higher prices. Thus, we have to weigh the benefits of a cleaner, safer environment against the costs of environmental protection.

Instinctively, most people don't like the idea of measuring the value of a cleaner environment in dollars and cents. But most people might also agree that spending $2 trillion to avoid a few cataracts is awfully expensive. There has to be *some* balance between the benefits of a cleaner environment and the cost of cleaning it up.

This chapter assesses our environmental problems from this economic perspective, considering three primary concerns:

- **How do (unregulated) markets encourage pollution?**
- **What are the costs of greater environmental protection?**
- **How can government policy best ensure an *optimal* environment?**

To answer these questions, we first survey the major types and sources of pollution. Then we examine the benefits and costs of environmental protection, highlighting the economic incentives that shape market behaviour.

12.1 THE ENVIRONMENTAL THREAT

The hole in the ozone layer and the earth's rising temperature are at the top of the list of environmental concerns. The list is much longer, however, and very old as well. As early as A.D. 61, the statesman and philosopher Seneca was complaining about the smoky air emitted from household chimneys in Rome. Lead emissions from ancient Greek and Roman silver refineries poisoned the air in Europe and the remote Arctic. And historians are quick to remind us that open sewers running down the street were once the principal mode of urban waste disposal. Typhoid epidemics were a recurrent penalty for water pollution. So we can't say that environmental damage is a new phenomenon or that it's now worse than ever before.

But we do know more about the sources of environmental damage than our ancestors did, and we can better afford to do something about it. Our understanding of the economics of pollution has increased as well. We've come to recognize that pollution impairs health, reduces life expectancy, and thus reduces labour-force activity and output. Pollution also destroys capital (such as the effects of air pollution on steel structures) and diverts resources to undesired activities (like car washes, laundry, and cleaning). Not least of all, pollution directly reduces our social welfare by denying us access to clean air, water, and beaches.

Air Pollution

Air pollution is as familiar as a smoggy horizon. But smog is only one form of air pollution.

Acid Rain. Sulfur dioxide (SO_2) is an acrid, corrosive, and poisonous gas that's created by burning high-sulfur fuels such as coal. As a contributor to acid rain, it destroys vegetation and forests. Electric utilities and industrial plants that burn high-sulfur coal or fuel oil are the prime sources of SO_2. Coal burning alone accounts for about 60 percent of all emissions of sulfur oxides. As the World View box on the next page illustrates, SO_2 pollution is a serious problem all over the world.

Smog. Nitrogen oxides (NO_x), another ingredient in the formation of acid rain, are also a principal ingredient in the formation of smog. Smog not only irritates the eyes and spoils the view, but it also damages plants, trees, and human lungs. Automobile emissions account for 40 percent of urban smog. Bakeries, dry cleaners, and production of other consumer goods account for an equal amount of smog. The rest comes from electric power plants and industrial boilers.

The Greenhouse Effect. The prime villain in the greenhouse effect is the otherwise harmless carbon dioxide (CO_2) that we exhale. Unfortunately, we and nature now release so much CO_2 that the earth's oceans and vegetation can no longer absorb it all. The excess CO_2 is creating a gaseous blanket around the earth that may warm the earth to disastrous levels. The burning of fossil fuels is a significant source of CO_2 buildup. The destruction of rain forests, which absorb CO_2, also contributes to the greenhouse effect.

Water Pollution

Water pollution is another environmental threat. Its effects are apparent in the contamination of drinking water, restrictions on swimming and boating, foul-smelling waterways, swarms of dead fish, and floating debris.

Organic Pollution. The most common form of water pollution occurs in the disposal of organic wastes from toilets and garbage disposals. The wastes that originate there are collected in sewer systems and ultimately discharged into the nearest waterway. The key question is whether the wastes are treated (separated and decomposed) before ultimate discharge. Sophisticated waste-treatment plants can reduce organic pollution up to 99 percent.

In addition to household wastes, our waterways must also contend with industrial wastes. Over half the volume of industrial discharge comes from just a few

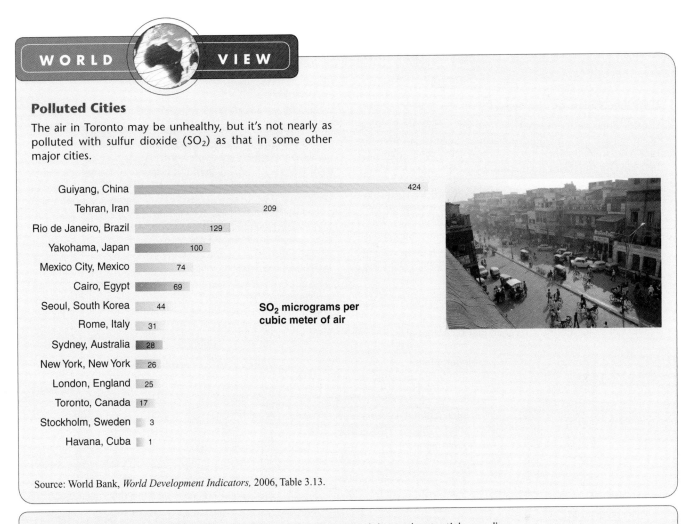

WORLD VIEW

Polluted Cities

The air in Toronto may be unhealthy, but it's not nearly as polluted with sulfur dioxide (SO_2) as that in some other major cities.

City	SO_2
Guiyang, China	424
Tehran, Iran	209
Rio de Janeiro, Brazil	129
Yakohama, Japan	100
Mexico City, Mexico	74
Cairo, Egypt	69
Seoul, South Korea	44
Rome, Italy	31
Sydney, Australia	28
New York, New York	26
London, England	25
Toronto, Canada	17
Stockholm, Sweden	3
Havana, Cuba	1

SO_2 micrograms per cubic meter of air

Source: World Bank, *World Development Indicators,* 2006, Table 3.13.

Analysis: Pollution is a worldwide phenomenon, with common origins and potential remedies.

---

industries—principally paper, organic chemicals, petroleum, and steel. Finally, there are the various forms of fertilizers (organic and chemical), pesticides, insecticides, and herbicides used by the agricultural sector. If improperly managed or stored, these chemical and organic wastes contaminate water supplies and trigger algae blooms that choke waterways and kill fish. Homeowners' lawn fertilizers and herbicides also contribute to the problem—to the point where a number of local authorities have passed bylaws prohibiting the use of chemicals on lawns and where lawn-care companies actively promote their "green" products. These forms of water pollution often result in the closure of waterways and beaches (see the Applications box).

Thermal Pollution. Thermal pollution is an increase in the temperature of waterways brought about by the discharge of steam or heated water. Heat discharges can kill fish, upset marine reproductive cycles, and accelerate biological and chemical processes in water, thereby reducing its ability to retain oxygen. Electric power plants account for over 80 percent of all thermal discharges, with primary metal, chemical, and petroleum-refining plants accounting for nearly all the rest.

Solid waste is yet another environmental threat. Solid-waste pollution is apparent everywhere, from the garbage can to litter on the streets and beaches, to debris in the water, to open dumps. According to Statistics Canada estimates, we generate over 30 million

WEB NOTE

For information on collaborative projects between the environmental agencies of the United States and Canada to help the Great Lakes, see http://binational.net/home_e.html.

Solid-Waste Pollution

APPLICATIONS

Can We Swim at the Beach?

Usually Great Lakes beaches are safe for swimming—unless health-related swimming advisories have been issued for bacterial contamination or other problems. These advisories may be issued for the following reasons.

- Combined sewage systems may overflow after a heavy rainfall, causing the direct or indirect discharge of raw sewage and stormwater into the Great Lakes.
- Improper storage and use of manure to fertilize agricultural fields, which can wash off into waterways.
- Onshore winds, which stir up bottom sediments containing bacteria.
- Wildlife waste on beaches (e.g., sea gulls, geese). Preliminary research has indicated that wildlife on beaches may be more of a contributing factor towards bacterial contamination of water and beaches than previously thought.

CP/Toronto Star/Jim Ross

Source: *State of the Great Lakes 2005,* http://binational.net. Produced by Environment Canada and the United States Environmental Protection Agency. Reproduced with the permission of the Minister of Public Works and Government Services Canada, 2007.

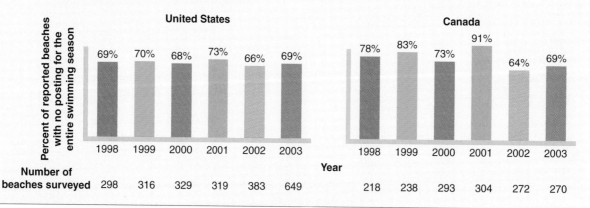

United States

69%	70%	68%	73%	66%	69%
1998	1999	2000	2001	2002	2003

Canada

78%	83%	73%	91%	64%	69%
1998	1999	2000	2001	2002	2003

Percent of reported beaches with no posting for the entire swimming season

Year

| Number of beaches surveyed | 298 | 316 | 329 | 319 | 383 | 649 | | 218 | 238 | 293 | 304 | 272 | 270 |

Analysis: High levels of water pollution often lead to closures of beaches. Who should bear that cost?

tonnes of solid waste each year.[1] Roughly half of this amount comes from residential sources in the form of organics (food/yard waste), paper, plastic (bottles, toys), glass, metal (appliances, electronics), and other products (tires, furniture, clothing, etc.). From 2000 to 2002, we observed a 1 million tonne increase in solid waste pollution. One of the reasons for this upward trend is that it is frequently less expensive to purchase a new product than to either repair or upgrade an existing product. However, the amount of solid waste originating in residential areas is often considered more dangerous than solid wastes originating in the agriculture sector (slaughter wastes, orchard prunings, harvest residues) or even in the mining sector (slag heaps, mill tailings), since it accumulates where people live. Larger cities such as Toronto have neither the land area nor the incinerators required for disposal of its solid waste, so in Toronto's case most of it is shipped off to the state of Michigan. This is not unique to Canadian cities. The city of London, England, for example, sends barges full of "rubbish" 50 kilometres down the River Thames to the wharf at Mucking, Essex. From here, they are transported a short distance by truck to one of the largest landfills in Western Europe. Not to be

[1]Statistics Canada (2005), *Human Activity and the Environment 2005,* "Solid Waste in Canada."

Toronto's Talkin' Trash

Toronto, Oct. 26—Currently, almost 60 percent of all of Toronto's garbage goes to landfills in Michigan, with over 700,000 tons of garbage shipped there last year alone. The great garbage debate was fuelled by Toronto's recent announcement of allocating a space near London, ironically entitled Green Land, as a future site of Toronto's garbage. The use of the 28-year-old Green Land dump will be sought after four years, when Michigan is set to close off its landfill to Toronto.

Local MPs in London are fighting to derail Toronto's current garbage claim in their city, citing possible toll booths and the closure of roads as a means to deter the city from dumping its garbage there.

"London is not Toronto's toilet," said local MPP for London's North Centre, Deb Matthews, who was quoted by the *London Free Press*. Other MPPs echoed Matthew's statement, claiming Toronto's need to stop finding other sites to place its garbage, and use their own sites for garbage disposal.

—Irisanne Fajardo

Source: "Toronto's Talkin' Trash," Irisanne Fajardo, October 23, 2006. University of Toronto, Medium II Publications, http://www.mediumonline.ca/.

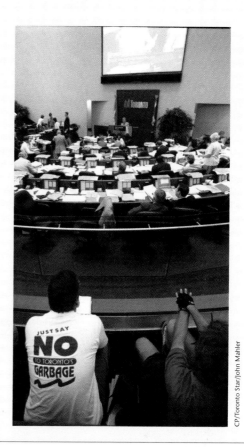

Analysis: The selection of disposal sites for solid wastes often creates negative externalities and leads to the NIMBY (Not In My Back Yard) syndrome. Who should bear that cost?

outdone, Philadelphia ships its garbage all the way to the country of Panama in Central America! As you might imagine, finding a suitable location to place all this solid waste can lead to the Not In My Back Yard (NIMBY) syndrome (see the Applications box above).

12.2 POLLUTION DAMAGES

Shipping garbage to Panama is an expensive answer to the waste disposal problem. But even those costs are a small fraction of the total cost of environmental damage. Much greater costs are associated with the damage to our health (labour), buildings (capital), and land. Even the little things count, like being able to enjoy a clear sunset or take a deep breath.

Although many people don't like to put a price on the environment, some monetary measure of environmental damage is important in decision making. Unless we value the environment above everything else, we have to establish some method of ranking the importance of environmental damage. Although it's tempting to say that clean air is priceless, ***we won't get clean air unless we spend resources to get it.*** This economic reality suggests that we begin by determining how much cleaner air is worth to us.

APPLICATIONS

Dirty Air Can Shorten Your Life

The largest study ever conducted on the health effects of airborne particles from traffic and smokestacks has found that people in the nation's most polluted cities are 15 to 17 percent more likely to die prematurely than those in cities with the cleanest air.

This form of pollution is killing citizens even in areas that meet Environmental Protection Agency air quality standards, said study coauthor Douglas Dockery of the Harvard School of Public Health, who said "the impact on life and health is more pervasive than previously thought."

In Washington, where levels of airborne particles fall in the low middle range for U.S. cities, the average long-term resident loses approximately one year of life expectancy compared to the average for such relatively pristine places as Topeka, Kan., or Madison, Wis., Dockery said. In highly polluted places like Los Angeles or Salt Lake City, the toll is much greater: Compared to people in the cleanest metropolitan areas, those exposed to the highest concentrations of particles run a risk of premature death about one-sixth as great as if they had been smoking for 25 years.

—Curt Suplee

Source: *The Washington Post*, March 10, 1995. © 1995 The Washington Post. Reprinted with permission. www.washingtonpost.com

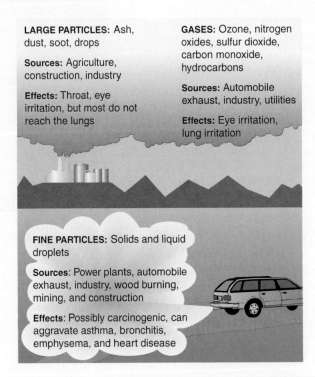

LARGE PARTICLES: Ash, dust, soot, drops

Sources: Agriculture, construction, industry

Effects: Throat, eye irritation, but most do not reach the lungs

GASES: Ozone, nitrogen oxides, sulfur dioxide, carbon monoxide, hydrocarbons

Sources: Automobile exhaust, industry, utilities

Effects: Eye irritation, lung irritation

FINE PARTICLES: Solids and liquid droplets

Sources: Power plants, automobile exhaust, industry, wood burning, mining, and construction

Effects: Possibly carcinogenic, can aggravate asthma, bronchitis, emphysema, and heart disease

Analysis: Pollution entails real costs, as measured by impaired health, reduced life spans, and other damages.

Assigning Prices

WEB NOTE

The Earth Policy Institute offers data on the costs of pollution at www.earth-policy.org.

In some cases, it's fairly easy to put a price on environmental damage. Scientists can measure the increase in cancer, heart attacks, and other disorders attributable to air pollution, as the United States' Environmental Protection Agency (EPA) does for air toxins (see the Applications box). Engineers and ecologists can also measure the rate at which buildings decay or forests and lakes die. Economists can then estimate the dollar value of this damage by assessing the economic value of lives, forests, lakes, and other resources. For example, if people are willing to pay $5,000 for a cataract operation, then the avoidance of such eye damage is worth at least $5,000. Saving a tree is worth whatever the marketplace is willing to pay for the products of that tree. Using such computations, the EPA estimates that air pollution alone inflicts health, property, and vegetation damage in excess of $50 billion ($US) a year.

The job of pricing environmental damage is much more difficult with intangible losses like sunsets. Nevertheless, when governmental agencies and courts are asked to assess the damages of oil spills and other accidents, they must try to inventory *all* costs, including polluted sunsets, reduced wildlife, and lost recreation opportunities. The science of computing such environmental damage is very inexact. Nevertheless, crude but reasonable procedures generate damage estimates measured in hundreds of billions of dollars per year.

One of the most frustrating things about all this environmental damage is that it can be avoided. The EPA estimates that *95 percent of current air and water pollution could be eliminated by known and available technology.* Nothing very exotic is needed: just simple things like auto-emission controls, smokestack cleaners, improved sewage and waste treatment facilities, and cooling towers for electric power plants. Even solid-waste pollution could be reduced by comparable proportions if we used less packaging, recycled more materials, or transformed our garbage into a useful (relatively low-polluting) energy source. The critical question here is, Why don't we do these things? Why do we continue to pollute so much?

Cleanup Possibilities

12.3 MARKET INCENTIVES

Previous chapters emphasized how market incentives influence the behaviour of individual consumers, firms, and government agencies. Incentives in the form of price reductions can be used to change consumer buying habits. Incentives in the form of high profit margins encourage production of desired goods and services. And market incentives in the form of cost differentials help allocate resources efficiently. Accordingly, we shouldn't be too surprised to learn that **market incentives play a major role in pollution behaviour.**

Imagine that you're the majority stockholder and manager of an electric power plant. Such plants are responsible for a significant amount of air pollution (especially sulfur dioxide and particulates) and nearly all thermal water pollution. Hence, your position immediately puts you on the most-wanted list of pollution offenders. But suppose you bear society no grudges and would truly like to help eliminate pollution. Let's consider the alternatives.

The Production Decision

As the owner-manager of an electric power plant, you'll strive to make a profit-maximizing *production decision.* That is, you'll seek the rate of output at which marginal revenue equals marginal cost. Let's assume that the electric power industry is still regulated so that the price of electricity is fixed, at least in the short run. The effect of this assumption is to render marginal revenue equal to price, thus giving us a horizontal price line, as in Figure 12.1*a.*

Figure 12.1*a* also depicts the marginal and average total costs (MC and ATC) associated with the production of electricity. By equating marginal cost (MC) to price (marginal revenue, MR), we observe (point *A*) that profit maximization occurs at an output of 1,000 kilowatt-hours per day. Total profits are illustrated by the shaded rectangle between the price line and the average total cost (ATC) curve.

The profits illustrated in Figure 12.1*a* are achieved in part by use of the cheapest available fuel under the boilers (which create the steam that rotates the generators). Recall that the construction of a marginal cost curve presumes some knowledge of alternative production processes. Recall too that the **efficiency decision** requires a producer to choose that production process (and its associated cost curve) that minimizes costs for any particular rate of output.

The Efficiency Decision

efficiency decision: The choice of a production process for any given rate of output.

Costs of Pollution Abatement. Unfortunately, the efficiency decision in this case leads to the use of high-sulfur coal, the prime villain in SO_2 and particulate pollution.

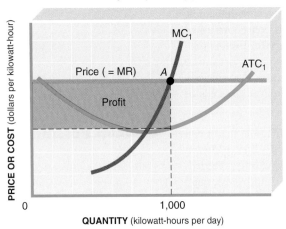

(a) Maximizing profits by using cheap but polluting process

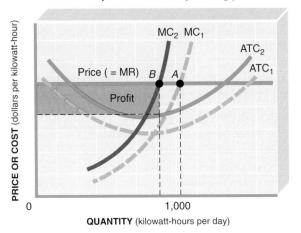

(b) Protecting the environment by using more expensive but less polluting process

FIGURE 12.1
Profit Maximization in Electric Power Production

Production processes that control pollution may be more expensive than those that don't. If they are, the MC and ATC curves will shift upward (to MC$_2$ and ATC$_2$). At the new profit-maximizing rate of output (point *B*), output and total profit shrink. Hence, a producer has an incentive to continue polluting, using cheaper technology.

Other fuels, such as low-sulfur coal, natural gas, and nuclear energy, cost considerably more. Were you to switch to one of them, the ATC and MC curves would both shift upward, as in Figure 12.1*b*. Under these conditions, the most profitable rate of output would be lower than before (point *B*), and total profits would decline (note the smaller profit rectangle in Figure 12.1*b*). Thus, ***pollution abatement can be achieved, but only at significant cost to the plant.***

The same kind of cost considerations lead the plant to engage in thermal pollution. Cool water must be run through an electric utility plant to keep the turbines from overheating. Once the water has run through the plant, it's too hot to recirculate. It must be either dumped back into the adjacent river or cooled off by being circulated through cooling towers. As you might expect, it's cheaper to simply dump the hot water in the river. The fish don't like it, but they don't have to pay the construction costs associated with cooling towers.

The big question here is whether you and your fellow stockholders would be willing to incur higher costs to cut down on pollution. Eliminating either the air pollution or the water pollution emanating from the electric plant will cost a lot of money. And to whose benefit? To the people who live downstream and downwind? We don't expect profit-maximizing producers to take such concerns into account. ***The behaviour of profit maximizers is guided by comparisons of revenues and costs, not by philanthropy, aesthetic concerns, or the welfare of fish.***

12.4 MARKET FAILURE: EXTERNAL COSTS

The moral of this story—and the critical factor in pollution behaviour—is that ***people tend to maximize their personal welfare, balancing private benefits against private costs.*** For the electric power plant, this means making production decisions on the basis of revenues received and costs incurred. The fact that the power plant imposes costs on others, in the form of air and water pollution, is irrelevant to its profit-maximizing decisions. Those costs are *external* to the firm and don't appear on its profit-and-loss statement. Those **external costs**—or *externalities*—are no less real, but they're incurred by society at large rather than by the firm.

external cost: Cost of a market activity borne by a third party; the difference between the social and private costs of a market activity.

Whenever external costs exist, a private firm won't allocate its resources and operate its plant in such a way as to maximize social welfare. In effect, society permits the power plant the free use of valued resources—clean air and clean water. The power plant has a tremendous incentive to substitute those resources for others (such as high-priced fuel or cooling towers) in the production process. The inefficiency of such an arrangement is obvious when we recall that the function of markets is to allocate scarce resources in accordance with the consumer's expressed demands. Yet here we are, proclaiming a high value for clean air and clean water and encouraging the power plant to use up both resources by offering them at zero cost to the firm.

The inefficiency of this market arrangement can be expressed in terms of a distinction between social costs and private costs. **Social costs** are the total costs of all the resources used in a particular production activity. On the other hand, **private costs** are the resource costs incurred by the specific producer.

Ideally, a producer's private costs will encompass all the attendant social costs, and production decision will be consistent with our social welfare. Unfortunately, this happy identity doesn't always exist, as our experience with the power plant illustrates. *When social costs differ from private costs, external costs exist. In fact, external costs are equal to the difference between the social and private costs*—that is,

$$\text{External costs} = \text{social costs} - \text{private costs}$$

When external costs are present, the market mechanism won't allocate resources efficiently. This is a case of *market failure.* The price signal confronting producers is flawed. By not conveying the full (social) cost of scarce resources, the market encourages excessive pollution. We end up with a suboptimal mix of output (too much electricity, too little clean air) and the wrong production processes.

The consequences of this market failure are illustrated in Figure 12.2, which again depicts the cost situation confronting the electric power plant. Notice that we use two different marginal cost curves this time. The lower one, the *private* MC curve, reflects the private costs incurred by the power plant when it operates on a profit-maximization basis, using high-sulfur coal and no cooling towers. It's identical to the MC curve in Figure 12.1*a*. We now know, however, that such operations impose external costs on others in the form of air and water pollution. These external costs must be added on to private marginal costs. When this is done, we get a *social* marginal cost curve that lies above the private MC curve.

Externalities in Production

> **social costs:** The full resource costs of an economic activity, including externalities.

> **private costs:** The costs of an economic activity directly borne by the immediate producer or consumer (excluding externalities).

"*Where there's smoke, there's money.*"

Analysis: If a firm can substitute external costs for private (internal) costs, its profits may increase.

FIGURE 12.2
Market Failure

Social costs exceed private costs by the amount of external costs. Production decisions based on private costs alone will lead us to point *B*, where private MC = MR. At point *B*, the rate of output is q_p.

To maximize social welfare, we equate *social* MC and MR, as at point *A*. Only q_s of output is socially desirable. The failure of the market to convey the full costs of production keeps us from attaining this outcome.

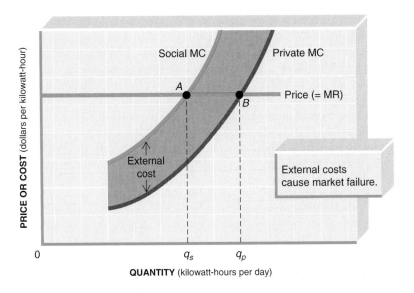

To maximize profits, private firms seek the rate of output that equates private MC to MR (price). ***To maximize social welfare, we need to equate social marginal cost to marginal revenue (price).*** This social optimum occurs at point *A* in Figure 12.2 and results in output of q_s. By contrast, the firm's private profit maximization occurs at point *B*, where q_p is produced. Hence, the private firm ends up producing more output than socially desired, while earning more profit and causing more pollution. As a general rule, ***if pollution costs are external, firms will produce too much of a polluting good.***

Externalities in Consumption

A divergence between private and social costs can also be observed in consumption. A consumer, like a producer, tends to maximize personal welfare. We buy and use more of those goods and services that yield the highest satisfaction (marginal utility) per dollar expended. By implication (and the law of demand), we tend to use more of a product if we can get it at a discount—that is, pay less than the full price. Unfortunately, the "discount" often takes the form of an external cost imposed on neighbours and friends.

Automobile driving illustrates the problem. The amount of driving one does is influenced by the price of a car and the marginal costs of driving it. People buy smaller cars and drive less when the attendant marginal costs (for instance, gasoline prices) increase substantially. But automobile use involves not only *private costs* but *external costs* as well. Auto emissions (carbon monoxide, hydrocarbons, and nitrogen oxides) are a principal cause of air pollution. In effect, automobile drivers have been able to use a valued resource, clean air, at no cost to themselves. Few motorists see any personal benefit in installing exhaust control devices because the quality of the air they breathe would be little affected by their efforts. Hence, low private costs lead to excessive pollution when high social costs are dictating cleaner air.

A divergence between social and private costs can be observed even in the simplest of consumer activities, such as throwing an empty soda can out the window of your car. To hang on to the can and later dispose of it in a trash barrel involves personal effort and thus private marginal costs. To throw it out the window not only is more exciting but also effectively transfers the burden of disposal costs to someone else. The resulting externality ends up as roadside litter.

The same kind of divergence between private and social costs helps explain why people abandon old cars in the street rather than haul them to scrapyards. It also explains why people use vacant lots as open dumps. In all these cases, ***the polluter benefits by substituting external costs for private costs.*** In other words, market incentives encourage environmental damage.

12.5 REGULATORY OPTIONS

The failure of the market to include external costs in production and consumption decisions creates a basis for government intervention. As always, however, we confront a variety of policy options. We may define these options in terms of *two general strategies for environmental protection:*

- *Alter market incentives* in such a way that they discourage pollution.
- *Bypass market incentives* with some form of regulatory intervention.

Market-Based Options

Insofar as market incentives are concerned, the key to environmental protection is to eliminate the divergence between private costs and social costs. The opportunity to shift some costs onto others lies at the heart of the pollution problem. If we could somehow compel producers to *internalize* all costs—pay for both private and previously external costs—the divergence would disappear, along with the incentive to pollute.

Emission Charges. One possibility is to establish a system of **emission charges,** direct costs attached to the act of polluting. Suppose that we let you keep your power plant and permit you to operate it according to profit-maximizing principles. The only difference is that we no longer agree to supply you with clean air and cool water at zero cost. From now on, we'll charge you for these scarce resources. We might, say, charge you 2 cents for every gram of noxious emission you discharge into the air. In addition we might charge you 3 cents for every gallon of water you use, heat, and discharge back into the river.

emission charge: A fee imposed on polluters, based on the quantity of pollution.

Confronted with such emission charges, you'd have to alter your production decision. *An emission charge increases private marginal cost and encourages lower output and cleaner technology.* Figure 12.3 illustrates this effect. Notice how the fee raises private marginal costs and induces a lower rate of (polluting) production (q_1 rather than q_0).

Once an emission fee is in place, a producer may also reevaluate the efficiency decision. Consider again the choice of fuels to be used in our fictional power plant. We earlier chose high-sulfur coal, for the very good reason that it was the cheapest fuel available. Now, however, there's an additional cost attached to burning such fuel, in the form of an emission charge. This added cost may encourage the firm to switch to cleaner sources of energy, which would increase private marginal costs but reduce emission fees.

An emission charge might also persuade a firm to incur higher fixed costs. Rather than pay emission charges, it might be more economical to install scrubbers and other

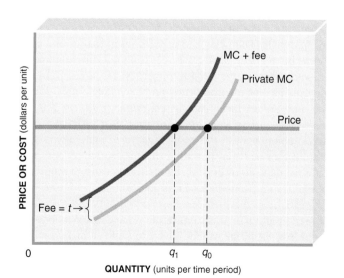

FIGURE 12.3
Emission Fees

Emission charges can be used to close the gap between marginal social costs and marginal private costs. Faced with an emission charge of t, a private producer will reduce output from q_0 to q_1. Emission charges may also induce different investment and efficiency decisions.

smokestack controls that reduce the volume of emissions from the burning of high-sulfur coal. This would entail additional capital outlays for the necessary abatement equipment but might not alter marginal costs. In this case, the fee-induced change in fixed costs might reduce pollution without any reduction in output.

The actual response of producers will depend on the relative costs involved. If emission charges are too low, it may be more profitable to continue burning and polluting with high-sulfur coal and simply pay a nominal fee. This is a simple pricing problem. We could set the emission price higher, prompting the behavioural responses we desire.

The same kind of relative cost considerations would apply to the thermal pollution associated with the power plant. The choice heretofore has been between building expensive cooling towers (and not polluting) or not incurring such capital costs (and simply discharging the heated water into the river). The profit-maximizing choice was fairly obvious. Now, however, the choice is between building cooling towers or paying out a steady flow of emission charges. The profit-maximizing decision is no longer evident. The decisive factor will be how high we set the emission charges. If the emission charges are set high enough, the producer will find it unprofitable to pollute.

Economic incentives can also change consumer behaviour. Over the years, regulatory agencies at the city, provincial, and national level have imposed deposits on beverage containers, encouraging consumers to return the containers for reuse or recycling. These include both alcoholic and non-alcoholic beverages and extend to glass bottles, cans, cardboard, and Tetra Pak containers; deposits typically range from 5¢ to 40¢ per container. Such deposits internalize pollution costs for the consumer and render the throwing of a beer can out the window equivalent to throwing away money. In Ontario, for example, the provincial "Beer Stores" operate a system-wide recovery and re-use program. They claim a 98 percent rate of return for the industry standard bottle (each bottle is reused 15 to 20 times).[2]

Some communities have also tried to reduce solid-waste processing by charging a fee for each bag of garbage collected and/or limiting the amount of garbage bags for the weekly collection. The City of Owen Sound, in Ontario, enforces both requirements: a limit of three bags per week, with each bag displaying a $2.00 tag. Bags in excess of the limit or not displaying a tag are simply not picked up!

In Charlotte, Virginia, U.S.A., a fee of 80 cents per 32-gallon bag of garbage had a noticeable impact on consumer behaviour. Economists Don Fullerton and Thomas Kinnaman observed that households reduced the weight of their garbage by 14 percent and the volume by 37 percent. As they noted, "Households somehow stomped their garbage to get more in a container and trim their garbage bill."

WEB NOTE

For more information on North American deposit systems, see the Grass Roots Recycling Network's website at: http://www.grrn.org/beverage/deposits/.

Recycling Materials. An important bonus that emission charges offer is an increased incentive for the recycling of materials. The glass and metal in used bottles and cans can be recycled to produce new bottles and cans. Such recycling not only eliminates a lot of unsightly litter but also diminishes the need to mine new resources from the earth, a process that often involves its own environmental problems. The critical issues are once again relative costs and market incentives. *A container producer has no incentive to use recycled materials unless they offer superior cost efficiency and thus greater profits.* The largest component in the costs of recycled materials is usually the associated costs of collection and transportation. In this regard, an emission charge such as the 5-cent container deposit lowers collection costs because it motivates consumers to return all their bottles and cans to a central location.

Higher User Fees. Another market alternative is to raise the price consumers pay for scarce resources. If people used less water, we wouldn't have to build so many sewage

[2]http://www.thebeerstore.ca/AboutUs/environmental_leadership.asp

APPLICATIONS

Quebec Imposes Carbon Tax: Motorists Wary of Pump Price

Quebecers will be distinct from other Canadians in another way starting this fall: They will have the country's first designated "carbon tax" to help fight global warming. The carbon tax is expected to raise $200 million a year to help finance Quebec's plan to reduce greenhouse-gas emissions and favour public transit.

Jack Star/PhotoLink/Getty Images

Natural Resources Minister Claude Bechard, who announced yesterday that a 0.8-cent-per-litre carbon tax will come into force on October 1, added that he hopes oil companies, which are reporting record profits, would absorb the tax and not pass it on to consumers.

"We hope at 0.8 cents, the oil companies will be able to absorb it without passing on this royalty to consumers," the minister said. "Especially when you realize that refinery profit margins have gone in the last three, four months from 8 cents a litre to about 19, 20, 22 cents a litre."

Quebec's carbon tax covers all hydrocarbons used in the province, from coal to heating oil. While the tax for gasoline is 0.8 cents a litre, the charge for diesel fuel is 0.9 cents, for light heating oil 0.96 cents, heavy heating oil one cent per litre, coke used in steel-making 1.3 cents per litre, coal $8 per tonne, and propane 0.5 cents per litre.

—Kevin Dougherty & Anne Sutherland

Source: Kevin Dougherty and Anne Sutherland, "Quebec Imposes Carbon Tax: Motorists Wary of Pump Price," *The Montreal Gazette,* Thursday, June 7, 2007. Material used with express permission of Montreal Gazette Group Inc., a CanWest Partnership.

Analysis: "Green" taxes not only help reduce the consumption of goods that pollute the atmosphere but also generate revenues for other pollution-abatement efforts.

---

treatment plants. In most communities, however, the price of water is so low that people use it indiscriminately. Higher water fees would encourage water conservation.

A similar logic applies to auto pollution. A cheap way to cut down on auto pollution is to drive less. Higher gasoline prices would encourage people to use alternative transportation and drive more fuel-efficient cars.

"Green" Taxes. Automakers don't want gasoline prices to go up; neither do consumers. So the government may have to impose *green taxes* to get the desired response. A green tax on gasoline, for example, raises the price of gasoline. The taxes not only curb auto emissions (less driving) but also create a revenue source for other pollution-abatement efforts. As the World View box on the next page indicates, other nations impose far more green taxes than does Canada.

In the above Application box, Quebec's Natural Resources Minister anticipates that, given the recent increase in refinery profit margins, oil companies will absorb the 0.8¢/litre carbon tax and refrain from passing it onto motorists. Do you think this will occur? If oil companies completely absorb the tax, there will be an increase in their private cost structure (small as it is) closer to the social cost structure (see Figure 12.2). If, however, the oil companies pass the tax fully onto consumers, our demand analysis in Chapter 2 suggests that consumers will purchase less gasoline as the price rises (again, as small at it is and everything else remaining constant). Either way, we should observe a reduction in the production/consumption of gasoline.

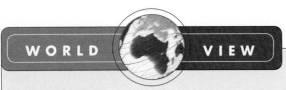

WORLD VIEW

Taxing Pollution

Economists have long argued that an efficient way to control pollution is to make those who cause it bear some of the costs via environmentally related or "green" taxes. These can run the gamut from retail taxes on gasoline to landfill charges on waste disposal.

By dint of its economic heft, the United States is commonly regarded as the world's biggest polluter. Yet the Organization for Economic Cooperation & Development reports that it imposes the lowest green taxes as a percent of gross domestic product of any industrial nation. While the average for OECD countries in 1998 was 2.7 percent of GDP, for example, the U.S. level was estimated at less than 1 percent.

Between 1994 and 1998, a majority of OECD members boosted their green-tax ratios, with Denmark's and Turkey's both rising by a full percentage point to 5 percent and 3 percent respectively. By contrast, the U.S., Germany, and France actually reduced their green-tax levels over the four-year period.

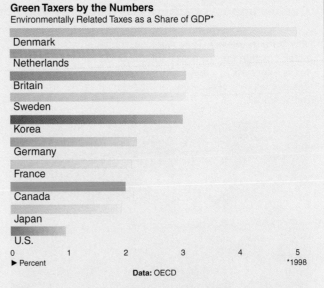

Green Taxers by the Numbers
Environmentally Related Taxes as a Share of GDP*

Denmark
Netherlands
Britain
Sweden
Korea
Germany
France
Canada
Japan
U.S.

0   1   2   3   4   5

► Percent   *1998

Data: OECD

Source: *BusinessWeek*, September 17, 2001. © 2001 The McGraw-Hill Companies, Inc. Reprinted with permission. www.businessweek.com

Analysis: "Green" taxes can be used to reduce the level of polluting consumption or production activities.

Pollution Fines. Not far removed from the concept of emission and user charges is the imposition of fines or liability for cleanup costs. In some situations, such as an oil spill, the pollution is so sudden and concentrated that society has little choice but to clean it up quickly. The costs for such cleanup can be imposed on the polluter, however, through appropriate fines. Such fines place the cost burden where it belongs. In addition, they serve as an incentive for greater safety, for such things as double-hulled oil tankers and more efficient safety mechanisms on offshore oil wells. When Royal Caribbean Cruises was fined $9 million in 1998 for dumping garbage and oil from its cruise ships, the firm decided to monitor waste disposal practices more closely. In the absence of such fines, firms have little incentive to invest in environmental protection.

Tradable Pollution Permits

Another environmental policy option makes even greater use of market incentives. Rather than penalize firms that have already polluted, let firms *purchase* the right to continue polluting. As crazy as this policy might sound, it can be highly effective in limiting environmental damage.

The key to the success of pollution permits is that they're bought and sold among private firms. The system starts with a government-set standard for pollution reduction. Firms that reduce pollution by more than the standard earn pollution credits. They may then sell these credits to other firms, who are thereby relieved of cleanup chores. ***The principal advantage of pollution permits is their incentive to minimize the cost of pollution control.***

To see how the permits work, suppose the policy objective is to reduce sulfur dioxide emissions by two tonnes. There are only two major polluters in the community: a copper smelter and an electric utility. Should each company be required to reduce its SO_2 emissions by one tonne? Or can the same SO_2 reduction be achieved more cheaply with marketable pollution rights?

Reduction in Emissions (in tonnes)	Marginal Cost of Pollution Abatement	
	Copper Smelter	Electric Utility
1	$200	$100
2	250	150
3	300	200

TABLE 12.1
Pricing Pollution Permits

If both firms reduce emissions by one tonne each, the cost is $300. If the utility instead reduces emissions by two tonnes, the cost is only $250. A permit system allows the smelter to pay the utility for assuming the added abatement responsibility.

Table 12.1 depicts the assumed cost of pollution abatement at each plant. The copper smelter would have to spend $200 to achieve a one-tonne reduction in SO_2 emissions. The utility can do it for only $100. Table 12.1 also indicates that the utility can attain a *second* tonne of SO_2 abatement for $150. Even though its marginal cost of pollution control is increasing, the utility still has lower abatement costs than the smelter. This cost advantage creates an interesting economic opportunity.

Recall that the policy goal is to reduce emissions by two tonnes. The copper smelter would have to spend $200 to achieve its share. But the utility can abate that second tonne for $150. Accordingly, the smelter would save money by *paying* the utility for additional pollution abatement.

How much would the smelter have to pay? The utility would want at least $150 to cover its own costs. The smelter would benefit at any price below $200. Accordingly, the price of this transaction would be somewhere between $150 (the utility's cost) and $200 (the smelter's cost). The smelter would continue to pollute, but total SO_2 emissions would still drop by two tonnes. Both firms and society would be better off.

At the first real U.S. auction of pollution credits the average price paid was $156 (see the Applications box). For this price a firm could pay someone else to reduce SO_2 emissions by one tonne rather than curb its own emissions. The Carolina Power and Light Company spent $11.5 *million* buying such permits.

U.S. Experience. Since they first became available in 1992, U.S. tradable pollution permits ("allowances") have become a popular mechanism for pollution control. Millions

APPLICATIONS

Auction: $156 to Emit a Ton of Pollutants

CHICAGO—The right to spew a ton of sulfur dioxide into the air in 1995 costs about $156. That was the average sale price Tuesday at the first auction of pollution credits.

Total sold: 150,010 permits for $21.4 million. Permits sold for the year 2000 were cheaper, an average $136.

Price range: $122 to $450.

The auction of credits, at the Chicago Board of Trade, is key to the Environmental Protection Agency's efforts to halve acid rain pollutants by 2010. . . .

Who sells credits? Utilities that have less pollution than allowed under EPA rules. Who buys? Utilities with pollution problems, or speculators.

Top buyer: Carolina Power & Light Co. spent $11.5 million. . . .

Consumers could gain: The program could halve the cost of anti-pollution rules for utilities, which could lower bills.

—Kevin Johnson

Source: *USA Today*, March 31, 1993. Copyright 1993, USA TODAY. Reprinted with permission. www.usatoday.com. For current price on pollution credits see www.epa.gov/airmarkets/trading/SO2 market.

Analysis: Marketable pollution permits encourage firms with more efficient pollution control technologies to overachieve, thereby earning pollution permits that can be sold to firms with more expensive pollution control technologies. Such trades reduce the *average* cost of pollution control.

WEB NOTE

The National Round Table on the Environment and the Economy spearheads much of the discussion and dissemination of information concerning emissions trading and other environmental issues. Visit their website at http://www.nrtee-trnee.ca/eng/index_eng.htm.

of allowances are now traded in the open market every year. Moreover, the permit market has gotten increasingly efficient, with visible bid and ask prices, broker specialists, and low transaction costs. In 2000, 12.7 *million* sulfur dioxide allowances were traded, each covering one ton of emission reduction. The price of a permit has also steadily declined, indicating that companies are discovering cheaper methods of pollution control. Entrepreneurs now have an incentive to discover cheaper methods for pollution abatement. They don't have to own a smelter or utility; they can now *sell* their pollution control expertise to the highest bidder. As the market for permits has expanded, the profit opportunities for environmental engineering firms have increased. This has accelerated productivity and reduced the cost of pollution abatement by 25 to 34 percent. In view of these results, the EPA extended the pollution-permit trading system to *water* pollution in 2003.

Canadian Experience. Compared to the United States, the Canadian trade in pollution permits (emissions trading system) is still in its infancy. There has been a considerable amount of analysis and consultation, a few voluntary trial programs involving public–private partnerships, and some private sector trades, but the federal government has not announced any clear emission trading rules or regulations.

The Ontario Pilot Emission Reduction Trading (PERT) project was a voluntary, industry-led initiative that provided credits to firms in the Windsor–Quebec corridor that reduced greenhouse gas (GHG) emissions below those established by the Ontario Ministry of Government. The Greenhouse Gas Emission Reduction Trading (GERT) pilots evaluated specific GHG reduction projects using tradable permits to measure and verify whether the emissions complied with baseline standards.[3] TransAlta and EPCOR in Alberta as well as Ontario Power Generation (OPG) are among a number of firms that have conducted voluntary emission trades both domestically and across the U.S. border over the years.

The Government of Ontario has taken the lead in tradable pollution permits by establishing Canada's first regulated emissions trading system. The trading system currently covers the acid rain and smog pollutants (SO_2 and NO_x) emitted by seven of the largest industrial sectors; electricity, iron and steel, cement, petroleum refining, pulp and paper, glass and carbon black. The provincial government has suggested that the emissions trading system could extend to other pollutants including GHGs (CO_2).

Command-and-Control Options

Public policy needn't rely on tradable permits or other market incentives to achieve desired pollution abatement. The government could instead simply *require* firms to reduce pollutants by specific amounts and even specify which abatement technology must be used. This approach is often referred to as the "command-and-control" option. The government *commands* firms to reduce pollution and then *controls* the process for doing so.

The potential inefficiency of the command-and-control strategy was outlined earlier in Table 12.1. Had the government required *each* firm to reduce pollution by one tonne, the total cost would have been $300. By allowing firms to use tradable permits, the cost of obtaining the same level of pollution abatement was only $250. The cost saving of $50 represents valuable resources that could be used to produce other desired goods and services.

Despite the superior efficiency of market-based environmental policies, the government often relies on the command-and-control approach. The 2006 Clean Air Act proposed by the minority Conservative government plans to reduce GHG emissions to approximately 45–60 percent of the 2003 levels (by 2050). This includes regulations on vehicle fuel consumption that will reduce GHGs by 5.3 megatonnes (by 2010) as well as a new regulatory framework for key industrial sectors (e.g., fossil-fuel–fired

---

[3]Other government initiatives to reduce GHGs without the use of tradable pollution permits include the Pilot Emission Removals, Reductions and Learnings (PERRL) Initiative. See Environment Canada's site http://www.ec.gc.ca/PERRL/about_e.html.

electricity generation, base metal smelters, forest products, and chemical production). The U.S. Clean Air Acts of 1970 and 1990, for example, mandated not only fewer auto emissions but also specific processes such as catalytic converters and lead-free gasoline for attaining them. Specific processes and technologies are also required for toxic waste disposal and water treatment. Laws requiring the sorting and recycling of trash are other examples of process regulation.

Although such command-and-control regulation can be effective, this policy option also entails risks. By requiring all market participants to follow specific rules, the regulations may impose excessive costs on some activities and too low a constraint on others. Some communities may not need the level of sewage treatment the federal government prescribes. Individual households may not generate enough trash to make sorting and separate pickups economically sound. Some producers may have better or cheaper ways of attaining environmental standards. *Excessive process regulation may raise the costs of environmental protection* and discourage cost-saving innovation. There's also the risk of regulated processes becoming entrenched long after they are obsolete. When that happens we may end up with worse outcomes than a less regulated market would have generated—that is, *government failure.*

Central Planning

Some of the worst government failure occurs in the most regulated economies. Prior to 1990, Eastern Europe relied on central planning to make production and investment decisions. There was no *market* incentive to pollute since there was no opportunity for private profit. On the other hand, the central planners had to set priorities. Their choice was to maximize production. Environmental concerns had lower priority. This set of priorities created an environmental catastrophe: polluted air and water, dying forests, poisoned food, and deteriorating human health. Poland, for example, produced six times more air pollution per unit of output than did Western Europe. Europe's largest coal-burning power plant, located in Belchatow, burns soft brown coal, covering the countryside with sulfur and soot. The world's largest single source of air pollution is the complex of ore smelters in Norilsk (central Siberia), which emits 2 *million* tonnes of sulfur a day. Cars made in Russia and Eastern Europe still burn leaded gas. The Volga River has been crippled by factory waste, untreated sewage, and hydroelectric dams, while the Black Sea has virtually been destroyed. The polluted environments of Eastern Europe and the former Soviet republics amply document that government-directed production isn't necessarily more environment-friendly than market-directed production.

12.6 BALANCING BENEFITS AND COSTS

Protecting the environment entails costs as well as benefits. Installing smokestack scrubbers on factory chimneys and catalytic converters on cars requires the use of scarce resources. Taking the lead out of gasoline wears out engines faster and requires expensive changes in technology. Switching to clean fuels requires enormous investments in technology, plants, and equipment.

Opportunity Costs

Whatever the exact costs of environmental protection, it's apparent that we're talking about an enormous reallocation of productive resources. Although cleaning up the environment is a universally acknowledged goal, we must remind ourselves that those resources could be used to fulfill other goals as well. The multibillion-dollar tab would buy a lot of subways and parks or build decent homes for the poor. If we choose to devote those resources instead to pollution-abatement efforts, we'll have to forgo some other goods and services. This isn't to say that environmental goals don't deserve that kind of priority but simply to remind us that any use of our scarce resources involves an *opportunity cost.*

Fortunately, the amount of additional resources required to clean up the environment is relatively modest in comparison to our productive capacity. Over a 10-year period we'll produce well over $10 trillion of goods and services (GDP). On this basis, the environmental expenditures contemplated by present environmental policies and goals represent only a small percent of total output.

The Optimal Rate of Pollution

optimal rate of pollution: The rate of pollution that occurs when the marginal social benefit of pollution control equals its marginal social cost.

Whether a small percentage of GDP is too much or too little to spend on environmental protection depends on the value we assign to other goods and services and to a cleaner environment. That is, the **optimal rate of pollution** occurs at the point at which the opportunity costs of further pollution control equal the benefits of further reductions in pollution. To determine the optimal rate of pollution, we need to compare the marginal social benefits of additional pollution abatement with the marginal social costs of additional pollution control expenditure. The optimal rate of pollution is achieved when we've satisfied the following equality:

$$\begin{array}{ccc} \text{Optimal} & \text{marginal benefit} & \text{marginal cost} \\ \text{rate of} & : \text{of pollution} & = \text{of pollution} \\ \text{pollution} & \text{abatement} & \text{abatement} \end{array}$$

This formulation is analogous to the utility-maximizing rule in consumption. If another dollar spent on pollution control yields less than a dollar of social benefits, then additional pollution control expenditure isn't desirable. In such a situation, the goods and services that would be forsaken for additional pollution control are more valued than the environmental improvements that would result. The Applications box below suggests that the United States may have already crossed that threshold in combating air pollution.

Although pollution abatement has been an economic success, that doesn't mean *all* pollution controls are desirable. The focus must still be on *marginal* benefits and costs. As the Applications box reports, the cost of cleaning up ground-level ozone exceeds resultant benefits by as much as 50:1. More generally, the formula for the optimal rate

APPLICATIONS

Two Economists Question Benefit of Cleaning Up a Major Air Pollutant

The health benefits of cleaning up a widespread urban air pollutant, ground-level ozone, may not be worth the price, two economists argue in a new study.

The economists at Resources for the Future, a respected nonadvocacy research institute in Washington, compared the costs of plans for Los Angeles and the nation as a whole to meet national air quality standards for ground-level ozone with their potential health benefits. In both cases, the most optimistic estimate of the costs fell far short of the most optimistic measure of the health benefits.

They chose to look at ground-level ozone because it is one of the most difficult air pollution problems to solve. They also said they believed they could effectively apply cost-benefit analysis to it.

According to cost estimates based on 1989 government data, they found the cost for the nation to meet the standards would be $8.8 billion to $12.8 billion through 2004 while health benefits would be $250 million to $1 billion. They

estimated that the cost of a more ambitious 1989 Los Angeles plan would be $13 billion through 2010 but that it would yield only $3 billion in health benefits.

Basis of Conclusions

The economists, Alan J. Krupnick and Paul R. Portney, concluded that air should be cleaned up in the most polluted areas but that investing billions of dollars to get people to quit smoking, control radon gas and provide better prenatal and neonatal care might contribute much more. . . .

"I don't expect people to like the conclusion," Mr. Portney said, "But this is not a justification for not cleaning up the air. It just says maybe we could get more health benefits for our money if we spent it someplace else."

The New York Times

Source: *The New York Times*, April 30, 1991. © 1991 The New York Times Company. Reprinted by permission. www.nytimes.com

Analysis: The costs of environmental protection are substantial and must be compared to the benefits. The *optimal* amount of pollution balances marginal benefits and costs.

of pollution implies that *a totally clean environment isn't economically desirable.* The marginal benefit of achieving zero pollution is infinitesimally small. But the marginal cost of eliminating that last particle of pollution will be very high. As we weigh the marginal benefits and costs, we'll conclude that *some* pollution is cost-effective.

Cost-Benefit Analysis

Although marginal analysis tells us that a zero-pollution goal isn't economically desirable, it doesn't really pinpoint the optimal level of pollution. To apply those guidelines we need to identify and evaluate the marginal benefits of any intervention and its marginal costs. Sometimes such calculations yield extraordinarily high cost-benefit ratios. According to researchers at the Harvard Center for Risk Analysis, the *median* cost per life-year saved by EPA regulations is $7.6 million. One of the highest cost-benefit ratios is attached to chloroform emission controls at pulp mills: The cost per life-year saved exceeds $99 billion. A human life may in fact be too precious to value in dollars and cents. But in a world of limited resources, the opportunity costs of every intervention need to be assessed. How many lives would be saved if we spent $99 billion on cancer or AIDS research?

In a number of communities, a similar cost-benefit analysis was performed on their recycling programs. Sure, everyone thinks that recycling is a good idea. But what happens when the opportunity costs associated with recycling exceed the benefits (see the Applications box)?

Who Will Pay?

The costs of pollution control aren't distributed equally. In New York City, the cost of the recycling program is borne by those who end up with fewer city services and amenities (opportunity costs). A national pollution-abatement program would target the relatively

---

APPLICATIONS

Forced Recycling Is a Waste

As New York City faces the possibility of painful cuts to its police and fire department budgets, environmentalists are belly-aching over garbage. Mayor Michael Bloomberg's proposed budget for 2003 would temporarily suspend the city's recycling of metal, glass and plastic, saving New Yorkers $57 million.

The city's recycling program—like many others around the country—has long hemorrhaged tax dollars. . . .

The city spends about $240 per ton to "recycle" plastic, glass, and metal, while the cost of simply sending waste to landfills is about $130 per ton.

You don't need a degree is economics to see that something is wrong here. Isn't recycling supposed to save money and resources? Some recycling does—when driven by market forces. Private parties don't voluntarily recycle unless they know it will save money, and, hence, resources. But forced re-cycling can be a waste of both because recycling itself entails using energy, water and labor to collect, sort, clean and pro-cess the materials. There are also air emissions, traffic and wear on streets from the second set of trucks prowling for recycla-bles. The bottom line is that most mandated recycling hurts, not helps the environment. . . .

"You could do a lot better things in the world with $57 million," says Mayor Bloomberg.

—Angela Logomasini

Source: *The Wall Street Journal,* March 19, 2002. Reprinted by permission of The Wall Street Journal and Angela Logomasini, © 2002 Dow Jones & Company. All rights reserved worldwide.

Analysis: Recycling uses scarce resources that could be employed elsewhere. The benefits of recycling may not exceed its (opportunity) costs.

WEB NOTE

Find out how economists
measure the costs and benefits
of environmental programs
at www.epa.gov. Click on
"Programs," then "Research,"
then "Office of Research and
Development."

small number of economic activities that account for the bulk of emissions and effluents. These activities will have to bear a disproportionate share of the cleanup burden.

To ascertain how the burden of environmental protection will be distributed, consider first the electric power plant discussed earlier. As we observed (Figure 12.2), the plant's output will decrease if production decisions are based on social rather than private marginal costs—that is, if environmental consequences are considered. If the plant itself is compelled to pay full social costs, in the form of either compulsory investment or emission charges, its profits will be reduced. Were no other changes to take place, the burden of environmental improvements would be borne primarily by the producer.

Such a scenario is unlikely, however. Rather than absorb all the costs of pollution controls themselves, producers will seek to pass on some of this burden to their customers in the form of higher prices. Their ability to do so will depend on the extent of competition in their industry, their relative cost position in it, and the price elasticity of consumer demand. In reality, the electric power industry isn't very competitive as yet, and its prices are still subject to government regulation. In addition, consumer demand is relatively price-inelastic. Accordingly, the profit-maximizing producer will appeal to the provincial or local power commission for an increase in electricity prices based on the costs of pollution control. Electric power consumers are likely to end up footing part or all of the environmental bill. The increased prices will more fully reflect the social costs associated with electricity use.

In addition to the electric power industry, the automobile, paper, steel, and chemical industries will be adversely affected by pollution controls. In all of these cases, the prices of the related products will increase, in some instances by significant percentages. These price increases will help reduce pollution in two ways. First, they'll help pay for pollution control equipment. Second, they'll encourage consumers to change their expenditure patterns in the direction of less polluting goods.

The Greenhouse Threat

Forget about littered beaches, smelly landfills, eye-stinging smog, and contaminated water. The really scary problem for the economy tomorrow is much more serious: Some scientists say that the carbon emissions we're now spewing into the air are warming the earth's atmosphere. If the earth's temperature rises only a few degrees, they contend, polar caps will melt, continents will flood, and weather patterns will go haywire (see the World View box on the next page). If things get bad enough, there may not be any economy tomorrow.

The Greenhouse Effect. The earth's climate is driven by solar radiation. The energy the sun absorbs must be balanced by outgoing radiation from the earth and the atmosphere. Scientists fear that a flow imbalance is developing. Of particular concern is a buildup of carbon dioxide (CO_2) that might trap heat in the earth's atmosphere, warming the planet.

The natural release of CO_2 dwarfs the emissions from human activities. But there's a concern that the steady increase in man-made CO_2 emissions—principally from burning fossil fuels like gasoline and coal—is tipping the balance.

The Skeptics. Other scientists are skeptical about both the temperature change and its causes. A 1988 National Oceanic and Atmospheric Administration study concluded that there's been no ocean warming in this past century. Furthermore, they say, the amount of CO_2 emitted into the atmosphere by human activity (about 7 billion tons per year) is only a tiny fraction of natural emissions from volcanoes, fires, and lightning (200 billion tons per year). Skeptics also point out that the same computer models predicting global warming in the next generation predicted a much larger increase in temperature for the previous century than actually occurred.

In mid-2001, the National Academy of Sciences resolved one of those issues. The Academy confirmed that the earth is warming, largely due to the increased buildup of greenhouse gas concentrations. A 2004 analysis by the U.S. National Center for Atmospheric Research concluded that natural climate changes were

WORLD   VIEW

Scientists Issue Dire Prediction on Warming

Faster Climate Shift Portends Global Calamity This Century

BEIJING, Jan. 22—In the most forceful warning yet on the threat of global warming, an international panel of hundreds of scientists issued a report today predicting brutal droughts, floods and violent storms across the planet over the next century because air pollution is causing surface temperatures to rise faster than anticipated.

The report, approved unanimously at a U.N. conference in Shanghai and described as the most comprehensive study on the subject to date, says that Earth's average temperature could rise by as much as 10.4 degrees [°F] over the next 100 years—the most rapid change in 10 millennia and more than 60 percent higher than the same group predicted less than six years ago.

If new scientific models are accurate, rising temperatures will melt polar ice caps and raise sea levels by as much as 34 inches, causing floods that could displace tens of millions of

people in low-lying areas—such as China's Pearl River Delta, much of Bangladesh and the most densely populated area of Egypt. Droughts will parch farmlands and aggravate world hunger. Storms triggered by such climatic extremes as El Niño will become more frequent. Diseases such as malaria and dengue fever will spread. . . .

The report cited "new and stronger evidence that most of the observed warming of the last 50 years is attributable to human activities," primarily the burning of oil, gasoline and coal, which produces carbon dioxide and other gases that trap heat in Earth's atmosphere. . . .

The global warming issue has proved highly contentious among environmental scientists, with many respected figures arguing that Earth undergoes periodic climatic changes with or without contributions from mankind.

—Philip P. Pan

Source: *The Washington Post*, January 23, 2001. © 2001 The Washington Post. Reprinted with permission. www.washingtonpost.com

Analysis: The external costs of consumption and production activities contribute to global environmental problems. What should be done to curb these global external costs?

responsible for the earth's warming from 1900 to 1950, but could not explain the continuing rise in the earth's temperature since then. Human activity seemed to be the only possible culprit.

In 2006, Sir Nicholas Stern, Head of the Government Economics Service for the U.K. government, presented the "Stern Review on the Economics of Climate Change." In the Review, Stern documents the stark prospects of climate change and identifies the increasing costs with delaying the reduction of GHGs. Using formal economic models, the costs of action, if promptly addressed, could be limited to 1 percent of global GDP each year. Alternatively, if no action is taken to reduce emissions, "the overall costs and risks of climate change will be equivalent to losing at least 5 percent of global GDP each year, now and forever. If a wider range of risks and impacts is taken into account, the estimates of damage could rise to 20 percent of GDP or more."

Global Externalities. Despite accumulating evidence, lingering uncertainty about the causes of the greenhouse effect has made policy decisions difficult. One thing is certain, however: ***CO_2 emissions are a global externality*** of industrial production and fuel consumption. Without some form of government intervention, there's little likelihood that market participants will voluntarily reduce CO_2 emissions.

Kyoto Protocol. In December 1997, most of the world's industrialized nations pledged to reduce CO_2 emissions. The Kyoto treaty they initialled in 1997 expressed an international commitment to reduce greenhouse emissions during the period 2008–2012. The world's industrialized nations promised to cut their emissions by 5.2 percent below 1990 levels. That would require some industries (e.g., automobile, steel, paper, electric power) to substantially alter production methods and, possibly, output. For their part, the developing nations of the world promised to curb their *growth* of emissions.

WEB NOTE

The full report, executive summary and FAQs of the Stern Review on the Economics of Climate Change can be seen at http://www.hm-treasury.gov.uk/. In the Search box, type in "Stern Review Index Page."

WEB NOTE

The United Nations provides information on climate change and emissions data for individual nations at www.unfccc.int.

After four years of design and debate, 178 nations signed the Kyoto Protocol at a June 2001 United Nations convention. Canada officially signed the Kyoto Protocol in April 1998, ratified the agreement in December 2002, and started the implementation process in February 2005 under the direction of the Minister of the Environment, Stéphane Dion. Canada pledged a 6 percent reduction in GHG emission targets for the 2008–2012 commitment period (from the 1990 baseline levels)—the equivalent of a nominal reduction of 270 megatonnes per year. To achieve this target, the government proposed a number of new initiatives. These included a market-based institution for the trading of pollution permits, a new regime for Large Final Emitters (LFEs), emission reductions from vehicles, and incentives for individual reductions through initiatives such as the One-Tonne Challenge Program.

Where are we now? Canada's emissions increased by 27 percent between 1990 and 2004. Our Kyoto commitment would imply a reduction of at least 33 percent—all to occur during the 2008–2012 period! The subsequent minority Conservative government of Stephen Harper viewed the Liberal plan as unrealistic and suggested replacing it with the Clean Air Act mentioned earlier in the chapter. A central focus of this Act is on "intensity-based" targets for reduction of GHGs. This involves the use of new technology and innovation to reduce the emissions per unit of energy produced at any level of output. Critics argue that an intensity-based approach will not necessarily lead to an overall reduction in GHG levels (a 10 percent improvement in emissions, for example, can be outweighed by a 15 percent increase in output).

While a number of signatories of the Kyoto Protocol continue toward their goals, two countries, Australia and the United States, have signed the treaty but refuse to ratify the agreement. In the case of the United States, the Bush administration argues that the implied costs of pollution abatement are far too high, especially in view of the uncertain payoff. President Bush also argues that the treaty puts the United States and other industrialized nations at a competitive disadvantage, since they (not the developing nations) have to absorb the higher pollution-abatement costs. Australia presents similar arguments and estimates that without the commitment of all major emitters (particularly the United States), the Protocol will deliver only about a 1 percent reduction in GHGs.[4]

With neither universal support nor enforcement mechanisms, the Kyoto Protocol will not achieve the target levels of pollution abatement. However, the treaty has increased public awareness of global environmental externalities and encouraged more efforts to control them. As with domestic policy, the challenge for the economy tomorrow is to find a policy mix that will generate the optimal level of global pollution.

[4]Although the Australian government refuses to ratify the Protocol it is on track to meeting their targeted commitment of limiting emissions to +8 percent of 1990 levels between 2008 and 2012. The estimated price tag is $1.62 billion ($Cdn).

SUMMARY

- Air, water, and solid-waste pollution impose social and economic costs. The costs of pollution include the direct damages inflicted on our health and resources, the expense of cleaning up, and the general aesthetic deterioration of the environment.
- Pollution is an external cost, a cost of a market activity imposed on someone (a third party) other than the immediate producer or consumer.
- Producers and consumers generally operate on the basis of private benefits and costs. Accordingly, a private producer

or consumer has an incentive to minimize his own costs by transforming private costs into external costs. One way of making such a substitution is to pollute—to use "free" air and water rather than install pollution control equipment, or to leave the job of waste disposal to others.

- Social costs are the total amount of resources used in a production or consumption process. When social costs are greater than private costs, the market's price signals are flawed. This market failure will induce people to harm the environment by using suboptimal processes and products.

- One way to correct the market inefficiency created by externalities is to compel producers and consumers to internalize all (social) costs. This can be done by imposing emission charges and higher user fees. Such charges create an incentive to invest in pollution abatement equipment, recycle reusable materials, and conserve scarce elements of the environment.
- Tradable pollution permits help minimize the cost of pollution control by (*a*) promoting low-cost controls to substitute for high-cost controls and (*b*) encouraging innovation in pollution control technology.
- An alternative approach to cleaning up the environment is to require specific pollution controls or to prohibit specific kinds of activities. Direct regulation runs the risk of higher cost and discouraging innovations in environmental protection.

- The opportunity costs of pollution abatement are the most desired goods and services given up when factors of production are used to control pollution. The optimal rate of pollution is reached when the marginal social benefits of further pollution control equal associated marginal social costs.
- In addition to diverting resources, pollution control efforts alter relative prices, change the mix of output, and redistribute incomes. These outcomes cause losses for particular groups and may thus require special economic or political attention.
- The greenhouse effect represents a global externality. Reducing global emissions requires consensus on optimal pollution levels (i.e., the optimal balance of pollution-abatement costs and benefits).

Key Terms

efficiency decision   255
external cost   256

social costs   257
private costs   257

emission charge   259
optimal rate of pollution   266

Questions for Discussion

1. What are the *economic* costs of the externalities caused by air toxins? Or beach closings? (See the Applications box, page 254.) How would you measure their value?
2. Should we try to eliminate *all* pollution? What economic considerations might favour permitting some pollution?
3. Why would auto manufacturers resist exhaust control devices? How would their costs, sales, and profits be affected?
4. Does anyone have an incentive to maintain auto-exhaust control devices in good working order? How can we ensure that they will be maintained?
5. Suppose we established a $10,000 fine for water pollution. Would some companies still find that polluting was economical? Under what conditions?

6. What economic costs are imposed by mandatory sorting of trash?
7. The issuance of a pollution permit is just a license to destroy the environment. Do you agree? Explain.
8. What opportunity costs of combating ozone pollution are identified in the Applications box on page 266?
9. If a high per-bag fee were charged for garbage collection, would illegal dumping increase?
10. Should Canada ratify the Kyoto treaty? What are the arguments for and against Canadian participation?

EXERCISES

PROBLEMS   The Student Problem Set to accompany this chapter can be found at the end of the book.

WEB ACTIVITIES   Web Activities to accompany this chapter can be found on the Online Learning Centre at **http://www.mcgrawhill.ca/olc/schiller**.

PART 5

Factor Markets: Basic Theory

actor markets operate like product markets, with supply and demand interacting to determine prices and quantities. In factor markets, however, resource inputs rather than products are exchanged. Those exchanges determine the wages paid to workers and the rent, interest, and profits paid to other inputs. The micro theories presented in Chapters 13 and 14 explain how those factor payments are determined.

The Labour Market

I n 2005, the Executive Chairman of Precision Drilling Trust—a Calgary-based oilfields services company—earned $840,000 in salary, a bonus of $3.3 million, "other" compensation equal to $15.6 million, and a whopping $55 million of option gains for a total financial remuneration of $74.8 million. The Prime Minister of Canada earned $288,600 (plus a car allowance of $2,122), while the average earnings of Canadian workers was roughly $38,000. Using a weighted average of the 10 provinces' minimum wages, the annual minimum wage earnings in 2005 amounted to $16,000. In addition, women in non-unionized jobs earned, on average, $4.50 per hour less than men working in non-unionized jobs.

What accounts for these tremendous disparities in earnings? Surely we can't hope to explain these differences on the basis of willingness to work. After all, most Canadians would be willing to work day and night for $75 million per year. For that matter, so would I. Accordingly, the earnings disparities can't be attributed simply to differences in the quantity of labour supplied. If we are going to explain why some people earn a great deal of income while others earn very little, we must consider both the supply and the demand for labour.

Institutional factors (e.g., rate of unionization and level of unemployment benefits) and geographic locations (e.g., small coal-mining town in the interior of British Columbia vs. Vancouver) can influence the employees' or employers' *market power*—the ability to alter market outcomes. Once again, the market structure plays an important role in determining both wages (price of labour) and the total amount employed in the market (quantity of labour). In this chapter, we examine the following questions:

- **How do people decide how much time to spend working?**
- **What determines the wage rate an employer is willing to pay?**
- **Why are some workers paid so much and others so little?**
- **How do large and powerful employers affect market wages?**
- **How do labour unions alter wages and employment?**
- **What outcomes are possible from collective bargaining between management and unions?**

To answer these questions we look at the behaviour of labour markets under both perfect and imperfect competition.

LEARNING OBJECTIVES

By the end of this chapter, you should be able to:

13.1 Understand how individuals derive their labour supply curve

13.2 Derive the market supply of labour

13.3 Explain the link between marginal physical product and marginal revenue product

13.4 Derive the demand for labour curve

13.5 Understand the market equilibrium for labour under perfect competition

13.6 Define cost efficiency and explain how a firm chooses between alternative production processes

13.7 Define monopsony, marginal factor cost (MFC), and bilateral monopoly

13.8 Explain how the market equilibrium for labour changes under conditions of imperfect competition

Analysis: The quantity of labour supplied at any given wage rate depends on the value of leisure and the desire for income. Even a seemingly low wage offer attracted a huge quantity of labour in Moscow.

13.1 INDIVIDUAL LABOUR SUPPLY

Our first concern in this chapter is to explain **labour supply** decisions. How do people decide how many hours to supply at any given wage rate? Do people try to maximize their total wages? If they did, we'd all be holding three jobs and sleeping on the commuter bus. Since most of us don't behave this way, other motives must be present. What are these other motivations, and how do they affect the quantity of labour supplied at various wage rates? (See the World View box.)

labour supply: The willingness and ability to work specific amounts of time at alternative wage rates in a given time period, *ceteris paribus.*

The reward for working comes in two forms: (1) the intrinsic satisfaction of working and (2) a paycheque. MBA grads in the United States say they care more about the intrinsic satisfaction than the pay (see the Applications box on the next page). They also get huge paycheques, however. Those big paycheques are explained in part by the quantity of labour supplied: MBA grads often end up working 60 or more hours a week. The reason people are willing to work so many hours is that they want more income.

Income vs. Leisure

Not working obviously has some value, too. In part, we need some nonwork time just to recuperate from working. We also want some time to watch television, go to a soccer game, or enjoy other goods and services we've purchased.

Our conflicting desires for income and leisure create a dilemma: The more time we spend working, the more income we have but also less time to enjoy it. Working, like all activities, involves an opportunity cost. Generally, we say that *the opportunity cost of working is the amount of leisure time that must be given up in the process.*

The inevitable trade-off between labour and leisure explains the shape of individual labour supply curves. As we work more hours, our leisure time becomes more scarce—and thus more valuable. Hence, *higher wage rates are required to compensate for the increasing opportunity cost of labour.* We'll supply a larger quantity of labour only if offered a higher wage rate. This is reflected in the labour supply curve in Figure 13.1.

The upward slope of the labour supply curve may be reinforced with the changing value of income. Those first few dollars earned on the job are really precious, especially if you have bills to pay. As you work and earn more, however, your most urgent

APPLICATIONS

MBA Grads Seek Challenge at Work, Not Just Big Bucks

Cynics might argue, but money apparently isn't what drives most graduate business students, *Inc.* magazine says. . . .

Inc. talked to 907 graduating MBA students at 10 schools this spring. Just 12 percent of those questioned said they went into graduate school primarily because of big salaries down the road. Only 24 percent rated a high salary as one of the most important considerations in choosing their next job.

Those answers don't surprise Teresa Miles, 23, who just earned her MBA at Duke University's Fuqua School of Business. "There are definitely some students who fit that greedy mold," says Miles, a native of Greenwich, Conn. "But it's such a stereotype I have to laugh at it."

Miles, who starts work June 15 at the Bank of New York's commercial lending department, will earn about $60,000 annually. But it was "a challenging experience and something that will do something for me" that led her to accept the bank's offer.

Most students think along those lines, says Associate Dean Dennis Weidenear at Purdue University's Krannert School of Management. "I don't think you should discount the pay they'll be getting because it is important," he says. "But they're not willing to walk over their grandmothers just to get a better salary."

Other poll results:

Challenging work was rated a "most important" job characteristic by 75 percent of the students; 44 percent ranked atmosphere first; 40 percent, location. . . .

—Mark Memmott

What MBAs at Some Top Schools Earn

School	Starting Salaries in 2003
Stanford	$107,320
Harvard	105,896
MIT	99,539
Northwestern	98,358
Chicago	97,872
Michigan	97,039
Dartmouth	96,714
Virginia	92,855

Source: *U.S. News & World Report,* April 12, 2004. Copyright 2004 U.S. News & World Report, L.P. Reprinted with permission. www.usnews.com

Source: *USA Today,* May 28, 1987. USA Today. Copyright 1987. Reprinted with permission (updated in 2001 by author). www.usatoday.com

Analysis: The quantity of labour supplied depends on the intrinsic satisfaction of working and the wages paid. MBA grads apparently work long hours for both high wages and job satisfaction.

needs will be satisfied. You may still want more things, but the urgency of your consumption desires is likely to be diminished. In other words, ***the marginal utility of income may decline as you earn more.*** If this happens, the wages offered for more work lose some of their allure. You may not be willing to work more hours unless offered a higher wage rate.

FIGURE 13.1
The Supply of Labour

The quantity of any good or service offered for sale typically increases as its price rises. Labour supply responds in the same way. At the wage rate w_1, the quantity of labour supplied is q_1 (point A). At the higher wage w_2, a worker is willing to work more hours per week, that is, to supply a larger quantity of labour (q_2).

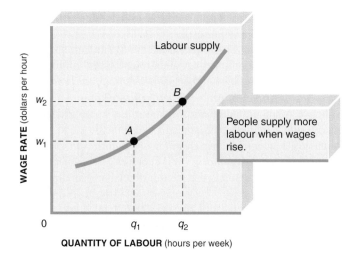

People supply more labour when wages rise.

The upward slope of an individual's labour supply curve is thus a reflection of two potential phenomena:

• The increasing opportunity cost of labour as leisure time declines.
• The decreasing marginal utility of income as a person works more hours.

Money isn't necessarily the only thing that motivates people to work. People *do* turn down higher-paying jobs in favour of lower-wage jobs that they like. Many parents forgo high-wage "career" jobs to have more flexible hours and time at home. Volunteers offer their services just for the sense of contributing to their communities; they don't need a paycheque. But money almost always makes a difference: People *do* supply more labour when offered higher wages.

13.2 MARKET SUPPLY

The **market supply of labour** represents the sum of all individual labour supply decisions. Although it's true that some individuals have backward-bending supply curves (see Appendix), these negative responses to higher wages are swamped by positive responses from the millions of individuals who participate in the Canadian labour market. As a result, the *market* supply curve is upward-sloping.

> **market supply of labour:** The total quantity of labour that workers are willing and able to supply at alternative wage rates in a given time period, *ceteris paribus.*

The upward slope of the labour supply curve doesn't imply that we'll all be working longer hours in the future. As time passes, the labour supply curve can *shift.* And it will whenever one of the underlying determinants of supply changes. ***The determinants of labour supply include***

• *Tastes* (for leisure, income, and work).
• *Income and wealth.*
• *Expectations* (for income or consumption).
• *Prices* of consumer goods.
• *Taxes.*

These shift factors determine the position and slope of the labour supply curve at any point in time. As time passes, however, these underlying determinants change, causing the labour supply curve to shift. This has evidently happened. In 1945—for employees paid by the hour—the average Canadian worker was employed for 44 hours a week at a wage rate of 85¢ per hour. By the end of 2006, the length of the work week for the average worker declined to 32 hours while earning a wage rate of $18.72 per hour. Contributing to this long-run leftward shift has been (1) the spectacular rise in living standards (a change in income and wealth), (2) the growth of income transfer programs that provide economic security when one isn't working (a change in income and expectations), and (3) the increased diversity and attractiveness of leisure activities (a change in tastes and other goods).

Elasticity of Labour Supply

Despite the evident long-run shifts of the labour supply curve, workers still respond positively to higher wage rates in the short run. To measure the resulting movements along the labour supply curve, we use the concept of elasticity. Specifically, **elasticity of labour supply** is the percentage change in the quantity of labour supplied divided by the percentage change in the wage rate—that is,

> **elasticity of labour supply:** The percentage change in the quantity of labour supplied divided by the percentage change in wage rate.

$$\text{Elasticity of labour supply} = \frac{\% \text{ change in quantity of labour supplied}}{\% \text{ change in wage rate}}$$

The elasticity of labour tells us how much more labour will be available if a higher wage is offered. If the elasticity of labour is 0.2, a 10 percent increase in wage rates will induce a 2 percent increase in the quantity of labour supplied.

The actual responsiveness of workers to a change in wage rates depends on the determinants of labour supply. Time is also important for labour supply elasticity, as individuals can't adjust their schedules or change jobs instantaneously.

Institutional Constraints

The labour supply curve and its related elasticities tell us how much time people would like to allocate to work. We must recognize, however, that people seldom have the opportunity to adjust their hours of employment at will. True, a Bill Gates or a Britney Spears can easily choose to work more or fewer hours. Most workers, however, face more rigid choices. They must usually choose to work at a regular job for eight hours a day, five days a week, or not to work at all. Very few firms are flexible enough to accommodate a desire to work only between the hours of 11 A.M. and 3 P.M. on alternate Thursdays. Adjustments in work hours are more commonly confined to choices about overtime work or secondary jobs (moonlighting) and vacation and retirement. Families may also alter the labour supply by varying the number of family members sent into the labour force at any given time. Students, too, can often adjust their work hours.

13.3 LABOUR DEMAND UNDER PERFECT COMPETITION

demand for labour: The quantities of labour employers are willing and able to hire at alternative wage rates in a given time period, *ceteris paribus*.

Regardless of how many people are *willing* to work, it's up to employers to decide how many people will *actually* work. That is, there must be a **demand for labour.** What determines the number of workers employers are willing to hire at various wage rates?

Derived Demand

In earlier chapters we emphasized that employers are profit maximizers. In their quest for maximum profits, firms seek the rate of output at which marginal revenue equals marginal cost. Once they've identified the profit-maximizing rate of output, firms enter factor markets to purchase the required amounts of labour, equipment, and other resources. Thus, ***the quantity of resources purchased by a business depends on the firm's expected sales and output.*** In this sense, the demand for factors of production, including labour, is a **derived demand;** it's derived from the demand for goods and services.

derived demand: The demand for labour and other factors of production results from (depends on) the demand for final goods and services produced by these factors.

Consider the plight of strawberry pickers. Strawberry pickers are paid very low wages and are employed only part of the year. But their plight can't be blamed on the greed of the strawberry growers. Strawberry growers, like most producers, would love to sell more strawberries at higher prices. If they did, the growers would hire more pickers and might even pay them higher wages. But the growers must contend with the market demand for strawberries: Consumers aren't willing to buy more strawberries at higher prices. As a consequence, the growers can't afford to hire more pickers or pay them higher wages. In contrast, information-technology (IT) firms are always looking for more workers and offer very high wages to get them. This helps explain why students who major in engineering, math, or computer science get paid a lot more than philosophy majors. IT specialists benefit from the growing demand for Internet services, while philosophy majors suffer because the search for the meaning of life is not a growth industry.

WEB NOTE

Average hourly earnings by occupation can be obtained from Statistics Canada's website (Table 281-0030) at http://www.statcan.ca.

The principle of derived demand suggests that if consumers really want to improve the lot of strawberry pickers, they should eat more strawberries. An increase in the demand for strawberries will motivate growers to plant more berries and hire more labour to pick them. Until then, the plight of the pickers isn't likely to improve.

The Labour Demand Curve

The number of strawberry pickers hired by the growers isn't completely determined by the demand for strawberries. The number of pickers hired will also depend on the wage rate. That is, ***the quantity of labour demanded depends on its price (the wage***

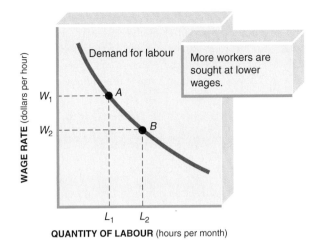

FIGURE 13.2
The Demand for Labour

The higher the wage rate, the smaller the quantity of labour demanded (*ceteris paribus*). At the wage rate W_1, only L_1 of labour is demanded. If the wage rate falls to W_2, a larger quantity of labour (L_2) will be demanded. The labour demand curve obeys the law of demand.

rate). In general, we expect that strawberry growers will be *willing to hire* more pickers at low wages than at higher wages. Hence, the demand for labour looks very much like the demand for any good or service (see Figure 13.2).

The fact that the demand curve for labour slopes downward doesn't tell us what quantity of labour will be hired. Nor does it tell us what wage rate will be paid. To answer such questions, we need to know what determines the particular shape and position of the labour demand curve.

A strawberry grower will be willing to hire another picker only if that picker contributes more to output than he or she costs. Growers, as rational businesspeople, recognize that *every* sale, *every* expenditure has some impact on total profits. Hence, the truly profit-maximizing grower will evaluate each picker's job application in terms of the applicant's potential contribution to profits.

Fortunately, a strawberry picker's contribution to output is easy to measure; it's the number of boxes of strawberries he or she picks. Suppose for the moment that Marvin, a college dropout with three summers of experience as a canoe instructor, is able to pick five boxes per hour. These five boxes represent Marvin's *marginal physical product (MPP).* In other words, Marvin's MPP is the *addition* to total output that occurs when the grower hires him for an hour:

$$\frac{\text{Marginal}}{\text{physical product}} = \frac{\text{change in total output}}{\text{change in quantity of labour}}$$

Marginal physical product establishes an *upper* limit to the grower's willingness to pay. Clearly the grower can't afford to pay Marvin more than five boxes of strawberries for an hour's work; the grower won't pay Marvin more than he produces.

Most strawberry pickers don't want to be paid in strawberries. At the end of a day in the fields, the last thing a picker wants to see is another strawberry. Marvin, like the rest of the pickers, wants to be paid in cash. To find out how much cash he might be paid, we need to know what a box of strawberries is worth. This is easy to determine. The market value of a box of strawberries is simply the price at which the grower can sell it. Thus, Marvin's contribution to output can be measured in either marginal physical product (five boxes per hour) or the dollar value of that product.

The dollar value of a worker's contribution to output is called **marginal revenue product (MRP).** Marginal revenue product is the change in total revenue that occurs when more labour is hired—that is,

$$\frac{\text{Marginal}}{\text{revenue product}} = \frac{\text{change in total revenue}}{\text{change in quantity of labour}}$$

Marginal Physical Product

Marginal Revenue Product

marginal revenue product (MRP): The change in total revenue associated with one additional unit of input.

In Marvin's case, the "change in quantity of labour" is one extra hour of picking strawberries. The "change in total revenue" is the *value* of the extra five boxes of berries Marvin picks in that hour. If the grower can sell strawberries for $2 a box, Marvin's marginal revenue product is simply five boxes per hour × $2 per box, or $10 per hour. We could have come to the same conclusion by multiplying marginal *physical* product times *price,* that is

$$MRP = MPP \times p$$

or

$$\$10 \text{ per hour} = 5 \text{ boxes per hour} \times \$2 \text{ per box}$$

We calculate MRP to determine how much Marvin should be paid. In compliance with the rule about not paying anybody more than he or she contributes, the profit-maximizing grower should be willing to pay Marvin up to $10 an hour. Thus, *marginal revenue product sets an upper limit to the wage rate an employer will pay.*

But what about a lower limit? Suppose that the pickers aren't organized and that Marvin is desperate for money. Under such circumstances, he might be willing to work—to supply labour—for only $4 an hour.

Should the grower hire Marvin for such a low wage? The profit-maximizing answer is obvious. If Marvin's marginal revenue product is $10 an hour and his wages are only $4 an hour, the grower will be eager to hire him. The difference between Marvin's marginal revenue product ($10) and his wage ($4) implies additional profits of $6 an hour. In fact, the grower will be so elated by the economics of this situation that he'll want to hire everybody he can find who's willing to work for $4 an hour. After all, if the grower can make $6 an hour by hiring Marvin, why not hire 1,000 pickers and accumulate profits at an even faster rate?

The Law of Diminishing Returns

The exploitive possibilities suggested by Marvin's picking are too good to be true. It isn't at all clear, for example, how the grower could squeeze 1,000 workers onto one acre of land and have any room left over for strawberry plants. There must be some limit to the profit-making potential of this situation.

A few moments' reflection on the absurdity of trying to employ 1,000 people to pick one acre of strawberries should be ample warning of the limits to profits here. You don't need two years of business school to recognize this. But some grasp of economics may help explain exactly why the grower's eagerness to hire additional pickers will begin to fade long before 1,000 are hired. The operative concept here is *marginal productivity.*

Diminishing MPP. The decision to hire Marvin originated in his marginal physical product—that is, the five boxes of strawberries he can pick in an hour's time. To assess the wisdom of hiring still more pickers, we have to consider how total output will change if additional labour is employed. To do so, we need to keep track of marginal physical product.

Figure 13.3 shows how strawberry output changes as additional pickers are hired. Marvin picks five boxes of strawberries per hour. Total output and his marginal physical product are identical, because he's initially the only picker employed. When the grower hires George, Marvin's old college roommate, we observe the total output increases to 10 boxes per hour (point *B* in Figure 13.3). This figure represents another increase of five boxes per hour. Accordingly, we may conclude that George's *marginal physical product* is five boxes per hour, the same as Marvin's. Given such productivity, the grower will want to hire George and continue looking for more pickers.

As more workers are hired, total strawberry output continues to increase but not nearly as fast. Although the later hires work just as hard, the limited availability of land and capital constrain their marginal physical product. One problem is the number of boxes. There are only a dozen boxes, and the additional pickers often have to wait

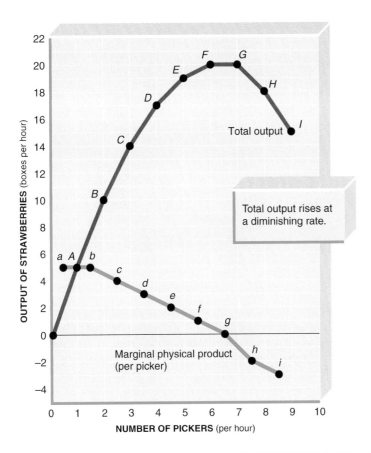

FIGURE 13.3
Diminishing Marginal Physical Product

The marginal physical product of labour is the increase in total production that results when one additional worker is hired. Marginal physical product tends to fall as additional workers are hired in any given production process. This decline occurs because each worker has increasingly less of other factors (e.g., land) with which to work.

When the second worker (George) is hired, total output increases from 5 to 10 boxes per hour. Hence, the second worker's MPP equals 5 boxes per hour. Thereafter, capital and land constraints diminish marginal physical product.

	Number of Pickers (per hour)	Total Strawberry Output (boxes per hour)		Marginal Physical Product (boxes per hour)
	0	0	>	5
A	1	5	>	5
B	2	10	>	4
C	3	14	>	3
D	4	17	>	2
E	5	19	>	1
F	6	20	>	0
G	7	20	>	−2
H	8	18	>	−3
I	9	15		

for an empty box. The time spent waiting depresses marginal physical product. The worst problem is space: As additional workers are crowded onto the one-acre patch, they begin to get in one another's way. The picking process is slowed, and marginal physical product is further depressed. Note that the MPP of the fifth picker is two boxes per hour, while the MPP of the sixth picker is only one box per hour. By the time we get to the seventh picker, marginal physical product actually falls to zero, as no further increases in total strawberry output take place.

Things get even worse if the grower hires still more pickers. If eight pickers are employed, total output actually *declines*. The pickers can no longer work efficiently under such crowded conditions. The MPP of the eighth worker is *negative*, no matter how ambitious or hardworking this person may be. Figure 13.3 illustrates this decline in marginal physical product.

TABLE 13.1
Diminishing Marginal Revenue Product

Marginal revenue product (MRP) measures the change in total revenue that occurs when one additional worker is hired. At constant product prices, MRP equals MPP × price. Hence, MRP declines along with MPP.

	Number of Pickers (per hour)	Total Strawberry Output (boxes per hour)	×	Price of Strawberries (per box)	=	Total Strawberry Revenue (per hour)		Marginal Revenue Product
	0	0		$2		0	>	$10
A	1 (Marvin)	5		2		$10	>	10
B	2 (George)	10		2		20	>	8
C	3	14		2		28	>	6
D	4	17		2		34	>	4
E	5	19		2		38	>	2
F	6	20		2		40	>	0
G	7	20		2		40	>	−4
H	8	18		2		36	>	−6
I	9	15		2		30		

Our observations on strawberry production are similar to those made in most industries. In the short run, the availability of land and capital is limited by prior investment decisions. Hence, additional workers must share existing facilities. As a result, *the marginal physical product of labour eventually declines as the quantity of labour employed increases.* This is the *law of diminishing returns* we first encountered in Chapter 5. It's based on the simple observation that an increasing number of workers leaves each worker with less land and capital to work with. At some point, this "crowding" causes MPP to decline.

Diminishing MRP. As marginal *physical* product diminishes, so does marginal *revenue* product (MRP). As noted earlier, marginal revenue product is the increase in the *value* of total output associated with an added unit of labour (or other input). In our example, it refers to the increase in strawberry revenues associated with one additional picker and is calculated as MPP × *p*.

The decline in marginal revenue product mirrors the drop in marginal physical product. Recall that a box of strawberries sells for $2. With this price and the output statistics in Figure 13.3, we can readily calculate marginal revenue product, as summarized in Table 13.1. As the growth of output diminishes, so does marginal revenue product. Marvin's marginal revenue product of $10 an hour has fallen to $6 by the time four pickers are employed and reaches zero when seven pickers are employed.

Note that the marginal revenue product would fall even faster if the price of strawberries declined as increasing quantities were supplied. Remember, however, that we're assuming the grower is a *competitive* producer. Therefore, changes in the grower's output do not influence the market price of strawberries.

13.4 A FIRM'S HIRING DECISION

The tendency of marginal revenue product to diminish will cool the strawberry grower's eagerness to hire 1,000 pickers. We still don't know, however, how many pickers will be hired.

The Firm's Labour Supply

Our earlier discussion of labour supply indicated that more workers are available only at higher wage rates. But that's true only for the *market* supply. A single producer may be able to hire an unlimited number of workers at the prevailing wage rate—if the firm is perfectly competitive in the labour market. In other words, *a firm that's a perfect competitor in the labour market can hire all the labour it wants at the prevailing market wage.*

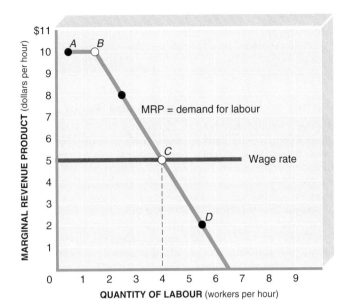

FIGURE 13.4
The Marginal Revenue Product Curve Is the Labour Demand Curve

The MRP curve tells us how many workers an employer would want to hire at various wage rates. An employer is willing to pay a worker no more than the marginal revenue product. In this case, a grower would gladly hire a second worker, because that worker's MRP (point *B*) exceeds the wage rate ($5). The sixth worker won't be hired at that wage rate, however, since the MRP (at point *D*) is less than $5. The MRP curve is the labour demand curve.

Let's assume that the strawberry grower is so small that his hiring decisions have no effect on local wages. As far as he's concerned, there's an unlimited supply of strawberry pickers willing to work for $5 an hour. His only decision is how many of these willing pickers to hire at that wage rate.

Figure 13.4 provides the answer. We already know that the grower is eager to hire pickers whose marginal revenue product exceeds their wage. He'll therefore hire at least one worker at that wage, because the MRP of the first picker is $10 an hour (point *A* in Figure 13.4). A second worker will be hired as well, because that picker's MRP (point *B* in Figure 13.4) also exceeds the going wage rate. In fact, *the grower will continue hiring pickers until the MRP has declined to the level of the market wage rate.* Figure 13.4 indicates that this intersection (point *C*) occurs when four pickers are employed. We can conclude that the grower will be willing to hire—will *demand*—four pickers if wages are $5 an hour.

The folly of hiring more than four pickers is also apparent in Figure 13.4. The marginal revenue product of the sixth worker is only $2 an hour (point *D*). Hiring a sixth picker will cost more in wages than the picker brings in as revenue. The *maximum* number of pickers the grower will employ at prevailing wages is four (point *C*).

The law of diminishing returns also implies that all four pickers will be paid the same wage. Once four pickers are employed, we can't say that any single picker is responsible for the observed decline in marginal revenue product. Marginal revenue product of labour diminishes because each worker has less capital and land to work with, not because the last worker hired is less able than the others. Accordingly, the "fourth" picker can't be identified as any particular individual. Once four pickers are hired, Marvin's MRP is no higher than any other picker's. *Each (identical) worker is worth no more than the marginal revenue product of the last worker hired, and all workers are paid the same wage rate.*

The principles of marginal revenue product apply to professional athletes as well as strawberry pickers. The Toronto Blue Jays are paying Vernon Wells, on average, $18 million per year to play baseball while the Los Angeles Galaxy are paying David Beckham approximately $1 million per week to play soccer. Both teams expect their new players to generate at least that much added revenue in extra ticket sales, merchandise sales, and advertising revenue (see the Applications box).

Whatever the explanation for the disparity between the incomes of baseball players and strawberry pickers, the enormous gap between them seems awfully unfair.

MRP = Firm's Labour Demand

APPLICATIONS

Blue Jays Sign Vernon Wells to Long-Term Contract

All-star Vernon Wells has signed a $126-million ($US), seven-year contract extension with the Toronto Blue Jays, the richest deal in franchise history.

"This is a huge commitment that obviously I'm going to honour and cherish and do my best to make this team a champion again," said Wells, a two-time Gold Glove winner.

Wells' deal ranks behind only those given to Alex Rodriguez ($252 million for 10 years), Derek Jeter ($189 million for 10 years), Manny Ramirez ($160 million for eight years), Todd Helton ($141.5 million for 11 years) and Alfonso Soriano ($136 million for eight years).

Source: December 18, 2006, CTV.ca News, http://www.ctv.ca/servlet/ArticleNews/story/CTVNews/20061218/vernon_wells_061218, accessed June 14, 2007.

David Beckham Scores Again—and Again

Goodbye, Madrid. And hellooo, Hollywood. English superstar David Beckham's decision to move there and play for the Los Angeles Galaxy of Major League Soccer was astonishing enough. But that gaudy five-year, $250 million deal left even the gimlet-eyed impresarios of Beverly Hills with their jaws hanging.

Along with wife Victoria (Posh of the Spice Girls), Beckham is a global marketing machine who hobnobs with the likes of Tom Cruise. His trademark kicks were immortalized in the film Bend It Like Beckham, and his face is plastered on billboards from Shanghai to São Paulo, selling everything from soda to cellphones.

Source: Based on Tim Smart, U.S. News and World Report, January 14, 2007, http://www.usnews.com/usnews/news/articles/070114/22week.htm, accessed June 14, 2007.

Analysis: Marginal revenue product measures what a worker is worth to an employer. The Toronto Blue Jays and the Los Angeles Galaxy are expecting a high MRP from the latest additions to their teams.

An obvious question then arises: Can't the number of pickers or their wages be increased?

Changes in Wage Rates

Suppose the government were to set a minimum wage for strawberry pickers at $7 an hour. At first glance this action would appear to boost the wages of pickers, who have been earning only $5 an hour. This isn't all good news for the strawberry pickers, however. ***There's a trade-off between wage rates and the number of workers demanded.*** If wage rates go up, growers will hire fewer pickers.

Figure 13.5 illustrates this trade-off. The grower's earlier decision to hire four pickers was based on a wage of $5 an hour (point *C*). If the wage jumps to $7 an hour, it no longer makes economic sense to keep four pickers employed. The MRP of the fourth worker is only $6 an hour. The grower will respond to higher wage rates by moving up the labour demand curve to point *G*. At point *G*, only three pickers are hired and MRP again equals the wage rate. If more workers are to be hired, the wage rate must drop.

Changes in Productivity

The downward slope of the labour demand curve doesn't doom strawberry pickers to low wages. It does emphasize, however, the inevitable link between workers' productivity and wages. ***To get higher wages without sacrificing jobs, productivity (MRP) must increase.***

Suppose Marvin and his friends all enroll in a local agricultural extension course and learn new methods of strawberry picking. With these new methods, the marginal physical product of each picker increases by one box per hour. With the price of strawberries still at $2 a box, this productivity improvement implies an increase in marginal *revenue* product of $2 per worker. This change causes an *upward shift* of the labour demand (MRP) curve equal to this $2 per worker at every quantity of labour demanded.

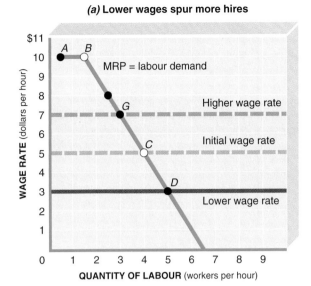

(a) Lower wages spur more hires

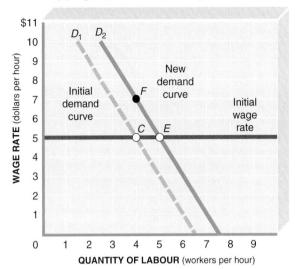

(b) Higher productivity also spurs more hires

FIGURE 13.5
Incentives to Hire

(a) **Lower wage** If the wage rate drops, an employer will be willing to hire more workers, *ceteris paribus*. At $5 an hour, only four pickers per hour would be demanded (point *C*). If the wage rate dropped to $3 an hour, five pickers per hour would be demanded (point *D*).

(b) **Higher productivity** If the marginal revenue product of labour improves, the employer will hire a greater quantity of labour at any given wage rate. The labour demand curve will shift up (from D_1 to D_2). In this case, an increase in MRP leads the employer to hire five workers (point *E*) rather than only four workers (point *C*) at $5 per hour.

Compare, for example, point *C* on the initial demand curve (D_1) in Figure 13.5*b* with point *F* on the new demand curve (D_2). Notice how the improvement in productivity has altered the value of strawberry pickers. The grower is now willing to pay a wage of $7 per hour for the four workers. Alternatively, the grower can employ more pickers at the original wage rate of $5, moving from point *C* to point *E*. *Increased productivity implies that workers can get higher wages without sacrificing jobs or more employment without lowering wages.* Historically, increased productivity has been the most important source of rising wages and living standards.

An increase in the price of strawberries would also help the pickers. Marginal revenue product reflects the interaction of productivity and product prices. If strawberry prices were to double, strawberry pickers would become twice as valuable, even without an increase in physical productivity. Such a change in product prices depends, however, on changes in the market supply and demand for strawberries.

Changes in Price

13.5 MARKET EQUILIBRIUM

The principles that guide the hiring decisions of a single strawberry grower can be extended to the entire labour market. This suggests that *the market demand for labour depends on*

- *The number of employers.*
- *The marginal revenue product of labour in each firm and industry.*

Increases in either the demand for final products or the productivity of labour will tend to increase the demand for labour.

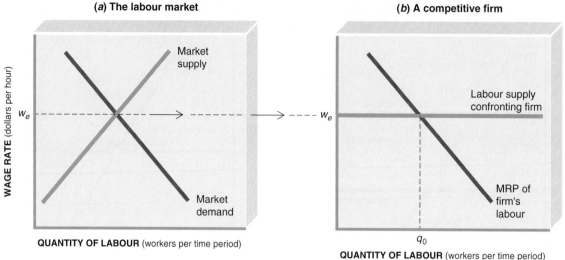

FIGURE 13.6
Equilibrium Wage

The intersection of *market* supply and demand determines the equilibrium wage in a competitive labour market. All the firms in the industry can then hire as much labour as they want at that equilibrium

wage. In this case, the firm can hire all the workers it wants at the equilibrium wage, w_e. It chooses to hire q_0 workers, as determined by their marginal revenue product within the firm.

On the supply side of the labour market we have already observed that ***the market supply of labour depends on***

- ***The number of available workers.***
- ***Each worker's willingness to work at alternative wage rates.***

The supply decisions of each worker are in turn a reflection of tastes, income, wealth, expectations, other prices, and taxes.

Equilibrium Wage

equilibrium wage: The wage rate at which the quantity of labour supplied in a given time period equals the quantity of labour demanded.

Figure 13.6 brings these market forces together. ***The intersection of the market supply and demand curves establishes the* equilibrium wage.** This is the only wage rate at which the quantity of labour supplied equals the quantity of labour demanded. Everyone who's willing and able to work for this wage will find a job.

If the labour market is perfectly competitive, all employers will be able to hire as many workers as they want at the equilibrium wage. Like our strawberry grower, every competitive firm is assumed to have no discernible effect on market wages. ***Competitive employers act like price takers with respect to wages as well as prices.*** This phenomenon is also portrayed in Figure 13.6.

13.6 CHOOSING AMONG INPUTS

One of the options employers have when wage rates rise is to utilize more machinery in place of labour. In most production processes there are possibilities for substituting capital inputs for labour inputs. In the long run, there are still more possibilities for redesigning the whole production process. Given these options, how should the choice of inputs be made?

Suppose a mechanical strawberry picker can pick berries twice as fast as Marvin. Who will the grower hire, Marvin or the mechanical picker? At first it would seem that the grower would choose the mechanical picker. But the choice isn't so obvious. So far, all we know is that the mechanical picker's MPP is twice as large as Marvin's. But we haven't said anything about the *cost* of the mechanical picker.

Suppose that a mechanical picker can be rented for $12 an hour, while Marvin is still willing to work for $5 an hour. Will this difference in hourly cost change the grower's input choice?

To determine the relative desirability of hiring Marvin or renting the mechanical picker, the grower must compare the ratio of their marginal physical products to their cost. This ratio of marginal product to cost expresses the **cost efficiency** of an input—that is,

$$\text{Cost efficiency} = \frac{\text{marginal physical product of an input}}{\text{cost of an input}}$$

Marvin's MPP is five boxes of strawberries per hour and his cost (wage) is $5. Thus, the return on each dollar of wages paid to Marvin is

$$\begin{array}{l}\text{Cost} \\ \text{efficiency} \\ \text{of labour}\end{array} = \frac{\text{MPP}_{\text{labour}}}{\text{cost}_{\text{labour}}} = \frac{5 \text{ boxes}}{\$5} = 1 \text{ boxes per } \$1 \text{ of cost}$$

By contrast, the mechanical picker has an MPP of 10 boxes per hour and costs $12 per hour; thus

$$\begin{array}{l}\text{Cost} \\ \text{efficiency of} \\ \text{mechanical} \\ \text{picker}\end{array} = \frac{\begin{array}{c}\text{MPP of} \\ \text{mechanical} \\ \text{picker}\end{array}}{\begin{array}{c}\text{cost of} \\ \text{mechanical} \\ \text{picker}\end{array}} = \frac{10 \text{ boxes}}{\$12} = 0.83 \text{ box per } \$1 \text{ of cost}$$

These calculations indicate that Marvin is more cost-effective than the mechanical picker. From this perspective, the grower is better off hiring Marvin than renting a mechanical picker.

From the perspective of cost efficiency, the cheapness of a productive input is measured not by its price but by the amount of output it delivers for that price. Thus, *the most cost-efficient factor of production is the one that produces the most output per dollar.*

The concept of cost efficiency helps explain why Canadian firms don't move en masse to Haiti, where workers are willing to work for as little as 80 cents an hour. Although this wage rate is far below the minimum wage in Canada, the marginal physical product of Haitian workers is even further below Canadian standards. Canadian workers remain more cost-efficient than the "cheap" labour available in Haiti, making it unprofitable to **outsource** Canadian jobs. So long as Canadian workers deliver more output per dollar of wages, they will remain cost-effective in global markets.

Typically a producer doesn't choose between individual inputs but rather between alternative production processes. General Motors, for example, can't afford to compare the cost efficiency of each job applicant with the cost efficiency of mechanical tire mounters. Instead, GM compares the relative desirability of a **production process** that is labour-intensive (uses a lot of labour) with others that are less labour-intensive. GM ignores individual differences in marginal revenue product. Nevertheless, the same principles of cost efficiency guide the decision.

Let's return to the strawberry patch to see how the choice of an entire production process is made. We again assume that strawberries can be picked by either human or mechanical hands. Now, however, we assume that one tonne of strawberries can be produced by only one of the three production processes described in Table 13.2. Process A is most *labour-intensive;* it uses the most labour and thus keeps more human pickers employed. By contrast, process C is *capital-intensive;* it uses the most mechanical pickers and provides the least employment to human pickers. Process B falls between these two extremes.

Cost Efficiency

Alternative Production Processes

The Efficiency Decision

TABLE 13.2
Alternative Production Processes

One tonne of strawberries can be produced with varying input combinations. Which process is most efficient? What information is missing?

	Alternative Processes for Producing One Tonne of Strawberries		
Input	Process A	Process B	Process C
Labour (hours)	400	270	220
Machinery (hours)	13	15	18
Land (acres)	1	1	1

Which of these three production processes should the grower use? If he used labour-intensive process A, he'd be doing the pickers a real favour. But his goal is to maximize profits, so we assume he'll choose the production process that best serves this objective. That is, he'll choose the *least-cost* process to produce one tonne of strawberries.

But which of the production processes in Table 13.2 is least expensive? We really can't tell on the basis of the information provided. To determine the relative cost of each process—and thus to understand the producer's choice—we must know something more about input costs. In particular, we have to know how much an hour of mechanical picking costs and how much an hour of human picking (labour) costs. Then we can determine which combination of inputs is least expensive in producing one tonne of strawberries—that is, which is most *cost-efficient.* Note that we don't have to know how much the land costs, because the same amount of land is used in all three production processes. Thus, land costs won't affect our efficiency decision.

Suppose that strawberry pickers are still paid $5 an hour and that mechanical pickers can be rented for $12 an hour. The acre of land rents for $500 per year. With this information we can now calculate the total dollar cost of each production process and quickly determine the most cost-efficient. Table 13.3 summarizes the required calculations.

The calculations performed in Table 13.3 clearly identify process C as the least expensive way of producing one tonne of strawberries. Process A entails a total cost of $2,656, whereas the capital-intensive process C costs only $1,816 to produce the same quantity of output. As a profit maximizer, the grower will choose process C, even though it implies less employment for strawberry pickers.

The choice of an appropriate production process—the decision about *how* to produce—is called the *efficiency decision.* As we've seen, a producer seeks to use the combination of resources that produces a given rate of output for the least cost. The efficiency decision requires the producer to find that particular least-cost combination.

TABLE 13.3
The Least-Cost Combination

A producer wants to produce a given rate of output for the least cost. Choosing the least expensive production process is the efficiency decision. In this case, process C represents the most cost-efficient production process for producing one tonne of strawberries.

Input	Cost Calculation
Process A	
Labour	400 hours at $5 per hour = $2,000
Machinery	13 hours at $12 per hour = 156
Land	1 acre at $500 = 500
	Total cost $2,656
Process B	
Labour	270 hours at $5 per hour = $1,350
Machinery	15 hours at $12 per hour = 180
Land	1 acre at $500 = 500
	Total cost $2,030
Process C	
Labour	220 hours at $5 per hour = $1,100
Machinery	18 hours at $12 per hour = 216
Land	1 acre at $500 = 500
	Total cost $1,816

APPLICATIONS

Stern Gets Sirius Payday: $83 Million

WASHINGTON—Everything is shocking about Howard Stern—even his pay.

Sirius Satellite Radio Inc., suffering steep losses and an ailing stock price has handed its star shock jock an $83-million ($US) stock bonus for helping the fledgling radio network exceed its subscriber target.

CP/AP/Richard Drew

The 52-year-old's raunchy antics have helped build an audience for Sirius. But the jury is still out on whether profanity and sexually-charged banter are the basis for a sustainable business. Even with Mr. Stern aboard, Sirius is losing hundreds of millions of dollars a year and remains stuck behind market leader XM Satellite Radio Holdings Inc.

Sirius chief executive officer Mel Karmazin is unapologetic about Mr. Stern's big payday. "The decision to bring Howard Stern to Sirius required a very significant commitment, and we are very pleased that our investment has dramatically paid off," he boasted yesterday. Mr. Stern, who signed a $500-million cash-and-stock contract to join Sirius in 2004, has been key to beating Wall Street expectations for revenue and subscribers, Mr. Karmazin pointed out.

Analysts had predicted Sirius would have about 3.5 millions subscribers by the end of 2006. Instead, it has almost twice that number, triggering Mr. Stern's payout. There were fewer than 600,000 when Mr. Stern joined.

—Barrie McKenna

Source: Barrie McKenna, "Stern gets Sirius payday: $83-million," *Globe and Mail* Jan 10, 2007, pg. B11. Reprinted with permission from *The Globe and Mail*.

Analysis: Companies find creative mechanisms to reward marginal revenue product. What portion of the increase in Sirius subscribers is specifically due to (1) Howard Stern, (2) the initial interest in a new product (satellite radio), or (3) the relative buoyancy of the economy (greater income)?

At the beginning of this chapter, we noted that the Executive Chairman of Precision Drilling Trust in Calgary received approximately $75 million for his annual remuneration—$20 million in salary, bonus, and "other compensation" plus $55 million in stock option gains. How was this figure determined?

One of the difficulties in calculating the appropriate level of CEO pay is the elusiveness of marginal revenue product. Should it be related exclusively to the value of the company's stock? Critics would argue that the price of a stock is not an adequate measure of a company's performance since much of its increase over the year was attributable to the general upswing in the stock market—the "all ships rise with the tide" argument. But clearly, a CEO is supposed to provide strategic leadership and a sense of mission. These are critical to a corporation's success but hard to quantify. Note that the remuneration for "shock jock" host, Howard Stern, is also based on performance (increased subscribers) but in the face of a falling stock price (see the Applications box).

Parliament has a similar problem in setting the Prime Minister's pay. We noted earlier that the Prime Minister earns slightly less than $300,000 per year. Can we argue that this salary represents the Prime Minister's marginal revenue product? The wage we pay our Prime Minister (and other public officials) is less a reflection of contribution to total output than a matter of custom. The salary also reflects the wage that voters believe is required to induce competent individuals to forsake private-sector jobs and assume the responsibilities of the Prime Minister. In this sense, the wage paid to public officials is set by their **opportunity wage**—that is, the wage they could earn in private industry.

Unmeasured MRP

WEB NOTE

Motivated by money? Check out the highest-paying occupations at www.higherbracket.ca.

opportunity wage: The highest wage an individual would earn in his or her best alternative job.

The same kinds of considerations influence the wages of professors. The marginal revenue product of a professor isn't easy to measure. Is it the number of students she teaches, the amount of knowledge conveyed, or something else? Confronted with such problems, most post-secondary institutions tend to pay professors according to their opportunity wages—that is, the amount the professors could earn elsewhere (after accounting for any differences in workplace environments). Opportunity wages also help explain the differences between the wage of a CEO and the workers who peddle their products. The lower wage of salesclerks reflects not only their marginal revenue product at the company they work for, but also the fact that they're not trained for many other jobs. That is, their opportunity wages are low. By contrast, most CEOs have accumulated impressive managerial skills that are in demand by many corporations; their opportunity wages are high.

13.7 IMPERFECT COMPETITION— LABOUR POWER

So far, our labour market analysis has been viewed from the perspective of a perfectly competitive market structure. How does the analysis change if either the suppliers of labour (i.e., the workers) or the demanders of labour (i.e., the employers) exert some sort of market power in the labour market? That is, in an *imperfectly competitive* labour market, what happens to our equilibrium wage rate and amount of labour employed?

Let's start the discussion with market power arising through the creation of labour unions.

Types of Unions

The immediate objective of labour unions is to alter the equilibrium wage and employment conditions in specific labour markets. ***To be successful, unions must be able to exert control over the market supply curve.*** That's why workers have organized themselves along either industry or occupational craft lines. *Industrial unions* include workers in a particular industry (the United Auto Workers, for example). *Craft unions* represent workers with a particular skill (like the International Brotherhood of Electrical Workers), regardless of the industry in which they work.

The purpose of both types of labour unions is to coordinate the actions of thousands of individual workers, thereby achieving control of market supply. If a union is able to control the supply of workers in a particular industry or occupation, the union acquires a *monopoly* in that market. Like most monopolies, unions attempt to use their market power to increase their incomes.

unionization rate: The percentage of the labour force belonging to a union.

The percent of the Canadian labour force belonging to a union—the **unionization rate**—has been on the decline for the past few decades; down from 38% in 1981 to 31% in 2004. And while union membership dropped in all provinces over this period, compared to other nations, Canada still has a relatively higher unionization rate (see the Applications box).

Union Objectives

A primary objective of unions is to raise the wages of union members. Union objectives also include improved working conditions, job security, and other nonwage forms of compensation, such as retirement (pension) benefits, vacation time, and health insurance. The Players Association and the National Football League have bargained about the use of artificial turf, early retirement, player fines, television revenues, game rules, the use of team doctors, drug tests, pensions, and the number of players permitted on a team.

Although union objectives tend to be as broad as the concerns of union members, we focus here on just one objective, wage rates. This isn't too great a simplification, because most nonwage issues can be translated into their effective impact on wage rates. What we seek to determine is whether and how unions can raise effective

APPLICATIONS

Union Membership

Union membership in France and the United States is far below that of other industrialized countries. While unionization rates have been declining in Canada, they've been rising in many other countries. In Sweden and Denmark nearly all workers belong to a union.

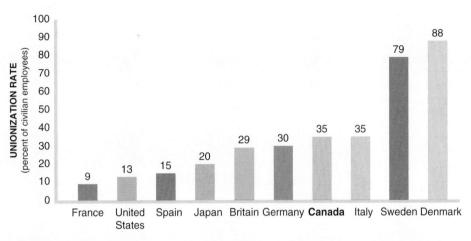

Source: European Foundation (2002 data).

Analysis: Unionization rates are comparatively high *but* declining in Canada. Unionization rates are still increasing in many other nations.

wage rates in a specific labour market by altering the competitive equilibrium depicted in Figure 13.6a.

In a competitive labour market, each worker makes a labour supply decision on the basis of his or her own perceptions of the relative values of labour and leisure. Whatever decision is made won't alter the market wage. One worker simply isn't that significant in a market composed of thousands. Once a market is unionized, however, these conditions no longer hold. A ***union evaluates job offers on the basis of the collective interests of its members.*** In particular, it must be concerned with the effects of increased employment on the wage rate paid to its members.

Like all monopolists, unions have to worry about the downward slope of the demand curve. In the case of labour markets, a larger quantity of labour can be "sold" only at lower wage rates. Suppose the workers in a particular labour market confront the market labour demand schedule depicted in Figure 13.7. This schedule tells us that employers aren't willing to hire any workers at a wage rate of $10 per hour (row Q) but will hire one worker per hour if the wage rate is $9 (row R). At still lower rates, the quantity of labour demanded increases; five workers per hour are demanded at a wage of $5 per hour.

An individual worker offered a wage of $5 an hour would have to decide whether such wages merited the sacrifice of an hour's leisure. But a union would evaluate the offer differently. A union must consider how the hiring of one more worker will affect the wages of all the workers.

The Marginal Wage

FIGURE 13.7
The Marginal Wage

The *marginal wage* is the change in *total wages* (paid to all workers) associated with the employment of an additional worker. If the wage rate is $8 per hour, only two workers will be hired (point *S*). The wage rate must fall to $7 per hour if three workers are to be hired (point *T*). In the process, *total wages* paid rise from $16 ($8 × 2 workers) to $21 ($7 × 3 workers). The *marginal* wage of the third worker is only $5 (point *t′*).

The graph illustrates the relationship of the marginal wage to labour demand. The marginal wage curve lies below the labour demand curve, because the marginal wage is less than the nominal wage.

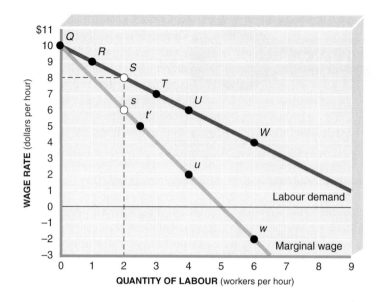

	Wage Rate (per hour)	×	Number of Workers Demanded (per hour)	=	Total Wages Paid (per hour)		Marginal Wage (per labour hour)
Q	10		0		$0		$9
R	9		1		9	>	7
S	8		2		16	>	5
T	7		3		21	>	3
U	6		4		24	>	1
V	5		5		25	>	−1
W	4		6		24	>	−3
X	3		7		21	>	

marginal wage: The change in total wages paid associated with a one-unit increase in the quantity of labour employed.

Total Wages Paid. Notice that when six workers are hired at a wage rate of $4 an hour (row *W*), total wages are $24 per hour. In order for a seventh worker to be employed, the wage rate must drop to $3 an hour (row *X*). At wages of $3 per hour, the *total* wages paid to the seven workers amount to only $21 per hour. Thus, total wages paid to the workers actually *fall* when a seventh worker is employed. Collectively the workers would be just as well off by sending only six people to work at the higher wage of $4 an hour and paying the seventh worker $3 an hour to stay home!

The basic mandate of a labour union is to evaluate wage and employment offers from this *collective* perspective. To do so, ***a union must distinguish the marginal wage from the market wage.*** The market wage is simply the current wage rate paid by the employer; it's the wage received by individual workers. The **marginal wage,** on the other hand, is the change in *total* wages paid (to all workers) when an additional worker is hired—that is,

$$\text{Marginal wage} = \frac{\text{change in total wages paid}}{\text{change in quantity of labour employed}}$$

The distinction between marginal wages and market wages arises from the downward slope of the labour demand curve. It's analogous to the distinction we made between marginal revenue and price for monopolists in product markets. The distinction simply reflects the law of demand: As wages fall, the number of workers hired increases. The marginal wage actually becomes negative at some point, when the implied wage loss to workers already on the job begins to exceed the wage of a new hired worker.

A union never wants to accept a negative marginal wage, of course. At such a point, union members would be better off paying someone to stay home. The question, then, is what level of (positive) marginal wage the union should accept.

We can answer this question by looking at the labour supply curve. The labour supply curve tells us how much labour workers are *willing to supply* at various wage rates. Hence, the labour supply curve defines the lowest wage *individual* union members would accept. If the union adopts a *collective* perspective on the welfare of its members, however, it will view the wage offer differently. From their collective perspective, the wage that union members are getting for additional labour is the *marginal* wage, not the nominal (market) wage. Hence, the marginal wage curve, not the labour demand curve, is decisive in the union's assessment of wage offers.

If the union wants to maximize the *total* welfare of its members, it will seek that level of employment which equates the marginal wage with the supply preferences of union members. In Figure 13.8, ***the intersection of the marginal wage curve with the labour supply curve identifies the desired level of employment for the union.*** This intersection occurs at point *s*, yielding total employment of two workers per hour.

The marginal wage at point *s* is $6. However, the union members will get a higher actual wage than that. Look up from point *s* on the marginal wage curve to point *S* on the employer's labour demand curve. Point *S* tells us that the employer is *willing to pay* a wage rate of $8 an hour to employ two workers. The union knows it can demand and get $8 an hour if it supplies only two workers to the firm.

What the union is doing here is choosing a point on the labour demand curve that the union regards as the optimal combination of wages and employment. In a competitive market, point *T* would represent the equilibrium combination of wages and employment. But the union forces employers to point *S*, thereby attaining a higher wage rate and reducing employment.

The union's ability to maintain a wage rate of $8 an hour depends on its ability to exclude some workers from the market. Figure 13.8 suggests that four workers are willing and able to work at the union wage of $8 an hour (point *N*), whereas only two are hired (point *S*). If the additional workers were to offer their services, the wage rate would be pushed down the labour demand curve (to $6 per hour). Hence, ***to maintain a noncompetitive wage, the union must be able to exercise some control over the labour supply decisions of individual workers.*** The essential force here is union

The Union Wage Goal

Exclusion

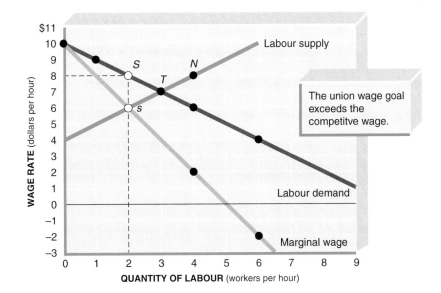

FIGURE 13.8
The Union Wage Objective

The intersection of the marginal wage and labour supply curves (point *s*) determines the union's desired employment. Employers are willing to pay a wage rate of $8 per hour for that many workers, as revealed by point *S* on the labour demand curve.

More workers (*N*) are willing to work at $8 per hour than employers demand (*S*). To maintain that wage rate, the union must exclude some workers from the market. In the absence of such power, wages would fall to the competitive equilibrium (point *T*).

solidarity. Once unionized, the individual workers in an industry or occupation must agree not to compete among themselves by offering their labour at nonunion wage rates. Instead, the workers must agree to withhold labour—to strike, if necessary—if wage rates are too low, and to supply labour only if a specified wage rate is offered.

13.8 IMPERFECT COMPETITION—EMPLOYER POWER

The power possessed by labour unions in various occupations and industries seldom exists in a power vacuum. Power exists on the demand side of labour markets, too. Labour markets with significant power on both sides, however, are common. To understand how wage rates and employment are determined in such markets, we have to assess the market power possessed by employers.

Monopsony

monopsony: A market in which there's only one buyer.

Power on the demand side of a market belongs to a *buyer* who is able to influence the market price of a good. With respect to labour markets, market power on the demand side implies the ability of a single employer to alter the market wage rate. The extreme case of such power is a **monopsony,** a situation in which one employer is the only buyer in a particular market. The classic example of a monopsony is a company town—that is, a town that depends for its livelihood on the decisions of a single employer.

There are many degrees of market power, and they can be defined in terms of *buyer concentration*. When buyers are many and of limited market power, the demand for resources is likely to be competitive. Between the two extremes lie the various degrees of imperfect competition, including the awkward-sounding but empirically important case of *oligopsony*. In an oligopsony (e.g., the auto industry), only a few firms account for most of the industry's employment.

The Potential Use of Power

Firms with power in labour markets generally have the same objective as all other firms—to maximize profits. What distinguishes them from competitive (powerless) firms is their ability to attain and keep economic profits. In labour markets, this means using fewer workers and paying them lower wages.

The distinguishing characteristic of labour market monopsonies is that their hiring decisions influence the market wage rate. In a competitive labour market, no single employer has any direct influence on the market wage rate; each firm can hire as much labour as it needs at the prevailing wage. But a monopsonist confronts the *market* labour supply curve. As a result, any increase in the quantity of labour demanded will force the monopsonist to climb up the labour supply curve in search of additional workers. In other words, *a monopsonist can hire additional workers only if it offers a higher wage rate.*

marginal factor cost (MFC): The change in total costs that results from a one-unit increase in the quantity of a factor employed.

Marginal Factor Cost. Any time the price of a resource (or product) changes as a result of a firm's purchases, a distinction between marginal cost and price (average cost) must be made. Making this distinction is one of the little headaches—and potential sources of profit—of a monopsonist. For labour, we distinguish between the **marginal factor cost (MFC)** of labour and its wage rate.

Suppose that Figure 13.9 accurately described the labour supply schedule confronting a monopsonist. It's evident that the monopsonist will have to pay a wage of at least $5 an hour if it wants any labour. But even at that wage rate, only one worker will be willing to work. If the firm wants more labour, it will have to offer higher wages.

Two things happen when the firm raises its wage offer to $6 an hour. First, the quantity of labour supplied increases (to two workers per hour). Second, the total wages paid rise by $7. This high *marginal* cost of labour is attributable to the fact that the first worker's wages rise when the wage rate is increased to attract additional workers. If all the workers perform the same job, the first worker will demand to be paid the new (higher) wage rate. Thus, *the marginal factor cost exceeds the wage rate, because additional workers can be hired only if the wage rate for all workers is increased.*

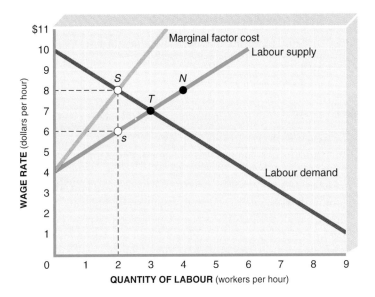

Wage Rate (per hour)	×	Quantity of Labour (workers per hour)	=	Total Wages Cost (per hour)		Marginal Factor Cost (per labour-hour)
4		0		$0		
5		1		5	>	$5
6		2		12	>	7
7		3		21	>	9
8		4		32	>	11
9		5		45	>	13

FIGURE 13.9
Marginal Factor Cost

More workers can be attracted only if the wage rate is increased. As it rises, all workers must be paid the higher wage. Consequently, the change in *total* wage costs exceeds the actual wage paid to the last worker. In the table, notice that, for example, the marginal factor cost of the second worker ($7) exceeds the wage actually paid to that worker ($6). Thus, the marginal factor cost curve lies above the labour supply curve.

In the graph, the intersection of the marginal factor cost and labour demand curves (point *S*) indicates the quantity of labour a monopsonist will want to hire. The labour supply curve (at point *s*) indicates the wage rate that must be paid to attract the desired number of workers. This is the monopsonist's desired wage ($6). In the absence of market power, an employer would end up at point *T* (the competitive equilibrium), paying a higher wage and employing more workers.

The Monopsony Firm's Goal. The marginal factor cost curve confronting this monopsonist is shown in the upper half of Figure 13.9. It starts at the bottom of the labour supply curve and rises above it. The monopsonist must now decide how many workers to hire, given the impact of its hiring decision on the market wage rate.

Remember that the labour demand curve is a reflection of labour's *marginal revenue product,* that is, the increase in total revenue attributable to the employment of one additional worker.

As we've emphasized, the profit-maximizing producer always seeks to equalize marginal revenue and marginal cost. Accordingly, the monopsonistic employer will seek to hire the amount of labour at which the marginal revenue product of labour equals its marginal factor cost—that is,

$$\text{Profit-maximizing level of input use} : \frac{\text{marginal revenue product of input}}{\text{(MRP)}} = \frac{\text{marginal factor cost of input}}{\text{(MFC)}}$$

In Figure 13.9, this objective is illustrated by the intersection of the marginal factor cost and labour demand curves at point *S*.

At point *S* the monopsonist is *willing to hire* two workers per hour at a wage rate of $8. But the firm doesn't have to pay this much. The labour supply curve informs us that two workers are *willing to work* for only $6 an hour. Hence, the firm first decides how many workers it wants to hire (at point *S*) and then looks at the labour supply curve (point *s*) to see what it has to pay them. As we suspected, a monopsonistic employer ends up hiring fewer workers at a lower wage rate than would prevail in a competitive market (point *T*).

13.9 COLLECTIVE BARGAINING

The potential for conflict between a powerful employer and a labour union should be evident:

- *The objective of a labour union is to establish a wage rate that's* **higher** *than the competitive wage (Figure 13.8).*
- *A monopsonist employer seeks to establish a wage rate that's* **lower** *than competitive standards (Figure 13.9).*

The resultant clash generates intense bargaining that often spills over into politics, the courts, and open conflict.

> **bilateral monopoly:** A market with only one buyer (a monopsonist) and one seller (a monopolist).

The confrontation of power on both sides of the labour market is a situation referred to as **bilateral monopoly.** In such a market, wages and employment aren't determined simply by supply and demand. Rather, economic outcomes must be determined by **collective bargaining**—that is, direct negotiations between employers and labour unions for the purpose of determining wages, employment, working conditions, and related issues.

> **collective bargaining:** Direct negotiations between employers and unions to determine labour market outcomes.

On occasion, negotiations break down; each side unwilling to move from its latest position. In the end, there will always be a settlement, but the process can sometimes involve a strike or lockout as the following Applications box outlines.

Possible Agreements

In a typical labour-business confrontation, the two sides begin by stating their preferences for equilibrium wages and employment. The *demands* laid down by the union are likely to revolve around point S in Figure 13.10; the *offer* enunciated by management is likely to be at point s.[1] Thus the boundaries of a potential settlement—a negotiated final equilibrium—are usually established at the outset of collective bargaining.

The interesting part of collective bargaining isn't the initial bargaining positions but the negotiation of the final settlement. The speed with which a settlement is reached and the terms of the resulting compromise depend on the patience, tactics, and

APPLICATIONS

Bettman Puts NHL on Ice

NHL commissioner Gary Bettman apologized to millions of hockey fans Wednesday afternoon while informing them the league has no choice but to lock out more than 600 players. The league's current collective bargaining agreement with the NHL Players' Association (NHLPA) expires Wednesday at midnight ET.

The two sides last met last Thursday, at which time the league rejected an offer from the union. The NHLPA proposed a four-point plan featuring a luxury tax, player salary rollbacks, changes to the entry-level player system and a revenue-sharing plan. But the NHL deemed the offer a "step back."

According to the players, the owners are determined to impose a salary cap which the NHLPA simply refuses to accept.

The NHL denies it covets a salary cap, instead asking only for "cost certainty." Bettman is looking for an agreement that would see a 60–40 split of player expenditures and revenue that is more in line with the three other major North American sports leagues—the NBA, NFL and Major League Baseball.

On Wednesday, Bettman stated NHL clubs have lost more than $1.8 billion ($US) during the current 10-year collective bargaining arrangement, while the average player salary has soared to $1.8 million from $733,000.

Source: Based on CBC Sports (with files from CP online), September 19, 2004, http://www.cbc.ca/sports/story/2004/09/14/nhllabour040914.html, accessed June 15, 2007.

Analysis: Under bilateral monopolies, wages and employment conditions are not determined by simple demand and supply but through collective bargaining. Reaching a settlement, however, may involve a strike or lockout.

---

[1] Even though points S and s may not be identical to the initial bargaining positions, they represent the positions of maximum attainable benefit for both sides. Points outside the demand or supply curve will be rejected out of hand by one side or the other.

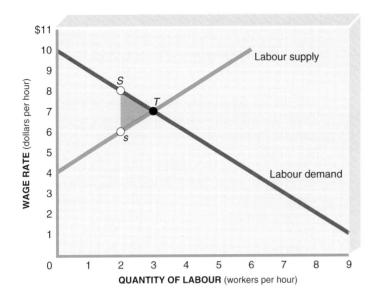

FIGURE 13.10
The Boundaries of Collective Bargaining

Firms with power in the labour market seek to establish wages and employment levels corresponding to point s (from Figure 13.9). Unions, on the other hand, seek to establish an equilibrium at point S (from Figure 13.8). The competitive equilibrium is at point T. The function of collective bargaining is to identify a compromise between these points—that is, to locate an equilibrium somewhere in the shaded area.

resources of the negotiating parties. ***The fundamental source of negotiating power for either side is its ability to withhold labour or jobs.*** The union can threaten to strike, thereby cutting off the flow of union labour to the employer. The employer can impose a lockout, thereby cutting off jobs and paycheques. The effectiveness of those threats depends on the availability of substitute workers or jobs.

Labour and management both suffer from either a strike or a lockout, no matter who initiates the work stoppage. The strike benefits paid to workers are rarely comparable to wages they would otherwise have received, and the payment of those benefits depletes the union treasury. By the same token, the reduction in labour costs and other expenses rarely compensates the employer for lost profits.

Because potential income losses are usually high, both labour and management try to avoid a strike or lockout if they can. In fact, a significant majority of all collective bargaining agreements are concluded without recourse to a strike and often without even the explicit threat of one.

The Pressure to Settle

The built-in pressures for settlement help resolve collective bargaining. They don't tell us, however, what the dimensions of that final settlement will be. All we know is that the settlement will be located within the boundaries established in Figure 13.10. The relative pressures on each side will determine whether the final equilibrium is closer to the union or the management position.

In the 2004–2005 National Hockey League lockout by the owners (see the Applications box), the pressures to settle were very one-sided. With the exceptions of large markets such as Toronto, Detroit, and New York, most teams were losing money and some were even losing less money during the lockout than during the regular season. In the end, the NHL and the player's union came to a six-year collective bargaining agreement that favoured the owner's position over the players. This included a 24 percent rollback on all existing player contracts as well as a team-by-team salary cap linked to projected revenues for the league (with no player earning more than 20 percent of his team's salary cap).

The final settlement almost always necessitates hard choices on both sides. Unions usually have to choose between increased job security or higher remuneration (wages, benefits, etc.). In some instances, they also must consider how management will react in the long run to higher wages, perhaps introducing a new technology that reduces dependence on labour. Employers are concerned whether productivity will suffer if workers are dissatisfied with their pay/benefit package.

The Final Settlement

SUMMARY

- The motivation to work arises from social, psychological, and economic forces. People need income to pay their bills, but they also need a sense of achievement. As a consequence, people are willing to work—to supply labour.
- There's an opportunity cost involved in working—namely, the amount of leisure time one sacrifices. By the same token, the opportunity cost of not working (leisure) is the income and related consumption possibilities thereby forgone. Thus each person confronts a trade-off between leisure and income.
- The supply of labour curve is upward-sloping, reflecting the higher wages necessary to compensate workers for the increasing opportunity cost of labour (i.e., the value associated with the reduction in leisure time).
- A firm's demand for labour reflects labour's marginal revenue product. A profit-maximizing employer won't pay a worker more than the worker produces.
- The marginal revenue product of labour diminishes as additional workers are employed on a particular job (the law of diminishing returns). This decline occurs because additional workers have to share existing land and capital, leaving each worker with less land and capital to work with.
- A producer seeks to get the most output for every dollar spent on inputs. This means getting the highest ratio of marginal product to input price. A profit-maximizing producer will choose the most cost-efficient input (not necessarily the one with the cheapest price).
- The efficiency decision involves the choice of the least-cost productive process and is also made on the basis of cost efficiency. A producer seeks the least expensive process to produce a given rate of output.
- Differences in marginal revenue product are an important explanation of wage inequalities. But the difficulty of measuring MRP in some jobs leaves many wage rates to be determined by opportunity wages or other mechanisms.
- Power in labour markets is the ability to alter market wage rates. Such power is most evident in local labour markets defined by geographical, occupational, or industrial boundaries.
- Power on the supply side of labour markets is manifested by unions, organized along industry or craft lines. The

basic function of a union is to evaluate employment offers in terms of the *collective* interest of its members.
- The downward slope of the labour demand curve creates a distinction between the marginal wage and the market wage. The marginal wage is the change in *total* wages occasioned by employment of one additional worker and is less than the market wage.
- Unions seek to establish that rate of employment at which the marginal wage curve intersects the labour supply curve. The desired union wage is then found on the labour demand curve at that level of employment.
- Power on the demand side of labour market is manifested in buyer concentrations such as monopsony and oligopsony. Such power is usually found among the same firms that exercise market power in product markets.
- By definition, power on the demand side implies some direct influence on market wage rates; additional hiring by a monopsonist will force up the market wage rate. Hence, a monopsonist must recognize a distinction between the marginal factor cost of labour and its (lower) market wage rate.
- The goal of a monopsonistic employer is to hire the number of workers indicated by the point at which the marginal factor cost of labour equals its marginal revenue product. The employer then looks at the labour supply curve to determine the wage rate that must be paid for that number of workers.
- The desire of unions to establish a wage rate that's higher than competitive wages directly opposes the desire of powerful employers to establish lower wage rates. In bilateral monopolies, in which power exists on both sides of the labour market, unions and employers engage in collective bargaining to negotiate a final settlement.
- Increases in wage rates induce people to work more—that is, to substitute labour for leisure. But this substitution effect may be offset by an income effect. Higher wages also enable a person to work fewer hours with no loss of income. When income effects outweigh substitution effects, the labour supply curve bends backward (see Appendix).

Key Terms

labour supply 275
market supply of labour 277
elasticity of labour supply 277
demand for labour 278
derived demand 278
marginal revenue product (MRP) 279
equilibrium wage 286

cost efficiency 287
outsourcing 287
production process 287
opportunity wage 289
unionization rate 290
marginal wage 292
monopsony 294

marginal factor cost (MFC) 294
bilateral monopoly 296
collective bargaining 296
substitution effect of wages (A) 300
income effect of wages (A) 301

Questions for Discussion

1. Would you continue to work after winning a lottery prize of $50,000 a year for life? Would you change schools, jobs, or career objectives? What factors besides income influence work decisions?
2. Is this course increasing your marginal productivity? If so, in what way?
3. How might you measure the marginal revenue product of (*a*) a quarterback and (*b*) the team's coach?
4. Explain why marginal physical product would diminish as
   (*a*) More secretaries are hired in an office.
   (*b*) More professors are hired in the economics department.
   (*c*) More construction workers are hired to build a school.
5. The minimum wage in Mexico is less than $1 an hour. Does this make Mexican workers more cost-effective than Canadian workers? Explain.
6. Collective bargaining sessions often start with unreasonable demands and categorical rejections. Why do unions and employers tend to begin bargaining from extreme positions?
7. Does a strike for a raise of 5 cents an hour make any sense? What kinds of long-term benefits might a union gain from such a strike?
8. Are large and powerful firms easier targets for union organization than small firms? Why or why not?
9. Why are farm workers much less successful than airplane machinists in securing higher wages?
10. How will union mergers affect the market power of unions?

E X E R C I S E S

PROBLEMS The Student Problem Set to accompany this chapter can be found at the end of the book.

WEB ACTIVITIES Web Activities to accompany this chapter can be found on the Online Learning Centre at **http://www.mcgrawhill.ca/olc/schiller**.

A P P E N D I X

A BACKWARD BENDING INDIVIDUAL SUPPLY CURVE?

In the text, we discussed how the individual supply curve for labour has the traditional upward-sloping shape of a supply curve. The force that drives people up the labour supply curve is the desire for more income—higher wages enable people to buy more goods and services. The quest for higher levels of consumption induces individuals to *substitute* labour for leisure.

At some point, however, additional goods and services will lose their allure. Individuals with extremely high incomes already have lots of toys. If they are offered a higher wage rate, the **substitution effect of wages** may not be persuasive. Rather than supplying *more* labour, they might even *reduce* the number of hours they work, thereby maintaining a high income *and* increasing their leisure (see the Applications box). While you might do cartwheels for $50 an hour, Bill Gates or Brad Pitt might not lift a finger for such a paltry sum. Muhammad Ali once announced that he wouldn't spend an hour in the ring

substitution effect of wages: An increased wage rate encourages people to work more hours (to substitute labour for leisure).

APPLICATIONS

Canada Ranks High on the List of the Work-Shy

UNITED NATIONS—More than a fifth of the world's workforce spends "excessively long" hours on the job, but Canadians are among the most work-shy, a United Nations study released Thursday shows.

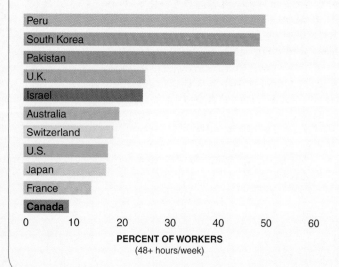

PERCENT OF WORKERS
(48+ hours/week)

Canadians rank well behind those countries' workers and are also behind the Israelis, Australians, Swiss, Americans, Japanese and even the French, who are famous for their adherence to the 35-hour work week before overtime kicks in.

"In Canada, just 10.6 per cent of the workforce works more than what we call excessive hours—anything over 48 hours," said Jon Messenger, one of the authors of Working Time Around the World.

Despite Canada's designation as a relatively leisure-loving society, one benefit is Canadian workers are more likely to retain good health than workers elsewhere.

"The rate of accidents goes through the roof when you go above 60 hours a week," said Messenger. "So does the rate of depression. The Japanese have done many studies on this, and they even coined the term 'karoshi'—which means death from overwork.'"

Source: Steven Edwards, CanWest News Service, June 8, 2007, http://www.canada.com/vancouversun/news/story.html?id=44b403f3-f1c3-43a6-b4e1-e57f6d63b9dd, accessed June 14, 2007. Or http://working.canada.com/toronto/resources/story.html?id=63027a09-806d-406e-909c-bb8ea696430d, accessed June 15, 2007. The UN Study is entitled "Working Time Around the World" and can be viewed at the International Labour Organization's site (under publications): http://www.ilo.org/global/What_we_do/Publications/lang—en/index.htm

Analysis: For some nations, income effects outweigh substitution effects in the labour-leisure trade-off.

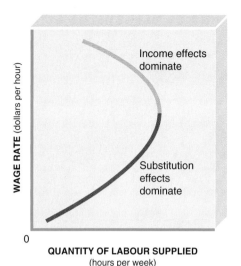

WAGE RATE (dollars per hour)

Income effects
dominate

Substitution
effects
dominate

0

QUANTITY OF LABOUR SUPPLIED
(hours per week)

FIGURE 13A.1
**The Backward-Bending
Supply Curve**

Increases in wage rates make additional hours of work more valuable, but also less necessary. Higher wage rates increase the quantity of labour supplied as long as substitution effects outweigh income effects. At the point where income effects begin to outweigh substitution effects, the labour supply curve starts to bend backward.

for less than $1 million and would box *less,* not more, as the pay for his fights exceeded $3 million. For him, the added income from one championship fight was so great that he felt he didn't have to fight more to satisfy his income and consumption desires.

A low-wage worker might also respond to higher wage rates by working *less,* not more. People receiving very low wages (such as migrant workers, household help, and babysitters) have to work long hours just to pay the rent. The increased income made possible by higher wage rates might permit them to work *fewer* hours. These *negative* labour supply responses to increased wage rates are referred to as the **income effect** of a wage increase.

A utility-maximizing individual will respond to these income and substitution effects by offering different quantities of labour at alternative wage rates. The *substitution effect* of high wages encourages people to work more hours. The *income effect,* on the other hand, allows them to reduce work hours without losing income. If substitution effects dominate, the labour supply curve will be upward-sloping. *If income effects outweigh substitution effects, an individual will supply* **less** *labour at higher wages.* This kind of reaction is illustrated by the backward-bending portion of the supply curve in Figure 13A.1.

income effect of wages: An increased wage rate allows a person to reduce hours worked without losing income.

Financial Markets

Christopher Columbus had a crazy entrepreneurial idea: He was certain he could find a new route to the Indies by sailing not east from Europe but west—around the world. Such a route, he surmised, would give Europe quicker access to the riches of the East Indies. Whoever discovered that western route could become very, very rich.

To find that route, Columbus needed ships, sailors, and tonnes of provisions. He couldn't afford to supply these resources himself. He needed financial backers who would put up the money. For several years he tried to convince King Ferdinand of Spain to provide the necessary funds. But the king didn't want to risk so much wealth on a single venture. Twice he'd turned Columbus down.

Fortunately, Genoese merchant bankers in Seville came to Columbus's rescue. Convinced that Columbus's "enterprise of the Indies" might bring back "pearls, precious stones, gold, silver, spiceries," and other valuable merchandise, they guaranteed repayment of any funds lent to Columbus. With that guarantee in hand, the Duke of Medina Sidonia, in April 1492, offered to lend 1,000 maravedis (about $5,000 in today's dollars) to Queen Isabella for the purpose of funding Columbus's expedition. With no personal financial risk, King Ferdinand then granted Columbus the funds and authority for a royal expedition.

Columbus's experience in raising funds for his expedition illustrates a critical function of financial markets, namely, the management of *risk*. This chapter examines how financial markets facilitate economic activities (like Columbus's expedition) by managing the risks of failure. Three central questions guide the discussion:

- **What is traded in financial markets?**
- **How do the financial markets affect the economic outcomes of WHO, WHAT, and FOR WHOM?**
- **Why do financial markets fluctuate so much?**

14.1 THE ROLE OF FINANCIAL MARKETS

A central question for every economy is WHAT to produce. In 1492, all available resources were employed in farming, fishing, food distribution, metalworking, and other basic services. For Columbus to pursue his quest, he needed some of those resources. To get them, he needed money to bid scarce resources from other pursuits and employ them on his expedition.

Entrepreneurs who don't have great personal wealth must get start-up funds from other people. There are two possibilities: either *borrow* the money, or invite other people to *invest* in the new venture.

How might you pursue these options? You could ask your relatives for a loan or go door-to-door in your neighbourhood seeking investors. But such direct fund-raising is costly, inefficient, and often unproductive. Columbus went hat in hand to the Spanish royal court twice, but each time he came back empty-handed.

The task of raising start-up funds is made much easier by the existence of **financial intermediaries**—institutions that steer the flow of savings to cash-strapped entrepreneurs and other investors. Funds flow into banks, pension funds, bond markets, stock markets, and other financial intermediaries from businesses, households, and government entities that have some unspent income. This pool of national savings is then passed on to entrepreneurs, expanding businesses, and other borrowers by these same institutions (see Figure 14.1).

Financial intermediaries provide several important services: They greatly reduce the cost of locating loanable funds. Their pool of savings offers a clear economy of scale compared to the alternative of door-to-door solicitations. They also reduce the cost to savers of finding suitable lending or investment opportunities. Few individuals have the time, resources, or interest to do the searching on their own. With huge pools of amassed savings, however, financial intermediaries have the incentive to acquire and analyze information about lending and investment opportunities. Hence, *financial intermediaries reduce search and information costs* in the financial markets. In so doing, they make the allocation of resources more efficient.

Although financial intermediaries make the job of acquiring start-up funds a lot easier, there's no guarantee that the funds needed will be acquired. First, there must be an adequate supply of funds available. Second, financial intermediaries must be convinced that they should allocate some of those funds to a project.

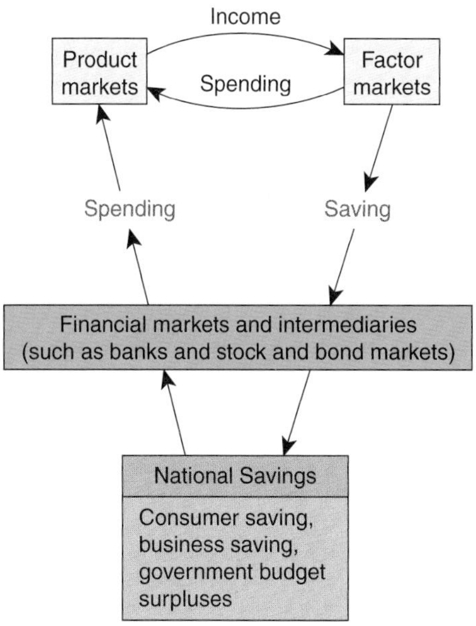

Financial Intermediaries

> **financial intermediary:** Institution (e.g., bank or the stock market) that makes savings available to borrowers (e.g., investors).

FIGURE 14.1

Mobilizing Savings

The central economic function of financial markets is to channel national savings into new investment and other desired expenditure. Financial intermediaries such as banks, insurance companies, and stockbrokers help transfer purchasing power from savers to spenders.

Venture Capitalists— Financing Tomorrow's Products

One of the proven paths to high incomes and wealth is entrepreneurship. Most of the great fortunes originated in entrepreneurial ventures, for example, building railroads, mass-producing automobiles, introducing new computers, or perfecting mass-merchandising techniques. These successful ventures all required more than just a great idea. To convert the original idea into actual output requires the investment of real resources.

Recall that Apple Computer started in a garage, with a minimum of resources (Chapter 7). The idea of packaging a personal computer was novel, and few resources were required to demonstrate that it could be done. But Steven Jobs couldn't have become a multimillionaire by building just a few dozen computers a month. To reap huge economic profits from his idea, he needed much greater production capacity. He also needed resources for marketing the new Apples to a broader customer base. In other words, Steven Jobs needed lots of economic resources—land, labour, and capital—to convert his entrepreneurial dream into a profit-making reality.

Steven Jobs and his partner, Steve Wozniak, had few resources of their own. In fact, they'd sold Jobs's Volkswagen and Wozniak's scientific calculator to raise the finances for the first computer. To go any further, they needed financial support from others. Loans were hard to obtain since the company had no assets, no financial history, and no certainty of success. Jobs needed people who were willing to share the *risks* associated with a new venture. He found one such person in A. C. Markkula, who put up $250,000 and became a partner in the new venture. Shortly thereafter, other venture capitalists provided additional financing. With this start-up financing, Jobs was able to acquire more resources and make the Apple Computer Company a reality.

This is a classic case study in venture capitalism. Venture capitalists provide initial funding for entrepreneurial ventures. In return for their financial backing, the venture capitalists are entitled to a share of any profits that result. If the venture fails, however, they get nothing. Thus, **venture capitalists provide financial support for entrepreneurial ideas and share in the risks and rewards.** Even Christopher Columbus needed venture capitalists to fund his risky expeditions to the New World.

Venture capital is as important to the economy today as it was to Columbus. In the immediate aftermath of the September 11, 2001, terrorist attacks, venture capitalists briefly withdrew their chequebooks (see the Applications box). This slowed the pace of entrepreneurship, innovation, and economic growth. For technology and entrepreneurship to continue growing, market conditions must be amenable to venture capitalists.

WEB NOTE

Canada's Venture Capital & Private Equity Association (CVCA) promotes the development of the Canadian venture capital industry through active advocacy and professional development activities. Visit http://www.cvca.ca/.

The Supply of Loanable Funds

As noted, the supply of loanable funds originates in the decisions of market participants to not spend all their current income. Those saving decisions are influenced by time preferences and interest rates.

Time Preferences. In deciding to *save* rather than *spend,* people effectively reallocate their spending over time. That is, people save *now* in order to spend more *later.* How much to save, then, depends partly on *time preference.* If a person doesn't give any thought to the future, she's likely to save little. If, by contrast, a person wants to buy a car, a vacation, or a house in the future, he's more inclined to save some income now.

Interest Rates. Interest rates also affect saving decisions. If interest rates are high, the future payoff to every dollar saved is greater. A higher return on savings translates into more future income for every dollar of current income saved. Hence, **higher interest rates increase the quantity of available savings (loanable funds).**

Risk. In the early 1990s, banks in Russia were offering interest rates on savings accounts of nearly 100 percent a year. In Latin America, banks have offered even higher interest rates on occasion. Yet few people rushed to deposit their savings in these banks. People worried that the banks might fail, wiping out their savings in the process. In other words, there was a high *risk* attached to those high interest rates.

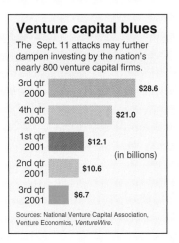

Venture Capital Falls 72 Percent from Last Year

SAN FRANCISCO—Venture capitalists, hunkered down because of the dot-com collapse, are tightening the financing spigot even more in the post-terrorist-attack economy.

"What's happened is so significant as to put . . . business on hold," says venture capitalist Richard Kramlich of New Enterprise Associates in Menlo Park.

Third-quarter venture investments totaled $6.7 billion, down 72 percent from the same quarter a year ago, says industry newsletter *VentureWire*. The number of private companies receiving venture capital dropped to 540, down 67 percent from a year earlier and down 39 percent from the second quarter.

—Jim Hopkins

Source: *USA Today,* October 8, 2001. USA TODAY. Copyright 2001. Reprinted with permission. www.usatoday.com

Venture capital blues

The Sept. 11 attacks may further dampen investing by the nation's nearly 800 venture capital firms.

3rd qtr 2000	$28.6
4th qtr 2000	$21.0
1st qtr 2001	$12.1
2nd qtr 2001	$10.6
3rd qtr 2001	$6.7

(in billions)

Sources: National Venture Capital Association, Venture Economics, *VentureWire*.

Analysis: Venture capital is a critical ingredient in entrepreneurship. When the flow of venture capital slows, so does the pace of technology and innovation.

Anyone who contemplated lending funds to Columbus confronted a similar risk. That was the dilemma King Ferdinand confronted. He had enough funds to finance Columbus's expedition, but he didn't want to risk losing so much on a single venture.

Risk Management. This is why the Genoese bankers were so critical: These financial intermediaries could spread the risk of failure among many individuals. Each investor could put up just a fraction of the needed funds. No one had to put all his eggs in one basket. Once the consortium of bankers agreed to share the risks of Columbus's expedition, the venture had wings. The Genoese merchant bankers could afford to take portions of the expedition's risks because they also financed many less risky projects. By diversifying their portfolios, they could select any degree of average risk they preferred. That is the essence of risk management.

Risk Premiums. Even though diversification permits greater risk management, lenders will want to be compensated for any above-average risks they take. Money lent to local merchants must have seemed a lot less risky than lending funds to Columbus. Thus no one would have stepped forward to finance Columbus if Columbus hadn't promised an *above-average* return upon the expedition's success. The difference between the rates of return on a safe (certain) investment and a risky (uncertain) one is called the **risk premium.** Risk premiums compensate people who finance risky ventures that succeed. Because these ventures are risky, however, investors often lose their money in such ventures too.

Risk premiums help explain why blue-chip corporations such as Microsoft can borrow money from a bank at the low "prime" rate while ordinary consumers have to pay much higher interest rates on personal loans. Corporate loans are less risky because corporations typically have plenty of revenue and assets to cover their debts. Consumers often get overextended, however, and can't pay all their bills. As a result,

risk premium: The difference in rates of return on risky (uncertain) and safe (certain) investments.

there's a greater risk that consumers' loans won't be paid back. It may also be more expensive to collect payments from consumers who fall behind. Banks charge higher interest rates on consumer loans to compensate for this risk.

14.2 THE PRESENT VALUE OF FUTURE PROFITS

In deciding whether to assume the *risk* of supplying funds to a new venture, financial intermediaries assess the potential *rewards*. People who are *demanding* funds must also have some sense of what the payoff to their venture will be. In Columbus's case, the rewards were the fabled treasures of the East Indies. Even if he found those treasures, however, the rewards would only come long after the expedition was financed. When Columbus proposed his East Indies expedition, he envisioned a round trip that would last at least six months. Were he successful in finding the fabled treasures of the East, he planned subsequent trips to acquire and transport his precious cargoes back home. Although King Ferdinand granted Columbus only one-tenth of any profits from the first expedition, Columbus had a claim on one-eighth of the profits of any subsequent voyages. Hence, even if Columbus succeeded in finding a shortcut to the East, he wouldn't generate any substantial profit for perhaps two years or more.

Suppose for the moment that Columbus expected no profit from the first expedition but a profit of $1,000 at the end of two years from a second voyage. How much was that future profit worth to Columbus?

Time Value of Money

To assess the value of *future* receipts, we have to consider the *time value* of money. A dollar received today is worth more than a dollar received two years from today. Why? Because a dollar received today can earn *interest*. If you have a dollar today and put it in an interest-bearing account, in two years you'll have your original dollar *plus* accumulated interest.[1] *As long as interest-earning opportunities exist, present dollars are worth more than future dollars.*

In 1492, there were plenty of opportunities to earn interest. Indeed, the Genoese bankers were charging high interest rates on their loans and guarantees. If Columbus had had the cash, he too could have lent money to others and earned interest on his funds.

To calculate the present value of future dollars, this forgone interest must be taken into account. This computation is essentially interest accrual in reverse. *We "discount" future dollars by the opportunity cost of money*—that is, the market rate of interest.

> **present discounted value (PDV):** The value today of future payments, adjusted for interest accrual.

Suppose the market rate of interest in 1492 was 10 percent. To compute the **present discounted value (PDV)** of future payment, we discount as follows:

$$\text{PDV} = \frac{\text{future payment}_N}{(1 + \text{interest rate})^N}$$

where N refers to the number of years into the future when a payment is to be made. If the future payment is to be made in 1 year, the N in the equation equals 1, and we have

$$\text{PDV} = \frac{\$1,000}{1.10}$$

$$= \$909.09$$

Hence, the present discounted value of $1,000 to be paid one year from today is $909.09. If $909.09 were received today, it could earn interest. In a year's time, the $909.09 would grow to $1,000 with interest accrued at the rate of 10 percent per year.

---

[1] Part of that interest payment will compensate for anticipated inflation; the remainder will compensate for the pure time value of money (postponed spending). Real (inflation-adjusted) interest rates express the time value of money.

Years in the Future	Future Payment ($ millions)	Present Value ($ millions)
0	$ 11.3	$ 11.30
1	11.3	10.82
2	11.3	10.35
3	11.3	9.91
4	11.3	9.49
5	11.3	9.08
*	*	*
*	*	*
*	*	*
25	11.3	3.79
	$294.0	$168.0

Note: The general formula for computing present values is $PDV = \Sigma \dfrac{\text{payment in year } N}{(1 + r)^N}$, where r is the prevailing rate.

TABLE 14.1
Computing Present Value

The present value of a future payment declines the longer one must wait for a payment. At an interest rate of 4.47 percent, $11.3 million payable in one year is worth only $10.82 million today. A payout of $11.3 million 25 years from now has a present value of only $3.79 million. A string of $11.3 million payments spread out over 25 years has a present value of $168 million (at 4.47 percent interest).

Suppose it would have taken Columbus two years to complete his expeditions and collect his profits. In that case, the present value of the $1,000 payment would be lower. The N in the formula would be 2 and the present value would be

$$PDV = \frac{\$1,000}{(1.10)^2} = \frac{\$1,000}{1.21} = \$826.45$$

Hence, *the longer one has to wait for a future payment, the less present value it has.*

Lottery winners often have to choose between present and future values. In July 2004, for example, Geraldine Williams, a housekeeper in Lowell, Massachusetts, won $294 million in a U.S. lottery. The $294 million was payable in 26 annual installments of $11.3 million. If the lucky winner wanted to get her prize sooner, she could accept an immediate but smaller payout rather than 25 future installments.

Table 14.1 shows how the lottery officials figured the present value of the $294 prize. The first installment of $11.3 million would be paid immediately. Mrs. Williams would have had to wait one year for the second cheque, however. At the then-prevailing interest rate of 4.47 percent, the *present* value of that second $11.3 million cheque was only $10.82 million. The *last* payoff cheque had even less value since it wasn't due to be paid for 25 years. With so much time for interest to accrue, that final $11.3 million payment had a present value of only $3.79 million. The calculations in Table 14.1 convinced lottery officials to offer an immediate payout of only $168 million on the $294 million prize. Mrs. Williams wasn't too disappointed.

The winner would have received even less money had interest rates been higher. At the time Mrs. Williams won the lottery, the interest rate on bonds was 4.47 percent. Had the rate been higher, the discount for immediate payment would have been higher as well. Table 14.2 indicates that Mrs. Williams would have received only $107 million had the prevailing interest rate been 10 percent. What Tables 14.1 and 14.2 illustrate, then, is that *the present discounted value of a future payment declines with*

- *Higher interest rates.*
- *Longer delays in future payment.*

The valuation of future payments must also consider the possibility of *non*payment. State governments are virtually certain to make promised lottery payouts, so there's little risk in accepting a promised payout of 25 annual installments. But what about the booty from Columbus's expeditions? There was great uncertainty that Columbus

Interest Rate Effects

Uncertainty

TABLE 14.2
Higher Interest Rates Reduce Present Values

Higher interest rates raise the *future* value of current dollars. The rates therefore reduce the *present* value of future payments. Shown here is the present discounted value of the July 2004 U.S. lottery prize of $294 million at different interest rates.

Interest Rate (%)	Present Discounted Value of $294 Million Lottery Prize ($ millions)
5.0%	$166.3
6.0	150.8
7.0	137.5
8.0	126.0
9.0	115.9
10.0	107.1

expected value: The probable value of a future payment, including the risk of nonpayment.

would ever return from his expeditions, much less bring back the "pearls, precious stones, gold, silver, spiceries" that people coveted. Investing in those expeditions was far riskier than deferring a lottery payment.

Expected Value. Whenever an anticipated future payment is uncertain, a risk factor should be included in present-value computations. This is done by calculating the **expected value** of a future payment. Suppose there was only a 50:50 chance that Columbus would bring back the bacon. In that event, the expected payoff would be

$$\text{Expected value} = (1 - \text{risk factor}) \times \text{present discounted value}$$

With a 50:50 chance of failure, the expected value of Columbus's first-year profits would have been

$$\text{Expected value} = (1 - 0.5) \times \$909.09$$
$$= \$454.55$$

Expected values also explain why people buy more lottery tickets when the prize is larger. The odds of winning the Lotto 649—where the winning ticket must match six numbers randomly drawn from numbers 1 through 49—are approximately *14 million* to 1. Given that the odds of being struck by lightening during any given year are roughly 600,000 to 1, it is no wonder that most individuals save their $2 for better purposes than buying a lottery ticket. With a typical $4 million prize, the *undiscounted* expected value of a $2 ticket is only 29 cents. When the lottery prize increases, however, the expected value of a ticket grows as well (there are still only 14 million possible combinations of numbers). When the grand prize reached $54 million in October 2005, the undiscounted value of a lone winning ticket jumped to close to $4. Millions of people decided that the expected value was high enough to justify playing the lottery. People took time off work, skipped classes and drove to the nearest lottery terminal to queue up for tickets (the prize was claimed by 17 oil workers from Camrose, Alberta). When the jackpot returns to its $4 million starting point, far fewer people buy tickets.

The Demand for Loanable Funds

People rarely borrow money to buy lottery tickets. But entrepreneurs and other market participants often use other people's funds to finance their ventures. ***How much loanable funds are demanded depends on***

*   ***The expected rate of return.***
*   ***The cost of funds.***

The higher the expected return, or the lower the cost of funds, the greater will be the amount of loanable funds demanded.

Figure 14.2 offers a general view of the loanable funds market that emerges from these considerations. From the entrepreneur's perspective, the prevailing interest rate represents the cost of funds. From the perspective of savers, the interest rate represents the payoff to savings. When interest rates rise, the quantity of funds supplied goes up

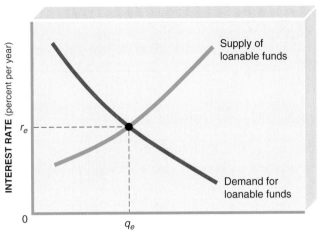

FIGURE 14.2
The Loanable Funds Market

The market rate of interest (r_e) is determined by the intersection of the curves representing supply of and demand for loanable funds. The rate of interest represents the price paid for the use of money.

and the quantity demanded goes down. The prevailing (equilibrium) interest rate is set by the intersection of these supply and demand curves.

14.3 THE STOCK MARKET

The concept of a loanable funds market sounds a bit alien. But the same principles of supply, demand, and risk management go a long way in explaining the action in stock markets. Suppose you had $1,000 to invest. Should you invest it all in lottery tickets that offer a multimillion-dollar payoff? Put it in a savings account that pays next to nothing? Or how about the stock market? The stock market can reward you handsomely; or it can wipe out your savings if the stocks you own tumble. Hence, stocks offer a higher average return than bank accounts but also entail greater average risk. People who bought Amazon.com stock in May 1997 got a 1,000 percent profit on their stock in only two years. But people who bought Amazon.com stock in December 1999 lost 90 percent of their investment in even less time. Canadians who invested in Nortel Networks—the Canadian telecommunications equipment giant—at the peak of its stock value in the summer of 2000, saw the value of their shares shrink precipitously from $124 to 0.69 cents over the next two years. Many Canadians had Nortel stock in their pension funds and the massive drop in the stock price wiped out a large portion of retiree's accounts.

When people buy a share of stock, they're buying partial ownership of a corporation. The three legal forms of business entities are

- Corporations
- Partnerships
- Proprietorships

Limited Liability. Proprietorships are businesses owned by a single individual. The owner-proprietor is responsible for all the business, including repayment of any debts. Members of a partnership are typically liable for all business debts and activities as well. By contrast, a **corporation** is a limited liability form of business. The corporation itself, not its individual shareholders, is responsible for all business activity and debts. As a result of this limited liability, you can own a piece of a corporation without worrying about being sued for business mishaps (like environmental damage) or nonpayment of debt. This feature significantly reduces the risk of owning corporate stock.

Shared Ownership. The ownership of a corporation is defined in terms of stock shares. Each share of **corporate stock** represents partial ownership of the business. Chipmaker Intel, for example, has nearly 6 *billion* shares of stock outstanding (that is, shares held by the public). Hence, each share of Intel stock represents less than one-sixth of one-billionth ownership of the corporation. Potentially, this means that

WEB NOTE

For a historical view of Nortel Networks stock prices, go to http://ca.finance.yahoo.com/, type in the stock symbol "NT," and choose "Canadian markets,"

Corporate Stock

corporation: A business organization having a continuous existence independent of its members (owners) and power and liabilities distinct from those of its members.

corporate stock: Shares of ownership in a corporation.

as many as 6 billion people could own the Intel Corporation. In reality, however, many individuals own hundreds of shares, and institutions may own thousands.

In principle, the owners of corporate stock collectively run the business. In practice, the shareholders select a board of directors to monitor corporate activity and protect their interests. The day-to-day business of running a corporation is the job of managers who report to the board of directors.

Stock Returns

If shareholders don't have any direct role in running a corporation, why would they want to own a piece of it? Essentially, for the same reason that the Genoese bankers agreed to finance Columbus's expedition: profits. Owners (shareholders) of a corporation hope to share in the profits the corporation earns.

Dividends. Shareholders rarely receive their full share of the company's profits in cash. Corporations typically use some of the profits for investment in new plants or equipment. They may also want to retain some of the profits for operational needs or unforeseen contingencies. ***Corporations may choose to retain earnings or pay them out to shareholders as* dividends.** Any profits not paid to shareholders are referred to as **retained earnings.** Thus,

> **dividend:** Amount of corporate profits paid out for each share of stock.

$$\text{Dividends} = \text{corporate profits} - \text{retained earnings}$$

> **retained earnings:** Amount of corporate profits not paid out in dividends.

In 2004, Intel paid quarterly dividends amounting to 4 cents per share for the year. But the company earned profits equal to $1.11 cents per share. Thus, shareholders received less than 5 percent of their accrued profits in dividend checks; Intel retained the remaining $1.07 per-share profit earned in 2004 for future investments. However, two years later, in 2006, Intel earned only 86 cents per share, yet announced a quarterly dividend of 11.5 cents per share payable on March 1, 2007. This increase from less than 5 percent of profits in the form of dividend cheques to over 13 percent illustrates the volatility of dividend returns in the high technology sector.

Capital Gains. If Intel invests its retained earnings wisely, the corporation may reap even larger profits in the future. As a company grows and prospers, each share of ownership may become more valuable. This increase in value would be reflected in higher market prices for shares of Intel stock. Any increase in the value of a stock represents a **capital gain** for shareholders. Capital gains directly increase shareholder wealth.

> **capital gain:** An increase in the market value of an asset.

Total Return. People who own stocks can thus get two distinct payoffs: dividends and capital gains. Together, these payoffs represent the total return on stock investments. Hence, ***the higher the expected total return (future dividends and capital gains), the greater the desire to buy and hold stocks.*** If a stock paid no dividends and had no prospects for price appreciation (capital gain, for example) you'd probably hold your savings in a different form (such as another stock or maybe an interest-earning bank account).

Initial Public Offering

When a corporation is formed, its future sales and profits are uncertain. When shares are first offered to the public, the seller of stock is the company itself. By *going public,* the corporation seeks to raise funds for investment and growth. A true *start-up* company may have nothing more than a good idea, a couple of dedicated employees, and Big Plans. To fund these plans, it sells shares of itself in an **initial public offering (IPO).** People who buy the newly issued stock are putting their savings directly into the corporation's accounts.[2] As new owners, they stand to profit from the corporation's business or take their lumps if the corporation fails.

> **initial public offering (IPO):** The first issuance (sale) to the general public of stock in a corporation.

[2]In reality, some of the initial proceeds will go to stockbrokers and investment bankers as compensation for their services as financial intermediaries. The entrepreneur who starts the company, other company employees, and any venture capitalists who help fund the company before the public offering may also get some of the IPO receipts by selling shares they acquired before the company went public.

In 1997, Amazon.com Inc. was still a relatively new company. Although the company had been in operation since 1994, its capacity to sell books on the Internet was limited. To expand, it needed more warehouse space, more computers, and additional staff. To finance this expansion, Amazon needed more money. The company could have *borrowed* money from a bank or other financial institution, but that would have saddled the company with debt and forced it to make regular interest payments. Lenders might have even wanted the officers of the company to guarantee repayment of the loan, burdening them with personal liability.

Rather than borrow money, Amazon's directors elected to sell ownership shares in the company. In May 1997, the company raised $54 million in cash by selling three million shares for $18 per share in its initial public offering.

Why were people eager to buy shares in Amazon.com Inc.? They certainly weren't buying the stock with expectations of high dividends. The company hadn't earned any profit in its first three years and didn't expect to earn a profit for at least another three years.

What might those future profits be worth? Suppose the company expected to earn profits of $1 per share in four years. What current value might those future profits have? In 1997, the prevailing long-term interest rate was close to 6 percent. Thus, the present discounted value of those future profits was

$$PDV = \frac{\$1}{(1 + 0.06)^4} = \frac{\$1}{1.262} = \$0.79$$

If you paid $18 for a share of stock that earned only 79 cents, you'd be paying a reasonable price for a share of company profits. This can be seen by computing the **price/earnings (P/E) ratio:**

$$P/E \ ratio = \frac{price \ of \ stock \ share}{earnings \ (profit) \ per \ share}$$

For Amazon.com in 1997,

$$P/E \ ratio = \frac{\$18}{0.79} = 22.8$$

In other words, investors were paying $22.80 for every $1 of discounted future profits. That implies a rate of return of $1 \div \$22.80$, or 4.4 percent. Compared to the interest rates banks were paying on deposit balances, Amazon.com shares looked like a good buy.

Risk Factors. The stock didn't look quite as cheap, however, when the risks of failure were considered. The 79 cents of discounted future profits were far from certain; they were merely a projection. In reality, the road to riches on the Internet is riddled with risks. Other companies (e.g., Chapters-Indigo) also sell books in cyberspace. Still more companies might enter the market if the outlook for profits improves. Technological advances might make Amazon.com's setup obsolete. Marketing and production costs may escalate. Any of these problems could jeopardize Amazon.com's future profits.

In view of these many risks, any projections of future profits must be adjusted for their uncertainty. If there's a 25 percent chance that Amazon.com will fail to hit the profit target, the *expected* value of future profits is

$$Expected \ value \ of \ profit = (1 - risk \ factor) \times PDV$$
$$= (1 - 0.25) \times 0.79$$
$$= 0.59$$

Secondary Trading

price/earnings (P/E) ratio: The price of a stock share divided by earnings (profit) per share.

From this perspective, the IPO price of Amazon.com wasn't quite so cheap. The expected rate of return was

$$\text{Expected rate of return} = \frac{\text{expected value of profit}}{\text{purchase price of stock}}$$

$$= \frac{\$0.59}{\$18.00} = 3.2\%$$

This was still better than most bank accounts but hardly exciting.

What *was* exciting about Amazon.com's IPO was the upside potential for growth. If e-commerce really took off, Amazon.com might generate exceptional profits, not a mere dollar or two. As people saw this potential unfold, they would surely want to buy shares of the company. As they did, the share price would increase, generating capital gains for those who bought earlier.

The prospect of such capital gains enticed a lot of stock buyers. On the first day of trading, the price of Amazon.com shares rose from the IPO price of $18 to as high as $30. Within a year the stock was selling for nearly $100. Within two years' time, the stock rose to $200 a share. This meteoric rise in the price of Amazon's stock represented a huge *capital gain* for its shareholders. The people who paid $200 a share were hoping for still higher share prices.

That post-IPO rise in Amazon's stock price had no direct effect on the company. A corporation reaps the proceeds of stock sales only when it sells shares to the public (the initial public offering). After the IPO, the company's stock is traded among individuals in the "aftermarket." Virtually all the trading activity on major stock exchanges consists of such aftermarket sales. Mr. Dow sells his Amazon share to Ms. Jones, who may later sell them to Destiny's Child. Such *secondary* trades may take place at the New York Stock Exchange (NYSE) on Wall Street. More and more secondary trading, however, occurs in computerized over-the-counter markets, or at other exchanges, such as Canada's Toronto Stock Exchange (TSX), with its listings of over 1,300 companies, and the U.S.'s National Association of Securities Dealers Automated Quotations system (NASDAQ) with its listing of over 3,000 companies.

Market Fluctuations

The price of a stock at any moment is the outcome of supply-and-demand interactions. I wouldn't mind owning a piece of Amazon.com. But since I think the current share price is too high, I'll buy the stock only if the price falls substantially. Even though I'm not buying any Amazon stock now, I'm part of the *market demand*. That is, all the people who are willing and able to buy Amazon.com stock at *some* price are included in the demand curve in Figure 14.3. The cheaper the stock, the more people will want to buy it, *ceteris paribus*. The opposite is true on the supply side of the market: Ever-higher prices are necessary to induce more shareholders to part with their shares.

Changing Expectations. In 2000–2001, investors reevaluated the profit prospects for Amazon.com and other dot.com companies. Several years of experience had shown that earning profits in e-commerce wasn't so easy. Projections of sales growth and future profits were sharply reduced. When Amazon.com failed to meet even those reduced expectations, its stock fell 20 percent in a single day. Figure 14.3 illustrates how this happened. The bad news reduced the demand for Amazon.com stock and increased the willingness of existing shareholders to sell. Such **changes in expectations imply shifts in supply and demand for a company's stock.** As Figure 14.3 illustrates, these combined shifts sent Amazon.com stock plummeting.

As Table 14.3 shows, the share price was $7.64 when the market closed on October 24, 2001. On that day, over 6 million shares of Amazon.com stock were traded. Along the path to the equilibrium closing price—the last trade of the day—the stock price fluctuated between a low ("Lo") of $7.15 and a high ("Hi") of $7.67. The price of Amazon.com stock fluctuated much more than that during the previous 52 weeks. As

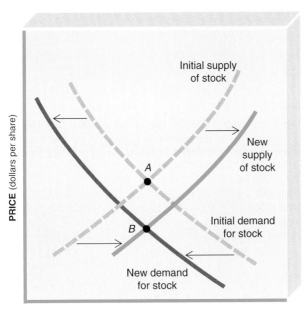

QUANTITY OF STOCK (shares per day)

FIGURE 14.3
Changing Expectations

The supply and demand for stocks is fueled in part by expectations of future profits. When investors concluded that Amazon.com's future profit potential wasn't so great, demand for the stock decreased, supply increased, and the share price fell.

Table 14.3 documents, the stock traded as high as $40.88 and as low as $5.51 during the year. What accounts for these dramatic price fluctuations?

The Value of Information. The abrupt rise and later plunge in the price of Amazon.com stock highlights a critical dimension of financial markets, namely, the value of information. People who bought Amazon.com shares on the way up were poorly informed about the prospects for e-commerce sales and profits. Had they known

TABLE 14.3
Reading Stock Quotes

The financial pages of the daily newspaper summarize the trading activity in corporate stocks. The following quotation summarizes trading in AT&T and Amazon.com shares on October 24, 2001.

52 Weeks							Vol				Net
Hi	Lo	Stock	Sym	Div	Yld%	P/E	100s	Hi	Lo	Close	Chg
25.15	14.75	ATT	T	.15	0.8	dd	142327	17.92	17.51	17.75	−.15
40.88	5.51	Amazon	AMZN	—	—	dd	66976	7.67	7.15	7.64	−1.91

The information provided by this quotation includes:
52-Weeks Hi and Lo: The highest and lowest prices paid for a share of stock in the previous year.
Stock: The name of the corporation whose shares are being traded.
Sym: The symbol used as a shorthand description for the stock.
Div: A dividend is the amount of profit paid out by the corporation in the preceding year for each share of stock.
Yld%: The yield is the dividend paid per share divided by the price of a share.
P/E: The price of the stock (P) divided by the earnings (profit) per share (E). This indicates how much a purchaser is effectively paying for each dollar of profits. Because Amazon.com had a loss in 1998, the P/E ratio is not computed.
Vol 100s: The number of shares traded in hundreds.
Hi: The highest price paid for a share of stock on the previous day.
Lo: The lowest price paid for a share of stock on the previous day.
Close: The price paid in the last trade of the day as the market was closing.
Net Chg: The change in the closing price yesterday vs. the previous day's closing price.

Growth Undergirds Google's Pricey IPO But Can It Keep Up?

INVESTORS HAD BETTER be feeling lucky about Google Inc.'s growth prospects.

Now that the Internet-search company has trotted out its own $35 billion or so estimate of its value, the challenge for those pondering whether to participate in Google's initial public offering of stock next month is to figure out how much longer the good times will last. Sure, the company is making money hand over fist, and it has juicy margins and profits that are expanding rapidly. But with its IPO shares likely to begin trading at expensive levels, Google is attractive only if it can maintain impressive growth.

In the near term, the acceleration likely will continue, analysts and industry specialists say. But some are concerned that growth in the search business and related advertising is slowing from its heady clip. Fewer people will be going online for the first time, they say, and those already on the Internet probably won't radically increase the number of searches they conduct. In the long run, Google likely will have to prove that it can continue to come up with new ways to profit from its dominant position in the Web-search business for its shares to be big winners.

"It all depends on how fast the growth momentum will come down," says Mark Mahaney, an analyst at American Technology Research, who says investors should put in bids of $115 a share for Google. "The question is how gracefully it exits hyper-growth."

Throughout the search industry there are indications that growth has slowed recently. Rival Internet titan Yahoo Inc., for instance, said earlier this month that the number of search queries was "pretty flattish" during the second quarter compared with the first period. Growth in the current quarter also should be flat, the company indicated. Ask Jeeves Inc., another search company, has seen its share price drop about 30% in the past four months amid investor worries.

—Gregory Zuckerman and Kevin J. Delaney

Analysis: People who buy a company's stock are betting on future sales and profits. If expectations change, the price of the stock will change as well.

WEB NOTE
You can retrieve the latest news about a stock on the Toronto Stock Exchange at www.tsx.com.

profits would be so hard to make, they wouldn't have paid so much for the stock. People who bought Google's IPO in 2004 hoped they wouldn't suffer a similar disappointment (see the Applications box). As it turns out, the market price for Google (stock symbol: GOOG) closed at $100.33 on its opening day and by January 2007 had hit the $500 mark—a 400 per cent increase in two and a half years.

The evident value of information raises a question of access. Do some people have better information than others? Do they get their information fairly? Or do they have "inside" sources (such as company technicians, managers, directors) who give them preferential access to information? If so, these insiders would have an unfair advantage in the marketplace and could alter the distribution of income and wealth in their favour. This is the kind of "insider trading" that got Martha Stewart into trouble (and jail).

The value of information also explains the demand for information services. People pay hundreds and even thousands of dollars for newsletters, wire services, and online computer services that provide up-to-date information on companies and markets. They also pay for the services of investment bankers, advisers, and brokers to help keep them informed. These services help disseminate information quickly, thereby helping financial markets operate efficiently (that is, they provide the best possible signal of changing resource values).

Booms and Busts. If stock markets are so efficient at computing the present value of future profits, why does the entire market make abrupt moves every so often? Fundamentally, the same factors that determine the price of a single stock influence the broader stock market averages as well. An increase in interest rates, for example, raises the opportunity cost of holding stocks. Hence, higher interest rates should cause stock prices to fall, *ceteris paribus.* Stocks might decline even further if higher interest rates are expected to curtail investment and consumption, thus reducing future sales and profits. Such a double whammy could cause the whole stock market to tumble.

Other factors also affect the relative desirability of holding stock. Federal budget and deficit decisions, monetary policy, consumer confidence, business investment plans, international trade patterns, and new inventions are just a few of the factors that may alter present and future profits. These ***broad changes in the economic outlook tend to push all stock prices up or down at the same time.***

Broad changes in the economic outlook, however, seldom occur overnight. Moreover, these changes are rarely of a magnitude that could precipitate a stock market boom or bust. In reality, the stock market often changes more abruptly than the economic outlook. These exaggerated movements in the stock market are caused by sudden and widespread changes in *expectations.* Keep in mind that the value of the stock depends on anticipated *future* profits and expectations for interest rates and the economic outlook. No elements of the future are certain. Instead, people use present clues to try to discern the likely course of future events. In other words, ***all information must be filtered through people's expectations.***

The central role of expectations implies that the economy can change more gradually than the stock market. If, for example, interest rates rise, market participants may regard the increase as temporary or inconsequential: Their expectations for the future may not change. If interest rates keep rising, however, investors may have greater doubts. At some point, the market participants may revise their expectations. Stock prices may falter, triggering an adjustment in expectations. A herding instinct may surface, sending expectations for stock prices abruptly lower (see cartoon).

Shocks. The September 11, 2001, terrorist attacks on the World Trade Center and the Pentagon illustrated how much faster expectations can change than does the real economy. The attacks paralyzed the U.S. economy for several days and made people fearful

WEB NOTE

Think you can make a profit in the stock market? Try the Stock Market Game, an electronic simulation of Wall Street trading, at www.smg2000.org.

Just a normal day at the nation's most important financial institution . . .

Analysis: Sudden changes in expectations can substantially alter stock prices.

Market Battered, but Intact

The Dow Jones industrial average suffered its worst one-day point loss ever on Monday as the stock market was swamped with selling on the first day of trading since last week's terrorist attacks.

Forecasts for today's trading were hard to find. In contrast, the market's first-day sell-off was widely expected in the aftermath of terrorists crashing hijacked airliners into the World Trade Center in New York and the Pentagon near Washington.

A sense that "everything had changed" pervaded Wall Street over the four days last week that the market was closed following the Sept. 11 attack. That was the longest market closing since World War I. Monday's session was a technical victory, given the damage to phone lines, computers and other equipment that had to be repaired. By day's end, the system handled a record 2.37 billion New York Stock Exchange shares.

The Dow's plunge of 684.81 points to 8,920.70 in Monday's trading eclipsed its previous one-day record loss of 617.78 points on April 14, 2000, at the beginning of the current bear market. But the percentage loss was not among the 10 worst of all time.

—Tom Walker

Source: *Atlanta Journal-Constitution*, September 18, 2001. Reprinted with permission. www.accessatlanta.com/ajc

Analysis: A sudden change in expectations can cause severe fluctuations in stock market values. The September 11 terrorist attacks created new uncertainties and reduced profit expectations.

for both their physical and economic security. People wanted to withdraw from the marketplace, taking their assets with them. When the U.S. stock exchanges opened several days after the attacks, stocks tumbled (see the Applications box). The Dow Jones industrial average (see Table 14.4) fell 685 points—its biggest loss ever. The NASDAQ Composite (Table 14.4) also plunged by more than 7 percent in one day. Within 10 days, the value of U.S. stocks had declined by more than $1 *trillion*.

The economy didn't fare nearly as badly as the stock market. Although the attacks were tragic in human terms, they made only a tiny dent in the economy's productive capacity. Quick responses by the government in defending the financial markets also dispelled fears of a financial meltdown. As people's worst fears subsided, the demand

Over 1,300 stocks are listed (traded) on the Toronto Stock Exchange (TSX), another 1,600 listed on the New York Stock Exchange (NYSE), and many times that are traded in other stock markets throughout the world. To gauge changes in so many stocks, people refer to various indexes such as Canada's S&P/TSX Composite Index and U.S.'s Dow Jones Industrial Average. These types of indexes help us keep track of the market's ups and downs. Some of the most frequently quoted indexes are

S&P/TSX Composite Index: An average of over 250 companies traded on the TSX. Membership is based on size and liquidity constraints.

S&P/TSX 60 Index: An average of 60 largest companies traded on the TSX. Membership is based on market capitalization (current stock price × outstanding shares).

Dow Jones Industrial Average: Arithmetic average of prices of 30 blue-chip industrial stocks traded on NYSE and NASDAQ. Membership is based on the largest, most liquid listed stocks.

New York Stock Exchange Composite Index: The "Big Board" index, which includes all 1,600-plus stocks traded on NYSE.

NASDAQ Composite: Measures all NASDAQ domestic- and international-based common type stocks (3,000+ companies). Companies must be exclusively listed on NASDAQ.

Nikkei 225: An index of 225 stocks traded on the Tokyo stock market. Membership is a function of liquidity and adequate representation of structural changes in the economy based on six sectors: technology, financial, consumer goods, materials, capital goods, transportation, and utilities.

TABLE 14.4
Stock Market Averages

for stocks picked up again. Within a month's time, the stock markets had fully recovered their post-attack losses. Along the way, however, changing expectations caused wild gyrations in stock prices.

Resource Allocations

Although it's fascinating and sometimes fun to watch stock market gyrations, we shouldn't lose sight of the *economic* role of financial markets. Columbus needed *real* resources—ships, men, equipment—for his expeditions. Five centuries later, Amazon.com also needed real resources—computers, labour, warehouse space—to get underway. To find the necessary economic resources, both Columbus and Amazon.com had to convince society to reallocate resources from other activities to their new ventures.

Financial markets facilitate resource reallocations. In Columbus's case, the Genoese bankers lent the funds that Columbus used to buy scarce resources. The funds obtained from Amazon.com's 1997 initial public offering served the same purpose. In both cases, the funds obtained in the financial markets helped change the mix of output. If the financial markets hadn't supplied the necessary funding, neither Columbus nor Amazon.com would have been able to get underway. The available resources would have been used to produce other goods.

14.4 THE BOND MARKET

The bond market is another mechanism for transferring the pool of national savings into the hands of would-be spenders. It operates much like the stock market. The major difference is the kind of paper traded. *In the stock market, people buy and sell shares of corporate ownership. In the bond market, people buy and sell promissory notes (IOUs).* A **bond** is simply an IOU, a written promise to repay a loan. The bond itself specifies the terms of repayment, noting both the amount of interest to be paid each year and the maturity date (the date on which the borrower is to repay the entire debt). The borrower may be a corporation (corporate bonds), local governments (municipal bonds), provincial governments (provincial bonds), the federal government (Treasury bills, Canada savings bonds), or other institutions.

bond: A certificate acknowledging a debt and the amount of interest to be paid each year until repayment; an IOU.

Bond Issuance

A bond is first issued when an institution wants to borrow money. Recall the situation Amazon.com faced in 1997. The company needed additional funds to expand its Internet operations. Rather than sell equity shares in itself, Amazon.com could have *borrowed* funds. The advantage of borrowing funds rather than issuing stock is that the owners can keep control of their company. *Lenders aren't owners, but shareholders are.* The disadvantage of borrowing funds is that the company gets saddled with a repayment schedule. Lenders want to be paid back—with interest. For a new company like Amazon.com, the burden of interest payments may be too great.

Ignoring these problems momentarily, let's assume that Amazon.com decided in 1997 to borrow funds rather than sell stock in itself. To do so, it would have *issued* bonds. This simply means that it would have printed formal IOUs called bonds. Typically, each bond certificate would have a **par value** (face value) of $1,000. The bond certificate would also specify the rate of interest to be paid and the promised date of repayment. An Amazon.com bond issued in 1997, for example, might specify repayment in 10 years, with annual interest payments of $100. The individual who bought the bond from Amazon.com would lend $1,000 for 10 years and receive annual interest payments of $100. Thus, *the initial bond purchaser lends funds directly to the bond issuer.* The borrower (such as Amazon.com, General Motors, or the Minister of Finance) can then use those funds to acquire real resources. Thus, the bond market also functions as a financial intermediary, transferring available savings (wealth) to those who want to acquire more resources (invest).

par value: The face value of a bond; the amount to be repaid when the bond is due.

As in the case of IPOs of stock, the critical issue here is the *price* of the bond. How many people are willing and able to lend funds to the company? What rate of interest will they charge?

default: Failure to make scheduled payments of interest or principal on a bond.

coupon rate: Interest rate set for a bond at time of issuance.

Bond Trading

liquidity: The ability of an asset to be converted into cash.

Current Yields

As we observed in Figure 14.2, the quantity of loanable funds supplied depends on the interest rate. At low interest rates no one is willing to lend funds to the company. Why lend your savings to a risky venture like Amazon.com when more secure bonds and even banks pay higher interest rates? Amazon.com might not sell enough books and may later **default** (not pay) on its obligations. Potential lenders would want to be compensated for this extra risk with above-average interest rates, that is, a risk premium. Remember that lenders don't share in any profits Amazon.com might earn. Hence, they'd want a hefty premium to compensate them for the risk of default.

Suppose that market participants will lend the desired amount of money to Amazon.com only at 16 percent interest. In this case, Amazon.com may agree to pay an interest rate—the so-called **coupon rate**—of 16 percent to secure start-up funding of $50 million. That means Amazon.com agrees to pay $160 of interest each year for every $1,000 borrowed and to repay the entire $50 million at the end of 10 years.

Once a bond has been issued, the initial lenders don't have to wait 10 years to get their money back. They can't go back to the company and demand early repayment, but they can sell their bonds to someone else. This **liquidity** is an important consideration for prospective bondholders. If a person had no choice but to wait 10 years for repayment, he or she might be less willing to buy a bond (lend funds). *By facilitating resales, the bond market increases the availability of funds to new ventures and other borrowers.* As is the case with stocks, most of the action in the bond markets consists of such aftermarket trades, that is, the buying and selling of bonds issued at some earlier time. The company that first issued the bonds doesn't participate in these trades.

The portfolio decision in the bond market is motivated by the same factors that influence stock purchases. The *opportunity cost* of buying and selling bonds is the best alternative rate of return—for example, the interest rate on other bonds or money market mutual funds. *Expectations* also play a role, in gauging both likely changes in opportunity costs and the ability of the borrower to redeem (pay off) the bond when it's due. *Changes in expectations or opportunity costs shift the bond supply and demand curves,* thereby altering market interest rates.

We've assumed that Amazon.com would have had to offer 16 percent interest to induce enough people to lend the company (buy bonds worth) $50 million. This was far higher than the 6 percent the Canadian government was paying on its bonds (borrowed funds) because lenders feared that Amazon.com might not be able to convert its great ideas into actual sales in a timely and profitable manner. In lending their funds to Amazon.com, they incur a risk of never getting their wealth back.

Suppose that Amazon.com actually got off to a good start and began selling books on the Web. The risk of a bond default would diminish, and people would be more willing to lend it funds. This change in the availability of loanable funds is illustrated in the rightward shift of the supply curve in Figure 14.4.

FIGURE 14.4
Shifts in Funds Supply

If lenders decide that a company's future is less risky, they will be more willing to lend it money or hold its bonds. This will raise the market price of existing bonds and lower current yields.

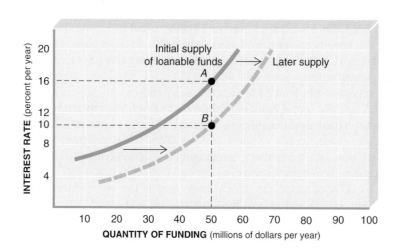

TABLE 14.5
Bond Price and Yields Move in Opposite Directions

Price of Bond	Annual Interest Payment	Current Yield
$ 600	$150	25.0%
800	150	18.8
1,000	150	15.0
1,200	150	12.5

The annual interest payments on a bond are fixed at the time of issuance. Accordingly, only the market (resale) prices of the bond can change. An increase in the price of the bond lowers its *effective* interest rate, or yield. The formula for computing the current yield on a bond is

$$\text{Current yield} = \frac{\text{annual interest payment}}{\text{market (resale) price of bond}}$$

Thus, higher bond prices imply lower yields (effective interest rates), as confirmed in the table above. Bond prices and yields vary with changes in expectations and opportunity costs.

The quotation below shows how changing bond prices and yields are reported. This General Motors (GM) 30-year bond was issue on July 15, 2003 with a coupon rate (nominal interest) of $8^{3/8}$ percent. Hence, GM promised to pay $83.75 in interest each year until it redeemed the (paid off) $1,000 bond on July 15, 2033. One year later, in July 2004, the market price of the bond was $1,032.4 (103.24), creating a yield of 8.112 percent. In June 2007, however, the market price of the bond dropped to $952.50 (95.25), giving a yield of 8.793 percent

Bond: GM $8^{3/8}$ 33		
Date	Price	Current Yield
July 2003	100.00	8.375
July 2004	103.24	8.112
June 2007	95.25	8.793

According to the new supply curve in Figure 14.4, Amazon.com could now borrow $50 million at 10 percent interest (point *B*) rather than paying 16 percent (point *A*). Unfortunately, Amazon.com already borrowed the funds and is obliged to continue paying $160 per year in interest on each bond. Hence, the company doesn't benefit directly from the supply shift.

The change in the equilibrium value of Amazon.com bonds must show up somewhere, however. People who hold Amazon.com bonds continue to get $160 per year in interest (16 percent of $1,000). Now there are lots of people who would be willing to lend funds to Amazon.com at that rate. These people want to hold Amazon.com bonds themselves. To get them, they'll have to buy the bonds in the market from existing bondholders. Thus, the *increased willingness to lend funds is reflected in an increased demand for bonds.* This increased demand will push up the price of Amazon.com bonds. As bond prices rise, their implied effective interest rate **(current yield)** falls. Table 14.5 illustrates this relationship.

Changing bond prices and yields are important market signals for resource allocation. In our example, the rising price of Amazon.com's bonds reflects increased optimism for the company's sales prospects. The collective assessment of the marketplace is that e-commerce will be a profitable venture. The increase in the price of Amazon.com bonds will make it easier and less costly for the company to borrow additional funds. The reverse scenario unfolded in 2000–2001. When investors concluded that e-commerce wasn't going to generate fast profits, the supply of funds to dot.coms dried up. That supply shift made it more difficult for firms to survive, much less expand e-commerce capacity.

current yield: The rate of return on a bond; the annual interest payment divided by the bond's price.

SUMMARY

- The primary economic function of financial markets is to help allocate scarce resources to desired uses. They do this by providing access to the pool of national savings for entrepreneurs, investors, and other would-be spenders.
- Financial markets enable individuals to manage risk by holding different kinds of assets. Financial intermediaries also reduce the costs of information and search, thereby increasing market efficiency.
- Future returns on investments must be discounted to present value. The present discounted value (PDV) of a future payment adjusts for forgone interest accrual.
- Future returns are also uncertain. The *expected* value of future payments must also reflect the risk of nonpayment.

- Shares of stock represent ownership in a corporation. The shares are initially issued to raise funds and are then traded on the stock exchanges.
- Changes in the value of a corporation's stock reflect changing expectations and opportunity costs. Share price changes, in turn, act as market signals to direct more or fewer resources to a company.
- Bonds are IOUs issued when a company (or government agency) borrows funds. After issuance, bonds are traded in the aftermarket (secondary market).
- The interest (coupon) rate on a bond is fixed at the time of issuance. The price of the bond itself, however, varies with changes in expectations (perceived risk) and opportunity cost. Yields vary inversely with bond prices.

Key Terms

financial intermediary 303
risk premium 305
present discounted value (PDV) 306
expected value 308
corporation 309
corporate stock 309

dividend 310
retained earnings 310
capital gain 310
initial public offering (IPO) 310
price/earnings (P/E) ratio 311
bond 317

par value 317
default 318
coupon rate 318
liquidity 318
current yield 319

Questions for Discussion

1. If there were no organized financial markets, how would an entrepreneur acquire resources to develop and produce a new product?
2. Why would anyone buy shares of a corporation that had no profits and paid no dividends? What's the highest price a person would pay for such a stock?
3. Why would anyone sell a bond for less than its par value?
4. If you could finance a new venture with either a stock issue or bonds, which option would you choose? What are their respective (dis)advantages?
5. Why is it considered riskier to own stock in a software company than to hold Government of Canada savings bonds? Which asset will generate a higher return?
6. How does a successful IPO affect WHAT, HOW, and FOR WHOM the economy produces?
7. What considerations might have created the difference between the coupon rate and current yield on GM bonds (Table 14.5)?
8. What is the price of Google stock now? What has caused the change in price since its 2004 IPO at $85 a share (Applications, p. 314)?

EXERCISES

PROBLEMS   The Student Problem Set to accompany this chapter can be found at the end of the book.

WEB ACTIVITIES   Web Activities to accompany this chapter can be found on the Online Learning Centre at **http://www.mcgrawhill.ca/olc/schiller**.

Distributional Issues

Efficiency and equity are central concerns of every society. Collectively, we seek to get as much output as possible from the resources we use. But we also care about how that output is distributed. We want some sort of fairness in the distribution of goods and services; that is to say, we want both *efficiency* in the production of goods and *equity* in their distribution. Unfortunately, these goals may conflict. If we use taxes to redistribute incomes, incentives to produce may be impaired. Similarly, if we provide income support for the poor, people may choose to work less. Chapters 15 and 16 examine these issues.

Taxes: Equity vs. Efficiency

Insistence on carving the pie into equal slices would shrink the size of the pie.
That fact poses the trade-off between economic equality and economic efficiency.
—Arthur M. Okun

S teve Jobs, chairman of Apple Computer, got a $90 million private jet as a pay bonus in 2001. That would have been enough income to lift nearly 50,000 poor Americans out of poverty. But Jobs didn't share his good fortune with those people, and they remained poor.

The market mechanism generated both Steve Jobs's extraordinary income and that of so many poor families. Is this the way we want the basic FOR WHOM question to be settled? Should some people own vast fortunes while others seek shelter in abandoned cars? Or do the inequalities that emerge in product and factor markets violate our notions of equity? If the market's answer to the FOR WHOM question isn't right, some form of government intervention to redistribute incomes may be desired.

The tax system is the government's primary lever for redistributing income. But taxing Peter to pay Paul may affect more than just income shares. If taxed too heavily, Peter may stop producing so much. Paul, too, may work less if assured of government support. The end result may be *less* total income to share. In other words: *Taxes affect production as well as distribution. This creates a potential trade-off between the goal of equity and the goal of efficiency.*

This chapter examines this equity-efficiency trade-off, with the following questions as a guide:

- **How are incomes distributed in Canada?**
- **How do taxes alter that distribution?**
- **How do taxes affect the rate and mix of output?**

After addressing these questions, we examine the allure of a "flat tax."

LEARNING OBJECTIVES

By the end of this chapter, you should be able to:

15.1   Define personal income, in-kind income, and wealth

15.2   Explain the economic importance of distribution of income and wealth

15.3   Explain how the Lorenz curve and Gini coefficient capture income inequality

15.4   Define a progressive tax, a regressive tax, and marginal tax rates

15.5   Explain how a progressive tax system reduces income inequality

15.6   Define vertical and horizontal equity, nominal tax rates, and effective tax rates

15.7   Explain how tax deductions, exemptions, and credits create equity concerns

15.8   Define tax incidence and understand its application to payroll taxes

15.9   Explain the trade-off between efficiency and equity associated with income redistribution

15.10   Discuss the arguments for and against the implementation of a flat tax system

15.1 WHAT IS *INCOME?*

Before examining the distribution of income in Canada, let's decide what to count as *income.* There are several possibilities. The most obvious choice is **personal income (PI)**—the flow of annual income received by households before payment of personal income taxes. Personal income includes wages and salaries, corporate dividends, rent, interest, pension benefits, welfare payments, and any other form of money income.

Personal income isn't a complete measure of income, however. Many goods and services are distributed directly as **in-kind income** rather than through market purchases. Many poor people, for example, live in public housing and pay little or no rent. As a consequence, they receive a larger share of total output than their money incomes imply. According to the Canadian Association of Food Banks, more than 750,000 people received food from a food bank in *one month* of 2006 (see the Applications box). In the United States there is a food stamp program that enables people with low incomes to purchase more food than their money incomes would allow. In this sense, food bank and food stamp recipients are better off than the distribution of personal income implies.

In-kind benefits aren't limited to low-income households. Students who attend public schools, colleges, and universities consume more goods and services than they directly pay for; public education is subsidized by all taxpayers. In most provinces, people over the age of 65 ("seniors") receive some form of compensation to reduce the cost of prescription drugs. And middle-class workers get noncash fringe benefits

Personal Income

personal income (PI): Income received by households before payment of personal taxes.

in-kind income: Goods and services received directly, without payment in a market transaction.

APPLICATIONS

More Working Poor Relying on Food Banks Despite an 8.5% Drop in Overall Use

OTTAWA, November 28, 2006—Even with employment, Canadians are struggling to stay above the poverty line and are increasingly turning to food banks to make ends meet, according to HungerCount 2006, the latest Canadian Association of Food Banks (CAFB) study.

StockFood Creative/Getty Images.

Charles Seiden, CAFB Executive Director, says the annual study shows the percentage of food bank clients who are part of Canada's workforce this year is 13.4%, up from 13.1% last year. "This increase has occurred in spite a welcome 8.5% drop in overall food bank use."

According to the survey, employed individuals continue to comprise the second largest group of food bank clients after social assistance recipients, which account for 53.5% of food bank clients nationally.

The study also showed children account for 41% of the estimated 753,458 food bank clients, although they make up only about a quarter of Canada's population.

A closer look at the drop in food bank recipients reveals that despite the overall decrease in food bank use "there was a 9% increase in the number of prepared meals served since last year"—food banks reported that the same clients were served more often.

Source: Canadian Association of Food Banks, November 28, 2006, http://www.cafb-acba.ca/english/1361.html.

Analysis: Regardless of whether their primary source of income was from employment or social assistance, more than 3/4 of a million Canadians received in-kind food benefits from food banks in 2006.

FIGURE 15.1

International Wealth Inequality

The top 10% of the wealthiest Canadians account for 53% of Canada's total wealth. This is slightly above the average of the 20 countries reporting information on wealth distribution.

Source: World Institute for Development Economics Research. James B. Davies, Susanna Sandstrom, Anthony Shorrocks, and Edward N. Wolf, International Wealth Inequality, Table 9, "Wealth shares for countries with wealth distribution data, official exchange rate basis," *The World Distribution of Household Wealth* (December 2006) p. 46. Used with permission.

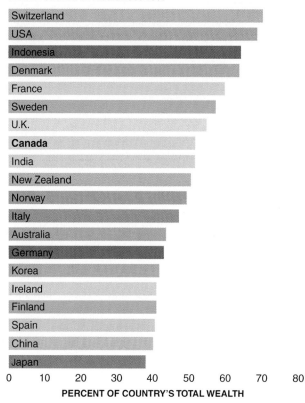

Wealth Shares of Wealthiest 10%

PERCENT OF COUNTRY'S TOTAL WEALTH

WEB NOTE

To view the latest issue of HungerCount, view the Canadian Association of Food Bank's Web site at http://www.cafb-acba.ca/ and look for "Research Studies."

(like health insurance, paid vacations, pension contributions) that don't show up in their paycheques.

So long as some goods and services needn't be purchased in the marketplace, *the distribution of money income isn't synonymous with the distribution of goods and services.* This measurement problem is particularly important when comparisons are made over time.

While Canada does not have an official poverty line, Statistics Canada's Low-Income Cut-offs (LICOs) are often cited as a benchmark for the poverty threshold. In 1980, the percentage of persons of low income (after tax, based on the 1992 Family Expenditure Survey) was 11.6 percent; in 2004 the percentage was relatively constant at 11.2 percent. At first glance, it would appear that not much has changed over the past twenty-five years. During this period, however, this percentage ranged from 10.2 to 15.7 percent. As Kerr and Michalski (2005) point out, an individual's "real" income or purchasing power can be influenced by three general events: (i) *demographic* factors (e.g., type of family structure, new immigrant, etc.), (ii) *economic* factors (e.g., availability of jobs and wage rates), and (iii) *political* factors (e.g., eligibility criteria for transfer payments).[1]

These political factors play an important role identifying the difference between the distribution of money income and the distribution of goods and services. In an effort to address budget deficits, both federal and provincial governments have reduced income support programs. Over this period, the number of food banks and charitable organizations that provide meals and other basic necessities have increased—effectively replacing the government income supports with in-kind benefits.

[1]Don Kerr and Joseph Michalski, "Income Poverty in Canada: Recent Trends Among Canadian Families 1981–2002," Discussion Paper no. 05-02, University of Western Ontario, 2005.

If our ultimate concern is access to goods and services, the distribution of wealth is also important. **Wealth** refers to the market value of assets (such as houses and bank accounts) people own. Hence, *wealth represents a stock of potential purchasing power; income statistics tell us only how this year's flow of purchasing power (income) is being distributed.* Accordingly, to provide a complete answer to the FOR WHOM question, we have to know how wealth, as well as income, is distributed. In general, wealth tends to be distributed much less equally than income. Using recent data from Statistics Canada, a special report by the TD Bank Financial Group estimates that the richest 20% of Canadians account for 44% of after-tax income but almost 70% of the total wealth in the economy.[2] While this wealth inequality might appear alarming to some, Canada ranks in the middle of the pack when compared to other countries reporting wealth distribution (see Figure 15.1).

15.2 THE SIZE DISTRIBUTION OF INCOME

Although incomes aren't a perfect measure of access to goods and services (much less happiness), they're the best single indicator of the FOR WHOM outcomes. The **size distribution of income** tells us how large a share of total personal income is received by various households, grouped by income class. Imagine for the moment that the entire population is lined up in order of income, with lowest-income recipients in front and highest-income recipients at the end of the line. We want to know how much income the people in front get in comparison with those at the back.

Table 15.1 shows the actual distribution of income in Canada in 2004. For this table, the entire population is sorted into five groups of equal size, ranked by income. Accordingly, the richest Canadians are in the top **income quintile;** the poor are in the lowest income quintile.

As a group, the lowest income quintile received, on average, an after-tax income of $12,200 in 2004. This represented only 4.8 percent of total after-tax income, despite the fact that it included 20 percent of all households (the lowest fifth). Thus the **income share** of the people in the lowest group (4.8%) was much smaller than their proportion in the total population (20%).

Wealth

wealth: The market value of assets.

size distribution of income: The way total personal income is divided up among households or income classes.

income quintile: One-fifth of the population, rank-ordered by income (e.g., lowest fifth).

income share: The proportion of total income received by a particular group.

TABLE 15.1
The Distribution of Income in Canada (2004)

The richest fifth of Canadian households receives about 45% of all the income—a considerable slice of the income pie. By contrast, the poorest fifth receives a mere sliver.

Source: Adapted from Statistics Canada CANSIM database table 202-0701. Statistics Canada information is used with the permission of Statistics Canada.

Income Quintile	Average Total Income (dollars)	Share of Average Total Income (percent)	Average After-Tax Income (dollars)	Share of Average After-Tax Income (percent)
Lowest fifth (poorest)	12,700	4.2	12,200	4.8
Second fifth	29,400	9.6	26,900	10.7
Third fifth	47,400	15.6	41,200	16.4
Fourth fifth	72,300	23.7	60,400	24.0
Highest fifth (richest)	143,200	46.9	110,700	44.0

[2]TD Financial Bank Group, "Lifestyles of the Rich and Unequal: An Investigation into Wealth Inequality in Canada," TD Economics Special Report, December 13, 2006. http://www.td.com/economics/special/dt1206_wealth.pdf.

FIGURE 15.2

The Lorenz Curve

The Lorenz curve illustrates the extent of income inequality. If all incomes were equal, each fifth of the population would receive one-fifth of total income. In this case, the diagonal line through point *C* would represent the cumulative size distribution of income. In reality, incomes aren't distributed equally. Point *A*, for example, indicates that the 20 percent of the population with the lowest income receives only 4.8 percent of total income.

Source: Table 15.1.

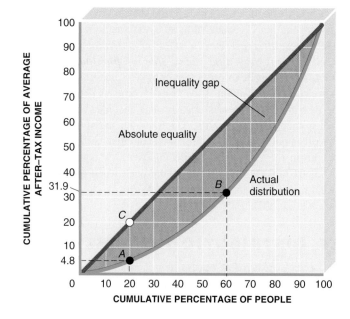

The Lorenz Curve

Lorenz curve: A graphic illustration of the cumulative size distribution of income; contrasts complete equality with the actual distribution of income.

Gini coefficient: A mathematical summary of inequality based on the Lorenz curve.

Moving to the other extreme, we observe that the top quintile received, on average, an after-tax income of $110,700 in 2004. More importantly, we see that the income share of individuals in this highest quintile (44%) is considerably larger than their proportion in the total population.

Similar to the wealth inequality comparisons in Figure 15.1, the distribution of income in Canada is not unique to our country: the distribution of income mirrors the distribution of wealth in most nations, but typically to a lesser degree.

The size distribution of income provides the kind of information we need to determine how total income (and output) is distributed. The **Lorenz curve** is a convenient summary of that information; it is a graphical illustration of the size distribution.

Figure 15.2 is a Lorenz curve for Canada. Our lineup of individuals is on the horizontal axis, with the lowest-income earners on the left. On the vertical axis we depict the cumulative share of average after-tax income received by people in our income line. Consider the lowest quintile of the distribution again. They're represented on the horizontal axis at 20 percent. If their share of income was identical to their share of population, they'd get 20 percent of total income. This would be represented by point *C* in the figure. In fact, the lowest quintile gets only 4.8 percent, as indicated by point *A*. Point *B* tells us that the *cumulative* share of income received by the lowest *three*-fifths of the population was 31.9 percent.

The really handy feature of the Lorenz curve is the way it contrasts the actual distribution of income with an absolutely equal one. If incomes were distributed equally, the first 20 percent of the people in line would be getting exactly 20 percent of all income. In that case, the Lorenz curve would run through point *C*. Indeed, the Lorenz "curve" would be a straight line along the diagonal. The actual Lorenz curve lies below the diagonal because our national income isn't distributed equally. In fact, the area between the diagonal and the actual Lorenz curve (the shaded area in Figure 15.2) is a convenient measure of the degree of inequality. ***The greater the area between the Lorenz curve and the diagonal, the more inequality exists.***

The visual summary of inequality the Lorenz curve provides is also expressed in a mathematical relationship. The ratio of the shaded area in Figure 15.2 to the area of the triangle formed by the diagonal is called the **Gini coefficient.** The higher the Gini coefficient, the greater the degree of inequality. Between 1981 and 2004, the Gini coefficient rose from 0.348 to 0.393. In other words, the shaded area in Figure 15.2 expanded by about 13 percent, indicating *increased* inequality. Although the

Robert Graysmith, © Graysmith.

Analysis: An increase in the size of the economic pie doesn't ensure everyone a larger slice. A goal of the tax system is to attain a fairer distribution of the economic pie.

size of the economic pie (real GDP) approximately *doubled* between 1981 and 2004, some people's slices got a lot bigger while other people saw little improvement, or even less (see cartoon).

To many people, large and increasing inequality represents a form of *market failure:* The market is generating a suboptimal (unfair) answer to the FOR WHOM question. As in other instances of market failure, the government is called on to intervene. The policy lever in this case is taxes. By levying higher taxes on the rich and providing more generous transfer payments to the poor, the government could promote greater equality.

The Call for Intervention

15.3 THE FEDERAL INCOME TAX

The federal income tax is designed for this redistributional purpose. Specifically, the federal income tax is designed to be **progressive**—that is, to impose higher tax *rates* on high incomes than on low ones. Progressivity is achieved by imposing increasing **marginal tax rates** on higher incomes. The *marginal* tax rate refers to the tax rate imposed on the last (marginal) dollar of income.

In 2006, the tax code specified the four tax brackets shown in Table 15.2. For an individual with a (taxable) income less than $36,378, the (federal marginal) tax rate was 15.25 percent. Any income in excess of $36,378 was taxed at a higher rate of

progressive tax: A tax system in which tax rates rise as incomes rise.

marginal tax rate: The tax rate imposed on the last (marginal) dollar of income.

Tax Bracket (Taxable Income)	Marginal Tax Rate
$0–$36,378	15.25%
$36,379–$72,756	22%
$72,757–$118,285	26%
over $118,285	29%

Source: Canada Revenue Agency (Web site), http://www.cra-arc.gc.ca/tax/individuals/faq/2006_rate-e.html. Accessed June 21, 2007. Reproduced with permission of the Minister of Public Works and Government Services Canada, 2006.

TABLE 15.2
Progressive Taxes

The federal income tax is progressive because it levies higher tax rates on higher incomes. The 2006 marginal tax rate started out at 15.25 percent for incomes below $36,378 and rose to 29 percent for incomes above $118,285.

22 percent. If an individual's income rose above $72,756, the amount between $72,756 and $118,285 was taxed at 26 percent. Any income greater than $118,285 was taxed at 29 percent.

To understand the efficiency and equity effects of taxes, we must distinguish between the *marginal* tax rate and the *average* tax rate. A person who earned $150,000 of taxable income in 2006 paid the 29 percent tax only on the income in excess of $118,285, that is, the last (marginal) $31,715. To find the average tax rate, we must calculate the income tax paid at the three tax rates assessed for income below $118,285.

Hence this individual's tax bill was

WEB NOTE

Current tax rate schedules are available from the Canada Revenue Agency at www.cra-arc.gc.ca/tax/individuals/faq/taxrates-e.html.

Marginal Tax Rate	Income		Tax
15.25% of	$ 36,378	=	$ 5,548
22% of	36,378	=	8,003
26% of	45,529	=	11,838
29% of	31,715	=	9,197
	$150,000		$34,586

The total tax of $34,586 represented only 23 percent of this individual's income. Hence, this person had a

- *Marginal* tax rate of 29 percent.
- *Average* tax rate of 23 percent.

The rationale behind this progressive system is to tax ever-larger percentages of higher incomes, thereby restraining inequalities. This makes the *after-tax* distribution of income more equal than the *before-tax* distribution. This is how *progressive taxes reduce inequality.*

Efficiency Concerns

Although the redistributive intent of a progressive tax system is evident, it raises concerns about efficiency. As noted in the chapter-opening quote, attempts to reslice the pie may end up reducing the size of the pie. The central issue here is incentives. Chapter 13 emphasized that the supply of labour is motivated by the pursuit of income. If the federal government takes away ever-larger chunks of income, won't that dampen the desire to work? If so, **the incentive to work more, produce more, or invest more is reduced by higher marginal tax rates.** This suggests that as marginal tax rates increase, total output shrinks, creating a basic conflict between the goals of equity (more progressive taxes) and efficiency (more output).

Tax Elasticity. How great the conflict is between the equity and efficiency depends on how responsive market participants are to higher tax rates. The Rolling Stones left Great Britain off their 1998–99 world tour because the British marginal tax rate was so high (see the World View box). Many other businesses relocate to low-tax nations for the same reason. For the typical household, however, the response to higher tax rates is limited to reducing hours worked. In all cases we can summarize the response with the **tax elasticity of supply;** that is,

tax elasticity of supply: The percentage change in quantity of hours supplied divided by the percentage change in tax rates.

$$\text{Tax elasticity of supply} = \frac{\text{\% change in quantity of hours supplied}}{\text{\% change in tax rate}}$$

If the tax elasticity of supply were zero, there'd be no conflict between equity and efficiency. But a zero tax elasticity would also imply that people would continue to work, produce, and invest even if the federal government took *all* their income in taxes. In today's range of taxes, the average household's elasticity of labour supply is

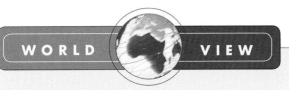

WORLD VIEW

Stones Keep England off '98 Tour to Avoid Tax

MUNICH, Germany, June 11—Mick Jagger said today that the Rolling Stones were disappointed they would not be playing in England this year, but the band looked forward to coming home for a series of concerts in 1999.

Lambasted by the British press for calling off a four-date tour at home because of a new tax law, members of the Stones said they opted out because the band stood to lose $19.6 million in taxes.

Under the previous tax code, Britons who lived and worked abroad for more than a year were exempt from British taxes on their earnings so long as they did not spend more than 62 days on native soil.

But the Labor government elected a year ago has scrapped that arrangement for everyone except some 10,000 seafarers. Now any citizen who works in Britain at all must pay tax on his or her entire year's earnings.

More than 300,000 tickets had been sold for the four British dates, which have been rescheduled for June 1999.

—Dorothee Stoewahse

Source: *The Washington Post*, June 12, 1998. © 1998 *The Washington Post*. Reprinted with permission. www.washingtonpost.com

Analysis: High tax rates deter people from supplying resources—in this case, staging a concert.

---

between −0.15 and −0.30. Hence, if tax rates go up by 20 percent, the quantity of labour supplied would decline by 3 to 6 percent.

As if the concern about efficiency weren't enough, critics also raise questions about how well the federal income tax promotes equity. What appears to be a fairly progressive tax in theory turns out to be a lot less progressive in practice. Hundreds of people with $1 million incomes pay no taxes. They aren't necessarily breaking any laws, just taking advantage of loopholes in the tax system.

Equity Concerns

Loopholes. The progressive ***tax rates described in the tax code apply to "taxable" income, not to all income.*** The so-called loopholes in the system arise from the way the Canada Revenue Agency defines taxable income. Computing taxable income under the current tax laws enables individuals to (i) exempt certain types of income, and (ii) subtract certain deductions from gross income; that is:

$$\text{Taxable Income} = \text{Gross Income} - \text{Non-taxable Income} - \text{Deductions}$$

Some of the non-taxable forms of income include gifts and inheritances, lottery winnings, strike pay, income of First Nations (if situated on a reserve), and capital gains on the sale of a taxpayer's principal residence. Some of the allowable deductions include contributions to Registered Retirement Savings Plans (RRSPs), child care expenses, and union and professional dues.

Once taxable income has been computed, the *tax payable before credits* is computed using the four tax brackets and tax rates in Table 15.2. Non-refundable tax credits are then deducted from tax payable before credits to reach the actual tax payable. These tax credits include a basic personal amount ($8,839 in 2006), Canadian Pension Plan (CPP) contributions, Employment Insurance (EI) premiums, tuition fees, education and medical expenses, charitable donations, and dividend tax credits (so that income is not taxed twice).

The purpose of these many *itemized deductions and tax credits* was to encourage specific economic activities and reduce potential hardship. The deduction for child care expenses, for example, helps relieve the financial burden for families where both spouses are working. The tax credit for tuition fees and education expenses not only partially relieves the burden of attending post-secondary institutions, but also encourages people to continue their education and training.

	Mr. Jones	Ms. Smith
1. Total income	$90,000	$30,000
2. Less exemptions and deductions	−$70,000	−$ 5,000
3. Taxable income	$20,000	$25,000
4. Tax	$ 2,400	$ 3,750
5. Nominal tax rate (= row 4 ÷ row 3)	12%	15%
6. Effective tax rate (= row 4 ÷ row 1)	2.7%	12.5%

vertical equity: Principle that people with higher incomes should pay more taxes.

horizontal equity: Principle that people with equal incomes should pay equal taxes.

nominal tax rate: Taxes paid divided by taxable income.

effective tax rate: Taxes paid divided by total income.

Whatever the merits of specific exemptions and deductions, they create potential inequities. People with high incomes can avoid high taxes by claiming large exemptions and deductions. Each year the Canada Revenue Agency discovers individuals earning million-dollar incomes and paying little or no taxes. They aren't doing anything illegal, just taking advantage of the many deductions. Nevertheless, this means that some people with high incomes could end up paying *less* tax than people with lower incomes. This would violate the principle of **vertical equity,** the progressive intent of taxing people on the basis of their ability to pay.

Table 15.3 illustrates vertical *in*equity. Mr. Jones has an income three times larger than Ms. Smith's. However, Mr. Jones also has huge deductions that reduce his *taxable* income dramatically. In fact, Mr. Jones ends up with less *taxable* income than Ms. Smith. As a result, he also ends up paying lower taxes.

The deductions that create the vertical inequity between Mr. Jones and Ms. Smith could also violate the principle of **horizontal equity**—as people with the *same* incomes end up paying different amounts of income tax. These horizontal *in*equities also contradict basic notions of fairness.

Nominal vs. Effective Tax Rates. Non-taxable income, deductions, and tax credits create a distinction between gross economic income and taxable income. That distinction, in turn, requires us to distinguish between nominal tax rates and effective tax rates. The term **nominal tax rate** refers to the taxes actually paid as a percentage of *taxable* income. By contrast, the **effective tax rate** is the tax paid divided by *total* economic income without regard to exemptions, deductions, credits, or other intricacies of the tax laws.

As Table 15.3 illustrates, a single individual with a gross income of $90,000 might end up with a very low *taxable* income, thanks to the benefits of various tax deductions and credits. Mr. Jones ended up with a taxable income of only $20,000 and a tax bill of merely $2,400. We could then characterize Mr. Jones's tax burden in two ways:

$$\text{Nominal tax rate} = \frac{\text{tax paid}}{\text{taxable income}}$$

$$= \frac{2{,}400}{\$20{,}000} = 12 \text{ percent}$$

or, alternatively,

$$\text{Effective tax rate} = \frac{\text{tax paid}}{\text{total economic income}}$$

$$= \frac{\$2{,}400}{\$90.000} = 2.7 \text{ percent}$$

This gap between the nominal tax rate (12 percent) and the effective tax rate (2.7 percent) is a reflection of the exemptions and deductions in the tax code. It's also the source of the vertical and horizontal inequities discussed earlier. Notice that Ms. Smith, with much less income, ends up with an effective tax rate (12.5 percent) that's more than four times higher than Mr. Jones's (2.7 percent).

Time Period	Number of Tax Brackets	Top Marginal Tax Rate	Minimum Income Threshold of Top Marginal Tax Rate
1976	13	47%	$ 78,000
1986	10	34%	$ 62,000
1996	3	29%	$ 59,000
2006	4	29%	$118,000

Source: Material based on Canada Revenue Agency, http://www.cra-arc.gc.ca/formspubs/t1general/allyears-e.html, and Tax Policy Center, http://www.taxpolicycenter.org/index.cfm. Reproduced with permission of the Minister of Public Works and Government Services Canada, 2006.

TABLE 15.4
Tax Reform in Canada

Over the past 30 years, the problems associated with a shrinking tax base, horizontal and vertical inequities, and tax-distorted resource allocations have been partially addressed through a reduction in marginal tax rates and fewer tax brackets.

Tax-Induced Misallocations. Tax exemptions and deductions not only foster inequity but encourage inefficiency as well. The optimal mix of output is the one that balances consumer preferences and opportunity costs. Exemptions and deductions, however, encourage a different mix of output. By offering preferential treatment for some activities, the tax code reduces their relative accounting cost. In so doing, *tax preferences induce resource shifts into tax-preferred activities.*

These resource allocations are a principal objective of tax preferences. Many tax experts warn of the inequities and inefficiencies that can occur if the accumulation of exemptions, deductions, and credits becomes so unwieldy and complex that tax considerations drive economic considerations in key investment and consumption decisions. They argue that the resulting mix of output is decidedly inferior to a *pure market outcome.*

A Shrinking Tax Base. There is another problem associated with exemptions and deductions. As the **tax base** gets smaller and smaller, it becomes increasingly difficult to sustain, much less increase, tax revenues. The tax arithmetic is simple:

$$\text{Tax revenue} = \frac{\text{average}}{\text{tax rate}} \times \frac{\text{tax}}{\text{base}}$$

As deductions, exemptions, and credits accumulate, the tax base (taxable income) keeps shrinking. To keep tax rates low—or to reduce them further—the federal government must avoid this potential erosion of the tax base.

Over the years, various federal governments have attempted to maintain the progressiveness of the federal income tax system and to avoid the potential inefficiencies discussed above. Table 15.4 illustrates major tax reforms with respect to marginal tax rates and threshold levels of income in Canada over the past thirty years.

15.4 PROVINCIAL, MUNICIPAL, AND PAYROLL TAXES

In addition to federal income tax, Canadian taxpayers must also pay provincial/territorial income taxes. Table 15.5 shows the highest marginal tax rate and associated income threshold for each province/territory as well as the highest total income tax rate for the combined federal and provincial/territorial income taxes. Other tax bills come from the provinces and municipal governments and also affect efficiency and equity.

With the exception of Alberta, *sales taxes* are a major source of revenue for provincial governments.[3] Municipal governments, on the other hand, rely on *property taxes* for the bulk of their tax receipts. Both taxes are **regressive:** They impose higher tax rates on lower incomes.

WEB NOTE

The Canadian Taxpayer's Association is an advocacy organization providing policies to "lower taxes, eliminate government waste, and hold politicians accountable." Visit their Web site at http://www.taxpayer.com/main/index.php.

tax base: The amount of income or property directly subject to nominal tax rates.

Sales and Property Taxes

regressive tax: A tax system in which tax rates fall as incomes rise.

[3]The goods and services tax (GST) collected by the federal government is also a sales tax.

TABLE 15.5
Combined Federal and Provincial/Territorial Marginal Tax Rates

Taxpayers in Canada also pay income taxes to the provinces or territories in which they reside. In 2006, the highest combined marginal tax rate varied from a minimum of 39% in Alberta to a maximum of 48.64% in Newfoundland.

Province/ Territory	Highest Marginal Tax Rate	Income Threshold	Combined Federal and Provincial/Territory Marginal Tax Rate
Newfoundland*	19.64%	$59,181	48.64%
Prince Edward Island*	18.37%	$61,500	47.37%
Nova Scotia*	19.25%	$93,001	48.25%
New Brunswick	17.84%	$108,769	46.84%
Quebec	24%	$57,431	48.22%
Ontario*	11.16%	$69,517	46.41%
Manitoba	17.4%	$65,001	46.4%
Saskatchewan	15%	$107,368	44.0%
Alberta	10%	All taxable income	39.0%
British Columbia	14.7%	$94,122	43.70%
Yukon	12.76%	$118,285	41.76%
Northwest Territories	14.05%	$112,358	43.05%
Nunavut	11.5%	$118,285	40.5%

*Each of these provinces has a surtax (i.e., additional tax) on top of their marginal tax rates.

Source: Provincial/Territorial tax rates (combined chart) 2006. http://www.cra-arc.gc.ca/tax/individuals/faq/taxrates-e.html#provincial. Reproduced with permission of the Minister of Public Works and Government Services Canada, 2006

At first glance, a 5 percent sales tax doesn't look very regressive. After all, the same 5 percent tax is imposed on virtually all goods. But we're interested in *people,* not goods and services, so **we gauge tax burdens in relation to people's incomes.** A tax is regressive if it imposes a proportionally *larger* burden on *lower* incomes.

This is exactly what a uniform sales tax does. To understand this concept, we have to look not only at how much tax is levied on each dollar of consumption but also at *what* percentage of income is spent on consumer goods.

Low-income families spend everything they've got (and sometimes more) on basic consumption. As a result, most of their income ends up subject to sales tax. By contrast, higher-income families save more. As a result, a smaller proportion of their income is subject to a sales tax. Table 15.6 illustrates this regressive feature of a sales tax. Notice that the low-income family ends up paying a larger fraction of its income (4.7 percent) than does the high income family (3 percent).

Property taxes are regressive also and for the same reason. Low-income families spend a higher percentage of their incomes for shelter. A uniform property tax thus ends up taking a larger fraction of their income than it does of the incomes of high-income families.

TABLE 15.6
The Regressivity of Sales Taxes

A sales tax is imposed on consumer purchases. Although the sales tax itself is uniform (here at 5 percent), the taxes paid represent different proportions of high and low incomes. In this case, the low-income family's *sales tax* bill equals 4.7 percent of its *income.* The high-income family has a sales tax bill equal to only 3 percent of its income.

	High-Income Family	Low-Income Family
Income	$100,000	$30,000
Consumption	$ 60,000	$28,000
Saving	$ 40,000	$ 2,000
Sales tax paid (5% of consumption)	$ 3,000	$ 1,400
Effective tax rate (sales tax ÷ income)	3.0%	4.7%

Tax Incidence. It may sound strange to suggest that low-income families bear the brunt of property taxes. After all, the tax is imposed on the landlords who *own* property, not on people who *rent* apartments and houses. However, here again we have to distinguish between the apparent payee and the individual whose income is actually reduced by the tax. **Tax incidence** refers to the actual burden of a tax—that is, who really ends up paying it.

In general, people who rent apartments pay higher rents as a result of property taxes. In other words, landlords tend to pass along to tenants any property taxes they must pay. Thus, to a large extent *the burden of property taxes is reflected in higher rents.* Tenants pay property taxes *indirectly* via these higher rents. The incidence of the property tax thus falls on renters, in the form of higher rents, rather than on the landlords who write cheques to the local tax authority.

Payroll taxes also impose effective tax burdens quite different from their nominal appearance. Consider, for example, Canada's Employment Insurance (EI) program. This is simply a payroll tax—financed by premiums paid by both employees and employers—designed to cover the funds paid to unemployed workers. Every worker currently sees $1.87 deducted from their pay for every $100 earned (employers contribute $2.62 per $100 paid to employees). But there's a catch: only wages below a legislated ceiling are taxable. In 2006, the wage ceiling was set at $39,000. Hence, a worker earning $100,000 paid the exact same EI tax ($729.30) as a worker earning $39,000. As a result, the tax rate (tax paid ÷ total wages) is lower for high-income workers than low- and middle-income workers. That is a *regressive* tax.

There is another problem in gauging the impact of the EI tax—namely, the tax incidence. Nominally, workers pay $1.87 out of the total $4.49 ($1.87 + $2.62) per $100 of payroll tax, or roughly 42%. But given that taxes will ultimately affect the equilibrium wage rate and quantity of labour hired, is it possible that employees pay more than this 42%? Will employers pay lower wages to compensate for their tax share?

Figure 15.3 illustrates how the tax incidence of a payroll tax is distributed when we have a competitive labour market. The supply of labour reflects the ability and willingness of people to work for various wage rates. Figure 15.3a assumes a relatively elastic supply of labour while Figure 15.3b assumes a relatively inelastic supply of labour. As we saw in Chapter 13, labour demand reflects the *marginal revenue product (MRP)* of labour; it sets a *limit* to the wage an employer is willing to pay.

Prior to the implementation of a payroll tax, the equilibrium wage rate and quantity of labour hired, in both diagrams, is w_0 and L_0 respectively. Like all excise taxes, a payroll tax drives a wedge between the wage paid by the firm, w_1, and the wage received by the worker, w_2. That is to say, there is only one equilibrium level of employment (L_1) where the difference between the wage paid by the firm and the wage received by the workers is exactly equal to the value of the payroll tax. In Figures 15.3a and b, the employer will pay the amount w_1, but part of that outlay ($w_1 - w_2$) will go to the government in the form of payroll taxes. Workers will receive only w_2 in wages. Thus, *fewer workers are employed, and the net wage is reduced when a payroll tax is imposed.*

What Figures 15.3a and b reveal, is how the true incidence of tax is distributed. With a relatively *elastic* supply of labour curve (Figure 15.3a), the burden of the payroll tax falls mainly on employers. Conversely, with a relatively *inelastic* supply of labour (Figure 15.3b), the tax incidence falls mainly on workers. So, to answer our question above: yes, it is possible that workers pay more than the current 42% of the EI tax when we compare the new equilibrium wage rate with the equilibrium wage without the payroll tax.

But regardless of how the burden of tax is divided between employers and workers or the degree of elasticity of supply, Figure 15.3 clearly shows the reduction in labour hired. In perfectly competitive labour markets, payroll taxes are often referred to as "job killers" since they increase a firm's labour cost and lead to a reduction in equilibrium quantity of labour exchanged.

tax incidence: Distribution of the real burden of a tax.

Payroll Taxes

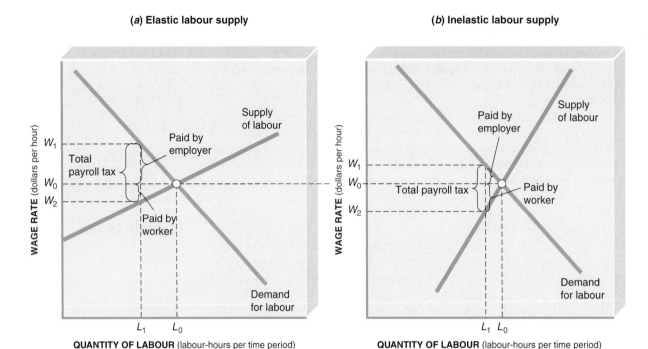

FIGURE 15.3

The Incidence of a Payroll Tax

Payroll taxes drive a wedge between the wage paid by the firm and the wage received by the worker. The equilibrium level of employment (L_1) occurs where the difference between the wage paid by the firm (w_1) and the wage received by the workers (w_2) is exactly equal to the value of the payroll tax. The incidence of a payroll tax will depend on the elasticity of supply. With a relatively *elastic* supply of labour curve (Figure 15.3a), the burden of the payroll tax falls mainly on employers. Conversely, with a relatively *inelastic* supply of labour (Figure 15.3b), the tax incidence falls mainly on workers. In both cases, however, we see that fewer workers are employed, and the net wage is reduced.

15.5 TAXES AND INEQUALITY

The regressivity of the Employment Insurance payroll tax and of many provincial and municipal taxes offsets most of the progressivity of the federal income tax. In a recent Statistics Canada study, tax filers were divided into three groups: the 10 percent with the highest incomes; the one-half with the lowest incomes; and the remaining 40 percent in the middle (intermediate group).[4] The top 10 percent group with the highest incomes received 36 percent of total income and paid 53 percent of total federal income tax (see Figure 15.4). On the other hand, the 50 percent of tax filers with the lowest incomes received 17 percent of total income but paid only 4 percent of total federal income tax. Hence the federal income tax is highly progressive despite existing levels of exemptions and deductions.

FIGURE 15.4

Income Tax Shares

Despite the current exemptions and deductions, the federal income tax remains highly progressive. The richest 10% of households pay over half of all federal income taxes, though they receive roughly a third of all income.

Source: Statistics Canada.

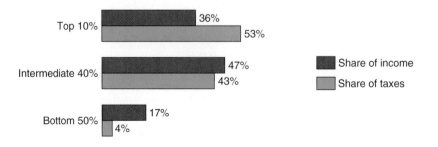

[4]Patrice Martineau, "Federal Personal Income Tax: Slicing the Pie," Statistics Canada, Catalogue No: 11-621-MIE2005024, 2005.

As we saw earlier in the chapter, however, the tax incidence associated with other federal taxes (e.g., Employment Insurance) will reduce the tax share of the 10 percent with the highest incomes. Adding provincial and municipal taxes reduces their tax share even further. The final result is that *the tax system, as a whole, ends up being much more proportional.*

The tax system tells only half the redistribution story. It tells whose income was taken away. Equally important is who gets the income the government collects. The government completes the redistribution process by *transferring* income to consumers. The **income transfers** may be explicit, as in the case of welfare benefits, Old Age Security payments, and unemployment insurance. Or the transfers may be indirect, as in the case of public schools, farm subsidies, and student loans. The direct transfers are more likely to be progressive, that is, to increase the income share of lower-income households. This progressivity results from the fact that low-income status is often a requirement for a direct income transfer. By contrast, most indirect transfers are ostensibly designed to fulfill other purposes, such as education and agricultural stability. As a consequence, they're less likely to be progressive and may even be regressive in some cases. We'll look more closely at income transfers in the next chapter.

To many people, the apparent ineffectiveness of the tax system in redistributing income is a mark of *government failure.* They want a much more decisive reslicing of the pie—one in which the top quintile gets a *lot* less than 47% of the pie and the poor get more than 4 percent (Table 15.1). But how much redistribution should we attempt? Rich people can rattle off as many good reasons for preserving income inequalities as poor people can recite for eliminating them.

Economists aren't uniquely qualified to overcome self-interest, much less to divine what a fair distribution of income might look like. But economists can assess some of the costs and benefits of altering the distribution of income.

The Costs of Greater Equality. The greatest potential cost of a move toward greater equality is the reduced incentives it might leave in its wake. People *are* motivated by income. In factor markets, higher wages call forth more workers and induce them to work longer hours. In fields where earnings are very high, as in the medical and legal professions, people are willing to spend many years and thousands of dollars acquiring the skills such earnings require. Could we really expect people to make such sacrifices in a market that paid everyone the same wage?

The Impact of Transfers

income transfers: Payments to individuals for which no current goods or services are exchanged, for example, Old Age Security payments, welfare, employment insurance payments.

What Is *Fair?*

"I suppose one could say it favors the rich, but, on the other hand it's a great incentive for everyone to make two hundred grand a year."

Analysis: Inequalities are an incentive for individuals to work and invest more.

The same problem exists in product markets. The willingness of producers to supply goods and services depends on their expectation of profits. Why should they work hard and take risks to produce goods and services if their efforts won't make them any better off? If incomes were distributed equally, producers might just as well sit back and enjoy the fruits of someone else's labour.

The essential economic problem absolute income equality poses is that it breaks the market link between effort and reward. If all incomes were equal, it would no longer pay to make an above-average effort. If people stopped making such efforts, total output would decline, and we'd have less income to share (a smaller pie). Not that all high incomes are attributable to great skill or effort. Such factors as luck, market power, and family connections also influence incomes. It remains true, however, that the promise of higher income encourages work effort. Absolute income equality threatens those conditions.

The argument for preserving income inequalities is thus anchored in a concern for productivity. From this perspective, income inequalities are the driving force behind much of our production. By preserving inequalities, we not only enrich the fortunate few, but also provide incentives to take risks, invest more, and work harder. In so doing, we enlarge the economic pie, including the slices available to lower-income groups. Thus, everyone is potentially better off, even if only a few end up rich. This is the rationale that keeps the top marginal tax rate in Canada below that in most other countries (see the World View box).

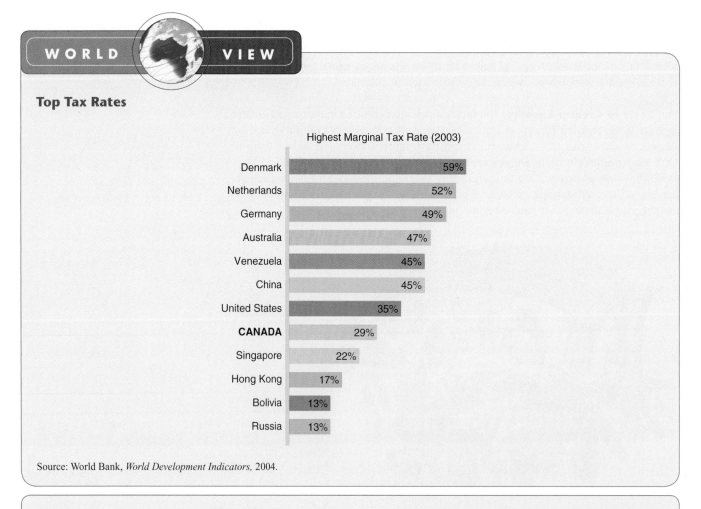

WORLD VIEW

Top Tax Rates

Highest Marginal Tax Rate (2003)

Country	Rate
Denmark	59%
Netherlands	52%
Germany	49%
Australia	47%
Venezuela	45%
China	45%
United States	35%
CANADA	29%
Singapore	22%
Hong Kong	17%
Bolivia	13%
Russia	13%

Source: World Bank, *World Development Indicators,* 2004.

Analysis: The highest marginal tax rate in Canada is lower than in most nations, but still higher than in some countries.

The Benefits of Greater Equality. Although the potential benefits of inequality are impressive, *there's a trade-off between efficiency and equality.* Moreover, many people are convinced that the terms of the trade-off are exaggerated and the benefits of greater equality are ignored. These rebuttals take the form of economic and non-economic arguments.

The economic arguments for greater equality also focus on incentives. The first argument is that the present degree of inequality is more than necessary to maintain work incentives. Upper-class incomes needn't be 11 times as large as those of the lowest-income classes; perhaps 4 times as large would do as well.

The second argument is that low-income earners might actually work harder if incomes were distributed more fairly. As matters now stand, the low-income worker sees little chance of making it big. Extremely low income can also inhibit workers' ability to work by subjecting them to poor health, malnutrition, or inadequate educational opportunities. Accordingly, some redistribution of income to the poor might improve the productivity of low-income workers and compensate for reduced productivity among the rich.

Finally, we noted that the maze of loopholes that preserves inequality also distorts economic incentives. Labour and investment decisions are influenced by tax considerations, not just economic benefits and costs. If greater equality were achieved via tax simplification, a more efficient allocation of resources might result.

Widespread dissatisfaction with the present tax system has spawned numerous reform proposals. One of the most debated proposals is to replace the current federal income tax with a **flat tax.** First proposed by Nobel Prize winner Milton Friedman in the early 1960s, the flat tax has been championed by many other economists over the years.

The key features of a "pure" flat tax include

A Flat Tax?

flat tax: A single-rate tax system.

- Replacing the current system of multiple tax brackets and rates with a single (flat) tax rate that would apply to all taxable income.
- Eliminating all deductions and credits.
- A large base exemption for individuals.

Simplicity. A major attraction of the flat tax is its simplicity. The current tax code that details all the provisions of the present system would be scrapped. The multitude of tax forms now in use would be replaced by a single, postcard-sized form.

Fairness. Flat-tax advocates also emphasize its fairness. They point to the rampant vertical and horizontal inequities created by the current tangle of tax exemptions. By scrapping all those deductions, the flat tax would treat everyone equally.

Moreover, the progressive nature of income taxes can be preserved with a flat tax through the inclusion of a large basic exemption. In a recently proposed U.S. version, the flat tax rate would be 17 percent, but one personal exemption would be maintained. Every adult would get a personal exemption of $13,100 and each child an exemption of $5,300. Accordingly, a family of four would have personal exemptions of $36,800. Hence, a family earning less than that amount would pay no income tax. *Effective* tax rates would increase along with rising incomes above that threshold.

Efficiency. Proponents of a flat tax claim it enhances efficiency as well as equity. Taxpayers now spend thousands of hours a year preparing tax returns. Legions of lobbyists, accountants, and lawyers devote their energy to tax analysis and avoidance. With a simplified flat tax, all those labour resources could be put to more productive use.

A flat tax would also change the mix of output. Consumption and investment decisions would be made on the basis of economic considerations, not tax consequences.

The Critique. As alluring as a flat tax appears, it has aroused substantial opposition. Firstly, on the political front, any major policy change will have winners and losers. The current tax system is thoroughly entrenched at both the institutional and personal level. All of the lobbyists, accountants, and lawyers mentioned above have a vested interest (i.e., their source of income) in maintaining the complexity of the current system. In addition, thousands of individuals are subsidized, both directly and indirectly, through the tax system. In the United States for example, interest payments on home mortgages are deductible; not only are home owners subsidized, but so too is the construction industry. Clearly, those individuals who benefit from the current system are not willing to change the current tax system and will apply significant pressure on the federal government to retain the status quo. Some *might* be willing to accept changes to the tax system if adequately compensated; but that leads to another series of hurdles, including negotiations of acceptable compensation for all those affected.

A number of proposed flat tax systems are "hybrid" forms of the pure system and introduce a certain regressive element into the tax system. For example, the above-mentioned U.S. proposal excludes taxing income on savings and investments (such as interest, dividends, and capital gains). The purpose of that exemption would be to encourage greater saving, investment, and economic growth. At the same time, however, such a broad exemption creates a whole new set of horizontal and vertical inequities. Someone receiving $1 million in interest and dividends could escape all income taxes, while a family earning $50,000 would have to pay.

Critics also object to the wholesale elimination of all deductions and credits. Many of those loopholes are expressly designed to encourage desired economic activity. Many tax cuts are explicitly designed to encourage education, family stability, and savings. By discarding all tax preferences, the flat tax significantly reduces the government's ability to alter the mix of output. Even if the current maze of loopholes exceeds the threshold of government failure, complete reliance on the market mechanism isn't necessarily appropriate. A careful pruning of the tax code rather than a complete uprooting might yield better results.

Finally, critics point out that the transition to a flat tax would entail a wholesale reshuffling of wealth and income. Home values in the United States, for example, would fall precipitously if the tax preference for homeownership were eliminated. That would hit the middle class particularly hard. Millionaires might benefit by sharply reduced tax burdens. Confronted with such adjustments, many people begin to have second thoughts about the desirability of adopting a flat tax in the economy tomorrow. Taxpayers seem to like the principle of a flat tax more than its actual provisions.

SUMMARY

- The distribution of income is a vital economic issue because incomes largely determine access to the goods and services we produce. Wealth distribution is important for the same reason.

- The size distribution of income tells us how incomes are divided up among individuals. The Lorenz curve is a graphic summary of the cumulative size distribution of income. The Gini coefficient is a mathematical summary.

- Personal incomes are distributed quite unevenly in Canada. At present, the highest quintile (the top 20 percent) gets nearly half of all income, and the bottom quintile gets 4 percent.

- The trade-off between equity and efficiency is rooted in supply incentives. The tax elasticity of supply measures how the quantity of resources (labour and capital) declines when tax rates rise.

- The progressivity of the federal income tax is weakened by various exemptions, deductions, and credits, which create a distinction between nominal and effective tax rates and cause vertical and horizontal inequities.

- Progressive federal income taxes are offset by regressive payroll, provincial, and municipal taxes. Overall, the tax system redistributes little income; most redistribution occurs through transfer payments.

- Tax incidence refers to the real burden of a tax. In many cases, reductions in wages, increases in rent, or other real income changes represent the true burden of a tax.
- There is a trade-off between efficiency and equality. If all incomes are equal, there's no economic reward for superior productivity. On the other hand, a more equal distribution of incomes might increase the productivity of lower income groups and serve important noneconomic goals as well.

- A flat tax is a nominally proportional tax system. A "pure" flat tax system with a large basic exemption leads to a progressive tax system. A "hybrid" flat tax system, such as one that excludes capital income, can lead to a more regressive tax system. A flat tax reduces the government's role in resource allocation (the WHAT and HOW questions).

Key Terms

personal income (PI) 323
in-kind income 323
wealth 325
size distribution of income 325
income quintile 325
income share 325
Lorenz curve 326

Gini coefficient 326
progressive tax 327
marginal tax rate 327
tax elasticity of supply 328
vertical equity 330
horizontal equity 330
nominal tax rate 330

effective tax rate 330
tax base 331
regressive tax 331
tax incidence 333
income transfers 335
flat tax 337

Questions for Discussion

1. What goods or services do you and your family receive without directly paying for them? How do these goods affect the distribution of economic welfare?
2. Why are incomes distributed so unevenly? Identify and explain three major causes of inequality.
3. Do inequalities stimulate productivity? In what ways? Provide two specific examples.
4. How would the wealth and income of Canadians be affected by a flat tax system that was not revenue-neutral but resulted in a federal budget deficit?
5. How might a flat tax affect efficiency? Fairness?
6. If a new tax system encouraged more output but also created greater inequality, would it be desirable?

7. If the tax elasticity of supply were zero, how high could the tax rate go before people reduced their work effort? How do families vary the quantity of labour supplied when tax rates change?
8. Is a new tax deduction for tuition likely to increase post-secondary enrollments? How will it affect horizontal and vertical equities?
9. If tax breaks for the rich really stimulated investment and growth, wouldn't everyone benefit from them? Why would anyone oppose them?
10. What share of taxes *should* the rich pay (see Figure 15.4)?

EXERCISES

PROBLEMS   The Student Problem Set to accompany this chapter can be found at the end of the book.

WEB ACTIVITIES   Web Activities to accompany this chapter can be found on the Online Learning Centre at **http://www.mcgrawhill.ca/olc/schiller**.

Transfer Payments: Social Assistance and Social Insurance

Cnadians are compassionate. Public opinion polls reveal that an overwhelming majority of the public wants to "help the needy." Most Canadians say they're even willing to pay more taxes to help fund aid to the poor. But their compassion is tempered by caution: Taxpayers don't want to be ripped off. They want to be sure their money is helping the "truly needy," not being squandered by deadbeats, drug addicts, shirkers, and "welfare queens."

The conflict between compassion and resentment affects not only welfare programs for the poor but also social assistance for the aged, unemployment insurance benefits for the jobless, and even disability benefits for injured workers. In every one of these programs, people are getting money without working. *Transfer payments* are payments to individuals for which no current goods or services are exchanged. In effect, they're a "free ride." The risk of providing a free ride is that some of the people who take it could have gotten by without it. As the American humorist Dave Barry observed, if the government offers $1 million to people with six toes, a lot of people will try to grow a sixth toe or claim they have one. Income transfers create similar incentives: They encourage people to change their behaviour to get a free ride.

This chapter focuses on how income transfer programs change not only the distribution of income, but also work incentives and behaviour. Central questions include

- **How much income do income transfer programs redistribute?**
- **How are transfer benefits computed?**
- **How do transfer payments alter market behaviour?**

LEARNING OBJECTIVES

By the end of this chapter, you should be able to:

16.1 Define and identify the two major types of transfer payments

16.2 Explain the major goal of transfer programs and some unintended consequences

16.3 Explain the difference between demographic-based, event-based, and needs-tested transfers

16.4 Discuss the ways in which social assistance and social insurance programs reduce work incentives

16.5 Identify the core policy dilemma of all income transfer programs

16.1 MAJOR TRANSFER PROGRAMS

Roughly 50 cents out of every federal tax dollar now is devoted to income transfers. That amounts to more than *$100 billion* a year in transfer payments (see Figure 16.1). Who gets all this money?

The easy answer to this question is that almost every household gets some of the transfer money. There are dozens of federal income transfer programs. Students get tuition grants and subsidized loans. Farmers get crop assistance. Homeowners get disaster relief when their homes are destroyed. Veterans get benefit cheques and subsidized health care. People over age 65 get Old Age Security benefits. And poor people get welfare cheques and subsidized housing.

Although income transfers are widely distributed, not everyone shares equally in the tax-paid bounty. As Figure 16.2 shows, just three of the myriad federal income transfers programs to individual Canadians account for over 75 percent of total outlays. The largest program, Old Age Security pensions, accounts for 43 percent of the transfer budget all by itself. Employment Insurance and Child Tax benefits absorb another 33 percent. By contrast, pensions to war veterans account for only 2%.

Income transfers do not always entail cash payments. Most of the transfer payments to provinces and territories are provided to support (i) health care (Canada Health Transfer), and (ii) education and social services (Canada Social Transfer). In Canada, universal coverage for medically necessary health care services is provided on the basis of need, rather than the ability to pay—hospital and doctors' bills are covered by these programs. Similarly, the cost of post-secondary education is partially subsidized by the government. Hence the benefits are paid *in-kind*, not in cash. Such programs provide **in-kind transfers,** that is, direct transfers of goods and services rather than cash. Legal aid, food stamps (in the United States), subsidized housing, resettlement assistance for new immigrants, and skills development programs are all in-kind programs. By contrast, Employment Insurance payments are **cash transfers** because the beneficiaries receive cheques, not services.

The provision of in-kind benefits rather than cash is intended to promote specific objectives. Few taxpayers object to feeding the hungry. But they bristle at the thought that social assistance (welfare) recipients might spend the income they receive on something potentially harmful like liquor or drugs or on nonessentials like cars or fancy clothes. To minimize that risk, taxpayers offer coupons, not cash, thereby limiting

WEB NOTE

To view a map identifying Canadian federal government transfer payments as a proportion of total income, visit http://atlas.nrcan.gc.ca/sites/english/maps/economic/income/income2001/transfer.

Cash vs. In-Kind Benefits

in-kind transfers: Direct transfers of goods and services rather than cash; examples include food stamps, legal aid, and housing subsidies.

cash transfers: Income transfers that entail direct cash payments to recipients, for example, Old Age Security, social assistance, and employment insurance benefits.

FIGURE 16.1
Federal Spending: Direct Program Expenses vs. Income Transfer Payments

The federal government has two major spending categories. Direct program expenses (e.g., purchase of military vehicles, wages for civil services, etc.) are payments for goods and/or services received, while income transfer payments (e.g., Old Age Security, Employment Insurance, etc.) are payments for which no current goods or services are exchanged. In 2006, over 50% of total tax revenues were spent on major transfers to persons and provinces/territories. Including minor transfer payments, the dollar value of this spending category exceeds $100 billion.

Source: Based on material from the Department of Finance. http://www.fin.gc.ca/ec 2006/pdf/ec2006e.pdf, pages 38, 46, and 50.

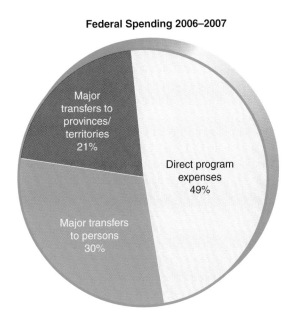

Federal Spending 2006–2007

Major transfers to provinces/territories 21%
Direct program expenses 49%
Major transfers to persons 30%

FIGURE 16.2
Federal Government Transfer Payments to Persons

There are dozens of federal transfer programs that remit income directly to individuals. Just three programs, however, account for over 75% of all transfers; Old Age Security payments, Employment Insurance benefits, and Child Tax Benefits.

Source: Adapted from Statistics Canada Web site http://www40.statcan.ca/l01/cst01/govt05a.htm. Statistics Canada information is used with the permission of Statistics Canada.

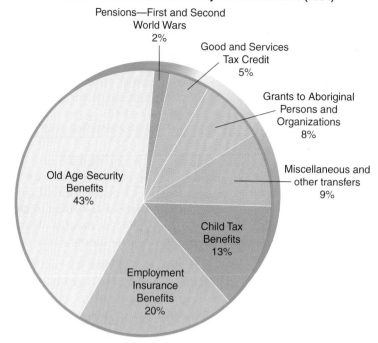

Federal Government Transfer Payments to Persons (2004)

Pensions—First and Second World Wars 2%
Good and Services Tax Credit 5%
Grants to Aboriginal Persons and Organizations 8%
Miscellaneous and other transfers 9%
Child Tax Benefits 13%
Employment Insurance Benefits 20%
Old Age Security Benefits 43%

---

target efficiency: The percentage of income transfers that go to the intended recipients and purposes.

the recipient's consumption choices. This helps reassure taxpayers that their assistance is being well spent.

The **target efficiency** of a transfer program refers to how well income transfers attain their intended purpose. In-kind housing transfers are more target-efficient than cash transfers because recipients would use equivalent cash transfers for other purposes. Food stamps are more target-efficient than cash in reducing hunger for the same reason. If given cash rather than coupons, recipients would spend less than 70 cents of each dollar on food.

Social Insurance vs. Social Assistance

You may have noted by now that not all income transfers go to the poor. A lot of student loans go to middle-class college students. And disaster relief helps rebuild both mansions and trailer parks. Such income transfers are triggered by either *demographics* or *events,* not the recipient's income. Other programs, such as the Child Tax Credit and the Guaranteed Income Supplement, are *income-tested* programs: they provide graduated benefits to those whose incomes are below a specified qualifying level. Finally, social assistance programs are *needs-tested* programs where beneficiaries' needs, incomes, and other assets are taken into consideration.[1]

Social assistance programs always entail some kind of income eligibility text. To receive income transfers or subsidized housing, a family must prove that it has too little income to fend for itself. In the United States, the food stamp program is an in-kind **social assistance program** because only poor families are eligible.[2]

social assistance programs: Needs-tested income transfer programs, for example, welfare and food stamps.

Employment Insurance and Old Age Security aren't *social assistance* programs because recipients don't have to be poor. In the case of Employment Insurance, the event of losing one's job is the criterion that makes one eligible for these benefits. And being part of the "senior citizen" *demographic* ensures one's eligibility for Old Age Security retirement benefits; at age 65, everyone—whether rich or poor—is entitled to these income transfers. These demographic- and event-conditioned benefits are the hallmark of **social insurance programs:** They insure people against the costs of old

social insurance programs: Event- and demographic-conditioned income transfers intended to reduce the costs of specific problems, for example, Old Age Security and Employment Insurance.

---

[1]For many countries, the definition of means-tested programs is identical to Canada's needs-tested criteria.
[2]In 2004, a family of four in the United States was considered poor if it had less than $18,900 ($US) of income.

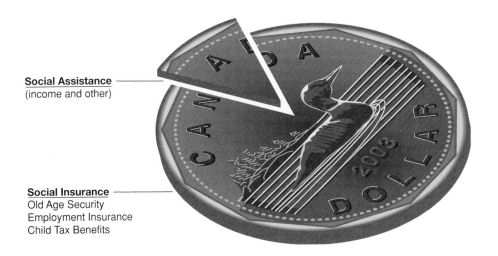

Social Assistance
(income and other)

Social Insurance
Old Age Security
Employment Insurance
Child Tax Benefits

FIGURE 16.3
Social Insurance vs. Social Assistance

Social insurance programs provide *demographic*—or *event*-based transfers—for example, upon reaching the age of 65 or becoming unemployed or disabled. Social assistance programs offer benefits only to those in need; they're *needs-tested*. Social insurance transfers greatly outnumber social assistance transfers.

Source: Adapted from Statistics Canada Web site http://www40.statcan.ca/l01/cst01/govt05a.htm. Statistics Canada information is used with the permission of Statistics Canada.

age, illness, disability, unemployment, and other specific problems. As Figure 16.3 illustrates, ***most income transfers are for social insurance programs, not social assistance.***

If the market sliced up the economic pie in a manner that society deemed fair, there would be no need for all these government-provided income transfers. Hence, the mere existence of such programs implies a *market failure*—an unfair market-generated distribution of income. When the market alone slices up the pie, some people get too much and others get too little. Notice that the concept of "fairness" is a *normative* issue. Different individuals have different beliefs regarding what constitutes a fair or equitable division of the economic pie. Therefore, we can expect that *society's values* will play a relatively important role in the economic analysis and formation of policy. To redress this inequity, we ask the government to play Robin Hood—taking income from the rich and giving it to the poor. Thus, ***the basic goal of income transfer programs is to reduce income inequalities.***

Transfer Goals

FOR WHOM. Transfer programs do in fact significantly change the distribution of income. Old Age Security alone redistributes $28 billion a year from workers to retirees. Those Old Age Security cheques account for a substantial portion of all the income older people receive. Without those cheques, some of the elderly population would be officially classified as poor. More generally, income transfers reduce Canadian inequality by approximately 16 percent (as measured by the Gini coefficient).

WHAT to Produce. In the process of redistributing incomes, income transfers also change the mix of output. The goal of food stamps, for example, is to increase food consumption by the poor. The strategy isn't to take food off rich people's plates, however. Instead, it is expected that the additional food purchases of the poor will encourage more food *production,* thereby changing the mix of output. Housing subsidies and free health care have similar effects on the mix of output. So do student loans: If more students end up going to post-secondary institutions, the mix of output changes in favour of educational services.

Although income transfers change the distribution of income and mix of output in desired ways, they are not costless interventions. The Law of Unintended Consequences rears its ugly head here: Income transfers often change market behaviour and outcomes in unintended (and undesired) ways.

Unintended Consequences

Reduced Output. First, the provision of transfer payments may dull work incentives. If you can get paid for *not* working (via a transfer payment), why would you go to

FIGURE 16.4
Reduced Labour Supply and Output

Transfer payments may induce people to supply less labour at any market wage rate. If this happens, the supply of labour shifts to the left and the economy's production possibilities shrink. We end up with less total output.

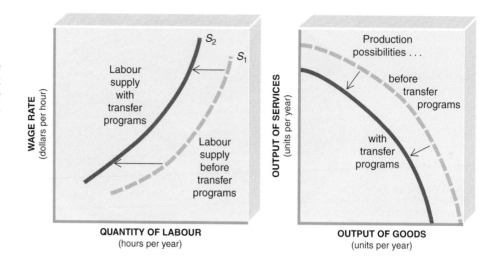

work? Why endure 40 hours of toil for a paycheque when you can stay home and collect a social assistance cheque, an unemployment cheque, or Old Age Security? If the income transfers are large enough, I'll stay home too. When people reduce their *labour supply* in response to income transfers, total output will shrink. Figure 16.4 shows that ***attempts to redistribute income may reduce total income.*** In other words, the pie shrinks when we try to reslice it.

Undesirable Behaviour. A reduction in labour supply isn't the only unintended consequence of income transfer programs. People may also change their *nonwork* behaviour. Social assistance benefits give women a (small) incentive to have more children and teen moms to establish their own households. Free health services encourage people to overuse health care services and neglect the associated costs. Employment Insurance benefits encourage workers to stay jobless longer. And, as Dave Berry noted at the beginning of the chapter, disability payments encourage people to grow a sixth toe. Although the actual response to these incentives is hotly debated, the existence of the undesired incentives is unambiguous.

16.2 SOCIAL ASSISTANCE PROGRAMS

To understand how income transfer programs change market behaviour and outcomes, let's look closer at how social assistance programs operate. From a jurisdictional perspective, the design, delivery, and administration of social assistance programs fall under the purview of the individual provinces and territories. Hence, the governments of the provinces and territories decide who receives social assistance, under what conditions, and for how long. As we shall see, all of these programs confront a central dilemma: how to help the poor without encouraging undesired market behaviour. The financing of these programs, however, comes from both the provinces and the federal government (Canada Social Transfer).

While "need" is the only eligibility requirement for social assistance, the application process and the determination of benefits is a multi-step course of action. First, applicants must complete the administrative requirements to assess initial eligibility: fill out prescribed forms; provide supporting documents such as proof of age, bank statements, and pay stubs; and meet with departmental representatives, etc. Applicants who successfully fulfill the administrative conditions proceed to the financial eligibility requirements. This is the "*needs test*" where the basic needs and the financial resources available to individuals are reviewed. Financial resources are divided into assets and income. Some of these resources are exempt from the calculations (Child Tax Benefits,

Maximum Basic Social Assistance Income Transfers		
Province or Territory	**Single (Employable)**	**Couple (Two children)**
Newfoundland & Labrador	$ 7,200	$11,900
Prince Edward Island	6,000	14,700
Nova Scotia	5,200	11,700
New Brunswick	3,200	9,900
Quebec	6,700	10,400
Ontario	6,400	12,200
Manitoba	5,600	14,100
Saskatchewan	6,300	12,500
Alberta	4,800	13,000
British Columbia	6,100	11,900
Yukon	12,000	21,300
Northwest Territories	13,300	25,100
Nunavut	10,700	31,500

Source: National Council of Welfare, *Welfare Incomes 2005*, http://www.ncwcnbes.net/documents/researchpublications/ResearchProjects/WelfareIncomes/2005Report_Summer2006/ReportENG.pdf, accessed February 24, 2007.

TABLE 16.1
Basic Social Assistance Benefits in Canada

The maximum basic social assistance income transfers in Canada vary by family type and by province or territory. In 2005, a family of four in British Columbia eligible for basic social assistance could receive a maximum income transfer of $11,900.

Goods and Services Tax rebates, compensation payments to those who have conditions such as HIV and Hepatitis C, etc.) while the remaining resources are deducted dollar for dollar from social assistance entitlements (see Table 16.1 for recent basic social assistance benefits).

The **budget deficit method** is used to determine the precise dollar amount of benefits. By definition, a budget deficit occurs when the amount of available financial resources is less than the provincial–territorial amount of social assistance for that family type. The Jones family (couple with two children) living in Vancouver could receive up to $11,900 depending on their needs and total value of their financial resources—after deducting exempt assets and income.

Suppose that the provincial government in British Columbia guaranteed all families the maximum $11,900 in basic social assistance benefits while earning up to a maximum of $10,000 a year in wages. The Jones family could potentially earn a total annual income of $21,900 while on social assistance.[3]

There are two potential problems with such a policy. Firstly, some struggling working families would have a strong incentive to start collecting social assistance. Why try to support a family of four by working full time with a paycheque of $20,000 when you can quit, work part-time (up to $10,000 per year) and receive basic social assistance benefits that, combined, provide you with a higher income?

Recall from Chapter 13 that the decision to work is largely a response to both the financial and psychological rewards associated with employment. People in dull, dirty, low-paying jobs get little of either. By quitting their jobs, declaring themselves poor, and accepting a guaranteed income transfer, they would gain much more leisure at little financial or psychological cost. In the process, total output would shrink (Figure 16.4).

The second potential problem affects the work behaviour of people who were poor to begin with. Assume that the Jones family was earning $10,000 before they got a social assistance cheque. The question now is whether the social assistance cheque will change their work behaviour.

budget deficit method: The shortfall between the amount of available financial resources and the provincial–territorial amount of social assistance for that family type.

The Work Incentive Problem

WEB NOTE

The National Council of Welfare's most recent report on each provincial–territorial social assistance program can be found at http://www.ncwcnbes.net/en/research/welfare-bienetre.html.

[3]The government of British Columbia may base the combined value of $21,900 on Statistic Canada's Low-Income Cut-offs (LICOs) poverty threshold values—see Chapter 15.

Suppose that family gets an opportunity to earn an extra $1,000 a year by working overtime. Should they seize that opportunity? Consider the effect of the higher *wages* on the family's *income*. Before working overtime, the Jones family earned

INCOME WITHOUT OVERTIME WAGES

Wages	$10,000
Welfare benefits	11,900
Total income	21,900

If they now work overtime, their income is

INCOME WITH OVERTIME WAGES

Wages	$11,000
Welfare benefits	10,900
Total income	$21,900

Something is wrong here: Although *wages* have gone up, the family's *income* hasn't.

Marginal Tax Rates. The failure of income to rise with wages is the by-product of how social assistance benefits were computed. ***If social assistance benefits are set equal to the maximum allowable, every additional dollar of wages reduces social assistance benefits by the same amount.*** In effect, the Jones family confronts a *marginal tax rate* of 100 percent: Every dollar of wages results in a lost dollar of benefits. Provincial and territorial governments aren't literally raising the family's taxes by a dollar. By reducing benefits dollar for dollar, however, the end result is the same.

With a 100 percent marginal tax rate and maximum allowable benefits, a family can't improve its income by working more. Thus, we end up with a conflict between compassion and work incentives. By guaranteeing a poverty-level income, we destroy the economic incentive of low-income workers to support themselves. This creates a **moral hazard** for welfare recipients; that is, we encourage undesirable behaviour. The moral hazard here is the temptation not to support oneself by working—choosing social assistance cheques instead.

> **moral hazard:** An incentive to engage in undesirable behaviour.

To reduce this moral hazard, most provinces have changed the way benefits are computed. To encourage social assistance recipients to lift their own incomes above the fixed-level income, a portion of their monthly earnings incomes are exempt. For example, in Quebec, the first $300 is completely exempt. Over the course of the year, this would amount to an additional $3,600 per family of four. Each province and territory has its own specific monthly earnings exemptions.[4] ***These exemptions effectively reduce the marginal tax rate from 100 per cent to a lower value.*** To illustrate how this incentive operates, consider the following simplified example.

Suppose Ms. Jones, a single employable person, receives the maximum allowable basic social assistance benefit of $8,000 per year and that *any* income earned is taxed at 67 percent. Her total annual income can be calculated as follows:

$$\frac{\text{Total}}{\text{income}} = \frac{\text{Wages}}{\text{earned}} + \frac{\text{Social assistance}}{\text{benefits}}$$

where her social assistance benefits are equal to:

$$\frac{\text{Social assistance}}{\text{benefits}} = \frac{\text{Maximum allowable}}{\text{benefit}} - \frac{2}{3}[\text{Wages earned}]$$

Figure 16.5 illustrates how a lower marginal tax rate alters the relationship of total income to wages. The black line in the figure shows the total wages Ms. Jones could earn at $8 per hour. She could earn nothing by not working or as much as $16,000 per year by working full time (point *F* in the figure).

---

[4]British Columbia is the only province that currently has no earnings exemptions.

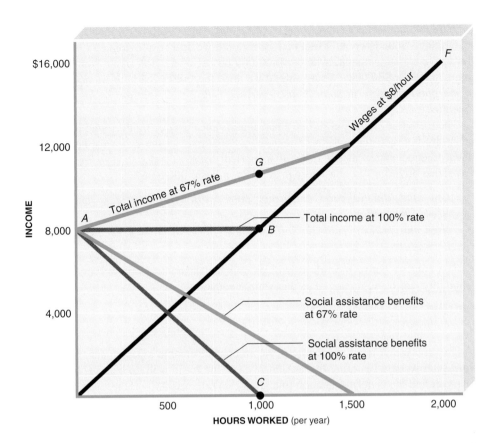

FIGURE 16.5
Work (Dis)Incentives

If social assistance benefits are reduced dollar for dollar as wages increase, the implied marginal tax rate is 100 percent. In that case, total income remains at the benefit limit of $8,000 (point *A*) as work effort increases from 0 to 1,000 hours (point *B*). There is no incentive to work in this range. When the marginal tax rate is reduced to 67 percent, total income starts increasing as soon as the social assistance recipient starts working. At 1,000 hours of work, total income is $10,226 (point *G*).

The brown lines in the figure show what happens to her welfare benefits and total income when a 100 percent marginal tax rate is imposed. At point *A* she gets $8,000 in social assistance benefits and total income because she's not working at all.

Now consider what happens to her total income if Ms. Jones goes to work. If she works 1,000 hours per year (essentially half-time), she could earn $8,000 (point *B*). But what would happen to her income? If the social assistance department cuts her benefit by $1 for every dollar she earns, her benefit cheque slides down the brown "welfare benefits" line to point *C*, where she gets nothing from welfare. By working 1,000 hours per year, all Ms. Jones has done is replace her social assistance cheque with a paycheque. That might make taxpayers smile, but Ms. Jones will wonder why she bothered to go to work. With a 100 percent tax rate, her total income doesn't rise above $8,000 until she works more than 1,000 hours.

The green lines in Figure 16.5 show how work incentives improve with a lower marginal tax rate. Now welfare benefits are reduced by only 67 cents for every $1 of wages earned. As a result, total income starts rising as soon as Ms. Jones goes to work. If she works 1,000 hours, her total income will include

Wages	$ 8,000	
Welfare benefit	2,667	= $8,000 − 2/3 ($8,000)
Total income	$10,667	

Point *G* on the graph illustrates this outcome.

It may be comforting to know that Ms. Jones can now increase her income to $10,667 by working 1,000 hours per year. But she still faces a higher marginal tax rate (67 percent) than rich people (the top marginal tax rate on federal income taxes is 29 percent). Why not lower their marginal tax rate even further, thus increasing both their work incentives and their total income?

Unfortunately, a reduction in the marginal tax rate would also increase welfare costs. Suppose we eliminated the marginal tax rate altogether. Then, Ms. Jones could

Incentives vs. Costs

earn $8,000 *and* keep welfare benefits of $8,000. That would boost their total income to $16,000. Sounds great, doesn't it? But should we still be providing $8,000 in welfare payments to someone who earns $8,000 on her own? How about someone earning $20,000 or $30,000? Where should we draw the line? Clearly, *if we don't impose a marginal tax rate at some point, everyone will be eligible for social assistance benefits.*

The thought of giving everyone a social assistance cheque might sound like a great idea, but it would turn out to be incredibly expensive. In the end, we'd have to take those cheques back, in the form of increased taxes, in order to pay for the vastly expanded program. We must recognize, then, a basic dilemma:

- *Low marginal tax rates encourage more work effort but make more people eligible for welfare.*
- *High marginal tax rates discourage work effort but make fewer people eligible for welfare.*

The conflict between work incentives and the desire to limit welfare costs and eligibility can be summarized in this simple equation:

$$\text{Breakeven level of income} = \frac{\text{basic benefits}}{\text{marginal tax rate}}$$

> **breakeven level of income:** The income level at which welfare eligibility ceases.

The **breakeven level of income** is the amount of income a person can earn before losing all welfare benefits. In Ms. Jones' case, the basic welfare benefit was $8,000 per year and the benefit-reduction (marginal tax) rate was 0.67. Hence, she could earn as much as

$$\text{Breakeven level of income} = \frac{\$8,000}{0.67} \text{ per year}$$

$$\approx \$12,000$$

before losing all welfare benefits. Thus, *low marginal tax rates encourage work but make it hard to get completely off welfare.*

If the marginal tax rate were 100 percent, the breakeven point would be $8,000 divided by 1.00. In that case, people who earned $8,000 on their own would get no assistance from welfare. Fewer people would be eligible for welfare, but those who drew benefits would have no incentive to work. If the marginal tax rate were lowered to 0, the breakeven point would rise to infinity ($8,000 divided by 0)—and we'd all be on welfare.

As this arithmetic shows, *there's a basic conflict between work incentives (low marginal tax rates) and welfare containment (smaller welfare rolls and outlays).* We can achieve a lower breakeven level of income (less welfare eligibility) only by sacrificing low marginal tax rates or higher income floors (basic benefits). Hence, welfare costs can be minimized only if we sacrifice income provision or work incentives.

Tax Elasticity of Labour Supply. The terms of the trade-off between more welfare and less work depend on how responsive people are to marginal tax rates. As we first noted in Chapter 15, the **tax elasticity of labour supply** measures the response to changes in tax rates; that is,

> **tax elasticity of labour supply:** The percentage change in quantity of labour supplied divided by the percentage change in tax rates.

$$\text{Tax elasticity of labour supply} = \frac{\% \text{ change in quantity of hours supplied}}{\% \text{ change in tax rate}}$$

If the tax elasticity of labour supply were zero, it wouldn't matter how high the marginal tax rate was: People would work for nothing (100 percent tax rate). In reality, the tax elasticity of labour supply among low-wage workers is more in the range of –0.2 to –0.4, so marginal tax rates *do* affect work effort.

16.3 SOCIAL INSURANCE–PENSION PLANS

Like social assistance programs, all the Canadian social insurance programs were developed to redistribute incomes. The programs with the greatest amounts of transfers—namely the Old Age Security (OAS) pension and the Canadian and Quebec Pension Plans (CPP/QPP)—are demographic-conditioned benefits; *age,* not income, is the primary determinant of eligibility. Other programs such as Employment Insurance (EI) are event-conditioned benefits, while the Canada Child Tax Benefit program distributes funds based on both demographics (families with children under 18) and income tests (families with incomes above the threshold do not receive any benefits).

Government transfer payments in the form of pensions account for almost one-half of all federal, provincial, and local government payments to individuals—over $58 billion in 2004 (see Figure 16.6). Given the relative importance of pension plans as a government transfer payment, let's examine whether we have the same policy conflicts between the goals of compassion, work incentives, and program costs that we observed with our social assistance programs.

OAS Program Features

The Old Age Security pension is available to all Canadians citizens 65 year of age or older who have lived in Canada for at least 10 years after reaching age 18. For each complete year of residence after the age of 18, an individual earns 1 of the 40 "portions of the pie"—partial pensions can be allotted to those who have lived in Canada for less than 40 years. In 2007, the maximum annual OAS payment was $5,903.16. Pensioners with an individual net income above a threshold value of $63,511, however, must repay 15 percent of the difference between this threshold value and their income.[5] Since the threshold for repayment is relatively high, the OAS, by itself, does not provide a significant incentive to retire; a 65-year old worker earning $60,000 per year receives the same maximum amount as a 65-year old pensioner with an annual income of $35,000.

The Earnings Test. Low-income OAS recipients, however, may be eligible for additional income under the Guaranteed Income Supplement (GIS) program. These

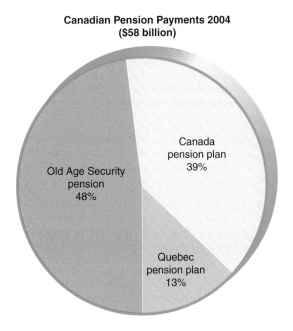

Canadian Pension Payments 2004
($58 billion)

Old Age Security pension 48%

Canada pension plan 39%

Quebec pension plan 13%

FIGURE 16.6
Canadian Pension Payments

In 2004, total federal, provincial, and local government payments to persons amounted to $130 billion. Almost one-half of these expenditures (over $58 billion) were in the form of pensions.

Source: Adapted from Statistics Canada CANSIM database table 384-0000. http://www40.statcan.ca/l01/cst01/govt05a.htm. Statistics Canada information is used with the permission of Statistics Canada.

[5]A pensioner earning $75,000 would have to repay ($75,000 − $63,511) × 0.15 = $1,723.35. The full OAS pension is eliminated when a pensioner's net income is $102,865 or above.

additional benefits are a function of income earned; a maximum of $7,450 per year for no income (OAS benefits are excluded in the calculation), reduced to zero for any income above $15,000. The federal government imposes an *earnings test* to determine the amount of retirement benefits a low-income OAS recipient can collect while still working. The earnings test is very similar to the formula used to compute social assistance benefits. The formula establishes a maximum benefit amount and a marginal tax rate that reduces benefits as wages are earned:

$$\text{Benefit amount} = \text{OAS award} + \text{Maximum GIS award} - 0.5(\text{wages earned})$$

Consider the case of Leonard, a 65-year-old worker contemplating retirement. Suppose Leonard's wage history entitles him to the maximum OAS award of $6,000 plus the maximum GIS award of $7,500 for a total pension of $13,500 per year. But he wants to keep working to supplement his social insurance benefits with wages. What happens to his benefits if he keeps working?

The benefit formula is

$$\text{Benefit amount} = \$6,000 + \$7,500 - 0.5(\text{wages earned})$$

The Work Disincentive. He faces the same kind of incentives that Ms. Jones had when on social insurance. The formula indicates that his benefits will drop by 50 cents for every dollar earned. Hence the implicit marginal tax rate is 50 percent. The federal government is effectively getting half of any wages Leonard earns. If he earns $15,000 in wages, he completely eliminates his GIS portion of the pension benefits and only raises his income from $13,500 to $21,000.

In reality, the marginal tax rate on Leonard's wages is even higher. If he works, Leonard will have to pay federal taxes (15.25 percent), provincial income taxes (say, another 10 percent), and the Employment Insurance payroll tax (1.8 percent). Hence the full burden of taxes and benefit losses includes

ITEM	MARGINAL TAX RATE
Social Insurance benefit loss	50.00%
Federal income tax	15.25
Provincial income tax	10.00
EI payroll tax	1.80
Total	77.05%

As a consequence, Leonard's income goes up only by 22.95 cents with every $1 he earns.

CPP/QPP Program Features

The other publicly funded pension plan is the Canadian Pension Plan (CPP); its sister plan in Quebec (QPP) operates in much the same fashion. These are compulsory public insurance plans whose purpose is to provide persons who work in Canada (Québec) and their families with basic financial protection in the event of retirement, death, or disability. The pension was designed to replace approximately 25 percent of the earnings on which a person's lifetime contributions were based.

Workers can qualify for a CPP retirement pension as early as 60 years of age. For younger workers (between the ages of 60 to 64) to be eligible for CPP benefits they must (i) stop working, *or* (ii) earn less than the current monthly maximum CPP retirement pension payment (currently $863.75 in 2007). The amount received is based on how much, and for how long an individual contributed to the plan—the average monthly benefit in 2006 was $473.

Typically, a person's CPP/QPP retirement pension starts the month after they reach their 65th birthday. There is a certain amount of flexibility built into the program whereby one can start collecting as early as the age of 60 or as late as the age of 70. For every month before or after a worker's 65th birthday, the CPP adjusts the amount of the pension by 0.5 percent. Therefore, a person starting their pension at age 60 receives a monthly payment that is 30 percent *lower* than if they waited until their

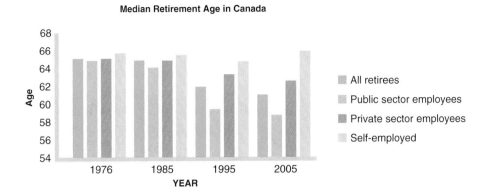

FIGURE 16.7
Median Retirement Ages

Since 1976, with the exception of self-employed workers, the median retirement age has seen a significant decline. Public sector workers, many with generous employer pension plans, have seen the greatest decline—from 64.8 to 58.7 years of age.

Source: Adapted from Statistics Canada CANSIM database table 282-0051. Statistics Canada information is used with the permission of Statistics Canada.

65th birthday. Similarly, a person who delays receiving their pension until the age of 70 receives a monthly payment that is 30 percent *greater* than if they collected it at age 65. The monetary incentive of delaying CPP benefits, however, does not seem attractive given that approximately two-thirds of Canadians now retire before the age of 65.

In addition to Old Age Security benefits and Canada Pension Plan benefits, about 40 percent of Canadians are currently covered by an employer pension plan—down from over 50 percent about twenty years ago. Depending on the class of worker, coverage ranges from 100 percent (public sector employees) to about 30 percent (private sector workers). Not surprisingly, therefore, we observe those with the greatest amount of pension benefits are also those who have the earliest retirement dates (see Figure 16.7).

Like social assistance recipients, older people are quick to realize that, in many cases, work no longer pays. Not surprisingly, a large percentage of workers approaching the official Canadian retirement age of 65 have exited the labour market in droves. The **labour-force participation rate** measures the percentage of the population that is either employed or actively seeking a job (unemployed). Figure 16.8 shows how precipitously the labour force participation rate for Canadian males aged 60–64 declined from 1976 to 1995. The overall general decline in labour-force participation rates among older workers during this 20-year time frame was not unique to Canada (See the World View box).

Since 2000, however, this participation rate has rebounded in Canada. Part of this can be explained by the buoyant Canadian economy (more available jobs), part by the increase in the willingness of older workers to engage in part-time work. Interestingly, the increase in female participation rates for women aged 60–64 has also increased significantly since 2000.

Declining Labour Supply

labour-force participation rate: The percentage of the working-age population working or seeking employment.

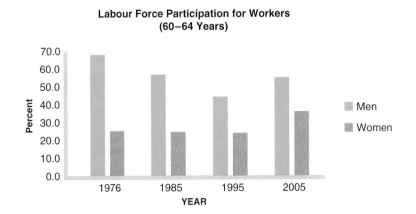

FIGURE 16.8
Labour-Force Participation Rates (60–64 years)

The ability to collect pensions, both public (CPP/QPP) and private, before the age of 65 has provided a monetary incentive for men aged 60–64 to reduce their labour-force participation rates.

Source: Adapted from Statistics Canada CANSIM database table 282-0002. Statistics Canada information is used with the permission of Statistics Canada.

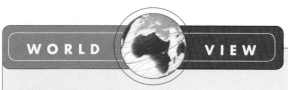

WORLD VIEW

An Aging World

Richer Countries Aging Fastest

The whole world is aging, but the trend is most pronounced in developed countries, where elders frequently outnumber youths.

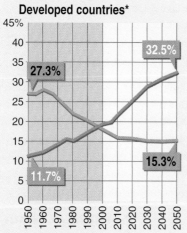

Legend:
- Percentage 14 and younger
- Percentage 60 and older

Developed countries*

(chart values: 27.3%, 32.5%, 11.7%, 15.3%; x-axis years 1950–2050; y-axis 0–45%)

*(Includes North America, Japan, Europe, Australia, New Zealand)

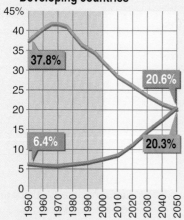

Developing countries

(chart values: 37.8%, 20.6%, 6.4%, 20.3%; x-axis years 1950–2050; y-axis 0–45%)

Source: *U.S. News & World Report*, March 1, 1999. Copyright 1999 U.S. News & World Report, L. P. Reprinted with permission. www.usnews.com

Workers have been retiring earlier . . .
Average age of retirement for men in industrialized countries

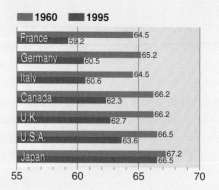

Legend: 1960, 1995

Country	1960	1995
France	59.2	64.5
Germany	60.5	65.2
Italy	60.6	64.5
Canada	62.3	66.2
U.K.	62.7	66.2
U.S.A.	63.6	66.5
Japan	66.5	67.2

. . . but fewer workers will be supporting retirees in the future . . .
Average number of contributors per retiree in public pension systems

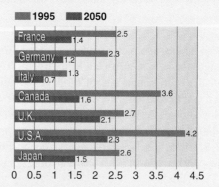

Legend: 1995, 2050

Country	1995	2050
France	2.5	1.4
Germany	2.3	1.2
Italy	1.3	0.7
Canada	3.6	1.6
U.K.	2.7	2.1
U.S.A.	4.2	2.3
Japan	2.6	1.5

. . . which could lead to higher taxes
Projected payroll tax rates needed to cover all retirees

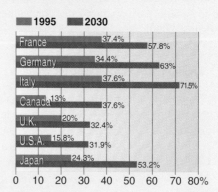

Legend: 1995, 2030

Country	1995	2030
France	37.4%	57.8%
Germany	34.4%	63%
Italy	37.6%	71.5%
Canada	13%	37.6%
U.K.	20%	32.4%
U.S.A.	15.8%	31.9%
Japan	24.8%	53.2%

Analysis: The aging of the world's population implies an increasing income transfer burden. As older workers choose to retire earlier, the burden increases still further.

The primary economic cost of Social Insurance programs isn't the benefits it pays but the reduction in total output that occurs when workers retire early. In the absence of Social Insurance benefits, millions of older workers would still be on the job, contributing to the output of goods and services. When they instead retire—or simply work less—total output shrinks.

The economic cost of Social Insurance is increased further by a labour supply reduction among *younger* workers. The Old Age Security payments are financed from Government of Canada general tax revenues, but the Canada and Québec Pension Plans are financed through payroll taxes. The payroll taxes levied on employees and employers increase the cost of labour and discourage people from working more, which further reduces total output. As the behaviour of both older and younger workers changes, ***the economic pie shrinks as we try to redistribute it from younger to older workers.***

Trade-Offs. Just because the intergenerational redistribution is expensive doesn't mean we shouldn't do it. Going to college or university is expensive too, but you're doing it. The real economic issue is benefits versus costs. Compassion for older workers is what motivates Social Insurance transfers. Presumably, society gains from the more equitable distribution of income that results (a revised FOR WHOM). The economic concern is that we *balance* this gain against the implied costs.

One way of reducing the economic cost of the Social Insurance program would be to eliminate the earnings test. If the earning test were eliminated, the marginal tax rate on the wages of older workers would drop from 50 percent to 0. In a flash, the work disincentive would vanish, and older workers would produce more goods and services.

There's a downside to this reform, however. If the earnings test were eliminated, all older individuals would get their full retirement benefit, even if they continued to work. This would raise the budgetary cost of the program substantially. To cover that cost, payroll taxes would have to increase. Higher payroll taxes would in turn reduce supply and demand for *younger* workers. Hence, the financial burden of eliminating the work test might actually *increase* the economic cost of Social Insurance.

There's also an equity issue here. Should we increase payroll taxes on younger low-income workers to give higher Social Insurance benefits to older workers who still command higher salaries? In 2000, the U.S. Congress gave a very qualified "yes" to this question. The earnings test was eliminated for workers over age 70 and a tax-free income threshold was set at $30,000 for workers aged 65–69. The marginal tax rate for workers aged 65–69 was also reduced to 33.3 percent. The lower earnings test and 50 percent marginal tax rate were left intact, however, for people aged 62–64, the ones for whom the retirement decision is most pressing. The *budget* cost of greater work incentives for "early retirees" was regarded as too high.

As we saw, all income transfer programs entail a redistribution of income. In the case of Social Insurance, the redistribution is largely intergenerational: Payroll taxes levied on younger workers finance retirement benefits for older workers. The system is financed on a pay-as-you-go basis; future benefits depend on future taxes. This is very different from private pension plans, whereby you salt away some wages while working to finance your own eventual benefits. Such private plans are advance-*funded.*

Many people say we should run the Social Insurance system the same way. They want to "privatize" Social Insurance by permitting workers to establish their own retirement plans. Instead of paying payroll taxes to fund someone else's benefits, you'd make a contribution to your own pension fund.

Compassion, Incentives, and Cost

Privatize Social Insurance?

The case for privatizing Social Insurance is based on both efficiency and equity. The efficiency argument reflects the core laissez-faire argument that markets know best. In a privatized system, individuals would have the freedom to tailor their consumption and saving choices. The elimination of mandatory payroll taxes and the earnings test would also lessen work disincentives.

Advocates of privatization also note how inequitable the existing program is for younger workers. The people now retired are getting a great deal: They paid relatively low payroll taxes when young and now receive substantial benefits. In part this high payoff is due to demographics. Fifteen years ago there were four workers for every retired person. By the time the post–World War II baby boomers retire, the ratio of workers to retirees will be a lot lower. By the year 2011, there will be only two workers for every retiree. As a result, the tax burden on tomorrow's workers will have to be a lot higher, or the baby boomers will have to accept much lower Social Insurance benefits. Either way, some generation of workers will get a lot less than everyone else. If Social Insurance is privatized, tomorrow's workers won't have to bear such a demographic tax burden.

As alluring as these suggestions sound, the privatization of Social Insurance would foster other inequities. The primary goal of Social Insurance is to fend off poverty among the aged. Social Insurance does this in two ways: by (1) transferring income from workers to retirees and (2) redistributing income from high-wage workers to low-wage workers in retirement with progressive benefit reductions. In these ways the program changes market outcomes. By contrast, a privatized system would let the market alone determine FOR WHOM goods are produced. Low-income workers and other people who saved little while working would end up poor in their golden years. In a privatized system, even some high earners and savers might end up poor if their investments turned sour. Would we turn our collective backs on these people? If not, then the government would have to intervene with *some* kind of transfer program. The real issue, therefore, may not be whether a privatized Social Insurance system would work but what kind of *public* transfer program we'd have to create to supplement it. Then the choice would be either (1) Social Insurance or (2) a privatized retirement system plus a public social assistance program for the aged poor. Framed in this context, the choice for the economy tomorrow is a lot more complex.

SUMMARY

- Income transfers are all payments for which no current goods or services are exchanged. They include both cash payments such as social assistance cheques and in-kind transfers such as food stamps and subsidized housing.
- Most transfer payments come from social insurance programs that cushion the income effects of specific events, for example, aging, illness, or unemployment. Social assistance programs are needs-tested; they pay benefits only to the poor.
- The basic goal of transfer programs is to alter the market's FOR WHOM outcome. Attempts to redistribute income may, however, have the unintended effect of reducing total income.
- Social assistance programs reduce work incentives in two ways. They offer some income to people who don't work at all, and they also tax the wages of recipients who do work via offsetting benefit reductions.
- The benefit reduction that occurs when wages increase is an implicit marginal tax. The higher the marginal tax rate, (1) the less the incentive to work but (2) the smaller the welfare caseload.
- The Social Insurance retirement program creates similar work disincentives. It provides an income floor for people who don't work and imposes a high marginal tax rate on workers aged 60–64.
- The core policy dilemma is to find an optimal balance between compassion (transferring more income) and incentives (keeping people at work contributing to total output).

Key Terms

in-kind transfers 341

cash transfers 341

target efficiency 342

social assistance programs 342

social insurance programs 342

budget deficit method 345

moral hazard 346

breakeven level of income 348

tax elasticity of labour supply 348

labour-force participation rate 351

Questions for Discussion

1. If we have to choose between compassion and incentives, which should we choose? Do the terms of the trade-off matter?

2. What's so hard about guaranteeing everyone a minimal level of income support? What problems arise?

3. If poor people don't want to work, should they get welfare? What about their children?

4. In the United States, once someone has received Temporary Aid to Need Families (TANF) social assistance benefits for a total of five years, they are permanently ineligible for more TANF benefits. Should they receive any further assistance? How will work incentives be affected?

5. In what ways do younger workers pay for Social Insurance benefits received by retired workers?

6. Should the Social Insurance earnings test be eliminated? What are the benefits and costs of doing so?

7. How would the distribution of income change if Social Insurance were privatized?

8. Who pays the economic cost of Social Insurance? In what ways?

EXERCISES

PROBLEMS

The Student Problem Set to accompany this chapter can be found at the end of the book.

WEB ACTIVITIES

Web Activities to accompany this chapter can be found on the Online Learning Centre at **http://www.mcgrawhill.ca/olc/schiller**.

PART 7

The Foreign Market

Our interactions with the rest of the world have a profound impact of the mix of output produced, the methods of production, and the distribution of income. Although Canada throughout its history has been a relatively large trading nation, recent advances in communications and transportation have only increased the globalization of the goods and services we buy and sell. And globalization itself has become a controversial issue.

This chapter on international trade takes a look at current trade patterns and discusses the motivation to trade. There is also a consideration of the pressures for trade protection and the effects of trade policy that create barriers to trade. Finally, there is a brief look at the intent and purpose of international institutions with respect to trade and Canada.

International Trade

Free trade, one of the greatest blessings a government can confer on a people, is in almost every country unpopular.

Thomas Babington Macaulay,
English historian and statesman, (1824)

In 2006, Canadians imported some $487.7 billion dollars worth of goods and services. We enjoy pineapples from Hawaii, cars from Japan, movies from the United Kingdom and t-shirts from China. And yet, free trade, as Macaulay suggests, is unpopular. We also sold about $524.7 billion dollars worth of Canadian produced goods and services to households in other countries in 2006, and no one is concerned because that production represents our jobs and our income So perhaps it isn't "free trade" that is the issue so much as "free imports". And perhaps that's understandable. After all, imports compete with goods and services that we have, or do, or could produce ourselves. In other words, imports compete with domestic jobs! So, we're left with exports, good; and imports, bad. But wait a minute. Our exports must then also be competition for, and replacements of, jobs in other countries. Would these other countries be better off not buying Canadian goods and services? Well, you see the problem. So, after all this, we are back to examining Macaulay's original proposition that if free trade is a blessing, why isn't it more popular?

Let's begin here by introducing—without discussion—a few of the arguments economists often put forward in favour of a free trade regime. At the conclusion of this chapter, you can look back and see if these arguments are persuasive.

As we noted above, increased trade leads to increased competition in many markets. Increased competition leads to the most efficient allocation of resources and therefore aids economic growth. Jagdish Bhagwati, in his book *In Defense of Globalization*, writes that the "freeing of trade is pursued because it is argued on both theoretical and empirical grounds, that it produces prosperity and has a favorable impact on poverty as well."[1] Amartya Sen expresses the importance of trade as one "freedom" that is fundamental to development in less developed countries.[2] He suggests that "the ability of the market mechanism to contribute to high economic growth and to overall economic progress has been widely—and rightly—acknowledged in the contemporary development literature."

[1] Jagdish Bhagwati, *In Defense of Globalization* (Oxford University Press: New York, 2004), p. 82.
[2] Amartya Sen, *Development as Freedom* (Anchor Books: New York, 1999), p. 6.

LEARNING OBJECTIVES

By the end of this chapter, you should be able to:

17.1 Describe the importance of trade to Canada's economy

17.2 Demonstrate the motivation to trade using a production possibility curve model and the mutual gain that arises from trade

17.3 Explain the concepts of absolute and comparative advantage and why absolute costs don't matter but comparative costs do

17.4 Explain why protectionist pressure arises in the economy and describe several arguments used to promote trade protection

17.5 Describe several barriers to trade and demonstrate the impact of barriers to trade through supply and demand

17.6 Describe the evolution of Canada's trade agreements, the WTO, and NAFTA

Therefore, the argument concludes, trade can make Canadians better off, can increase economic growth, can lead to a reduction in poverty, and can assist and accelerate development in emerging economies. The purpose of this chapter, then, is to explain how these advantages of international trade arise.

This chapter begins with a survey of international trade patterns—what goods and services we trade, and with whom. Then we address basic issues related to such trade:

- **What benefit, if any, do we get from international trade?**
- **How much harm do imports cause, and to whom?**
- **Should we protect ourselves from "unfair" trade by limiting imports?**

After examining the arguments for and against international trade, we draw some general conclusions about trade policy. As we'll see, international trade tends to increase *average* incomes, although it may diminish the job and income opportunities for specific industries and workers.

17.1 TRADE PATTERNS

In 2005 the United States imported $1,732.4 billion ($US) worth of merchandise (goods) from around the world.[3] This represented approximately 21 percent of the world's total merchandise imported. Compare this to Canada's total **imports** of $388.2 billion ($Cdn) (about $319.7 billion ($US)), or about 3.9 percent of the world's total. This large difference in dollar value, however hides the relative importance of imports in the two economies. In Canada, imports represent about 28 percent of total GDP, whereas in the United States, imports make up about one-half of that amount.

In 2006, although imports represented 34 percent of total gross domestic product, they accounted for even larger shares of specific product markets. Coffee is a familiar example. Since all coffee is imported, Canadians would have a harder time staying awake without imports. Likewise, there'd be no aluminum if we didn't import bauxite, no chrome bumpers if we didn't import chromium, no tin cans without imported tin, and a lot fewer computers without imported components.

We import *services* as well as *goods*. If you fly to Europe on Virgin Airways you're importing transportation services. If you stay in a London hotel, you're importing lodging services. When you go to Barclay's Bank to cash traveller's cheques, you're importing foreign financial services. These and other services now account for approximately 17 percent of total Canadian imports, or about $79.5 billion ($Cdn) in 2005.

While we're buying goods (merchandise) and services from the rest of the world, global consumers are buying our **exports.** In 2005, Canada exported $453.1 billion ($Cdn) worth of goods, including wheat, softwood lumber, cars and car parts, crude petroleum, aluminum, and natural gas.[4] We also exported approximately $66.6 billion in services, for example software licenses, tourism, engineering, and financial services.

In the case of *exports,* in 2005 Germany was the world's largest exporter of goods in dollar terms with sales of $969.9 billion ($US). The United States ranked second at $904.4 billion ($US). Although Canada ranked 9th in dollar terms, this hides the importance of exports as a proportion of our total GDP. In 2005, exports of goods represented a little more than 33 percent of total GDP compared to the U.S. ratio of

imports: Goods and services purchased from international sources.

Exports

exports: Goods and services sold to foreign buyers.

[3]World Trade Organization, "Leading Exporters and Importers in World Merchandise Trade: Table 1.6," *World Trade in 2005—Overview,* http://www.wto.org/english/res_e/statis_e/its2006_overview_e.htm, accessed February 24, 2007.

[4]World Trade Organization, "Leading exporters and importers in world merchandise trade: Table 1.6," *World Trade in 2005—Overview,* (2006) http://www.wto.org/english/res_e/statis_e/its2006_e/its06_overview_e.htm, accessed February 24, 2007.

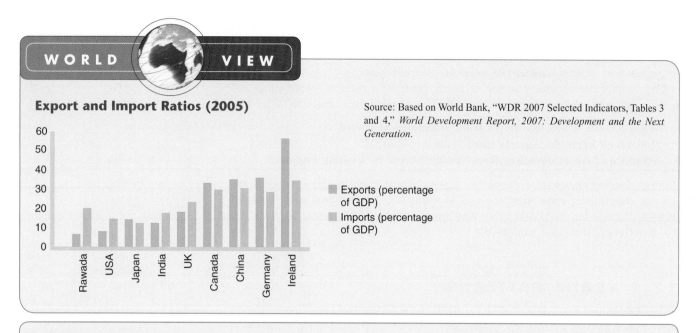

WORLD **VIEW**

Export and Import Ratios (2005)

Source: Based on World Bank, "WDR 2007 Selected Indicators, Tables 3 and 4," *World Development Report, 2007: Development and the Next Generation.*

- Exports (percentage of GDP)
- Imports (percentage of GDP)

Countries (left to right): Rawada, USA, Japan, India, UK, Canada, China, Germany, Ireland

Analysis: The relatively low export and import ratio of the United States and Japan reflects the relatively large size of their domestic economies and their ability to produce a broader range of goods. The higher ratios of Canada, China, Germany, and particularly Ireland illustrate a greater importance of trade as a component of GDP.

a little greater than 7 percent of GDP. If we include exported services as well, Canada's proportion to GDP increases to almost 38 percent.

The World View box illustrates the proportion of GDP represented by exports and imports for a number of countries. Ireland is one of the most export-oriented countries, with a ratio of goods exports to GDP of almost 56 percent. Since Ireland is also a large tourist destination, adding in tourism services can push its export ratio over 90 percent! By contrast, Rwanda exports very little as a proportion of GDP; less than 6 percent. This reality may indicate that Rwanda has few goods to sell to other countries, or that other countries may not allow Rwanda to sell goods in their markets. Where the latter is the case—due to government policy—Sen's freedom to trade is violated and Rwandan development may be hindered and delayed.

Trade Balances

Although we export a lot of goods, we also import other goods and these two values may not be equal, resulting in an imbalance in our trade. The trade balance is simply the difference between the value of exports and the value of imports, that is,

$$\text{Trade balance} = \text{Exports (X)} - \text{Imports (Im)}$$

In 2006, our total exports exceeded our total imports by $37 billion, meaning that Canada had a positive trade balance or **trade surplus** for this year.

trade surplus (deficit): The amount by which the value of exports exceeds (is less than) the value of imports in a given time period.

Although the overall trade balance includes both goods and services, these international flows are usually reported separately, with the *merchandise* trade balance distinguished from the *services* trade balance. As Table 17.1 shows, Canada had a merchandise trade surplus of $51.3 billion in 2005 but a trade deficit in services of $14.3 billion, adding up to the overall $37 billion surplus.

When Canada has a trade surplus with the rest of the world, other countries must have an offsetting trade deficit. On a global scale, imports must equal exports, since every good exported by one county must be imported by another. Hence, *any imbalance in Canada's trade must be offset by reverse imbalances elsewhere.*

Even when Canada's overall balance in the trade account is in surplus, the bilateral balance—that is, accounts with other individual countries—varies greatly. Table 17.2,

Product Category	Exports, X ($ billions)	Imports, Im ($ billions)	Surplus (Deficit)
Merchandise (goods)	$455.696	$404.391	$51.305
Services	69.010	83.269	(14.259)
Total Trade	$524.706	$487.660	$37.046

Source: Adapted from Statistics Canada Web site http://www40.statcan.ca/01/cst01/econ04.htm and also available from Statistics Canada CANSIM database table 380-0017. Statistics Canada information is used with the permission of Statistics Canada.

TABLE 17.1

Canada's Trade Balance, 2006

Both merchandise (goods) and services are traded between countries. Canada typically has a merchandise surplus and a services deficit. When combined, they resulted in an overall trade surplus in 2006.

Canada's Trade by Country or Country Group	Exports to ($ billions)	Imports from ($ billions)	Merchandise Trade Balance ($ billions)
United States	$360.963	$264.889	$96.024
Japan	$10.455	$11.882	−$1.427
United Kingdom	$11.560	$9.543	$2.016
Other EU Countries	$21.270	$32.495	−$11.224
Other OECD Countries	$17.561	$23.683	−$6.123
Other Countries	$33.887	$61.902	−$28.015

Notes: 1. United States includes Puerto Rico and Virgin Islands.
2. Other OECD countries excludes the United States, Japan, United Kingdom, and other EU (European Union) countries.
3. Other countries are countries not included in OECD or EU.

Source: Adapted from Statistics Canada Web site http://www40.statcan.ca/101/cst01/gblec02a.htm. Statistics Canada information is used with the permission of Statistics Canada.

TABLE 17.2

Canada's Bilateral Merchandise Trade Balances, 2006

The Canadian trade surplus is the net result of trade surpluses and trade deficits with individual countries. Canada had a huge merchandise trade surplus with the United States, which was reduced by merchandise trade deficits in much of the rest of the world.

for example, shows that our 2006 aggregate merchandise trade surplus ($51.3 billion) included a huge bilateral surplus with the United States ($96.0 billion) and bilateral deficits with Japan and the European Union countries taken together.

17.2 MOTIVATION TO TRADE

Many people wonder why we trade so much, particularly since (1) we import many of the things we also export (like computers, airplanes, clothes), (2) we *could* produce many of the other things we import, and (3) we worry so much about trade imbalances. Why not just import those few things that we can't produce ourselves, and export just enough to balance that trade?

Although it might seem strange to be importing goods we could produce ourselves, such trade is entirely rational. Our decision to trade with other countries arises from the same considerations that motivate individuals to specialize in production: satisfying their remaining needs in the marketplace. Why don't you become self-sufficient, growing all your own food, building your own shelter, recording your own songs? Presumably because you've found that you can enjoy a much higher standard of living (and better music) by working at just one job then buying other goods in the marketplace. When you do so, you're no longer self-sufficient. Instead, you are *specializing* in production, relying on others to produce the array of goods and services you want. When countries trade goods and services, they are doing the same thing—*specializing* in production, then *trading* for other desired goods. Why do they do this? Because ***specialization increases total output.***

To see how nations benefit from trade, we'll examine the production possibilities of two countries. We want to demonstrate that two countries that trade can together produce more output than they could in the absence of trade. If they can, ***the gain***

Specialization

from trade is increased world output and a higher standard of living in all trading countries. This is the essential message of the *theory of comparative advantage.*

Production and Consumption without Trade

Consider the production and consumption possibilities of just two countries—say, Canada and France. For the sake of illustration, assume that both countries produce only two goods: bread and wine. Let's also set aside worries about the law of diminishing returns and the substitutability of resources, thus transforming the familiar *production possibilities* curve into a straight line, as in Figure 17.1.

The "curves" in Figure 17.1 suggest that Canada is capable of producing much more bread than France. With our labour, land, and other resources, we assume that Canada is capable of producing up to 100 zillion loaves of bread per year. To do so, we would have to devote all our resources to that purpose. This capability is indicated by point *A* in Figure 17.1*a* and in row *A* of the accompanying production possibilities schedule. France (Figure 17.1*b*), on the other hand, confronts a *maximum* bread production of only 15 zillion loaves per year (point *G*).

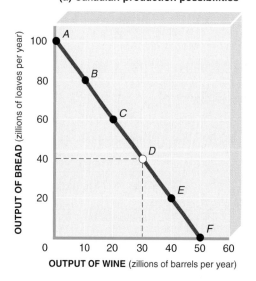

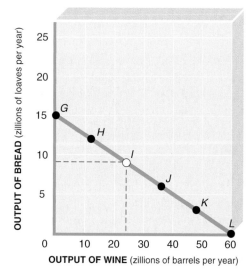

Canadian Production Possibilities		
	Bread (zillions of loaves) +	Wine (zillions of barrels)
A	100 +	0
B	80 +	10
C	60 +	20
D	40 +	30
E	20 +	40
F	0 +	50

French Production Possibilities		
	Bread (zillions of loaves) +	Wine (zillions of barrels)
G	15 +	0
H	12 +	12
I	9 +	24
J	6 +	36
K	3 +	48
L	0 +	60

FIGURE 17.1

Consumption Possibilities Without Trade

In the absence of trade, a country's consumption possibilities are identical to its production possibilities. The assumed production possibilities of Canada and France are illustrated in the graphs and the corresponding schedules. Before entering into trade, Canada chose to produce and consume at point *D*, with 40 zillion loaves of bread and 30 zillion barrels of wine. France chose point *I* on its own production possibilities curve. By trading, each country hopes to increase its consumption beyond these levels.

The capacities of the two countries for wine production are 50 zillion barrels for Canada (point *F*) and 60 zillion for France (point *L*), largely reflecting France's greater experience in tending vines. Both countries are also capable of producing alternative *combinations* of bread and wine, as evidenced by their respective production possibilities curves (points *A–F* for Canada and *G–L* for France).

In the absence of contact with the outside world, the production possibilities curve for each country would also define its **consumption possibilities.** Without imports, a country cannot consume more than it produces. Thus, the only immediate issue in a closed economy is which mix of output to choose—*what* to produce and consume—out of the domestic choices available.

Assume that Canadians choose point *D* on their production possibilities curve, producing and consuming 40 zillion loaves of bread and 30 zillion barrels of wine. The French, on the other hand, prefer the mix of output represented by point *I* on their production possibilities curve. At that point they produce and consume 9 zillion loaves of bread and 24 zillion barrels of wine.

To assess the potential gain from trade, we must focus the *combined* output of Canada and France. In this case, total world output (points *D* and *I*) comes to 49 zillion loaves of bread and 54 zillion barrels of wine. What we want to know is whether world output would increase if France and Canada abandoned their isolation and started trading. Could either country, or both, consume more output by engaging in a little trade?

Because both countries are saddled with limited production possibilities, trying to eke out a little extra wine and bread from this situation might not appear very promising. Such a conclusion is unwarranted, however. Take another look at the production possibilities confronting Canada, as reproduced in Figure 17.2*a*. Suppose Canada were to produce at point *C* rather than point *D*. At point *C* we could produce 60 zillion loaves of bread and 20 zillion barrels of wine. That combination is clearly possible, since it lies on the production possibilities curve. We didn't choose that point earlier because we assumed the mix of output at point *D* was preferable. The mix of output at point *C* could be produced, however.

We could also change the mix of output in France. Assume that France moved from point *I* to point *K*, producing 48 zillion barrels of wine and only 3 zillion loaves of bread.

> **consumption possibilities:** The alternative combinations of goods and services that a country could consume in a given time period.

Production and Consumption with Trade

(a) Canadian production and consumption

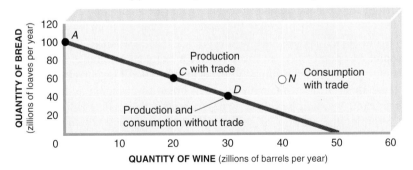

(b) French production and consumption

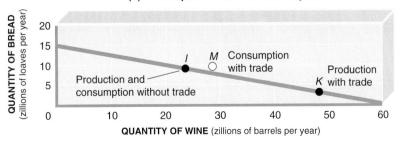

FIGURE 17.2
Consumption Possibilities with Trade

A country can increase its consumption possibilities through international trade. Each country alters its mix of domestic output to produce more of the good it produces best. As it does so, total world output increases, and each country enjoys more consumption. In this case, trade allows Canada's consumption to move from point *D* to point *N*. France moves from point *I* to point *M*.

Two observations are now called for. The first is simply that output mixes have changed in each country. The second, and more interesting, is that total world output has increased. When Canada and France were at points *D* and *I*, their *combined* output consisted of

	Bread (zillions of loaves)	Wine (zillions of barrels)
Canada (at point *D*)	40	30
France (at point *I*)	9	24
Total pretrade output	49	54

After moving along their respective production possibilities curves to points *C* and *K*, the combined world output becomes

	Bread (zillions of loaves)	Wine (zillions of barrels)
Canada (at point *C*)	60	20
France (at point *K*)	3	48
Total output with trade	63	68

Total world output has increased by 14 zillion loaves of bread and 14 zillion barrels of wine. ***Just by changing the mix of output in each country, we've increased total world output.*** This additional output creates the potential for making both countries better off than they were in the absence of trade.

Canada and France weren't producing at points *C* and *K* before because they simply didn't want to *consume* those particular output combinations. Nevertheless, our discovery that points *C* and *K* allow us to produce *more* output suggests that everybody can consume more goods and services if we change the mix of output in each country. This is our first clue as to how specialization and trade can benefit an economy.

Suppose we're the first to discover the potential benefits from trade. Using Figure 17.2 as our guide, we suggest to the French that they move their mix of output from point *I* to point *K*. As an incentive for making such a move, we promise to give them 6 zillion loaves of bread in exchange for 20 zillion barrels of wine. This would leave them at point *M*, with as much bread to consume as they used to have, plus an extra 4 zillion barrels of wine. At point *I* they had 9 zillion loaves of bread and 24 zillion barrels of wine. At point *M* they can have 9 zillion loaves of bread and 28 zillion barrels of wine. Thus, by altering their mix of output (from point *I* to point *K*) and then trading (point *K* to point *M*), the French end up with more goods and services than they had in the beginning. Notice in particular that this new consumption possibility (point *M*) lies *outside* France's domestic production possibilities curve.

The French will be quite pleased with the extra output they get from trading. But where does this leave Canada? Does France's gain imply a loss for us? Or do we gain from trade as well?

Mutual Gains   As it turns out, *both* Canada and France gain by trading. Canada, too, ends up consuming a mix of output that lies outside our production possibilities curve.

Note that at point *C* we produce 60 zillion loaves of bread per year and 20 zillion barrels of wine. We then export 6 zillion loaves to France. This leaves us with

TABLE 17.3
Gains from Trade

When nations specialize in production, they can export one good and import another and end up with more goods to consume than they had without trade. In this case, Canada specializes in bread production.

	Production	+	Imports	−	Exports	=	Consumption	Production and Consumption with No Trade
			Production and Consumption with Trade					
Canada at . . .	Point C						Point N	Point D
Bread	60	+	0	−	6	=	54	40
Wine	20	+	20	−	0	=	40	30
France at . . .	Point K						Point M	Point I
Bread	3	+	6	−	0	=	9	9
Wine	48	+	0	−	20	=	28	24

54 zillion loaves of bread to consume. In return for our exported bread, the French give us 20 zillion barrels of wine. These imports, plus our domestic production, permit us to *consume* 40 zillion barrels of wine. Hence, we end up consuming at point N, enjoying 54 zillion loaves of bread and 40 zillion barrels of wine. Thus, by first changing the mix of output (from point D to point C), then trading (point C to point N), we end up with 14 zillion more loaves of bread and 10 zillion more barrels of wine than we started with. International trade has made us better off, too.

Table 17.3 recaps the gains from trade for both countries. Notice that Canadian imports match French exports and vice versa. Also notice how the trade-facilitated consumption in each country exceeds no-trade levels.

There's no sleight of hand going on here; the gains from trade are due to specialization in production. When each country goes it alone, it's a prisoner of its own production possibilities curve; it must make production decisions on the basis of its own consumption desires. When international trade is permitted, however, each country can concentrate on the exploitation of its production capabilities. ***Each country produces those goods it makes best and then trades with other countries to acquire the goods it desires to consume.***

The resultant specialization increases total world output. In the process, each country is able to escape the confines of its own production possibilities curve, to reach beyond it for a larger basket of consumption goods. ***When a country engages in international trade, its consumption possibilities always exceed its production possibilities.*** These enhanced consumption possibilities are emphasized by the positions of points N and M outside the production possibilities curves (Figure 17.2). If it weren't possible for countries to increase their consumption by trading, there'd be no incentive for trading, and thus no trade.

17.3 PURSUIT OF COMPARATIVE ADVANTAGE

Although international trade can make both countries better off, it's not so obvious which goods should be traded, or on what terms. In our previous illustration, Canada ended up trading bread for wine in terms that were decidedly favourable to us. Why did we export bread rather than wine, and how did we end up getting such a good deal?

Opportunity Costs

comparative advantage: The ability of a country to produce a specific good at a lower opportunity cost than its trading partners.

The decision to export bread is based on **comparative advantage,** that is, the *relative* cost of producing different goods. Recall that we can produce a maximum of 100 zillion loaves of bread per year or 50 zillion barrels of wine. Thus, the domestic *opportunity cost* of producing 100 zillion loaves of bread is the 50 zillion barrels of wine we forsake to devote our resources to bread production. In fact, at every point on Canada's production possibilities curve (Figure 17.2a), the opportunity cost of a loaf of bread is $\frac{1}{2}$ barrel of wine. We're effectively paying half a barrel of wine to get a loaf of bread.

Although the cost of bread production in Canada might appear outrageous, even higher opportunity costs prevail in France. According to Figure 17.2b, the opportunity cost of producing a loaf of bread in France is a staggering four barrels of wine. To produce a loaf of bread, the French must use factors of production that could otherwise be used to produce four barrels of wine.

Comparative Advantage. A comparison of the opportunity costs prevailing in each country exposes the nature of comparative advantage. Canada has a comparative advantage in bread production because less wine has to be given up to produce bread in Canada than in France. In other words, the opportunity costs of bread production are lower in Canada than in France. *Comparative advantage refers to the relative (opportunity) costs of producing particular goods.*

A country should specialize in what it's *relatively* efficient at producing, that is, goods for which it has the lowest opportunity costs. In this case, Canada should produce bread because its opportunity cost ($\frac{1}{2}$ barrel of wine) is less than France's (four barrels of wine). Were you the production manager for the whole world, you'd certainly want each country to exploit its relative abilities, thus maximizing world output. Each country can arrive at that same decision itself by comparing its own opportunity costs to those prevailing elsewhere. *World output, and thus the potential gains from trade, will be maximized when each country pursues its comparative advantage.* Each country does so by exporting goods that entail relatively low domestic opportunity costs and importing goods that involve relatively high domestic opportunity costs. That's the kind of situation depicted in Table 17.3.

Absolute Costs Don't Matter

absolute advantage: The ability of a country to produce a specific good with fewer resources (per unit of output) than other countries.

In assessing the nature of comparative advantage, notice that we needn't know anything about the actual costs involved in production. Have you seen any data suggesting how much labour, land, or capital is required to produce a loaf of bread in either France or Canada? For all you and I know, the French may be able to produce both a loaf of bread and a barrel of wine with fewer resources than we're using. Such an **absolute advantage** in production might exist because of their much longer experience in cultivating both grapes and wheat or simply because they have more talent.

We can envy such productivity, and even try to emulate it, but it shouldn't alter our production or trade decisions. All we really care about are *opportunity costs*—what *we* have to give up in order to get more of a desired good. If we can get a barrel of wine for less bread in trade than in production, we have a comparative advantage in producing bread. As long as we have a *comparative* advantage in bread production we should exploit it. It doesn't matter whether France could produce either good with fewer resources. For that matter, even if France had an absolute advantage in *both* goods, we'd still have a *comparative* advantage in bread production, as we've already confirmed. The absolute costs of production were omitted from the previous illustration because they were irrelevant.

17.4 TERMS OF TRADE

terms of trade: The rate at which goods are exchanged; the amount of good A given up for good B in trade.

It definitely pays to pursue one's comparative advantage by specializing in production. It may not yet be clear, however, how we got such a good deal with France. We're clever traders, but beyond that, is there any way to determine the **terms of trade,** the quantity of good A that must be given up in exchange for good B? In our previous illustration, the terms of trade were very favourable to us; we exchanged only 6 zillion loaves of bread for 20 zillion barrels of wine (Table 17.3). The terms of trade were thus 6 loaves = 20 barrels.

The terms of trade with France were determined by our offer and France's ready acceptance. But why did France accept those terms? France was willing to accept the offer because the terms of trade permitted France to increase its wine consumption without giving up any bread consumption. The offer of 6 loaves for 20 barrels was an improvement over France's domestic opportunity costs. France's domestic possibilities required it to give up 24 barrels of wine to produce 6 loaves of bread (see Figure 17.2*b*). Getting bread via trade was simply cheaper for France than producing bread at home. France ended up with an extra 4 zillion barrels of wine (Table 17.3).

Our first clue to the terms of trade, then, lies in each country's domestic opportunity costs. ***A country won't trade unless the terms of trade are superior to domestic opportunities.*** In our example, the opportunity cost of 1 barrel of wine in Canada is 2 loaves of bread. Accordingly, we won't export bread unless we get at least 1 barrel of wine in exchange for every 2 loaves of bread shipped overseas.

All countries want to gain from trade. Hence, we can predict that ***the terms of trade between any two countries will lie somewhere between their respective opportunity costs in production.*** That is, a loaf of bread in international trade will be worth at least $\frac{1}{2}$ barrel of wine (Canada's opportunity cost) but no more than 4 barrels (the French opportunity cost). In our example, the terms of trade ended up at 1 loaf = 3.33 barrels (that is, at 6 loaves = 20 barrels). This represented a very large gain for Canada and a small gain for France. Figure 17.3 illustrates this outcome and several other possibilities.

Limits to the Terms of Trade

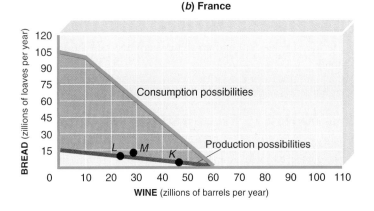

(a) Canada

(b) France

FIGURE 17.3
Searching for the Terms of Trade

Assume Canada can produce 100 zillion loaves of bread per year (point *A*). If we reduce output to only 85 zillion loaves, we could move to point *X*. At point *X* we have 7.5 zillion barrels of wine and 85 zillion loaves of bread.

Trade increases consumption possibilities. If we continued to produce 100 zillion loaves of bread, we could trade 15 zillion loaves to France in exchange for as much as 60 zillion barrels of wine. This would leave us *producing* at point *A* but *consuming* at point *Y*. At point *Y* we have more wine and no less bread than we had at point *X*.

A country will end up on its consumption possibilities curve only if it gets *all* the gains from trade. It will remain on its production possibilities curve only if it gets *none* of the gains from trade. The terms of trade determine how the gains from trade are distributed, and thus at what point in the shaded area each country ends up.

Note: The kink in the consumption possibilities curve at point *Y* occurs because France is unable to produce more than 60 zillion barrels of wine.

The Role of Markets and Prices

WEB NOTE

Find out more about Canada's trade negotiations and agreements at Foreign Affairs and International Trade Canada: http://www.international.gc.ca/tna-nac/menu-en.asp.

Relatively little trade is subject to such direct negotiations between countries. More often than not, the decision to import or export a particular good is left up to the market decisions of individual consumers and producers.

Individual consumers and producers aren't much impressed by such abstractions as comparative advantage. Market participants tend to focus on prices, always trying to allocate their resources to maximize profits or personal satisfaction. Consumers tend to buy the products that deliver the most utility per dollar of expenditure, while producers try to get the most output per dollar of cost. Everybody's looking for a bargain.

So what does this have to do with international trade? Well, suppose that Henri, an enterprising Frenchman, visited Canada before the advent of international trade. He observed that bread was relatively cheap while wine was relatively expensive—the opposite of the price relationship prevailing in France. These price comparisons brought to his mind the opportunity for making a fast euro. All he had to do was bring over some French wine and trade it in Canada for a large quantity of bread. Then he could return to France and exchange the bread for a greater quantity of wine. *Alors!* Were he to do this a few times, he'd amass substantial profits.

Henri's entrepreneurial exploits will not only enrich him but will also move each country toward its comparative advantage. Canada ends up exporting bread to France, and France ends up exporting wine to Canada, exactly as the theory of comparative advantage suggests. The activating agent isn't the Ministry of Trade and its 620 trained economists but simply one enterprising French trader. He's aided and encouraged, of course, by consumers and producers in each country. Canadian consumers are happy to trade their bread for his wines. They thereby end up paying less for wine (in terms of bread) than they'd otherwise have to. In other words, the terms of trade Henri offers are more attractive than the prevailing (domestic) relative prices. On the other side of the Atlantic, Henri's welcome is equally warm. French consumers are able to get a better deal by trading their wine for his imported bread than by trading with the local bakers.

Even some producers are happy. The wheat farmers and bakers in Canada are eager to deal with Henri. He's willing to buy a lot of bread and even to pay a premium price for it. Indeed, bread production has become so profitable in Canada that a lot of people who used to grow and mash grapes are now growing wheat and kneading dough. This alters the mix of output in the direction of more bread, exactly as suggested in Figure 17.2a.

In France, the opposite kind of production shift is taking place. French wheat farmers are planting more grape vines so they can take advantage of Henri's generous purchases. Thus, Henri is able to lead each country in the direction of its comparative advantage while raking in a substantial profit for himself along the way.

Where the terms of trade and the volume of exports and imports end up depends partly on how good a trader Henri is. It will also depend on the behaviour of the thousands of individual consumers and producers who participate in the market exchanges. In other words, trade flows depend on both the supply and the demand for bread and wine in each country. ***The terms of trade, like the price of any good, depend on the willingness of market participants to buy or sell at various prices.*** All we know for sure is that the terms of trade will end up somewhere between the limits set by each country's opportunity costs.

17.5 PROTECTIONIST PRESSURES

Although the potential gains from world trade are impressive, not everyone will participate in the celebration. On the contrary, some people will see the threat in establishing new trade routes. These people and groups will not only boycott the celebration but actively seek to discourage Canadians from continuing to trade at all!

APPLICATIONS

Chrysler Deals to Get Small Cars from China

The Chrysler Group has agreed in principle to import Chinese-built subcompact cars to North America and Europe, a milestone that could lead to the first Chinese cars on North American roads if Chinese automakers don't act on their own faster.

The deal between Chrysler and Chery Automobile Co., if approved by the DaimlerChrysler supervisory board this month, would give Chrysler a subcompact model it lacks.

While a domestic automaker importing Chinese vehicles may raise some political concerns, Chrysler CEO Tom LaSorda has said such a partnership is the only way Chrysler could sell a vehicle profitably.

Source: Based on Justin Hyde, Joe Guy Collier, and Jason Roberson, "Chrysler deals to get small cars from China," *National Post* (January 5, 2007), p. DT2.

Analysis: Goods imported from other countries compete with the same or similar goods produced in Canada and can alter the mix of production in both countries.

Microeconomic Pressures

Consider, for example, the auto workers at DaimlerChrysler in Windsor. As the Applications box above explains, DaimlerChrysler has agreed to a deal to sell cars imported from China in North America. Suppose Canadians are able to buy cars more cheaply from China than they can from Windsor. Before long we begin to hear talk about unfair foreign competition, or about the higher quality of the Canadian-built cars, or about the desire for "fair" trade. The car industry may also emphasize the importance of maintaining an adequate production of cars and a strong automobile industry here at home, just in case other countries use our lack of car production to force us to agree to other deals.

Import-Competing Industries. Joining with the auto workers will be the other automotive parts producers and merchants whose livelihood depends upon the domestic Canadian car industry. If they are clever enough, the auto workers will also get the Premier of Ontario to join their demonstration. After all, the Premier must recognize the needs of the local constituents, and there are almost certainly no Ontarians producing cars in China. Canadian consumers are, of course, benefiting from these reduced car prices, but they're unlikely to demonstrate over a couple of hundred dollars on the price of a car. On the other hand, those few hundred dollars per car translate into millions of dollars for the domestic car companies and their workers.

Of course, while Canadian consumers are buying cars made in China, Chinese consumers are buying goods and services from Canada. And the affected Chinese industries and workers are no happier about international trade than are the Canadian auto workers. They would dearly love to sink all those boats bringing Canadian goods and services from Canada, thereby protecting their own market position.

If we're to make sense of trade policies, then, we must recognize one central fact of life: Some producers have a vested interest in restricting international trade. In particular, ***workers and producers who compete with imported products—who work in import-competing industries—have an economic interest in restricting trade.*** This helps explain why Canadian auto workers are unhappy with DaimlerChrysler's deal with China and why the domestic car industry is unhappy with car imports. It also explains why farmers in the United States are unhappy with imports of Canadian wheat for pasta production, or why U.S. lumber producers are unhappy with imports of Canadian softwood lumber for home construction.

Export Industries. Although imports typically mean fewer jobs and less income for some domestic industries, exports represent increased jobs and income for other industries. Producers and workers in export industries gain from trade. Thus, on a microeconomic level there are identifiable gainers and losers from international trade. *Trade not only alters the mix of output but also redistributes income from import-competing industries to export industries.* This potential redistribution is the source of political and economic friction. It is this friction that makes the case for Macauley's contention that we began this chapter with, that free trade is "in almost every country, unpopular."

Net Gain. We must be careful to note, however, that the microeconomic gains from trade are greater than the microeconomic losses. It's not simply a question of robbing Peter to enrich Paul. We must remind ourselves that consumers in general enjoy a higher standard of living as a result of international trade. As we saw earlier, trade increases world efficiency and total output. Accordingly, we end up slicing up a larger pie rather than just reslicing the same old smaller pie.

This point is made by U.S. economist Paul Krugman when he describes the perspectives of business people and economists. Business people tend to focus on the impact of individual exports or imports, often a win–lose situation for any particular industry. The focus of economists is on the "gains from trade," the fundamental increase in total world spending described above.

> Why don't economists subscribe to what sounds like common sense to businesspeople? The idea that free trade means more global jobs seems obvious: More trade means more exports and therefore more export-related jobs. But there is a problem with that argument. Because one country's exports are another country's imports, every dollar of export sales is, as a matter of sheer mathematical necessity, matched by a dollar of spending shifted from some country's domestic goods to imports. Unless there is some reason to think that free trade will increase total world spending, overall world demand will not change.[5]

That total world spending will increase is, in fact, the point made with comparative advantage. As countries shift their resources towards goods and services in which they have comparative advantage, total world production can rise, thus increasing income and spending. In other words, trade is beneficial because it increases total production (and thereby additional employment and consumption).

The gains from trade will mean nothing to workers who end up with a smaller slice of the (larger) pie. It's important to remember, however, that the gains from trade are large enough to make everybody better off. Whether we actually choose to distribute the gains from trade in this way is a separate question, to which we shall return shortly. Note here, however, that *trade restrictions designed to protect specific microeconomic interests reduce the total gains from trade.* Trade restrictions leave us with a smaller pie to split up.

Additional Pressures

Import-competing industries are the principal obstacle to expanded international trade. Selfish micro interests aren't the only source of trade restrictions, however. Other arguments are also used to restrict trade.

National Security. The national security argument for trade restrictions is twofold. We can't depend on foreign suppliers to provide us with essential defense-related goods, it is said, because that would leave us vulnerable in time of war. The domestic agricultural industry often promotes a similar argument. If Canada was to become dependant on foreign sources of food, we could be "made" to make decisions we otherwise wouldn't make at the threat of the food being withheld.

---

[5]Paul Krugman, "A country is not a company," *Harvard Business Review,* (96)2, pp. 40–47.

APPLICATIONS

U.S. Appliance Firms Guilty of Dumping in Canada

OTTAWA—Prices for some major appliances could more than double as a result of a ruling that the U.S. companies behind Whirlpool, Frigidaire, Kelvinator and Amana have unfairly dumped exports on the $1-billion-a-year Canadian appliance market.

The Canadian International Trade Tribunal has confirmed a ruling from the Canadian Customs and Revenue Agency that refrigerators, dishwashers and dryers were sold at below-market prices.

Camco Inc. of Hamilton, which makes appliances under the GE, Hotpoint, Kenmore, Beaumark and other brand names, complained last November that it was losing sales to unfair competition from White Consolidated Industries Inc. and Whirlpool Corp., two major U.S. manufacturers.

A four-month investigation, following a probe by customs officials, confirmed the goods had been sold for less than the price in the home [U.S.] market or at a loss.

"It [the ruling] will have a substantial positive impact for Camco. We're confident we will regain a substantial share of the profit we've lost over the past two years," James Fleck, Camco president, said yesterday. "It's a level playing field and an opportunity to regain the market share we've lost."

Depending on the model, prices will have to increase anywhere from a few dollars to almost 150%.

Source: Ian Jack, "U.S. appliance firms guilty of dumping in Canada," *National Post,* August 9, 2000, p. C3. Material reprinted with the express permission of National Post Company, a CanWest Partnership.

Analysis: Dumping results in unfair competitive pressure as selling prices don't necessarily reflect market conditions or costs. These and other pressures in the appliance industry caused the Hamilton Camco plant to close in 2004, while the company itself was sold to Controladora Mabe SA. a Mexico-based company.

Dumping. Another argument against free trade arises from the practice of **dumping.** Foreign producers "dump" their goods when they sell them in Canada at prices lower than those prevailing in their own country, perhaps even below the costs of production.

> **dumping:** The sale of goods in export markets at prices below domestic prices.

Dumping may be unfair to import-competing producers, but it isn't necessarily unwelcome to the rest of us. As long as foreign producers continue dumping, we're getting foreign products at low prices. How bad can that be? There's a legitimate worry, however. Foreign producers might hold prices down only until domestic producers are driven out of business. Then we might be compelled to pay the foreign producers higher prices for their products. In that case, dumping could consolidate market power and lead to monopoly-type pricing. The fear of dumping, then, is analogous to the fear of predatory pricing. The Applications box illustrates both the concern of manufacturers and the benefit to consumers. The loss of market share and profitability to Camco Inc. may result in a reduction in production, or a complete cessation. Consumers, on the other hand, will pay "from a few dollars to almost 150%" more for their refrigerators, dishwashers, or dryers as additional duties are imposed.

The potential costs of dumping are serious. It's not always easy to determine when dumping occurs, however. Those who compete with imports have an uncanny ability to associate any and all low prices with predatory dumping.

Infant Industries. Actual dumping threatens to damage already established domestic industries. Even normal import prices, however, may make it difficult or impossible for a new domestic industry to develop. Infant industries are often burdened with abnormally high startup costs. These high costs may arise from the need to train a whole workforce and the expenses of establishing new marketing channels. With time to grow, however, an infant industry might experience substantial cost reductions and establish a comparative advantage. When this is the case, trade restrictions might help nurture an industry in its infancy. Trade restrictions are justified, however, only if there's tangible evidence that the industry can develop a comparative advantage reasonably quickly.

Improving the Terms of Trade. A final argument for restricting trade rests on how the gains from trade are distributed. As we observed, the distribution of the gains from trade depends on the terms of trade. If we were to buy fewer imports, foreign producers might lower their prices. If that happened, the terms of trade would move in our favour, and we'd end up with a larger share of the gains from trade.

One way to bring about this sequence of events is to put restrictions on imports, making it more difficult or expensive for Canadians to buy foreign products. Such restrictions will reduce the volume of imports, thereby inducing foreign producers to lower their prices. Unfortunately, this strategy can easily backfire: Retaliatory restrictions on imports, each designed to improve the terms of trade, will ultimately eliminate all trade and therewith all the gains people were competing for in the first place.

17.6 BARRIERS TO TRADE

The microeconomic losses associated with imports give rise to a constant clamour for trade restrictions. People whose jobs and incomes are threatened by international trade tend to organize quickly and air their grievances. The World View box below depicts the efforts of farmers in Montana and North Dakota to limit imports of Canadian wheat and livestock. They hope to convince Congress to impose restrictions on imports. More often than not, Congress grants the wishes of these well-organized and well-financed special interests.

Embargoes

embargo: A prohibition on exports or imports.

The surefire way to restrict trade is simply to eliminate it. To do so, a country need only impose an embargo on exports or imports, or both. An **embargo** is nothing more than a prohibition against trading particular goods.

As the World View on the next page illustrates, some embargo decisions arise not from a concern for domestic jobs, but more from domestic sensibilities. While the reason underlying the decision may be valid, the article makes the point that economic consequences are still imposed on both potential consumers—replacement with more expensive or less desirable products—and on the export producers—loss of jobs, incomes, and way of life.

Tariffs

tariff: A tax (duty) imposed on imported goods.

A more frequent trade restriction is a **tariff,** a special tax imposed on imported goods. Tariffs, also called *customs duties,* were once the principal source of revenue for governments. In modern times, tariffs have been used primarily as a means to protect specific industries from import competition. In Canada, while most tariffs are imposed

WORLD VIEW

Farmers Stage Protests over Import of Products

Farmers claiming that imports of Canadian grain and other agricultural products are depressing U.S. prices threatened on Tuesday more blockades at border crossings unless the U.S. government acts to slow the flow of goods.

Farmers also want Canadian wheat and livestock tested for diseases and additives that are banned here.

Blockades and other protests have appeared at various border crossings in North Dakota and Montana for several days. In Montana, 20 long-haul truckers were ticketed Monday, the first day of a state crackdown on border inspections. And farmers in North Dakota dumped grain on U.S. Highway 281, stopping truck traffic for eight hours.

"We've got an oversupply of wheat, hogs and cattle already," said Curt Trulson, a farmer in Ross, N.D. "We don't need any more foreign commodities."

Source: *USA Today,* September 23, 1998. USA TODAY. © 1998, USA Today. Reprinted with permission. www.usatoday.com

Analysis: Import-competing industries cite lots of reasons for restricting trade. Their primary concern, however, is to protect their own jobs and profits.

Inuit Call for Rethink of Seal-Ban Proposal

A council representing Inuit from Canada, Russia, Alaska and Greenland has warned European legislators that a renewed push to ban seal products could devastate native communities.

Some members of the European Parliament say the annual seal hunt in Canada is cruel and unsustainable and they've passed a non-binding declaration calling for a ban on imports of seal products. It will be up to the European Commission to determine whether it becomes law.

Meanwhile, the German Parliament unanimously endorsed an import ban the day after the Inuit Circumpolar Council,

which represents 150,000 Inuit living in the Arctic, sent a letter asking legislators to rethink their position.

"The proposed legislation would hurt our Inuit economy, our Inuit culture, and our Inuit spirituality in unimaginable ways," council chairwoman Patricia Cochran said in a letter dated Oct. 18.

"Inuit base their hunt, all hunts, on the principle of sustainable use, not on the principle of subjective 'public decency' as some European governments seem to be doing," she wrote.

Source: *The Globe and Mail* (October 31, 2006), p. A15. Used with permission of the Canadian Press.

Analysis: Although bans, or embargoes, may have more to do with political, social, or cultural sensibilities, the economic impacts are no less consequential.

on goods coming from other countries, in some cases there are also tariffs for goods moving from one province to another.

The tariff imposed on imported goods is also dependent on the particular country of origin. In the most recent customs tariff provided by the Canada Border Services Agency, countries are separated into four categories (although an individual country can be simultaneously in more than one category). Some countries have been designated for a General Preferential Tariff treatment, some countries are beneficiaries of the Least Developed Country tariff treatment, some countries are designated beneficiary countries for purposes of the Commonwealth Caribbean Countries tariff treatment, and others receive no beneficial treatment and are subject to the full tariff.[6]

The attraction of tariffs to import-competing industries should be obvious. *A tariff on imported goods makes them more expensive to domestic consumers and thus less competitive with domestically produced goods.* Among tariffs in place for Canada in 2007 were $0.374 per litre on sparkling wine and $0.2816 per litre on cider. These tariffs enable Canadian-produced sparkling wine and cider to sell at a higher price, and therefore contribute higher sales revenue and profits for domestic producers. In the same manner, ski jackets (made from synthetic material) face a tariff of 18 percent while a new guitar has 6 percent added.[7] In each case, domestic producers in import-competing industries gain. The losers are domestic consumers, who end up paying higher prices.

"Beggar Thy Neighbour." Microeconomic interests aren't the only source of pressure for tariff protection. Imports represent leakage from the domestic circular flow and a potential loss of jobs at home. From this perspective, the curtailment of imports looks like an easy solution to the problem of domestic unemployment. Just get people to "buy Canadian" instead of buying imported products, so the argument goes, and domestic output and employment will surely expand.

Tariffs designed to expand domestic employment are more likely to fail than to succeed. If a tariff wall does stem the flow of imports, it effectively transfers the

WEB NOTE

For more information about Canada's most recent customs tariffs, go to the Canada Border Services Agency site at http://www.cbsa-asfc.gc.ca/trade-commerce/tariff-tarif/menu-e.html#current.

[6]See the Canada Border Services Agency Web site at http://www.cbsa-asfc.gc.ca/menu-eng.html for more information.
[7]All tariff amounts have been taken from documents on the Canada Border Services Agency Web site. These are from the Departmental Consolidation of the Customs Tariff, 2007. http://www.cbsa-asfc.gc.ca/general/publications/tariff2007/01-99/tblmod-1-e.html, accessed March 2, 2007.

"Beggar-Thy-Neighbour" Policies in the 1930s

President Herbert Hoover, ignoring the pleas of 1,028 economists to veto it, signed the Smoot-Hawley Tariff Act on June 17, 1930. It was a hollow celebration. The day before, anticipating the signing, the stock market suffered its worst collapse since November 1929, and the law quickly helped push the Great Depression deeper.

The new tariffs, which by 1932 rose to an all-time high of 59 percent of the average value of imports (today it's 5 percent), were designed to save American jobs by restricting foreign competition. Economists warned that angry nations would retaliate, and they did.

- Spain passed the Wais tariff in July in reaction to U.S. tariffs on grapes, oranges, cork, and onions.
- Switzerland, objecting to new U.S. tariffs on watches, embroideries, and shoes, boycotted American exports.
- Italy retaliated against tariffs on hats and olive oil with high tariffs on U.S. and French automobiles in June 1930.
- Canada reacted to high duties on many food products, logs, and timber by raising tariffs threefold in August 1932.

- Australia, Cuba, France, Mexico, and New Zealand also joined in the tariff wars.

From 1930 to 1931 U.S. imports dropped 29 percent, but U.S. exports fell even more, 33 percent, and continued their collapse to a modern-day low of $2.4 billion in 1933. World trade contracted by similar proportions, spreading unemployment around the globe.

In 1934 the U.S. Congress passed the Reciprocal Trade Agreements Act to empower the president to reduce tariffs by half the 1930 rates in return for like cuts in foreign duties on U.S. goods. The "beggar-thy-neighbour" policy was dead. Since then, the nations of the world have been reducing tariffs and other trade barriers.

Source: World Bank, *World Development Report 1987;* and *The Wall Street Journal,* April 28, 1989, Reprinted by permission of The Wall Street Journal, © 1989 Dow Jones & Company. All rights reserved. www.worldbank.org; www.wsj.com

Analysis: Tariffs inflict harm on foreign producers. If foreign countries retaliate with tariffs of their own, world trade will shrink and unemployment will increase in all countries.

unemployment problem to other countries, a phenomenon often referred to as "beggar thy neighbour." The resultant loss of business in other countries leaves them less able to purchase our exports (see the World View box).

Quotas

quota: A limit on the quantity of a good that may be imported in a given time period.

Tariffs reduce the flow of imports by raising import prices. The same outcome can be attained more directly by imposing import **quotas,** numerical restrictions on the quantity of a particular good that may be imported. As explained in the Applications box on the next page, the intention to limit the importation of milk-protein concentrates will increase the revenue of dairy fanners in Canada by $2-million a month, but might result in a reduction of cheese production in Canada or higher prices faced by consumers. Although quotas restrict the quantity of imports while tariffs increase the price of importing, both result in the same effect—protection of the domestic producer and higher domestic prices for consumers.

Comparative Effects

Quotas, like all barriers to trade, reduce world efficiency and invite retaliatory action. Moreover, their impact can be even more damaging than tariffs. To see this, we may compare market outcomes in four different contexts: no trade, free trade, tariff-restricted trade, and quota-restricted trade.

No-Trade Equilibrium. Figure 17.4a depicts the supply-and-demand relationships that would prevail in an economy that imposed a trade *embargo* on foreign textiles. In this situation, the *equilibrium price* of textiles is completely determined by domestic demand and supply curves. The no-trade equilibrium price is p_1, and the quantity of textiles consumed is q_1.

APPLICATIONS

Ottawa Moves on Dairy Protection: Import Restriction

OTTAWA—The federal Conservative government has moved to restrict the import of a key ingredient used to make cheese.

The decision, announced yesterday by Agriculture Minister Chuck Strahl, came about due to the failure by the country's dairy processors to resolve a dispute regarding the import of milk-protein concentrates. Dairy farmers claimed they lost, collectively, about $2-million a month in sales in the last fiscal year because of increased imports of milk-protein substitutes, and have called on Ottawa to restrict imports of the product for the past three years.

"We are very pleased with the outcome," said Jacques Laforge, president of the 16,000-member Dairy Farmers of Canada. "It stops the erosion of our revenue. What we've lost, we've lost. But this freezes the damage."

Don Jarvis, president of the Dairy Processors Association of Canada, said his members—such as Saputo Inc., Kraft Canada Inc. and Agripur—bought milk-protein from abroad because it is not readily available in Canada and was in most cases cheaper. He said yesterday's decision could have an impact on the availability and pricing of cheese.

Source: P. Vieira, "Ottawa moves on dairy protection: Import restriction," *National Post* (February 8, 2007), p. FP7. Material reprinted with the express permission of National Post Company, a CanWest Partnership.

Analysis: The quote from the president of the Dairy Farmers of Canada crystallizes the point here: "it stops the erosion of our revenue." Dairy farmers are able to receive higher prices for milk-protein concentrates because the restriction on imports imposed by the federal government reduces supply and thereby raises the price of imported substitutes.

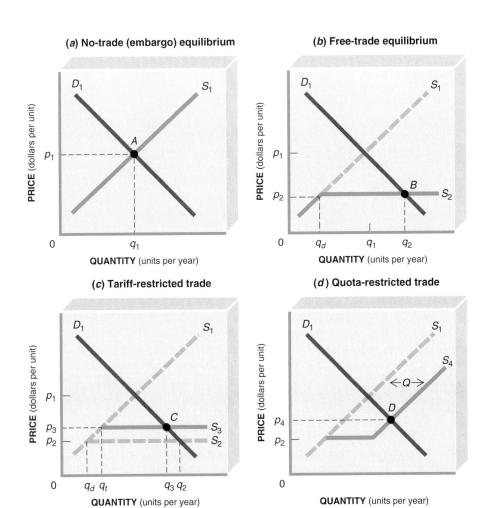

FIGURE 17.4

The Impact of Trade Restrictions

In the *absence of trade,* the domestic price and sales of a good will be determined by domestic supply and demand curves (point A in part a). Once trade is permitted, the market supply curve will be altered by the availability of imports. With *free trade* and unlimited availability of imports at price p_2, a new market equilibrium will be established at world prices (point B).

Tariffs raise domestic prices and reduce the quantity sold (point C). *Quotas* put an absolute limit on imported sales and thus give domestic producers a great opportunity to raise the market price (point D).

Free-Trade Equilibrium. Suppose now that the embargo is lifted. The immediate effect of this decision will be a rightward shift of the market supply curve, as foreign supplies are added to domestic supplies (Figure 17.4b). If an unlimited quantity of textiles can be bought in world markets at a price of p_2, the new supply curve will look like S_2 (infinitely elastic at p_2). The new supply curve (S_2) intersects the old demand curve (D_1) at a new equilibrium price of p_2 and an expanded consumption of q_2. At this new equilibrium, domestic producers are supplying the quantity q_d while foreign producers are supplying the rest ($q_2 - q_d$). Comparing the new equilibrium to the old one, we see that *free trade results in reduced prices and increased consumption.*

Domestic textile producers are unhappy, of course, with their foreign competition. In the absence of trade, the domestic producers would sell more output (q_1) and get higher prices (p_1). Once trade is opened up, the willingness of foreign producers to sell unlimited quantities of textiles at the price p_2 puts a lid on domestic prices.

Tariff-Restricted Trade. Figure 17.4c illustrates what would happen to prices and sales if the United Textile Producers were successful in persuading the government to impose a tariff. Assume that the tariff raises imported textile prices from p_2 to p_3, making it more difficult for foreign producers to undersell domestic producers. Domestic production expands from q_d to q_t, imports are reduced from $q_2 - q_d$ to $q_3 - q_t$, and the market price of textiles rises. Domestic textile producers are clearly better off, whereas consumers and foreign producers are worse off. In addition, the government will collect increased tariff revenues.

Quota-Restricted Trade. Now consider the impact of a textile *quota*. Suppose we eliminate tariffs but decree that imports can't exceed the quantity Q. Because the quantity of imports can never exceed Q, the supply curve is effectively shifted to the right by that amount. The new curve S_4 (Figure 17.4d) indicates that no imports will occur below the world price p_2 and above that price the quantity Q will be imported. Thus, the *domestic* demand curve determines subsequent prices. Foreign producers are precluded from selling greater quantities as prices rise further. This outcome is in marked contrast to that of tariff-restricted trade (Figure 17.4c), which at least permits foreign producers to respond to rising prices. Accordingly, *quotas are a greater threat to competition than tariffs, because quotas preclude additional imports at any price.* Suppose that restricting the imports of milk-protein concentrates—as suggested in the Applications box—increases the price of cheese by 20 percent. This would result in $10 worth of cheese now being priced at $12. Canadian consumers end up paying more for cheese, and having fewer dollars remaining to buy other goods and services.

"TELL ME AGAIN HOW THE QUOTAS ON JAPANESE CARS HAVE PROTECTED US"

—from *Herblock at Large* (Pantheon Books, 1987).

Analysis: Trade restrictions that protect import-competing industries also raise consumer prices.

Voluntary Restraint Agreements

voluntary restraint agreement (VRA): An agreement to reduce the volume of trade in a specific good; a voluntary quota.

A slight variant of quotas has been used in recent years. Rather than impose quotas on imports, the government asks foreign producers to "voluntarily" limit their exports. A form of this **"voluntary restraint agreement"** was part of the Canada–United States softwood lumber agreement negotiated in Fall 2006. One of the options in the agreement was for producers to "restrain" exports to a maximum market share of between 30 and 34 percent, depending upon the prevailing market price in the United States.

In the 1980s, Canada negotiated with Japanese automakers to "voluntarily" limit their sales of cars in Canada. The result was a shortage of Japanese cars in the market, and higher prices (and profit margins) for each car than they otherwise would have been.

All these voluntary export restraints, as they're often called, represent an informal type of quota. The only difference is that they're negotiated rather than imposed. But these differences are lost on consumers, who end up paying higher prices for these goods.

Nontariff Barriers

Tariffs and quotas are the most visible barriers to trade, but they're only the tip of the iceberg. Indeed, the variety of protectionist measures that have been devised is testimony to the ingenuity of the human mind. At the turn of the twentieth century, the Germans were committed to a most-favoured-nation policy, a policy of extending equal treatment

WORLD VIEW

High Court Opens U.S. Roads to Mexican Trucks

The Supreme Court ruled yesterday that the Bush administration can open U.S. roads to Mexican trucks as soon as it wants, overruling a lower court judgment that the government must first study the environmental effects.

Under NAFTA, which went into effect in 1994, the United States was supposed to phase out restrictions on Mexican trucks crossing the border by 2000, provided those trucks meet U.S. safety standards. But under pressure from members of Congress and the Teamsters union, which feared losing jobs to low-wage Mexican drivers, the Clinton administration maintained the existing barriers, citing safety concerns. As a result, Mexican trucks have been confined to a 20-mile zone along the border, where they transfer their loads to U.S. carriers in cities such as San Diego and Laredo, Tex.

The Bush administration vowed to open the border in 2001 after a NAFTA panel held that Washington was violating the agreement.

—Paul Blustein

Source: *The Washington Post,* June 8, 2004. © 2004 The Washington Post. Reprinted with permission. www.washingtonpost.com.

Analysis: Nontariff barriers like extraordinary safety requirements on Mexican trucks limit import competition.

---

to all trading partners. The Germans, however, wanted to lower the tariff on cattle imports from Denmark without extending the same break to Switzerland. Such a preferential tariff would have violated the most-favoured-nation policy. Accordingly, the Germans created a new and higher tariff on "brown and dappled cows reared at a level of at least 300 meters above sea level and passing at least one month in every summer at an altitude of at least 800 meters." The new tariff was, of course, applied equally to all countries. But Danish cows never climb that high, so they weren't burdened with the new tariff.

With the decline in tariffs over the last 20 years, nontariff barriers have increased. Canada uses product standards, licensing restrictions, restrictive procurement practices, and other nontariff barriers to restrict imports.

APPLICATIONS

B.C. Premier Shines Spotlight on Free Trade

It wasn't even on the agenda, but the seemingly dry subject of provincial free trade stole some of the spotlight at a meeting between western premiers yesterday. "When are we going to decide we are a country? When are we going to decide that the free movement of goods and people and services is something that is part of what a national identity should be?" British Columbia Premier Gordon Campbell told reporters after the annual conference wrapped up in Iqaluit.

B.C. and Alberta signed a first-of-its-kind interprovincial trade agreement that began coming into effect this spring. The deal, which is opposed by unions in both provinces, aims to slash trade barriers and red tape and increase labour mobility in a bid to create the country's second-largest economic trade zone, behind Ontario. Both governments were confident that the Trade, Investment and Labour Mobility Agreement (TILMA) would become an example for the rest of the country. However, no other provinces have acted on it or joined it.

Source: Katherine Harding, "B.C. Premier shines spotlight on free trade," *The Globe and Mail* (July 7, 2007), p. A7.

Analysis: Barriers to trade are not only an international concern, many barriers exist between provinces across the country, and the motivation, benefits, and costs of reducing or eliminating them are the same as in the international sphere.

An Increasingly Global Market

17.7 INTERNATIONAL INSTITUTIONS

Proponents of free trade and representatives of special interests that profit from trade protection are in constant conflict. But most of the time the trade-policy deck seems stacked in favour of the special interests. Because the interests of import-competing firms and workers are highly concentrated, they're quick to mobilize politically. By contrast, the benefits of freer trade are less direct and spread over millions of consumers. As a consequence, the beneficiaries of free trade are less likely to monitor trade policy—much less lobby actively to change it. Hence, the political odds favour the spread of trade barriers.

Multilateral Trade Pacts

Despite these odds, the long-term trend is toward *reducing* trade barriers, thereby increasing global competition. Two forces encourage this trend. The principal barrier to protectionist policies is worldwide recognition of the gains from freer trade. Since world nations now understand that trade barriers are ultimately self-defeating, they're more willing to rise above the din of protectionist cries and dismantle trade barriers. They diffuse political opposition by creating across-the-board **trade pacts** that seem to spread the pain (and gain) from freer trade across a broad swath of industries. Such pacts also incorporate multiyear timetables that give affected industries time to adjust.

> **trade pact:** A negotiation or agreement between countries governing trade; *bilateral* trade pacts involve two countries, and *multilateral* trade pacts involve more than two countries.

The opposition of import-competing industries to these multilateral, multiyear trade pacts is countered by a second force: the interests of *export*-oriented industries and other multilateral firms. Restrictions on imports of milk-protein concentrates in Canada may result in retaliation by the countries that sold us the concentrates and a reduction in Canadian exports to those countries. Tariffs or export charges, such as in the 2006 Softwood Lumber agreement, increases the price of lumber in the U.S. market, making buildings and housing more expensive for U.S. consumers. An increasing popular awareness of such damage has created a political climate for freer trade.

Global Pacts: GATT and WTO

The granddaddy of the multilateral, multiyear free-trade pacts was the 1947 **General Agreement on Tariffs and Trade (GATT).** Twenty-three nations pledged to reduce trade barriers and give all GATT nations equal access to their domestic markets.

> **General Agreement on Tariffs and Trade (GATT):** A trade pact that covered the rules and regulations governing the international trade in goods; now part of the World Trade Organization, WTO.

Since the first GATT pact, seven more "rounds" of negotiations have expanded the scope of GATT: 117 nations signed the 1994 pact. As a result of these GATT pacts, average tariff rates in developed countries have fallen from 40 percent in 1948 to less than 4 percent today.

WTO. The 1994 GATT pact also created the **World Trade Organization (WTO)** to enforce free-trade rules. If a nation feels its exports are being unfairly excluded from another country's market, it can file a complaint with the WTO. In April 2006 Canada joined the European Union and the United States in complaining about the way China imposes tariffs on imported car parts. In September 2006 the WTO created a panel drawn from other WTO members to make a decision about the complaint. If the panel finds in Canada's favour, they may enable Canada to impose retaliatory tariffs on some Chinese goods or services.

> **World Trade Organization (WTO):** A global international institution that deals with the rules of trade among nations.

On the other side, in November 2006 the European Union filed a complaint with the WTO regarding Canada's unequal tax treatment of domestically produced versus imported wine and beer. At this stage, the European Communities are asking for "consultations" with Canada. If these consultations prove fruitless, the complaint could move to a "third-party" panel for an adjudication, and if the European Communities were successful, the ability to impose retaliatory tariffs on other Canadian goods or services.

In effect, the WTO is now the world's trade police force. It is empowered to cite nations that violate trade agreements and even to impose remedial action when violations persist. Why do sovereign nations give the WTO such power? Because they are all convinced that free trade is the surest route to GDP growth.

APPLICATIONS

DOHA Talks in Danger of Collapse; Subsidies at Issue: Rich, Poor Countries Remain at Odds

WASHINGTON—Global trade talks [the Doha Round] launched six years ago appear to be sliding quickly into a coma with the world's wealthiest countries fearing there may not be any quick recovery. Trade ministers from Canada, the United States and leading Asian countries wrapped up another stalled set of trade negotiations in Australia yesterday by complaining there appears to be little chance for trade breakthroughs globally, . . . or among Asia–Pacific countries any time soon.

The Doha Round launched in 2001 and aimed at reducing farm subsidies among the richer countries and making it easier

for poorer countries to trade, has virtually gone nowhere in the past six years. The rich and poor countries are still at odds, leading to a near collapse last month in Germany at a meeting of the so-called G4 countries, which are the U.S., the European Union, Brazil and India.

Source: Peter Morton, "DOHA talks in danger of collapse; Subsidies at issue: rich, poor countries remain at odds," *National Post* (July 7, 2007), p. FP7. Material used with express permission of Montreal National Post Company, a CanWest Partnership.

Analysis: Multilateral trade negotiations are complex. Although "rich" countries have pledged to reduce subsidies that distort trade, political consequences and internal lobbies have made it difficult to actually do so.

WTO Protests. Although freer trade clearly boosts economic growth, some people say that it does more harm than good. Environmentalists question the very desirability of continued economic growth. They worry about the depletion of resources, congestion and pollution, and the social friction that growth often promotes. Labour organizations worry that global competition will depress wages and working conditions. And many Third World nations are concerned about playing by trade rules that always seem to benefit rich nations (e.g., copyright protection, import protection, farm subsidies).

Despite some tumultuous street protests (e.g., Seattle in 1999), WTO members continue the difficult process of dismantling trade barriers. The latest round of negotiations began in Doha, Qatar, in 2001. The key issue in the "Doha Round" has been farm subsidies in rich nations. Poor nations protest that farm subsidies in the United States and Europe not only limit their exports but also lower global farm prices (hurting farmers in developing nations). By the end of 2004, the WTO had secured pledges to reduce those farm subsidies (see the Applications box).

Because worldwide trade pacts are so complex, many nations have also pursued *regional* free-trade agreements. In December 1992, the United States, Canada, and Mexico signed the **North American Free Trade Agreement (NAFTA),** a 1,000-page document covering more than 9,000 products. The ultimate goal of NAFTA is to eliminate all trade barriers in goods and services between these three countries. At the time of signing, intraregional tariffs averaged 11 percent in Mexico, 5 percent in Canada, and 4 percent in the United States. NAFTA requires that all tariffs between the three countries be eliminated by 2007. The pact also requires the elimination of specific nontariff barriers. But NAFTA does not enable labour mobility which was included in the British Columbia–Alberta agreement (see the Applications box on page 377).

The NAFTA-initiated reduction in trade barriers substantially increased trade flows between Mexico, Canada, and the United States. It also prompted a wave of foreign investment in Mexico, where both cheap labour and NAFTA access were available. Overall, NAFTA accelerated economic growth and reduced inflationary pressures in all three nations. In the first 10 years of the agreement (1994–2004), Canada's exports by value to its NAFTA partners increased by 87 percent.[8] Over this same period, exports from the

Regional Pacts: NAFTA and EU

North American Free Trade Agreement (NAFTA): A regional agreement among Canada, the United States, and Mexico to implement a free trade area.

[8]Government of Canada, *NAFTA: A decade of strengthening a dynamic relationship,* http://www.dfait-maeci.gc.ca, accessed March 3, 2007.

APPLICATIONS

Regional and Bilateral Free Trade Initiatives

Canada is exploring, negotiating, or has recently completed free trade agreements with a number of countries or country-groups around the world. The purpose of these agreements is to "enhance [Canada's] economic prosperity and provide the foundation for sustainable economic, social and cultural development." The latest agreement announced on June 7, 2007, was with the European Free Trade Association (EFTA), which includes Switzerland, Norway, Iceland, and Liechtenstein. As a trading group, the EFTA would represent Canada's 8th largest export market.

The Minister of International Trade, David Emerson, has also announced the start of negotiations toward free trade agreements with Columbia, Peru, and the Dominican Republic. As well, negotiations are continuing with South Korea, Jordon, and Singapore as well as with larger trade groups such as the Central America Four (CA4) including El Salvador, Guatemala, Honduras, and Nicaragua; the Caribbean Community (CARICOM); and the Andean countries.

Source: Based on Foreign Affairs and International Trade Canada, http://www.international.gc.ca/trade/tna-nac/efta-en.asp, accessed November 14, 2007.

Analysis: One trade strategy has been to negotiate smaller bilateral deals and knit them into a larger framework later on. Part of the motivation for this has been the difficulties in large scale negotiations such as the WTO's Doha Round (see the Applications box on page 379).

WEB NOTE

For more information regarding Canada and the North American Free Trade Agreement (NAFTA), go to http://www.dfait-maeci.gc.ca/nafta-alena/menu-en.asp. For information on APEC, go to http://apec.org/.

WEB NOTE

To see what's new, check out the Foreign Affairs and International Trade Canada site on current trade negotiations and agreements, http://www.international.gc.ca/tna-nac/what-en.asp.

United States to Canada and Mexico increased by almost 70 percent and Mexican exports to Canada and the United States increased by more than 200 percent.

As we discussed earlier, exports are only half of the exchange since Mexican and U.S. exports become Canadian imports. Since imports represent, at least in some cases, a replacement of goods that were previously produced in Canada by Canadian workers, one criticism of NAFTA was fear of increased unemployment in the Canadian economy. Canadian economist Richard Harris looked at the evidence across a number of studies and found that the FTA and NAFTA had no significant impact on job losses in Canada and offered one study suggesting that increased trade had accounted for 23 percent of the jobs created between 1971 and 1991.[9] He also quotes economic historian Douglas Irwin, that:

> In fact, the overall effect of trade on the number of jobs is best approximated as zero. Total employment is not a function of international trade, but the number of people in the labour force.

In 1989, Canada also began discussions with 12 other countries that border on the Pacific Ocean. This became the Asia-Pacific Economic Cooperation (APEC) group and has since grown to 21 countries. The purpose of the group is to reduce tariffs and other barriers to trade, to increase investment, and aid economic reform. Through these measures economists expect more efficiency and stronger economic growth.

Since 1994, Canada has concluded agreements with Chile, Costa Rica, and Israel, and continues to negotiate with members of the Caribbean Community (CARICOM) and members of the ANDEAN community in South America, as well as other individual countries.

The *European Union* is another regional pact, but one that virtually eliminates national boundaries among 25 countries. The EU not only eliminates trade barriers but also enhances full intercountry mobility of workers and capital. In 1999, the EU nations also created a new currency (the euro) that has replaced the German mark, the French franc, and other national currencies. In effect, Europe has become one large, unified market. As trade barriers continue to fall around the world, the global marketplace is

[9]Richard Harris, *The economic impact of the FTA and NAFTA agreements for Canada: A review of the evidence. included in NAFTA@IO.* J. M. Curtis and A. Sydor, (eds.) Public Works and Government Services Canada, http://www.dfait-maeci.gc.ca, accessed March 3, 2007.

APPLICATIONS

Free Trade, Human Rights Top Harper's Colombian Agenda

Free trade talks, human rights and Colombia's efforts to end its decades-old civil war will top the agenda today as Prime Minister Stephen Harper gets down to business on the first stop on his four-nation tour of Latin America and the Caribbean.

Canada is intent on signing a free-trade deal with Colombia, a growing economy that despite its internal strife and notoriety as the world's no. 1 cocaine producer is a increasingly attractive investment destination for Canadian companies, particularly in the mining and oil and gas sectors.

A coalition of Canadian groups ranging from the Canadian Labour Congress to the Canadian chapter of Amnesty International last week called on Mr. Harper to stop all trade talks with Colombia until the issue is fully debated in Canada. "Canada must send a strong message in the Americas that it puts human rights first—for trade deals, investment, development assistance and diplomatic policy—and expects other governments to do the same," the coalition said in a statement.

Source: Alan Freeman, "Free Trade, Human Rights Top Harper's Colombian Agenda," *The Globe and Mail* (July 16, 2007), p. A4. Reprinted with permission of the Globe and Mail.

Analysis: Trade deals can be seen to legitimize foreign governments but can also increase the international scrutiny, comment, and criticism of their actions as well.

likely to become more like an open bazaar as well. The resulting increase in competition should spur efficiency and growth in the economy tomorrow.

Although the focus of this chapter has largely been of the market benefits from trade, we should recognize that a considerable amount of the debate around trade and trade agreements arises from "non-market" concerns. Examples of these would be the human rights records of potential partners, the perception of an unequal distribution of benefits particularly between rich and poor countries, and potential environmental consequences of transporting goods around the world.

As the Applications box above discusses, a potential free trade deal between Columbia and Canada has been criticized for putting trade opportunities before human rights concerns, suggesting that "Canada must send a strong message in the Americas that it puts human rights first—for trade deals. . . ." In other words, that trade deals should be a reward after repairing human rights records rather than come before.

A Broader View of Trade

APPLICATIONS

The "100-Mile" Diet

This "diet" isn't about reducing your weight or improving your health, but, rather, is a response to the greenhouse gasses emitted as food is transported around the world. The salad we have with dinner may include lettuce from California, mangoes from Australia, and sweet peppers from Mexico. Our morning ritual may include coffee grown in India or Guatemala and fruit delivered in the midst of the northern winter from

countries in the southern hemisphere. Alisa Smith and James McKinnon wrote *The 100-mile diet: A year of local eating* about their experiment to shop for food and drink that comes from within 100-miles of their Vancouver apartment.

Source: Based on Alisa Smith and James MacKinnon, *The 100-mile diet: A year of local eating*, (Toronto: Random House Canada, 2007), http://100milediet.org/category/about/.

Analysis: Transportation costs are often assumed away in economic analysis, and the fact that the price of transportation has become so inexpensive makes this assumption reasonable. But the externalities of transportation are also ignored, and these may be becoming more important.

As the Applications box at the bottom of the previous illustrates, trade requires the transportation of goods and services from where they are produced to where they will be consumed. The externality of transportation, using trains, airplanes, trucks, and ships, may be increased pollution or greenhouse gas emissions. The "100-mile diet" is a response to the distance some goods travel and an attempt to use producers closer to home.

SUMMARY

- International trade permits each country to specialize in areas of relative efficiency, increasing world output. For each country, the gains from trade are reflected in consumption possibilities that exceed production possibilities.
- One way to determine where comparative advantage lies is to compare the quantity of good A that must be given up in order to get a given quantity of good B from domestic production. If the same quantity of B can be obtained for less A by engaging in world trade, we have a comparative advantage in the production of good A. Comparative advantage rests on a comparison of relative opportunity costs.
- A country with absolute advantage is able to produce some good or service with fewer resources (per unit of output). Patterns of trade are not determined by absolute advantage but rather by comparative advantage. Absolute costs don't count!
- The terms of trade—the rate at which goods are exchanged—are subject to the forces of international

supply and demand. The terms of trade will lie somewhere between the opportunity costs of the trading partners. The terms of trade determine how the gains from trade are shared.
- Resistance to trade emanates from workers and firms that must compete with imports. Even though the country as a whole stands to benefit from trade, these individuals and companies may lose jobs and incomes in the process.
- Trade barriers take many forms. Embargoes are outright prohibitions against import or export of particular goods. Quotas limit the quantity of a good imported or exported. Tariffs discourage imports by making them more expensive. Other nontariff barriers make trade too costly or time-consuming.
- The World Trade Organization (WTO) seeks to reduce worldwide trade barriers and enforce trade rules. Regional accords such as the European Union (EU) and North American Free Trade Agreement (NAFTA) pursue similar objectives among fewer countries.

Key Terms

imports 359
exports 359
trade surplus (deficit) 360
consumption possibilities 363
comparative advantage 366
absolute advantage 366
terms of trade 366

dumping 371
embargo 372
tariff 372
quota 374
voluntary restraint agreement (VRA) 376
trade pact 378

General Agreement on Tariffs and Trade, GATT 378
World Trade Organization, WTO 378
North American Free Trade Agreement, NAFTA 379

Questions for Discussion

1. Suppose a lawyer can type faster than any secretary. Should the lawyer do her own typing? Can you demonstrate the validity of your answer?
2. What would be the effects of a law requiring bilateral trade balances?
3. If a nation exported much of its output but imported little, would it be better or worse off? How about the reverse, that is, exporting little but importing a lot?

4. How does international trade restrain the price behaviour of domestic firms?
5. Suppose we refused to sell goods to any country that reduced or halted its exports to us. Who would benefit and who would lose from such retaliation? Can you suggest alternative ways to ensure import supplies?
6. Domestic producers often base their claim for import protection on the fact that workers in country X are

paid substandard wages. Is this a valid argument for protection?

7. Based on the Applications box on page 369, what might be the impact of the DaimlerChrysler deal on Chrysler workers in Canada? What might be the impact on potential purchasers of these Chrysler products?

8. If Canada was to ask Chrysler to "voluntarily" restrict the export of these Chinese-produced cars, what would be the impact in the Canadian market? What would be the effect on Canadian workers? On Canadian buyers?

9. The B.C. Fruit Growers Association (BCFGA) has alleged that Washington state farmers dumped apples into the B.C. market during 2004. What would be the effect of a countervailing duty or tariff on Washington's apples?

10. Canada is currently negotiating trade agreements with several countries. These negotiations generally rely on each country "giving up" some protection. What if Canada simply unilaterally removed all tariffs and non-tariff barriers? Who would lose? Who would win? What would be the net effect on the economy as a whole?

EXERCISES

PROBLEMS   The Student Problem Set to accompany this chapter can be found at the end of the book.

WEB ACTIVITIES   Web Activities to accompany this chapter can be found on the Online Learning Centre at **http://www.mcgrawhill.ca/olc/schiller**.

GLOSSARY

Note: Numbers in parentheses indicate the page numbers on which the definitions appear.

absolute advantage: The ability of a country to produce a specific good with fewer resources (per unit of output) than other countries. (366)

antitrust: Government intervention to alter market structure or prevent abuse of market power. (188)

average fixed cost (AFC): Total fixed cost divided by the quantity produced in a given time period. (113)

average physical product (APP): The average productivity of a factor of production—calculated by dividing total output by total units of input. (106)

average total cost (ATC): Total cost divided by the quantity produced in a given time period. (112)

average variable cost (AVC): Total variable cost divided by the quantity produced in a given time period. (113)

barriers to entry: Obstacles, such as patents, that make it difficult or impossible for would-be producers to enter a particular market. (154)

bilateral monopoly: A market with only one buyer (a monopsonist) and one seller (a monopolist). (296)

bond: A certificate acknowledging a debt and the amount of interest to be paid each year until repayment; an IOU. (317)

breakeven level of income: The income level at which welfare eligibility ceases. (348)

budget constraint: A line depicting all combinations of goods that are affordable with a given income and given prices. (97)

budget deficit method: The shortfall between the amount of available financial resources and the provincial–territorial amount of social assistance for that family type. (345)

capital: Final goods produced for use in the production of other goods, e.g., equipment, structures. (6)

capital gain: An increase in the market value of an asset. (310)

cartel: A group of firms with an explicit, formal agreement to fix prices and output shares in a particular market. (209)

cash transfers: Income transfers that entail direct cash payments to recipients, e.g., Old Age Security, social assistance, and employment insurance benefits. (341)

ceteris paribus: The assumption of nothing else changing. (19)

collective bargaining: Direct negotiations between employers and unions to determine labour market outcomes. (296)

combine laws (competition policy): Government intervention to alter market structure or prevent abuse of market power. (231)

comparative advantage: The ability of a country to produce a specific good at a lower opportunity cost than its trading partners. (366)

competition policy: Government policies and laws identifying and regulating the competitive process. (58)

competitive firm: A firm without market power, with no ability to alter the market price of the goods it produces. (135)

competitive market: A market in which no buyer or seller has market power. (154)

complementary goods: Goods frequently consumed in combination; when the price of good X rises, the demand for good Y falls, *ceteris paribus*. (34)

concentration ratio (CR): The proportion of total industry output produced by the largest firms (usually the four largest). (194)

constant returns to scale: Increases in plant size do not affect minimum average cost; minimum per-unit costs are identical for small plants and large plants. (119)

consumption possibilities: The alternative combinations of goods and services that a country could consume in a given time period. (363)

contestable market: An imperfectly competitive industry subject to potential entry if prices or profits increase. (187)

corporate stock: Shares of ownership in a corporation. (309)

corporation: A business organization having a continuous existence independent of its members (owners) and power and liabilities distinct from those of its members. (309)

cost efficiency: The amount of output associated with an additional dollar spent on input; the MPP of an input divided by its price (cost). (287)

coupon rate: Interest rate set for a bond at time of issuance. (318)

cross-price elasticity of demand: Percentage change in the quantity demanded of X divided by percentage change in price of Y. (71)

cross-subsidization: Use of high prices and profits on one product to subsidize low prices on another product. (240)

current yield: The rate of return on a bond; the annual interest payment divided by the bond's price. (319)

default: Failure to make scheduled payments of interest or principal on a bond. (318)

demand: The willingness and ability to buy specific quantities of a good at alternative prices in a given time period, *ceteris paribus*. (31)

demand curve: A curve describing the quantities of a good a consumer is willing and able to buy at alternative prices in a given time period, *ceteris paribus*. (33)

demand for labour: The quantities of labour employers are willing and able to hire at alternative wage rates in a given time period, *ceteris paribus*. (278)

demand schedule: A table showing the quantities of a good a consumer is willing and able to buy at alternative prices in a given time period, *ceteris paribus*. (32)

derived demand: The demand for labour and other factors of production results from (depends on) the demand for final goods and services produced by these factors. (278)

dividend: Amount of corporate profits paid out for each share of stock. (310)

dumping: The sale of goods in export markets at prices below domestic prices. (371)

economic cost: The value of all resources used to produce a good or service; opportunity cost. (130)

economic growth: An increase in output (real GDP); an expansion of production possibilities. (12)

economic profit: The difference between total revenues and total economic costs. (131)

economics: The study of how best to allocate scarce resources among competing uses. (4)

economies of scale: Reductions in minimum average costs that come about through increases in the size (scale) of plant and equipment. (119)

effective tax rate: Taxes paid divided by total income. (330)

efficiency: Maximum output of a good from the resources used in production. (10)

efficiency decision: The choice of a production process for any given rate of output. (255)

elasticity of labour supply: The percentage change in the quantity of labour supplied divided by the percentage change in wage rate. (277)

embargo: A prohibition on exports or imports. (372)

emission charge: A fee imposed on polluters, based on the quantity of pollution. (259)

entrepreneurship: The assembling of resources to produce new or improved products and technologies. (6)

equilibrium price: The price at which the quantity of a good demanded in a given time period equals the quantity supplied. (42)

equilibrium wage: The wage rate at which the quantity of labour supplied in a given time period equals the quantity of labor demanded. (286)

expected value: The probable value of a future payment, including the risk of nonpayment. (308)

explicit costs: A payment made for the use of a resource. (130)

exports: Goods and services sold to foreign buyers. (359)

external costs: Cost of a market activity borne by a third party; the difference between the social and private costs of a market activity. (256)

externalities: Costs (or benefits) of a market activity borne by a third party; the difference between the social and private costs (benefits) of a market activity. (56)

factor market: Any place where factors of production (e.g., land, labour, capital) are bought and sold. (29)

factors of production: Resource inputs used to produce goods and services, e.g., land, labour, capital, entrepreneurship. (6)

financial intermediary: Institution (e.g., a bank or the stock market) that makes savings available to dissavers (e.g., investors). (303)

fixed costs: Costs of production that don't change when the rate of output is altered, e.g., the cost of basic plant and equipment. (110)

flat tax: A single-rate tax system. (337)

free rider: An individual who reaps direct benefits from someone else's purchase (consumption) of a public good. (53)

game theory: The study of decision making in situations where strategic interaction (moves and countermoves) between rivals occurs. (204)

General Agreement on Tariffs and Trade (GATT): A trade pact that covered the rules and regulations governing the international trade in goods; now part of the World Trade Organization. (378)

Gini coefficient: A mathematical summary of inequality based on the Lorenz curve. (326)

government failure: Government intervention that fails to improve economic outcomes. (17)

horizontal equity: Principle that people with equal incomes should pay equal taxes. (330)

implicit cost: The value of resources used, even when no direct payment is made. (130)

imports: Goods and services purchased from international sources. (359)

income effect of wages: An increased wage rate allows a person to reduce hours worked without losing income. (301)

income elasticity of demand: Percentage change in quantity demanded divided by percentage change in income. (89)

income quintile: One-fifth of the population, rank-ordered by income (e.g., lowest fifth). (325)

income share: The proportion of total income received by a particular group. (325)

income transfers: Payments to individuals for which no current goods or services are exchanged, e.g., Old Age Security payments, welfare, employment insurance payments. (335)

indifference curve: A curve depicting alternative combinations of goods that yield equal satisfaction. (96)

indifference map: The set of indifference curves that depicts all possible levels of utility attainable from various combinations of goods. (97)

inferior good: Good for which demand decreases when income rises. (90)

inflation: An increase in the average level of prices of goods and services. (62)

initial public offering (IPO): The first issuance (sale) to the general public of stock in a corporation. (310)

in-kind income: Goods and services received directly, without payment, in a market transaction. (323)

in-kind transfers: Direct transfers of goods and services rather than cash; examples include food stamps, legal aid, and housing subsidies. (341)

investment decision: The decision to build, buy, or lease plant and equipment; to enter or exit an industry. (145)

labour supply: The willingness and ability to work specific amounts of time at alternative wage rates in a given time period, *ceteris paribus*. (275)

labour-force participation rate: The percentage of the working-age population working or seeking employment. (351)

laissez faire: The doctrine of "leave it alone," of nonintervention by government in the market mechanism. (14)

law of demand: The quantity of a good demanded in a given time period increases as its price falls, *ceteris paribus*. (33)

law of diminishing marginal utility: The marginal utility of a good declines as more of it is consumed in a given time period. (73)

law of diminishing returns: The marginal physical product of a variable input declines as more of it is employed with a given quantity of other (fixed) inputs. (107)

law of supply: The quantity of a good supplied in a given time period increases as its price increases, *ceteris paribus*. (39)

liquidity: The ability of an asset to be converted into cash. (318)

long run: A period of time long enough for all inputs to be varied (no fixed costs). (117)

long-run competitive equilibrium:
$p = MC = $ minimum ATC. (161)

Lorenz curve: A graphic illustration of the cumulative size distribution of income; contrasts complete equality with the actual distribution of income. (326)

macroeconomics: The study of aggregate economic behaviour, of the economy as a whole. (18)

marginal cost (MC): The increase in total cost associated with a one-unit increase in production. (108)

marginal cost pricing: The offer (supply) of goods at prices equal to their marginal cost. (166)

marginal factor cost (MFC): The change in total costs that results from a one-unit increase in the quantity of a factor employed. (294)

marginal physical product (MPP): The change in total output associated with one additional unit of input. (105)

marginal rate of substitution: The rate at which a consumer is willing to exchange one good for another; the relative marginal utilities of two goods. (99)

marginal revenue (MR): The change in total revenue that results from a one-unit increase in the quantity sold. (138)

marginal revenue product (MRP): The change in total revenue associated with one additional unit of input. (279)

marginal tax rate: The tax rate imposed on the last (marginal) dollar of income. (327)

marginal utility: The change in total utility obtained by consuming one additional (marginal) unit of a good or service. (73)

marginal wage: The change in total wages paid associated with a one-unit increase in the quantity of labour employed. (290)

market demand: The total quantities of a good or service people are willing and able to buy at alternative prices in a given time period; the sum of individual demands. (36)

market failure: An imperfection in the market mechanism that prevents optimal outcomes. (16)

market mechanism: The use of market prices and sales to signal desired outputs (or resource allocations). (13)

market power: The ability to alter the market price of a good or service. (58)

market share: The percentage of total market output produced by a single firm. (197)

market shortage: The amount by which the quantity demanded exceeds the quantity supplied at a given price; excess demand. (43)

market structure: The number and relative size of firms in an industry. (134)

market supply: The total quantities of a good that sellers are willing and able to sell at alternative prices in a given time period, *ceteris paribus*. (38)

market supply of labour: The total quantity of labour that workers are willing and able to supply at alternative wage rates in a given time period, *ceteris paribus*. (277)

market surplus: The amount by which the quantity supplied exceeds the quantity demanded at a given price; excess supply. (43)

microeconomics: The study of individual behaviour in the economy, of the components of the larger economy. (18)

mixed economy: An economy that uses both market signals and government directives to allocate goods and resources. (16)

monopolistic competition: A market in which many firms produce similar goods or services but each maintains some independent control of its own price. (218)

monopoly: A firm that produces the entire market supply of a particular good or service. (58)

monopsony: A market in which there's only one buyer. (294)

moral hazard: An incentive to engage in undesirable behaviour. (346)

natural monopoly: An industry in which one firm can achieve economies of scale over the entire range of market supply. (58)

nominal tax rate: Taxes paid divided by taxable income. (330)

normal good: Good for which demand increases when income rises. (90)

normal profit: The opportunity cost of capital: zero economic profit. (132)

North American Free Trade Agreement (NAFTA): A regional agreement among Canada, the United States, and Mexico to implement a free trade area. (379)

oligopolist: One of the dominant firms in an oligopoly. (197)

oligopoly: A market in which a few firms produce all or most of the market supply of a particular good or service. (193)

opportunity cost: The most desired goods or services that are forgone in order to obtain something else. (7)

opportunity wage: The highest wage an individual would earn in his or her best alternative job. (289)

optimal consumption: The mix of consumer purchases that maximizes the utility attainable from available income. (77)

optimal mix of output: The most desirable combination of output attainable with existing resources, technology, and social values. (52)

optimal rate of pollution: The rate of pollution that occurs when the marginal social benefit of pollution control equals its marginal social cost. (266)

outsourcing: The relocation of production to foreign countries. (287)

par value: The face value of a bond; the amount to be repaid when the bond is due. (317)

perfect competition: A market in which no buyer or seller has market power. (134)

personal income (PI): Income received by households before payment of personal taxes. (323)

predatory pricing: Temporary price reductions designed to alter market shares or drive out competition. (209)

present discounted value (PDV): The value today of future payments, adjusted for interest accrual. (306)

price ceiling: Upper limit imposed on the price of a good or service. (61)

price discrimination: The sale of an identical good at different prices to different consumers by a single seller. (182)

price elasticity of demand: The percentage change in quantity demanded divided by the percentage change in price. (80)

price floor: Lower limit imposed on the price of a good or service. (60)

price leadership: An oligopolistic pricing pattern that allows one firm to establish the (market) price for all firms in the industry. (209)

price/earnings (P/E) ratio: The price of a stock share divided by earnings (profit) per share. (311)

price-fixing: Explicit agreements among producers regarding the price(s) at which a good is to be sold. (208)

private costs: The costs of an economic activity directly borne by the immediate producer or consumer (excluding externalities). (257)

private good: A good or service whose consumption by one person excludes consumption by others. (53)

product differentiation: Features that make one product appear different from competing products in the same market. (199)

product market: Any place where finished goods and services (products) are bought and sold. (30)

production decision: The selection of the short-run rate of output (with existing plant and equipment). (136)

production function: A technological relationship expressing the maximum quantity of a good attainable from different combinations of factor inputs. (102)

production possibilities: The alternative combinations of final goods and services that could be produced in a given time period with all available resources and technology. (8)

production process: A specific combination of resources used to produce a good or service. (287)

productivity: Output per unit of input, e.g., output per labour-hour. (103)

profit: The difference between total revenue and total cost. (107)

profit per unit: Total profit divided by the quantity produced in a given time period; price minus average total cost. (158)

profit-maximization rule: Produce at that rate of output where marginal revenue equals marginal cost. (140)

progressive tax: A tax system in which tax rates rise as incomes rise. (327)

public choice: Theory of public-sector behaviour emphasizing rational self-interest of decision makers and voters. (65)

public good: A good or service whose consumption by one person does not exclude consumption by others. (53)

quota: A limit on the quantity of a good that may be imported in a given time period. (374)

regressive tax: A tax system in which tax rates fall as incomes rise. (331)

regulation: Government intervention to alter the behaviour of firms, e.g., in pricing, output, or advertising. (231)

retained earnings: Amount of corporate profits not paid out in dividends. (310)

risk premium: The difference in rates of return on risky (uncertain) and safe (certain) investments. (305)

scarcity: Lack of enough resources to satisfy all desired uses of those resources. (5)

shift in demand: A change in the quantity demanded at any (every) given price. (35)

short run: The period in which the quantity (and quality) of some inputs can't be changed. (104)

short-run competitive equilibrium: $p = $ MC (160)

shutdown point: That rate of output where price equals minimum AVC. (145)

size distribution of income: The way total personal income is divided up among households or income classes. (325)

social assistance programs: Needs-tested income transfer programs, e.g., welfare and food stamps. (342)

social costs: The full resource costs of an economic activity, including externalities. (257)

social insurance programs: Event- and demographic-conditioned income transfers intended to reduce the cost of specific problems, e.g., Old Age Security and Employment Insurance. (342)

substitute goods: Goods that substitute for each other; when the price of good X rises, the demand for good Y increases, *ceteris paribus*. (33)

substitution effect of wages: An increased wage rate encourages people to work more hours (to substitute labour for leisure). (300)

supply: The ability and willingness to sell (produce) specific quantities of a good at alternative prices in a given time period, *ceteris paribus*. (31)

supply curve: A curve describing the quantities of a good a producer is willing and able to sell (produce) at alternative prices in a given time period, *ceteris paribus*. (147)

target efficiency: The percentage of income transfers that go to the intended recipients and purposes. (342)

tariff: A tax (duty) imposed on imported goods. (372)

tax base: The amount of income or property directly subject to nominal tax rates. (331)

tax elasticity of labour supply: The percentage change in quantity of labour supplied divided by the percentage change in tax rates. (348)

tax elasticity of supply: The percentage change in quantity of hours supplied divided by the percentage change in tax rates. (328)

tax incidence: Distribution of the real burden of a tax. (333)

terms of trade: The rate at which goods are exchanged; the amount of good A given up for good B in trade. (366)

total cost: The market value of all resources used to produce a good or service. (110)

total revenue: The price of a product multiplied by the quantity sold in a given time period. (86)

total utility: The amount of satisfaction obtained from entire consumption of a product. (73)

trade pact: A negotiation or agreement between countries governing trade; *bilateral* trade pacts involve two countries, and *multilateral* trade pacts involve more than two countries. (378)

trade surplus (deficit): The amount by which the value of exports exceeds (is less than) the value of imports in a given time period. (360)

transfer payments: Payments to individuals for which no current goods or services are exchanged, like the Canada Pension Plan, welfare, unemployment benefits. (59)

unemployment: The inability of labour-force participants to find jobs. (62)

unionization rate: The percentage of the labour force belonging to a union. (290)

unit labour cost: Hourly wage rate divided by output per labour-hour. (121)

utility: The pleasure or satisfaction obtained from a good or service. (72)

variable costs: Costs of production that change when the rate of output is altered, e.g., labour and material costs. (110)

vertical equity: Principle that people with higher incomes should pay more taxes. (330)

voluntary restraint agreement (VRA): An agreement to reduce the volume of trade in a specific good; a "voluntary" quota. (376)

wealth: The market value of assets. (325)

World Trade Organization (WTO): A global international institution that deals with the rules of trade among nations. (378)

Abitibi-Consolidated Inc., 125
absolute advantage, 366
Abu Dhabi Water and Electricity Authority, 117
Abuse Guidelines, 214
Acer, 156
acid rain, 250
acquisition, 184, 211–212
ad spending per capita, 92
administrative costs, 235–236
Adolph Coors Co., 211
advertising, 91–93, 93*f*, 212, 224–225
aging, and richer countries, 352
Agripur, 375
Air Canada, 202, 210, 243
air pollution, 250, 254
Airline Deregulation Act, 242
airline industry, 182, 209, 242–243
Alaron Trading Corp., 206
Alberta, 34, 41, 61, 183, 200, 245, 246, 264, 331, 377
Alberta Energy, 211
Alcan Aluminum Ltd., 48, 117, 244
Alling, William R., 185
allocation of market shares, 209
allocative efficiency, 165–166
alternative production processes, 287
Aluminum Company of America (Alcoa), 214
Amana, 371
Amazon.com Inc., 149, 225, 309, 311, 312–313, 313*f*, 317
America Online, 128, 155, 225
American Airlines, 202
American Home Products, 208
American Technology Research, 314
Amnesty International, 381
AMR Corp., 202
ANDEAN Community, 380
Anheuser-Busch Cos., 211
"animal spirits," 6
antitrust, 188
    contestability, 214–215
    described, 188–190
    enforcement, 213–215
    industry behaviour, 213
    industry structure, 213
    objections to, 214
    paucity of antitrust resources, 213
    structure guidelines, 214
antitrustinstitute.org, 190
Apple Computer Inc., 155, 156–157, 159, 162, 165, 167, 168, 189, 192, 220, 304, 322
arc, 81*n*
Asia-Pacific Economic Cooperation (APEC), 380
Associated Press, 195
AST, 164
Atari, 156, 164
AT&T, 189, 240, 313*f*
auction commissions, 209
auction of pollution credits, 263
Auditor General, 63
Australia, 270
automobile driving, 258
automobile industry, 212
autoweb.com, 39
average costs
    average fixed cost (AFC), 113
    average total cost (ATC), 112, 116–117, 231–232, 232*f*
    average variable cost (AVC), 113
    described, 112–114, 112*f*
    long-run average costs, 118–119
    minimum average cost, 114, 119
average fixed cost (AFC), 113
average hourly earnings, 278
average physical product (APP), 105*f*, 106–107, 109
average productivity, 105–107
average tax rate, 328
average total cost (ATC), 112, 116–117, 231–232, 232*f*
average variable cost (AVC), 113, 144–145

B2B solutions, 122–123
baby formula, 208
backward bending individual supply curve, 300–301, 301*f*
Badillo, Frank, 219
ballot box economics, 65
Bank of Canada Act, 17
Bank of New York, 276
Barguzin, 174
Barnes and Noble, 149
barriers to entry, 154
    competitive markets, 154
    microcomputer industry, 159
    monopolistic competition, 218–219
    monopoly, 179, 182–184
    oligopoly, 210–215
    patents, 174
barriers to trade. *See* trade barriers
Barry, Dave, 340, 344
Bastos of Canada Ltd., 194
BBC, 188
Beaudoin, Laurent, 125
Bechard, Claude, 261
Becker, Gary, 20, 85
Beckham, David, 283, 284
Beckham, Victoria, 284
"beggar thy neighbour," 373–374
Bell, 226, 241
benefits, external, 57–58
Benson & Hedges Incorporated, 194
Bentham, Jeremy, 73
Bettman, Gary, 296
Bhagwati, Jagdish, 358
Bharat Aluminum Co., 11
bilateral monopoly, 296
Bill C-68, 63
bin Dhaen al-Hamili, Mohammed, 206
bloated costs, 234
Bloomberg, Michael, 85, 267
BMO Financial Group, 226
Board of Railway Commissioners, 237
Board of Transport Commissioners, 242
Bombardier Inc., 125
bond, 317
    coupon rate, 318
    current yields, 318–319, 319*t*
    default, 318
    liquidity, 318
    par value, 317
    price, 319*t*
bond issuance, 317–318
bond market
    bond issuance, 317–318
    bond trading, 318
    current yields, 318–319
    described, 317
bond trading, 318
bookfinder.com, 39
Boxing Day, 44
Branca, Michael, 211
brand image, 92, 219
brand loyalty, 220–221, 221
brand names, 226
Brazil, 240, 379
breakeven level of income, 348
Bristol-Myers Squibb, 208
British Airways, 209
British Columbia, 346*n*, 377
British Petroleum, 196
British Telecommunications, 240
Buchanan, James, 66
budget constraint, 97, 97*f*
budget deficit method, 345
Bush, George, 270, 377
bush airlines, 242
"but for" test, 214–215
buyer concentration, 294

Cable News Network. *See* CNN
Calgary Taxi Commission, 212*n*
California, 233, 244
California electricity crisis (2000–2001), 27, 61–62
Camco Inc., 371
Campbell, Gordon, 377
Canada
    basic social assistance benefits, 345*t*
    bilateral merchandise trade balances, 361*t*
    Chinese tariffs, complaints, 378
    consumption patterns, 71
    deregulation in. *See* deregulation
    exports, 359–360
    ice storm, 48
    imports, 358, 359
    income distribution in, 325*t*
    manufacturing markets, 195*f*
    market reforms, 15
    monetary policy, 125
    most valuable brands, 226
    North American Free Trade Agreement
        (NAFTA), 379–380
    Prime Minister of Canada, 274
    productivity in, 122
    recent mergers, 211
    tax reform, 331*t*
    trade balance, 361*t*
    tradable pollution permits, 263
    typical consumer, 71
    unionization rate, 291
    unit labour costs, 124
    work hours in, 300
Canada Border Services Agency, 373
Canada Firearms Centre, 63
Canada Pension Plan (CPP), 329, 349, 350–351
Canada Revenue Agency, 328, 329, 330, 371
Canada Social Transfer, 344
Canada Trust, 211
Canada–U.S. Free Trade Agreement, 380
Canadian Airways, 242, 243
Canadian Association of Food Banks, 323, 324
Canadian Broadcasting Corporation, 64
Canadian Cancer Society, 83, 84
Canadian Coffee Drinking Study, 218
Canadian Customs and Revenue Agency. *See* Canada
    Revenue Agency
Canadian Dairy Commission, 211–212
Canadian dollar, 125
Canadian Institute for Health Information (CIHI), 7
Canadian International Trade Tribunal, 371
Canadian National Railways, 238, 242
Canadian Pacific Railway (CPR), 238, 242
Canadian Press, 195
Canadian Radio-television and Telecommunications
    Commission (CRTC), 239, 241
Canadian Taxpayer's Association, 331
Canadian Tire, 226
Canadian Transportation Act, 238
CanJet, 210, 243
capital, 6, 12
Capital Cities/ABC Inc., 188
capital gains, 310, 312
capital-intensive production process, 287
carbon dioxide emissions, 268–270
carbon tax, 261
CARICOM, 380
Carroll, Cynthia, 117
cartel, 209
Cascades Fine Papers Group Inc., 208
cash transfers, 341–342
Casio, 159
catfish farming, 141, 151, 152
Catfish Institute, 154
causation, 26
centrally planned economies, 10, 265
Centre for Regulatory Innovation, 246

CEO pay, 274, 289
ceteris paribus, **19**
  and demand, 34–35
  optimal consumption, 79
  price, and supply decisions, 147
  price, and utility, 74
  shifts of supply, 40–41
  stock prices and high interest rates, 315
Chan, Eddie, 165
changes in demand, 36
changes in quantity demanded, 36
changes in quantity supplied, 40
changes in supply, 40, 41
Chapters-Indigo, 311
Charlotte, Virginia, 260
cheap foreign labour, 121
Chery Automobile Co., 369
Chicago Board of Trade, 263
Child Tax Benefits, 341, 344
Child Tax Credit, 342
Chile, 240
China, 15, 17, 18, 240, 369, 378
chlorofluorocarbons (CFCs), 249
choice
  consumer choice. *See* consumer choice
  mechanisms of choice, 13–17
Chrétien, Jean, 63
Christie's, 209
Chrysler Group, 369
cigarette industry, 212
cigarette taxes, 85
circular flow
  dollars, and exchange, 30–31
  factor markets, 29–30
  illustration, 29*f*
  locating markets, 30
  product markets, 30
  two markets, 29–30
City Brewery, 200
Clean Air Act, 270
cleanup, 255
Clear Channel Entertainment, 179, 183, 210
climate change, 268–270
Clinton, Bill, 85, 377
close substitutes, 183
CNN, 187, 188
Coca-Cola Co., 192, 204, 219, 220, 225, 226
Coca-Cola Enterprises Inc., 204
Cochran, Patricia, 373
The Coffee Company, 218
collective bargaining, 296–297, 297*f*
Colombia, 380, 381
Columbus, Christopher, 302, 306
combine laws, 231
command-and-control options, 264–265
command economies, 14
Commonwealth Caribbean Countries tariff treatment, 373
communism, 17
Communist Manifesto (Marx), 14
Compaq, 164
comparative advantage, 365–366
compassion, 353
competition
  see also perfect competition
  and e-commerce, 149
  imperfect competition. *See* imperfect competition
  nonprice competition, 212
  oligopoly, 199
Competition Act, 208, 209, 213
Competition Bureau, 58, 59, 187, 208, 210, 211, 214, 241
competition policy, 58, 231
Competition Tribunal, 186, 214
competitive firm, 135
  see also perfect competition
  determinants of supply, 146–149
  investment decision, 145–146
  long-run competitive equilibrium, 160–161, 161*f*
  long-run costs, 146
  marginal cost curve, 147
  vs. monopoly, 180–184
  production decision, 136–137
  profit maximization rule, 138–143, 140*f*
  short-run competitive equilibrium, 160, 161*f*
  short-run supply curve, 147*f*

shutdown decision, 143–145
supply shifts, 147
tax effects, 147–149
total revenue curve, 136, 136*f*
competitive markets, 154
  competitive process, 165–168
  exit, 153
  market entry, 153, 153*f*
  market supply curve, 152–154
  microcomputer industry, 154–164
  zero profits, tendency towards, 153–154
competitive process
  allocative efficiency, 165–166
  production efficiency, 166
  sequence of events, 167
  summary of, 166*f*
  zero economic profit, 166
complementary goods, 34, 90–91
compliance costs, 236
computer industry. *See* microcomputer industry
concentration ratio (CR), 194, 218
La Connivence, 49
conspiracy, 208
constant opportunity costs, 10*n*
constant-quality units, 106*n*
constant returns to scale, 119
consumer behaviour, 71–72
  see also consumption
consumer buying intentions, 33
consumer choice
  advertising and, 91–92
  economic explanation, 72
  equilibrium outcomes, 79–80
  indifference curves, 95–100
  marginal utility *vs.* price, 75–77
  price changes, responses to, 87, 88*f*
  sociopsychiatric explanation, 71
  utility maximization, 77–78
  utility-maximizing rule, 78–79
  wants, 92–93
consumer-choice theory, 75–76
consumption
  Canada's consumption patterns, 71
  effects of, 56
  externalities, 258
  optimal consumption, 77–79, 95, 98, 98*f*
  with trade, 363–364
  without trade, 362–363
consumption possibilities
  with trade, 363–364, 363*f*
  without trade, 362–363, 362*f*
contestability, 214–215
contestable markets, 187–188, 194
Continental Airlines, 202
coordination problems, 207–209
corporate loans, 305–306
corporate stock, 309–310
corporation, 309
cost-benefit analysis
  environmental protection, 267
  government failure, 64–65
cost curves, 116*f*
cost cushion, 205, 207*f*
cost-driven production decisions, 16
cost efficiency, 287
costs
  absolute costs, 366
  administrative costs, 235–236
  average costs, 112–114, 112*f*
  average fixed cost (AFC), 113
  average total cost (ATC), 112, 116–117
  average variable cost (AVC), 113
  bloated costs, 234
  cheap foreign labour, 121
  competitive firm, 136–137
  competitive markets, 158*t*
  compliance costs, 236
  economic cost, 130–131
  economies of scale, 121–123
  efficiency, 236
  and exchange rates, 124–125
  explicit costs, 130
  external costs, 56–57, 256–258
  factor costs, 38

fixed costs, 110
  of funds, 308
  of greater equality, 335–337
  implicit cost, 130
  key measures of, 115*t*
  long-run average costs, 118–119
  long-run costs, 117–119, 146
  marginal cost (MC), 108–109, 114
  marginal factor cost (MFC), 294, 295*f*
  opportunity cost. *See* opportunity cost
  and output, 136–137
  pollution abatement costs, 255–256
  private costs, 257
  production costs. *See* production costs
  and productivity improvements, 122*f*
  and profit, 130–133
  of regulation, 235–237
  resource costs, 107–109
  social assistance programs, 347–348
  social costs, 257
  social insurance programs, 353
  total cost, 110–111, 137*f*
  unit costs, 124–125
  unit labour costs, 121–122, 124
  variable costs, 110–111
coupon rate, 318
craft unions, 290
Crosby, Sidney, 91
cross-price elasticity of demand, 90–92, **91**
cross-subsidization, 240
Crown corporations, 236
Crow's Nest Pass Agreement, 238
Cuba, 14, 15
Cuette, Pierre, 49
Cunningham, Rob, 84
currency fluctuations, 125
current yields, 318–**319,** 319*t*
customs duties, 372–374

DaimlerChrysler, 196, 369
Dairy Farmers of Canada, 375
Dairy Processors Association, 375
dairy protection, 375
damage from pollution, 253–255
Das Kapital (Marx), 14
Davis, Grey, 27, 30, 62
decisions
  cost-driven production decisions, 16
  economic questions, 12–13
  hiring decision, 282–285
  investment decision, 145–146
  output decision, 115
  production decisions. *See* production decision
  shutdown decision, 143–145
  tax effects, 147–149
default, 318
Dell, Michael, 165
Dell Computer, 155, 156, 164, 165, 220, 221
Delta Air Lines, 202
demand, 31
  ceteris paribus, 34–35
  changes in demand, 36
  changes in quantity demanded, 36
  consumer buying intentions, 33
  cross-price elasticity of demand, 90–92
  demand curve. *See* demand curve
  derived demand, 278
  determinants of demand, 33–34, 35, 71–72
  elastic demand, 82–83
  existence of, 31
  firm *vs.* industry demand, 171*f*
  income elasticity of demand, 89–90, 89*f*
  individual demand, 31–33
  inelastic demand, 82–83
  influencing demand, 91–92
  law of demand, 33
  loanable funds, 308–309
  market demand, 36
  market demand curve, 36–38, 37*f*
  point elasticity of demand, 81*n*
  price elasticity of demand. *See* price elasticity of demand
  shift, and equilibrium price, 45
  shifts in, 35–36, 35*f*

shifts *vs.* movements, 35*f,* 36
social demand, 57–58
demand curve, 33
and advertising campaigns, 92, 93*f*
downward-sloping demand curve, 171
illustration, 32*f*
indifference curves, 99–100
individual's demand curve, 81*f*
kinked demand curve, 200–202, 200*f,* 206, 206*f*
labour demand curve, 278–279, 283*f*
market demand curve, 36–38, 37*f,* 135, 135*f,* 181
origins of, 94–95
price elasticity changes, 88*f*
shifts, 35
social demand curve, 56–57, 57*f*
and utility theory, 72–80
demand for labour, 278
derived demand, 278
diminishing marginal physical product, 280–282, 281*f*
diminishing marginal revenue product, 282
and hiring decision, 283–284
illustration, 279*f*
labour demand curve, 278–279
law of diminishing returns, 280–282
marginal physical product, 279
marginal productivity, 280–282
marginal revenue product, 279–280
under perfect competition, 278–282
demand schedule, 32–33, 32*f,* 35, 100
Denmark, 377
Department of Agriculture, Food and Rural
Development (Alberta), 41
deregulation
airline industry, 242–243
electric industry, 244–246
in practice, 237–247
railroad industry, 237–239
telephone industry, 239–241
deregulation movement, 65
derived demand, 278
determinants of demand
changes in, 89
constant, 35
described, 33–34
economic explanation, 72
sociopsychiatric explanation, 71
supply shifts, 147
determinants of elasticity, 83–85
determinants of labour supply, 277
determinants of market power, 193–194
determinants of supply
competitive firm, 146–149
described, 38–39
short-run determinants, 146–147
differentiated oligopoly, 198
Digital Equipment, 159
diminishing marginal physical product, 280–282, 281*f*
diminishing marginal returns, 106–107
diminishing marginal revenue product, 282
diminishing marginal utility, 73–74
Dion, Stéphane, 270
discretionary income, 71
diseconomies of scale, 121
Disney, 226
Disneyland, 131
distribution control, 210–211
dividends, 310
division of labour, 121
Dockery, Douglas, 254
Doha Round, 379
dollar
Canadian dollar, 125
and exchange, 30–31
Dominican Republic, 380
Domtar Inc., 208
Dow Jones Industrial Average, 316
downward-sloping demand curve, 171
Duke of Medina Sidonia, 302
Duke University, 276
dumping, 371
duopoly, 134

e-commerce, 149
earnings test, 349–350

Earth Policy Initiative, 254
Eastern Europe, 265
Eastman Kodak, 183
economic cost, 130
economic freedom, 14–15
economic growth, 12, 12*f*
economic profits, 130–132, **131,** 132*t,* 221, 223
economic questions
how, 13
market mechanism, 47–48
what, 12
for whom, 13
economics, 4
end *vs.* means, 17
macroeconomics, 18–19
microeconomics, 18–19
and politics, 20
purpose of studying, 17–20
theory *vs.* reality, 19–20
economies
centrally planned economies, 10
command economies, 14
market economy, 13–14
mixed economy, 16–17
understanding how they function, 17–20
economies of scale, 119
B2B solutions, 122–123
cheap foreign labour, 121
constant returns to scale, 119
described, 120–121
diseconomies of scale, 121
illustration, 120*f*
increasing returns to scale, 120–121
market power, 186–187
monopoly, 175, 184, 186–187
natural monopoly, 186–187
productivity and costs, 121–123
unit labour costs, 121–122
the economy, 4–5
effective tax rate, 330
efficiency, 10
see also inefficiency
allocative efficiency, 165–166
cost efficiency, 287
costs, 236
and federal income tax, 328–329
flat tax, 337
government waste, 64
price efficiency, 233
production efficiency, 166, 234
production function, 103–104
and production possibilities curve, 10
and size, 121
trade-off with equality, 337
efficiency decision, 255–256, 287–288
elastic demand, 82–83
elasticity
cross-price elasticity of demand, 90–92
elasticity of labour supply, 277–278
income elasticity of demand, 89–90, 89*f*
price elasticity of demand. *See* price elasticity of demand
shifts *vs.* movements, 89
tax elasticity of labour supply, 348
tax elasticity of supply, 328–329
elasticity of labour supply, 277–278
electricity industry, 244–246
embargoes, 372
Emerson, David, 380
emission charges, 259–260, 259*f*
employer pension plans, 351
employer power, 294–295
Employment Insurance, 148, 329, 333, 334, 341, 342
Employment Insurance Act, 148
EnCana, 211
endorsement deals, 91
Entel, 240
entrepreneurship, 6
economic profits, 133
as factor of production, 6
incentive of, and market power, 186
entry
see also barriers to entry
competitive markets, 153, 153*f*
long-run rules, microcomputer industry, 161*t*

market *vs.* firm effects, monopolistic
competition, 223*f*
monopolistic competition, 221–222
entry barriers. *See* barriers to entry
environmental damage, 254–255
environmental protection
auction of pollution credits, 263
balance of benefits and costs, 265–270
carbon dioxide emissions, 268–270
central planning, 265
chlorofluorocarbons (CFCs), 249
cleanup, 255
climate change, 268–270
command-and-control options, 264–265
cost-benefit analysis, 267
distribution of costs, 267–268
efficiency decision, 255–256
emission charges, 259–260, 259*f*
external costs, 256–258
global warming, 268–270
"green" taxes, 261
greenhouse effect, 268–270
Kyoto Protocol, 269–270
market-based regulation, 259–262
market failure, 256–258
market incentives, 255–256, 259
opportunity cost, 265–266
optimal rate of pollution, 266–267
pollution abatement costs, 255–256
price on environmental damage, 254–255
production decision, 255
recycling, 260, 267
regulatory options, 259–265
sulfur dioxide allowances, 264
taxes on pollution, 261, 262
tradable pollution permits, 262–265, 263*t*
user fees, 260–261
Environmental Protection Agency, 254, 263, 268
environmental threats
acid rain, 250
air pollution, 250, 254
greenhouse effect, 250
Not In My Backyard (NIMBY) syndrome, 253
organic pollution, 250–251
polluted cities, 251
pollution damages, 253–255
smog, 250
solid-waste pollution, 251–253
thermal pollution, 251
water pollution, 250–251
EPCOR, 264
equilibrium
free-trade equilibrium, 376
labour market equilibrium, 285–286
long-run, in monopolistic competition, 222–223
monopolistic competition, 222*f*
no-trade equilibrium, 374
outcomes, 79–80
short-run competitive equilibrium, 160, 161*f*
zero-profit equilibrium, 223
equilibrium price, 42
changes in equilibrium, 45–47, 46*f*
demand shift, 45
illustration, 42*f*
invisible hand, 43
long-run competitive equilibrium, 160–161, 161*f*
market clearing, 42–43
market shortage, 43–44
market supply curve, 152
market surplus, 43
self-adjusting prices, 44–45
simultaneous shifts, 45–47, 47*f,* 47*n*
supply shift, 45
equilibrium wage, 286, 286*f*
European Communities, 378
European Free Trade Association, 380
European Union, 190, 196, 240, 246, 379, 380–381
excess capacity, 223–224
exchange
constraints leading to, 28–29
and dollars, 30–31
and markets, existence of, 30
exchange rates, 124–125
executive pay, 274, 289

exit
  competitive markets, 153
  long-run rules, 161t
  microcomputer industry, 164
  monopolistic competition, 221–222
expectations
  and bond supply and demand, 318
  as determinant of demand, 33, 39, 72
  as determinant of labour supply, 277
  as determinant of market supply, 38
  and stock market fluctuations, 312–313, 313f, 315
expected gain (loss), 203–204
expected rate of return, 308
expected value, 308
explicit costs, 130
export industries, 370
exports, 359–360
external benefits, 57–58
external costs, 56–57, **256**–258
externalities, 56
  carbon dioxide emissions, 269
  in consumption, 258
  external benefits, 57–58
  external costs, 56–57
  illustration, 57f
  and market failure, 55–58
  in production, 57, 257–258
  transportation externalities, 381
ExxonMobil, 196

factor costs, 38
factor markets, 29–30
factors of production, 6
fairness, 335–337, 337
Fanning, Shawn, 54
Fantasma Productions, 179
Farm Fresh Catfish Co., 141, 152
farm size, 120
Federal Court of Appeal, 186
federal departments and agencies, 236
Federal Energy Regulatory Commission (FERC), 27
federal income tax
  see also taxes
  average tax rate, 328
  effective tax rate, 330
  efficiency concerns, 328–329
  equity concerns, 329–331
  horizontal equity, 330
  income tax shares, 334f
  itemized deductions, 329
  loopholes, 329–330
  marginal tax rates, 327, 332t
  nominal tax rate, 330
  progressive tax, 327, 327t
  tax base, 331
  tax credits, 329
  tax elasticity of supply, 328–329
  tax-induced misallocations, 331
  tax reform in Canada, 331t
  taxable income, 329
  vertical equity, 330
  vertical inequity, 330t
Federal Motor Carrier Safety Administration, 236
Ferdinand, King of Spain, 302, 305, 306
final settlement, 297
financial intermediaries, 303, 310n
  see also financial markets
financial markets
  bond market, 317–319
  demand for loanable funds, 308–309
  economic role, 317
  expected value, 308
  financial intermediaries, 303
  interest rate effects, 307
  mobilization of savings, 303f
  present value of future profits, 306–309
  risk management, 305
  risk premiums, 305–306
  role of, 303–306
  stock market, 309–317
  supply of loanable funds, 304–306
  time value of money, 306–307
  uncertainty, and future payments, 307–308
  venture capitalists, 304

firm demand, 171f
firm demand curve, 135, 135f
First Nations, 329
fixed costs, 110
flat tax, 337–338
flawed price signals, 224
Fleck, James, 371
Flickinger, Burt P. III, 219
Flynn, Phil, 206
food banks, 323
for whom question, 13
Ford Motor, 196
Foreign Affairs and International Trade Canada, 368, 380
foreign labour, cheap, 121
former Soviet Union, 14
France, 240, 291
franchises, monopoly, 183
Fraser, Sheila, 63
free rider, 53
free trade, 381
free-trade equilibrium, 376
Freudian perspective, 71
Frigidaire, 371
Frito-Lay, 210, 211
fuel-efficiency rebate, 16
Fujishige, Hiroshi, 131
Fullerton, Don, 260
Fuqua School of Business, 276
fur, 174
future profits/payments. See present value of future profits

G4 countries, 379
gains from trade, 364–365, 365t, 370
game theory, 204
  described, 202
  expected gain (loss), 203–204
  payoff matrix, 202–203, 203t
  Prisoner's Dilemma, 203
Gandhi, Mahatma, 11
Gates, Bill, 189
Gateway, 164, 220
Gatorade, 91
General Agreement on Tariffs and Trade (GATT), 378
General Electric Co., 188, 196, 226
General Motors Corp., 145, 196, 287
General Preferential Tariff treatment, 373
Germany, 145, 240, 359, 372, 376–377
Gilson, Edith, 221
Gini coefficient, 326
global brands, 226
global perspective. See world view
global warming, 268–270
Godsmack, 179
goods
  complementary goods, 34, 90–91, 91f
  inferior good, 90
  luxury goods, 83–84
  multiple goods, 75, 79
  necessities, 83–84
  normal good, 90
  other goods, 33, 38, 39, 72
  private goods, 53, 55
  public goods, 53–55
  substitute goods, 33–34, 84, 90, 91f
Goods and Services Tax rebates, 345
Google, 314
Gorky Park, 174
Government Economics Service (UK), 269
government failure, 17
  ballot box economics, 65
  central planning, 265
  cost-benefit analysis, 64–65
  described, 62–63
  excessive process regulation, 265
  illustration, 63f
  ineffectiveness of tax system, 335
  opportunity cost, 63–64
  perceptions of waste, 63
  public-choice theory, 65–66
  valuation problems, 64–65
government intervention
  goal of, 62–63
  government failure. See government failure
  and mechanisms of choice, 14

minimum wage, 60
  resource allocation, influence on, 16
Government of Canada, 162
government regulation. See regulation
government size, 64
Graitcer, Kellam, 220
Grand River Enterprises, 194
graphs
  causation, 26
  linear curves, 25–26
  negative slope, 23
  nonlinear curves, 25–26, 26f
  positive slope, 23
  shifts, 24–25
  slope, 23–24, 25f
  using graphs, 22–26
Grass Roots Recycling Network, 260
Great Britain, 240, 329
Great Depression, 374
Great Lakes, 251, 252
green revolution, 2
"green" taxes, 261
greenhouse effect, 250, 268–270
Greenhouse Gas Emission Reduction Trading (GERT), 264
growth
  economic growth, 12, 12f
  population growth, 12
Guaranteed Income Supplement, 342, 349–350
gun registry, 63

Hall, Maria C., 133
Harmony Airways, 243
Harper, Stephen, 6, 15, 20, 270, 381
Harris, Richard, 380
Harvard Center for Risk Analysis, 267
Hasegawa, Ken, 206
Health Canada, 247
Helton, Todd, 284
Heritage Foundation, 15
Hewlett-Packard, 156, 165, 220, 221
higherbracket.ca, 289
Himawari CX, 206
hiring decision
  alternative production processes, 287
  choice among inputs, 286–290
  cost efficiency of input, 287
  efficiency decision, 287–288
  incentives to hire, 285f
  and labour demand, 283–284
  and labour supply, 282–283
  least-cost combination, 288f
  and market equilibrium, 285–286
  outsourcing, 287
  price, changes in, 285f
  productivity changes, 284–285
  unmeasured marginal revenue product, 289–290
  wage rate changes, 284
Hoffman, James, 141
Hollingsworth, Steve, 141
Hong Kong, 14
Hoover, Herbert, 374
horizontal equity, 330
how question, 13
human rights, 381
HungerCount, 323, 324

IBM, 2, 159, 164, 189, 212, 225, 226
IBM-Levano, 156
ice storm, 48
Iceland, 380
ICG Propane, 187
IDC, 165
imperfect competition
  advertising wars, 225
  described, 134, 192, 193
  labour power, 290–294
  monopolistic competition. See monopolistic competition
  monopsony, 294–295
  oligopoly. See oligopoly
  oligopsony, 294
imperfect knowledge, 20
Imperial Tobacco Canada, 194
implicit cost, 130
import-competing industries, 369

imports, 359
In Defense of Globalization (Bhagwati), 358
in-kind income, 323
in-kind transfer, 341–342
Inc. magazine, 276
incentives
    vs. costs, 347–348
    entrepreneurial incentives, 186
    to hire, 285*f*
    social insurance programs, 353
    work incentive problem, 345–347, 347*f*, 350
income
    after-tax distribution *vs.* before-tax distribution, 328
    breakeven level of income, 348
    as determinant of demand, 33, 72
    as determinant of labour supply, 277
    discretionary income, 71
    distribution in Canada, 325*t*
    in-kind income, 323
    inequality. *See* inequality
    vs. leisure, 275–277
    Lorenz Curve, 326–327, 326*f*
    marginal utility of, 276
    meaning of, 323–325
    personal income (PI), 323
    poverty in Canada, 324
    redistribution, 59–60
    size distribution of income, 325–327
    taxable income, 329
income effect of wages, 301
income elasticity of demand, 89–90, 89*f*
income quintile, 325
income share, 325
income transfers, 335
    see also transfer payments
increasing returns to scale, 120–121
Independent Electricity System Operator (IESO), 246
Index of Economic Freedom, 14, 15
India, 11, 14, 379
indifference curves, 96
    budget constraint, 97, 97*f*
    construction of, 95–97
    demand curve, deriving, 99–100
    described, 94–95
    illustration, 96*f*
    indifference map, 96–97, 96*f*
    marginal rate of substitution, 99
    marginal utility and price, 98–99
    optimal consumption, 98, 98*f*
    slope, 99
    utility maximization, 97–99
indifference map, 96–97, 96*f*
individual demand, 31–33
industrial unions, 290
industry demand, 171*f*
industry marginal cost curve, 166
inefficiency
    see also efficiency
    command-and-control strategy, 264
    consequences of inefficient production, 10, 11*f*
    excess capacity, 223–224
    monopolistic competition, 223–224
    and production possibilities curve, 10
    tax-induced misallocations, 331
inelastic demand, 82–83
inequality
    after-tax distribution *vs.* before-tax distribution, 328
    costs of greater equality, 335–337
    federal income tax, and equity concerns, 329–331
    Gini coefficient, 326–327
    income inequality, 325–327
    international wealth inequality, 324
    Lorenz Curve, 326–327
    as market failure, 327
    taxes, 334–338
inequity
    federal income tax, and equity concerns, 329–331
    and market failure, 59–62
    market output, 60–61
    minimum wage, 60
    price ceilings, 61–62
    price floors, 60
    transfer payments, 59–60
    vertical inequity, 330*t*

infant industries, 371
inferior good, 90
Infineon, 209
inflation, 62
initial public offering (IPO), 310–311
inputs
    choice among, by employees, 286–290
    control of key inputs, 183–184
    cost efficiency, 287
    varying input levels, 102–103
Institute of Public Administration of Canada (IPAC), 246
Intel Corporation, 2, 3, 189, 225, 226, 309–310
interbrand.com, 225
interest rate effects, 307
interest rates, 304, 308*t*, 315
International Brotherhood of Electrical Workers, 290
International Business Machines Corp. *See* IBM
international institutions
    General Agreement on Tariffs and
        Trade (GATT), 378
    global trade pacts, 378–379
    multilateral trade pacts, 378
    North American Free Trade Agreement
        (NAFTA), 379–380
    World Trade Organization (WTO), 378–379
international trade
    absolute advantage, 366
    barriers to trade, 372–377
    broader view of trade, 381–382
    Canada
        bilateral merchandise trade balances, 361*t*
    comparative advantage, 365–366
    exports, 359–360
    gains from trade, 364–365, 365*t*
    global trade pacts, 378–379
    imports, 359
    international institutions, 378–381
    motivation to trade, 361–365
    multilateral trade pacts, 378
    mutual gains, 364–365
    production and consumption with trade, 363–364
    production and consumption without trade, 362–363
    protectionist pressures, 368–372
    specialization, 361–362
    terms of trade, 366–368, 367*f*
    trade balances, 360–361, 361*t*
    trade patterns, 359–361
    trade surplus (deficit), 360–361
    world view
        export and import ratios, 360
international wealth inequality, 324
Internet, 122–123, 149
Inuit, 373
Inuit Circumpolar Council, 373
investment decision, 145–146
invisible hand, 13–14, 43
iPods, 167–168
Ireland, 360
Irwin, Douglas, 380
Isabella, Queen of Spain, 302
Ivan the Terrible, 174

J. Walter Thompson, 221
Jackson, Thomas Penfield, 189
Jagger, Mick, 329
Japan, 196, 211, 240, 300
Jarvis, Don, 375
Jeter, Derek, 284
Jobs, Steve, 156, 168, 304, 322
Johnston, Summerfield K. Jr., 204
Joseph Huber Brewery, 200
JTI-Macdonald, 194

Karmazin, Mel, 289
"karoshi," 300
Kelman, Steven, 65
Kelvinator, 371
Kerr, Don, 324
Keynes, John Maynard, 14
kinked demand curve, 200–202, 200*f*, 206, 206*f*
Kinnaman, Thomas, 260
Klein, Ralph, 34
Kraft Canada Inc., 375
Kraft Foods Inc., 219

Kramlich, Richard, 305
Krannert School of Management, 276
Krugman, Paul, 370
Krupnick, Alan J., 266
Kyoto Protocol, 269–270

Labatt Breweries of Canada, 59, 192, 194, 200
labour
    see also labour market
    cheap foreign labour, 121
    demand. *See* demand for labour
    as factor of production, 6
    and immigration increase, 12
    minimum wage, 60
    and population growth, 12
    quality-adjusted units of labour, 106*n*
    quality of, 12
    unit labour costs, 121–122, 124
labour demand. *See* demand for labour
labour demand curve, 278–279, 283*f*
labour-force participation rate, 351, 351*f*
labour-intensive production process, 287
labour market
    backward bending individual supply curve, 300–301, 301*f*
    bilateral monopoly, 296
    choice among inputs, 286–290
    demand. *See* demand for labour
    employer power, 294–295
    equilibrium wage, 286, 286*f*
    firm's hiring decision. *See* hiring decision
    income effect of wages, 301
    labour power, 290–294
    market equilibrium, 285–286
    monopsony, 294–295
    substitution effect of wages, 300–301
    supply. *See* labour supply
    unions. *See* unions
labour power, 290–294
    see also unions
labour supply, 275
    backward bending individual supply curve, 300–301, 301*f*
    determinants of labour supply, 277
    elasticity of labour supply, 277–278
    and hiring decision, 282–283
    illustration, 276*f*
    income *vs.* leisure, 275–277
    institutional constraints, 278
    market supply of labour, 277–278
    retirement, 351
    tax elasticity of labour supply, 348
labour supply curve, 275–276
Laforce, Jacques, 375
laissez faire, 14
land, 6
Large Final Emitters (LFEs), 270
laser eye surgery, 209
LaSorda, Tom, 369
Latin America, 304
law of demand, 33
law of diminishing marginal utility, 73–74
law of diminishing returns, 107, 136, 280–282
law of increasing opportunity cost, 10
law of supply, 39
lawsuits, 184
Least Developed Country Tariff treatment, 373
Leichtenstein, 380
leisure, 275–277
Libya, 15
limited liability, 309
limits to output, 6–7
linear curves, 25–26
liquidity, 318
Liquor Control Board of Ontario (LCBO), 170, 183
Live Nation Inc., 183
    see also Clear Channel Entertainment
loanable funds
    demand, 308–309
    market, 308–309, 309*f*
    supply of, 304–306
local markets, 195
London, 253
long-distance services, 240, 241
long run, 117
long-run average costs, 118–119

long-run competitive equilibrium, 160–161
long-run costs, 117–119, 146
long-run marginal costs, 119
loopholes, 329–330
Lorenz Curve, 326–327, 326*f*
Los Angeles Galaxy, 283, 284
lottery winners, 307
Lotus Development Corporation, 212
low concentration ratios, 218
Low-Income Cut-offs (LICOs), 324
luxury goods, 83–84

Macaulay, Thomas Babington, 358
MacKenzie, Denyse, 59
Mackenzie King, William Lyon, 242
macro instability, 62
macroeconomics, 18–19
Magnetek Inc., 185
Mahaney, Mark, 314
Major League Soccer, 284
Malthus, Thomas, 2
Manitoba, 200
manufacturing markets, 195*f*
marginal cost curve, 147
marginal cost (MC), 108
  vs. average total cost, 116–117
  computation of, 114
  described, 108–109
  illustration, 115*f*
  long-run marginal costs, 119
  and output, 142
  and payroll taxes, 148
  profit-maximizing rule, 138–139
marginal cost pricing, 180–181, 224
marginal factor cost (MFC), 294, 295*f*
marginal physical product (MPP), 105–107, 105*f*,
    108–109, 108*f*, 121, 279, 280–282, 281*f*
marginal productivity, 105–107, 280–282
marginal rate of substitution, 99
marginal revenue curve, 206*f*
marginal revenue (MR), 138
  and microcomputer industry, 176–177
  and price, in monopoly, 171–173, 172*f*
  and total revenue, 138*t*
marginal revenue product, 279–280, 282,
    283–284, 289–290, 295
marginal revenue product curve, 283*f*
marginal tax rates, 327, 332*t*, 346–347, 348
marginal utility, 73, 74–77, 74*f*, 98–99
marginal wage, 291–**292**, 292*f*
Maritz Research, 218
market activity, 28
market-based environmental regulation, 259–262
market demand, 36
  see also demand
market demand curve, 36–38, 37*f*, 135, 135*f*, 181
market economy, 13–14
market failure, 16
  causes, 53
  described, 52–53
  environmental threats, 256–258
  external costs, 256–258
  externalities, 55–58
  illustration, 52*f*
  inequality, 327
  inequity, 59–62
  macro instability, 62
  market power, 58
  and market power, 213
  maximization of social welfare, 258*f*
  public goods, 53–55
market incentives (pollution), 255–256, 259
market mechanism, 13
  and basic economic questions, 47–48
  failure of, 16
  government influence on resource allocation, 16
  as invisible hand, 43
  market failure. *See* market failure
market outcomes, 47–49
market participants
  industry behaviour, 213
  maximizing behaviour, 28
  specialization, 28–29
  who participates, 28

market power, 58
  Canadian manufacturing markets, 195*f*
  comparative perspective, 180–184
  concentration ratio (CR), 194
  contestable markets, 187–188
  described, 170, 171
  determinants of, 193–194
  downward-sloping demand curve, 171
  economies of scale, 186–187
  employer power, 294–295
  entrepreneurial incentives, 186
  firm size, 194–195
  labour power, 290–294
  limits to power, 181–182
  and market failure, 58, 213
  measurement of, 194–195
  measurement problems, 195
  in microcomputer industry, 174–179
  monopolistic competition, 218
  and monopoly, 171
    see also monopoly
  and perfect competition, 134
  vs. political power, 181
  price and marginal revenue, 171–173
  and profit maximization, 173–174, 173*f*
  pros and cons, 184–190
  research and development, 184–186
  restricted supply, 58
market reforms, 15
market share, 197–198, 209
market shortage, 43–44, 61*f*
market structures, 134
  characteristics, 193*t*
  degrees of power, 193
  determinants of market power, 193–194
  extremes, 134
  illustration, 134*f*
  market behaviour and outcomes, effect on, 196
  monopolistic competition. *See* monopolistic competition
  monopoly. *See* monopoly
  natural monopoly. *See* natural monopoly
  oligopoly. *See* oligopoly
  perfect competition, 134
    see also competitive firm
market supply, 38
  see also supply
  changes in quantity supplied, 40
  changes in supply, 40, 41
  construction of, 39
  determinants of supply, 38–39
  of labour, 277–278
  microcomputer industry, 159–161, 162–163
  restricted supply, 58
  sellers' intentions, 39
  shift, and equilibrium price, 45
  shifts of supply, 40–41
market supply curve, 39, 40*f*, 152–154, 152*f*
market supply of labour, 277–278
market surplus, 43
  and price floors, 60*f*
market transactions, 30
market wage, 292
markets
  bond market, 317–319
  competitive markets. *See* competitive markets
  contestable markets, 187–188, 194
  exchange and, 30
  factor markets, 29–30
  financial markets. *See* financial markets
  labour market. *See* labour market
  loanable funds market, 308–309, 309*f*
  local markets, 195
  locating markets, 195
  manufacturing markets, 195*f*
  market clearing, 42–43
  microcomputer industry. *See* microcomputer industry
  national markets, 195
  product markets, 30
  role of, and terms of trade, 368
  stock market. *See* stock market
Markkula, A. C., 304
Martin, Paul, 20
Marx, Karl, 14
"Math Skills for Introductory Economics," 26

Mattel, 164
Matthews, Deb, 253
MBA students, 276
McDonald's, 218, 226, 275
McGraw-Hill, 58
McMaster University, Department of Economics, 14
means, 17
means-tested program, 342*n*
measurement of market power, 194–195
mechanisms of choice
  balance, 17
  command economies, 14
  government failure, 17
  government intervention, 14
  invisible hand of market economy, 13–14
  mixed economy, 16–17
medallion system, 212
median retirement ages, 351*f*
memory chips, 209
Mercedes, 226
mergers, 211–212
Metro, 145
Mexico, 124, 238, 240, 377, 379
Michalski, Joseph, 324
Microcell Telecommunications Inc. (Fido), 241
microcomputer industry
  barriers to entry, 179
  economic profits, 158
  exits, 164
  home computers *vs.* personal computers, 161–162
  initial equilibrium, 157*f*
  long-run competitive equilibrium, 160–161, 161*f*
  low entry barriers, 159
  lure of profits, 158–159
  and marginal revenue, 176–177
  market characteristics of perfect competition, 154–155
  market evolution, 155–156
  market power, 174–179
  market supply, shift of, 159–161, 162–163
  monopoly, 174–179
  monopoly price, 177
  monopoly profits, 177–179, 178*f*
  oligopoly, 197–199
  personal computer market, 164
  price competition, 162
  production decision, 157–158, 176–177
  profit calculations, 158
  reduced output, 177
  revenue, costs and profits, 158*t*
  short-run competitive equilibrium, 160, 161*f*
  shutdowns, 163–164
microeconomic protectionist pressures, 369–370
microeconomics, 18–19
Micron, 209
Microsoft Corporation, 133, 168, 188–190, 192, 212,
    225, 226
Middle East, 117
Miles, Teresa, 276
Minhas, Manjit, 200
Minhas, Ravinder, 200
Minhas Creek Brewing Co., 200
minimum average cost, 114, 119
minimum-service regulation, 234–235, 235*f*
minimum wage, 60
Mississippi, 141, 152
mixed economy, 16
mobile wireless services, 241
mobilization of savings, 303*f*
models, 19–20
Molson Coors Brewing Co., 192, 194, 211
Molson Inc. *See* Molson Coors Brewing Co.
monopolistic competition, 218
  advertising wars, 224–225
  behaviour, 219–225
  brand image, 219
  brand loyalty, 220–221, 221
  described, 134
  economic profits, 221, 223
  entry, 221–222
  equilibrium, 222*f*
  excess capacity, 223–224
  exit, 221–222
  flawed price signals, 224
  independent production decisions, 218

inefficiency, 223–224
long-run equilibrium, 222–223
long-run profits, lack of, 222–223
low concentration, 218
low entry barriers, 218–219
market power, 218
market *vs.* firm effects of entry, 223*f*
vs. perfect competition, 224*f*
product differentiation, 219
short-run price and output, 221
structural characteristics, 218–219
zero-profit equilibrium, 223
monopoly, 58
see also market power
acquisition, 184
barriers to entry, 179, 182–184
bilateral monopoly, 296
vs. competitive industry, 180–184
contestable markets, 187–188
control of key inputs, 183–184
economies of scale, 175, 184, 186–187
entrepreneurial incentives, 186
as extreme, 134
franchises, 183
lawsuits, 184
limits to power, 181–182
and marginal cost pricing, 180–181
marginal revenue, 171–173, 172*f*
and market power, 171
and microcomputer industry, 174–179
mix of output, 180–181
natural monopoly. *See* natural monopoly
patents, 174, 183
political power, 181
power plant monopolies, 244
price, 171–173, 172*f*, 177
price discrimination, 182
and price elasticity of demand, 181–182
productivity advances, 180
profit maximization, 171–172, 173–174, 173*f*
profits, 177–179, 178*f*
research and development, 184–186
telephone monopolies, demise of, 240
monopsony, 294–295
Montreal Economic Institute, 183
moral hazard, 346
Moscow, 275
most-favoured-nation policy, 376–377
most valuable brands, 226
motivation, 129, 363–364
motivation to trade
gains from trade, 364–365, 365*t*
mutual gains, 364–365
production and consumption without trade, 362–363
specialization, 361–362
Mountain Crest Brewing Co., 200
movements, 35–36, 89
Mulroney, Brian, 20
multilateral trade pacts, 378
multiple goods, 75, 79
municipal taxes, 331–333
Murdoch, Rupert, 188
mutual gains, 364–365

Naimi, Ali, 206
Napster, 54
NASDAQ (National Association of Securities Dealers Automated Quotations System), 312
NASDAQ Composite, 316, 316*f*
nation-building, 237
National Academy of Sciences, 268
National Council of Welfare, 345
National Football League, 290
National Football Players Association, 290
National Hockey League, 91
national markets, 195
National Oceanic and Atmospheric Administration, 268
National Round Table on the Environment and the Economy, 264
national security argument, 370
National Transportation Act, 238
natural gas rebates, 61
natural monopoly, 58
see also regulation

administrative costs of regulation, 235–236
bloated costs, 234
call for regulation, 235
characteristics of, 231, 232*f*
compliance costs, 236
costs of regulation, 235–237
declining ATC curve, 231–232
economies of scale, 186–187
efficiency costs of regulation, 236
minimum-service regulation, 234–235, 235*f*
output regulation, 234–235
price efficiency, 233
price regulation, 233–234
production efficiency, 23
profit regulation, 23
regulation of, 231–233
regulatory options, 233–235
subsidy, 233–234
unregulated behaviour, 232–233
NatWest Securities, 211
NBC, 188
necessities, 83–84
needs test, 344–345
needs-tested criteria, 342, 342*n*
negative marginal utility, 73
negative slope, 23
net gain, 370
network economies, 212–213
New Brunswick, 48
New Canadian Air Policy, 243
New Enterprise Associates, 305
New York City, 85, 267
New York Mercantile Exchange, 206
New York Stock Exchange Composite Index, 316*f*
New York Stock Exchange (NYSE), 312
News Corp., 188
news industry, 188
NHL Players' Association, 296
Nigeria, 206
Nikkei 225, 316*f*
Nintendo, 192
Nippon Telegraph & Telephone, 240
no-trade equilibrium, 374
Nokia, 226
nominal tax rate, 330
nonlinear curves, 25–26, 26*f*
nonpayment possibility, 307
nonprice competition, 199, 212
nontariff barriers, 376–377
normal good, 90
normal profit, 132
normative statements, 19
Nortel Networks, 309
North American Free Trade Agreement (NAFTA), 238, 377, **379–380**
North American Industry Classification Structure (NAICS), 194*n*
North Korea, 14
Northwest Airlines, 202
Norway, 246, 380
Not In My Backyard (NIMBY) syndrome, 253
Nova Scotia, 48
NPD Group, 155
number of buyers, 33
number of sellers, 38

Old Age Security, 341, 342, 349–350
oligopolist, 197
oligopoly, 193
advertising, 212
allocation of market shares, 209
antitrust enforcement, 213–215
barriers to entry, 210–215
battle for market shares, 197–198
behaviour, 196–199
cartel, 209
collective interests, 203
vs. competition, 204–207
coordination problems, 207–209
cost cushion, 205, 207*f*
described, 134
differentiated oligopoly, 198
distribution control, 210–211
expected gain (loss), 203–204

game theory, 202–204
government regulation, 211–212
joint *vs.* individual interests, 207
kinked demand curve, 200–202, 200*f*, 206, 206*f*
marginal revenue curve, 206*f*
mergers and acquisitions, 211–212
network economies, 212–213
nonprice competition, 199, 212
output, 205
patents, 210
payoff matrix, 202–203, 203*t*
predatory pricing, 209
prevailing market price, 198
price, 205
price-fixing, 208–209
price leadership, 209
product differentiation, 199
profit maximization, 205*f*
pure oligopoly, 198
reduced prices, 198
retaliation, 198–199
rivals' response to price increases, 201–202
rivals' response to price reductions, 201
sticky prices, 205–207
training, 212
oligopsony, 294
Oman Oil Company (S.A.O.C.), 117
One-Tonne Challenge Program, 270
Ontario, 48, 170, 183, 245, 246
Ontario Energy Board, 245
Ontario Pilot Emission Reduction Trading (PERT), 264
Ontario Power Generation (OPG), 264
Oogav, Shy, 133
OPEC, 205, 206, 208
opportunity cost, 7
and bond supply and demand, 318
constant opportunity costs, 10*n*
environmental protection, 265–266
and government actions, 64
and government failure, 63–64
government waste, 64
illustration of, 7
increasing, 9–10
international trade, 366
law of increasing opportunity cost, 10
and production possibilities curve, 8, 9–10
and scarcity, 7
opportunity wage, 289
optimal consumption, 77–79, 95, 98, 98*f*
optimal mix of output, 52
optimal outcomes, 48–49
optimal rate of pollution, 266–267
organic pollution, 250–251
Organization for Economic Cooperation & Development (OECD), 262
other goods, 33, 38, 39, 72
"other things remaining equal." *See* ceteris paribus
Ottawa, 375
output
allocative efficiency, 165–166
competitive firm, 136–137
and costs, 136–137
and income transfers, 343–344, 344*f*
inequities in market output, 60–61
limits to output, 6–7
and marginal cost, 142
monopoly, 180–181
oligopoly, 205
optimal mix of output, 52
profit-maximizing rate, 139–142
regulation of, 234–235
and revenues, 136
short-run, in monopolistic competition, 221
output decision, 115
outsourcing, 287
Owen Sound, City of, 260

Pacific Gas and Electric, 245
packaging, 49
PanCanadian Energy, 211
par value, 317
patents, 174, 183, 210
payoff matrix, 202–203, 203*t*
payroll taxes, 148, 333, 334*f*

PCjr, 164
peer-to-peer (P2P) online distribution, 54
Penn World Tables, 20
pension plans, 349–354
PepsiCo Inc., 192, 204, 219, 220
perceptions of waste, 63, 219
perfect competition, 134
    see also competitive firm; competitive markets
    demand for labour, 278–282
    firm demand curve, 135, 135*f*
    market characteristics of, 154–155
    market demand curves, 135, 135*f*
    vs. monopolistic competition, 224*f*
    vs. oligopoly, 204–207
    price takers, 134–135
    structure, 134–135
personal computer market, 164
personal income (PI), 323
Peru, 380
Peter the Great, 174
Petro-Canada, 226
Pilot Emission Removals, Reductions and Learnings
    (PERRL) Initiative, 264*n*
plate system, 212
point elasticity of demand, 81*n*
Polaroid Corporation, 183
political power, 181
politics, 20
polluted cities, 251
pollution. *See* environmental protection; environmental
    threats
pollution abatement costs, 255–256
pollution damages, 253–255
pollution permits, 262–265, 263*t*
population growth, 12
Portney, Paul R., 266
positive slope, 23
positive statements, 19
poverty threshold, 324
power
    employer power, 294–295
    labour power, 290–294
    market power. *See* market power
    political power, 181
    potential use of power, 294–295
power plant monopolies, 244
Precision Drilling Trust, 274, 289
predatory pricing, 209, 210
predictions, 3
preferences, 95
    see also tastes
present discounted value (PDV), 306
present value of future profits
    computation of, 307
    demand for loanable funds, 308–309
    expected value, 308
    higher interest rates, 308*t*
    interest rate effects, 307
    present discounted value (PDV), 306
    time value of money, 306–307
    uncertainty, and future payments, 307–308
price
    vs. average variable cost, 144–145
    bonds, 319*t*
    changes in, and hiring decision, 285*f*
    competitive price and profit squeeze, 159*f*, 160*f*
    consumer response to changes, 87, 88*f*
    as determinant of labour supply, 277
    efficiency, 233
    on environmental damage, 254–255
    equilibrium price, 42–47
    flawed price signals, 224
    marginal cost pricing, 180–181
    and marginal revenue curve, 171–173
    vs. marginal utility, 75–77, 98–99
    as market mechanism, 13
    and market power, 171–173
    and monopoly, 171–173, 172*f*
    oligopoly, 205
    of other goods, 38, 39
    pollution permits, 263*t*
    prevailing market price, 198
    reduced prices, 198, 201
    relative price, 84–85

role of, and terms of trade, 368
self-adjusting prices, 44–45
short-run, in monopolistic competition, 221
stability, 205
sticky prices, 205–207
and utility, 74–75
wheat prices, 41
price ceiling, 61–62, 61*f*
price discrimination, 182
price/earnings (P/E) ratio, 311
price elasticity of demand, 80, 181
    computation of, 80–83
    described, 80
    determinants of elasticity, 83–85
    elastic demand, 82–83
    elasticity estimates, 83*f*
    extremes of elasticity, 82*f*
    inelastic demand, 82–83
    long-run *vs.* short-run, 85
    and market demand curve, 181
    and total revenue, 86–87, 86*f*, 87*t*, 88*f*
price-fixing, 208–209
price floors, 60, 60*f*
price leadership, 209, 213
price regulation, 232*f*, 233–234
price takers, 134–135
Priceline.com, 36
Prime Minister of Canada, 274
Prisoner's Dilemma, 203
private costs, 257
private goods, 53, 55
privatization, 353–354
privatized companies, 10–11
Procter & Gamble, 225
product differentiation, 199, 219
product markets, 30
production
    efficiency, 166, 234
    externalities in, 57, 257–258
    with trade, 363–364
    without trade, 362–363
production costs
    average costs, 112–114, 112*f*
    average fixed cost (AFC), 113
    average total cost (ATC), 112, 116–117
    average variable cost (AVC), 113
    cost curves, 116*f*
    cost summary, 114–117
    dollar costs, 109–117
    economies of scale, 119–123
    fixed costs, 110
    key measures of costs, 115*t*
    long-run average costs, 118–119
    long-run costs, 117–119
    long-run marginal costs, 119
    marginal and average productivity, 105–107
    marginal cost (MC), 108–109, 114
    production function, 102–104
    resource costs, 102, 107–109
    total cost, 110–111
    variable costs, 110–111
production decision, 136–137, 157–158, 176–177, 218, 255
production function, 102
    capacity of single firm, 102*n*
    efficiency, 103–104
    and productivity advances, 122
    short-run, 104, 104*f*
    table, 102*t*
    varying input levels, 102–103
production possibilities, 8
    consumption possibilities, 362–364
    economic growth, 12, 12*f*
    efficiency, 10
    inefficiency, 10
    and opportunity costs, 8, 9–10
    production possibilities curve, 8, 9*f*
    production possibilities schedule, 8*t*
    scarce resources, 8
    underproduction of public goods, 55*f*
    unemployment, 11
production possibilities curve, 8, 9*f*
    see also production possibilities
production possibilities schedule, 8*t*
production process, 287

productivity, 103
    advance, 122
    average productivity, 105–107
    changes in, and hiring decision, 284–285
    cheap foreign labour, 121
    economies of scale, 121–123
    and exchange rates, 124–125
    improvements, and costs, 122*f*
    marginal physical product (MPP). *See* marginal
        physical product (MPP)
    marginal productivity, 105–107, 280–282
    and monopolies, 180
professional athletes, 283
profit, 107
    competitive markets, 158*t*
    and costs, 130–133
    economic profits, 130–132, 132*t*, 221
    entrepreneurship, 133
    monopolistic competition, and long-run profits,
        222–223
    monopoly, 177–179, 178*f*
    motive, 129
    normal profit, 132
    present value of future profits, 306–309
    public opinion about, 130
    regulation, 23
    and risk, 133
    taxes, 149
    total profit, 137*f*, 142*f*
    zero profits, 153–154, 166
profit maximization
    electric power production, 256*f*
    goals of, 28
    monopoly, 171–172, 173–174, 173*f*
    oligopoly, 205*f*
profit maximization rule, 140
    adding up profits, 142–143
    illustration, 140*f*
    marginal cost, 138–139
    marginal revenue (MR), 138
    and monopolies, 172
    oligopoly, 205
    rate of output, 139–142
profit per unit, 158
progressive tax, 327, 327*t*
property taxes, 147–148, 331–333
prosperity cheques, 34
protectionist pressures
    described, 368
    dumping, 371
    export industries, 370
    import-competing industries, 369
    infant industries, 371
    microeconomic pressures, 369–370
    national security, 370
    net gain, 370
    terms of trade, 372
provincial taxes, 331–333
public choice, 65–66
public goods, 53
    free-rider dilemma, 53–54
    income redistribution, 60
    and market failure, 53–55
    no exclusion, 53, 54
    relief of misery, 59
    technical considerations, 54
    underproduction, 54–55, 55*f*
public-sector activity. *See* government intervention
public services, 64–65
    see also government failure
Purdue University, 276
pure oligopoly, 198

quality-adjusted units of labour, 106*n*
quality deterioration, 234–235
quantity, 74–75
Quebec, 48, 170, 183, 261
Quebec Pension Plan (QPP), 349, 350–351
quota-restricted trade, 376
quotas, 374

railroad industry, 237–239
Railway Abandonment Regulations, 238
Railway Act, 237

Railway Association of Canada (RAC), 238, 239*t*
Ralph bucks, 34
Ramirez, Manny, 284
rational behaviour, 76
RBC Financial Group, 225, 226
RealNetworks Inc., 189
Reciprocal Trade Agreements Act, 374
recycling, 260, 267
redistribution of income, 59–60
Reebok, 91
regional trade pacts, 379–381
Registered Retirement Savings Plans (RRSPs), 329
regressive tax, 331–332, 332*t*
regulated rate plan (RPP), 245
regulation, 231
  administrative costs, 235–236
  balance of benefits and costs, 237
  vs. competition policy, 231
  compliance costs, 236
  costs of regulation, 235–237
  critics, 6
  deregulation. *See* deregulation
  efficiency costs, 236
  environmental protection. *See* environmental protection
  imperfect answers, 235
  minimum-service regulation, 234–235, 235*f*
  natural monopoly, 231–233
  necessity of, 246–247
  oligopoly, 211–212
  output regulation, 234–235
  price regulation, 232*f,* 233–234
  profit regulation, 23
  quality deterioration, 234–235
  regulatory options, 233–235
  unregulated behaviour, 232–233
relative price, 84–85
research and development, 184–186
resource allocation
  financial markets, 317
  government influence on, 16
  stock market, 317
resource constraints, 107
resource costs, 102, 107–109
resources
  scarcity. *See* scarcity
  specialized resources, 9
restricted supply, 58
Retail Forward Inc., 219
retained earnings, 310
retaliation, 198–199
retirement, 351
revenue
  competitive markets, 158*t*
  marginal revenue (MR). *See* marginal revenue (MR)
  marginal revenue product, 279–280, 282, 283–284, 289–290, 295
  total revenue. *See* total revenue
Riesman, David, 71
risk
  high interest rates, 304
  and profit, 133
  stock, 311–312
  and supply of loanable funds, 304–305
risk management, 305
risk premiums, 305–306
Rodriguez, Alex, 284
Rogers Wireless Communications Inc., 241
Rolling Stones, 329
Roots Air, 243
Rothmans, 194
Royal Airlines, 243
Royal Bank of Canada, 225
Royal Caribbean Cruises, 262
Royal Dutch/Shell, 196
Russia, 14–15, 275, 304
Rwanda, 360

sales taxes, 331–333, 332*t*
Samsung, 209
Sandberg, Annette, 236
Sapporo, 211
Saputo Inc., 375
Saskatchewan farm size, 120
Saudi Arabia, 206

savings, 303*f*
scarcity, 5
  core problem, 5–7
  factors of production, 6
  issues, 4
  limits to output, 6–7
  and opportunity cost, 7
  and production possibilities curve, 8
Schimberg, Henry A., 204
Schumpeter, Joseph, 6
Scotiabank, 226
seal bans, 373
Second Cup, 218
second-hand smoke, 56
secondary trading, 311–312
self-adjusting prices, 44–45
sellers' intentions, 39
September 11, 2001, 70, 315–316
settlement pressures, 297
shared ownership, 309–310
Sharp, 159
shifts, 35
  changes in demand, 36
  changes in quantity demanded, 36
  changes in supply, 40, 41
  in demand, 35–36, 35*f,* 45
  described, 24–25
  vs. movements, 35*f,* 36, 89
  simultaneous shifts, 45–47, 47*f,* 47*n*
  of supply, 40–41, 45, 147
  shocks, 315–317
Shoppers Drug Mart, 226
short run, 104, 117
short-run competitive equilibrium, 160, 161*f*
short-run determinants of supply, 146–147
short-run production function, 104, 104*f*
shortage. *See* market shortage
Shourie, Arun, 11
shutdown decision, 143–145, 163–164
shutdown point, 144, 145
simultaneous shifts, 45–47, 47*f,* 47*n*
Singapore, 380
Sirius Satellite Radio Inc., 289
size, and efficiency, 121
size distribution of income, 325–327
Sleeman's, 211
slope, 23–24, 25*f,* 99
Smart Meter price, 245
SmartTape™, 246
Smith, Adam, 13, 14, 16, 43
smog, 250
Smoot-Hawley Tariff Act, 374
social assistance programs, 342
  basic social assistance benefits, 345*t*
  breakeven level of income, 348
  budget deficit method, 345
  described, 344–345
  earnings exemptions, 346
  incentives *vs.* costs, 347–348
  marginal tax rates, 346–347, 348
  needs test, 344–345
  vs. social insurance programs, 342–343
  tax elasticity of labour supply, 348
  work incentive problem, 345–347, 347*f*
social costs, 257
social demand, 57–58
social demand curve, 56–57, 57*f*
social insurance programs, 342
  Canada Pension Plan (CPP), 349, 350–351
  compassion, 353
  costs, 353
  declining labour supply, 351
  described, 349
  earnings test, 349–350
  incentives, 353
  median retirement ages, 351*f*
  Old Age Security, 349–350
  pension plans, 349–354
  privatization, 353–354
  Quebec Pension Plan (QPP), 349, 350–351
  vs. social assistance programs, 342–343
  trade-offs, 353
Société des alcools du Québec (SAQ), 170, 183
sociopsychiatric explanation, 71

solid-waste pollution, 251–253
Sony, 192
Soriano, Alfonso, 284
Sotheby's, 209
South Korea, 380
South Padre Island, 133, 149
Soviet Union, 174
S&P/TSX 60 Index, 316*f*
S&P/TSX Composite Index, 316*f*
specialization
  constraints leading to, 28–29
  farms and, 121
  motivation to trade, 361–362
specialized resources, 9
Standard Oil, 189
Starbucks Corp., 218, 219
Statistics Canada, 71, 84, 120, 251, 278, 324, 325, 334
Statoil, 211
Stern, Howard, 289
Stern, Sir Nicholas, 269
Stern Review on the Economics of Climate Change, 269
Stevens, C. R., 185
sticky prices, 205–207
stock market
  averages, 316*f*
  booms and busts, 314–315
  corporate stock, 309–310
  expectations, changes in, 312–313. 313*f*
  initial public offering (IPO), 310–311
  market fluctuations, 312–317
  price/earnings (P/E) ratio, 311
  resource allocations, 317
  secondary trading, 311–312
  shocks, 315–317
  stock quotes, 313*f*
  stock returns, 310
  total return, 310
  value of information, 313
Stock Market Game, 315
stock quotes, 313*f*
stock returns, 310
Stoll, Jon, 179
Strahl, Chuck, 375
Strategic Resource Group, 219
subsidies
  as determinant of market supply, 38
  government provision of, 61
  price regulation, 233–234
substitute goods, 33–34, 84, 90, 91*f*
substitution effect of wages, 300–301
sulfur dioxide allowances, 264
Summit Technology, 209
Superior Propane, 187
supply, 31
  see also market supply
  labour supply, 275–277
  law of supply, 39
  loanable funds, 304–306
  tax elasticity of supply, 328–329
supply curve, 147, 147*f*
  see also market supply curve
surplus. *See* market surplus
Switzerland, 377, 380

t-shirt shops, 133
Tabac ADL, 194
target efficiency, 342
Tariff Rate Quotas (TRQ), 211*n*
tariff-restricted trade, 376
tariffs, 372–374
tastes, 33, 72, 91, 95, 277
tax base, 331
tax burdens, 332
tax credits, 329
tax effects, 147–149
tax elasticity of labour supply, 348
tax elasticity of supply, 328–329
tax incidence, 333
tax reform, 331*t*
taxable income, 329
taxes
  carbon tax, 261
  cigarette taxes, 85
  competitive firm, 147–149

taxes (*cont.*)
  costs of greater equality, 335–337
  as determinant of labour supply, 277
  as determinant of market supply, 38
  fairness, 335–337
  federal income tax. *See* federal income tax
  flat tax, 337–338
  "green" taxes, 261, 262
  impact on business decisions, 148*f*
  income transfers, 335
  and inequality, 334–338
  marginal tax rates, 332*t*
  municipal taxes, 331–333
  payroll taxes, 148, 333, 334*f*
  on pollution, 262
  on profit, 149
  progressive tax, 327, 327*t*
  property taxes, 147–148, 331–333
  proportional tax system, 335
  provincial taxes, 331–333
  redistribution of income, 59–60
  regressive tax, 331–332, 332*t*
  sales taxes, 331–333, 332*t*
  supply, effect on, 147–149
  tariffs, 372–374
  top tax rates, globally, 336
TD Bank Financial Group, 325
TD Canada Trust Bank, 211, 226
technology, 38
teen smoking rate, 84
Telebras, 240
telephone industry, 239–241
Telus, 226, 241
terms of trade, 366–368, 367*f*, 372
terrorist attacks, 70, 315–316
Texas Instruments, 163
theories, 19–20
thermal pollution, 251
Ticketmaster, 179, 183, 210
Tim Hortons, 218, 226
time, 85
time preferences, 304
time value of money, 306–307
Toronto, 253
Toronto Blue Jays, 283, 284
Toronto-Dominion Bank, 211
Toronto Stock Exchange (TSX), 312, 314
Toshiba, 156
total cost, 110–111, 137*f*
total profit, 137*f*, 142*f*
total return, 310
total revenue, 86
  competitive firm, 136, 136*f*
  and marginal revenue, 138*t*
  and price elasticity, 86–87, 86*f*, 87*t*, 88*f*
total revenue curve, 136, 136*f*
total utility, 73, 74*f*
Toyota, 196, 226
tradable pollution permits, 262–265, 263*t*
trade. *See* international trade
Trade, Investment and Labour Mobility Agreement (TILMA), 377
trade balances, 360–361, 361*t*
trade barriers
  "beggar thy neighbour," 373–374
  comparative effects, 374–376
  described, 372
  embargoes, 372
  free-trade equilibrium, 376
  impact of trade restrictions, 375*f*
  no-trade equilibrium, 374
  nontariff barriers, 376–377
  quota-restricted trade, 376
  quotas, 374
  tariff-restricted trade, 376
  tariffs, 372–374
  voluntary restraint agreement (VRA), 376
trade-offs, 4, 284, 337, 353
trade pact, 378
  global trade pacts, 378–379
  multilateral trade pacts, 378
  regional trade pacts, 379–381
trade patterns, 359–361
trade surplus (deficit), 360–361

training, 212
Trans-Canada Airlines, 242
TransAlta, 264
transfer payments, 59
  cash transfers, 341–342
  described, 59–60, 340
  federal spending, 341*f*
  goals, 343
  in-kind transfer, 341–342
  income-tested programs, 342
  major transfer programs, 341–344, 342*f*
  needs-tested criteria, 342, 342*n*
  pension plans, 349–354
  as proportion of total income, 341
  reduced output, 343–344, 344*f*
  social insurance *vs.* social assistance, 342–343, 343*f*
  target efficiency, 342
  undesirable behaviour, 344
  unintended consequences, 343–344
Transportation Act of 1938, 242
transportation externalities, 381
trucking industry, 236
Trulson, Curt, 372
trustbusters, 187
tshirtmall.com, 149
Turner Broadcasting System, 188
Tyler, Aleamer, 152

uncertainty, 307–308
unemployment, 11, 62
unionization rate, 290
unions
  collective bargaining, 296–297, 297*f*
  craft unions, 290
  exclusion, 293–294
  industrial unions, 290
  and marginal wage, 291–292, 292*f*
  membership, 291
  and monopoly on market, 290
  objectives, 290–291
  types of unions, 290
  wage goal, 293, 293*f*
Unisource Canada, Inc., 208
unit costs, 124–125
unit labour costs, 121–122, 124
United Airlines, 202
United Arab Emirates, 206
United Auto Workers, 290
United Nations, 2, 269, 270, 300
United States
  Chinese tariffs, complaints, 378
  deregulation of airline industry, 242–243
  deregulation of electric industry, 246
  farmers' protests, 373
  as G4 country, 379
  imports, 359
  and Kyoto Protocol, 270
  largest firms, 196
  Mexican trucks, 377
  North American Free Trade Agreement (NAFTA), 379–380
  optimal rate of pollution, 266
  scrutiny of subsidization, 238
  telephone monopolies, demise of, 240
  tradable pollution permits, 263–264
  union membership, 291
  War on Poverty, 65
Universal Manufacturing Corp., 185
unmeasured marginal revenue product, 289–290
U.S. Bureau of Labor Statistics, 122
U.S. Clean Air Acts, 265
U.S. Department of Justice, 188, 190
U.S. Department of Transportation, 236
U.S. Federal Trade Commission, 209
U.S. National Center for Atmospheric Research, 268–269
US Airways, 202
user fees, 260–261
Utilitarianism, 73
utility, 72
  diminishing marginal utility, 73–74
  marginal utility, 73, 74*f*, 75–77, 98–99
  measurement of, 72–73
  multiple goods, 75

  price and quantity, 74–75
  total utility, 73, 74*f*
utility maximization
  budget constraint, 97, 97*f*
  described, 77–80
  goals of, 28
  indifference curves, 97–99
  optimal consumption, 98, 98*f*
  utility-maximizing rule, 78–79
utility theory, 72–75, 79

variable costs, 110–111
Vehicle Efficiency Incentive, 15
venture capital, 304, 305
Venture Capital & Private Equity Association, 304
VentureWire, 305
Verizon Wireless Ampitheatre, 179
vertical equity, 330
vertical inequity, 330*t*
Vietnam, 151, 152
VISX, 209
vitamins, 208
Voice over Internet Protocol (VoIP), 240
voluntary restraint agreement (VRA), 376

wages
  CEO pay, 289–290
  income effect of wages, 301
  marginal wage, 291–292, 292*f*
  market wage, 292
  minimum wage, 60
  opportunity wage, 289
  substitution effect of wages, 300–301
  union wage goal, 293, 293*f*
  wage rate changes, 284
Wal-Mart Stores, 145, 165, 196
wants, 92–93
war veterans, 341
Wardair, 243
Warner, Lloyd, 71
waste, perceptions of, 63–64
water pollution, 250–251
wealth, 277, 325
Wealth of Nations (Smith), 13
Weaver, John, 125
Weidenear, Dennis, 276
welfare benefits. *See* social assistance programs
welfare maximization, 28
Wells, Vernon, 283, 284
Western Grain Transportation Act, 120, 238
WestJet, 202
what question, 12
wheat prices, 41
Whirlpool Corp., 371
White Consolidated Industries Inc., 371
Williams, Geraldine, 307
Winders, Mark, 210
work incentive problem, 345–347, 347*f*, 350
World Trade Centre, 70, 315–316
World Trade Organization (WTO), 238, 378–379
world view
  ad spending per capita, 92
  aging, and richer countries, 352
  best Canadian and global brands, 226
  China, and private property, 18
  export and import ratios, 360
  Index of Economic Freedom, 15
  international trade. *See* international trade
  international wealth inequality, 324
  largest firms in the world, 196
  polluted cities, 251
  taxes on pollution, 262
  top tax rates, 336
Wozniak, Steven, 156, 304
wrong predictions, 3

Xerox, 159

Yahoo!, 225

zero-profit equilibrium, 223
zero profits, 153–154, 166

Problems for Chapter 1

Name: _____

1. According to Table 1.1 (or Figure 1.1), what is the opportunity cost of the
   - (a) Third metric tonne of wheat? _____
   - (b) Fourth metric tonne of wheat? _____

2. (a) According to Figure 1.2, what is the opportunity cost of Canada's wheat production at point *C*?
   (b) What would be the gain to Canada's softwood lumber production if Canada cut the output of wheat from three metric tonnes per year to two metric tonne per year (that is, move from point *C* to point *B*)?

3. How much money would be available to spend on health care if the current spending on national defence is reduced from 1% of the $1.5 trillion economy to ½ %?

4. What is the opportunity cost (in dollars) to attend an hour-long econ lecture for
   - (a) A minimum-wage teenager $_____
   - (b) A $100,000 per year corporate executive $_____

5. Suppose either computers or televisions can be assembled with the following labour inputs:

Units produced	1	2	3	4	5	6	7	8	9	10
Total labour used	3	7	12	18	25	33	42	54	70	90

   (a) Draw the production possibilities curve for an economy with 54 units of labour. Label it P54.
   (b) What is the opportunity cost of the eighth computer?
   (c) Suppose immigration brings in 36 more workers. Redraw the production possibilities curve to reflect this added labour. Label the new curve P90.
   (d) Suppose advancing technology (e.g., the miniaturization of electronic circuits) increases the productivity of the 90-labourer workforce by 20 percent. Draw a third production possibilities curve (PT) to illustrate this change.

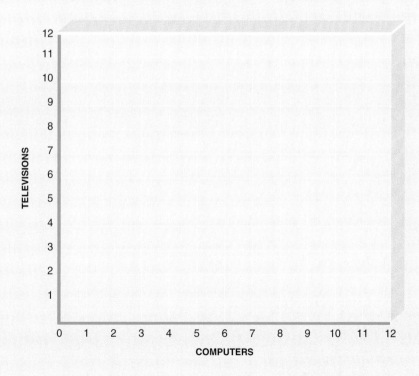

TELEVISIONS (vertical axis, 1–12)

COMPUTERS (horizontal axis, 0–12)

6. Suppose there's a relationship of the following sort between study time and grades:

	(a)	(b)	(c)	(d)	(e)
Study time (hours per week)	0	2	6	12	20
Grade-point average	0	1.0	2.0	3.0	4.0

If you have only 20 hours per week to use for either study time or fun time,

(a) Draw the (linear) production possibilities curve on the graph below that represents the alternative uses of your time.

(b) What is the cost, in lost fun time, of raising your grade-point average from 2.0 to 3.0? Illustrate this effort on the graph (point C to point D).   _____

(c) What is the opportunity cost of increasing your grades from 3.0 to 4.0? Illustrate as point D to point E.   _____

(d) Why does the opportunity cost change? _____

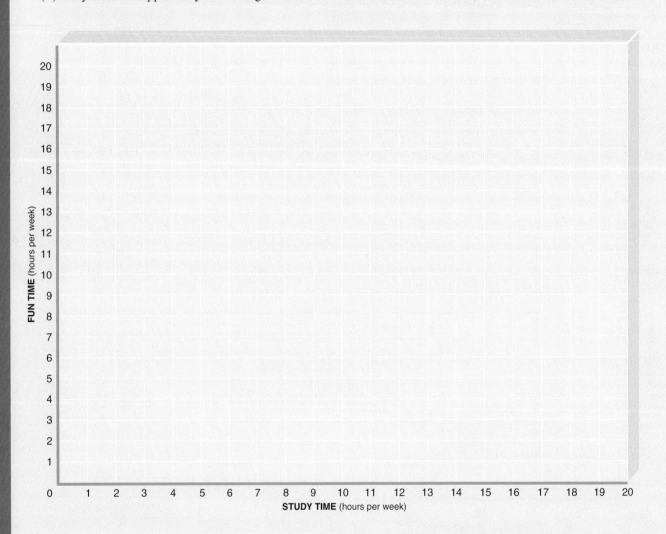

Problems for Chapter 2

Name: _____

1. According to Figure 2.3, at what price would Tom buy 15 hours of web tutoring?

      (*a*) Without a lottery win.   _____

      (*b*) With a lottery win.   _____

2. According to Figures 2.5 and 2.6, what would the new equilibrium price of tutoring services be if Ann decided to stop tutoring?   _____

3. Given the following data, identify the amount of shortage or surplus that would exist at a price of

      (*a*) $5.00   _____

      (*b*) $3.00   _____

      (*c*) $1.00   _____

A. Price	$5.00	$4.00	$3.00	$2.00	$1.00			$5.00	$4.00	$3.00	$2.00	$1.00
B. Quantity demanded							C. Quantity supplied					
Al	1	2	3	4	5		Alice	3	3	3	3	3
Betsy	0	1	1	1	2		Butch	7	5	4	4	2
Casey	2	2	3	3	4		Connie	6	4	3	3	1
Daisy	1	3	4	4	6		Dutch	6	5	4	3	0
Eddie	1	2	2	3	5		Ellen	4	2	2	2	1
Market total	__	__	__	__	__		Market total	__	__	__	__	__

4. Graph the official and equilibrium prices for upscale clothes in Vancouver on Boxing Day (see Application, p. 44).

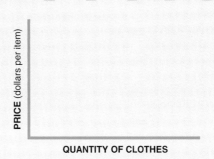

5. In the World View on page 49, menu prices are continuously adjusted. Graph the initial and final (adjusted) prices for the following situations. Be sure to label axes and graph completely.

(*a*) **Customers are ordering too little haddock.**

(*b*) **The kitchen is running out of beef ribs.**

6. As a result of the ice storm in Eastern Canada, the demand for generators increased, driving up the price of generators in this market. What effect, if any, do you think this may have had on the market for generators in other parts of Canada?

Problems for Chapter 2 (cont'd)

Name: _____

7. Biofuels derived from agricultural products such as corn, canola, soybeans, and wheat have received considerable interest as an alternative to fossil fuels since many scientists believe that they reduce greenhouse gases. On the following three graphs, show how an increase in demand for biofuel (say wheat)—*ceteris paribus*—will affect the equilibrium for (*a*) biofuel wheat, (*b*) pasta, and (*c*) coal.

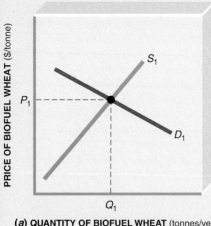 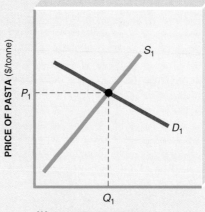 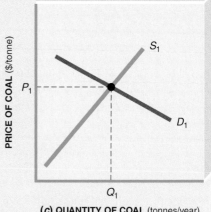

(*a*) QUANTITY OF BIOFUEL WHEAT (tonnes/year)   (*b*) QUANTITY OF PASTA (tonnes/year)   (*c*) QUANTITY OF COAL (tonnes/year)

8. Suppose the population for the city of Calgary has increased dramatically over the past year. In addition, the union representing construction workers has negotiated a 20% increase in the hourly wages paid to carpenters, plumbers, and drywallers.

    Given the above information, if we examine the market for single family housing, which curve will directly affected by

           (*a*) the increase in population?   _____

           (*b*) the increase in hourly wage rates?   _____

On the following graphs, illustrate the three possible outcomes associated with this simultaneous shift in the market for single family housing.

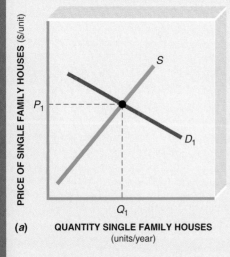 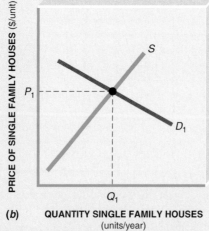 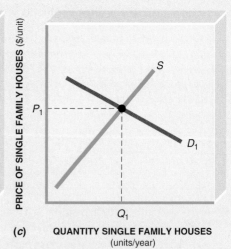

(*a*)   QUANTITY SINGLE FAMILY HOUSES (units/year)   (*b*)   QUANTITY SINGLE FAMILY HOUSES (units/year)   (*c*)   QUANTITY SINGLE FAMILY HOUSES (units/year)

Problems for Chapter 3

Name: _____

1. In Figure 3.2, by how much is the market
   (a) Overproducing private goods?   _____
   (b) Underproducing public goods?   _____

2. Assume that the product depicted below generates external costs in consumption of $5 per unit.
   (a) Draw the social demand curve.   _____
   (b) What is the socially optimal output?   _____
   (c) By how much does the market overproduce this good?   _____

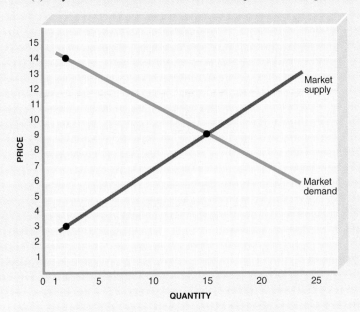

3. In the previous problem's market equilibrium, what is
   (a) The market value of the good?   _____
   (b) The social value of the good?   _____

4. Suppose the following data represent the market demand for college education:

Tuition (per year)	$1,000	2,000	3,000	4,000	5,000	6,000	7,000	8,000
Enrollment demanded (in millions per year)	8	7	6	5	4	3	2	1

   (a) If tuition is set at $5,000, how many students will enroll?   _____

   Now suppose that society gets an external benefit of $1,000 for every enrolled student.

   (b) Draw the social and market demand curves for this situation on the graph below.
   (c) What is the socially optimal level of enrollments at the same tuition price of $5,000?   _____
   (d) How can this optimal enrollment level be achieved?_____

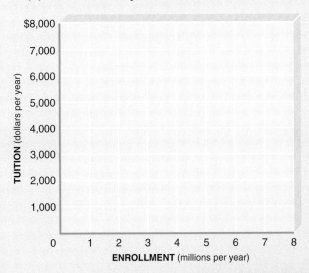

Name: _____

5. What is the relationship of Quebec power to Ontario power? (circle one)

(*a*) Complementary good   (*b*) Substitute good

Illustrate on the graphs below the impacts of a Ontario price ceiling (at P_c) on the Ontario and Quebec electricity markets.

(*c*) Which determinant of demand for Quebec electricity changes in this case? _____

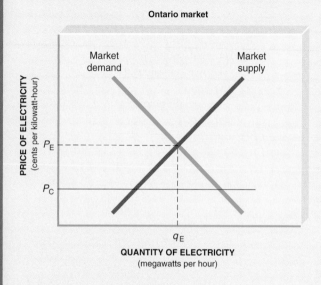

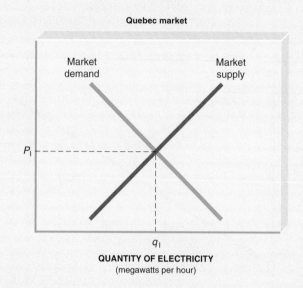

6. Use the following data to draw supply and demand curves on the accompanying graph.

Price	$ 8	7	6	5	4	3	2	1
Quantity demanded	2	3	4	5	6	7	8	9
Quantity supplied	10	9	8	7	6	5	4	3

(*a*) What is the equilibrium price? _____

(*b*) If a *minimum* price (price floor) of $6 is set, what disequilibrium results? _____

(*c*) If a *maximum* price (price ceiling) of $3 is set, what disequilibrium results? _____

Illustrate these answers.

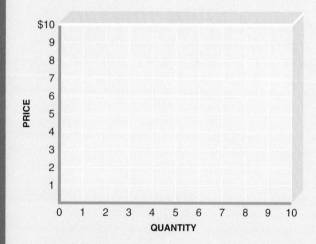

Problems for Chapter 4

Name: _____

1. Illustrate the following demand on the accompanying graph:

Price (per pair)	$100	$80	$60	$40	$20
Quantity demanded (pairs per day)	10	14	18	22	26

(a) How many pairs will be demanded when the price is $70? _____

(b) How much money will be spent on shoes at a price of $50? _____

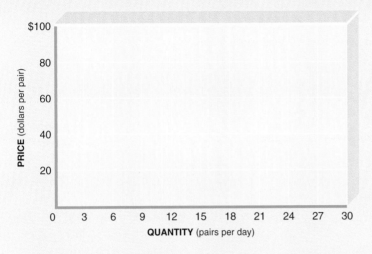

2. According to the Applications box on page 84, Statistics Canada reports that teenage smoking has fallen approximately by 27 percent from 2002 to 2003 (*i.e.*, from 22 percent in 2002 to 18 percent in 2003). Assuming that all of this decrease was due to an increase in the price of cigarettes, use the elasticity value of cigarettes from Table 4.3 to estimate the percentage increase in the price. _____%

3. Suppose consumers buy 10 million packs of cigarettes per month at a price of $2 per pack. If a $1 tax is added raising the price to $3,

(a) By what percent does price change? (Use midpoint formula on p. 82.) _____%

(b) By what percent will cigarette sales decline in the short run? (See Table 4.3 for clue.) _____%

(c) According to Gary Becker, by how much will sales decline in the long run? (See Applications, page 85.) _____%

4. From Figure 4.5, compute (a) the price elasticity between each of the following points and (b) the total revenue at each point.

	Price Elasticity		Total Revenue
Point *D* to *E*	_____	At point *D*	_____
		E	_____
G to *H*	_____	*G*	_____
		H	_____

5. What is the price elasticity of demand for New York City cigarettes? (See Applications, page 85.) _____

6. According to the calculation on p. 90, by how much will popcorn sales increase if average income goes up by 2.0 percent? _____%

7. Use the following table to compute the income elasticity of the demand for air travel:

	Income (per year)	Vacations (per year)		Income Elasticity of Demand
a.	$ 20,000	0		
b.	50,000	1	*b* to *c*	_____
c.	100,000	3	*c* to *d*	_____
d.	200,000	5		

8. Suppose the following table reflects the total satisfaction derived from consumption of pizza slices and Pepsis. Assume that pizza costs $1 per slice and a large Pepsi costs $2. With $20 to spend, what consumption mix will maximize satisfaction? _____

Quantity consumed	1	2	3	4	5	6	7	8	9	10	11	12	13	14
Total units of pleasure from pizza slices	47	92	132	166	196	224	251	271	288	303	313	315	312	300
Total units of pleasure from Pepsis	111	200	272	336	386	426	452	456	444	408	340	217	92	−17

9. Use the following data to illustrate the (*a*) demand curve and (*b*) total revenue curve:

Price	$1	2	3	4	5	6	7	8	9	10
Quantity	18	16	14	12	10	8	6	4	2	0

(*a*) At what price is total revenue maximized?
(*b*) At that price what is the elasticity of demand?
(*c*) Indicate the elastic and inelastic regions of each curve on the graphs.

$ _____

$E =$ _____

(a) Demand curve

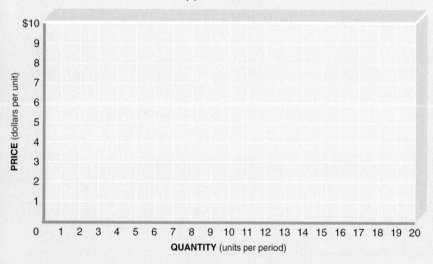

(b) Total revenue curve

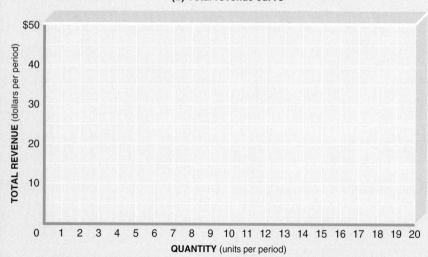

Problems for Chapter 5

Name: _____

1. (*a*) Complete the following cost schedule:

Rate of Output	Total Cost	Marginal Cost	Average Fixed Cost	Average Variable Cost	Average Total Cost
0	$100				
1	110				
2	130				
3	165				
4	220				
5	300				

(*b*) Use the cost data to plot the ATC and MC curves on the accompanying graph.

(*c*) At what output rate is ATC minimized? _____

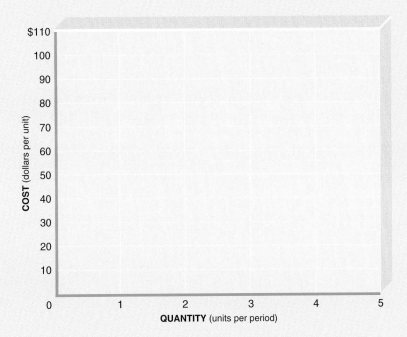

2. Based on Figure 5.2, the lowest cost per unit will occur when
   (*a*) we move from _____ worker(s) to _____ worker(s) and,
   (*b*) we move from _____ units of output to _____ units of output.

3. Refer to the production table for jeans (Table 5.1). Suppose a firm had three sewing machines and could vary only the amount of labour input.
   (*a*) Graph the production function for jeans given the three sewing machines.
   (*b*) Compute and graph the marginal physical product curve.
   (*c*) At what amount of labour input does the law of diminishing returns first become apparent in your graph of marginal physical product? _____
   (*d*) Is total output still increasing when MPP begins to diminish? _____
   (*e*) When total output stops increasing what is the value of MPP? _____

Problems for Chapter 5 (cont'd)

Name: _____

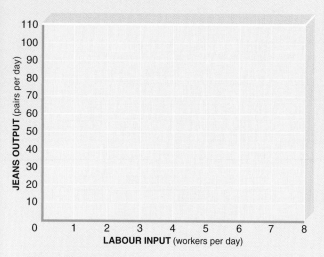

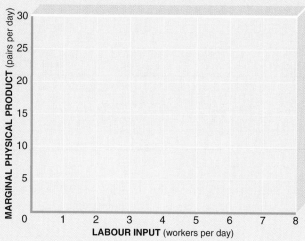

4. The following table indicates the average total cost of producing varying quantities of output from three different plants:

Rate of output	10	20	30	40	50	60	70	80	90	100
Average total cost										
Small firm	$ 600	$500	$400	$500	$600	$700	$800	$900	$1,000	$1,100
Medium firm	800	650	500	350	200	300	400	500	600	700
Large firm	1,000	900	800	700	600	500	400	300	400	500

(a) Plot the ATC curves for all three firms on the graph.
(b) Which plant(s) should be used to produce 40 units?   _____
(c) Which plant(s) should be used to produce 100 units?   _____
(d) Are there economies of scale in these plant-size choices?   _____

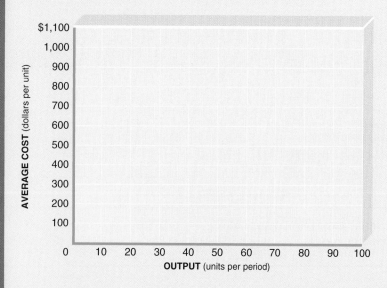

5. According to the Applications on page 120, what percentage change has occurred to the "Total number of farms in Saskatchewan" over the past 25 years?   _____

6. Suppose (A) the hourly wage rate is $15 in Canada and $1 in China, and (B) productivity is 20 units per hour in Canada and 1 unit per hour in China. What are unit labour costs in
   (a) Canada?   _____
   (b) China?   _____

Problems for Chapter 6

Name: _____

1. If the owner of the Table 6.1 drugstore hired a manager for $10 an hour to take his place, how much of a change would show up in

   (a) Accounting profits?   _____
   (b) Economic profits?   _____

2. Suppose a company incurs the following costs: labour, $400; equipment, $300; and materials, $100. The company owns the building, so it doesn't have to pay the usual $800 in rent.
   (a) What is the total accounting cost?   _____
   (b) What is the total economic cost?   _____
   (c) How would accounting and economic costs change if the company sold the building and then leased it back?   _____

3. If the price of catfish fell from $13 to $7 per bushel, use Figure 6.7 to determine the

   (a) Profit-maximizing output.   _____
   (b) Profit or loss per bushel.   _____
   (c) Total profit or loss.   _____

4. (a) Complete the following cost and revenue schedules:

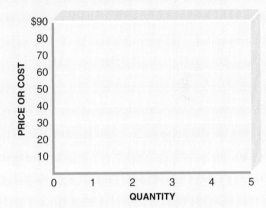

Quantity	Price	Total Revenue	Total Cost	Marginal Cost
0	$80	_____	$ 50	_____
1	80	_____	60	_____
2	80	_____	90	_____
3	80	_____	190	_____
4	80	_____	210	_____
5	80	_____	300	_____

   (b) Graph MC and P.
   (c) What rate of output maximizes profit?   _____
   (d) What is MC at that rate of output?   _____

5. Complete the following cost schedule:

Quantity	0	1	2	3	4	5	6	7
Total cost	$10	$12	$16	$21	$30	$40	$54	$72
ATC	____	____	____	____	____	____	____	____
MC		____	____	____	____	____	____	____

Assuming the price of this product is $12, at what output rate is

   (a) Total revenue maximized?   _____
   (b) ATC minimized?   _____
   (c) Profit per unit maximized? _____
   (d) Total profit maximized?   _____

6. Assume that the price of silk ties in a perfectly competitive market is $15 and that the typical firm confronts the following costs:

Quantity (ties per day)	0	1	2	3	4	5	6	7	8	9	10
Total cost	$10	$18	$28	$40	$54	$70	$88	$108	$130	$154	$180

   (a) What is the profit-maximizing rate of output for the firm?   _____
   (b) How much profit does the firm earn at that rate of output?   _____
   (c) If the price of ties fell to $11, how many ties should the firm produce?   _____
   (d) At what price should the firm shut down?   _____

7. Using the data from Problem 6 (at the original price of $15), determine how many ties the producer would supply if
   (*a*) A tax of $2 per tie were collected from the producer.   _____
   (*b*) A property tax of $2 was levied.   _____
   (*c*) Profits were taxed at 50 percent.   _____

8. Suppose labour is the only variable cost in fish farming and that a new minimum-wage law increases wages by 40 percent.
   (*a*) What will the new output rate be for the firm in Figure 6.7?   _____
   (*b*) How much profit will it make?   _____

9. Complete the following table:

Output	Total Cost	Marginal Cost	Average Total Cost	Average Variable Cost
0	$100			
6	110	_____	_____	_____
12	130	_____	_____	_____
18	170	_____	_____	_____
24	220	_____	_____	_____
30	290	_____	_____	_____
36	380	_____	_____	_____
42	490	_____	_____	_____

   According to the table above,
   (*a*) If the price is $8, how much output will the firm supply?
   (*b*) How much profit or loss will it make?   _____
   (*c*) At what price will the firm shut down?   _____
                                                                                   _____

9. A firm has leased plant and equipment to produce video game cartridges, which can be sold in unlimited quantities at $21 each. The following figures describe the associated costs of production:

Rate of output (per day)	0	1	2	3	4	5	6	7	8
Total cost (per day)	$50	$55	$62	$75	$92	$117	$150	$189	$248

   (*a*) How much are fixed costs?
   (*b*) Draw total revenue and cost curves on the graphs below.   _____
   (*c*) Draw the average total cost (ATC), marginal cost (MC), and demand curves of the firm.
   (*d*) What is the profit-maximizing rate of output?
   (*e*) Should the producer stay in business?   _____
   (*f*) What is the size of the loss if production continues?   _____
   (*g*) How much is lost if the firm shuts down?   _____
                                                                                   _____

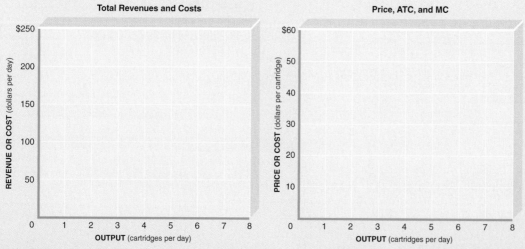

Problems for Chapter 7

Name: _____

1. According to Table 7.1,
   (a) What were the fixed costs of production for the firm? _____
   (b) At what rate of output was profit per computer maximized? _____
   (c) At what output rate was total profit maximized? _____

2. Suppose the following data summarize the costs of a perfectly competitive firm:

Quantity	0	1	2	3	4	5	6	7	8
Total cost	$100	102	105	109	114	120	127	135	144

   (a) Draw the firm's MC curve on the graph on the left below.
   (b) Draw the market supply curve on the right graph, assuming 8 firms identical to the one above.
   (c) What is the equilibrium price in this market? _____

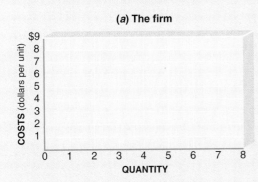

(a) The firm

(b) The market

3. Suppose the following data describe the demand for liquid-diet beverages:

Price	$11	$10	$9	$8	$7	$6	$5	$4	$3	$2
Quantity demanded	9	12	15	18	21	24	27	30	33	36

Four identical, perfectly competitive firms are producing these beverages. The cost of producing these beverages at each firm are the following:

Quantity produced	0	1	2	3	4	5	6	7	8	9	10
Total cost	$5	$8	$10	$13	$17	$22	$28	$36	$45	$55	$67

   (a) What price will prevail in this market? _____
   (b) What quantity is produced? _____
   (c) How much profit (loss) does each firm make? _____
   (d) What happens to price if two more identical firms enter the market? _____

4. Suppose the typical catfish farmer was incurring an economic loss at the prevailing price p_1.
   (a) Illustrate these losses on the firm and market graphs. (b) What forces would raise the price? What price would prevail in long-term equilibrium? Illustrate your answers on the graphs.

(a) The market

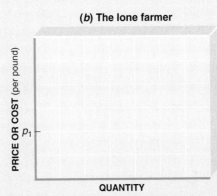

(b) The lone farmer

Problems for Chapter 7 (cont'd)

Name: _____

5. According to Table 7.1,
   (*a*) What was the prevailing computer price in 1978? _____
   (*b*) How much total profit did the typical firm earn? _____
   (*c*) At what price would profits have been zero? _____
   (*d*) At what price would the firm have shut down? _____

6. Suppose that the monthly market demand schedule for Frisbees is

Price	$8	$7	$6	$5	$4	$3	$2	$1
Quantity demanded	1,000	2,000	4,000	8,000	12,000	18,000	26,000	35,000

Suppose further that the marginal and average costs of Frisbee production for every competitive firm are

Rate of output	100	200	300	400	500	600
Marginal cost	$3.00	$2.00	$3.00	$5.00	$7.00	$12.00
Average total cost	6.00	4.00	4.00	4.00	6.00	8.00

Finally, assume that the equilibrium market price is $6 per Frisbee.
   (*a*) Draw the cost curves of the typical firm and identify its profit-maximizing rate of output and its total profits. Remember to plot MC at mid-points.
   (*b*) Draw the market demand curve and identify market equilibrium.
   (*c*) How many Frisbees are being sold? _____
   (*d*) How many (identical) firms are initially producing Frisbees? _____
   (*e*) How much profit is the typical firm making? _____
   (*f*) In view of the profits being made, more firms will want to get into Frisbee production. In the long run, these new firms will shift the market supply curve to the right and push price down to average total cost, thereby eliminating profits. At what equilibrium price are all profits eliminated? _____
   (*g*) How many firms will be producing Frisbees at this price? _____

(a) The firm

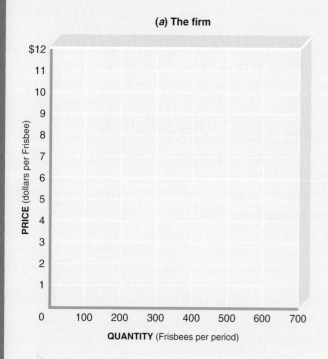

(b) The market

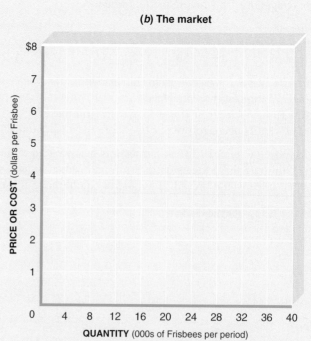

Problems for Chapter 8

Name: _____

1. Use Figures 8.2 and 8.3 to answer the following questions:
   (a) What is the highest price the monopolist could charge and still sell fish? _____
   (b) What is total revenue at that highest price? _____
   (c) What rate of output maximizes total revenue? _____
   (d) What is marginal revenue at that rate of output? _____
   (e) What is price at that rate of output? _____
   (f) What rate of output maximizes total profit? _____
   (g) What is MR at that rate of output? _____
   (h) What is price? _____

2. (a) Complete the following table:

Price	$15	$13	$11	$9	$7	$5	$3	$1
Quantity demanded	2	4	6	8	10	12	14	16
Marginal revenue		___	___	___	___	___	___	___

   (b) If marginal cost is constant at $7, what is the profit-maximizing rate of output? Assume that "odd" quantities can be produced. _____
   (c) What price should be charged at that rate of output? Assume that "even" prices can be charged. _____

3. The following table indicates the prices various buyers are willing to pay for a Miata sports car:

Buyer	Maximum Price	Buyer	Maximum Price
Buyer A	$50,000	Buyer D	$20,000
Buyer B	40,000	Buyer E	10,000
Buyer C	30,000		

   The cost of producing the cars includes $10,000 of fixed costs and a constant marginal cost of $20,000.
   (a) Graph below the demand, marginal revenue, and marginal cost curves.
   (b) What is the profit-maximizing rate of output and price for a monopolist? How much profit does the monopolist make?

   Output _____
   Price _____
   Profit _____

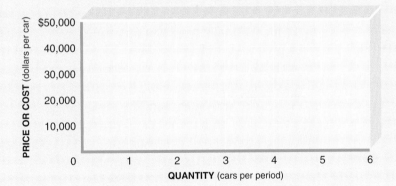

4. If the on-campus demand for soft drink is as follows:

Price (per can)	$0.25	0.50	0.75	1.00	1.25	1.50	1.75	2.00
Quantity demanded (per day)	100	90	80	70	60	50	40	30

   and the marginal cost of supplying a soft drink is 75 cents, what price will students end up paying in
   (a) A perfectly competitive market? _____
   (b) A monopolized market? _____

Problems for Chapter 8 (cont'd)

Name: _____

5. The following table summarizes the weekly sales and cost situation confronting a monopolist:

Price	Quantity Demanded	Total Revenue	Marginal Revenue	Total Cost	Marginal Cost	Average Total Cost
$20	0			$ 16		
18	2			28		
16	4			44		
14	6			64		
12	8			88		
10	10			116		
8	12			148		
6	14			184		
4	16			224		
2	18			297		

(a) Complete the table.
(b) Graph the demand, MR, and MC curves on the graph below.
(c) At what rate of output is total revenue maximized within this range? _____
(d) What are the values of MR and MC at the revenue-maximizing rate of output?   MR _____
                                                           MC _____
(e) At what rate of output are profits maximized within this range? _____
(f) What are the values of MR and MC at the profit-maximizing rate of output?   MR _____
                                                           MC _____
(g) What are total profits at that output rate? _____
(h) If a competitive industry confronted the same demand and costs, how much output would it produce in the short run? _____
(i) What would happen to long-run price if the market became perfectly competitive?

_____

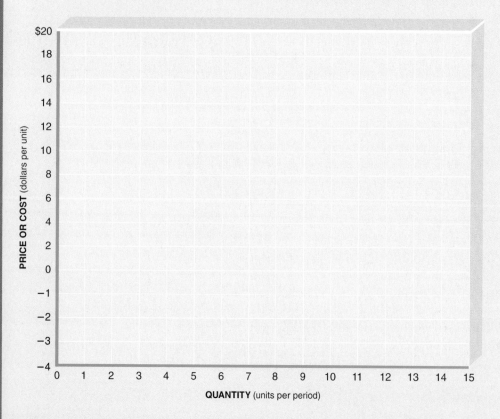

Problems for Chapter 9

Name: _____

1. According to Figure 9.1, which Canadian manufacturing sectors have 4-firm concentration ratios greater than 70 percent?

_____   _____   _____

_____   _____   _____

_____   _____   _____

2. According to the Applications box on page 202,
   (*a*) increases in airfares for WestJet and Air Canada were _____

                                                          (cost-related / advertising-related)
   (*b*) major U.S. airlines _____ Delta Airlines 25 percent cut in fares.
                    (matched / did not match)

3. Assume an oligopolist confronts *two* possible demand curves for its own output, as illustrated below. The first (*A*) prevails if other oligopolists don't match price changes. The second (*B*) prevails if rivals *do* match price changes.

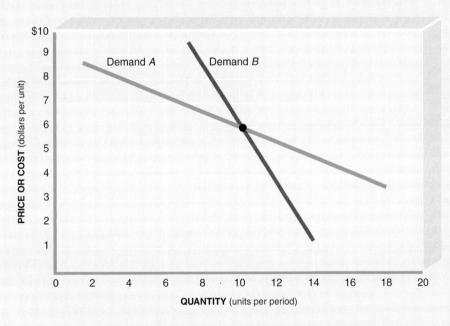

   (*a*) By how much does quantity demanded change if price is reduced from $6 to $4 and
       (*i*) Rivals match price cut?   _____
       (*ii*) Rivals don't match price cut?   _____
   (*b*) By how much does quantity demanded change when price is raised from $6 to $8 and
       (*i*) Rivals match price hike?   _____
       (*ii*) Rivals don't match price hike?   _____

4. How large would the probability of a "don't match" outcome have to be to make a universal price cut statistically worthwhile? (See expected payoff, p. 203.)   _____

5. Suppose the payoffs to each of four strategic interactions is as follows:

	Rival Response	
Action	**Reduce Price**	**Don't Reduce Price**
Reduce price	Loss = $200	Gain = $20,000
Don't reduce price	Loss = $5,000	No loss or gain

    (*a*) If the probability of rivals matching a price reduction is 99 percent, what is the expected
        payoff to a price cut?   _____

    (*b*) If the probability of rivals reducing price even though you don't is 5 percent, what is the
        expected payoff to *not* reducing price?   _____

    (*c*) What should you do?   _____

6. Suppose that the following schedule summarizes the sales (demand) situation confronting an
   oligopolist:

Price (per unit)	$8	$10	$12	$14	$16	$17	$18	$19	$20
Quantity demanded (units per period)	9	8	7	6	5	4	3	2	1

Using the graph below,
    (*a*) Draw the demand and marginal revenue curves facing the firm.
    (*b*) Identify the profit-maximizing rate of output in a situation where marginal cost is constant at
        $10 per unit.   _____

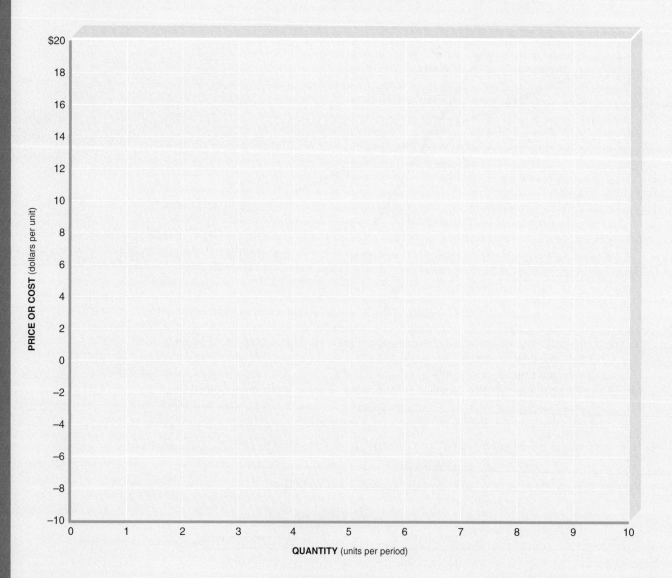

7. What is the price elasticity of demand in Figure 9.2?   _____

1. In Figure 10.1*b*,
   (*a*) At what output rate is economic profit equal zero?   _____
   (*b*) At what output rate(s) are positive economic profits available?   _____
   (*c*) At what output rate(s) do economic losses occur?   _____

2. (*a*) Use the accompanying graph to illustrate the short-run equilibrium of a monopolistically
        competitive firm.
   (*b*) At that equilibrium, what is   (*i*) Price?   _____
                                                         (*ii*) Output?   _____
                                                         (*iii*) Total profit? _____

   (*c*) Identify the long-run equilibrium of the same firm.
   (*d*) In long-run equilibrium, what is   (*i*) Price?   _____
                                                         (*ii*) Output?   _____
                                                         (*iii*) Total profit? _____

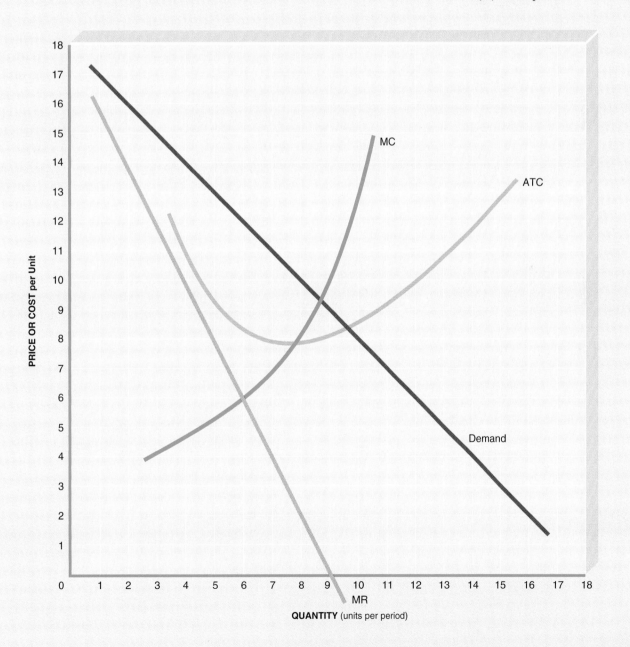

Problems for Chapter 10 (cont'd)   Name: _____

3. (*a*) In the *short*-run equilibrium of the previous problem, what is
       (*i*) The price of the product?   _____
       (*ii*) The opportunity cost of producing the last unit?   _____
   (*b*) In *long*-run equilibrium what is
       (*i*) The price of the product?   _____
       (*ii*) The opportunity cost of producing the last unit?   _____

4. According to the Applications box on p. 219,
   (*a*) By how much could unit sales at Starbucks decline after the 2004 price increase without
      reducing total revenue?   _____%
   (*b*) If the price elasticity of demand for Starbucks is 0.10, by how much would unit sales have
      fallen?   _____%

5. On the accompanying graph, identify each of the following *market* outcomes:
   (*a*) Short-run equilibrium output in competition.
   (*b*) Long-run equilibrium output in competition.
   (*c*) Long-run equilibrium output in monopoly.
   (*d*) Long-run equilibrium output in monopolistic competition.

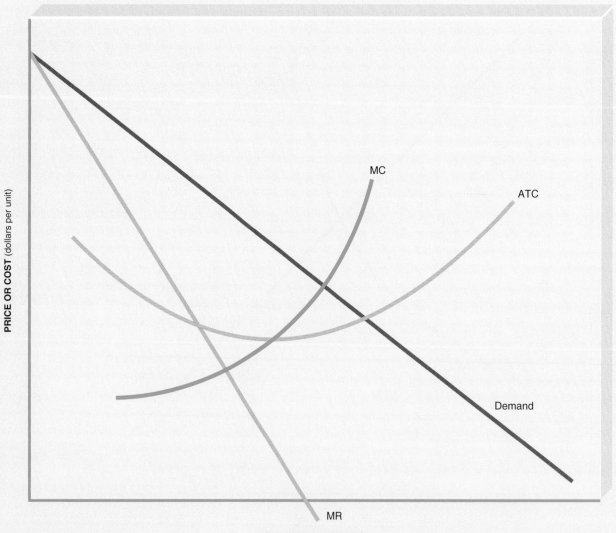

Problems for Chapter 11

Name: _____

1. In Figure 11.1, what would be the equilibrium level of output if
   (*a*) prices were regulated at zero-profit (economic)? _____
   (*b*) prices were regulated at marginal costs? _____
   (*c*) the market was unregulated? _____

2. What happens to total profits when new technology reduces average total costs (shifts ATC downward in Figure 11.1) in
   (*a*) An unregulated natural monopoly? _____
   (*b*) A price(=MC)-regulated natural monopoly? _____
   (*c*) A profit-regulated natural monopoly? _____

3. Suppose a natural monopolist has fixed costs of $30 and a constant marginal cost of $2. The demand for the product is as follows:

Price (per unit)	$10	$9	$8	$7	$6	$5	$4	$3	$2	$1
Quantity demanded (units per day)	0	2	4	6	8	10	12	14	16	18

Under these conditions,
   (*a*) What price and quantity will prevail if the monopolist isn't regulated? _____
   (*b*) What price-output combination would exist with efficient pricing (MC = p)? _____
   (*c*) What price-output combination would exist with profit regulation (zero economic profits)? _____
   Illustrate your answers on the graph below.

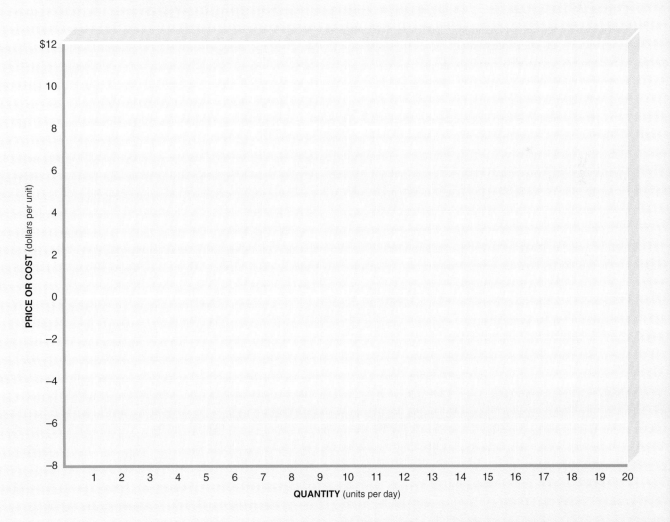

4. According to the Applications box on p. 236, how much will annual shipping costs increase for each saved life?   _____

5. In the long-distance telephone industry, three new transmission technologies—microwave, satellite, and fibre-optic cable—have replaced the traditional coaxial cable made of copper. The following schedule indicates the costs of the different technologies. (Although similar to the actual figures, the data have been altered to ease calculation and graphing.) Voice circuits indicate the number of phone conversations that can be carried simultaneously. Costs are given in thousands of dollars per month.

Number of voice circuits	50	100	500	1,000	1,500
Total cost of					
Fibre-optic cable	$60	$100	$250	$300	$337
Microwave	40	45	150	250	375
Satellite	35	50	200	350	525

(a) Compute and graph (in a single diagram) the average costs of each technology.

(b) Draw the long-run average cost curve facing a long-distance telecommunication company that's deciding what transmission technology to use.

(c) Are there economies, diseconomies, or constant returns to scale?   _____

(d) In the long run, how many firms would you expect to provide long-distance service over any given route between two cities? (Base your answer on the long-run average cost curve you drew.)   _____

(e) With microwave technology, what would be the smallest number of voice circuits that a company could provide and still achieve minimum average cost?   _____

(f) What kind of technology would be most appropriate if only 50 voice circuits were needed between two towns?   _____

(g) What if between 100 and 1,000 voice circuits were needed?   _____

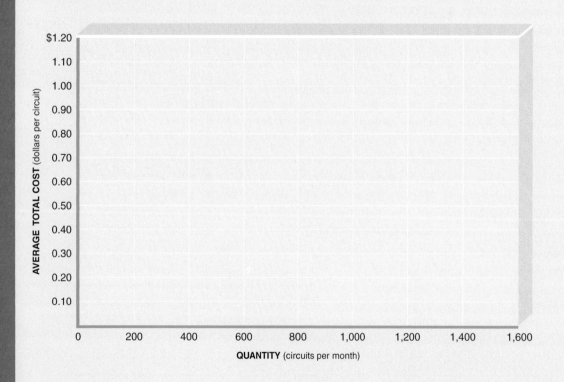

Problems for Chapter 12

Name: _____

1. How many tons of SO$_2$ emissions did the Carolina Power and Light Company buy in 1993? See the Applications box, page 263. _____

2. In some states, mining for coal leaves large mounds of rubble, which poses flooding problems, causes land damage, and is unsightly. The following table shows the estimated annual social benefits and costs of restoring various amounts of such land:

Land restored (in acres)	0	100	200	300	400	500
Social benefits of restoring land	0	$70	$120	$160	$190	$220
Social costs of restoring land	0	$10	$40	$80	$140	$230

(*a*) Compute the marginal social benefits and the marginal social costs for each restoration level.

Land restored (in acres)	0	100	200	300	400	500
Marginal benefit	_____	_____	_____	_____	_____	
Marginal cost	_____	_____	_____	_____	_____	

(*b*) What is the optimal rate of restoration? _____

3. Most people pay nothing for each extra pound of garbage they create. Yet the garbage imposes external costs on a community. In view of this factor, what's an appropriate price for garbage collection? Answer the questions based on the following graph.
   (*a*) What is the quantity of garbage collection now demanded? _____
   (*b*) How much would be demanded if a fee of $2 per pound were charged? _____
   (*c*) Draw the social demand curve when an external benefit of $3 per pound exists.
   (*d*) If the marginal cost of collecting garbage were constant at $5 per pound, what would be the socially optimal level of garbage collection? _____

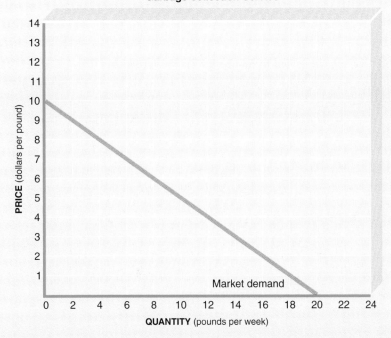

Garbage-collection Service

4. Using the estimated costs and health benefits for the Los Angeles plan to clean up ground-level ozone pollutants from 1989–2010 (Applications box, p. 266), what is the net benefit? _____

5. How much more per ton is New York City paying to recycle rather than just dump its garbage (Applications box, p. 267)? _____

Problems for Chapter 12 (cont'd)   Name: _____

6. Suppose three firms confront the following costs for pollution control:

Emissions Reduction (tonnes per year)	Total Costs of Control		
	Firm A	Firm B	Firm C
1	$ 50	$ 60	$ 40
2	100	140	150
3	180	230	300
4	300	350	600

(a) If each firm must reduce emissions by 1 tonne, how much will be spent?   _____

(b) If the firms can trade pollution rights, what would be the cheapest way of attaining a net 3-tonne reduction?   _____

(c) How much would a pollution permit trade for?   _____

Now suppose the goal is to reduce pollution by 6 tonnes.

(d) If each firm must reduce emissions by 2 tonnes, how much will be spent?   _____

(e) If the firms can trade permits, what is the cheapest way of attaining a 6-tonne reduction?   _____

(f) How much will a permit cost?   _____

7. The following cost schedule depicts the private and social costs associated with the daily production of apacum, a highly toxic fertilizer. The sales price of apacum is $20 per ton.

Output (in tons)	0	1	2	3	4	5	6	7	8
Total private cost	$5	7	13	23	37	55	77	103	133
Total social cost	$7	15	31	55	87	127	175	231	295

Answer the questions using this schedule, and graph on the figure below.

(a) Graph the private and social marginal costs associated with apacum production.

(b) What is the profit-maximizing rate of output?   _____

(c) How much profit is earned at that output level?   _____

(d) What is the socially optimal rate of output?   _____

(e) How much profit is there at that output level?   _____

(f) How much of a "green tax" per tonne would have to be levied to induce the firm to produce the socially optimal rate of output?   _____

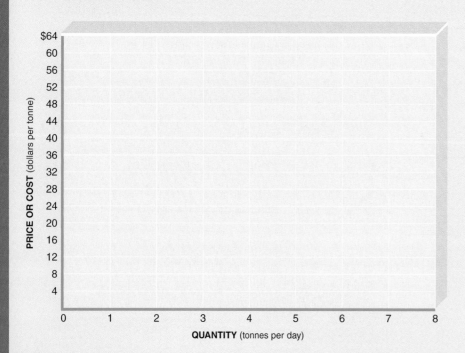

PRICE OR COST (dollars per tonne)

$64, 60, 56, 52, 48, 44, 40, 36, 32, 28, 24, 20, 16, 12, 8, 4

0 1 2 3 4 5 6 7 8

QUANTITY (tonnes per day)

Problems for Chapter 13

Name: _____

1. Apples can be harvested by hand or machine. Handpicking yields 40 pounds per hour, mechanical pickers yield 70 pounds per hour. If the wage rate of human pickers is $6 an hour and the rental on a mechanical picker is $15 an hour,
   (*a*) Which is more cost-effective? _____
   (*b*) If the wage rate increased to $8 an hour, which would be more cost-effective? _____

2. The following table depicts the number of grapes that can be picked in an hour with varying amounts of labour:

Number of pickers (per hour)	1	2	3	4	5	6	7	8
Output of grapes (in flats)	20	38	53	64	71	74	74	70

   (*a*) Illustrate the supply and demand of labour for a single farmer, assuming that the local wage rate is $10 an hour and a flat of grapes sells for $2.
   (*b*) How many pickers will be hired? _____
   (*c*) If the wage rate doubles, how many pickers will be hired? _____
   (*d*) If the productivity of all workers doubles, how many pickers will be hired at a wage of $20 an hour? _____
   (*e*) Illustrate your answers on the graph below.

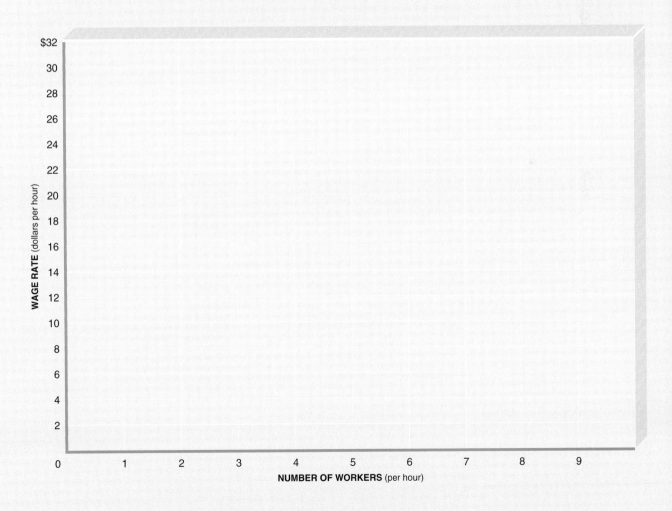

3. Suppose the following supply-and-demand schedules apply in a particular labour market:

Wage rate (per hour)	$4	$5	$6	$7	$8	$9	$10
Quantity of labour supplied (workers per hour)	0	2	4	6	8	10	12
Quantity of labour demanded (workers per hour)	12	10	8	6	4	2	0

Graph the relevant curves and identify the
(*a*) Competitive wage rate.   _____
(*b*) Union wage rate.   _____
(*c*) Monopsonist's wage rate.   _____

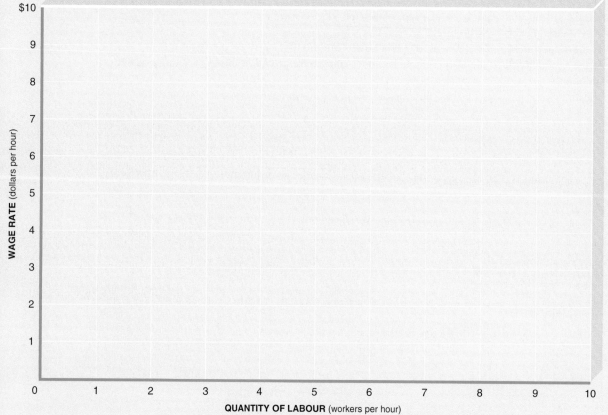

WAGE RATE (dollars per hour)

QUANTITY OF LABOUR (workers per hour)

4. As a result of the collective bargaining between the owners of National Hockey League clubs and the players' union, the 2005 agreement included:
(*a*) a(n) _____ in existing players contracts by 24 percent;
                                        (increase/decrease)
(*b*) no player earning more than _____ of the team's salary cap.
                                        (15%/20%/25%)

Problems for Chapter 14

Name: _____

1. If a $48 stock pays a quarterly dividend of $1, what is the implied rate of return?   _____

2. If a $32 per share stock has a P/E ratio of 20 and pays out 40 percent of its profits in dividends, what is the implied rate of (dividend) return on the stock?   _____

3. If the market rate of interest is 5 percent, what is the present discounted value of $1,000 that will be paid in

                                        (*a*) 1 year?   _____
                                          (*b*) 5 years?   _____
                                          (*c*) 10 years?   _____

4. What is the present discounted value of $10,000 that is to be received in five years if the market rate of interest is

                                          (*a*) 0 percent?   _____
                                          (*b*) 5 percent?   _____
                                          (*c*) 10 percent?   _____

5. Compute the expected return on Columbus's expedition assuming that he had a 50 percent chance of discovering valuables worth $1 million, a 25 percent chance of bringing home only $10,000, and a 25 percent chance of sinking.   _____

6. Locate the stock quotation for General Motors Corporation at http://finance.yahoo.com. Type "GM" in the get quotes box. From the information provided, determine
   (*a*) Yesterday's percentage change in the price of GM stock.   _____
   (*b*) How much profit (earnings) GM made last year for each share of stock?   _____
   (*c*) How much of that profit was paid out in dividends.   _____
   (*d*) How much profit GM retained for investment.   _____
   (*e*) What was the 52 week range for the price of GM stock?   _____

7. Compute the market price of the GM bonds described in Table 14.5 if the yield goes to 9 percent.   _____

8. What is the current yield on a $1,000 bond with a 6 percent coupon if its market price is
                                           (*a*) $900?   _____
                                             (*b*) $1,000?   _____
                                             (*c*) $1,100?   _____

9. How much interest accrued each day on the cash payoff of the U.S. lottery jackpot? (See Table 14.1.)   _____

Problems for Chapter 14 (cont'd)

Name: _____

10. Illustrate the impact of the following events on stock prices:

(a) A federal court finds Microsoft guilty of antitrust violations.

Microsoft stock

PRICE (dollars per share)

QUANTITY (shares per day)

(b) Intel announces a new and faster processor.

Intel stock

PRICE (dollars per share)

QUANTITY (shares per day)

(c) Corporate executives announce they intend to sell a large block of stock.

Company stock

PRICE (dollars per share)

QUANTITY (shares per day)

(d) AOL's competitors cut Internet-access prices.

AOL stock

PRICE (dollars per share)

QUANTITY (shares per day)

Problems for Chapter 15

Name: _____

1. Using the tax rates in Table 15.2, consider an individual earning $100,000 in 2006. Assuming no tax deductions,
   (a) how much income tax did this person pay?   _____
   (b) what was their marginal tax rate?   _____
   (c) what was their average tax rate?   _____

2. Using Table 15.2, compute the taxable income and taxes for the following taxpayers:

Taxpayer	Gross Income	Exemptions and Deductions	Taxable Income	Tax
A	$ 20,000	$ 7,000	_____	_____
B	30,000	4,000	_____	_____
C	40,000	28,000	_____	_____
D	70,000	32,000	_____	_____
E	200,000	80,000	_____	_____

Which taxpayer has
   (a) The highest nominal tax rate?   _____
   (b) The highest effective tax rate?   _____
   (c) The highest marginal tax rate?   _____

3. If the tax elasticity of supply is −0.30, by what percentage will the quantity of labour supplied decrease when the marginal tax rate increases from 40 to 50 percent?   _____

4. By what percentage would the quantity of labour supplied increase if the tax elasticity of supply is −0.15 and the marginal tax rate fell from 22 to 19 percent?   _____

5. If the tax elasticity of labour supply was −0.15, by how much would the quantity of labour supplied increase among people in the top Canadian tax bracket if the highest marginal tax rate in Canada were reduced to the level of Hong Kong's (World View, p. •••)?   _____

6. Based on the data from Table 15.5, in 2006, which province or territory has the
   (a) maximum value for the highest marginal tax rate?   _____
   (b) minimum value for the highest marginal tax rate?   _____
   (c) lowest income threshold for the highest marginal tax rate?   _____
   (d) highest income threshold for the highest marginal tax rate?   _____

7. Consider the recently proposed flat tax rate discussed in the text. Under this scenario, the flat tax is set at 17%, each adult receives a $13,100 personal exemption, and each child receives an exemption of $5,300. Accordingly, a family of four (2 adults, 2 children) would have personal exemptions equaling $36,800. What would be the effective tax rate for a family of four with earnings of
   (a) $30,000?   _____
   (b) $60,000?   _____
   (c) $90,000?   _____

8. Following are hypothetical data on the size distribution of income and wealth for each quintile (one-fifth) of a population:

Quintile	Lowest	Second	Third	Fourth	Highest
Income	5%	10%	15%	25%	45%
Wealth	2%	8%	12%	20%	58%

   (a) On the graph on the next page, draw the line of absolute equity; then draw a Lorenz curve for income, and shade the area between the two curves.
   (b) In the same diagram, draw a Lorenz curve for wealth. Is there more inequality in the distribution of wealth than of income, or less? How do you know?
   (c) The difference in inequality between income and wealth is quite typical of most economies. What might be the reason?   _____

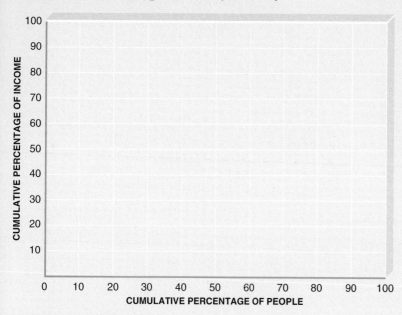

9. (a) On the graph below, draw the supply and demand for labour represented by the following data:

Wage	$1	2	3	4	5	6	7	8	9	10	11	12
Quantity of labour												
Supplied	1	2	3	4	5	6	8	10	12	14	17	20
Demanded	20	18	16	14	12	10	8	6	5	4	3	2

(b) How many workers are employed in equilibrium?

(c) What wage are they paid?   _____

(d) Now suppose a payroll tax of $2 per worker is imposed on the workers (i.e., "suppliers" of labour). Draw the "supply + tax" graph that results.

(e) How many workers are now employed?   _____

(f) How much is the employer paying for each worker?   _____

(g) How much is each worker receiving?   _____

For the incidence of this tax,

(h) What is the increase in unit labour cost to the employer?   _____

(i) What is the reduction in the wage paid to labour?   _____

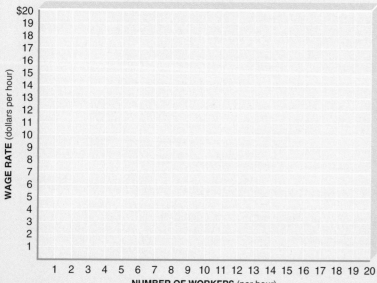

Problems for Chapter 16

Name: _____

1. Suppose the social assistance benefit formula is

$$\text{Benefit} = \$6,000 - 2/3 \,(\text{wages} > \$4,000)$$

   (a) What is the marginal tax rate? _____

   (b) How large is the benefit if wages equal

   (i) $0? _____
   (ii) $4,000? _____
   (iii) $9,000? _____

   (c) What is the breakeven level of income in this case? _____

2. A social assistance recipient can receive food stamps as well as cash welfare benefits. If the food stamp allotment is set as follows,

$$\text{Food stamps} = \$5,000 - 0.30 \,(\text{wages})$$

   (a) How high can wages rise before all food stamps are eliminated? _____

   (b) If the social assistance cheque formula in Problem 1 applies, what is the *combined* marginal tax rate of both welfare and food stamps for wages above $4,000? _____

3. Draw a graph showing how benefits, total income, and wages change under the following conditions:

$$\text{Wages rate} = \$10 \text{ per hour}$$

$$\text{Welfare benefit} = \$6,000 - 0.5 \,(\text{wages} > \$3,000)$$

   Label the following points:
   A—welfare benefit when wages = 0
   B—welfare benefit when wages = $10,000
   C—breakeven level of income

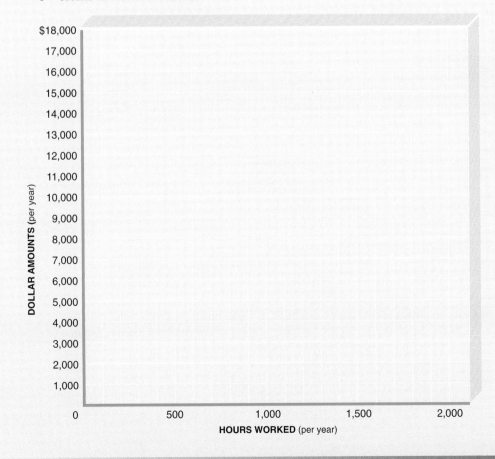

DOLLAR AMOUNTS (per year)

HOURS WORKED (per year)

4. Consider the case of Martha, a 65-year old worker contemplating retirement. Suppose her wage history entitles her to a maximum Old Age Security (OAS) pension of $6,000 plus the maximum Guaranteed Income Supplement (GIS) of $7,500 for a total pension of $13,500 per year. If she wants to supplement her benefits by working part-time, how many hours of work, at a wage rate of
   (a) $10/hour, will she require to earn a combined total income of $20,000?   _____
   (b) $16.25/hour, will she require to earn a combined total income of $20,000?   _____
   (c) $15/hour, will reduce her GIS award to $0?   _____

5. Consider the case of Graeme, a 60-year old worker contemplating retirement. Suppose his wage history enables him to earn the maximum monthly Canada Pension Plan (CPP) payment of $900. What will be his monthly CPP payment if he decides to retire
   (a) now?   _____
   (b) at aged 65?   _____
   (c) at aged 70?   _____

6. (a) On the graph below, depict the case of Martha, our 65-year old worker contemplating retirement from Problem 4. Assume she can work for $10/hour, is entitled to the maximum OAS pension of $6,000 plus the maximum GIS of $7,500 for a total pension of $13,500 per year. Draw in her wage income line, pension benefit line and total income line.
   (b) What is her total income if she works 500 hours?   _____
   (c) What is her total income if she works 1,000 hours?   _____
   (d) What is her total income if she works 2,000 hours?   _____
   (e) She completely eliminates her GIS payment when she works _____ hours.

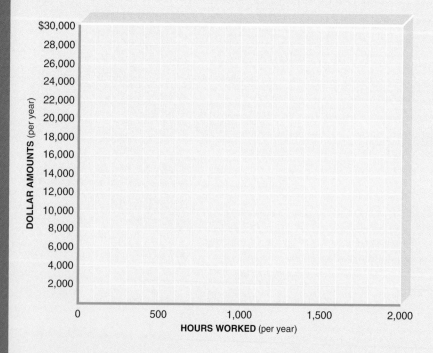

7. If older workers have a tax elasticity of labour supply equal to −0.20, by how much will their work activity decline when they hit the Social Insurance earnings-test limit where the marginal tax rate is 50 percent? (Assume explicit taxes of 30 percent below that limit.)   _____%

Problems for Chapter 17

Name: _____

1. Suppose Canada can produce a maximum of 200,000 hybrid sport coupes or 160,000 barrels of Okanagan wine. (If we assume a constant opportunity cost):
   (a) What is the opportunity cost of one barrel of wine? _____
   (b) If another country offers to trade six hybrid sport coupes for four barrels of Okanagan wine, should Canadians accept the offer? _____
   (c) What are the implied terms of trade in part "b" above? _____

2. What if you are able to cook a meal in 60 minutes or clean the house in 90 minutes while your roommate is able to cook a meal or clean the house in 45 minutes:
   (a) Who has the absolute advantage in cooking meals? In cleaning the house? _____
   (b) Who has the comparative advantage in cooking meals? In cleaning the house? _____

3. If it takes 64 farm workers to harvest one tonne of strawberries and 16 farm workers to harvest one tonne of wheat, what is the opportunity cost of five tonnes of strawberries? _____

4. Alpha and Beta, two tiny islands off the east coast of Tricoli, produce pearls and pineapples. The following production possibilities schedules describe their potential output in tonnes per year.

Alpha		Beta	
Pearls	Pineapples	Pearls	Pineapples
0	30	0	20
2	25	10	16
4	20	20	12
6	15	30	8
8	10	40	4
10	5	45	2
12	0	50	0

   (a) Graph the production possibilities confronting each island.
   (b) What is the opportunity cost of pineapples on each island (before trade)?   Alpha: _____
   Beta: _____

   (c) Which island has a comparative advantage in pearl production? _____
   (d) Graph the consumption possibilities of each island with free trade.

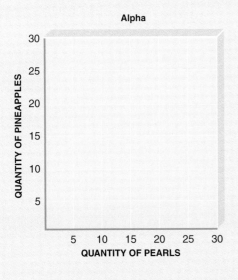

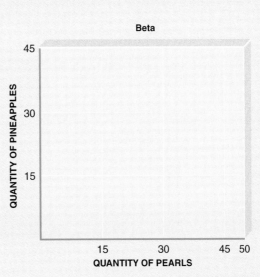

5. In 2004, Canadian cheese producers made about 830 million kilograms of cheese (according to numbers on the Dairy Processors Association home page at http://www.dpac-atlc.ca/english/). The Applications box on page 375 presents the federal government's decision to "restrict the import of a key ingredient used to make cheese." Don Jarvis, president of the Dairy Processors Association suggested that the "decision could have an impact on the availability and pricing of cheese."

   (a) If the restriction on imported milk-protein concentrates increases the price of cheese by $0.75 per kilogram and Canadian consumers bought 700 million kilograms of cheese, what is the cost of the restriction to Canadian consumers each year?   _____

   (b) If Canadian dairy farmers are "losing" $2 million per month because of the trade in milk-protein concentrates, what is the cost of the imports to dairy farmers each year?   _____

   (c) Could consumers pay the farmers their annual loss and still be better off?   _____

6. Suppose the two islands in Problem 4 agree that the terms of trade will be one for one and exchange 10 pearls for 10 pineapples.   _____

   (a) If Alpha produced 6 pearls and 15 pineapples while Beta produced 30 pearls and 8 pineapples before they decided to trade, how much would each be producing after trade? Assume that the two countries specialize just enough to maintain their consumption of the item they export, and make sure each island follows its comparative advantage.

   (b) How much would each island be consuming after specializing and trading?   Alpha: _____
                                                                                        Beta: _____

   (c) How much would the combined production of pineapples increase for the two islands due to trade? _____

   (d) How much would the combined production of pearls increase? _____

   (e) How could both countries produce and consume even more? _____
   _____

   (f) Assume the two islands are able to trade as much as they want with the rest of the world, with the terms of trade at one pineapple for one pearl. Draw the ultimate consumption possibilities curve for each island.

7. Suppose the following table reflects the domestic supply and demand for compact disks (CDs):

Price ($)	16	14	12	10	8	6	4	2
Quantity supplied	8	7	6	5	4	3	2	1
Quantity demanded	2	4	6	8	10	12	14	16

   (a) Graph these market conditions and identify the equilibrium price and sales.   Price/sales: _____

   (b) Now suppose that foreigners enter the market, offering to sell an unlimited supply of CDs for $6 apiece. Illustrate and identify
       (i) The market price   _____
       (ii) Domestic consumption   _____
       (iii) Domestic production   _____

   (c) If a tariff of $2 per CD is imposed, what will happen to
       (i) The market price?   _____
       (ii) Domestic consumption?   _____
       (iii) Domestic production?   _____
   Graph your answers.

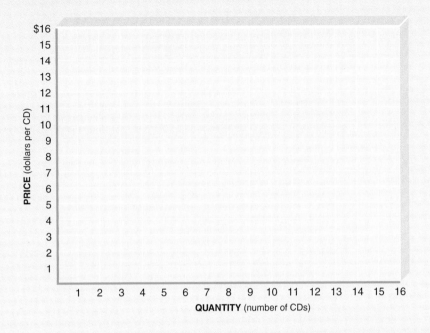

8. Go to the website: http://www.international.gc.ca/tna-nac/reg-en.asp, which provides information on the "regional and bilateral initiatives" of the Government of Canada. Pick one of the links to Canada's "Free trade negotiations and discussions" and write a paragraph giving the Canadian perspective of the proposed agreement.   _____

9. The Applications box on page 379 suggests that the latest round of WTO negotiations—the DOHA round—are in danger of collapse because of subsidies paid to farmers in "rich" countries. Using a supply and demand format graph to illustrate, explain the impact of rich country subsidies on the willingness and ability to supply agricultural goods and the impact on potential "poor" country exporters.   _____

10. The Applications box on page 377 talks about establishing free trade within Canada as well as between Canada and other countries. Go to the Alberta Trade, Investment and Labour Mobility Agreement, TILMA website at http://www.tilma.ca/ and write a paragraph giving the purpose of TILMA and the potential impact in the Alberta and British Columbia economies.   _____